SORTITION AND DEMOCRACY

HISTORY, TOOLS, THEORIES

Edited by
Liliane Lopez-Rabatel
and Yves Sintomer

SORTITION &
PUBLIC POLICY
the luck of
the draw

imprint-academic.com

Published in the UK by
Imprint Academic, PO Box 200, Exeter EX5 5YX, UK

Distributed in the USA by
Ingram Book Company,
One Ingram Blvd., La Vergne, TN 37086, USA

ISBN 9781788360166 paperback
ISBN 9781788360159 cloth

A CIP catalogue record for this book is available from the
British Library and US Library of Congress

Contents

Acknowledgments

This book is partly the outcome of a conference organized at the École française d'Athènes in October 2015 with the title: 'Tirage au sort et démocratie directe. Les témoignages antiques et leur postérité.' We would like to thank Alexandre Farnoux, the director of the Athens French school, Julien Fournier, who was at that time the director of the Ancient Studies department, Nolween Grémillet, responsible for the communication, and Évi Platanitou, administrative assistant.

We are also grateful to the institutions that have given their financial support for the conference or for the book: the Groupement d'Intérêt Scientifique Démocratie et Participation; the École française d'Athènes; the research programme 'Political Representative Claims: A Global View—France, Germany, Brazil, China, India' (CLAIMS), funded by a joint programme of the Agence Nationale pour la Recherche (ANR) and the Deutsche Forschungsgemeinschaft (DFG); the Association Française de Science Politique (AFSP); the Institut de Recherche sur l'Architecture Antique (IRAA); the Centre de Recherches Sociologiques et politiques de Paris (CRESPPA); the Centre Marc Bloch (Berlin); the AFSP Standing group 'La représentation politique: histoire, théories, mutations contemporaines' (GRePo); the Laboratoire de recherche historique Rhône-Alpes (LAHRA); the research team 'Espace, pratiques sociales et images dans les mondes grec et romain' (ESPRI—ArScAn, Archéologies et Sciences de l'Antiquité).

Our thanks to the translator, Sarah-Louise Raillard, for the great work she has done and her remarkable patience and sympathy; to Charlotte Fouillet, our research assistant; and to the authors for their collaboration and their trust.

Liliane Lopez-Rabatel and Yves Sintomer

Liliane Lopez-Rabatel
and Yves Sintomer

Introduction
The History of Sortition in Politics: Instruments, Practices, and Theories

Tranlsated by Sarah-Louise Raillard

Since the 1990s, historians, sociologists, and political scientists have all shown renewed interest in sortition, a device which has also resurfaced in public discussions in many countries around the world.[1] However, this ancient form of decision-making and designation—which many believed had been relegated to the dustbin of history—was rediscovered along two relatively distinct trajectories by historians on the one hand, and sociologists and political scientists on the other.

The Return of Sortition

While historiography has devoted a certain amount of attention to the use of sortition in politics, in particular during Greek and Roman Antiquity as well as during the Middle Ages in Italy and Spain, such interest was relatively incidental. Over the years, the studies that focused on random selection in politics were few and far between. If we look at European Antiquity specifically, there are no more than half a dozen important contributions to list: Fustel de Coulanges (1891) and John Wycliffe Headlam (1891) at the beginning of the 1890s, Victor Ehrenberg (1923) in the 1920s, Christian Meier (1956), then Lili Ross

---

[1]   This volume is partially drawn from a conference organized by Liliane Lopez-Rabatel and Yves Sintomer, held in October 2015 at the *École Française d'Athènes* [French School of Athens] in collaboration with the *Institut de Recherche sur l'Architecture Antique* [Research Institute on Ancient Architecture], CNRS-MSH MOM (*Université Lumière Lyon* 2), CSU-CRESPPA (CNRS-Université Paris 8), the *GIS Démocratie et Participation* [Scientific Interest Group in Participatory Democracy] and the *Association Française de Science Politique* [French Political Science Association]. The theme of the conference was 'Random selection and direct democracy: Ancient accounts and their legacy'.

Taylor (1966), and finally Eastland Stuart Staveley (1972) a few decades later.

Renewed interest in random selection in politics

Starting in the 1990s, and drawing on advances made in the fields of historiography, archaeology, and epigraphy, the number of studies on sortition began to proliferate and break new ground. Mogens H. Hansen's seminal work (1995) marked a turning point in research on Ancient Athens and was quickly followed by other studies (cf. in particular Boegehold, 1995; Demont, 2003, drawing on the pioneering work done by Dow, 1937). A parallel movement took place with regard to studies on Ancient Rome, with publications by Claude Nicolet (1976), Claude Nicolet and Azedine Beschaouch (1991), and Roberta Stewart (1998), as well as synthesis like the one elaborated by Frédéric Hurlet (2006). Interestingly enough, there was also renewed interest in the Italian Communes, especially following the publication of John N. Najemy's work (1982), and some general comparisons have begun to be published (Tanzini, 2014; Keller, 2015) rather than only monographs. This movement has expanded outside of the West, including in countries such as China (Will, 2002; Wang, 2018) and Mexico (Aguilar Rivera, 2000). More generally, sortition has been examined in various studies that seek to deconstruct different modes of designation and appointment (Ruffini, 1977; Schneider and Zimmermann, 1990; Dartmann *et al.*, 2010), whereas its uses in divinatory practices and pre-modern politics have already been the subject of a preliminary overview (Cordano and Grottanelli, 2001).

At the same time, interest in random selection has resurfaced, growing exponentially within activist circles and in the domain of political science research. First mentioned by a few pioneers in the late 1960s and early 1970s (Dahl, 1970), the political use of random selection was then further studied in Germany, where Peter Dienel proposed the use of 'planning cells', or *Planungszellen*, in 1969, the first of which were tried out in the winter of 1972–73; and concurrently in the United States, where Ned Crosby created a very similar mechanism in 1974 that he called 'citizen juries'. The latter term would be broadly disseminated, whereas Dienel's 'planning cells' would largely remain a German use (Dienel, 1997; Crosby, 1975). In 1988, James Fishkin invented deliberative polling, testing the process out for the first time in 1994 in Great Britain (Fishkin, 1997). Militant authors such as John Burnheim (1985), Benjamin Barber (1997), Lynn Carson and Brian Martin (1999), and Barbara Goodwin (2005) also helped to popularize the idea. In France, the seminal work of Bernard Manin (1997) on representative government played a crucial role in rousing activist interest in sortition, even despite a certain misunderstanding of Manin's arguments, given that the author is far from supporting this form of decision-making (Hayat, 2019). The French blogger Étienne Chouard and the Belgian intellectual David Van Reybrouck (2016) also published a number of very popular essays on the subject. Other academics, whether active in politics or not, helped to rehabilitate the concept of sortition, including John Gastil (2000), Philippe C. Schmitter and Alexander H. Trechsel (2004), Dominique Bourg *et al.* (2011), and Jon Elster (2013); this trend even reached countries as distant from Europe as China (Wang, 2018). The British publisher Imprint Academic has played a significant role in this regard, republishing recent titles that were already out of print, as well as new works in the field (Callenbach and Phillips, 2008; Barnett and Carty, 2008; Sutherland, 2008; Delannoi and Dowlen, 2010). As Julien Talpin demonstrates in this volume, there has been fruitful cross-pollination between theoretical work on deliberative democracy and research on randomly selected minipublics, leading to an explosion in the number of publications on the subject, as well as the proliferation of democratic experiments in the use of random selection across the Global North and beyond. A number of collective manifestos were published at the end of the 2010s, with contributions from Erick O. Wright, the former president of the American Sociological Association, and Jane Mansbridge, the former president of the American Political Science Association (Gastil and Wright, 2018; 2019).

An unprecedented historical panorama

At the turn of the 2000s and 2010s, four political scientists and sociologists — Anja Röcke (2005), Yves Sintomer (2007, 2011), Oliver Dowlen (2008), and Hubertus Buchstein (2009) — published historical surveys of the use of random selection in politics. At the same time, archaeological studies (Lopez-Rabatel, 2011) and the experimental reconstruction of an Ancient Greek *kleroterion* under the aegis of the IRAA by Nicolas Bresch in Paris allowed us to finally understand the true uses of the famous 'lottery machine' described by Aristotle in his work *The Athenian Constitution*. The material conditions of this form of decision-making have thus been greatly elucidated. By situating itself at the intersection of these two avenues of research, this volume seeks to build upon the significant advances made in studies on sortition. It contains an unprecedented overview of the theories, uses, and instruments of political sortition from Antiquity to the present day. It sheds new light on the historical, ideological, and institutional foundations of random selection, as well as on the material conditions of its practice.

To this day, no equivalent overview exists at the international level. The fact that this volume brings together leading specialists studying a wide variety of different time periods and geographical regions means that it can go further, in terms of both depth and precision, than the aforementioned studies which sought to provide a panoramic overview of the historical uses of random selection. Conversely, sortition has until now generally been the subject of very narrow studies focusing on specific periods and cultural areas. The extreme level of specialization of such studies has not allowed their authors to venture interpretations about other peoples and places, and has therefore stymied a global understanding of the uses of sortition. This text is therefore unique in more than one way, as it seeks to be interdisciplinary and trans-historical. Its innovation lies in the interdisciplinary approach used by experts in different academic fields who examine random selection in all its theoretical, procedural, and physical dimensions. While the approaches used by political scientists, historians, philosophers, political sociologists, archaeologists, and philologists are different both within and across disciplines, they remain largely complementary and therefore all add to the immense value of this volume.

The composition of this volume is governed by both chronological and geographical factors. For the first time, studies are brought together that stretch from Greek Antiquity to the present day and from all four corners of the globe. While the chapters which focus on the Ancient World, the Middle Ages, and the modern period mostly concern Mediterranean Europe, with a few incursions into East Asia, France, and Switzerland, the scope of the volume as a whole is much broader, including a study of China's use of sortition from the very end of the 16th century to the beginning of the 20th century. Looking at very recent history, a number of authors in this volume also analyse the numerous experiments in random selection that have been conducted in Western Europe as well as Iceland, British Columbia, and several American states during the 21st century.

In this volume, three dimensions of sortition are investigated: the instruments used to implement sortition and the role they played; the various practices of random selection and their historical and political context; and the theoretical principles that helped to promote, or on the contrary hinder, the use of sortition in politics. Given these different concerns, varying types of sources are used as applicable: literary and philosophical texts ranging from Greco-Roman Antiquity to the present day; epigraphic texts and archaeological vestiges (for the Athenian and

Roman periods); sociological studies, observations, and analyses of contemporary practices; iconographic documents; and statistical data. These sources – which differ in their accessibility, readability, and completeness, depending on the period in question – are compared and contrasted with other sources from an interdisciplinary and transhistorical perspective which drew significantly on a number of thematic conferences that were held during the writing of this volume.

Given that they stem from the nature of the sources and the academic disciplines from which they are drawn, the methods used in this volume are diverse. Studying the vocabulary of sortition offers a kind of lexical framework to look at the physical tools and logistical procedures employed in Greco-Roman Antiquity (Milano, Lopez-Rabatel) and during the Middle Ages (Tanzini); this is complemented by an analysis of archaeological vestiges and their representations. While the research focuses on the terms used to describe the tools of sortition, it also includes generic terms describing 'random selection' and 'election', two concepts that are not as mutually exclusive as is often imagined. In the absence of technical texts, cross-reference with institutional or philosophical works sometimes allows for a better understanding of the political contexts in which sortition was used. Conversely, but in the same vein, philosophical writings from Antiquity, while sometimes the primary subject of a study (Macé), are also pitted against political realities or material circumstances. Such writings are likewise referenced to determine the nature of their contribution to theories of modern and contemporary political philosophy, in particular with regard to the role played by sortition (Moreno Pestaña). In the fields of science and political sociology, fieldwork examines the political scope and functioning of deliberative minipublics (Fourniau, Dowlen), various mechanisms of democratic deliberation, and the many guises of random selection both inside and outside of the political sphere (Courant). Ultimately, the 'survival' of random selection in politics is interpreted in an unprecedented fashion using A. Warburg's concept of the 'pathos formula'(Sintomer).

Divinatory Sortition and Distributive Sortition: The Historical Construction of Random Selection in Politics as a Specific Practice

In our contemporary world, the fact that most uses of random selection for political, scientific, and entertainment purposes have been secularized means that we assume there is an essential difference between secular and religious uses of sortition, without even questioning the historical pertinence of such a distinction. This volume doubtless partly rests upon this assumption—aside from the chapter by Romain Loriol, most of the essays contained herein focus on practices that we would today designate as 'political' in nature and only mention the divinatory uses of sortition in passing, if at all. While the practice of divinatory sortition was used in a wide variety of civilizations, the political use of random selection was largely (though not exclusively) developed in the West, where it became particularly widespread and increasingly rationalized (Hacking, 1990). To our knowledge (although a systematic investigation of non-Western sources would likely produce a few surprises), only China under the Ming and Qing dynasties witnessed a similar development of sortition practices, as discussed in the chapter by Pierre-Étienne Will.

Religious and political

Nevertheless, the dichotomy between political and religious sortition was—and is—not a self-evident one. The question of the relationship between random selection and religion is therefore examined in a number of the studies contained in this volume, in different contexts ranging from Antiquity to the modern era. In the Near East, in Greece and in Rome, no hard-and-fast distinction was made between religion and politics: religion was a civic engagement and many political acts were embedded within religious rituals. Random selection was included in a broad range of activities, including both divinatory practices and what we might today call political practices, but whose religious or at least ritual dimensions remained nonetheless significant. At first glance, the similarities between the instruments first used in the Near East, Ancient Greece, and Ancient Rome are striking, in terms of both political and divinatory uses of drawing lots. In Rome especially, all political acts were ritualized. Although some authors now distinguish between random selection in terms of pure chance and random selection as revealing the divine will, it may be that this distinction had little significance during some periods in the Ancient World.

The religious dimension of random selection is illustrated in the Homeric epics, where the procedure is accompanied by a prayer to the gods. For a long time, and in the wake of the arguments made by Fustel de Coulanges (1891), the idea that random selection in Antiquity was predominantly a religious matter prevailed. This situation began to change, however, with the work of Hansen (1999). While today the common view is that the practice of random selection was completely detached from religious signification by the time it was employed in the radical democracy of 4th-century BCE Athens, some scholars have argued that the matter is perhaps not so cut and dried. In his *Laws*, Plato differentiates between two kinds of sortition. One form, based on 'proportional' equality and equity, is the expression of divine will; the other is used for the 'seventh form of rule', which is more trivial and allows for the allocation of public offices. In the latter case, prayers are addressed to the gods so that they may guide chance appropriately. Arnaud Macé argues that Plato attributes a religious dimension to chance by incorporating the question of divine approval into the process. As a staunch opponent of democracy, Plato grants the use of random selection in the ideal city a value that it probably did not have in his contemporary democratic Athens. Lotteries were held in the Theseion as early as the 4th century BCE, and the description of the random selection of members of the people's jury by the author of *The Athenian Constitution* illustrate a ritualized civic procedure. Moreover, in the 2nd century CE, several *kleroteria* were displayed in the sanctuary where lotteries took place. While these elements all suggest that we cannot overlook the ritual dimension of the procedure, they do not imply that when Athenians proceeded to randomly select citizens for public offices, they believed they were revealing the will of the gods. In fact, Plato's text suggests quite the opposite. The lotteries used to distribute political duties gradually lost their initially religious signification. This evolution can be seen in Athens starting in the 5th century, and in Rome after the fall of the Republic. Although the ritual dimension continued to be important, perhaps even fundamental, the idea that the will of the gods was expressed every time public offices were randomly allocated was no longer a belief shared by the majority of citizens (or, if we are to believe Cicero (1923), by the majority of educated citizens). From this point of view, it is significant that the lottery machine, the *kleroterion* (starting in the 4th century BCE) as well as the rotating urn, the *urna versatilis* (starting in the 1st century BCE), were never used for divinatory purposes, according to extant sources. Nevertheless, it was only during the Christian Middle Ages that the norms governing religious practices and political acts were to diverge radically with regard to the use of sortition; it was likewise only at this point that the distinction between the two uses began to be theorized.

Thomas Aquinas: Sors divisoria *vs.* sors divinatoria

By investigating the distinction between political and religious uses of chance, we are revisiting a traditional argument dating back to the Christian Middle Ages. Thomas Aquinas was the first to establish a rigorous classification of the different uses of sortition. In the section on divination in his *Summa Theologica* (2007 [1269–72]) and a short treatise called *De Sortibus* (1963 [1270–71]), Aquinas explains that 'there are three kinds of divination. The first is when the demons are invoked openly, this comes under the head of "necromancy"; the second is merely an observation of the disposition or movement of some other being, and this belongs to "augury"; while the third consists in doing something in order to discover the occult; and this belongs to "sortilege"' (2007, volume 3, p. 1596).

The rationales for the first two kinds of divination are at antipodes from each other. The first, which is illicit, consists of directly invoking demons, illegitimately trying to discern the divine will, and possibly giving into superstition – the last two practices ultimately amount to letting demons act surreptitiously. In opposition to this demonic form of divination, condemned for both theological and rationalist reasons (which had already been established by Cicero, 1923), Thomas Aquinas describes a licit form of divination, essentially what is practised by augurs. It consists of analysing and interpreting certain natural phenomena in order to predict the future. According to Aquinas, it is both useful and necessary to consult the movement of the stars to better manage agricultural cycles, either by directly analysing causal chains (the movement of the stars leading, for example, to eclipses and thus exerting a direct influence over natural bodies), or by looking for clues of causal dynamics not immediately perceptible (the flight paths of birds or the behaviour of animals in general could reveal ongoing natural events that humans could not detect directly (Aquinas, 2007 [1269–72])). This kind of divination could be subject to a process of rationalization.

The third kind of divination, using lots, deserves a description of its own: it is a kind of halfway point between the other two forms. In the *Summa Theologica*, it is defined as a process 'practised by observing certain things done seriously by men in the research of the occult, whether by drawing lots, which is called "geomancy"; or by observing the shapes resulting from molten lead poured into water; or by observing which of several sheets of paper, with or without writing upon them, a person may happen to draw; or by holding out several unequal sticks and noting who takes the greater or the lesser; or by throwing dice, and observing who throws the highest score; or by observing what catches the eye when one opens a book, all of which are named "sortilege"' (Aquinas, 2007 [1269–72], article 3, p. 1596).

In *De Sortibus* (1963 [1270–1271]), Aquinas further develops his reflections on the subject. Aquinas gives a new theological foundation to the condemnation of chance-based divinatory practices (*sors divinatoria*, or *sortes sanctorum*), which the Church had outlawed since the Council of Vannes in 462, but which widely remained in practice (as can be observed in the life of Saint Francis of Assisi, 1180–1226) (Courcelles, 1963). The *Decree of Gratian (Decretum Gratiani)*, written between 1139 and 1158 and which had helped to establish canon law, likewise condemned the practice. In the context of a discussion on divinatory practices, Gratian comments on the idea that 'chance was not evil; it was something that indicated the divine will amidst human doubt'. Gratian also writes: 'we respond thusly: before the Gospels flourished, many things were permitted, that have since been completely eradicated in our era of more perfect discipline. For example, the marriage of priests, or of related persons, was not forbidden by ancient laws, the laws of the Gospel, or the laws of the Apostles, but is nevertheless completely forbidden by ecclesiastical law. Moreover, we recognize that there is no harm in the [act of drawing] lots, but the practice is forbidden to the faithful, so that they are not tempted to return to the old idolatries under the guise of practicing divination' (*Decretum Gratiani,* Question II, C. I; see also C. VII).

Thomas Aquinas's originality lies elsewhere, however. He takes into account the growing use of random selection for magistrates in the Italian Communes, as the latter were rediscovering a procedure that had apparently disappeared for centuries. He also argues for the banning of random selection procedures for official Church positions. His contemporary political context was quite unique: the use of random selection for public offices was widespread in Northern and Central Italy, where in most cases it was combined with various forms of co-option and election, with the result that this reintroduction of chance into politics is now seen as the primary procedural contribution of the Italian Communes to political history (Keller, 2015). Although the practice was tolerated for a long time,[2] in 1223 (several decades before Aquinas was writing), Pope Honorius III ultimately decided to prohibit random selection for Episcopal nomination procedures; two years later, he extended this prohibition to other ecclesiastical offices (Keller, 2015). Whereas the use of sortition in the political sphere sought precisely to distribute power and avoid its monopolization by a single individual or

---

[2] According to Saint Jerome, several passages in the *Decretum Gratiani* define the clergy, etymologically speaking, as *kleros*, or those whose lot has been dedicated to God. In the medieval context, however, this was no longer a reference to sortition strictly speaking, but to chance in the sense of destiny and divine election. Nonetheless, the *Decretum* does not refer to the prohibition of random selection for religious offices. Cf. *Decretum Gratiani*, Distinctio XXI, C. I; Pars secunda, Cause XII, Question I, C. V and C VII. We would like to thank Julien Théry for his insightful commentary on these points.

faction, its transfer into the religious sphere ran counter to the predomi-
nant trend of entrenching Church hierarchies and firmly establishing
the Pope's authority, an ambition illustrated by the 11th-century
Gregorian Reforms. The principle of resorting to a higher authority in
the case of a disagreement at any given level of the hierarchical pyra-
mid was thus clearly reinforced.

By distinguishing three different types of sortition, Thomas Aquinas
provided a theological basis for the prohibition on sortition in canon
law. The first kind, which he called *sors divisoria* ('distributive
sortition'), he deemed the most legitimate. This procedure could be
used in secular affairs, when it was necessary to distribute goods or
attribute functions. But since the Church had become an institution, it
was forbidden from using such expedient measures: to do so would be
to offend the Holy Spirit and the wisdom with which it had endowed
its clerics, its bishops in particular. Hierarchy could always be relied on
in cases of disagreement. The second type of selection, 'consultative
sortition' (*sors consultatoria*), was also permitted in secular affairs alone:
it consisted of leaving a decision to chance when it was unclear which
side to take after exhausting one's reasoning capacities. The third kind
of random selection, called 'divinatory sortition' (*sors divinatoria*),
entailed unduly soliciting God's judgment by the use of divination
techniques. Here Thomas Aquinas reiterated his prohibition and even
expanded it, arguing that divinatory sortition could only entail a pact
with the Devil or, at the very least, could allow demons to intervene in
human affairs; the seriousness of the sins involved depended on the
kind of divination practised.

A typology of the different uses of sortition

By freely drawing on Aquinas's analysis and the various other attempts
to classify the different uses of sortition that began to emerge in the
Middle Ages, we can today use, with slight modifications, the typology
proposed by Cristiano Grottanelli (2001, p. 158). From the perspective
of 21st-century scholars, the uses of random selection can be divided
into three major categories: (1) *sors divisoria* (distributive sortition),
which consists of randomly distributing goods or functions; (2) *sors
divinatoria* (cleromancy), a specific kind of divination (or, to use a
different kind of vocabulary, of 'mantic', or knowledge of the divine)
using the drawing of lots; and (3) games of chance. To be truly
systematic, a fourth category should be added: the scientific and
statistical use of chance to calculate probabilities; however, we shall
leave this category aside as it is not pertinent here.

These three categories can in turn be subdivided. Distributive sortition (*sors divisoria*) can entail distributing goods (and different kinds of goods), or functions. Cleromancy (*sors divinatoria*) can entail revealing someone's destiny or the expression of a divine will—the two not being the exact same thing. In fact, destiny can refer to a supernatural realm or a cosmic order that does not involve the personal will of a deity, and the idea of destiny or fate can persist in ritual uses even when secularization and rationalization have discredited belief in the direct intervention of the gods down on earth. Cleromancy can moreover refer to a number of various techniques. And finally, games of chance can be divided into many different categories, in particular depending on the instruments used (cf. Figure 1).

Distribution of goods and functions: distributive sortition (*sors divisoria*)		Cleromancy: divinatory sortition (*sors divinatoria*)		Games of chance
Distribution of goods in lots: land, territories, loot, real estate, rare healthcare items, etc. 'Negative' distribution: punishments, decimation, conscription, taxes, etc.	Distribution of functions: political, military or religious positions	Reveals a destiny	Expresses the divine will	Games of dice and anklebones (several millennia BCE); lotteries (China 200 BCE, Roman Empire, 15th-century Europe); card games (China 9th century, Europe 14th century); lotto (Genoa 16th century), etc.
Distribution of political powers seen as properties over the governed and their goods		Extraction of an object (*sors, kleros*—cleromancy in the strictest sense), of cards (cartomancy), random selection of a book page (bibliomancy); divination using dice or astragals (astragalomancy), small sticks (achilleomancy); the burning of turtle scales (cheloniomancy); etc.		
Distribution of goods and functions as revealed destiny or the expression of divine will				
		Interpretation of fortune or misfortune in games as a sign of fate or (more rarely) divine will		
Potential use of the same instruments for distributive sortition, cleromancy, and games of chance, shifting techniques from one realm to another				

Figure 1: The uses of random selection. (Source: Sintomer, 2020).

These distinctions are of course largely analytical. Any use of this typology must of course take into account that it has been elaborated in the current climate, where the religious and political uses of random selection are generally distinct practices — which was not the case in Antiquity. In historical practice, the different domains influenced each other and transfers frequently occurred. The original unity of distributive sortition (*sors divisoria*) stemmed from a view of power as a sort of property over people, territories, and movable objects. In that regard, it was logical to confuse the distribution of goods with the allocation of functions. Moreover, the revelation of destinies and expressions of divine will often have shifting borders, especially in societies where belief in the voluntary action of supernatural forces remains strong. The idea that distributive sortition drew its significance from divine intervention or some other manifestation of a deity was likewise very widespread throughout history. Finally, the techniques and instruments used to operate random selection procedures were often the same as those used in games of chance, cleromancy, and politics; conversely, the creation of specific tools like the *kleroterion* generally marked one realm's growing autonomy from another, and in particular the growing autonomy of politics with regard to religion.

Three Lessons

What are the main lessons imparted by this volume, regarding the political uses of distributive sortition? Below, we shall outline what we believe to be our three primary conclusions.

Random selection, a political procedure that was widespread throughout history

Our first conclusion, which becomes apparent thanks to the cumulative effect of the contributions in this volume, nonetheless runs counter to the common perception of 21st-century citizens — and doubtless that of the majority of political researchers. In addition to election, dynastic succession, and patronage, random selection was in fact one of the most widespread procedures used to designate public offices throughout history. A number of comparative studies on election as a designation procedure have been published recently, focusing on both the Ancient World (Borlenghi *et al.*, 2019) and contemporary society (Deloye and Ihl, 2008). These studies have allowed us to historically contextualize the institutional mechanism of election by examining how it operates in the real world, which practices give it meaning, and what ideological universes it helps to establish. Such studies have moreover investigated the continuities and turning points in the history of election. It is high time that random selection received a similar treatment.

In fact, the procedural importance of random selection across a wide variety of contexts is striking. Its role in democratic Athens is relatively well known, and the chapters provided herein by Liliane Lopez-Rabatel, Arnaud Macé, and Paul Demont further develop this line of inquiry. The phenomenon of Athenian sortition, examined in all its complexity — including its lexicon, its material requirements, its location, its non-political uses, and its institutional and theoretical frameworks — paints the picture of a society whose organizational processes largely relied on the use of lot. With the exception of a handful of specialists, however, few are aware that sortition was, as Lucio Milano demonstrates, equally present in the Middle East, and that it likewise played a major role in Republican Rome and during the Principate. In this regard, the chapters contributed by Virginie Hollard, Julie Bothorel, Wolfgang Blösel, and Romain Loriol provide an unprecedented historical perspective. Analysing the lexicon of sortition highlights the omnipresence of lot in Rome, whether it was a question of playing games or managing everyday life. The use of random selection by institutions can be interpreted, depending on the case and point of view, as an avatar of republicanism, or on the contrary, as forming part of the sovereign's system of tyrannical power.

The importance of random selection in the Italian Communes, a topic which has doubtless received less attention than Ancient Athens by activists in the public sphere interested in the return to politics of sortition procedures, is nonetheless an important historical subject. The chapter penned by Lorenzo Tanzini provides an unparalleled analysis of sortition's use in different Italian cities during the Middle Ages, while the chapter written by Claire Judde de Larivière looks at the Venetian history of random selection and illustrates the wide variety of popular uses of sortition, uses that go far beyond the well-known election of the Doge. Looking at the modern period, the chapter provided by Yann Lignereux on French town magistrates of the 17th century illustrates that the use of chance was far from being an exclusively Italian procedure during that period. Raphaël Barat (writing about the Republic of Geneva at the end of the 17th and during the 18th century), and Antoine Chollet and Aurèle Dupuis (discussing the canton of Glaris from the 17th to the beginning of the 19th century) demonstrate to what extent the random selection of town magistrates, variously coupled with election and/or direct democracy, constituted a crucial procedure in Switzerland during the modern era. This remained the case until the revolutionary period at the end of the 18th century, which saw the birth of the Helvetic Republic, a period examined by Maxime Mellina.[3]

It is perhaps surprising for contemporary French readers to realize that the political use of random selection was far from being limited to Christian Europe. Sortition was a widespread practice throughout Imperial China during more than three centuries, where it was used to distribute provinces amongst high-ranking civil servants who had passed the imperial examination. This arrangement, astutely analysed by Pierre-Étienne Will, harks back to the mode of allocating the different Roman provinces amongst consuls and other high magistrates. The Chinese coupling of random selection and competitive examinations was unique, however, and was not replicated anywhere in European history.

Next, the chapters which look at the contemporary period shed new light on the return of random selection to the political sphere today. José Luis Moreno Pestaña accounts for the rather limited interpretation of sortition by Jacques Rancière and Cornélius Castoriadis, authors for whom it nonetheless remains crucial to refer to Ancient Athens when discussing democratic theories.[4] How sortition has worked in practice is elucidated in a particularly innovative way by Dimitri Courant, who describes the instruments used to draw lots in the contemporary world. Jean-Michel Fourniau similarly peers into the 'black box' of the allegedly random selection of contemporary minipublics and analyses how the recruitment of such participants is not a simple act of sortition. Oliver Dowlen looks at the stated objectives of random selection and compares them with the different ways of conducting sortition procedures. In a synoptic essay, Julien Talpin analyses randomly selected minipublics in light of various theories of deliberative democracy, highlighting just to what extent this encounter has been circumstantial, and could end up merely being a transitional phase.

Two concluding essays round out the volume. First, Yves Sintomer examines the historical occurrences of the figure of the child drawing lots, from Antiquity to the present day, and its fluctuating significance. Yves Deloye then draws a number of methodological and historiographical conclusions from studies on voting in order to determine the

---

[3]   A collective work edited by Antoine Chollet has even more systematically illustrated the role of random selection in politics, as well as the importance of transfers between Swiss cantons (cf. for a preliminary overview, Chollet and Dupuis, 2019).

[4]   This contribution is part of a larger collective research project which also gave rise to the publication of a special issue of the journal *Daimon: Revista Internacional de Filosofía* on random selection (Costa *et al.*, 2017).

pertinence, scope, and limits of the perspectives on random selection contained in this volume.

The significance of instruments

Drawing on developments in France in the fields of the sociology of science (Callon and Latour, 1991) and the historical sociology of politics, one significant element that emerges from all the essays contained in this volume is the physical importance of the various instruments without which sortition would remain unfeasible. The instruments used to conduct random selection procedures are linked to the various social interests that govern their use, and which they in turn embody and promote.

Analysing the material conditions of random selection is fruitful in this regard, as such an approach highlights strong elements of continuity as well as two major turning points in the procedure's historical evolution. On the one hand, such an analysis underscores the formal similarities exhibited by the different objects and procedures used over long periods of time. The original set-up for sortition included a receptacle (*hydria,* vase, cylinder, drum, etc.) which held the lots (cubes, wax or cloth balls, gold or silver marbles, coins, straws, slips of paper, pieces of bamboo, etc.) that were then publicly extracted to designate the person who would occupy the public office in question. This process was streamlined over the years, with the objects used being increasingly refined and manufactured, and the practices gradually losing their magical character, while still remaining heavily ritualized. The equipment used for sortition could include both naturally occurring and manufactured objects that could be employed for a variety of purposes; overall, the instruments used exhibit an undeniable continuity, even today. Many activist movements currently use random selection in a way that does not differ fundamentally from the procedure as it was used several millennia ago.

Nevertheless, the history of sortition witnessed two important technical innovations, which represented turning points with regard to the political significance of random selection. The first turning point, analysed in depth by Liliane Lopez-Rabatel, occurred during the Classical era. The Greek invention of the lottery machine, or *kleroterion,* attests to the new needs that arose thanks to the exponential use of lottery practices in Athens and a few other politically similar cities. The *kleroterion* was a tangible manifestation of a political logic that preceded it: while the random selection of political offices was a common enough practice in Archaic Greece and the Classical Middle East (cf. Milano), the practice took on a radically new democratic significance in Athens during the 5th century BCE. The larger number of people included in the drawing pool, as well as the greater number of public offices that had to be filled by lottery, led to the technical invention of the lottery machine. In turn, the *kleroterion* helped to standardize the procedure while highlighting both its impartial and democratic aspects. It is interesting to note that the tools of sortition exhibit a certain degree of inertia: just as the original instruments continued to be used for several decades after the establishment of a radical democracy, so the gradual decline of the latter did not bring out about immediate disappearance of the *kleroterion*, which continued to be used well into the 2nd century BCE. The fact that archaeological remains of *kleroteria* were only identified in the 20th century cannot be the sole explanation for why the machine had no heir or equivalent in later societies, from Republican Rome until the 19th century. Being based, procedurally speaking, on rotating mandates, random selection, and a full citizen assembly, Athenian radical democracy has no historical parallel, even if we look at the Italian Communes (which entailed a certain degree of self-governance). In later experiments with sortition, the tools were first borrowed from the *instrumentum* of everyday, as had been the case during the Homeric era—they were drawn from craftsmen's tools or the implements employed in games of chance. The procedure was not refined much further, except in Switzerland during the 18th century (Chollet and Dupuis, 2018). And when random selection machines were reinvented in the modern era, in order to distribute lots amongst a much larger number of people, they were primarily used for lotteries. Their function would thus remain overwhelmingly limited to the sphere of entertainment (and indirectly, finance), with little technical transfer towards the world of politics until the end of the 20th century.

The turning point illustrated by the advent of the *kleroterion* nonetheless finds a parallel occurrence during the last third of the 20th century, with the transition from mechanical tools to digital ones. This second technical innovation—which has not, however, completely eliminated the use of older technologies—is analysed in depth by Dimitri Courant. To conduct opinion polls and also to create deliberative minipublics, sophisticated computer programs have been developed which allow for recruitment to occur from millions of potential participants. It may seem strange that digital technologies are used alongside artisanal selection methods, based on integer tables and various demographic constraints (age, geographic location, gender, etc.), to 'hand-pick' individuals. However, this baffling situation can be explained by the new function performed by random selection whenever it is used to establish a representative sample—or at least a fair cross-section of the people, to use the words of the United States Supreme Court.[5] The concept of the representative sample may be well-known to 21st-century readers, who have been bombarded with decades of statistics and opinion polls. However, it was only invented at the end of the 19th century, and it was only used to establish mini-publics during the 1970s. Consequently, before the invention of the representative sample, no relationship could have been established between random selection and descriptive representation, a situation where representatives are endowed with social characteristics that are similar to those they represent (Sintomer, 2020). For all of the experiments described in this volume, including those occurring at the beginning of the 19th century, the idea that random selection could create a sample that statistically resembles the people was not yet scientifically conceivable. It was only when this notion was theoretically and empirically verified that the use of digital tools took off, thanks to the growing presence of information technologies in everyday life. However, when the stated goal is to achieve a representative sample or at least a diverse cross section of the people, random selection can give way to the creation of quota-based samples, thanks to stratified random selection (generally used by pollsters) and quasi-artisanal methods which, as Jean-Michel Fourniau convincingly argues, help to 'correct' the vagaries of chance using a limited pool of people, especially when financial incentives are absent and such mechanisms lack real power.

If we set aside these technical innovations and the turning points they marked, the parameters that matter when we are examining the political significance of random selection methods are less the relatively minor variations in the instruments used than the fact that the procedures are performed by 'incorruptible' individuals in a public and ritualized manner. In fact, historical continuity can be observed with regard to the individuals in charge of performing sortition procedures. In Ancient Greece, randomly selected officers, or *archons,* were deemed to be honest, impartial, and above all accusations of wrongdoing. In other contexts, special civil servants were responsible for the extraction of the lots. Likewise, even if it was not systematically applied, the use of a child to draw lots was widespread in political contexts from the 13th to the 18th century, with the result that it can be seen as a paradigmatic representation of the action of drawing lots. Sortition, whose most famous depiction is likely the complex procedure used to elect the

---

5   *The Jury Selection and Service Act,* 28, United States Supreme Court, sections 1861–69.

Doge in Venice, developed from a base of pagan, Christianized and then secularized practices that used a child to draw lots in the context of both games and divination.

The different experiments in random selection analysed in this volume are all ritualized procedures. They present a number of functional similarities, despite being codified according to their specific historical contexts and being necessarily dependent on the equipment and the locations available. In this regard, it is notable that lottery drawings in Ming China were organized by the Ministry of Rites. The key element of these ceremonies lay in the performance of transparency and impartiality, which required a certain degree of public openness (note that it is only thanks to modern information technologies that random selection can now take place in a black box). The spaces where random selection takes place are part of the procedure's ritual staging, insofar as they define a specific trajectory for the candidates and those randomly selected, whether such spaces are public (as in Athens, where sortition took place in front of one of the ten entrances to the People's Court, or in the Theseion); closed (as in Venice, in the Grand Council chamber); or in small spaces (as in Geneva, where ballots were filled out 'between the two doors'). Random selection can also take place in courtrooms, to select jurors, or in political meeting halls, as in the case of the Mexican political party Morena. In most cases, random selection procedures are subject to a certain degree of performative staging, expressed by a contrast between inside and outside, the entrance and exit of candidates and elected officials (here again, however, some contemporary procedures are exceptions). No buildings seem to have ever been specifically devoted to random selection; in fact, many accounts tell us that sortition generally occurred in places which primarily served other purposes (including, for instance, to hold meetings of the bodies in question). When the performative staging of sortition was pushed to the extreme, as was the case in Lyon and Marseilles in the 17th century, the procedure was sometimes stripped of its original purpose, becoming another tool for the political elites to confiscate and then consolidate power. How sortition locations are configured depends in large part on the degree of transparency required with regard to both procedure and results—and hence, on the most effective way to prevent potential fraud. Regardless of whether a limited group of people or a large public is concerned, the key requirement is portraying impartiality so that the process and its results will be judged favourably by the group in question.

One procedure, different meanings

In the political realm, the highly self-reflexive society of Ancient Greece produced philosophical inquiries into the nature of random selection as early as the 4th century BCE, with the emergence of Plato and Aristotle's unprecedented reflections on the subject. Setting aside the wide variety of practices and historical contexts, should we conclude that there exists an essential meaning to the practice of random selection? While such a question may seem suspicious to historians, it should nevertheless be asked, especially when considering whether random selection is a more democratic mechanism than election. This argument comes from a reading (too cursory, as demonstrated by Buchstein, 2015) of Aristotle's famous statement 'it is thought to be democratic for the offices to be assigned by lot, for them to be elected oligarchic' (1932, IV, 9, 1294-b). This hypothesis, which may seem counter-intuitive to most citizens and political leaders today, was nonetheless revisited by Bernard Manin (1997) and has in fact played an important role with regard to the current popularity of random selection among sortition activists.

Nevertheless, this volume illustrates that this hypothesis (that random selection is inherently more democratic than election) does not withstand historical scrutiny. In reality, sortition has no more of an 'essential' meaning than election does; it never exists independently of a historical and political context. Moreover, democratic objectives seem to have only been at play in a minority of the cases studied in this volume. From a comparative sociological perspective drawing on the work of Max Weber, the most we can do is elaborate a handful of ideal-type reasons for using sortition, keeping in mind that their value is analytic and that historically they have been combined in various ways (Sintomer, 2020). In the first ideal-type scenario, which is particularly common in contexts where religion and politics do not represent two distinct spheres of activity, using random selection to attribute public offices reveals the will of the gods (or at least fate), which would other-wise remain unknown to human minds. Democratic objectives did play an important role in Athens, since random selection helped to expand the recruitment base and the number of citizens performing a public duty. Under the attenuated form of republican self-government, which opened up the process to a somewhat larger group of active citizens, the same democratic logic can also be found in the Italian Communes of the Middle Ages and the Renaissance. And in the 21st century, the democratic virtues of sortition have been touted in militant circles, as mentioned above. Random selection is often seen as ensuring equality, since each individual has an equal chance of being selected to perform a public duty. The logic governing the selection of jurors preserves this value of equality, despite being subtly different. In fact, jury selection is less concerned with rotating public offices amongst citizens who can adopt general laws that apply to the whole public, than it is with ensuring that every individual is capable of passing judgment on particular cases. The reasoning behind contemporary minipublics is different yet again. Minipublics are based on representative samples (or at least fair cross-sections) of the people and, in addition to this 'descriptive' value, their legitimacy is closely linked to the fact that they provide the locus for deliberations conducted in quasi-ideal situations — which was far from being the case in past experiments with sortition. While such mechanisms of democratic deliberation help to develop collective intelligence with regard to negotiation and decision-making skills, they also run the risk of turning the democratic deliberations of a small group of selected citizens against mass democracy, thus only ensuring the civic participation of the majority by proxy. Minipublics do not truly encourage access to deliberation for those who already engage in it the least, as they are neither spaces where public duties are attributed nor where decisions are made. In that regard, they help to redefine the relationship between random selection and democracy.

The studies contained in this volume nonetheless point to the special importance of impartiality. Although it would be overreaching to make impartiality the essential or exclusive characteristic of random selection in politics, it can nonetheless be observed across all the mechanisms analysed. Consequently, one can conclude that the use of sortition operates as a fundamental element of social cohesion, as it entrusts to an impartial mechanism the task to select without provoking conflict and power struggles that would threaten group unity. Throughout history, the unifying function of impartiality has been associated with the use of random selection, which assigns the non-human mechanism with the responsibility for managing any 'divisions' that may arise within a group seeking to divide and attribute goods and functions in a consensual manner (see Thomas Aquinas's category of *ars divisoria,* for example). Since time immemorial, the pacifying role of random selection has been recognized. In *The Iliad,* for instance, Zeus, Hades, and Poseidon receive their respective realms via sortition; random selection also acts as an urban planning tool and a social demiurge in Plato's ideal city. The use of sortition outside of politics is attested to during all eras and in a wide variety of domains, not just in religious contexts as its ritual dimension might otherwise suggest.

Embodying a sort of collective resolve to achieve a shared objective according to the rules established by the group (and accepted by the individuals), the ritualization and solemnity of sortition procedures ensure the legitimacy of their results and help individuals to feel like they belong to a common social, religious, civil, and/or political community. Sortition is supposed to transform political rivals into the civil servants. It attributes a social or political role to participation in a shared 'mission'.

Conclusion:
An Uncertain Fate for Random Selection

The renewed interest in random selection that we see today cannot be understood unless we also consider the deep-seated crisis of representative democracy in the 21st century. Free and fair elections held between political rivals had long been seen as the be-all and end-all of democracy. After the fall of the Berlin Wall, some intellectuals even proclaimed 'the end of history', arguing that this political event marked the culmination of humanity's ideological evolution. More than three decades later, the political landscape looks very different. The competitive party system in old democracies is suffering from a growing lack of legitimacy, while new authoritarian and proto-Fascist tendencies are popping up everywhere. On the other hand, China, which is now the second largest world power, seems to offer a functionally effective political model but can hardly be characterized as democratic, regardless of how one chooses to define the term.

Amidst this context, an increasing number of democratic innovators are turning to sortition, whether to create deliberative minipublics or to mitigate factional tensions within political parties (Sintomer, 2018). The idea of institutionalizing this new selection method, including for instance by using it to create a new legislative chamber, has gained popularity among activist circles (Van Reybrouck, 2016) and in academia (Gastil and Wright, 2018; 2019). Although it had fallen into disuse with the rise of representative government, sortition has now resurfaced in theories of deliberative democracy.

This volume looks at both the return to politics of random selection mechanisms and the major trends in the academic field studying this mode of designation. The chapters in this book were contributed by researchers whose objective was first and foremost to gain a deeper understanding of the instruments, practices, and theories of random selection throughout the ages. This volume consequently provides a vast overview of random selection in politics, looking at its material conditions, its staging, and the ideal frameworks that give it meaning.

Although the studies here mainly focus on the Western world, several forays are made into other regions, in support of a more systematic global analysis of sortition.

While some of the authors may also have militant objectives, this volume primarily seeks to make an interdisciplinary contribution to academic research. However, this contribution may likewise be useful to current social and political discussions of the crisis and renewal of democracy. This illustrates one of the main values of the social and human sciences: by meticulously analysing concepts, practices, and tools, such studies can enrich public discussion of political issues and help individuals and groups to make more informed decisions. Thanks to its impartiality — at a time when politics is everywhere suspected of only serving the particular interests of the professional politicians in power, random selection seems like a promising method to a growing number of actors. While its use in the radical democratic sense is far from being a historical constant, it is evident that this potential accounts for sortition's newfound popularity today. The good deliberation achieved by randomly selected minipublics is increasingly linked to decision-making processes in contexts that are typical of traditional representative democracy, but also of direct or participatory democracy. Recent experiments in randomly allocating the right to speak in the 'Occupy movements' in Greece and Spain illustrate that random selection can take place within the exercise of a radical deliberative democracy.

In the 21st century, the tools used for random selection hark back to two sometimes complementary and sometimes contradictory dimensions. On the one hand, sortition today continues to use some traditional implements, everyday objects, and mechanical lotteries. On the other, the advent of the digital age has marked a turning point in sortition procedures. For now, the two kinds of sortition tools co-exist and are deployed to varying ends. It can be argued that the use of the *kleroterion* died out more for political reasons than because the machine no longer met the technical requirements of the age. Digital sortition poses a similar political question: under what conditions can the undeniable technical efficiency of digital sortition be compatible, in the medium and long term, with the injunctions of impartiality and transparency expressed by the calls to reintroduce random selection into politics? To what extent will new practices need to be ritualized in order to ensure the procedure's legitimacy?

This volume hopes to shed light on these questions, by offering studies that have all the rigour of academia but may also be of interest to intellectuals and activists who advocate for the return of random selection, to practitioners who currently use sortition, and to the wider public interested in understanding how politics and citizen participation function today.

References

Aguilar Rivera, J. (2000) *En pos de la quimera. Reflexiones sobre el experimento constitucional atlántico*, Mexico: CIDE/FCE.

Aquinas, T. (1963), *Liber de sortibus ad dominum Iacobum de Tonengo* (1270-1271), Carey, P.B. (trans.) Dover: Dominican House of Philosophy.

Aquinas, T. (2007) *Summa Theologica*, 2007 [1269-1272], Fathers of the English Dominican Province (trans.), New York: Cosmo Classics.

Aristotle (1932) *Politics*, Cambridge: Harvard University Press.

Barnett, A. & Carty, P. (2008 [1998]) *The Athenian Solution*, Exeter: Imprint Academic.

Barber, B. (1997 [1984]) *Une démocratie forte*, Paris: Desclée de Brouwer.

Boegehold, A.L., Camp, J.M.K., Crosby, M. & Lang, M.L. (1995) *The Athenian Agora XXVIII, The Lawcourts at Athens, Sites, Buildings, Equipment, Procedure, and Testimonia*, Princeton, NJ: American School of Classical Studies.

Borlenghi, A., Chillet, Cl., Hollard, V., Lopez-Rabatel, L. & Moretti, J.-Ch. (eds.) (2019) *Voter dans l'Antiquité. Pratiques, lieux et finalités en Grèce, à Rome et en Gaule*, Lyon: Éditions de la Maison de l'Orient et de la Méditerranée.

Bourg, D. (ed.) (2011) *Pour une sixième République écologique*, Paris: Odile Jacob.

Buchstein, H. (2009) *Demokratie und Lotterie. Das Los als politisches Entscheidungsinstrument von der Antike bis zu EU*, Frankfurt: Campus.

Buchstein, H. (2015) Countering the 'Democracy Thesis' — Sortition in Ancient Greek political theory, *Redescriptions*, 18 (2), pp. 126-157.

Burnheim, J. (1985) *Is Democracy Possible?*, Cambridge: Polity Press.

Callenbach, E. & Phillips, M. (2008 [1985]) *A Citizen Legislature*, Exeter: Imprint Academic.

Callon, M. & Latour, B. (eds.) (1991) *La science telle qu'elle se fait. Anthologie de la sociologie des sciences de langue anglaise*, Paris: La Découverte.

Carson, L. & Martin, B. (1999) *Random Selection in Politics*, Westport, CT: Praeger Publishers.

Cicero (1923) *De Divinatione*, Cambridge, MA: Harvard University Press.

Chollet, A. & Fontaine, A. (eds.) (2018) *Expériences du tirage au sort en Suisse et en Europe (16e-21esiècles)/Erfahrungen des Losverfahrens in der*

Schweiz und in Europa (16.-21. Jahrhundert), Schriftenreihe der Bibliothek am Guisanplatz (BiG), n° 74.

Cordano, F. & Grottanelli, C. (eds.) (2001) *Sorteggio Pubblico e Cleromanzia dall'Antichità all'Età Moderna*, Milan: Edizioni Et.

Costa Delgado, J., Lopez-Rabatel, L., Moreno Pestaña, J.L. & Sintomer, Y. (eds.) (2017) Sorteo y democracia/Sortition and democracy, *Daimon: Revista Internacional de Filosofia*, thematic issue, Ediciones de la Universidad de Murcia, 72, September–December.

Courcelles, P. (1963) L'enfant et les 'sorts bibliques', *Vigiliae Christianae*, 7, Amsterdam: North Holland Publishing Company, pp. 194–220.

Crosby, N. (1975) *In Search of the Competent Citizen*, Working Paper, Plymouth, Center for New Democratic Processes.

Dahl, R.A. (1970) *After the Revolution? Authority in a Good Society*, New Haven, CT: Yale University Press.

Dartmann, Ch., Wassilowsky, G. & Weller, Th. (eds.) (2010) *Technik und Symbolik vormoderner Wahlverfahren (Beihefte der Historischen Zeitschrift)*, Munchen: Oldenbourg.

Delannoi, G. & Dowlen, O. (eds.) (2010) *Sortition: Theory and Practice*, Exeter: Imprint Academic.

Déloye, Y. & Ihl, O. (2008) *L'acte de vote*, Paris: Presses de Sciences Po.

Demont, P. (2003) Le Klèrôtérion ('machine' à tirer au sort) et la démocratie athénienne, *Bulletin Association G. Budé*, pp. 26–52.

Dienel, P. (1997) *Die Planungszelle*, Wiesbaden: Westdeutscher Verlag.

Dow, S. (1937) *Prytaneis: A Study of the Inscriptions Honoring the Athenian Councillors, Hesperia* Suppl. I., Athens: American School of Classical Studies.

Dowlen, O. (2008) *The Political Potential of Sortition: A Study of the Random Selection of Citizens for Public Offices*, Exeter: Imprint Academic.

Elster, J. (2013) *Securities Against Misrule: Juries, Assemblies, Elections*, Cambridge: Cambridge University Press.

Ehrenberg, V. (1923) Losung, in *Paulys Real-Enzyklopädie der klassischen Altertumswissenschaft.*

Fishkin, J. (1997) *The Voice of the People: Public Opinion & Democracy*, New Haven, CT: Yale University Press.

Fustel de Coulanges, N.-D. (1891) Recherches sur le tirage au sort appliqué à la nomination des archontes athéniens, in *Nouvelles recherches sur quelques problèmes d'histoire*, revues et complétées d'après les notes de l'auteur par Camille Jullian, Paris: Hachette, pp. 145–179.

Gastil, J. (2000) *By Popular Demand: Revitalizing Representative Democracy through Deliberative Elections*, London: University of California Press.

Gastil, J. & Wright, E.O. (eds.) (2018) Politics and Society, 46 (3), special issue, *Legislature by Lot: Transformative Designs for Deliberative Governance*.

Gastil, J. & Wright, E.O. (eds.) (2019) *Legislature by Lot: An Alternative Design for Deliberative Governance*, London: Verso.

Goodwin, B. (2005 [1992]) *Justice by Lottery*, New York: Harvester Wheatsheaf.

Grottanelli, C. (2001) La cléromancie ancienne et le dieu Hermès, in Cordano, F. & Grottanelli, C. (eds.) *Sorteggio Pubblico e Cleromanzia dall'Antichità all'Età Moderna*, Milan: Edizioni Et, pp. 155–196.

Hacking, I. (1990) *The Taming of Chance*, Cambridge: Cambridge University Press.

Hansen, M.H. (1999 [1991]) *Athenian Democracy in the Age of Demosthenes*, Oxford: Blackwell Publishers.

Hayat, S. (2019) La carrière militante de la référence à Bernard Manin dans les mouvements français pour le tirage au sort, in Lopez-Rabatel, L. & Sintomer, Y. (eds.) *Tirage au sort et démocratie. Histoire, instruments, théories, Participations*, Special issue, 2019, pp. 437–452.

Headlam, J.W. (1891) *Election by lot in Athens*, Cambridge: Cambridge University Press, reprint 1931.

Hurlet, F. (2006) *Le proconsul et le prince d'Auguste à Dioclétien*, Bordeaux: Ausonius Editions.

Keller, H. (2015) Electoral systems and conceptions of community in Italian Communes (12th–14th centuries), *Revue française de science politique*, English edition, November 2015.

Lopez-Rabatel, L. (2011) *Klêrôtèria. Le tirage au sort dans le monde grec antique. Machines, institutions, usages*, doctoral dissertation in Ancient languages, history and civilization languages, Université Lumière Lyon 2.

Manin, B. (1997) *Principles of Representative Government*, Cambridge: Cambridge University Press.

Meier, Ch. (1956) Praerogativa Centuria, in *Paulys Real-Enzyklopädie der klassischen Altertumswissenschaft*, Supplementband VIII, Munich, pp. 569–598.

Najemy, J.N. (1982) *Corporatism and Consensus in Florentine Electoral Politics, 1280–1400*, Chapel Hill, NC: University of North Carolina Press.

Nicolet, C. (1976) *Le métier de citoyen dans la Rome républicaine*, Paris: Seuil.

Nicolet, C. & Beschaouch, A. (1991) Nouvelles observations sur la 'Mosaïque des chevaux' et son édifice à Carthage, in *Comptes rendus des séances de l'Académie des Inscriptions et Belles-Lettres*, 135 (3), pp. 471–507.

Röcke, A. (2005) *Losverfahren und Demokratie. Historische und demokratietheoretische Perspektiven*, Munster: LIT.

Ruffini, E. (1977) Sistemi di deliberazione collettiva nel medioevo italiano, in *La ragione dei più. Ricerche sulla storia del principio magoritario*, Bologna: Il Mulino.

Schmitter, P.C. & Trechsel, A.H. (eds.) (2004) *The Future of Democracy in Europe*, A Green Paper for the Council of Europe.

Schneider, R. & Zimmermann, H. (eds.) (1990) *Wahlen und Wählen im Mittelalter*, Sigmaringen: Jan Thorbecke.

Sintomer, Y. (2007) *Le pouvoir au peuple. Jurys citoyens, tirage au sort et démocratie participative*, Paris: La Découverte.

Sintomer, Y. (2011) *Petite histoire de l'expérimentation démocratique. Tirage au sort et politique d'Athènes à nos jours*, Paris: La Découverte.

Sintomer, Y. (2018) From deliberative to radical democracy? Sortition and politics in the 21st century, *Politics and Society*, 46 (3), pp. 337–357.

Sintomer, Y. (2020) *Between Radical and Deliberative Democracy: Random Selection in Politics from Athens to Contemporary Experiments*, Cambridge: Cambridge University Press.

Staveley, E.S. (1972) *Greek and Roman Voting and Elections*, London: Thames and Hudson.

Stewart, R. (1998) *Public Office in Early Rome: Ritual Procedure and Political Practice*, Ann Arbor, MI: Michigan University Press.

Sutherland, K. (2008) *A People's Parliament*, Exeter: Imprint Academic.

Tanzini, L. (2014) *A consiglio. La vita politica nell'Italia dei comuni*, Bari: Laterza.

Taylor, L.R. (1966) *Roman Voting Assemblies from the Hannibalic War to the Dictatorship of Caesar*, Ann Harbor, MI: University of Michigan Press.

Van Reybrouck, D. (2016) *Against Elections: The Case for Democracy*, New York: Penguin Random House.

Wang, S. (2018) *Sortition, Democracy and Republic: From Athens to Venice* (in Chinese), Beijing: CITIC Press.

Will, P.-E. (2002) Creation, conflict, and routinization: The appointment of officials by drawing lots, 1594–1700, in Santangelo, P. (ed.) *Ming Quing Yanjiu*, Naples: Università degli Studi di Napoli 'L'Orientale'.

Part I:
Ancient Worlds

Lucio Milano

Destiny, the Drawing of Lots, and Divine Will in Ancient Near Eastern Societies

Translated by Alta L. Price

From there we departed, and came upon a deep ditch, utterly
despoiled, emptied, and annihilated.
There, nothing could be heard but cries and screams.
There lurked lions and leopards,
and speckled scorpions.
The Man said to me: 'This is called the Land of Forgetting,
or Lowly Abyss,
and it is the realm of gamblers, dice throwers,
those who have said "God cannot see."
Their blood deserves to be spilled,
hence the Lord's hand strikes them
in both body and soul
and then, because they turned back toward Heaven as if it were a gamble
and blessed God with mouth and heart
when their plans turned out to be failures:
hence they measure their actions in their own bosoms
and shall receive no pity in the Last Judgment.'
—Immanuel of Rome, *Ha-Tofet ve-ha-Eden* (109–114)

While gathering material for this presentation I came across an intriguing 17th-century text.[1] It only marginally touches upon my topic, but seemed like a good way to spark reflection on the meaning (perhaps taken for granted by many) often attributed to our ideology of 'fate' or 'destiny' in both historical and anthropological terms, starting

---

[1] This essay is drawn from a conference paper, hence both author and editors have chosen to leave its conversational tone intact. (This English title was chosen for fluidity, and could just as accurately have been rendered as 'Fate, Sortition, and Divine Will in Ancient Near Eastern Societies' — trans.)

with the cultural parameters expressed in biblical and above all rabbinical tradition.[2] The text in question is *Chayye Yehuda*, the Hebrew-language autobiography written by Leon of Modena (or Leon Modena of Venice, the name he himself preferred), an eminent Venetian rabbi whose life spanned from the late 16th century to the mid-17th century (1571–1648).[3] His character was complex and his works prolific (Adelmann, 1985): he not only wrote in Hebrew, but also published several successful books in Italian (including a history of Jewish rituals and a Hebrew–Italian dictionary for translators titled *Galut Yehuda*); he divided his time between studying and gambling—as he frequently mentions in his autobiography, he developed an almost uncontrollable addiction to the latter, especially during hard times. In the embittered existential inventory of his life, gambling came to represent 'his sin', Yehuda's sin: a vice encouraged by Satan, and perhaps connected to astral configurations; in any case, it resulted in actual, real-world ruin as he lost one of his daughters' intended dowries and nearly his entire savings.

Gambling and Divine Will:
Preliminary Reflections

But, beyond these admittedly intriguing biographical details, the point I would like to highlight here is that Leon of Modena—author of refined exegeses, a manual of magical formulas, and a collection of rabbinical maxims—also, in his youth, wrote an operetta about gambling. Titled *Sur me-Ra* ('Far from Evil'), it was published in Venice in 1595 and must have been a success, as it was then reissued in Prague in 1615, in Leiden in 1656, and subsequently translated into Latin and German. It is a dialogue between two characters, Eldad and Medad, who carry out a classic talmudic debate to develop several arguments both in favour of and against gambling—a pursuit that ultimately forces human beings to squarely face the ups and downs of life and, in a certain sense, *reveals* people to themselves, confronting them with God's will.

This viewpoint strikes me as emblematic of a specific, decidedly pre-modern way of seeing nature, and the theoretical foundations of *destiny* or *fate*, on the eve of the major scientific revolution that was about to arrive with the advent of calculated probability in the mid-17th

---

2   I would like to thank Giovanni Levi for having brought Leon Modena's auto-biography to my attention, and for having discussed the author's peculiar personality with me.

3   See Cohen (1988), which includes an extensive bibliography.

century (Hald, 1990). Whereas the works of many 17th-century mathe-maticians focused primarily on the algebraic aspects of the problem (e.g. the *Liber de Ludo Aleae* by Gerolamo Cardano, another avid gambler),[4] Leon of Modena's operetta was still steeped in moral—*qualitative* rather than *quantitative*—judgment. This viewpoint was typical of pre-modern epistemological thought, which did not under-estimate the *practical* mechanisms of action guided by a roll of the dice but, above all else (and in significantly dialogical and dialectical ways), emphasized the philosophical implications of the decision to make gambling a way of life. This same judgment had shaped the work of the late 13th-century Jewish poet Immanuel of Rome (Manoello Romano), whose Dantesque poem placed dice-rolling gamblers in hell (*tofet*), in a ditch of lions, leopards, and scorpions.[5]

Bad luck, dark destiny, an awareness of sin, and the manifestation of divine will are recurring themes in Modena's autobiography (e.g. 'In Kislev 5374 I returned to my bad old ways, gambling, and from then on I found myself surrounded solely by Evil'); and I believe that his por-trayal of several other events in his own life are heavily tinged by the same mental outlook. Two examples will suffice. First, the relationship between luck, destiny, and magic. Leon himself writes of the mis-fortune that occurred as a result of his own alchemical experiments: having set up a laboratory with one of his sons in order to obtain ten times an amount of silver starting with an alloy of silver and lead, the fumes ended up killing his son, casting Leon into deep distress and another bout of gambling, which became a self-castigation of sorts.[6] Indeed, gambling follows the same binary logic that underlies many magical procedures, catalysing divine action and repeatedly placing the human practitioner at a juncture. Nevertheless, unlike the exploration

---

[4] We do not know whether Leon of Modena was familiar with Cardano's work, which was posthumously published in 1663 but presumably written around 1565 and used Niccolò Tartaglia's methods for solving cubic equations. In any case, Cardano's text mirrors a field of research that could not have been entirely unknown to Modena—especially since his death in 1648 occurred well after Galileo wrote *Sopra le scoperte dei dadi* ('A Discovery Concerning Dice'), generally dated to the period between 1613 and 1623 (despite first being published in 1718).

[5] Immanuel of Rome's *Ha-Tofet ve-ha-Eden* ('Inferno and Paradise'), the last (28a) of his *maḥberot* or 'conversations', was recently translated into Italian by E. Weiss Levi: see Immanuello Romano, edited by G. Battistoni (2000). The passage on gamblers, cited at the beginning of this chapter, appears on lines 109–115 of the Italian transla-tion (page 165 of the Hebrew text).

[6] Re. this event and the interest in alchemy, as well as talmudic study, that it sparked over the next three generations of the Modena family, see Scholem (2006).

of magic, 'indulgence' in gambling is necessarily conditioned by moral condemnation, negative judgment, and a sense of guilt.

Second, the relationship between fate and dreams, a connection that is only indirectly touched upon in Modena's autobiography but is unique and notable because the bad luck brought on by gambling is often followed by a series of premonition-laden dreams. Here, too, the connection is significant because it points toward an interdependence between two only apparently spurious situations, ultimately linked by the fact that both are dominated by attempts to forecast the future — namely, gambling (through the chance roll of the dice) and divination (through dream interpretation). The collection of magical formulas Modena published — and in which, as previously mentioned, he appears to have been particularly invested — also reflects a 'technical' conception of such processes, which couldn't be farther from a casual or episodic conception of either gambling or divination.[7]

Yaḥalu's Cube

Leon Modena's case, as mentioned earlier, is emblematic — not so much of a *reflection* on the concept of 'fate' or 'luck' (which has, as we well know, illustrious antecedents, starting with Plato and Aristotle), but certainly of a practice that quite directly links 'fate' and 'luck' (in the sense of gaming and gambling) and divine judgment, according to a perspective that was widespread, albeit far from unequivocal, in the Ancient World. And since my topic today centres on destiny, the drawing of lots, and divine will in Ancient Near Eastern societies, I hope to prove that in this context, as well, the connection between fate and divine manifestation is strong, although this particular take on it is culturally structured. I shall, naturally, limit my examples to just a few, drawn from the Ancient Mesopotamian, Jewish, and Hittite worlds.

A.L. Oppenheim, one of the Assyriologists most attuned to anthropological perspectives within the study of Ancient Sumerian-Akkadian civilization, has been one of the few to examine sortition in Mesopotamia; and his work has focused, not coincidentally, on divination. In his view, the problem could be distilled in the following, rather

---

[7] The fact that Leon Modena chose a Jewish nanny who was also an expert in natural medicine to care for one of his sons is also interesting. Such an expertise — amid the rapid passage from empirical approaches based on combinations of medicine and magic to a more generalized interest in chemistry and medicine — was common in many early 17th-century Jewish communities (and also evident in the large number of Jewish medical students enrolled at the University of Padua): see Sigmund (1996).

minimalist terms, which I'll quote directly from a passage in his *Ancient Mesopotamia*:

> Of the three operational practices mentioned, the throwing of lots, the observation of oil in water (lecanomancy), and the observation of smoke from incense (libanomancy), the first had no cultic status in Mesopotamia. We know from legal documents that in the Old Babylonian period and in Susa lots were used to assign the shares of an estate to the sons. We learn from later documents that shares of temple income were originally distributed by lot to certain officials of the sanctuary. In these instances the throwing of lots — marked sticks of wood — was to establish a sequence among persons of equal status that would be acceptable, as divinely ordained, to all participants. This is also the case with the Assyrian custom used to select the official who was to give his name to the new year by means of clay dice. The method of casting lots, however, is not mentioned in the compendia as a means of obtaining knowledge of the future. One exception comes from an isolated text from Assur, which speaks of the use of two stone lots, apparently furnishing positive or negative answers. This indicates that the throwing of stone lots was used in Mesopotamia, but rarely and probably on an unofficial level. There is more evidence from Boghazkeui. A small group of omen texts, written characteristically enough in Hittite, speak of divination by means of lots (written KIN, Hittite reading and meaning unknown). The Hittite and the Assyrian evidence suggest the possibility of a substratum influence in this type of divination; it is possible that the local practices of the northwestern periphery succeeded in reaching the level of literature in these isolated instances. (Oppenheim, 1977, pp. 208–209)

Selection of the eponym in Assyria, *limmu*[8] — the term might derive from the root *lwy*, 'follow one another (in an official role)',[9] or be related to the term for 'thousand', *līmu*, which, just as in Hebrew and Ugaritic (*lim*) would indicate a 'group of people' and, by extension, 'a thousand, leader of a thousand' (del Olmo Lete and Sanmartin, 2003, under *lim* [I]) — is the most interesting case Oppenheim cites as an example of the practice of sortition, and is also the one that brings us closest to the issue of *public sortition* we're dealing with in this seminar. However, contrary to his analysis, this is in no way whatsoever a sortition carried out among subjects of equal status, comparable to the type of sortition used to divvy up inheritances (see §3), but rather a type of sortition whose results had to correspond, at least from a certain period onward, to specific, predetermined criteria. In fact, under some of the rulers, the sequence of eponyms wasn't left to chance, and was

---

8 Cf. CAD L, 194ff; Ahw 554, see *limu(m)* I, *limmu*.
9 Cf. Akkadian *lawûm*, *lamû* II (AHw 541; CAD L, 69ff) and the related noun — Hebrew *lwh*, Aramaic *lwy*, Ugaritic *lwn(y)*.

instead (pre)set, at least for the first few years—and then in later years the selection of a governor from one province as opposed to another as eponym was evidently subject to criteria shaped by political opportunity or convenience. The issue of sortition when applied to eponym selection is therefore more complex than it might initially seem.

But let's stick to logical order, and before all else have a look at how the sortition and alternation of the *limmu* are documented.

There are several well-documented chronicles and lists of these eponyms and their set sequence—albeit rife with interruptions—dating back to the Old Assyrian period (ca. 1850 BC). Documentation of the circumstances and ways in which they were nominated are, on the other hand, extremely rare. Of the few to be found, one is particularly valuable: a clay cube (2.8 × 2.7 cm) of unknown provenance and now part of the Yale Babylonian Collection (YBC 7058), with an inscription running horizontally along four of its sides. It was published by F.J. Stephens in 1937 (YOS 9, plates XXVII, XLV, no. 73). The inscription's content, as more recently reconsidered by A. Millard (1994, pp. 7-9; previously in Michel, 1949, pp. 261-264)—reads as follows:

I.	*aš-šur bēlu rab[û]*	O Aššur, great lord!
	^{d}*adad bēlu rabû*	O Adad, great lord!
	pu-ú-ru	(This is) the lot
	šá ^{m}*ia-ḫa-li*	of Yaḫalu,
	[m]asenni rabî	the great chamberlain
II.	*šá* ^{md}*šùl-*	of Shal-
	ma-nu-ašarēd	maneser,
	šar₄ ^{mat}*aš-šur*	king of Assyria,
	^{amēl}*šá-kìn*	the governor of
	^{āl}*kip-šu-ni*	Kipshuni,
	^{mat}*qu-me-[n]I*	of Qumeni,
III.	^{mat}*me-eḫ-ra-ni*	Mehrani,
	^{mat}*ú-q[i]*	Uqi,
	^{ša}*de-ri-ni[m]*	the Cedar Mountain
	ráb ka-a-ri	customs officer.
	ina li-mì-šú	In his eponymate,
	pu-ri- šú	his lot,
IV.	*ebūr* ^{mat}*aš-šur*	may the crops of Assyria
	lišir ^{lid}*lidmiq*	grow well and soundly.
	ina pāni aš-šur	Before Aššur
	^{d}*adad*	and Adad
	pu-ur-šu	may his lot
	li-l[i]-a	come up (*or* fall out).

Since we don't know where the cube came from—be it from a temple, a tomb, a building either public or private—it's impossible to say whether it was actually used for the sortition of the *limmu*, or was instead considered a votive or propitiatory object, inscribed to record or foretell the actual election of Yaḫalu. What is certain, however, is that according to the Canon of Eponyms, Yaḫalu, the governor of Kipshuni, in the upper Tigris region, served three terms as eponym under Shalmaneser III's reign: in 833, 824, and 821 BC (Millard, 1994, p. 124). Whether this cube was used to actively select the leader or was created with a celebratory inscription after the fact (I am inclined to believe the latter), it is in any case plausible that the sortition was carried out by placing one or more cubes or dice[10] with the names of each candidate and a well-wishing phrase of the sort we see on Yaḫalu's cube into a container. The verb *elû*, used in the last line to indicate how the lot was to be drawn, literally means 'to go (come) up', from which one could conclude that such cubes or 'lots' (*pūru*) were probably '(taken) up',[11] or drawn directly from the container, rather than rolled or tossed.[12]

Pūru, the 'Lot' of the Assyrian Eponym

The sortition of the eponym generally isn't recorded in the narrative texts, with the exception of two passages from the Annals of Shalmaneser III. In particular, the inscription of the Black Obelisk (Schramm, 1973, pp. 79–81) records the circumstances as follows:

> *ina 31 palêya šanûtēšu pūru īna pān Aššur Adad akururu*
>
> 'in the thirty-first year of my reign (*palû*) I cast the lots (*pūru akuru*) for the second time before Aššur and Adad.'[13]

In this case, the verb used to refer to the 'lots' or dice is not *elû*, but *karāru*, 'to lay down, toss', which—not having been documented elsewhere in association with *pūru*—has generally been translated with the generic 'to cast (the lot)'.[14] Since the king became eponym in the second

---

10   In cases where multiple eponyms were to be selected at one time, see below.

11   Another recent reading suggests *li-l[a]-a, lilâ*, with the contraction in the last syllable, *-ia*, becoming *-â* (Yamada, 2000, p. 324).

12   The hypothesis that they were rolled or tossed was proposed by Hallo (1983, p. 20), which reads the last line as *li-[da]-a, liddâ*, 'may it fall', followed by Finkel and Reade (1995, p. 167).

13   Ann. 13, II. 174ff. This account is nearly identical to that of the statue of Shalmaneser III in Nimrud (Ann. 14, II. 320ff): cf. A.K. Grayson, *RIMA* 3 (A.O. 102.16), wherein the previous eponymate is not referred to. On the historical implications of this discrepancy, cf. Yamada (2000, pp. 333–334).

14   Cf. CAD K, 209a.

year of his reign, the first and second eponymate of Shalmaneser III would essentially correspond to the second and thirty-second years of his reign (857 and 827).

The Annals' formulation, however, remains quite problematic, both in terms of its interpretation as well as its historical and chronological implications. By underlining the possibility that the Assyrian king returned to the role of eponym after thirty years' rule—a period that could plausibly correspond to a generational cycle—A.R. Millard suggested that this practice dated all the way back to the era of Tiglath-pileser II, and that clues of its continuation could even be found in the era of Ashurbanipal (Millard, 1994, p. 14). This point of view has recently been challenged by Sh. Yamada and E. Weissert,[15] who maintain that the thirty-first eponymate referred to on the Black Obelisk is actually tied to the thirty-third year of Shalmaneser III's reign (826) and that the eponym in question isn't the king, but rather the *turtānu* ('commander-in-chief') Dayyān-Aššur, who—as we know from the *Eponym Canon*—served two terms as eponym (Millard, 1994, pp. 27 and 30). Furthermore, the meaning of *pūru karāru* is not 'to cast the lot', but rather 'to place (= dedicate) the lot (before god)', as is shown by the use of *karāru* in other ritual contexts.[16]

According to Yamada and Weissert, the inscription on the Black Obelisk is a celebratory text, commissioned by Dayyān-Aššur to commemorate himself, in which the scribe or stone carver must have interpolated the ruler's declarations as declarations of Dayyān-Aššur. The first phrase ('in the thirty-first year of my eponymate') would be attributed to the ruler, while the second ('I placed the lots for the second time before Aššur and Adad') would be attributed to Dayyān-Aššur. And those would be followed by another declaration by the ruler:

> At the time, when I was in the city of Kalḫu, I gave orders and sent Dayyān-Aššur, commander-in-chief (*turtānu*), wise leader of my army, to the head of my army and encampment. He went to the cities of Data, the man of Hubushkia.

---

15 Cf. Yamada (2000, pp. 333–334, Appendix B, in collaboration with E. Weissert, 'The Commemoration of Dayyan-Ashur's Second Eponymate in the Black Obelisk and the Calah Statue').

16 E.g. UZU.KA.IZI *labakte ina* IGI EN *ikarrarūni* 'roasted, marinated meat they placed before Bel' (A. Livingstone, SAA 3, no. 35, I, 26). Other examples involve the dedication of salt, or a goblet of wine or beer: cf. CAD K, 208ff, under *karāru* 1 and 2.

The later report of this military campaign was ultimately given by Dayyān-Aššur in the first person: 'I received his tribute. I went to Zapparia, a walled city in the land of Muṣaṣir, etc...'

The Assyrian *turtānu*, who had already served a term as eponym in 853, would then have the obelisk placed in the main square of Nimrud, probably along with a statue of himself.[17]

Yamada and Weissert's reconstruction strikes me as philologically and etymologically convincing, and carries with it two significant consequences for our investigation. If placed in relation to Yaḫalu's 'cube', above all else it reinforces the interpretation of the object as a votive gift with a celebratory inscription. But there's more: if, in fact, the inscription of the eponym's 'fate' in the Annals of Shalmaneser III refers not to the sovereign, but to one of his highest officers, one could surmise that, unlike the selection of a sovereign's eponymate, the selection of the eponym's officer needed an explicit 'recognition' from the gods. The invocations of Aššur and Adad (the national god of Assyria and the god of storms—but also of prosperity and abundance —respectively), found both in the cube's inscription as well as in the text of the Annals, is in this respect highly significant and must not be underestimated.

It has been shown that the drawing of the eponyms was carried out a year after the new sovereign took the throne, as he himself fulfilled the role of eponym during the first year;[18] and this system is known to have changed over time, both in terms of the sovereign's eponymate— which, between Shalmaneser III and Shalmaneser V, moved from the first to the second year of rule[19]—and the succession of official eponyms. But where did this ceremony take place, and how many of the following eponyms were drawn on that single occasion? Millard mentions the possibility that the drawing took place during the New Year's celebrations (*akītu*)—so it is apt to note that the Jewish celebration of Purim (see below) has the same timing—but we might also add that, most likely, it took place in Assur, the religious capital of the

---

[17] As Yamada and Weissert suggest (2000, p. 333, no. 30), this was likely the statue discovered and published by Gadd (1936, pl. 8, no. 2).

[18] This seems to have been the case during the period that spanned from Tiglath-pileser I to Aššur-dan II (ca. 1186–932 BC), for which there is a highly incomplete list of eponyms documented in the poorly preserved manuscript A7 (cf. Millard, 1994, pp. 7–8, 18).

[19] This approach was explicitly documented in the *Canon of Eponyms* for Tiglath-pileser III, who was said to have taken the throne during the eponymate of Nabu-belu-usur, whose first year of rule was during the eponymate of Bel-dan, and was eponym during the second year of rule (in 743).

Assyrian kingdom. In the case of Shalmaneser III, who lived in Kalḫu/Nimrud, the king would have gone to Assur, and probably to the temple of Assur where, under the protection of the eponymous god, the sortition of one or a series of eponyms destined to determine the following years of leadership took place. The hypothesis that the institution of the *limmu* was originally connected to the upkeep of the sanctuary and the cult of the divine Assur is nothing new, either, as A. Poebel had suggested the possibility as early as the 1940s.[20]

We know the list of Assyrian eponyms, whose names were often used by scribes to date letters and legal documents, through two main sources: the Canon, which was reconstructed through various lists and chronicles, and covers the period from 910 to 649 BC;[21] and through individual records (e.g. the eponyms of the paleo- and middle-Assyrian periods[22]) or chronicles from specific periods (such as those of the eponyms of the reign of Šamši-Adad I found in Mari and Tell Leilan; Whiting, 1990, pp. 167–218). Although little can be said about the criteria determining the sequence of eponyms in post-canonical periods, the canonical list, beginning with Shalmaneser III, displays a coherent system of succession: as previously noted, the king comes first, followed by the army commander (*turtānu*), and — in variable order — the chief cupbearer (*rab šāqê*), palace herald (*nāgir ekalli*), and treasurer (*masennu*). These were then followed by the provincial governors, whom it is hard to believe would have been in a purely chance order — it is more likely that they respected a hierarchy determined by political events and changes in the organizational structure of the empire.

The nomination of these imperial officials to the eponymate must have taken such differences into consideration. The system of drawing lots might have become necessary at a certain point (both Yaḫalu's 'cube' and references in the Annals date back to the period of Shalmaneser III) and the drawing itself may have been considered 'guided' — not by people, of course, but by the righteous will of the gods (Aššur and Adad) under whose auspices it was carried out.[23] The

---

20 Cf. JNES I (1942), 280.
21 For the reconstruction of the list, see Millard (1994, pp. 17–54).
22 Cf., for the former, Larsen (1976, pp. 192–223) and Veenhof (1985, pp. 191–218); for the latter, Saporetti (1979).
23 The hypothesis that the system for selecting the eponyms was predetermined was first suggested by Forrer (1920), and more recently supported by Finkel and Reade (1995, p. 170): 'Was there still an element of chance in the choice? Status and power certainly decided the identity of many eponyms, possibly all of them. The number of visible regularities in the sequence increases through different reigns from

pūru of the eponym allowed for a *divine recognition* of the governor – or a limited number of governors – who were in fact *predestined* to fulfil the role.

Although the sortition of the eponym is not directly related to cleromancy, there are doubtless ties between this particular institution and divinatory practices, as evidenced by the fact that the gods are involved in providing implicit approval for the outcome of the selection. Divination by sortition is broadly documented in Mesopotamia and must have influenced the institutional practices of sortition. For example, the two aforementioned texts discovered in Assur and quoted by Oppenheim, in which mention is made of the use of stone dice that give their roller a negative or positive response.[24] And I do not believe, as Oppenheim claims, that this was a rare and unofficial use (even if it is, admittedly, true that the Babylonian manuals on divination do not mention cleromancy). Indeed, a passage of the *Lugal-e*, a Sumerian poem that recounts the actions of the god Ninurta, actually presumes a widespread knowledge of the use of stone dice in divination. In the section of the poem that lists various blessings and curses for such stones, the na-stone – the die used to decide the fate of the battle – is cursed:[25]

> My King turned to the na stone.
> He [scraped the surface of[26]] the *na* stone.
> Ninurta son of Enlil cursed it:
> 'Stone, since you said, "If only it had been me";
> *na* stones, since you dared chance against [giš-šub = *isqu*] my privileges
> [to take them for your own[27]] –
> lie down there, you, to be worked on like a pig.

Shalmaneser III on. By the time of Tiglath-pileser III, it was possible to determine which official would probably be eponym many years in advance. The formal decision was presumably taken by the king, relying on precedent and other considerations...' According to the authors, Yaḫalu's cube has nothing to do with a royal sortition: 'In our view it was made as the one lot that could qualify in a formal election, distantly recalling an older genuine lottery. As such it would have been used in an appropriate ceremony, which demonstrated divine approbation of the predetermined choice...' The inscription on the cube would, therefore, be 'an invocation suitable for recitation at the telling moment, just before the eponymate of Yaḫalu began'.

24 LKA 137 and 138: see J. Nougayrol, in OLZ 51 (1956), 41.
25 Cf. van Dijk (1983, II. pp. 479–486), which includes a (slightly modified) translation.
26 Cf. Bottéro and Kramer (1989, p. 359).
27 na₄-na me-ǧá (/ mè-mu) ǧiš ba-e-šub-bu-za-na-gim (/ ǧiš-šub-šu[b...]). The Akkadian text reads: NA₄[11] *ša ana ta-ḫa-zi-ya is-qa t[a-ad-du]-ú*, therefore cf. CAD I, 199b: 'you, na-stone, who have been cast as a lot (to determine the outcome of) the battle against me.'

Be discarded, be used for nothing, end up by being reduced to tiny fragments [as plaster?]. He who knows you shall reduce you to liquid" [as a stucco].'

Isqu, the 'Part' Drawn from Among Equals

In the Akkadian version of the passage quoted above, 'fate' or 'lots' are not defined as *pūru*, but as *isqu* (GIŠ.ŠUB.BA), which is the term generally used to indicate not only the procedure of sortition, but also the 'part' or 'quota' drawn and, in some cases, the 'prebend'; *pūru*, on the other hand, designates the eponym's 'fate' or 'lot', and is rarely used outside this specific context (a few records indicate its use regarding the division of fields in the neo-Assyrian period, and silver in the Old Assyrian period).

A quick consultation of the *Chicago Assyrian Dictionary* (CAD) provides sufficient proof that the use of *isqu* (along with the verbs *leqû*, *nadû*, *zâzu*, or *maqātu*) is common in legal contexts dealing with the division or assignment of property and real estate. There are well-established examples from the Old Babylonian period such as: 'The division was decided by mutual agreement (*ina mitgurtišunu*), by drawing lots (*isqam iddûma*)'; 'The sons of so-and-so took (such-and-such parts) by mutual agreement by drawing lots (*ina mitgurtišunu… ina isqim ilqû*)';[28] '(Having established the quantity of goods) divide it in two, and give one part to one man, the other to the other man, according to the lots drawn (*ana šēna zūzama ina isqim ana* PN *u* PN₂ *idna*)'; or, as in a text from Susa, 'We have received (our parts) as they were divided, and we are satisfied by what our fathers decided by drawing lots… and we adhered to what our fathers set forth by drawing lots (*ša abbūni… isqāti iddûma u nīnu warki isqāti ša abbūni iddûšu nittalak kīma zīzānuma zīzānu*);[29] etc.

In the same way it pertains to the human realm, sortition pertains to the divine realm as well, as seen in the opening poem of Atraḫasis. The gods, having taken the container of dice, 'drew lots and went on to divide' (*isqam iddû ilū izzūzu*) the realms of heaven, earth, and the zone

---

28   Cf. CAD I, 198b–199a, entry 1.

29   Cf. CAD I, 199a, entry 1. For a synonym of *isqu* in a similar context, cf. the entry for *kipputtātu* (CAD K, 400; Ahw, 483a), perhaps connected to *kippatu*, 'circle, ring', *kapāpu*, 'bend over, kneel', which appears repeatedly in another text from Susa (MDP 22, 21 line 2, 14): 'before these eleven witnesses they took (their parts) by drawing lots and *counting in a circle*(?)', *ina isqi u kipputtāti*.

between them among Anu, Ellil, and Enki.[30] And it is precisely this nexus between divine action and its effects on human beings' happenstance—expressed through the gods' many epithets—that sometimes shifts the meaning of *isqu* from 'fate' as a worldly notion to 'destiny' as a divine determination. In these instances, the god might appear as *mussiq / mu'addu / mukīn isqête*, 'he who assigns destinies', or *muza' iz isqête*, 'he who distributes fates'.[31]

Assyrian royal inscriptions show that it is usually the king whose 'destiny' (*isqu*) is predetermined by the gods, but there is no shortage of broader uses of the term (as in the scholastic saying 'To be a scribe is a good destiny', *isiq damāqi*[32]), which can also end up taking on broader knowledge-related meanings (e.g. 'Accept your destiny and make your mother happy! Run fast and make your god happy'; Alster, 1997, pp. 29, 1,145).

As previously mentioned, however, *isqu* can also refer to the goods divided up by sortition: the inherited 'part' (of a field or other real estate), or simply one part of a whole, and by extension a type of income, expenditure, or revenue—such as, to take an example from the neo- and late-Babylonian period, the offerings set aside for the gods or prebends assigned to temple officials for their own sustenance. In this case, the *isqu* can refer to sources of nourishment including portions of sacrificial meat or libations.

As for our specific interests here, the *isqu*, the 'portion', refers—at least in the original sense—to an egalitarian criterion for the division of goods, even if, over time, this meaning expanded to include any part. This usage comes, as we shall soon see, from the same semantic field as the Hebrew term *gôral*, which, like the Akkadian *isqu*, refers to sortition as applied to an inheritance, while at the same time carrying strong religious implications.

Purim, 'Lots' in the *Book of Esther*

This is the perfect time to have a look back at the other Akkadian term for 'lots', *pūru*, one example of which, as we've seen, is found in the inscription on Yaḫalu's cube. Indeed, this term, which is relatively well-documented in Akkadian, also appears in the Hebrew bible, but just

---

[30] *Atraḫasis*, I, 11–16. Dalley (1989, p. 36, no. 4). This passage naturally brings to mind a comparison with the division of the cosmos among Zeus, Poseidon, and Hades as described in the *Iliad* XV, 187–193; cf. the commentary by W. Bukert (1983, p. 53).

[31] Re. the notion of the gods' 'establishing fate, destiny', cf. *šimta / šimāti šâmu* and their related usages.

[32] Cf. the documentation provided in CAD I, 201, entry 3.

once—in the *megillah* of Esther, which includes an account of how the festival of Purim came to be. The connection between the ceremony for drawing lots to determine the Assyrian eponym and the festival of Purim has been repeatedly emphasized, beginning with the fact that both events took place in the month of Addaru, which immediately preceded Nisannu, which marked the start of the new year.[33]

The tale of Esther takes place in the Persian city of Susa, and its narrative emblematically unfolds through a series of 'revelations' triggered by fate. Esther is a young woman from a Jewish family who, not having revealed her background, enters into King Ahasuerus's harem and from there is chosen to be queen, taking the place of Vashti, his previous wife. A plot is hatched by Ahasuerus's viceroy, Haman, against Mordecai, Esther's cousin and caretaker: because Mordecai—descendant of a Jewish family that had been deported from Jerusalem to Babylonia—refused to bow down before Haman, the latter convinces the king to issue an official decree ordering the extermination of Persia's entire Jewish population. Mordecai informs Esther of the decree, and she manages to thwart the massacre by denouncing Viceroy Haman, who had previously plotted to kill the king. Haman is then sentenced to death, and the day that had been selected by sortition for the extermination of all Persian Jews—the 13th of Adar—is declared a holiday and called *pûrim*, 'lots'.

In the biblical account, the singular term *pûr* is glossed with the Hebrew term *gôral*—literally 'sortition, drawing by lot'—as it is clearly a non-Hebrew term. The day of the extermination was, therefore, chosen by drawing lots, a procedure that harkens back to the Assyrian use of sortition (*pūru*), described in Esther 3:7 as follows:

> In the first month, that is, the month of Nisan, in the twelfth year of King Ahasuerus, pur—which means 'the lot'—was cast before Haman concerning every day and every month, [until it fell on] the twelfth month, that is, the month of Adar.

The festival's etymology is explicitly laid out at the end of the story, referring to the use of sortition (*pûr*), from which Purim (pl.), the festival of 'lots', takes its name (Esther 9:20–24):

> Mordecai recorded these events. And he sent dispatches to all the Jews throughout the provinces of King Ahasuerus, near and far, charging them to observe the fourteenth and fifteenth days of Adar, every year— the same days on which the Jews enjoyed relief from their foes and the

---

[33] Cf. Hallo (1983, pp. 19–29). Previously: Lewy (1939a, pp. 127–151, and 1939b, pp. 117–124).

same month which had been transformed for them from one of grief and mourning to one of festive joy. They were to observe them as days of feasting and merrymaking, and as an occasion for sending gifts to one another and presents to the poor.

The Jews accordingly assumed as an obligation that which they had begun to practice and which Mordecai prescribed for them. For Haman son of Hammedatha the Agagite, the foe of all the Jews, had plotted to destroy the Jews, and had cast pur—that is, the lot—with intent to crush and exterminate them. But when [Esther] came before the king, he commanded: 'With the promulgation of this decree, let the evil plot, which he devised against the Jews, recoil on his own head!' So they impaled him and his sons on the stake. For that reason these days were named Purim, after pur.

The etymological complexity of *pûrim* has led to several unique interpretations (or misunderstandings?), both in the LXX as well as in Flavius Josephus, *Antiquities of the Jews,* where *pûrim* is translated as *phrourai*, literally 'guards'[34]—perhaps thinking of the Aramaic term *prwr'*, from the root *prr*, 'to destroy', but nevertheless leaving out any reference to 'fate' or 'destiny'.

The roots of this particular story—which, in establishing the festival of Purim, presumably draws upon mythical elements (as can be seen even in the protagonists' names, Esther/Ishtar, Mordecai/Marduk, etc.)—have repeatedly been traced to both Persian and, later, Babylonian influences (the New Year's festival and the use of sortition to determine various characters' destinies); such aspects could have inspired, among other things, the incorporation of the critical commentary included in the passages quoted above (Esther 3, 7, and 9, 20:32; De Vaux, 1973, pp. 514–517). But what is most important to note here is that, in the biblical text—despite the aetiological explanation provided at the end of the story—the theme of 'fate' and its connection to 'lots' is played out in much broader terms than the mere use of sortition to select a certain day or date. In fact, the story's central thread is a *reversal of fortunes*: the prophesy of the Jews' extermination as invoked by the fateful day chosen by sortition turns into its exact opposite—namely, a massacre of Persians and the resulting celebration. It is as if sortition simultaneously served as an institutional expedient, to arrive at an apparently neutral outcome, and as a trial by ordeal-type procedure, the vehicle of a strongly weighted prophesy, i.e. the successful outcome of events. Such a result is, in a certain sense, a given—but sortition gives it a blessing of sorts in the form of apparent legitimacy, the idea that justice has finally been done.

---

[34] *Ant.* XI VI 13.

Gôral, Qesem, and Sortition in the Bible

This is the perfect moment to look a little deeper into the use of the term *gôral* in the bible and its potentially problematic implications with regard to cleromancy, since in this context they seem, as a whole, rather more persuasive than in most Mesopotamian accounts. Divination based on 'lots' has been well-documented and amply studied in the Hebrew bible; however, the term technically used to define it is not *gôral*, but rather *qesem*. One key example, from among many, is Ezekiel's prophecy regarding the destruction of Jerusalem (Ezekiel 21:23–28), which includes a discussion of divinatory practices, including sortition (*qesem*), used to decide the outcome of battle:

> The word of the LORD came to me: And you, O mortal, choose two roads on which the sword of the king of Babylon may advance, both issuing from the same country; and select a spot, select it where roads branch off to [two] cities. Choose a way for the sword to advance on Rabbah of the Ammonites or on fortified Jerusalem in Judah. For the king of Babylon has stood at the fork of the road, where two roads branch off, to perform divination (*liqsam qesem*): He has shaken arrows, consulted teraphim, and inspected the liver.
>
> In his right hand came up the omen against Jerusalem (*qesem Yerušalayim*) — to set battering rams, to proclaim murder, to raise battle shouts, to set battering rams against the gates, to cast up mounds, to erect towers. In their eyes, the oaths they had sworn to them were like empty divination (*qesem šawe'*); but this shall serve to recall their guilt, for which they shall be taken to task.

The relationship between consulting oracles and the outcome (favourable or unfavourable) of a battle is a common theme in nearly all Near-Eastern historiographic literature — and Mesopotamian accounts in particular; Liverani has done excellent research to cast light on its aims and by what exact mechanisms they were reached: it is absolutely clear that such mechanisms served to 'establish' correct models of behaviour in specific contexts (above all, regarding the king; Liverani, 1985, pp. 31–45), through the use of a fairly standardized repertoire of ideologically connoted situations and expressions. The dialectics resulting from the king's conduct with regard to prophesies (obedience/disobedience), the nature of the prophesies themselves (positive/negative), and the selection criteria (human suggestion/divine prophesy) become behavioural models to be followed in certain situations — be they favourable or unfavourable, normal or exceptional — as exemplified by pseudo-historiographic texts in various settings, from the legends of Akkadian rulers to the feats of Israel's judges and kings.

In this context, sortition is an infrequent yet significant divinatory practice that, as shown in the passage from Ezekiel quoted earlier, settles things once and for all (the arrow's[35] selection overrules hepato-mancy [divination by liver] and the consultation of oracles), and in other cases has clear connections with the 'acknowledgment' or 'recognition' granted following a trial by ordeal. See, for instance, 2 Kings 17:17, where the impieties committed by the Israelites lead to the Assyrians' destruction of Samaria; their cruel deeds range from trial by ordeal (passing through fire) and divination by sortition (*qesem*).

Using *gôral* to mean 'fate' or 'lots' is by its very nature more complex and ambiguous, because it can refer to both the apportioning of goods (and in this sense it partially overlaps with the semantic field of the Akkadian *isqu*) as well as the selection of institutional figures (the sortition of high priests and, with the establishment of royalty in Ancient Israel, the sortition of a king), just as we have already seen for the Akkadian *pūru*. A line from Proverbs (16:33) would seem to leave no doubt that this type of sortition depends upon divine will:

[From the bag] (*ḥēq*) The lot is cast (*gôral*) into the lap; but the whole disposing thereof (*mišpāṭ*) is of the LORD.

The 'bag of the *gôral*', where the lots were shaken prior to being cast and read as divinatory signs (*mišpāṭ*), was usually worn along with the priestly breastplate (*ḥošen hamišpāṭ*), in which objects called *urim* and *tummim* were placed.[36] The priestly breastplate was worn atop the ephod (*'epôd*), a garment presumably used in connection with oracular practices, which has a long history,[37] and is described in minute detail in Exodus 28:6–14. The complex philological and exegetical questions tied to this and other types of priestly divination, not to mention its instruments, would carry us far off topic: that said, it is worth noting that the idea that *urim* and *tummim* (the 'light and perfect' objects) actually referred to the two faces of a coin—and therefore provided a binary, 'yes/no' response[38]—probably is not accurate, and should be

---

[35] On the parallel many believe exists between this practice and the later Arab practice of divination using arrows and sticks, cf. the ample bibliography in the *Jewish Encyclopedia* (specifically under 'Lots').

[36] Cf. Ex. 28:29–30; Lev. 8:8.

[37] Cf. del Olmo Lete and Sammartín (2003, vol. I, under *'ipd*). Comparing this with references to an *epattum* in paleo-Assyrian texts, where the garment always has a connection with the city of Talḫât ('Talḫayum' in Mari), one can reasonably conclude that it has north-Syrian origins, which makes the reference to the Israelite ephod more understandable (Durand, 1990, pp. 661–662).

[38] As, to name just one of many, R. de Vaux claims in *Ancient Israel*. *Urim* and *tummim* certainly were not positive and negative oracles, respectively. Their use is discussed in 1 Samuel 14:40–42 (reconstructed on the basis of the LXX), where Saul invites the people to judge the sin committed by Jonathan during the war with the Philistines:

discarded. They are, instead, used in a strictly wartime divinatory practice, based on the 'enlightenment' provided each time by what are best understood as precious gems contained in the high priest's breastplate (Batsch, 1999). In this type of divination, sortition would carry little weight and make little sense. Its relationship to other prophetic techniques, on the other hand, is clear — and explicitly mentioned in a passage from Samuel (I Samuel 28:6). Saul, attacked by the Philistines, questions the Lord, but receives no answer, 'neither by dreams, nor by Urim, nor by prophets' — that is, no answer came from any of the means by which he could establish an accurate line of communication with the divine (Grottanelli, 1998, pp. 244-247).

The phraseology and expressions associated with *gôral*, in addition to the term itself (which in Arabic refers to a pebble, and in a passage of Hosea seems to refer to a 'staff' or 'divinatory rods' used for sortition[39]), instead recall the systematic procedure of drawing lots (with the verb *nāpal*) in the various fields it applies to: judicial, institutional, and divinatory. The first is typically associated with references to tracts of land being 'divided by lots' (*ḥālaq be-gôral*) among the tribes of Israel in the book of Joshua,[40] which we also find in Numbers 26:52-56 with a technical formulation echoing language commonly used on documents of inheritance, even from the Mesopotamian traditions (cf., therefore, *isqu*):

> The LORD spoke to Moses, saying, 'Among these shall the land be apportioned as shares [*nahala*, literally, 'portion'], according to the listed names: with larger groups increase the share, with smaller groups reduce the share. Each is to be assigned its share according to its enrollment. The land, moreover, is to be apportioned [*ḥālaq*] by lot [*gôral*]; and the allotment shall be made according to the listings of their ancestral

---

'Then said he [Saul] unto all Israel, Be ye on one side, and I and Jonathan my son will be on the other side. And the people said unto Saul, Do what seemeth good unto thee. Therefore Saul said unto the Lord God of Israel, Give a perfect lot. And Saul and Jonathan were taken [*urim*]: but the people escaped [*tummim*]. And Saul said, Cast lots between me and Jonathan my son. And Jonathan was taken.' According to de Vaux the two objects — *urim* and *tummim* — had purely conventional values, set each time by the respective parties. And so the oracle's response would always be either yes or no, and the selection would be carried out by elimination or successive clarification. One example is when David consults the oracle in Keilah to enquire whether Saul would destroy the city or if its inhabitants would hand David over to Saul, and the priestly ephod provides a two-part answer: first, 'He will come down', and second, 'They will deliver thee up' (1 Samuel 23:9-12).

[39]   Hosea 4:12.

[40]   Cf. Joshua 13:6, 14:2, 15:1, 17:1, 18:6-10, 19:15, and 23:4.

tribes. Each portion shall be assigned by lot [*teḥalleq naḥalatô*], whether
for larger or smaller groups.'

In other cases, as was hinted at earlier, the use of sortition (*gôral*) is
applied to institutional mechanisms of the sort used for Assyrian
eponyms—albeit almost exclusively for templar roles, as is the case
with sortition of priestly roles in the temple in Jerusalem. The twenty-
four priestly divisions fulfilled by the descendants of Aaron—as well as
by the Levites and the families of cantors, musicians, and temple gate-
keepers—are assigned their turn of service (*pequdat 'avodā*) by a public
drawing, carried out before the king and high priests.[41] Each candidate
is represented by a lot (*gôral*), which is presumably taken (*yāṣa'*) from a
preset, numbered series. Not unlike the practice carried out for
Assyrian eponyms, here, too, fate and the drawing of lots acts as a
revelation of divine will that had been explicitly announced, in advance,
to Aaron. In some respects this is the same institutional procedure that,
with a greater emphasis on its divinatory aspects, leads to Saul's
election in 1 Samuel 10:17-27—one of the many stories of the establishment of royalty in Ancient Israel. Here, too, sortition by successive
clarification—from tribe (*šēbeṭ*) to family (*mišpaḥā*) to individual (Saul)
—leads to the sole possible choice, because it is guided by the divine
hand. Since Saul, selected by sortition to become king, then cannot be
found, the need to consult (*šā' al*) divine authority arises once again;
this time, the reply is that Saul has hidden among the baggage. Once he
has finally been found, his remarkable height proves that the king can
be no one but him. Technically speaking, the oracle supplements the
sortition, but the two procedures effectively complement one another,
unfolding in tandem.

The KIN Oracle in Hittite Anatolia:
Sortition and Divination

As we near the end of this brief overview, I would be remiss to neglect
Oppenheim's reference to sortition as one of the technical means
deployed in Hittite divination,[42] since it is as emblematic as it is
culturally and geographically circumscribed. If indeed, amidst their
many discrepancies, the documentation from both Mesopotamian texts
and the Hebrew bible share an inconsistent use of sortition in fields
relating to religion and magic—instead showing a consistent intervention of fate solely in 'civil' contexts (legal practice, institutional

---

[41]   1 Chronicles 24-26.
[42]   See §2 above.

roles) — then Hittite documentation attests to sortition's status as one of
the canonical systems of forecasting and interpreting the future. This
so-called KIN oracle (the term appears to generically refer to 'magic'[43])
is listed alongside ornithomancy, lecanomancy, and extispication as
one of the methods of divination by which favourable or unfavourable
oracular responses may be obtained.[44] In this process the enquirer, a
sorceress (salŠU.GI),[45] formulates a question for which an oracular
response is desired; the response is then provided by the fortuitous
configuration of a series of symbols placed within a set divinatory
space, and through a set number of successive moves. In Archi's
description of the process, 'the symbols represent human beings, gods,
and other positive or negative entities, some of whom are agents that
actively affect other passive entities, resulting in the latter's being
pushed or pulled toward other symbols, which represent the final goal
of the procedure' (Archi, 1974, p. 115). A response is solicited through
the expressions 'may it be favourable!' (SIG_5-*ru*) or 'may it be
unfavourable!' (NU.SIG_5-*du*), depending on whether the situations in
question are positive or negative; the final response, after the enquirer's
examination, is formulated with the expression 'favourable' or
'unfavourable', which then either confirms or denies the initial
question. Thus, in the following example (KUB V 24 I 58–60), a request
for confirmation is ultimately contradicted by the oracle's unfavourable
result:

> and may the KIN be [favourable]! The king
> took the favour and the blood, and (placed them) at the light illness;
> (2nd:) the man in question [literally, 'standing in front'], the (his)
>   'heart' <catch> fire and give it to the community. Not [favourable].[46]

The response derives from the symbols' complex combinations, which
are presumably moved by an animal who is repeatedly allowed into
the 'magical space'. Because certain details are expected — symbols'
actions ('taken', 'given', etc.) and their movements ('entering', 'exiting',
'crossing', etc.) — it is entirely possible that, for each move, the animal
took on the name of a certain symbol depending upon the point at
which it entered the space: from that point ('the king', 'the god', or

---

43 KIN is the equivalent of *anijatt-* in Hittite and *šipru* in Akkadian.
44 A. Goetze was the first to interpret the KIN oracle as *Losorakel*; see *Kleinasien*[2], 140ff.
    Detailed studies can also be found in Archi (1974, pp. 113–144); Ünal and
    Kammenhuber (1974, pp. 157–180); and Soysal (2000, pp. 85–122).
45 On the political role of 'sorceresses' in the Hittite court and their predominantly
    Luwian and Hurrian heritage, see de Martino (1989, pp. 18–21).
46 For text and translation, see Archi (1994, p. 117).

other figure) the animal brushed up against the passive symbols, then exited the space from another point, which in turn determined to whom the moved symbols were then 'given'.

In one of the best-preserved texts (KUB V 1, II 60–72) the operation can be analytically followed, in response to two successive questions (distinguished from one another by a separating line on the tablet) regarding plans for a military campaign against the Nerik region:

'His Majesty will reach Nerik, will carry out Pitamna's deed, Ḫaršama's deed,

he will not retreat from Tanizila, and will fight the mountain people of Ḫarḫawa; he will also fight Kammama (and) Šaqamaḫa. May (all) this be favourable!

The goddess Ḫannaḫanna stood, took the town's well-being and prosperity, and the god Zababa, and they(!) are set to the right of the men of Ḫatti;

2nd: the men of Ḫatti took the favour, vigour, resistance, the king's mission, and the well-being, and (gave them) to the gods;

3rd: the enemy took the battle and the entire soul, and they(!) (are) given(!) back to the enemy. (Result:) favourable.

His Majesty will succeed in Nerik, and will then fight (the people of) Ḫarḫawa, attack Kammama, Šaqamaḫa, Tašmaḫa, and Ḫarna,

will not carry out Pitamna's deed, Ḫaršama's deed, Tanizila's deed.

May (all) this be favourable! The king took the community(?), the attack, the mission, Ḫatti's fire, arms,

and crossed over the wall, and they(!) are set before the enemy (near) the fault; 2nd: Ḫatti's men took the disgrace, the strength, the year, and the protection, and they(!) (are) given(!) to the goddess Ḫannaḫanna;

3rd: the enemy took the battle and the entire soul, and they(!) (are) given(!) to the friend. (Result:) favourable.[47]

One might think, as an alternative to Archi's interpretation, that the progression of expected moves within the KIN oracle's use was instead determined by a roll of the dice, or another type of numerical combination determining the symbol's movements like chess pieces on a game board: but, for various reasons, this hypothesis is unlikely. The fact remains that, even above and beyond the operative logic of this divinatory practice, it is the only one (of the many we have considered) that is a *formalized* case of predicting the future through the intervention of fate.

With regard to the many cases examined over the course of this study, the Anatolian one — which comes from an ancient and absolutely

---

[47] For text and translation, see *ibid.* (pp. 113–115).

local tradition[48] — is a case unto itself. Human behaviour and the gods' judgment of it, as well as the very ideal of justice — be it in the practice of law or in the determination of institutional roles (of king or eponym) — which are of fundamental importance in the logic determining biblical and Mesopotamian sortition, do not seem to play even the slightest part here: to the contrary, they constitute a relatively unified horizon of cleromantic practices in the rest of the Near East.

References

Adelmann, H.E. (1985) *Success and Failure in the Seventeenth-Century Ghetto of Venice: The Life and Thought of Leon da Modena, 1571–1648*, PhD dissertation, Brandeis University.

Alster, B. (1997) *Proverbs of Ancient Sumer*, vol. I, Bethesda: Capital Decisions Ltd.

Archi, Al. (1974) Il sistema KIN della divinazione ittita, in *OrAnt*, 13, pp. 113–144.

Batsch, Ch. (1999) Ourîm et toummîm, un oracle de guerre dans le judaïsme du second temple, in Batsch, Ch., Egelhaaf-Gaiser, U. & Stepper, R. (eds.) *Zwischen Krise und Alltag. Antike Religionen im Mittelmeerraum*, Stuttgart: Steiner.

Bottero, J. & Kramer, S.N. (1989) *Lorsque les dieux faisaient l'homme*, Paris: Gallimard.

Bukert, W. (1983) Oriental Myth and Literature in the Iliad, in Hägg, R. (ed.) *The Greed Renaissance of the Eighth Century B.C.: Tradition and Innovation. Proceedings of the Second International Symposium at the Swedish Institute in Athens, 1–5 June, 1982*, Stockholm: Paul Åströms.

Cohen, M.R. (1988) *The Autobiography of a Seventeenth-Century Venetian Rabbi: Leon Modena's 'Life of Judah'*, Princeton, NJ: Princeton University Press.

Dalley, S. (1989) *Myths from Mesopotamia: Creation, The Flood, Gilgamesh, and Others*, London/Oxford: Oxford University Press.

De Martino, S. (1989) Hattušili I e Haštayar: un problema aperto, in *OrAnt*, 28, pp. 1–24.

Del Olmo Lete, G. & Sanmartín, J. (2003) *A Dictionary of the Ugaritic Language in the Alphabetic Tradition*, vol. I, Leiden: Brill.

De Vaux, R. (1973) *Ancient Israel: Its life and Institutions*, London: DLT.

---

[48] Cf. Archi (1974, pp. 131ff.). Regarding the probable introduction of sorceresses' (sal.mešŠU.GI) oracular divinations in the era of Hattušili I, see de Martino (1989, p. 21). Regarding their origin, in addition to de Martino's reference to their probable Luwian and Hurrian heritage, Soysal (2000, pp. 155–156) has recently hypothesized that they instead had a Hattic background.

Durand, J.M. (1990) Review of Ribichini S. & Xella P., *La Terminologica dei Tessili nei Testi di Ugarat*, Roma, 1985, in *MARI: Annales de Recherches Interdisciplinaires*, 6, pp. 659–664.

Finkel, I.L. & Reade, J.E. (1995) Lots of Eponyms, *Iraq*, 57, pp. 167–172.

Forrer, E. (1920) *Die Provinzeinteilung des assyrischen Reiches*, Leipzig: Hinrichs.

Gadd, C.J. (1936) *The Stones of Assyria: The Surviving Remains of the Assyrian Sculpture, Their Recovery, and Their Original Positions*, London: Chatto and Windus.

Grayson, A.K. (1996) *Assyrian Rulers of the Early First Millennium BC II (858–745 BC)*, Toronto, ON: Toronto University Press.

Grottanelli, C. (1998) *Sette storie bibliche*, Brescia: Paideia.

Hallo, W.W. (1983) The First Purim, *Biblical Archaeologist*, 46, pp. 19–29.

Hald, A. (1990) *A History of Probability and Statistics and Their Applications before 1750*, New York: Wiley.

Larsen, M.T. (1976) *The Old Assyrian City-State and its Colonies*, Copenhagen: Akademisk Forlag.

Romano, Immanuello, ed. by Battistoni, G. (2000) *L'inferno e il Paradiso [Ha-tofet ve-ha-Eden]*, Weiss Levi, E. (trans.) Florence: Giuntina.

Lewy, J. (1939a) The Feast of the 14th Day of Adar, in *HUCA* 14.

Lewy, J. (1939b) Old Assyrian *puru'um* and *pūrum*, in *RHA* 5.

Liverani, M. (1985) Naram-Sin e i presagi difficili, in Fales, F.M. & Grottanelli, C. (eds.) *Soprannaturale e potere nel mondo antico e nelle società tradizionali*, Milan: Franco Angeli.

Michel, E. (1949) Die Assur-Texte Shalmanesers III (858–824), 8: Fortsetzung, in *Die Welt des Orients 1*, 4, pp. 231–233.

Millard, A. (1994) *The Eponyms of the Assyrian Empire 910–612 BC* (=SAAS II), Helsinki: The Neo-Assyrian Text Corpus Project.

Oppenheim, A.L. (1977) *Ancient Mesopotamia: Portrait of a Dead Civilization*, rev. ed. completed by Reiner, E., Chicago, IL, and London: University of Chicago Press.

Saporetti, C. (1979) *Gli eponimi medio-assiri*, Malibu, CA: Undena.

Schramm, W. (1973) *Einleitung in die Assyrischen Königsinschriften, II. Teil, 934–722 v.Chr.*, Leiden: Brill.

Scholem, G. (2006) *Alchemy and Kabbalah*, New York/Washington, DC: Spring.

Sigmund, S. (1996) La vita nei ghetti, in Vivanti, C. (ed.) *Gli ebrei in Italia (Storia d'Italia, Annali, 11)*, vol. II, Turin: Einaudi.

Soysal, O. (2000) Analysis of a Hittite Oracular Document, in ZA 90.

Ünal, A. & Kammenhuber, A. (1974) Das Althethitische Losorakel Kbo XVIII 151, in KZ 88.

Van Dijk, J. (1983) *LUGAL UD ME-LÁm-bi NIR-GÁL, I.* 'Introduction, texte composite, traduction', Leiden: Brill.

Veenhof, K.R. (1985) *Eponyms of the 'Later Old Assyrian Period' and the Mari Chronology*, in MARI 4.

Whiting, R.M. (1990) Tell Leilan/ Šubat Enlil: Chronological Problems and Perspectives, in Eichler, S., Wäfler, M. & Warburton, D. (eds.) *Tall al-Hamīdīya 2*, Freiburg: Vandenhoeck & Ruprecht.

Yamada, S. & Weissert, E. (2000) The Commemoration of Dayyan-Ashur's Second Eponymate in the Black Obelisk and the Calah Statue, in Yamada, S., *The Construction of the Assyrian Empire*, Leiden: Brill.

Yamada, S. (2000) *The Construction of the Assyrian Empire*, Leiden: Brill.

Liliane Lopez-Rabatel

Drawing Lots in Ancient Greece – Vocabulary and Tools

Translated by Catherine Delcroix-Howell and William Howell
in collaboration with Sarah-Louise Raillard

The birth of Athenian democracy is generally situated at the very end of the 6th century BCE, a period of political unrest during which the Greek city, newly freed from tyranny, struggled to determine the nature of its future government.[1] The main factions among the nobility were embodied by Cleisthenes, on one side, who favoured a 'democratic programme', and by Isagoras, on the other, who looked for Spartan support to impose an oligarchic regime. Bolstered by the support of the Areopagus, once the Council of the Archons had been stripped of all its responsibilities, Cleisthenes gained power and established what the Ancient Greeks variably called democracy (the government of the people) or *isonomia* (the equality of political rights), the first elements of which originated in the 7th century BCE with Solon's laws (*nomoi*) and were followed by numerous other attempts to redefine the body politic during the 6th century BCE.

By analogy with the philosophical movements of the late Archaic period, namely Pythagoreanism and the cosmology of Anaximander (a pre-Socratic philosopher from Asia Minor active at the end of 7th and the beginning of 6th centuries BCE), Cleisthenes imagined, as a 'harmoniser of the City', an 'in-between' regime (Ismard, 2011, pp. 173–174), with the aim of preventing the return of tyranny. He reorganized the civic territory, securing spaces designed to integrate the ancient social divisions in order to guarantee *isonomia*. He thus created new

[1] This chapter was written in collaboration with the research engineer Nicolas Bresch, who contributed to the study of material remains and proposed reproductions. My thanks to Yves Sintomer for his careful proofreading and constructive remarks.

administrative entities across the whole of Attica, the *demes*, the geographic repartition of which enabled access to citizenship for non-Athenians and freed slaves. Cleisthenes also replaced the four Ionian tribes with ten tribes, each one composed of three 'trittyes', or population divisions (one trittys each for coastal, inland, and urban areas), and from which the recruitment of the members of the Boule (the Council of Five Hundred) was operated. Cleisthenes' democratic programme relied upon the enlargement of the body politic, which would weaken the power of the aristocracy embodied by the Areopagus to the benefit of the Boule, the Ecclesia (the People's Assembly), and the Heliaia (the People's Court). This reform also incorporated procedures aimed at broadening the role of the people, both in the decision-making process and in the designation of its leaders. It is at this time that the bouleutic calendar—a new political calendar based on the decimal system—appeared and was superimposed over the solar calendar. The bouleutic calendar was composed of 10 periods of time, during which each of the 10 tribes would take turns presiding over the Council of Five Hundred. Without going into the various debates regarding when exactly the lottery system was introduced as a modality used to allocate different public offices, it is undeniable the establishment of the Council of Five Hundred was a crucial moment in the history of Athenian democracy. After that point, the attribution and rotation of posts was entirely decided by drawing lots, a practice which had already been in use for the law courts since the Solonian period, but not for the archons (the 10 main magistrates), who were elected until 487–486 BCE. Whereas voting remained the means by which the people expressed their decision-making power, the use of random selection to designate magistrates consistently increased up until the 4th century BCE, a period which is often referred to as 'radical' or 'extreme' democracy.

It is therefore useful to study the relationship between the Athenian democratic system and its main means of implementation, the lottery system. Attempting to identify the essential stages in the history of the lottery in Ancient Greece requires examining both archaeological remains and the lexicon used to describe the instruments of random selection. In so doing, a historical turning point comes to the fore: the invention of the *kleroterion*, the lot-drawing machine attested to by both literature and archaeology, marked a decisive inflection point in the evolution of political instruments aimed at serving the democratic ideal.

The world of Homer provides us with the first documentation of codified procedures, depicting the archetypical instruments used to

draw lots. Poetic texts from the classical period depict the first evolution undergone by these tools. They were shaped, both in terms of their
name and their function, by the existing gap between the time of
history and the time of writing (particularly important in the works of
the tragic poets): a gap henceforth rooted in the political context of the
Ancient Greek city. Moreover, it is in oratories and the philosophical
treatises of the 5th and 4th centuries BCE that the names of the first
manufactured objects of random selection appeared. These objects
paved the way for instrument standardization and procedural regulation, culminating in the invention of the *kleroterion,* an ingenious
machine for drawing lots, as well as the concrete result of the democratic ideal as developed over the course of the 5th and 4th centuries
BCE. Archaeologists have unearthed the remnants of some of these
sortition machines. The method used to study and subsequently
describe the operation of these machines demonstrates the complexity
of the relationship between the lexicon of sortition and the objects it
designates, and attests to the need to compare textual sources with
archaeological remains in order to lay the groundwork for a political
history of sortition in Ancient Greece.

In what way does archaeology, specifically the discovery of *kleroteria*
fragments in Athens and in the Cyclades, facilitate access to a better
understanding of Ancient Greek lottery procedures, and, consequently,
of their role in the democratic system? Does the sole study of material
remains enable us to accurately date the evolution of their usage and to
conclude (or not) that the procedure was used for exclusively democratic purposes? Did this technical revolution mark a rupture between
conflicting underlying and period-dependant political significations or,
on the contrary, was it embedded within a continuity of practices that
functioned independently of the given system of government?

The present chapter presents the results of an enquiry which first
analysed the vocabulary associated with the drawing of lots and
secondly studies the instruments used to draw lots through the words
used to refer to them. Rather than focusing on the different institutional
aspects highlighted by the lexical field of sortition, we shall attempt to
outline the history of the lottery in the Greek world through practical
analysis, starting from the idea that words are as much descriptive
tools as they are 'forms of experiencing the world and a means to act
within and upon it' (Topalov *et al.*, 2010, p. xviii).

Our main objective is scrutinizing the lexicon associated with
random selection instruments and demonstrating how this lexicon
depends on the technical evolution of an ancient practice, a practice
which consistently grew more complex and culminated in the creation

of the *kleroterion*. The second part of this chapter will be entirely dedicated to the study of the form and shape of the machine, as well as its operation and usage.

The First Lottery Devices

Given that the most ancient evidence of lottery procedures is exclusively literary in nature, we are forced to rely on abstract references to these practices and hunt down clues regarding their materiality in a variety of texts.

The vocabulary of lottery

Ancient Greeks seldom used the abstract term of 'drawing lots', be it as the noun *klerosis* (κλήρωσις) or any of its derived forms. The concept of random selection, traditionally opposed to that of 'election', the *hairesis* (αἵρησις), only appeared sporadically before the philosophical literature of the 4th century BCE: we find one reference in Euripides (*Andromache*, 384), and one in Isocrates (*Areopagiticus*, 23-3). There are very few epigraphic testimonials of the word *klerosis* or any of its derived forms; the first appears in an honorific decree dated from 327–366 BCE.[2] The derived words *apoklerosis, diaklerosis, epiklerosis* are seldom found in Athenian sources from the classical period, although the term *epiklerosis* appears in numerous inscriptions from the Hellenistic period in Asia Minor.

On the other hand, the verbs which derive from the root noun *kleros* (κλῆρος = chance) such as *kleroo* (κληρόω = to draw lots), *apokleroo* (ἀποκληρόω = to eliminate by drawing lots), *diakleroo* (διακληρόω = to sort out two parties by drawing lots), and *epikleroo* (ἐπικληρόω = to draw a deputy) (Laffon, 2016) occur much more frequently. They attest to a more practical vision, inasmuch as they refer to the procedure itself, rather than the multiple occurrences of the verb *lanchano* (λαγχάνω) which evoke, without providing details regarding their reality, the recourse to sortition, and, above all, its end result (Perpillou, 1966, in particular chapter 9).

---

[2]   The decree honours the *thesmothete* Teleskopos for successfully carrying out the drawing of lots for the court magistrates and jury members. Together with their secretary, the six thesmothetes and the three archons were the 10 main Athenian magistrates nominated by drawing of lots every year (Woodhead, 1997, no. 85).

Drawing the short straw

The use of drawing lots was recorded since the time of the great epics: the *Iliad* provides us with six different references,[3] the *Odyssey* with three. These scenes serve a variety of purposes: determining a particular order for taking action, appointing one or more representatives of a group, and awarding or sharing property between equals.

Klerous pallein (Κλήρους πάλλειν)

Paul Demont (2000) has demonstrated that these rare scenes depict a rigorously ritualized procedure. Although none of these scenes describe the entire process of random selection from start to finish, they nonetheless form a small corpus which, as a whole, allows us to piece together the standard procedure used to draw lots in Homeric texts.

The first, essential stage consists of choosing objects and marking them with a sign (*sema*, σῆμα), by means of an engraving (*epigrapsas*, ἐπιγράψας).[4] In the second stage, the heroes toss their tokens (*kleroi*, κλῆροι) into a helmet. Thirdly, while raising their hands towards the sky, the heroes address the gods with an individual prayer, in which the audience sometimes joins, thus placing the drawing of lots under the sign of a divine authority. The fourth action, which can be simultaneous or have already occurred, consists of shaking the tokens in the helmet to ensure that the protagonists are acting in good faith. Finally, as if suddenly animated by some external force, the tokens break out from the helmet to designate the lucky chosen one (Demont, 2000).

In two passages (*Iliad* III, v. 316 and XXIII, v. 861), a standard verse appears: they 'took the lots and shook them in the bronze-wrought helmet' (*klerous en kynee chalkerei pallon helontes*, κλήρους ἐν κυνέῃ χαλκήρεϊ πάλλον ἑλόντες) which informs us of the vocabulary used in Homeric texts to designate lottery instruments and actions. These tools include the *kleroi*, which were natural objects from the plant world rather than the mineral environment. The substantive *kleros* (κλῆρος) probably stems from an Indo-European etymology, borrowing the verb *klao* (κλάω) meaning 'to break' (Chantraine, 1968a). These small pieces of purposefully broken wood remind us of drawing straws, or perhaps the stick in La Fontaine's fable, *The Gout and the Spider*. Always near to

---

[3] *Iliad*, III, 314–324; VII, 179–192; XV, 189–192; XXIII, 352–357 and 861–862; XXIV, 400. *Odyssey*, IX, 331; X, 205–209; 207–209.

[4] This stage is mentioned only once, in book VII of the *Iliad* (v. 179–192), in the scene where Nestor must choose which of the seven warriors will have to fight against Hector.

hand, the hero's helmet (*kynee*) is used as the recipient. The etymology of the word used to indicate this manufactured object, the 'dog skin', indicates that it must have included at least some leather, probably the padding within the skullcap.

In Homer's epic, the process of drawing lots thus includes five main steps: (1) choosing a natural object to represent each hero: the verb *haireo* (to take, to hold) is often used here; (2) affixing a distinctive sign, a *sema*, on the *kleros*: indicated by the verbs *semaino* (to mark with a distinctive mark) and *epigrapho* (to inscribe); (3) mixing the lots: designated by the verb *pallo* (to shake, to brandish the lots); (4) praying; and (5) extracting the lots from the recipient (the helmet in this case) which is described in three passages using the verb *throsko* (to jump), later replaced by the verb *orouo* (to launch oneself). When this last stage is not mentioned, it is the result — the selection of a person or position by lot — that is underscored by the use of expressions including the verb 'to obtain by the lots, to obtain from the gods' (*lanchano*), an expression which is used in the aorist tense and indicative mood to insist on the achieved action. The procedure of drawing lots can sometimes successively appoint several persons. In the *Odyssey* (XXIII, v. 352–357), Nestor, Eumelos, Menelaus, and then Meriones are appointed. Only the designation of Nestor, the first among them, is explicitly conducted by lot. For the subsequent individuals, the poet repeats the verb *lanchano* three times. Most often, this result expresses the consensus between the wishes of the participants and the divine will; for example, the drawing of the lots appointed Ajax, the champion 'the lot that themselves desired' (*Iliad* VII, v. 182) and the companions whom Ulysses 'would fain have chosen' to help him to blind Polyphemos (*Odyssey* IX, v. 334).

In these canonical scenes of random selection, the lexicon used to name the basic equipment and the main actions related to this practice anticipate the tools and procedures which are attested to in later periods. Whereas we do not find in Homer the verb *kleroo* (drawing the lots) as used by the tragic poets and Aristophanes in his comedies, the noun form *kleros* is central to the epic language used to describe the drawing of lots. It is used in the nominative case (*Iliad* III, v. 316; VII, v. 175; XXIII, v. 352, 861; *Odyssey* X, v. 206) when, as if animated by a life of its own, the lot jumps or expels itself from the helmet. It is used in the accusative case (*Iliad* VII, v. 171; XXIII, v. 81; and XXIV, v. 400; *Odyssey* IX, v. 331) as the direct object of the verbs *haireo* (to take), *semaino* (to mark with a sign), *ballo* (to throw), and *pallo* (to shake). *Kleros* is also used in the dative case as 'a tool' in two lexicalized verbal expressions (*Iliad* VII, v. 171; XXIII, v. 861; XXIV, v. 400; *Odyssey* IX, v.

331) meaning 'to draw the lots' (*kleroi lachen*, κλήρῳ λάχεν, and *kleroi pepalasthai*, κλήρῳ πεπαλάσθαι).

The *kleros/pallo* linguistic pair is thus the characteristic expression used to describe the process of drawing lots in Homeric language. Two hapax logomena, terms which have only been found to occur a single time each, and which in this case are compound words using elements from both the *kleros* and *pallo* lexical families, appear in the *Homeric Hymn to Hermes* (v. 127) and in a fragment attributed to the poet Stesichoros (7th–6th centuries BCE), respectively:[5] the adjective *kleropales* (κληροπαλής) describes the pieces of flesh which have been 'drawn' by the god Hermes, and *kleropaledon* (κλαροπαληδὸν) acts as a adverb derived from the adjective *kleropales*.

Paloi lachein/palos (Πάλῳ λαχεῖν/πάλος)

In poetry and tragedies from the 6th–5th centuries BCE, the verb *pallo*, which we have found in only one occurrence in Aeschylus, disappears to the benefit of the verb *kleroo*. However, *klero* (in its noun form *kleros*) is often replaced by the noun *palos*, itself derived from *pallo*. There is no trace of the noun *palos* in epigraphic texts and it occurs extremely rarely in literary texts from the classical epoch. The word appears for the first time in the 7th century BCE in a fragment attributed to the poet Sappho (7th–6th century BCE) (frag. 33, v. 2). It is used in a polysemic way just like the French word 'sort' or the English word 'lot'. The *Seventh Olympic* written by the poet Pindar in the 5th century BCE (VII, IV, v. 106–116) provides us with another hapax logomenon, the adjective *ampalon* (ἄμπαλον for ἀναπάλον) which means 'drawn once more by the lots' according to the scholiast's commentary, in which he uses the verb *anakleroo* to specify its meaning.

A good example of the evolution of random selection-related vocabulary is provided by a passage from *The Seven against Thebes* (v. 456–458), in which Aeschylus (5th century BCE) refers to the drawing of lots conducted by Eteocles to attribute the seven gates of Thebes to himself and his six companions. Having found refuge in Argos after the death of his father Oedipus, Polyneices returns to take Thebes back from his brother Eteocles. A messenger reports to the latter that Polyneices and the six Argive warriors who accompany him have attributed each of the seven gates to themselves by drawing lots. He then describes the enemies, then Eteocles assigns to each of his own six companions an adversary in accordance with his capacity. In order to

---

[5]   Stesichoros, *P. Lille* 73 and 76, v. 218–224 (Meillier, 1978).

describe this action, the poet associates the verb *kleroo* (to draw lots) with the expression *paloi lachein* (literally, 'to draw by means of a lot') in a redundant phrase which nonetheless specifies the practicalities of drawing lots.

In spite of lexical evolution, this passage presents itself as a quotation from the Homeric scene of drawing of lots: an upside-down helmet is used and an object jumps out of it, a *palos*. The adjective *tritos*, indicating that the lot is the third one, attests to a multi-phased procedure. This is an isolated example among the rare occurrences of this phrase found in the tragic and lyrical corpus. The lots are no longer animated and no longer jump out spontaneously from the helmet. They are taken out, as illustrated, for example, in the passage from *Agamemnon* by Aeschylus (v. 332–335), in which the verb *spao* is used, with the meaning 'to take out from, to remove from', thus indicating human intervention. We can thus present a more nuanced conclusion to the ongoing debate over the relationship between sortition and divination, launched in the modern era by Fustel de Coulanges and persisting to this day (Fustel, 1884; cf. Demont's chapter in the present work, pp. 112–129): that is, whereas historically the practice was tightly linked to divination rituals, this no longer appears to have been the case during the classical era.

Depending on the case, the term *palos* could thus refer to the lot in its material reality, the tool metonymically representing the practice (Euripides, *The Children of Heracles*, v. 543–547), or the 'lot of fate' as the result of the process, particularly in the phrases where it is used in the dative case with the verb *lachein* (Aeschylus, *The Seven against Thebes*, v. 55 and 128). With Euripides (*Ion*, v. 416) a tragic poet from the 5th century BCE, the word *palos* is associated with the verb *kleroo* to evoke the drawing of lots of the 'internal service' which 'speaks for the god' in the temple at Delphi.

Moreover, in Aeschylus's *Eumenides* (v. 741–758), the *palos* is assimilated to the *psephos*, the water-polished pebble which, during the classical era that followed, referred to the ballot token (*psephos demosia*) utilized in public voting procedures. The ballots cast to determine Orestes' guilt were either referred to by the noun *palos* — in a bit of Homeric reminiscence — or by the noun *psephos*, which evoked the political context in which democratic practices were developing. However, this ambivalence was probably due to the natural origin of both voting implements and sortition instruments. The small piece of wood, the Homeric accessory for the drawing of lots, came from the plant world whereas, with the water-polished pebbles, the mineral world supplied the first voting instruments.

Outside of the tragic genre, it should be observed that, during the classical period, three mentions of the word *palos* can be found from the 5th century BCE, in Herodotus's *Histories* (III, 80, 128; IV, 94) and one from the 4th century BCE, in Aeneas Tacticus's *On the Defence of Fortified Positions* (20.2). The word *palos* never appears in inscriptions, whether made by orators or by philosophers who allude to the drawing of lots with the verb *kleroo*. During the 2nd century BCE, Pausanias (IV, *Messenia*) uses this term, perhaps with an archaic purpose, to refer to tokens fashioned out of clay and dried by the sun or cooked in the fire, in the episode where Messenia is attributed to Aristodemos's and Krespontes' children by the drawing of lots. The term is also found in the work of lexicographers, for the most part dependant on the work of Pollux of Naucratis (2nd century BCE). As the holder of the Athenian chair of philosophy, Pollux of Naucratis composed an anthology of Greek words for the emperor Commodus: the *Onomasticon*, a sort of textbook designed to enable the Emperor to compose the beautiful speeches required by his function. Pollux associates the noun *palos* with the verbs *lanchano* and *kleroo*, thus encapsulating the early history of the words associated with drawing lots.

In epic poems or in tragic works, when the latter present themselves as references to an epic works, the recipient used to collect the lots was the warrior's helmet. During the classical period, a 'generic' recipient appears, generally borrowed from the domestic sphere. In Aeschylus, urns (*teuche*, τεύχη), are found; *hydria* (ὑδρία), narrow-necked clay pots with three handles utilized for water storage, a material reality reflected in its etymology, are also found in an Athenian decree from 352–351 BCE. The decree refers to the consultation of an oracle to solve a quarrel between Athens and Megara regarding the sacred land of Eleusis (*IG* II², 1, 37; Clinton, 2005, no. 144). Boxes (*kibotia*, κιβώτια) are also mentioned in *The Constitution of the Athenians* (64, 1).[6] A variant of the *hydria*, the two-handled silver *kalpis* (κάλπις), is found in the *Hermotimus* (40) where Lucian (2nd century BCE) describes a procedure for drawing lots to match up competitors in the gymnic contests at Olympia. The way these various recipients were referred to varied according to context and time, but their designations did not, at least at the time, seem to indicate that they were specifically designed for drawing of lots, no more so than the lots themselves.

---

[6]   The attribution of the text to Aristotle is not formally established. It may well have been written by one of his disciples. For convenience's sake, however, we shall consider that Aristotle was the author. The text is dated around 320 BCE.

To conclude regarding the use of the noun *palos*, we can say that it appears somewhat later than the verb from the same root, *pallesthai*, which is essentially found in Homeric texts, whereas *palos* is used by the tragic poets: Herodotus in the 5th century BCE and rare later authors, who utilized it as an archaic turn of phrase. The natural object, singled out by a sign (*sema*), thus becomes a cultural personal object. The references in Aeschylus's work indicate that the word *palos*, interchangeable with the word *psephos*, rapidly acquired a generic meaning. Finally, the word could present a figurative sense, polysemic in a similar fashion to the word 'lot'. The texts in which it appears never provide a description of the object, and we must therefore deduce its material and shape from context. In the lottery process as described in the sources, the step of shaking and mixing up the lots is emphasized much more than the aleatory extraction of a single lot from the recipient.

Drawing beans

We have seen that, as early as in time of Homer, the drawing of lots could be evoked in two different manners: either by the verb *pallo* associated with the noun *kleros*, referring primarily to the practice or to the procedure, or by the verb *lanchano*, in the aorist tense to highlight the situation or result. In the language of the classical era, it is the verb *kleroo*, alongside the verb *lanchano*, which therefore came to refer to the action of drawing lots.

By the 5th century BCE, an expression had appeared: 'to draw the bean' (*kuamoi lachein*, κυάμῳ λαχεῖν, also found in the form *kuameuo*, κυαμεύω), which reveals the evolution of the instruments used in the lottery: twigs or pebbles gave way to beans. In comparison with the large numbers of texts which evoke the drawing of lots using the verbs *kleroo* or *lanchano*, those in which the expression *kuamoi lachein* or the verb *kuameuo* can be found are not so numerous. They almost all date from the 5th century BCE (Herodotus, VI, 109; Thucydides, VIII, 66, 1 and 69, 4; Aristophanes, *Birds*, v. 1022; Xenophon, *Memorabilia*, I, 2, 9). In epigraphic texts, the occurrences of this expression are even fewer and only present in the 5th century BCE. The expression also appears in an Athenian decree to the city of Erythrea (*IG* I 3 14, 1, 9 and 13; 465–450 BCE; Brun 2005, no. 6), imposing, among other measures, the establishment of random selection for the Council of 120 members. It again appears in a decree from a *deme* of Plotheiea, regarding the drawing of lots for financial magistrats (*IG* II² 1172, 1, 11–14, 420–390 BCE; Brun 2005, no. 138). In the first of two decrees by Callias (*IG* I³ 52, side A, I, 13) which dictated the financing of embellishments to the

Acropolis at the end of the 5th century BCE , the random selection of treasurers is mentioned using a compound of the verb *kuameuo*.[7]

In the 4th century BCE, we note only four occurrences of this verb: one in Andocides (*On the Mysteries*, 96), one in Demosthenes, quoting an ancient text (*Against Timocrates*, 14-151), and two in *The Constitution of the Athenians* (8, 1 and 32, 1). Moreover, the use of beans for the lottery appears to have enhanced Aristophanes' lexical creativity. In *The Knights* (v. 40-44), the people are ironically mocked as 'bean eaters' (*kuamotrox*, κυαμοτρώξ) because of their sickening compulsion for participating in politics. We find the same image in *Lysistrata* (v. 537) with the use of the expression 'bean-eater' (*kuamous trogon*, κυάμους τρώγων). While the expression was obsolete by the end of the 4th century BCE, '*kuamoi lachein*' reappears in Plutarch, a Roman writing in Greek at the end of the 1st century and the beginning of the 2nd century CE. The author was perhaps using the phrase in an attempt to adapt his lexicon to the context of reference: the *Life of Aristides* (I.8), who was born around 530 BCE and died in 467 BCE, and the *Life of Pericles* (27, 1), a strategist and influential statesman from the 5th century BCE.

The presence of the expression *kuamoi lachein* and the verb *kuameuo* in literary and epigraphic texts from the 5th century BCE seems to coincide with the period during which beans were used for lotteries and random selection procedures. Of course, we do not possess any material remains of this sort, given that this equipment would have been perishable, but the first archaeological traces of objects used for lotteries — clay tokens and bronze tablets from the first quarter of the 4th century BCE — suggest that these tools rather abruptly replaced beans. In Plutarch, there is a reference to the possibility of drawing a white bean (*Life of Pericles*, 27, 1) using the word *phryctos* (φρυκτὸς) in a context of cleromancy (casting lots for the purpose of divination) (*On brotherly love*, 492b). This usage is possibly referring to a rather large bean, roasted to distinguish it from the others, which would have been the precursor to the black and white cubes mentioned in *The Constitution of the Athenians*.

The First Tools Engraved for Drawing Lots

By affixing a personal sign to the Homeric lots, such as by roasting the beans in the case of cleromancy, the transformation of natural objects into cultural objects demonstrates the need to rationalize lottery

---

[7] Let us also cite, in a context where reproductions are more significant: *IG* I³ 41, 1.105 (446/5?) and *IG* I³, 1,7 (425/4).

procedures. This led to the production, at the beginning of the 4th century BCE, of manufactured tokens as mentioned in Aristophanes' *Wealth* (v. 277–8; 972; 1164–67), which were either referred to as a *symbolon* (ξύμβολον, meaning 'token'), or by metonymy, as a *gramma* (γράμμα, letter). In a passage of *Assemblywomen* (v. 675–690), Aristophanes mocks the designation by lottery of jury members in various courts. Praxagora has imagined a new constitution, according to which each citizen will be randomly assigned not to a magistrates' court, but to a place to have dinner, by drawing 'letters' which correspond to the first letter of the various place names. The three letters mentioned in this passage from Aristophanes, the beta, the theta, and the kappa, recall the 24 letters of the alphabet as well as the *sampi* which appears on bronze and lead tokens from the beginning of the 4th century BCE, and which were contemporaneous with *Assemblywomen* and *Wealth* (Boegehold, 1984). Such tokens were revealed by archaeological excavations of the Athenian Agora. According to Boegehold, who presents the catalogue, the number 25 allows for the division of all the courts into equal parts, regardless of their composition: 200, 400, and 500 jury members. Thus, these letters could have been used to randomly assign sections of courts to jurors for an entire year, before the first quarter of the 1st century BCE saw the creation of a daily lottery system to select jurors for each day. Because the last letter mentioned by Aristophanes was the letter *kappa*, which is the tenth letter of the Greek alphabet, Boegehold argues that these letters could announce the letters of the court sections engraved onto the *pinakia*, the citizens' bronze identity plates used in subsequent lottery procedures. However, it is entirely possible that Aristophanes could have been referring to the 25 letters of the preserved bronze tokens, without necessarily subscribing to Boegehold's interpretation, given that the use of these 'letter tokens' still remains rather obscure.

Among the random selection equipment used by the People's Court and as described by Aristotle (*The Constitution of the Athenians*, 63, 2), we find the term *balanos* (βάλανος), which could refer to an acorn or a chestnut, on which the letters corresponding to the various courts were engraved. We do not know whether the term *balanoi* was used in fact to refer to terracotta marbles, nor can we reject the possibility that natural objects such as acorns were used, since sticks painted with the colour of the various courts were also in use at the time in the same context.

Let us also point to a particularity uncovered in the decree of Athens regarding the sacred land of Eleusis. While we cannot devote much time in this chapter to the complex process of random selection as a means of pacification, it is nonetheless interesting to note that for the oracular consultation, which was one stage of the procedure, the questions were engraved on two thin strips of tin (1, 37: *karriteros*), in either positive or negative etching, strips which were then rolled up in wool and placed inside two *hydriai*. The contents of the two *hydriai* were then drawn by lot.

The transition from the Homeric twig onto which a *sema* was applied to the various manufactured engraved objects gave birth to a word found only once in the extant literature, the present participle *klarographesantes* (κλαρογραφησάντες) from the verb *klarographo* which means 'to inscribe on a lot'. This term is found in a decree issued by the city of Nacona in Sicily around 300 BCE which established the terms of reconciliation between rival factions. After a civil war, the authorities decided to restore peace and to reorganize the body politic by proceeding to homologous pairings monitored by arbiters from Segesta. The lottery was performed using 'inscribed lots'. The random selection was operated by simultaneously extracting a name from each vase until the lots were used up: 'pairs of brothers' were thus formed. As expected, the recipients used for this lottery were *hydriai;* we do not know the shape of the tokens, but since they were supposed to display a name, it is probable that they resembled the Athenian identity plates (Demont, 2010; Lopez-Rabatel, 2011).

From the classical period onwards, the drawing of lots is referred to as *kleroo* and its result continues to be expressed by the verb *lanchano*, or by the compound verb *synlanchano*, as in the Nacona decree where the process was designed to pair up 'brothers' from two different civil factions (*oi synlachontes adelphoi*). However, the vocabulary referring to the tools in use displays the great diversity of natural materials exploited; materials that were then modified and sealed with a human mark. The recipients were always domestic objects of various shapes and materials.

However, the diversity of these tools should not cause us to overlook the continuity of practices, particularly regarding the four fundamental stages of the lottery process: i.e. choosing or making the lots with the inscription of a mark or of a name; placing them in the recipient; jumbling them up; and finally drawing the lots as such. In comparison with the Homeric procedure, the disappearance of the prayer phase is notable. It reveals the absence of any strong religious symbolism in the lottery procedure during the classical period, even though the intricate links between political and religious matters during that era are well known, including in procedures considered to be exclusively democratic. The purification of the enclosure of the

Pnyx, performed by spreading the blood of a sacrificed piglet, is a significant example of such a link.

The invention of the kleroterion

The expansion of random selection procedures which accompanied the advent of democracy during the first decades of the 5th century BCE led to the modification of lottery equipment. With the progressive enlargement of the citizenry, membership to which all census classes were eligible, as well as the rise of the democratic notions that all citizens should have access to public office and that increased power should be devolved to the People's Court, it became necessary to perform more frequent lotteries for larger groups. The Ancient Greeks were therefore forced to design machines which met three essential requirements: the machines had to guarantee equality among all, avoid fraud, and allow for a faster and more complex selection than the individual drawing of lots.

The kleroterion and its accessories

The tool that was ultimately designed, and whose purpose was only identified many years after its discovery, was called a *kleroterion* (κληρωτήριον). The oldest reference to one appears in *The Wasps* by Aristophanes (v. 698). This word is composed of the stem of the verb *kleroo* (κληρόω), 'to draw lots', derived from the noun *kleros,* probably originally referring to the object which was drawn, a pebble or a piece of wood (Chantraine, 1968a), and of the derivative suffix -*terion,* used to form the names of instruments, places, and religious ceremonies (Chantraine, 1968b, pp. 62–66; Demont, 2003, p. 27); or even, as recently evidenced by an inscription at Kyme (Frölich, 2004), to moments during a procedure. This semantic range explains the variety of earlier commentaries regarding the term *kleroterion* and the differing translations that preceded the identification of any archaeological remains.

In Aristophanes' *Assemblywomen* (v. 681–686), the referent was likely a transportable object which Praxagora, in order to set up the new constitution she imagined based on the concept of communal ownership, seeks to position on the Agora in order to choose, by lottery, the places to which citizens will be assigned for their dinner. In his *Onomasticon* Book IX (44), the lexicographer Pollux of Naucratis (2nd CE) mentions the *kleroterion* in a list of public buildings, as a place where the *klerotai* sat (the randomly selected citizens or jurors). While Pollux concedes that the latter is also a location attested to in a lost play by

Aristophanes, *The Geras* (*The Old Woman*),[8] the term *kleroterion* also figures as a recipient, *aggeion* (ἀγγεῖον) in the inventory of words related to the judicial equipment listed in Book X (61), alongside the clepsydra and the voting tokens.

The first translations of *The Constitution of the Athenians*, the papyrus bearing the manuscript of which was discovered in 1891 (Kenyon, 1891), reproduced the multiple meanings found in Aristophanes and Pollux. The word *kleroterion* was translated by the term 'urns for random selection' (Reinach, 1891) then by 'premises for random selection' (Haussoullier and Mathieu, 1912), thus indicating that the actual referent had not yet been identified.

Sterling Dow (1937) is to be credited with having connected the word to the object itself. Dow published the first overview of the *kleroteria* in a compilation of decrees in honour of the *prytaneis* – the fifty advisors drawn by lots from the Council of 500 – that was discovered during the excavations of the Athenian Agora undertaken by the American School in 1931. Two of these relatively incomplete inscriptions shed a significant light on the history of the *kleroteria*. They were engraved on steles, one side of which showed columns of slots carved into the stone (Dow, 1937, pp. 142–146, no. 79 and 80) and on which the decree was ordered to be transcribed onto a '*kleroterion* of stone'. This is how Dow first identified as *kleroteria* the steles unearthed between 1830 and 1920 by excavations supervised by the Greek Archaeological Service (Thompson 1972, p. 220) and, after 1837, carried out by the Greek Archaeological Society, as well as the steles later discovered by the American School in 1931. From then on, Dow argued that in *The Constitution of the Athenians*, the word *kleroterion* unambiguously referred to a random selection machine. Whereas the possible reference to a place cannot be rejected outright, be it from a linguistic perspective or from the (albeit rare) viewpoint of literary testimony, it is the meaning of the *kleroterion* as a tool which is of interest here. In a riddle written by the poet Eubulus in the middle of the 4th century BCE (PCG V, F106 = Athenaeus, *The Learned Banqueters* 10, 450b-c), the mysterious object is referred to by a kind of 'doublet', the word *kleroterion* and the nominal adjective *klerotikon* (κληρωτικὸν). Otherwise unknown, this term is probably a poetic invention, whose suffix allows the author to emphasize the idea that the object was

---

[8] Under the entry '*kleroteria*' and about the same fragment, Phrynichos the Atticist, a grammarian and lexicographer from the same period, wrote that it referred to the 'location where the dikastes [jurymen] are drawn by lottery' (*Praeparatio sophistiqua*, Epitome, Aristophanes fr. 146).

destined for, or otherwise related to, random selection. The poet uses the word *kleroterion* in another passage (PCG V, F74 = Athenaeus, *The Learned Banqueters* 14, 640b–c), in a heterogeneous list of goods, objects, and persons that can be found in Athens. Lastly, the ancient commentaries of verses 674 and 752 from *The Wasps* mention another noun of the same etymology, the *klerotris* (κληρωτρίς), a 'ballot urn', topped with a *ketharion* (κηθαρίον), a sort of basket or funnel through which ballots were inserted. Although the commentator is speaking about drawing lots, he uses the term *psephos*, which very early on in Greek literature had come to refer to ballot tokens. Moreover, the grammarian Hesychius of Alexandria employed the same term in the 4th century BCE when he wrote about the *ketion*, a 'large-sized' tool used to 'push the ballots into the *kleroteria*' (*Lexicon, s. v.* κήτειον). In the *Souda*, a Greek encyclopaedia from the 10th century CE, an equivalence is established between the *kleroteria* and the *klerotrides* (plural of *klerotris*), considered as public offices filled by random selection procedures. It is significant that, even in contemporary sources, references confuse voting materials and random selection. This confusion can be explained by a shift towards the generic designation of objects that were all of natural origin. This was the case for the word *psephos*, as well as *palos*, which were reserved during the Homeric era for the drawing of lots but later used by the tragic poets to refer to ballot tokens (Laffon, 2016; Lopez-Rabatel, 2019). The term *kleroterion* could likewise refer to the lottery machine, as well as to the public institutions or the gathering places associated with the drawing of lots. This polysemy stems equally from metonymy and synecdoche, as evidenced by a passage from a short essay by Plutarch, in which the *kleroteria* symbolize political or judicial activity (*Whether an Old Man Should Engage in Public Affairs* 793d): 'But for a man who is quite old, even if you subtract the lack of glory, that love of office that always responds at every *kleroterion*, that busy restlessness that lies in wait for every chance to serve in a lawcourt or synedrion, are toilsome and miserable.'

Outside of Athens, the word was used in a decree of political association between the cities of Smyrna and Magnesia on the Meander, dated 243–242 BCE (*IK* 8,1 = Ihnken, 1978 and *IK* 24, 573 = Petzl, 1987; Rhodes, Osborne, 2003) and in the first Edict of Cyrene issued by Emperor Augustus around 7–6 BCE (de Visscher, 1965, pp. 16–19 and 69–73) to refer to instruments of a somewhat different configuration than those used for lottery procedures.

Although we now know that *kleroteria* were familiar to Athenians in their daily life, until Dow's pioneering studies, historians long remained ignorant of their material reality. Dow briefly described the fragments already published and introduced some unpublished fragments as recently discovered during the excavations of the Agora. He suggested a formal and functional reconstruction of the machines used in a judicial context from information contained in the *Constitution of the Athenians* (62–68). Through a comparative study of material remains, Dow was also able to show that the use of *kleroteria* went far beyond the judicial framework: these machines were likely also used to draw lots for a great number of magistracies and lower-level public offices.

When an exhaustive and meticulous study of the *pinakia*, the bronze tablets that were inserted in the slots of the *kleroteria*, was published by Kroll (1972), this marked a notable advance in our understanding of the institutional function of the random selection procedures used to appoint magistrates and jurors in the People's Court. The Athenian literary and epigraphic attestations of *kleroteria* were compiled by Boegehold *et al.* (1995) in a volume from *The Athenian Agora* collection devoted to the law courts in Athens. The study of the material corpus, taken up by Dow again in 1969, was left unfinished. After Dow's death, the unpublished *kleroteria* corpus as well as Dow's archives were first transferred to J. Kroll, then graciously shared with me during my doctoral research.[9] In this context, I studied the remains and undertook experimental archaeological work in collaboration with Nicolas Bresch, with whom I am currently pursuing this research and preparing the publication of the *kleroteria* discovered in Athens, Delos, and Paros. This publication will be complemented by an overview of the material and institutional aspects of random selection and lottery procedures in the Greek world.[10]

---

[9] I would like to express my sincere thanks to Professor Kroll and Professor Camp, Director of the Excavations of Athenian Agora, for allowing this dossier to be entrusted to me for publication, with authorization from the First Ephoria of Prehistorical and Classical Antiquity (the Greek Ministry for Culture and Sports). My gratitude also goes to the French School of Athens, to whom I owe the ability to undertake several field missions to study the material in Athens and Delos, and which has also acted as an intermediary in all administrative dealings with Greek officials.

[10] The arguments and provisional conclusions presented in this article stem jointly from research undertaken towards a doctoral dissertation in Languages, History and Civilization of Ancient Worlds titled '*Kleroteria*. The Drawing of Lots in the Ancient Greek World: Machines, Institutions and Use', supervised by Professor Moretti, University of Lyon 2 (2011), and from ongoing experimental archaeology studies presented at the *Salon Innovatives* held in Marseille on 17 and 18 May 2017 (https://lejournal.cnrs.fr/videos/la-machine-qui-tirait-au-sort-les-citoyens-

The use of *pinakia* in the Greek world beyond Athens is attested from the Hellenistic to the Imperial period, notably in Rhodes (Fraser, 1972). In 1998, Müller (1998, pp. 167–172) described two *kleroteria* fragments that were recycled as the uprights of a church window in the town of Paroikia (on the island of Paros); in 2001, four fragments found on Delos island and studied by Moretti (2001, pp. 133–143) confirmed the use of lottery procedures outside of Athens, employing tools that were relatively similar to the equipment used in Athens.

Shape and operation of the kleroteria

The Athenian *kleroteria* corpus includes fewer than 40 fragments from 17 different machines, in varying states of conservation. To these we can add four other fragments from three different machines discovered on the island of Delos, as well as two more fragments from the same *kleroterion* recycled in the church window in Paros. *Kleroteria* were discovered in two different places in Athens, the Ancient Agora and the Roman Agora; both correspond to significant phases in the history and civic life of the city. The location of the various fragments in one or the other agora is not without effect regarding the definition of their use — even if none of these remains were found in place, and even if it is quite probable that a certain number of the fragments were displaced, at least within a limited perimeter.

The first collection, constituted between 1831 and 1920, was discovered outside of the Ancient Agora, on the Acropolis, and in the zone of the Roman Agora and Hadrian's Library. The elements of the second collection, which comprises newly discovered fragments, were found on the Ancient Agora between 1935 and 1953. The concerned zones are, by order of frequency: the region of the Odeon of Agrippa, which corresponds to a construction-free zone during in the classical era; the north-east of the Agora, around the Stoa of Attalos; the south-western sector, around the Metroon (between the new Bouleuterion, the Metroon, and the Tholos) and then the Monument of the Eponymous Heroes; the south of the Agora (in the region of the middle Stoa and of civic buildings from the Roman period and north of the Aiakeion); and, finally, the south-east of the Agora, where the double-sided *kleroterion* that holds a very important place in the history of this research was discovered. However, we do not know the provenance of the fragment which first led to the identification of the *kleroteria*, and

---

dathenes). The complete corpus of *kleroteria* and a synthesis of their use will be presented in a forthcoming publication.

which bears the unique un-reconstructed mention of the word *kleroterion*.

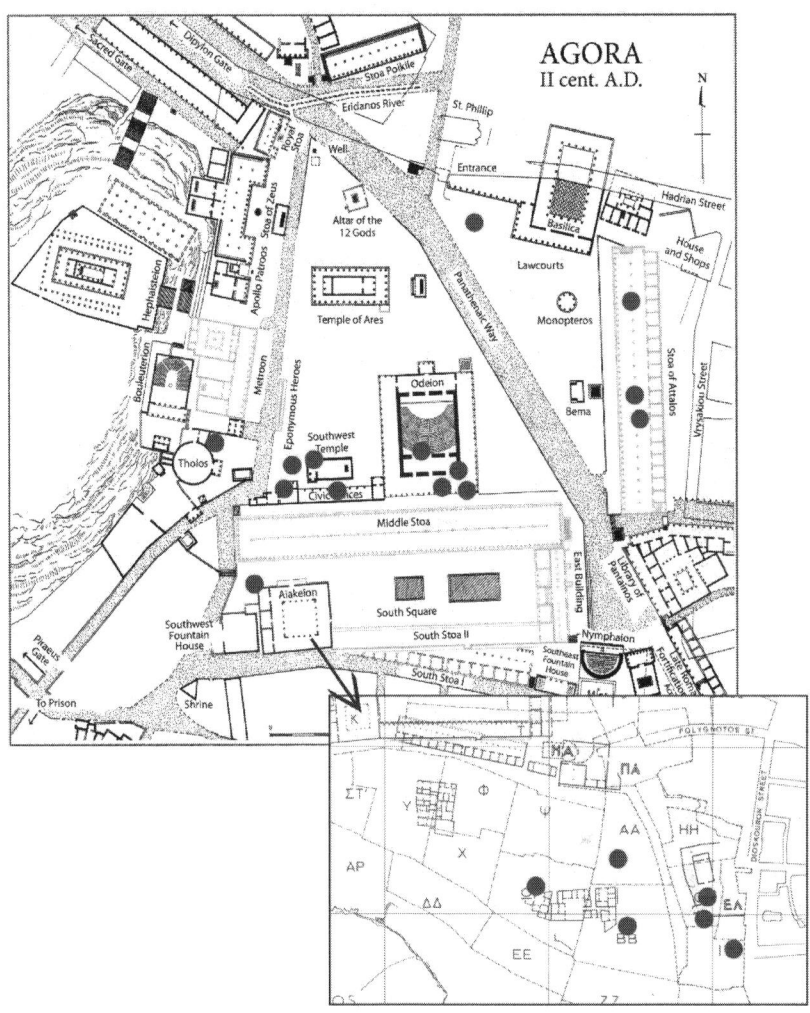

Figure 1: Discovery sites of the *kleroteria* on the Ancient Agora: produced by the author L. Lopez-Rabatel, IRAA (from Mauzy, *Agora Excavations 1931–2006, A Pictorial History*, p. 9, The American School of Classical Studies at Athens, Athens, 2006, and Kroll, *The Athenian Agora: Results of excavations*, Vol. XXVI: The Greek Coins, Princeton, 1993, plate 35, plan of the Athenian Agora *ca.* 100 BCE, showing excavation sections and grid).

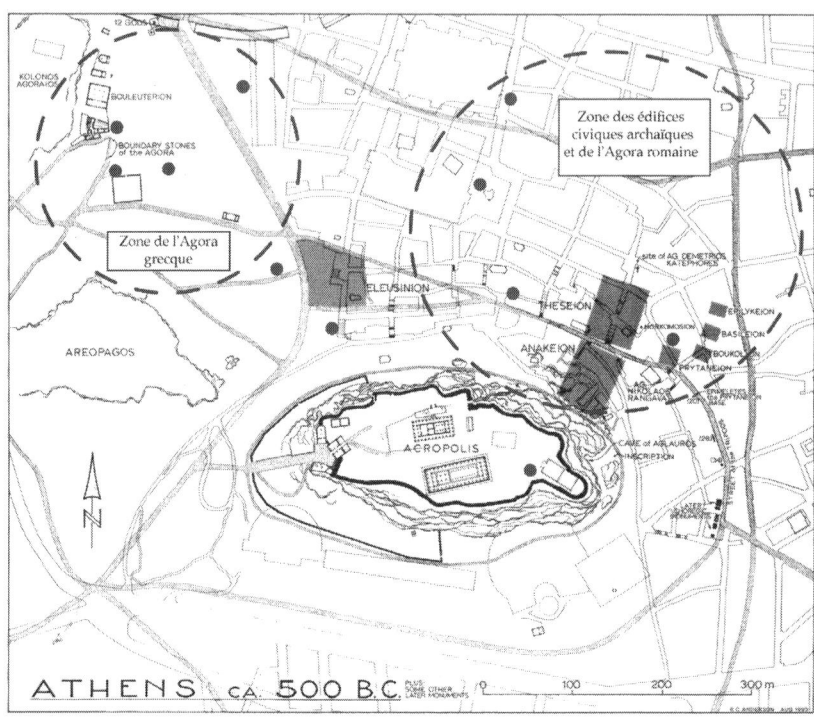

Figure 2: Athens, discovery sites of the *kleroteria* on the Ancient Agora and the Roman Agora: produced by the author L. Lopez-Rabatel, IRAA (from Shear, 1994, fig. 1: Acropolis and Agora, ca. 500 BCE, showing locations of earliest civic buildings, sanctuaries, and streets in relation to modern city blocks).

The *kleroteria* which have come down to us are all made of marble, the vast majority of them in Pentelic marble; some are in blue-grey marble from Mount Hymette. From the similar features observed while studying the fragments, we can establish a general idea of what the machine must have looked like. It resembles a stone stele similar to the funerary tombstones shaped like small temples which proliferated in Attica from around 450 BCE to the end of the 4th century BCE.

Figure 3: Photograph of *kleroterion* no. 1 (Epigraphic Museum of Athens, EM 8984). Photograph Ph. Collet, EFA.

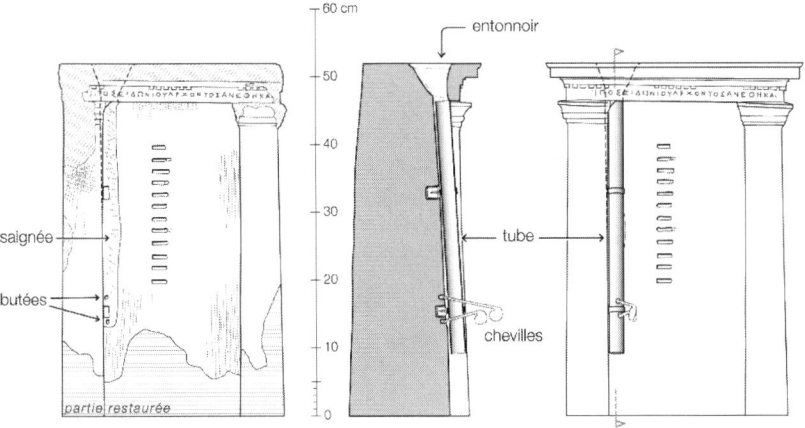

Figure 4: Nomenclature of kleroterion elements (Bresch, IRAA Paris).

The *kleroterion* is built within an architectural frame composed of two pilasters topped with capitals and a flat capstone of Doric style in which a funnel-like hole is carved. The funnel empties against the left pilaster, above a vertical groove. On two preserved fragments, mortises and smaller cavities are present beneath the groove. Slots are drilled in rows and columns on the front side of the steles, the number of which varies. A few fragments possess an inscription, a dedication engraved on the architrave, or a decree in honour of the *prytaneis* on one of its two sides. It is by confronting these remains with the passage of the *Constitution of the Athenians* describing the process of random selection in the courts that Dow was able to begin reconstructing these machines. Paragraphs 63 and 64 offer us, in a non-linear order, information regarding the form and operation of *kleroteria* at the end of the 4th century BCE, used almost daily (about 200 days a year) to randomly select jurors for the *dikasteria* (popular courts).

> **63.1.** The nine archons by tribes fill the dikasteria, and the secretary of the thesmothetai represents the tenth tribe.
> **2.** There are ten entrances to the dikasteria, one for each tribe, and twenty kleroteria, two for each tribe, and one hundred boxes, ten for each tribe, and other boxes where they put the pinakia of the dikasts [judges] who have been chosen by lot, and two hydriai. [...]
> **4.** Each dikast has his boxwood pinakion inscribed with his name, patronymic, and deme, and one letter of [the alphabet] up to kappa, for the dikasts are divided into ten sections distributed over the tribes, with about the same number in each letter [section].
> **5.** After the thesmothetes has chosen by lot the letters which are to be attached to the dikasteria, the attendant takes the allotted letter and places it on the proper dikasterion.

64.1. The ten boxes lie in front of the entrance for each tribe. On them are inscribed the letters as far as kappa. After the dikasts have thrown their pinakia into the box on which is written the same letter as is on the pinakion itself, the attendant shakes them, and the thesmothetes draws one pinakion from each box.

2. This dikast is called the inserter (empektes), and he inserts the pinakia from the box into the column of slots on which is the same letter as that on the box. He [the inserter] is chosen by lot, so that the same person does not always insert the pinakia and cheat. There are five columns of slots in each of the kleroteria.

3. When he has thrown in the dice, the archon draws lots for tribe members on the kleroterion. The dice are bronze, black and white; as many white ones are thrown in as [the number of] dikasts needed to be chosen, a single white one for each five pinakia; and the black dice in the same way. After he draws out the cubes, the herald calls those who have been allotted to serve. The inserter is included in the number [of those accepted as dikasts]. (Aristotle, *Constitution of the Athenians*, trad. Boegehold, 1995, pp. 207–208; 232)

The *kleroterion* was endowed with *stoicheia* (στοιχεῖα), rows of slots distributed in five *kanonides* (κανονίδες) which probably corresponded to a vertical alignment, if we refer to the mention of letters that are placed 'above them' (ἐφ᾽ ἧς ...). Various accessories were used: the *pinakia*, boxwood plates inscribed with a letter, bronze, black, or white cubes, and finally boxes bearing a letter corresponding to one of those engraved on the *pinakia*, as well as on the top on the columns. The main actors involved in the procedure were the *dikastes*, the potential judges who participated in the drawing of lots, the archon, the main magistrate who supervised the operations on behalf of a given tribe and proceeded to the random selection by 'taking the cubes out', as well as the *empektes* who inserted the *pinakia* in the *kleroterion* and who sat among the jurors nominated for that the day. The procedure is only partially described in the text. The *dikastes* running for office first put their *pinakion* in a box bearing the same letter as the one engraved on the plate. The *empektes* draws the plates out of the box to insert them in the column above which the same letter is engraved. Then the archon 'puts' the cubes in a proportionate number corresponding to one-fifth of the number of candidates to select—one cube, be it black or white, for every five *pinakia*. The archon 'pushes' (the cubes) down and out of the *kleroterion* in order to proceed to the selection. The lottery for the constitution of peoples' juries thus unfolds, for each of the ten Athenian tribes, in front of each of the ten tribunal entrances respectively appointed, and on the threshold of which two *kleroteria* are placed.

This elliptic text, which only presents an incomplete description of the machines and the procedure, can be clarified despite a number of chronological inconsistencies (to which we will return later), by establishing a comparison with the material remains of *kleroteria* and their main accessory, the *pinakia*, of which large numbers were excavated.

The vertically aligned rows of slots observable on the fragments correspond to the *stoicheia* and the *kanonides*. As we know through the texts but also thanks to archaeological discoveries, the *pinakia* that were inserted inside were engraved with a citizen's name, his patronym, and his demotic (that is, the place of origin of his family), as well as a letter — the so-called 'section letter'; which, as demonstrated by Kroll (1972), corresponded to a decimal subdivision of each of the ten tribes. Basing his study of Aristotle's text, Dow argues that the trunk of the upside-down funnel, hollowed out into the front side of the machine, was made to receive the cubes inserted by the archon. He then suggested that the cubes passed through a tube which was placed against the groove dug alongside the left pilaster (see Figure 4), running vertically from the funnel. This hypothesis was confirmed by the presence of two mortises observed along the groove of the two fragments, *kleroterion* no. 1 and *kleroterion* no. 2, and which could have served to affix the tube, as well as by the presence of two small cavities, located both above and underneath the lower mortise and most probably linked to the functioning of the cube-evacuation device.

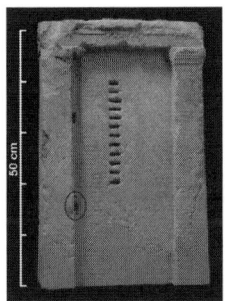

Figure 5: Photograph of *kleroterion* no. 1 (Epigraphic Museum of Athens, EM 8984); from a photograph by Ph. Collet, EFA, revised by N. Bresch (IRAA).

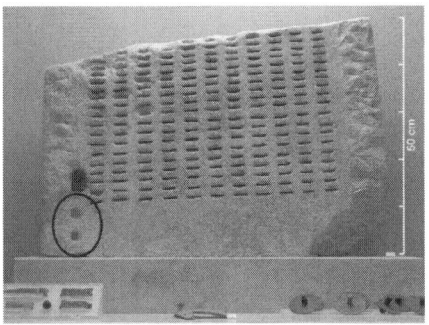

Figure 6: Photograph of *kleroterion* no. 2 (Athenian Agora Excavations, Museum, inv. I 3967 (B 1725/I 396); N. Bresch and L. Lopez-Rabatel [IRAA]).

The mechanism of the *kleroteria* was explored by Dow in *Prytaneis* (1937), as well as in his last unpublished work. This investigation was then furthered by Bishop (1970), who put forward the hypothesis that the small cavities found on *kleroterion* no. 1 and on *kleroterion* no. 2 could have served as recesses for rods that went through the tube from end to end and were taken out alternately to isolate the lower lot and expel it from the tube. For this study, Bishop took into account the gap between the recesses, the presumed diameter of the tube, and the likely size of the lots, deduced from the diameter of the funnel's mouth.

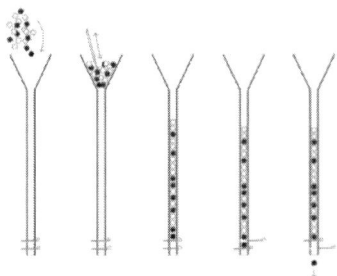

Figure 7: Diagram for the staggered extraction of cubes, based on Bishop's (1970) hypothesis; N. Bresch (IRAA).

Without negating the significant contributions made by Dow and Bishop, it was necessary to test this theoretical system while taking into account two elements which we argue had not been sufficiently addressed by these authors: the shape and mass of the lots inserted into the machine.[11] Starting from the premise that cubes cannot go through a circular tube, Dow and Bishop had deduced that only spherical balls could have been used in the *kleroteria*. Consequently, they argued that the term *kybos* was not appropriately employed and was in fact just a semantically weakened generic term. Our first objective was thus to demonstrate that it was possible to use cubes in the *kleroteria*, whatever the cross-section of the tube, whether rectangular or curvilinear, which could indeed vary according to the groove against which it rested. Stemming from the first objective, our second goal was to test the validity of the theoretical staggered extraction system suggested by Bishop, taking into account the constraints linked to the mass of the material used, bronze. It was necessary to verify that it was possible, with only one rod going throughout the tube, to lift a pile of bronze

---

[11] This work of experimental archaeology was undertaken in collaboration with N. Bresch.

cubes, as this operation would have been required to ensure the progressive extraction of the cubes.

The first experiment was undertaken on a cardboard model reproducing the full-scale *kleroterion* no. 1, and including all the necessary elements: a funnel dug into the front side with an opening of a diameter indicating the maximal dimension of the lots; a groove alongside the left-hand pilaster provided the measurements of the tube that must be reconstructed; mortises designed for affixing; and finally, recesses dug at the base of the groove, allowing us to deduce the gap between the pegs used for the staggered extraction of the cubes. A transparent tube was used to observe the behaviour of the cubes as they fell down through the tube and when they were isolated between the two rods before their extraction.

Figure 8: *Kleroterion* no. 1 (Epigraphic Museum of Athens, inv. EM 8984) and its reproduction by N. Bresch (IRAA), with the necessary accessories to demonstrate its functioning, presented during a conference at the Epigraphic Museum of Athens, May 2013.[12]

It is outside the scope of this chapter to outline all the steps of this experiment in a detailed fashion. We shall therefore directly present the conclusions that we have reached thus far.

1. We have been able to define the maximum diameter of the tube by taking into account the funnel's mouth, as well as the measurements of the opening of the groove at the top. This result gives a

[12] Conference held in the context of epigraphic sessions organized in Athens by the French School at Athens, British School at Athens, and the Epigraphic Museum of Athens.

tube of a diameter that is narrower than the one reconstructed by
Bishop.

2. Using the diameter of the tube, we have been able to determine
   the maximum size of the lots by preserving two hypotheses: as
   balls, the data indicate their diameter; as cubes, the data indicate
   their axial or interior diagonal, rather than the diagonal of one of
   their faces. We can observe that after eventually flipping themselves over — and thus behaving just like balls — the cubes come to
   rest with one face towards the bottom and pile up one on top of
   each other, a phenomenon which is confirmed by the law of stable
   equilibrium.

3. The maximum size of the lots therefore must be refined according
   to the space available between the rods designed to allow for the
   extraction of the cubes, a space which is defined by the gap
   between the cavities found at the bottom of the groove. It became
   apparent in the course of the tests we carried out with lots of
   varying sizes that the rods that go through the tube can be neither
   parallel nor horizontal in relation to each other, as the uppermost
   rod, if placed too high, cannot lift the second cube from the
   bottom in order to isolate the lower cube (hypothesis 2).

4. Given that no tube has been conserved, it was possible to imagine
   another orientation of the pegs without, however, changing the
   placement of their exit towards the stone. Different tests led to the
   conclusion that the rods had to be placed in a converging position,
   with one rod inclined towards the top, the other towards the
   bottom. In order to accomplish this, it was necessary to space the
   holes vertically on the external side of the tube.

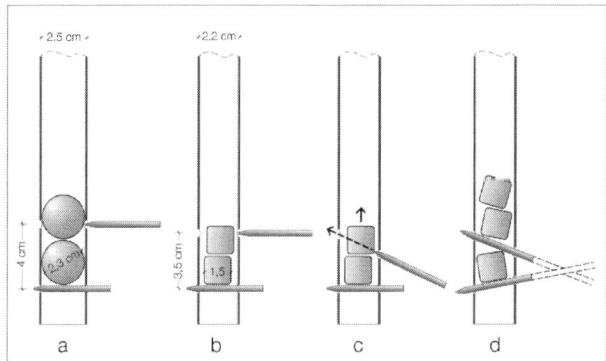

Figure 9: Diagram depicting the successive hypotheses regarding the staggered
cube extraction mechanism (N. Bresch and L. Lopez-Rabatel [IRAA]): (a) Bishop's
hypothesis (1970); (b) Bishop's hypothesis with cubes (1970); (c) hypothesis with
inclined upper peg; (d) hypothesis with both inclined pegs.

It was then possible to take into account the mass of the cubes, a factor that had hitherto been overlooked both theoretically and experimentally. To do so, we inserted a tin ballast into the tube, weighing the same as the 12 cubes combined.[13] The process becomes less smooth but remains possible.

These hypotheses were then tested directly on *kleroterion* no. 1, conserved at the National Epigraphic Museum in Athens.[14] The form of the cavities presented at the base of the groove confirmed the orientation of the pegs as had been hypothesized. By means of a last series of tests using a plastic tube, we were able to verify the staggered lot extraction method as reconstructed using the amended Bishop hypothesis. Using the *kleroterion*, we have moreover been able to prove that the funnel can contain the 12, 1.5-cm cubes that we had reproduced, but that it was occasionally necessary to stir the cubes for them to travel smoothly through the tube. This therefore confirms the necessity of the tool mentioned in the literature, the *ketion*, or 'stirring stick', the function of which was doubtless to orient the cubes and force them to enter the tube with a side flat towards the bottom. (Eubulus, *PCG* V, F. 106 = Athenaeus, *The Deipnosophistae* 10,450 b–c; Hesychius, *Lexicon*, *s.v.* κήτειον). Similar experiments undertaken with marbles have revealed the superiority of using cubes, insofar as cubes can be easily exhibited on a horizontal stand during counting operations and thus remain visible throughout the whole lottery process.

The conclusions of these experiments undertaken on *kleroterion* no. 1 still need to be analysed in comparison with data from other machines, but none of the other extant *kleroteria* provide all the necessary elements: the size of the funnel's mouth, the maximal measurements of the groove for the tube, and the presumed centre distance of the pegs inserted inside the tube. It is, however, possible to theoretically apply this procedure to all the *kleroteria*.

Although this experimental archaeological study has led to a notable breakthrough in our understanding of how the *kleroteria* functioned, their contextualization in turn raises questions which are sometimes impossible to resolve.

The major difficulty when comparing material remains with testimonial accounts lies in the chronological gaps. We have texts at our

---

[13]   From a ridge about 1.5 cm long, according to the composition of bronze in those days (approximately 140 grams).

[14]   This study was conducted at the National Epigraphic Museum of Athens, which we wish to thank here for having granted us the authorization to examine the conserved materials and for providing us with an extremely warm welcome.

disposal which date mostly from the 5th and 4th centuries BCE. There are also some inscriptions from the 3rd and 2nd centuries BCE in which *kleroteria* are mentioned, but those machines probably did not have the same shape as those reproduced according to Aristotle's text and which were in use at the end of the 4th century BCE. Excavations revealed some 300 bronze *pinakia* dating back to the first three-quarters of the 4th century BCE in Athens. It seems that these *pinakia* could not have been used in such machines, contrary to what has been assumed until now. They were replaced by boxwood *pinakia*, of which there are no remains left. The 'sections' represented by the first ten letters of the alphabet on the bronze *pinakia* seem, however, to have been created in the context of civil reforms specifically designed to address the needs of a random selection mechanism whose oldest material reality nonetheless eludes us. It is not implausible that the two types of *pinakia* (in bronze and in boxwood) may have co-existed for different purposes, used variably to draw lots for public offices and to select jury members.[15]

Figure 10: *Pinakion* belonging to Meidonides, Meidon's son from the *deme* of Kephisia, the sole owner (Kroll, 1972, no. 20 and p. 127).

Figure 11: *Pinakion* belonging to Philomnestos from the *deme* of Ikarion, the sixth owner (Kroll, 1972, no. 96 and p. 196).

---

[15] This hypothesis, which is based on Kroll's conclusions in his study on the *pinakia*, cannot be fully elaborated within the limits of this chapter. It shall be presented in the forthcoming work mentioned in note 10.

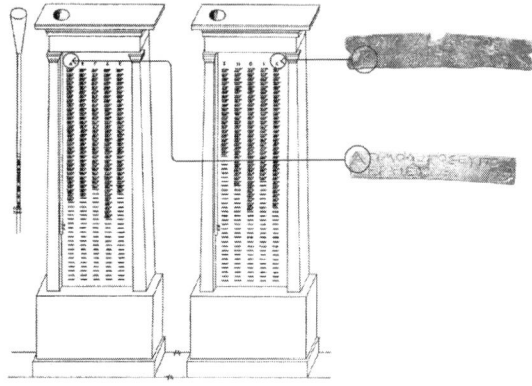

Figure 12: Matching between the section letters engraved on the *pinakia* and those appearing above the columns of grooves (produced by Lopez-Rabatel from a reproduction from Rhodes, 1981, p. 707, and Kroll, 1972, no. 37 and 96).

Among the *kleroteria* which have survived, the ones bearing inscriptions provide us with elements that help to date them more precisely. These apparatuses date from the 2nd century BCE and more precisely from the years 189–188 and 162–161 BCE. Other *kleroteria* without inscriptions can be cautiously dated by the number of columns they have: *kleroterion* no. 3, dated according to its inscription as from 164–163 BCE, possesses six columns. Supposing that a twin *kleroterion* may have been used in the same context, there would have been 12 columns in total, which correspond to the 12 tribes that Athens recognized between 200 and 127 BCE.

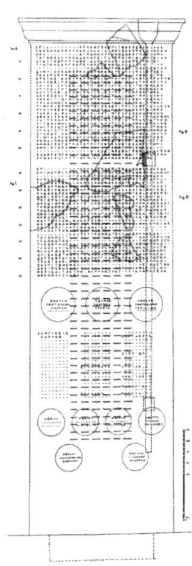

Figure 13: *Kleroterion* no. 3, reproduction of the stele based on fragments conserved, showing the back side with grooves superimposed over the front side with inscriptions (Dow, 1937, p. 206).

The eleven-columned *Kleroterion* no. 2 (in Figure 6), on display in the Agora Museum, may have been designed and used during a very short period of time from the year 201 to the spring of 200 BCE, a short interval during which there were 11 tribes in Athens. These observations illustrate the difficulties involved in applying 4th-century BCE institutional realities to the 2nd century BCE, about which we know much less. The continued existence of an apparatus, which may or may not have resembled the one used two centuries earlier, does not guarantee institutional continuity. It appears here that the number of columns of the *kleroteria* no longer corresponds to the 100 sections of Athenian society from the 4th century BCE but to the number of tribes, after 200 BCE, a date after which quotas regarding the representation of the *demes* were abolished. At the time of Cleisthenes' reform in 508 BCE, the territory of Attica had been divided into 139 *demes*, geographical and administrative entities of different sizes, and grouped within 10 unequal tribes. For the random selection of Council members, a system of representational quotas was instituted for each *deme*, according to its demographic weight and geographical location (by the sea, inland, urban). For any given tribe, lots were not drawn for the same number of candidates within each *deme*. From 200 BCE on, fifty councillors per tribe were drawn by lottery, without taking into account their *deme* of origin. This change in the configuration and use of *kleroteria* likely accounts for the disappearance of random selection as a specifically democratic mechanism, in the service of the principle of equal opportunity for all citizens to participate in public life.

Kleroteria: uses and locations

In an attempt to review the various uses of the *kleroterion* in democratic Athens, it is necessary to return to the end of the 6th century BCE and to the first decades of the 5th century BCE, a time when the durable foundations of social and political organization were being implemented, thus allowing for the rise and the subsequent development of the democratic regime during the 5th and 4th centuries BCE.

Illustrated in 487 BCE by the abrupt change how the archons were designated — rather than being elected as before, the archons were henceforth randomly selected — the growing use of sortition to the detriment of election prompted a change in equipment. We demonstrated a similar evolution in vocabulary by describing the *kleroteria* and their functioning. The widespread adoption of random selection is alluded to in the *Constitution of the Athenians* through the description of the lottery procedure at the People's Court during the last quarter of the 4th century BCE. However, thanks to another passage from this text, as well as a number of other sources, we know that a considerable number of political offices (around 700 magistracies and lower-ranking public offices) were also assigned by lottery for varying lengths of time ranging from one day to one year.

Reviewing the political positions assigned by lottery in literary and epigraphic sources enables us to suggest the specifications characterizing the design of the *kleroteria* according to different circumstances, to clarify the frequency of random selection procedures and to establish the composition of the body of candidates. It thus appears, with a variable degree of certainty, that random selection largely corresponded to annual positions. Annual lotteries were used every year to select the panel of 6,000 potential jury members, the 500 Council members (the *bouleutes*), and around 700 other public positions, all composed of voluntary citizens (*ex apanton*: from the whole, i.e. from the whole citizenry). In addition, for each *prytany* (a period of time that was one-tenth of the bouleutic year), a lottery took place monthly to select the 50 councillors from one of the ten tribes who would exercise the presidency of the Council in turns, thus acting as the councillor for a period of 36 to 37 days. Starting some time between 403 and 379 BCE, institutional changes led to the creation of a new office, the nine *proedroi*, who were selected by drawing lots among the 450 Councillors who were not exercising the *prytany* at that time. That lottery occurred daily. As for the *dikastes*, they were selected by lottery to constitute the Jury of the People's Court for about 200 days per year.

Whatever the size of the group within which the selection took place, the number of columns on the machine used always depended on the number of tribes, whereas the number of rows could be further indicated when the body of candidates was defined, such as was the case when drawing lots for the *prytany*. Among all of the existing *kleroteria*, only *kleroterion* no. 1 has preserved its number of rows. For the other material remains, it is necessary to infer, according to their size and use, the number of rows that they originally possessed, which occasionally raises unsolvable problems. *Kleroterion* no. 2, which displays 11 columns of grooves, was most probably used to randomly select the 550 *bouleutes* in 200 BCE. We can therefore deduce that it contained at least 50 rows of slots ($50 \times 11 = 550$) corresponding to the selected candidates, marked by 50 white cubes inserted into the funnel. In order to guarantee the random nature of the lottery, a certain number of rows corresponding to the rejected candidates (and an equivalent number of black cubes) was added. We can only speculate regarding the total number of grooves needed (70? 100?), since it was not possible to predict the number of candidates. However, we can estimate a number by taking into account the measurements of the stele. In most cases, when the number of columns was not preserved we are led to reconstitute a number comprised between 10 and 12 (or half of that number if taking into account the hypothesis of twin *kleroteria*), representing the number of tribes. This number varied during the Hellenistic era, which, while it no longer enjoyed a demo-cratic government, had not altogether abandoned the procedure of drawing lots. We therefore end up reconstructing large-scale machines which reach up to 1.60 m in height, thus posing a certain number of questions regarding the modalities of their use.

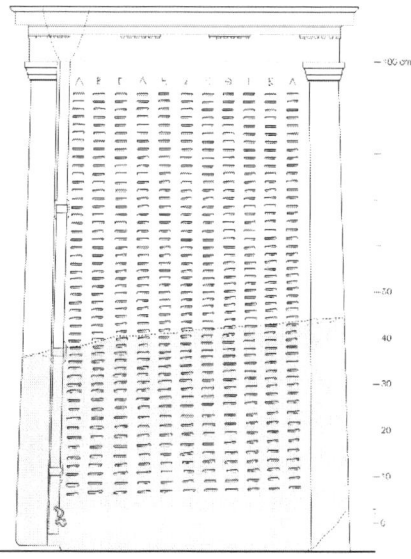

Figure 14: Reconstruction of *kleroterion* no. 2, N. Bresch and L. Lopez-Rabatel (IRAA). Athenian Agora Excavations, Museum, inv. I 3967 (B 1725/I 396).

With the advent of the *kleroterion*, the implementation of the democratic ideal experienced unprecedented technical development. This new tool satisfied the need to combine a preliminary sorting with the simulta-neous selection of numerous candidates, in particular for the random selection of court jurors. The sorting process was conducted according to the information provided by the *Constitution of the Athenians*, by filling up the grooves vertically according to the section letter which appeared on each citizen's *pinakion*. When a white or black cube was expelled from the tube, a complete row was selected; several candi-dates were therefore chosen at once, from 6 to 12 depending on the machine.

As early as the classical period, however, the *kleroterion* was also used in situations when it was not indispensable. According to Aristotle (*Constitution of the Athenians*, 66.1), the presidency of various court chambers was assigned to the archons by means of two *kleroteria*: cubes of the colour corresponding to that of the court were poured into the first machine, while cubes with the name of magistrates were inserted in the second machine. *Pinakia* were not used in this case and one cube was extracted simultaneously from each machine in order to match archons and courts, a result which could have been obtained by just drawing from two recipients. At a later period, the use of one *kleroterion* made with only one column (*kleroterion* no. 1) in a situation where simple rudimentary equipment (recipients and lots) would have been sufficient and quicker likely indicates that the *kleroterion* had a symbolic as well as practical function. From this point of view, it is not unfounded, despite their dissimilarities, to establish a parallel between the small *kleroteria* marked with a dedication and the large *kleroteria* with a *prytany*'s decree inscribed on them. It is interesting to note that these inscriptions are all dated from between 189 and 162 BCE, reflecting a unique political context of Athenian assertiveness in regard to the city's identity and its democratic values. These characteristics were also expressed, *inter alia*, by the reorganization of the Theseia, the ceremony in honour of Theseus, the legendary hero and founder of the city of Athens. It is notable that these machines present a number of archaic traits. For instance, the first series have a partially conserved Doric entablature at the top of the stele (with *guttae* associated or not with a *regula*), which is deemed to be the most ancient of the decorative orders in Greek mythology. Similarly, on *kleroterion* no. 3 from the second series, the positioning of the inscription in *stoichedon* — engraving the letters in a grid — is a design element no longer attested to after 276–275 BCE (Tracy, 1995). These particular traits which recall the ancient and glorious past of Athens, at that point under Roman rule, raise the question of whether these machines, emblematic of democracy, were being used as tools for propaganda.

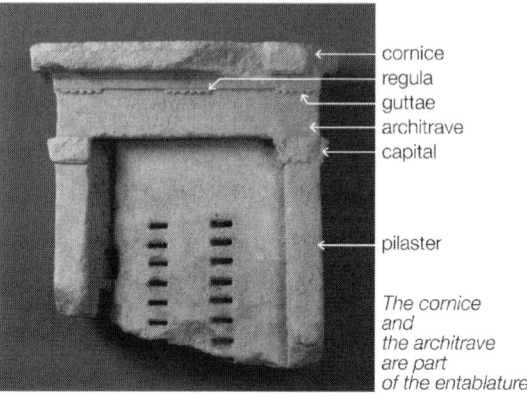

Figure 15: Nomenclature of the architectural elements of *kleroteria* (*kleroterion* no. 4, conserved at the Epigraphic Museum of Athens, EM 13255). (Photograph by Ph. Collet, revised by N. Bresch, IRAA.)

Textual documentation and archaeological remains provide very little information on the sites in which the lotteries took place in Athens. The study of the various functions assigned by drawing lots, the localization of the premises of the assemblies (the Bouleuterion for the Council, the Pnyx for the People's Assembly and Courts), the frequency of selections procedures and meetings, as well as the physical space required for lotteries to be held mean that the *kleroteria* may have been used in four different areas.

For the first of these areas, the *Constitution of the Athenians* explicitly indicates that the random selection of jurors for the People's Court took place in front of the *dikasteria*, a cluster of courtrooms that Rhys Townsend (1995) has identified with the remains of buildings located in the north-east of the Agora, on the site of the Stoa of Attalos. This identification raises some unsolvable problems given our present-day sources. Despite the discovery in this zone of a certain number of tokens which were used in court, if this hypothesis is conceivable for the period of activity for edifices A to D which date from the end of the 5th century BCE to *circa* 350 BCE, it is impossible for the Square Peristyle, which was only erected around 300 BCE and ultimately remained unfinished. Secondly, we find allusions in Aristophanes' *Assemblywomen* (v. 675–690) to the use of *kleroteria* in the north-west of the Agora. Finally, for the last two sites, two inscriptions dating from around 350 BCE mention that trials were held in the Stoa Poikile and in the Parabyston (*IG* II 1641 side b, 1 and 1646, I 8–12).

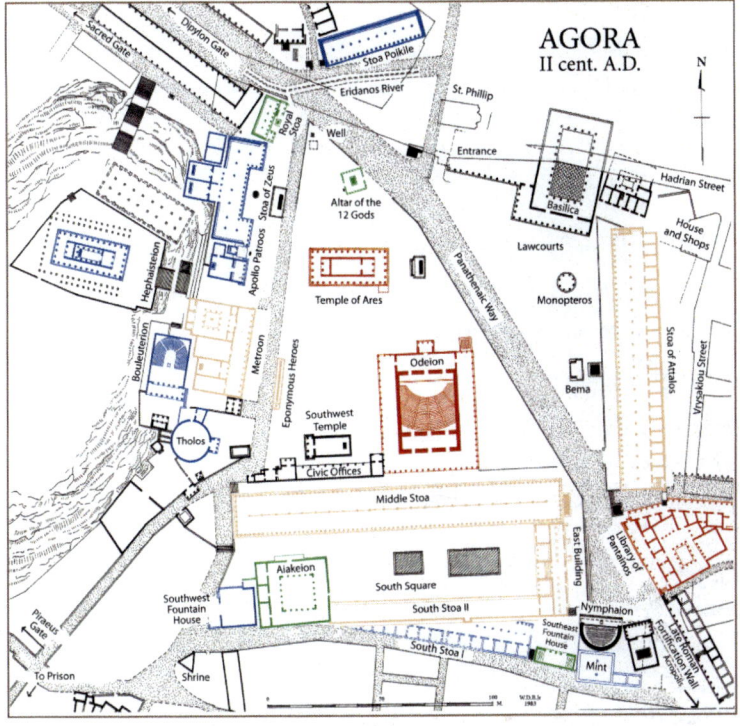

10. Plan of the Agora at the height of its development in ca. A.D. 150

Archaic
Classical
Hellenistic
Roman

Figure 16: Ancient Agora of Athens (in Mauzy, *Agora Excavations 193–2006, A Pictorial History*, p. 9, The American School of Classical Studies at Athens, Athens, 2006).

Among the sites where *kleroteria* fragments were discovered, various areas stand out on account of the density of the discovered fragments: the Bouleuterion site south-west of the Agora, and the area encompassing the Roman Agora and Hadrian's library. The first site could have housed daily or monthly lotteries inside the Prytaneion, the enclosure around the Bouleuterion and the Tholos inside of which inscribed steles were erected. In the area of Hadrian's library, a series of small, identical *kleroteria* were discovered that raise certain problems of interpretation, but more importantly attest to the continuity of customs inherited from democratic Athens during the Roman era.

We know from Aristotle (*Constitution of the Athenians*, 62, 1) and from Aeschines (*Against Ctesiphon*, 13) that, in the 4th century BCE, lottery procedures were conducted in the authentic Theseion,[16] a sanctuary which was presumably located to the north-east of the Acropolis (see map above), although no remains exist today. The enclosure of the Theseion appears to have encompassed an area large enough to hold large-scale lotteries for numerous candidates, including for the yearly selection, which did not require meeting places nearby but did on the other hand demand a certain solemnity. At the end of the 2nd century BCE, it was in this sanctuary built around 450 BCE and dedicated to Athens' founding father that two of the large *kleroteria* were erected, with inscriptions providing fairly reliable evidence that the drawing of lots took place within the *temenos*, the sacred enclosure. It is possible that, during the late Hellenistic period, the area including the Theseion and the Prytaneion could have been, as it had been in the 5th century BCE, an emblematic place of the Athenian identity in which a number of civic activities took place.

While we can cautiously identify the areas in which lotteries were held in classical Athens, including up until the late Hellenistic era, we are currently unable to offer a precise description of their arrangement, which must have been composed of mobile and temporary devices.

Conclusion

Such as we can glean from the combined study of archaeological remains and the vocabulary used to describe random selection instruments, the history of drawing lots in the Ancient Greek world was characterized by a gap between political innovations and the equipment that could enable such innovations to be implemented.

The discontinuity between the Homeric era and the democratic period did not lie solely in the disappearance of prayers to the gods as an essential stage of all sortition procedures. It was also marked by the transition from improvised and spontaneous lotteries among small groups to a system of random selection designed to meet clearly expressed political aims that were part of an institutionalized time-frame. Because it applied, theoretically, to all citizens, the democratic lottery system led to the search for more sophisticated instruments and the implementation of more rigorously defined procedures.

---

[16] The building in question should not be confused with the Hephaisteion, situated north-west of the Agora and provisonally called the Theseion before being formally identified as the Temple of Hephaestus.

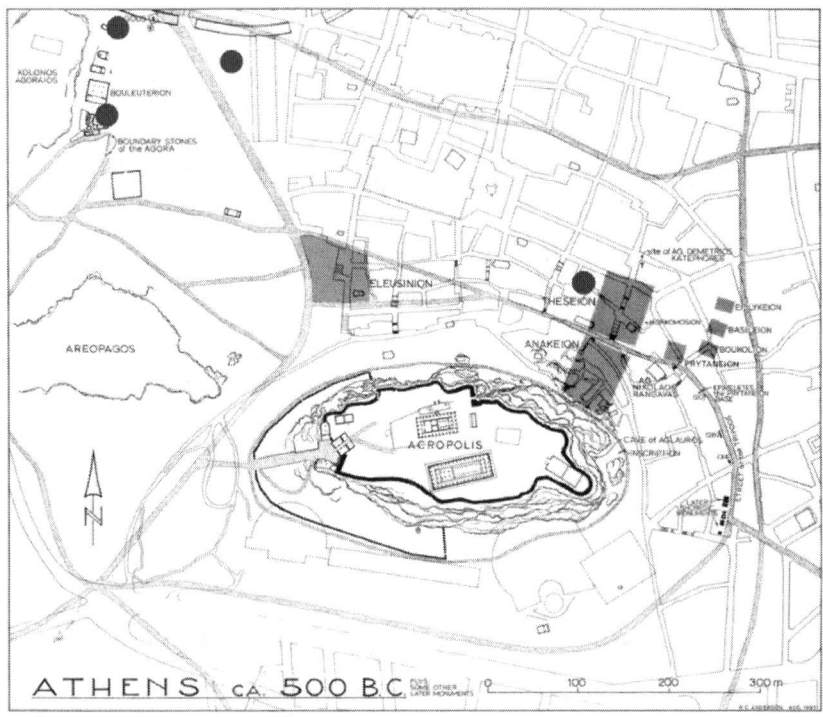

Figure 17: Areas where *kleroteria* were used in Athens, from the end of the 4th century to the 2nd century BCE (from Shear, 1994, fig. 1: Acropolis and Agora, ca. 500 BCE, showing locations of earliest civic buildings, sanctuaries, and streets in relation to modern city blocks).

In the Homeric world, the lots came from the natural environment, while the recipient was from the very beginning a manufactured object. The complexity of the reforms undertaken during the early democratic period contrasted with the rudimentary nature of the implements still in use during the 5th century BCE, such as beans for random selection and pebbles for voting. The supremacy of sortition over voting awarded by radical democracy manifested itself through the differential evolution of the instruments used for each of these procedures respectively. Voting equipment underwent a gradual transformation, with manufactured standard ballot tokens more or less reproducing the primitive tools originally borrowed from the natural world. Under the democratic regime, the voting pebbles and the circular bronze tokens were referred to using the same term *psephos,* and further described as *demosia* (literally 'of the people', i.e. public).

The equipment used to conduct lotteries experienced a much more radical transformation with the invention of the *kleroterion,* or 'lottery machine', which appears in textual sources more than one century after Cleisthenes' reforms. The Homeric-era twigs marked with a distinctive sign gave way in the 4th century BCE to the *pinakia*, bronze plates marked with the essential elements of a citizen's identity. These plates were uniquely both personal objects while also the property of the state, which controlled their production and guaranteed their authenticity. Helmets and water vases were replaced by a stele marked with grooves which preserved the original function of the receptacle, but also become a machine for both sorting and drawing lots. The *kleroterion* was not an *ex-nihilo* invention: in fact, it was the adaptation of an existing object, the funerary stele (which could also bear inscriptions to be exposed to the public), reformulated to satisfy the needs of a complex procedure. Thus, the evolution of the practice of drawing lots led to great technical as well as lexical innovation, illustrating the 'craftiness of intelligence' cherished by Détienne and Vernant.

The *a posteriori* reconstruction by historians of lottery procedures and processes rests on the one hand on the insights afforded by the foundational text of the *Constitution of the Athenians*, and on the other on the archaeological analysis of the manufactured objects used to accomplish those processes. The study of *kleroteria* and the context of their use uncovers a number of hypotheses of varying degrees of credibility and provides some breakthroughs in our understanding of how they functioned. The main difficulty encountered when confronting archaeological remains with literary testimonies resides in the chronological gaps. For the most part, the extant texts date from the 5th and 4th centuries BCE, while a few inscriptions date from the 3rd and 2nd centuries BCE, and most remains are from the 4th century BCE (for the *pinakia*) and the 2nd century BCE (for the *kleroteria* with elements that can be precisely dated). There may be some risks involved in applying the institutional realities of the 4th century BCE to the 2nd century BCE, a period about which we know much less. The continued existence of certain implements, which we cannot be certain were identical to the implements in use two centuries earlier, does not entail a similar institutional continuity. But progress also stems from examining these overlapping co-existences. Moreover, reflecting on lottery practices and procedures necessarily raises questions regarding the places where these practices and procedures took place; here again, our hypotheses remain tentative, even though we can be relatively certain that the Bouleuterion and the Theseion hosted random selection procedures.

However, it appears that we have made progress in understanding the mechanism behind the extraction of the lots. Experientially, we were able to demonstrate that the lottery procedure could be accomplished with cubes. In addition, the need to take the measurements of each of the machines into account leads us to conclude that each *kleroterion* was equipped with its own accessories. The results of our study of the epigraphic and literary sources mentioning the public offices which were filled by random selection enables us to have a more complete idea of the types of machines required (size, number of columns and rows), according to the organization of the civic body at a given time and depending on the different lotteries which structured the political life of Athenians during the classical period.

This ingenious political machine, the *kleroterion*, only appeared during the latter part of the democratic era and, even then, only in a form that literary sources shroud in some mystery. The democratic system, which from the beginning reflected a complex and thorough theoretical development, was immediately materialized in fundamental reforms affecting the very fabric of society. Finding adequate tools to uphold a new governing paradigm was a challenging endeavour, however, and it was only after more than a century of democracy — and the numerous failed attempts mentioned by the texts — that the *kleroterion*, this 'democratic machine', was invented. Exposed in full view of the public, it served to guarantee the honesty of random selection procedures, while dispelling the dark side of sortition. It ultimately became an essential component of the ritualized theatricalization of public life.

The discrepancy observed between political innovations and the creation of appropriate tools, conversely, finds an echo in the 'abusive' use of the machine in circumstances which did not require its complexity and for which only a limited range of its possibilities were required, for instance when only one tube and one column were used.

The democratic phenomenon exhibits a discrepancy between the history of politics and the history of technical innovation: tools are the product of political innovations but in return, once they are invented, constitute powerful instruments which operate in service of a given political logic and even continue to embody such logic long after the golden age of democracy has passed.

References

N.B. Except where indicated to the contrary, the references to Greek texts pertain to those from the Collections des Universités de France (CUF), les Belles Lettres, Paris.

Austin, C. & Kassel, R. (1986) *Poetae comici graeci*, vol. V, Berlin: W. de Gruyter (= PCG V).

Bishop, J.D. (1970) The Cleroterium, *JHS*, no. 90, Cambridge: Cambridge University Press, pp. 1–14.

Boegehold, A.L., *et al.* (1995) *The Athenian Agora XXVIII, The Lawcourts at Athens: Sites, Buildings, Equipment, Procedure, and Testimonia*, Princeton, NJ: American School of Classical Studies.

Boegehold, A. (1984) Many letters: Aristophanes Plutus 1166–1167, in Boegehold, A., *et al.* (eds.) *Studies Presented to Sterling Dow on his Eightieth Birthday* (GRBM 10), Durham, NC: Duke University, pp. 23–29.

Brun, P. (2005) *Impérialisme et démocratie à Athènes. Inscriptions de l'époque classique*, Paris: Armand Colin.

Chantraine, P. (1968a) *Dictionnaire étymologique de la langue grecque: Histoire des mots*, Paris: Klinksieck.

Chantraine, P. (1968b) *La formation des noms en grec ancien*, 2nd ed., Paris: Klinksieck.

Clinton, K. (2005) *Eleusis: The Inscriptions on Stone: Documents of the Sanctuary of the Two Goddesses and Public Documents of the Deme*, vol. IA (text)-IB (plates), Athens: Archaeological Society at Athens.

Coulson, W.D.E., *et al.* (1994) *The Archaeology of Athens and Attica under the Democracy: Proceedings of an International Conference Celebrating 2500 Years since the Birth of Democracy in Greece*, held at the American School of Classical Studies at Athens, 4–6 December 1992, Oxford.

Demont, P. (2003) Le *klèrôtèrion* et la démocratie athénienne, *Bulletin de l'Association G. Budé*, Paris: Les Belles Lettres, pp. 26–52.

Demont, P. (2000) Lots héroïques: remarques sur le tirage au sort de l'*Iliade* aux *Sept contre Thèbes d'Eschyle*, *REG*, no. 113, Paris: Les Belles Lettres, pp. 299–325.

Demont, P. (2010) Tirage au sort et démocratie en Grèce ancienne, *La Vie des idées*, 22 June 2010, [Online], http://www.laviedesidees.fr/Tirage-au-sort-et-democratie-en-Grece-ancienne.html.

Dow, S. (1937) *Prytaneis: A Study of the Inscriptions Honoring the Athenian Councillors, Hesperia*, Suppl. I., Athens: American School of Classical Studies.

De Visscher, F. (1965) *Les Édits d'Auguste découverts à Cyrène*, Osnabruck: O. Zeller.

Fraser, P.M. (1972) Notes on two Rhodian institutions. II. The Rhodian jury-system, *ABSA*, no. 67, London: British School at Athens, pp. 119–124.

Fröhlich, P. (2004) *Logistèrion*, à propos d'une inscription de Kymè récemment publiée, *REG*, no. 117, Paris: Les Belles Lettres, pp. 59–81.

Fustel de Coulanges, N.D. (1864) *La Cité antique*, Paris: Flammarion.

Hansen, M.H. (1993) *La démocratie athénienne à l'époque de Démosthène: structure, principes et idéologie*, Paris: Les Belles Lettres.

Haussoullier, B. & Matthieu, G. (1922) *La Constitution d'Athènes*, Paris: Les Belles Lettres.

Homer (1924) *The Iliad*, Murray, A.T. (trans.), Cambridge, MA: Harvard University Press.

Homer (1919) *The Odyssey*, Murray, A.T. (trans.), Cambridge, MA: Harvard University Press.

Ihnken, Th. (ed.) (1978) *Die Inschriften von Magnesia am Sipylos: mit e. Kommentar zum Sympolitievertrag mit Smyrna*, Inschriften griechischer Städte aus Kleinasien, Bd. 8, Bonn: Habelt.

Ismard, P. (2011) Les associations et la réforme clisthénienne: le politique 'par le bas', in Azoulay, V. & Ismard, P. (eds.) *Clisthène et Lycurgue d'Athènes. Autour du politique dans la cité classique [issu d'un colloque tenu à Paris, dans les locaux de l'Institut National d'Histoire de l'Art, les 30 et 31 janvier 2009]*, Paris: Publications de la Sorbonne.

Kenyon, F.G. (1891) *On the Constitution of Athens*, London: British Museum.

Kroll, J.H. (1972) *Athenian Bronze Allotment Plates*, Cambridge, MA: Harvard University Press.

Kroll, J.H. (1993) *The Athenian Agora XXVI: The Greek Coins*, Princeton, NJ: American School of Classical Studies at Athens.

Laffon, A. (2016) La désignation des suppléants par tirage au sort (ἐπιλαχών) dans l'Athènes classique, *REG*, no. 129, Paris: Les Belles Lettres.

Lopez-Rabatel, L. (2011) *Klèrôtèria. Le tirage au sort dans le monde grec: machines, institutions et usages*, 2 vol., doctoral dissertation, Université Lyon 2 (unpublished).

Lopez-Rabatel, L. (2019) Le vote dans le monde grec: procédures et équipement, in Borlenghi, A., Chillet, Cl., Hollard, V., Lopez-Rabatel, L. & Moretti, J.-Ch. (eds.) *Voter en Grèce, à Rome et en Gaule. Pratiques, lieux et finalités*, Lyon: Maison de l'Orient et de la Méditerranée, pp. 53–84.

Mauzy, C. (2006) *Agora Excavations 1931–2006, A Pictorial History*, Athens: The American School of Classical Studies at Athens.

Meillier, Cl. (1978) La succession d'Œdipe d'après le P. Lille 76a + 73, poème lyrique probablement de Stésichore, *REG*, no. 91, Paris: Les Belles Lettres.

Moretti, J.-Ch. (2001) *Klèrôtèria* trouvés à Délos, *BCH*, no. 125, de Paris: Boccard, pp. 133–143.

Müller, Kl. (1998) Zwei Kleroterion-Fragmente auf Paros, *AA*, Berlin: W. de Gruyter, pp. 167–172.

Petzl, G. (1987) *Die Inschriften von Smyrna, II, 1,* Inschriften griechischer Städte aus Kleinasien, Bonn: Habelt.

Perpillou, J.-L. (1996) *Recherches lexicales en grec ancien, Étymologie, analogie, représentations,* Paris: Peeters.

Reinach, Th. (1891) *Aristote: la république athénienne,* Paris: Hachette.

Rhodes, P.J. (1981) *A Commentary on the Aristotelian 'Athenaion Politeia',* Oxford: Clarendon Press.

Rhodes, P.J. & Osborne, R. (2003) *Greek Historical Inscriptions 404–323 B.C.,* Oxford: Oxford University Press.

Sève, M. (2006) *Aristote, Constitution d'Athènes (trad.),* Paris: Le Livre de Poche.

Shear, T.L. (1994) σονόνους τ᾽Ἀθήνας ἐποιησάτην: The Agora and the Democracy, in Coulson, W.D.E., *et al.* (eds.) *The Archaeology of Athens and Attica under the Democracy: Proceedings of an International Conference Celebrating 2500 Years since the Birth of Democracy in Greece,* held at the American School of Classical Studies at Athens, 4–6 December 1992, Oxford.

Thompson, H.A. & Wycherley, R.E. (1972) *The Athenian Agora: Results of Excavations, vol. XIV, The Agora of Athens: The History, Shape and Uses of an Ancient City Center,* Princeton, NJ: American School of Classical Studies.

Topalov, Chr., *et al.* (eds.) (2010) *L'aventure des mots de la ville,* Paris: Robert Laffont.

Townsend, R.F. (1995) *The Athenian Agora: Results of Excavations, vol. XXVII, The East Side of the Agora. The Remains beneath the Stoa of Attalos,* Princeton, NJ: American School of Classical Studies.

Tracy, S.V. (1995) *Athenian Democracy in Transition: Attic Letter-Cutters of 340 to 290 B.C.,* Berkeley, CA: University of California Press.

Woodhead, A.G. (1997) *Inscriptions: The Decrees in the Athenian Agora,* vol. XVI, Princeton, NJ: American School of Classical Studies.

Arnaud Macé

Plato on Drawing Lots
The Foundation of the Political Community

Translation revised by Sarah-Louise Raillard

Plato provides us with a rich and detailed account of the various practices that involved sortition, or the drawing of lots, in Greek culture during the archaic and classical periods.[1] He confirms that the practice of drawing lots had, in the various societies of Ancient Greece, a wide anthropological scope that went beyond the strictly political realm. Even before selection by lot was used to distribute public offices, the procedure was used to attribute many other things: land, inherited property, loot, and hunting spoils, as well as the right to engage in a singular fight on behalf of the group, or the obligation to go establish a new colony (Borecký, 1965; Macé, 2014). Plato even adds to the list of cultural uses of selection by lot, for instance in the case of matching spouses or choosing future lives (Demont, 2014, pp. 151–152 and 154–159). He also attests to the fact that the political use of sortition extended well beyond the scope of the democratic regime. Of course, as Aristotle explained, it is 'thought to be democratic for the offices to be assigned by lot (*klerotas… tas arkhas*), for them to be elected, oligarchic'.[2] But this should not be seen as a strict dichotomy, and more as a matter of proportion. The Greek democracies for which we have historical sources, such as Athens, never stopped using elections to appoint important public officials, even when sortition also played a significant role in designation. We shall indeed be able to confirm that Plato's hostility towards Athenian democracy led him to limit the use of sortition for the designation of public officials. But we shall also be

---

[1] I would like to thank Sarah-Louise Raillard for her contribution to strengthening and clarifying my first English draft.

[2] Aristotle, *Politics* IV 9 1294 b7–9. All translations are taken from the edition mentioned in the bibliography.

forced to admit that democracy did not have a monopoly on the political use of sortition; in fact, Plato suggested extending the use of random selection to facets of the political sphere to which democracy did not dream of applying it.

If Plato marginalizes the use of sortition to attribute positions of political authority, believing that the use of random selection in such a context went against the principle of knowledge-based merit, he nonetheless stresses the importance of drawing lots to distribute goods and missions. In so doing, Plato refers back to the archaic tradition of drawing lots, which was viewed as the best procedure to distribute items or tasks among equals, as it allowed for the allocation of objects through individual shares in order to engender a feeling of community (Macé, 2014). Therefore, even as Plato limits the use of random selection as a means to appoint officials, he extends its scope as a tool for repartition, ultimately transforming it into the cornerstone of the political community. In fact, random selection was seen as fostering the sentiment of belonging to a civic community through the equality of received shares. The distribution of equal parts of a territory in particular allowed a body of citizens to believe that each and every one of them belonged to the same, larger whole. Moreover, the practice of drawing lots would inform the fundamental structure of any social body within which it occurred: in order to be able to receive equal shares of the resources or the roles that form part of an assigned mission, a given group must consent to being divided into smaller units and reconfigured in alternate groupings, according to the number of equal shares of the distributable object that exist at any given moment. Conceiving of the social body as the sum of the recipients of possible lots also means granting it a dynamic fluidity that will form the basis of its cohesion and of its capacity for action, regardless of whether a regime is democratic or not.

The Culture of Chance:
Accepting One's Fate

The drawing of lots was only one aspect of a wider culture that one might call the Greek culture of chance, particularly noticeable in the Greek penchant for games of chance such as games involving marbles, dice, or sherds (for the latter case, see Demont, 2013). The Greeks knew that in this realm, as in many others, they were only borrowing from their Eastern neighbours, the Lydians in particular. Herodotus reports that the Lydians invented all games of chance during a period of food shortages, in an attempt to forget that they were hungry. That is, all except one game, the game of *pessoi*, also called *petteia* (Herodotus,

Histories I 94, 12–16; Athenaeus, *Deipn.* I 19) a term which could have generically refered to all draught games, whether also involving dice or not (Kurke, 1999, p. 253; see diverging opinion in Schädler, 2009). The *pessoi*, Herodotus claims, was in fact a Greek invention; many say Palamedes came up with it (sometimes he is also said to have invented dice games), although Plato playfully attributes its invention to the Egyptian god Thoth (Gorgias DK B 11a30; Sophocles fr. 479 R; Plato *Phaedrus* 274d; Kurke, 1999, p. 250). Game practices were embedded in the warrior culture of the Greeks, as the mention of Palamedes suggests. This was an idea also illustrated by the portrait of the suitors in the *Odyssey*, who play *petteia* with a light heart as they wait for Penelope to pick one of them (*Odyssey*, I. 106).

Another illustration is the famous representation of Achilles and Ajax playing a sort of draughts game called 'five lines': once the dice were rolled, the player was supposed to move the draughts accordingly along five lines (Schädler, 2009; Dasen, 2015). Plato very clearly expressed the idea that one should accept the outcome of chance: 'To deliberate, I said, about what has happened to us, and, as it were in the fall of the dice, to determine the movements of our affairs with reference to the numbers that turn up, in the way that reason indicates would be the best, and, instead of stumbling like children, clapping one's hands to the stricken spot and wasting the time in wailing' (Plato, *Republic* X 604 c–d). The same idea is implied when Plato suggests that we should think of the immanent justice at work in the universe through analogy with the game of *petteia* (*Laws* X 903c–e). The gods first take into account the moral transformations that each soul has imposed on itself through the course of its own actions, becoming better or worse accordingly, and then move each soul towards a better or worse place. Throwing the dice, in the game, becomes an *analogon* of the moral transformation of individuals, which the gods accept as an event independent from their own actions, consequently moving their draughts accordingly (Macé, 2017). In the numerous analogies that refer to this game, which is a possible ancestor of backgammon, we repeatedly receive the same advice to accept what, in the course of events, does not depend on us. This is also what we find in Heraclitus fr. 52: 'Time is a child playing draughts (*petteia*).'

Accepting one's fate following the roll of the dice should be seen as a playful version of a more serious form of consent: sometimes it is the honour of risking one's life or changing it for ever that is decided by chance, whether one is chosen to join a new colony, accompany a war expedition, or engage in individual combat (Demont, 2010). Putting one's destiny in the hands of chance naturally comports a religious dimension, as evidenced by the prayers pronounced by the Homeric warriors before they drew lots from a helmet, to determine who would fight the other army's champion (Demont, 2000). To be selected by lot was to be chosen by the gods. This fundamental dimension of accepting chance was not, however, the only one.

Random Selection and Equality

Acceptance was also based on the perception of equality. This perception was at stake in a scene of the *Iliad* that describes the great division of the different realms of the universe among the three divine brothers—Poseidon, Zeus, and Hades:

> For three brethren are we, begotten of Cronos, and born of Rhea,—Zeus, and myself, and the third is Hades, that is lord of the dead below. And in three-fold wise are all things divided, and unto each hath been apportioned his own share (*time*). I verily, when the lots were shaken (*pallomenon*), won for my portion (*elakhon*) the grey sea to be my habitation for ever, and Hades won the murky darkness, while Zeus won the broad heaven amid the air and the clouds; but the earth and high Olympus remain yet common to us all.[3]

This scene illustrates the practices used to distribute loot, game, and inheritances attested in Ancient Greece (Borecký, 1965; Macé, 2014). The verb *pallo* (translated here as 'I shake the lots') is used in this sentence the same way as it is in many other descriptions of drawing lots (Demont, 2000). The *time* is the share (here a portion of the universe), which it is an honour to receive when one is recognized as eligible to take part in a random selection. Poseidon insists that such a division proves that he shares equal rights with Zeus: he is equal to him in dignity (*homotimos* 186), because he is equal in share (*isomoros* 209).

Plato also insists on the egalitarian aspect of sortition, taking this practice as an example and perhaps the best incarnation of equality (*isotes*): 'The one of these any State or lawgiver is competent to apply in the assignment of shares (*timas*),—namely, the equality determined by measure, weight and number,—by simply employing the lot (*klero*) to give even results in the distributions.'[4] Distributing lots (*kleroi*) means recognizing the two-fold equality that exists between all recipients: the equality between shares of equal measure or value, and the equality between the recipients themselves. The fact that no distinction of rank

---

[3]   Homer, *Iliad* XV 187–193, translation by Murray, slightly modified.
[4]   Plato, *Laws* VI 757 b, translation by Bury, slightly modified.

is made between recipients is precisely what differentiates this form of equality from the other kind, which 'dispenses more to the greater and less to the smaller, giving due measure to each according to nature' (*ibid.*, 757c). Merely by taking part in the process of drawing lots, one is recognized as an equal. Generally speaking, equality through the allotment of equal shares was, in Ancient Greece, an illustration of the principle of the common good: to be entitled to an equal share is to have something in common with the other recipients (Macé, 2014, pp. 458–468). And if not everyone receives a share, if there is only one indivisible item to be distributed – in cases where an individual is granted the honour of fighting the enemy's champion, for instance – everyone will still have been recognized as equally worthy of being chosen by the gods. Certain gods were also designated as 'common' in a particular sense, meaning 'impartial': so Ares was said to be 'common to all men' (*xunos anthropois*, Archilochus, fr. 110) since war spares no one.

Drawing Lots and Political Authority: Knowledge Prevails

The drawing of lots also appears in the context of designating those who will hold authority (*arkhe*). In a passage of the *Laws* (III 690 a–c), Plato lists seven claims for appearing as a legitimate commander among men, whether in small or big domains, that is, in families or states. They are as follows:

	1	2	3	4	5	6	7
Title	Filiation	Nobility	Age	Slavery	Force	Know-ledge	Lot
Relation-ship	Parent/child (father, mother)	Aristocrat/commoner	Old/young	Master/servant	Strong/weak	Wise/ignorant	The winners of lots/the losers of lots

One understands how the fact of being a parent, an aristocrat, an elder, a master, a powerful or a wise individual, or even the one selected by sortition might, in the right circumstances, allow one to claim authority over a child, a commoner, a young person, a slave, a weak or ignorant individual, or the losers of the drawing of lots. This is an empirical description of the rights or claims that men might invoke: the order of this list should not be read as conferring degrees of legitimacy to or establishing a hierarchy between those claims. Plato only goes so far here as to collect the various titles invoked by men in society. In due course, however, he will assess each claim and title critically.

The inclusion of sortition in the aforementioned list aligns with what we have already discussed. Thanks to chance, authority is marked by 'heaven's favour and good-luck': then the one who 'gains the lot (*lakhonta*) [...] will most justly be ruler' and the one who does not 'shall take his place among the ruled' (*Laws* III 690c 5-9). The Athenian speaking these words then cites the example of the Spartan ephors (the 'watchers'), a council of five officials elected annually who worked, together with other institutions, to temper the power of the Spartan kings. Most of the information regarding this institution seems to indicate that the ephors may have been elected rather than appointed by lot (Lévy, 2003, p. 198). However, it should be noted that Plato's Athenian only states that the power of the ephors 'was not far removed from government by lot' (692a). Perhaps he only meant that ephors were seen as being appointed by divine favour, as a government by lot might be, and that this granted them the authority to oppose kings' power, and even question royal actions.

Plato also places a high value on the sixth claim, which he sees as the most 'natural' of all. He quotes Pindar when he explains that this right 'is very prevalent among all kinds of creatures', being 'according to nature': it ordains that 'the wise man lead and rule'. It is an authority that is not 'against nature, but rather according thereto — the natural rule (*arkhe*) of law, without force, over willing subjects' (*Laws* III 690b6–c4). It is understandable that such a right, if it is the most natural of all, should correspond to the second form of equality mentioned above, 'the natural equality given on each occasion to things unequal' (VI 757d). Inequality in knowledge, which forms the basis of virtue, is precisely what Plato sees as the best example of 'the truest and best form of equality' (757b), the one that gives to all individuals in accordance with their nature.

Plato uses the example of ship captains and medical doctors to illustrate why the wise have a legitimate claim to ruling. Plato asks us to consider what a group might become if it decided to usurp the decision-making power of a ship captain or a doctor, proceeding to gather assemblies without distinction of competence, perhaps but not necessarily listening to the advice of doctors or captains, before making its final decisions in medical or sea matters and appointing, to implement such decrees, officials 'selected by lot' (*Statesman*, 298a–298d). In this passage of the *Statesman*, the same line of reasoning is playfully extended to all possible fields of knowledge, from carpentry to military strategy, even including cattle herding, *petteia*-playing, and doing arithmetic. In all these cases, replacing expert knowledge with written rules would ruin all knowledge (*ibid.*, 299e–300a; Demont, 2014, pp. 144–146). But for Plato, virtue is knowledge, and there is no political domain without expert knowledge. Political authority must therefore be placed under the second kind of equality, or, at least, this equality should play the greatest role in the designation of who shall make decisions and pass laws. Plato further elaborates on his theory of the two forms of equality as he discusses the designation of officials, whose purpose is precisely to make equality by lot subordinate to equality according to nature in this domain. In the case of the attribution of authority, equality by lot might only be used 'on account of the discontent of the masses, and in doing so to pray, calling upon God and Good Luck to guide for them the lot aright towards the highest justice'. In short: one will use both types of equality 'but that form, which needs good luck, we should employ as seldom as possible' (*Laws*, VI 757e–758a).

Marginalizing the Use of Sortition for Public Officers

The institutions described in the *Laws* systematically apply this hierarchy of equalities whenever political authority is concerned: sortition plays a more limited role for the designation of most offices than it would within democratic processes, while co-optation and election play a more extended role. Within the context of the *Laws*, co-optation would be mainly adopted for the selection of young people: when the officers of the Nocturnal Council, the highest institution in the city, would consequently be tasked with choosing young individuals (between 30 and 40 years old, see *Laws* XII 952ff.), or when young 'land-stewards' would be selected for each tribe (Brisson, 2000). The officers of the Nocturnal Council would include the ten oldest guardians of the laws, to which would probably be added the current guardian in charge of education and his predecessors, as well as the most distinguished examiners and supervisors. All these offices were to be filled by election, with selection by lot being either excluded or reduced to a minimal function.

The guardians of the laws would be elected according to a procedure described in Book VI (753b4–d6). All citizens who could bear arms would take part; that is, all adults, both male and female. The election would therefore be an act of the Assembly. The Assembly would not have the legislative power that it would have in a democracy, but nonetheless retain a few judiciary and administrative prerogatives. It would bring together the electors who designated the

guardians of the laws, as well as a large number of public officials—
'city-stewards', 'market-stewards', 'umpires of athletic contests',
'examiners', or 'administrators of the sacred treasury'. In the first
round, every person would go to the sanctuary and leave on the altar a
tablet that contained the name of their nominee, with their father's
name and that of their tribe and of the *deme* they belonged to. During a
whole month, everyone would be able to consult the tablets on the
altar, and, if any tablet was improperly written, it could be publicly
exposed. In such a way, one could denounce corruption, for instance
when an individual would have been forced to vote for someone to
whom they were indebted. The 300 names that received the greatest
number of votes—a significant portion of a population that only
included 5,040 households—would be exposed, and then the same
process of selection would be applied again. The best 100 were then
exposed again, and the best 37 would finally be elected after a third
round.

This election was in fact a virtue contest,[5] a competition where
virtue had to be performed and then recognized. That is, one must be
recognized by one's peers as having sufficient virtue to be designated,
and one must know how to recognize virtue amongst one's peers. The
publication of the votes leads us to consider that this was a pedagogical
tool to engage citizens in the search for virtue in their midst, with the
full knowledge that everyone's choices would be publicly scrutinized.
In doing so, the population would be training its ability to see what the
wise man recognizes with more clarity, as his eyes are guided by his
mind. The institution of new public and collective practices would
create the necessary conditions to develop shared knowledge and a
convergence of perceptions across all citizens, without reducing the
differences between various types of experience and knowledge: to the
contrary, those differences would inform different roles in the general
process of public participation.

The *Laws* envisioned the aforementioned contest happening every
twenty years, since the guardians were elected for a twenty-year
period. The virtue of a whole generation would therefore be assessed at
once. One might observe more frequent elections for the examiners,[6]

---

5   The idea of the virtue contest has been suggested by L. Brisson and J.-F. Pradeau
     with regard to the election of examiners, which we shall discuss below.
6   It is regarding these that L. Brisson and J.-F. Pradeau wrote: 'En fait, si on prend en
     considération les autres passages du dialogue relatifs aux concours et aux décrets
     honorifiques, il est clair que Platon a fait de ces élections un véritable concours de

three more of whom would be selected each year, after the designation of the first twelve, to reach the maximum number of 84.[7] The whole city would gather after the summer solstice 'at the common precincts of Helios and Apollo, there to present before the god the names of three out of their own number' (XII 945e). The process would start with an election among candidates that had not been previously announced, as with the guardians. Each citizen could propose the person that they believed to be the most virtuous ('each citizen proposing that man, not less than fifty years old, whom (with the exception of himself) he regards as in all respects the best', 946a). Half of the proposed individuals — those who received a greater number of votes — would stay in the race. If an odd number remained, the candidate with the least number of voices would be eliminated before the group was divided in half. And if there were too many individuals who were *ex aequo*, or tied, the youngest individuals would be eliminated. The voting process would continue until three candidates remained, each with a different number of votes; the three individuals would then become examiners, preserving the hierarchy of votes that existed between them. The 'three best citizens' of the city would then be crowned with olive leaves and presented to Apollo and Helios. They would become priests of Apollo; the citizen with the most votes would become a high priest. This electoral process, which expressed the enlightened choice made by all citizens, left only a residual role to chance in the situation where two of the three finalists, or all three, received the exact same number of votes. In such a case, 'they shall commit the matter to good luck and chance, and distinguish by lot between the first, the second, and the third' (*ibid.*, 946b). Selection by lot did not therefore interfere with the public's recognition of merit; the use of sortition to express good fortune was welcome. In this case, sortition was not used to designate an individual or to assign a task, but simply to break a tie and establish a hierarchy amongst equally deserving participants (a similar example can be

---

vertu, destiné à désigner chaque année les meilleurs des citoyens' (Brisson and Pradeau, 2007, p. 139).

7 L. Brisson and J.-F. Pradeau (2007, p. 139) put forward the number 75, which was indeed the maximum number for the 26th year, by which point the 12 initial examiners would have withdrawn (if they were 50 at the moment of their nomination, the youngest age possible for this function, they would have spent 25 years in office, until reaching the maximum age of 75). They would then leave the 75-person body of examiners otherwise composed of examiners elected every year during those 25 years. But according to this hypothesis, this means that, the year before their retirement, the body would have included 84 examiners, and 81 examiners two years prior, and 78 examiners three years before.

found in the *Iliad* when the competitors draw their place on the departure line in the funeral games (XXIII 352–357). When we refer back to Plato, this is the kind of random selection typically exemplified by the drawing of lots to determine the order in which souls will chose their new lives, when they come back after a thousand years in *Phaedrus* (249b), or according to the Myth of Er that concludes *The Republic* (Demont, 2014, pp. 154–159; Macé, 2016, pp. 78–79). In such examples, souls do not randomly select which life they will get to lead, but merely the order in which they are allowed to advance — the point being that if a soul was corrupt or ignorant, choosing first would be even worse than choosing last, because there will be too much tempta-tion to obtain riches or glory rather than virtue.

As we go down in the hierarchy of public offices, it appears that the role of sortition increases: we see its importance rise somewhat in the case of lower offices, typically those regarding positions in the *Boule* (or deliberative council). Unlike the Athenian Council, entirely designated through sortition of fifty *bouleutes* (councillors) per tribe, elections would be the principal mode of designation for the *Boule* as envisioned by the *Laws*. The council 'shall consist of thirty dozen — as the number 360 is well-adapted for the sub-divisions': the total was divided 'into four groups' of 90 councillors and '90 councillors shall be voted for from each of the property-classes' (*Laws* VI 756 b–c). The election would take place for each class over the course of four days, and all members would have to vote or face fines proportional to their class (the members of the lowest class did not face a fine if they did not vote). The names would be kept under seal until the fifth day, when they would be exposed for all to see. Everyone would vote again, and 'when they have selected 180 from each of the classes, they shall choose out by lot one-half of this number, and test them; and these shall be the Councillors for the year' (756e). Sortition was not merely ordinal here; it was effectively used to designate those who would be councillors from a pool of selected candidates. It is worth noticing that the Athenian stranger refers to the councillors who are selected for one year as magistrates selected by lot (XII 945b). All things considered, this procedure could be viewed as a mixture of monarchy and democracy, a mixture that combined the two kinds of equality and was designed to avoid dissension, without nonetheless placing individuals of different merit on the same level (VI 756e–757a). Other designation procedures for lower officials also utilized this hybrid form, including umpires for athletic contests, which were selected by a draw from a pre-selected group of candidates. Twenty candidates would be elected by a show of hands, then three of them selected by lot, and finally these would be submitted to the scrutineers for approval (765c–d).

Finally, although sortition is mentioned twice as a means of indirect selection, these are merely exceptions that confirm the rule. Certain priests and priestesses were envisioned for selection by lot (759b–c): in the case of lower religious offices (such as keeping the temples in good condition), random selection was seen as directly expressing the divine will ('by committing their appointment to the divine chance of the lot'). On the other hand, we have seen that high priests (the examiners) were to be selected through an elaborate electoral process designed to high-light individual merit. While some judges were destined to be selected by sortition (XII 956e), Plato drastically limited the democratic use of sortition to the selection of daily jurors. Only the tribal court would be concerned—that is, the second-level court for private affairs—whereas for all more important matters, the guardians of the laws and the judges elected among public officials would be appointed.

Drawing Lots and Repartition: Community Foundations

The subordination of sortition in the process of designation should not make us forget about the fundamental role played by random selection (the drawing of lots) in the *Laws*, especially when it is not a question of attributing political authority, but rather of allocating land, as in the great Homeric distribution of the realms of the universe for example. Territories would first be divided into three concentric regions (the agora, the city, and the countryside), which would in turn be divided into twelve parts that would be distributed among the twelve tribes. In the middle of his description of public offices, and with the purpose of introducing some of his most important positions, Plato introduces this complex division of territories. A great division into twelve shares (VI 758e2–3) had to be completed before certain of the aforementioned public offices could be filled. Those twelve regions would then be attri-buted, in turn, to twelve different but equal teams of guardians:

> We have marked out the whole country as nearly as possible into twelve
> equal portions: to each portion one tribe shall be assigned by lot, and it
> shall provide five men to act as land-stewards and phrourarchs ('watch-
> captains'); it shall be the duty of each of the Five to select twelve young
> men from his own tribe of an age neither under 25 nor over 30. To these
> groups of twelve the twelve portions of the country shall be assigned,
> one to each in rotation for a month at a time, so that all of them may
> gain experience and knowledge of all parts of the country. (VI, 760b–c)

If we examine the divisions that occurred at levels below the tribe, we can discover that each home would also receive a share of the territory, a 'lot' or *kleros*. It is notable that Plato choses the word *kleros* to refer to the patch of land distributed to each family, as he previously used the verbs *klero* and *lankano* to refer to the attribution and reception of shares drawn by lot, respectively: whoever 'buys or sells the house-plot or land-plot allotted to him must suffer the penalty attached to this sin' (V 741c). Since plots of land would be attributed by random selection, the plots had to be subdivided in order to be distributed 'as equally as we can' (V 737c). For instance, it was necessary to ensure that the portions of land were equal with regard to agricultural productivity, as stipulated in 745c. The two parts of each individual plot (one in the centre, the other on the outskirts of the territory) should also be equal in terms of productivity, by 'balancing the differences in size by differences in productivity' (V 745d). The attribution of plots, as equal shares, would establish the equality of rights among all citizens, much like when the divine brothers in the *Iliad* receive their equal shares of the universe. Plato scholars have insisted on the fundamental dimension of the attribution of a *kleros* to each family as being a foundational element on which the state relies (Pradeau, 2000). The conclusion to be gleaned here is that equality through lot is the kind of equality on which this fundamental dimension of the political community is based.

It is in relation to the *kleroi* that the Athenian stranger compares the city of Magnesia to the ideal city depicted in the *Republic*. In Book V 739a, the Athenian ranks the best forms of polities, hoping to provide wisdom to those founding new cities. The first kind of state described is one where 'friends have all things really in common' (739c); it closely resembles the regime described in the *Republic*. The things shared were, in that case, women, children, and wealth, and the intention was that shared possessions would engender a community of perception, action, and feelings: 'and so far as possible it is contrived that even things naturally "private" have become in a way "communized," – eyes, for instance, and ears and hands seem to see, hear, and act in common, – and that all men are, so far as possible, unanimous in the praise and blame they bestow, rejoicing and grieving at the same things' (739b–d). This kind of communal existence entailed the highest level of virtue; however, it was not an option for the project outlined in the *Laws*, which involved adult citizens already shaped by the customs of their original cities. But one could nonetheless hope to see a paler reflection of the *Republic* in this city, conceived of as second-best polity.

Of course, the most harmonious community could not be attained if citizens were allowed to 'portion out the land and houses' and if land was not farmed 'in common, since such a course is beyond the capacity of people with the birth, rearing and training we assume' (739e–740a). It was nevertheless possible to 'let the apportionment be made with this intention—that the man who receives the portion (*ton lakhonta*) should still regard it as common (*koinen*) property of the whole state, and should tend the land, which is his fatherland, more diligently than a mother tends her children, inasmuch as it, being a goddess, is mistress over its mortal population, and should observe the same attitude also towards the local gods and daemons' (740a). This begs the question: how does one create a feeling of community when individual portions are at stake, when undivided communal property (as in the best polity) has been replaced by the distribution of individual shares? In Ancient Greece, in addition to the *exclusive* common good that could only be enjoyed as an undivided whole—for example, the Earth or Mount Olympus in the distribution previously mentioned—there was also an *inclusive* type of common good that appeared whenever recipients had the sentiment that they had been granted the same object or responsibility, that they all shared equally in a larger concern (Macé, 2014). The equality underpinning the random attribution of plots to divide up a whole territory was a principle that allowed everyone to view their own individual plot as a share of the city's common property. Moreover, individuals were only allowed to take part in the distribution if they were willing to accept that 'the land [was] sacred to all the gods' (741c), a dedication emphasizing the unity of the whole territory.

The importance of maintaining the initial equality confirms this hypothesis. Complicated measures would indeed be implemented to ensure that the number of homes remained the same: owners could only leave their plot to one of their sons and were therefore forced to marry off their daughters and give their remaining sons to families deprived of heirs. In addition, birth control would be necessary when fertility rates were too high, while encouragement and stimulation of the birth rate would be necessary in the opposite situation. Emigration and immigration would be a last resort. No one would be allowed to become too rich; that is, they would never be worth more than four times the initial value of their plot, or otherwise they would be forced to marry their children off to impoverished families, to restore equilibrium (740b–741a). These stipulations reveal that differences of wealth—although present when the citizens arrived, as they in fact served to distribute them into four classes initially (Pradeau, 2000, see chart p. 30) —were to be maintained within the initial boundaries defined in relation to the value of the plot that was equally distributed to all. As no individual is supposed to ever amass more than four times the value of their initial plot, the plot thus becomes the standard against which to measure all subsequent differences. Despite their differences, citizens would always keep sight of the *isomoria* (equality of shares), which both measured and limited them. It was therefore essential to preserve real equality in the initial distribution, since that would be the condition according to which everyone would subsequently be able to believe that they possessed an equal share of the common territory that belonged to the city as a whole just as much as it belonged to them. Despite inequalities, everyone thereby possessed an equal and interchangeable share of the whole. In that respect, equality through allotment, as warranted by the gods, would be a core principle of the civic community.

This use of random selection to allocate shares went beyond the use of sortition as a means to compensate for reliance on merit within the designation process. It was the foundation of an entire political community, one based on the model of 'inclusive' or distributed common goods. That is, a community based on *isomoria*, on the fact that each member of a collective is given an identical share, precisely the kind of share that can be fairly attributed by lot. An illustration of such a community based on equally divided shares is provided when Plato proposes that the wall protecting the city should be formed by combining all of the gates and walls that families erect to protect their individual homes (VI 779a8–b7; Macé, 2014, p. 467).

What Kind of Social Body is Designed for Random Selection?

In order to conduct random selections, the social body must possess certain characteristics. For instance, the social body must contain an easily divisible number of citizens: 'Let us assume that there are—as a suitable number—5,040 men, to be land-holders and to defend their plots (*nome*); and let the land and houses be likewise divided into the same number of parts—the man and his allotment (*kleros*) forming together one division' (V 737e). Why this number, the Athenian asks? While Plato's character could not, of course, recognize the number as a factorial of seven ($7! = 7 \times 6 \times 5 \times 4 \times 3 \times 2 \times 1$), he nonetheless understands that this number can be divided by many other numbers. This number, the Athenian says 'contains the most numerous and most consecutive sub-divisions. Number as a whole comprises every division for all purposes; whereas the number 5,040, for purposes of war, and in peace for all purposes connected with contributions and distributions, will admit of division into no more than 59 sections, these being consecutive from one up to ten' (V 738 a–b). The social body would thus be divisible in many ways: 5,040 may be divided into 4 groups or into 12 (the tribes, which comprised 420 homes each), or any over the limit of its 59 divisors. To divide and combine again: 30 dozens (or 360) could be elected to the Counsel, which is 5,040 divided by 14, and this number could be converted by dividing it by the classes, as the Athenian does to organize the election of the Council (90 councillors designated in each of the 4 classes, as we have seen).

To put it in other words, although random selection was not favoured for designating public officials, it nonetheless governed, at a deep level, the organization of the social body. The community was structured as a body easily divided by the greatest possible number of divisors, thus lending itself to the distribution of tasks and assignments among equals. The civic body was thus easy to handle, functioning like trained troops who might be awarded loot, hunting spoils, or tasks, much like Homeric warriors complied with all attributions imposed by their chief, the 'shepherd of men'. Odysseus, arriving on the island of the Cyclops with twelve boats, divides his men into three groups to go hunting. Later, he redistributes the same men into twelve groups to divide the hunting spoils, a certain number of goats, into equal shares among them (*Odyssey*, IX, 157–160; Macé, 2014, p. 453).

Plato allows us to observe the internal structure imposed on a political body whose cohesion is based on repeated forms of distribution, which gives it a particularly dynamic form of fluidity. He indicates that this cohesion is most threatened by the potential loss of *isomoria*, or equality in constitutive shares, which provides citizens with the impression that they all equally share in the city. If we now turn to the question of democracy, it is evident that the debate shifts. Plato allows us to state that it is essential for a political community — whether democratic or not, insofar as public offices are concerned — to be designed and perceived as a community of recipients of lots and therefore as a community of equals, the equality in shares standing in for equal status within a community. But this equality of shares could be composed of shares of land rather than political prerogatives. One might wonder if, in the Athenian democracy, the revision of tribal and religious groups associated with the Reforms of Cleisthenes had a similar objective in mind: a structure allowing for the division and reconfiguration of the social body according to the various attributions of resources and tasks. Such a system would need to ensure that the distribution of public offices was such that it would allow a democratic population to perceive the social body as fit to be the recipient of political distributions. Plato thus opens up several new lines of analysis regarding how sortition — and the form of equality that the procedure entails—can help to shape a society and its potential for action. Such analysis could look at diverse political regimes, going beyond the specific form that their practices of equality might take.

References

Borecký, B. (1965) *Survivals of some tribal ideas in classical Greek: The use and the meaning of lagchanō, dateomai, and the origin of ison echein, ison nemein, and related idioms*, Acta Universitatis Carolinae, Philosophica et historica, Prague: Univerzita Karlova.

Brisson, L. (2000) Les magistratures non-judiciaires dans les Lois, *Cahiers Glotz*, pp. 85–101.

Brisson, L. & Pradeau, J.-F. (2007) *Les Lois de Platon*, Paris: PUF.

Dasen, V. (2015), Achille et Ajax: quand l'agôn s'allie à l'alea, *Revue du Mauss*, 46, pp. 81-98.

Demont, P. (2000) Lots héroïques: remarques sur le tirage au sort de l'*Iliade* aux *Sept contre Thèbes*, *Revue des études grecques*, pp. 299–325.

Demont, P. (2010) Tirage au sort et démocratie en Grèce ancienne, *La Vie des idées*, [Online], http://www.laviedesidees.fr/Tirage-au-sort-et-democratie-en.html.

Demont, P. (2013) Note sur un jeu enfantin avec tirage au sort chez Platon (*Phèdre* 241B4 et *République*, V, 521C), in Pino Campos, L.M. & Santana Henríquez, G. (eds.) Καλός καὶ ἀγαθὸς ἀνήρ διδασκάλου παράδειγμα. *Homenaje al Profesor Juan Antonio Lopez Ferez*, Madrid: Ed. clasicas, pp. 237–240.

Demont, P. (2014) Platon et le tirage au sort, in Fumaroli, M., Jouanna, J., Trédé-Boulmer, M., *et al.* (eds.) *Hommage à Jacqueline de Romilly: l'empreinte de son œuvre*, Paris : Académie des Inscriptions et Belles-Lettres, pp. 141–159.

Kurke, L. (1999) Ancient Greek board games and how to play them, *Classical Philology*, 94, pp. 247–267.

Lévy, E. (2003) *Sparte: Histoire politique et sociale jusqu'à la conquête romaine*, Paris: Éditions du Seuil.

Macé, A. (2014) Two forms of the common in Ancient Greece, *Les Annales. Histoire et Sciences sociales* (English edition), 69, pp. 441–469.

Macé, A. (2016) La circulation cosmique des âmes. Platon, le mythe d'Er, in Ducoeur, G. & Muckensturm-Poulle, C. (eds.) *La Transmigration des Âmes en Grèce et en Inde anciennes*, Besançon: Presses Universitaires de Franche-Comté, pp. 63–80.

Macé, A. (2017) La justice cosmique dans les *Lois*: Platon lecteur d'Homère et d'Anaxagore, in Crubellier, M., Jaulin, A. & Pellegrin, P. (eds.) *Philia/Dike. Aspects du lien social et politique en Grèce ancienne*, Paris: Classiques Garnier.

Pradeau, J.-F. (2000) Sur les « lots » de la cité des Lois. Remarques sur l'institution des KLHROI, *Cahiers du Centre G. Glotz*, pp. 25–36.

Schädler, U. (2009) *Pente grammai*: The Ancient Greek Board Game *Five Lines*, in Nuno Silva, J. (ed.) *Board Game Studies Colloquium XI (Proceedings)*, Lisbon: Associaçao Ludus, pp. 169–192.

Primary sources

Archilochus, *Iambi et elegi Graeci*, vol. 1, West, M.L. (ed.), Oxford: Clarendon Press, 1971.

Athenaeus, *Athenaei Naucratitae deipnosophistarum libri xv*, 3 vols., Kaibel, G. (ed.), Leipzig: Teubner, 1 xv 1887; 3: 1890, Repr. 1 1965; 3: 1966.

Aristotle, *Politics*, Rackham, H. (ed. & trans.), Cambridge: Cambridge University Press, 1944.

Gorgias, in *Die Fragmente der Vorsokratiker*, vol. 2, 6th edition, Diels, H. & Kranz, W. (eds.), Berlin: Weidmann, 1952.

Heraclitus, in *Die Fragmente der Vorsokratiker*, vol. 1, 6th edition, Diels, H. & Kranz, W. (eds.), Berlin: Weidmann, 1952.

Herodotus, *Histoires*, Legrand, P.-E. (ed. & trans.), Paris: les Belles Lettres, 9 volumes, 1932–1968.

Homer, *Homeri Odyssea*, von der Mühll, P. (ed.), Basel: Helbing & Lichtenhahn, 1962.

Homer, *The Iliad*, with an English translation, Murray, A.T. (trans.), 2 vols., Cambridge, MA: Harvard University Press; London: William Heinemann, Ltd., 1924.

Plato, *Laws*, in *Plato in Twelve Volumes*, Vols. 10 and 11, Bury, R.G. (trans.), Cambridge, MA: Harvard University Press; London: William Heinemann Ltd., 1967 and 1968.

Plato, *Republic*, in *Plato in Twelve Volumes*, Vols. 5 and 6, Shorey, P. (trans.), Cambridge, MA: Harvard University Press; London: William Heinemann Ltd., 1969.

Sophocles, *Tragicorum Graecorum fragmenta*, vol. 4, Radt, S. (ed.), Göttingen: Vandenhoeck & Ruprecht, 1977.

Paul Demont

Selection by Lot in Ancient Athens
From Religion to Politics

Translation revised by Sarah-Louise Raillard

The widespread use of selection by lot in classical Athenian democracy never fails to elicit the interest of contemporary political pundits, who see it as an example of democratic experimentation that is most likely to renew and enrich our Western representative systems of government (Sintomer, 2020). Before it attracted the attention of political scientists, however, the various uses of selection by lot were the subject of very different discussions of a rather theological nature. Such discussions first occurred in Greek Antiquity, accompanied by a gradual process of secularization, then re-emerged in the modern Western world, again alongside a process of secularization, albeit of a different nature, leading modern thinkers to frequently underestimate the role that religion played in sortition in classical Greece (Demont, 2010). In fact, most scholars today would argue that it is necessary to separate 'the origins of drawing by lots and its links with religion' from 'selection by lot as a political institution' (particularly in Athenian democracy), a distinction which is found in the greatest encyclopaedia of Antiquity (the *Real-Encyclopädie für Altertumswissenschaft*), under the entry *Losung* ('Drawing by lots', Ehrenberg, 1927).

In Ancient Greek polytheism, a man's 'fate' became assimilated with the 'lot' (in Greek, *moira*) which was spun for him by the Moirai (the Fates). According to Plato, this allotment relied on 'Necessity', the mother of the three Moirai (other sources refer to alternative genealogies). One of the Moirai is named Lachesis, 'The Allotter', the second Clotho, 'The Spinner', in charge of the logic behind one's fate, and the third one Atropos, 'The Inevitable', due to the inescapable nature of death. Greek polytheism did not, and in fact could not have, a dogmatic theology: depending on the text and on the era, the relationship between the Moirai and the other gods — and especially Zeus, some-times believed to be the father of the Moirai — is described in a variety of ways. Zeus himself, at any rate, is not almighty, since every god has his or her own exclusive powers and prerogatives — powers which, Homer explains, were distributed by lot, at least insofar as Zeus and his brothers were concerned. Thus, man could think of himself as receiving a share of fate, a lot that befell him unless he prayed to one god or another (or to the gods in general) in an attempt to influence destiny, as sometimes occurs in Homer and various Greek tragedies (Demont, 2000). This is also the case in a number of epic poems, where the hero must be divinely chosen to fight a duel (against an opponent who is equally appointed). On two occasions, the *Iliad* depicts a scene where lots are cast, accompanied by prayers to the gods. Fate and the gods usually select the most valiant candidate. In the *Seven Against Thebes* by Aeschylus, performed in Athens during the first half of the 5th century BCE[1] and which describes the seven duels pitting the best Thebans against their opponents, a contrast is drawn between the appointment of the heroes by King Eteocles on the Theban side, and the random selection by lots among equals, on the side of the Seven who attack Thebes with Eteocles' brother, Polynices. Bringing together these two modes of selection increases the dramatic tension and leads to an inevitable outcome. As the casting of lots unfolds, the audience gradually understands that the two brothers will inevitably be forced to confront each other: such is the will, in this tragic lottery, of the harsh allotter that is the god of war, Ares. Eteocles himself understands this and is unable (and unwilling) to oppose the will of the god. Sub-sequently, and according to the Athenian rules of inheritance between siblings which provide for a drawing by lots between equal shares, fate will bestow an equal lot upon the two brothers: death. The interplay between these two modes of selection — appointment by the chief and drawing by lots between equals — is represented here with its most tragic consequences. The process unfolds in democratic Athens, but without any reference to democracy, and is embedded within a con-ception of the world where the gods never cease to play their part. Divine intervention does not mean that men are not responsible for their actions and should not feel guilty for their crimes, however. The concept of 'double causality' or 'double motivation' was in fact elabora-ted by scholars in an attempt to clarify this point in a secularized world.

---

[1]   Penned in 467 BCE to be exact: at that time, the chief magistrates, or 'archons', were chosen each year by drawing lots amongst wealthy citizens.

This notion was not always the source of consensus, however. In Sophocles' works, the transition from *Oedipus Rex* — in which the role of the gods and the responsibility of man seem tragically intertwined — to *Oedipus at Colonus* — in which divine intervention appears to excuse man's failure, transforming it into an unintentional crime — corroborates this evolution (Saïd, 1978). Quite paradoxically, as the cult of a rather ambiguously defined goddess Τύχη ('Fortune') was spreading, fate increasingly seemed to be deprived of any religious value. As Headlam noted (albeit leading to somewhat excessive conclusions, as we shall argue below, 1891, p. 10), when Socrates strenuously condemned the democratic use of selection by lot, neither he nor his accusers made the slightest reference to its possibly divine origins (according to Xenophon and Plato). Plato strongly rejects fatalistic interpretations in the final myth of *The Republic* (see Demont, 2013 and 2014, and in the present volume, Macé, pp. 95-111). A (relatively) random distribution of shares between men does not by any means imply that man is absolved of all responsibility for his actions, Plato argues: quite the opposite. The essential moral choice rests entirely upon man. Moreover, choosing implies that one is refusing to surrender to the drawing of lots. Man must not let chance rule over him or over his City. Otherwise, in his soul as well as in the state, democracy would reign — democracy in this case being characterized by the growing number of magistracies selected by lot. According to Plato, due to the anarchy (the 'power vacuum') in every individual's soul, desires will quite randomly, and without any divine intervention, constantly give way to others, instead of being rebuked by reason with the help of the 'heart'. Similarly, in the City, by dint of being randomly shared again and again, power will no longer be truly exerted by anyone, instead of being wielded by the philosopher king with the help of the guardians. Conversely, if the necessity of reason prevailed, there would be no need for casting lots, except to have certain decisions accepted (and in that case, it would be possible to rig the mechanisms, if need be). Sortition thus appears to have grown increasingly secularized, while its use progressively became an almost exclusively democratic political practice. This evolution is well summed up by an Aristotelian formula: 'It is accepted as democratic when public offices are assigned by lot, and as oligarchic when they are filled by election' (*Politics*, 4.9, 1294b8).

In the monotheistic Christian civilization, with its rigid celestial hierarchy, it is somewhat simpler to analyse the use of selection by lot, because, according to an old adage given new life by Albert Einstein, '*God does not play dice*' (Gataker, 1627, p. 58). As Thomas Aquinas wrote in his short treaty about sortition (*De sortibus*, circa 1270, perhaps prompted by a debate regarding the use of sortition, with a view to settling the question of a contested episcopal appointment), certain things exist from necessity, and always exist, such as that God exists, for two and three to equal five, and for the sun to rise in the east. God brings all causes and consequences under control. Drawing lots makes sense only for humans and human affairs, Aquinas argues, especially when individuals cannot know or act efficiently on their own. The intervention of chance, which is ultimately of no great significance, fits into a complex hierarchy of causes that must not jeopardize either human free will or God's essential role (Porro, 2012). Then, on the express condition that he shall avoid resorting to the devil's work (Céard, 1996, pp. 111–114), man is allowed to resort to selection by lot on three grounds: *sors divisoria*, *sors consultoria*, and *sors divinatoria*. Sortition can be used to determine what individuals shall receive in terms of possessions, honours (when consensus did not exist), or even punishments (*communium rerum diuisio*, or the 'distribution of common things' was the most authorized way of drawing lots), to determine the best course of action or to predict the future. Of course, the democratic use of sortition was not even mentioned by Thomas Aquinas as such. Had it been, it would only have been envisioned as a subset of the *communium rerum diuisio*. In order to authorize a moderate use of drawing by lots, Thomas Aquinas comments on what Saint Augustine had said about *Psalm* 30: '"My lots are in thy hands": the lot is no evil thing, but it is what indicates the Divine Will in human doubt' (in *The City of God*, chapter 5).[2] Aquinas is somewhat more tolerant than Gratian, however, who, while observing that certain examples in the Old Testament (and even a handful in the New Testament: *Luke*, I, 9, *Acts* I, 26) demonstrate that the use of sortition is not inherently wicked, nevertheless distinguishes what happened before the Gospel from the official Christian doctrine, which favours the free will of human determination (Causa XXVI, *Decretum*).

Therefore, using random selection can only be religiously permitted when it is absolutely necessary: that is, when it is accompanied by

---

[2] A similar argument is also found in Rabelais' *Tiers Livre*: '*Comme disent les Talmudistes en sort n'estre aucun mal contenu: seulement par sort estre, en anxiété et doubte des humains, manifestée la volunté divine*' ('As the Talmudists say, there is no evil in lot: it is whence the Divine Will manifests itself in the anxiety and doubt of human wits', *Tiers Livre*, 44, with Jean Céard's note in the *Pochothèque* edition: 'In attributing the sentence to the "Talmudists", Epistemon recalls that it is also quoted by the Decretists [see chap. XXXIX, n. 7]', that is to say in Gratian's *Decretum*, causa XVI, quaestio 2, canon 'Chance').

prayers to distribute possessions or to designate an official or volunteer (particularly with a view to avoiding popular dissension), with the proviso that it must not supplant the recognition of the action of the Holy Spirit. Thus, selecting a bishop by drawing lots, when the election demonstrates divine will through the agency of the Holy Spirit, is wrong (St Thomas Aquinas, question 95, article 8; Porro, 2012, n. 54), whereas drawing lots for a civil office is, on the contrary, acceptable. But one must not, under any circumstances, acknowledge random selection as fortuitous, or consider that human reason rules more or less successfully over the fate of men without divine intervention, or conclude that human things are not always steered by a superior instance — arguments which would ultimately limit the power of divine Providence and eliminate the cult of religion as well as the fear of God.[3]

As the moderate puritan minister, Thomas Gataker, observed (Boyle, 2013, p. 62; see also Céard, 1996, 114 no. 58), the Thomistic doctrine continued to be accepted after the Protestant Reformation, especially by so-called 'Popish writers'. Nevertheless, religious debates on the different uses of random selection underwent a remarkable evolution owing to the work of the aforementioned Thomas Gataker, in particular *Of the Nature and Use of Lots: A Treatise Historical and Theological* (1619, a second revised edition was published in 1627 to address various objections).[4] This work is worthy of a brief examination since it has long been considered as an important step towards the perceived secularization of sortition, and it provides a highly interesting historical analysis. It is important to note that Gataker developed his theories before the advent of probability calculus and the Age of Enlightenment; as a result, his text relies more on philosophical theology marked by the debates of the Protestant Reformation than on a truly scientific study of chance. Being opposed to the outright condemnation of games of chance, Gataker argues from his faith, constantly quoting the Bible (often in Hebrew) and the Church Fathers; he also draws on his extensive knowledge of Antiquity, likewise quoting

---

3   Manin (2012, pp. 120–121) refers to the *Summa Theologica* commenting, perhaps with an overly worldly perspective, on a decretal issued by Pope Honorius III in 1223: 'So, the Church voiced no objections to the purely secular use of lot, that is, where it was not given supernatural significance.' See also Porro (2012), in particular p. 429: 'It is the Divine Governance of the world that founds, in the final analysis, the possibility to resort to any type of lot, in order to divide, to question, to predict the future.'

4   A modernized English version was published in 2008 by Conall Boyle and includes a very well-documented preface. It is now also available in e-book format (2013, in particular pp. 8, 19, 61–64).

classical writers from Aristophanes to Lactantius, directly in Greek and Latin, and displaying remarkable erudition overall.[5] In Gataker, Cicero, Plutarch, and Thomas Aquinas are often cited in support of each other. If Gataker chose to write his treatise in English (unlike his works of exegesis and erudition in Latin, among which we find a commented edition of Marcus Aurelius), it is because of the debates that arose following several sermons he gave on this topic. In fact, the question of morality and devotion with regard to games of chance (cards, dice, etc. — what the Puritans called 'lusurious lots'), the practice of astrology, as well as random methods for the allocation of possessions, were still important subjects of practical, everyday concern for Gataker's parishioners (Boyle, 2013, pp. 9–11). The minister's thesis, which he recalls in the foreword of the second edition, was that it is wrong to believe that the hand and providence of God could be found behind every lot cast. The Scriptures and the Church Fathers, as well as Seneca, teach that 'God is the author of all things, be they casual or other' (*ibid.*, p. 44), and there are instances when the drawing of lots is warranted by God to serve certain specific and 'special' purposes. However, as Gataker explains, one must not mistake the divine point of view for the human point of view, and, on the other hand, 'as the Schoolman [Thomas Aquinas] not unfairly said, that *"there might be some use of some kind of Lot, although there were no providence at all to guide it"* for the decision of the matter in question is referred wholly [...] to the casual motion of the creature, without any special providence of the Creator required' (p. 50). Therefore, Gataker reaches a second conclusion in chapter 2: 'the casualty of an event does not simply of itself make it a work of God's special or immediate providence.'

From this perspective of secularization, the subject of many contemporary discussions (Duxbury, 1999, pp. 20–22), Gataker endeavours to carry out the first thorough historical survey of selection by lot. He hopes that by demonstrating that the uses of random selection are varied, common, and long-established, it will be more difficult for his opponents to associate them all with Providence. History and theology are intertwined, as the title of Gataker's book suggests (*A Treatise Historical and Theological*). He begins by describing the different classifications proposed by theorists, among which we can see the category of 'Civil or Politic Lots' explicitly emerge: to put an end to strife and lawsuits, to divide up possessions, and to assign offices. Such a

---

[5] The modernized version has deliberately set aside this erudition, for it is not accessible to today's reader anymore.

category, Gataker notes, is acknowledged by many as useful and legitimate, an opinion he shares. He even inserts it into his own classification under the name of 'Ordinary Lots Serious', and devotes chapters 4 and 5 to the matter, which we shall focus on here.[6] If he qualifies this use of lots as 'ordinary', it is in the strongest sense of the word, as opposed to the 'special' events likely to fall within the purview of Providence: 'no extraordinary power or providence is required [...] in these Ordinary, Civil, Divisory Lots' (Boyle, 2013, pp. 66–67).

The use of lots is attested to in the Bible, for the assignment of sacred offices (as far as the Levites are concerned), as well as for the assignment of civil charges. Here is a noteworthy example: a drawing by lots is organized among the tribes of Israel with a view to deciding who will go to war and who will support the war (*Judges*, 20.9). Gataker approvingly notes the explanation given by a commentator from the end of the 16th century: 'the State there was then popular, as one of them well noted: and therefore it seemed best to decide by Lot [on what] without much tumult in an Anarchy could not easily have been determined otherwise' (pp. 72–73). The Platonic association between a popular system of government and anarchy, as well as its link with the use of sortition, appear here as commonplaces. The sole value of resorting to lottery is avoiding insolvable strife in the absence of any valid authority.

Soon afterwards, Gataker moves on to the example of the Greeks. Exceptionally enough, he begins with the political theory — which clearly shows the significant influence Ancient Greek political thought had on him — before examining a number of concrete cases. Referring to Herodotus, Plato, and to Aristotle's *Politics* in particular,[7] Gataker notes that selection by lot is a key feature of democracy and of popular systems of government more broadly, for the process entails 'the most equality and indifferency that might be'. This lack of differentiation and total equality are not always to be desired, he adds, because they do not necessarily amount to 'equity'.[8] From a theoretical standpoint, there is no inherent link between democracy and selection by lot, since drawing by lots is accepted in 'the best ordered Estates'. Gataker relies here on

---

[6] The second chapter is entitled: 'Of the Lawfulness of Such Lots: with Cautions to be observed in the use of them.'

[7] These references, though perfectly accurate, can be found only in the original edition, pp. 68–69.

[8] This is an adaptation of the distinction, established by Greek theoreticians who were hostile to extreme democracy, between 'arithmetical' equality (which gives an equal share to each individual) and 'geometrical' equality (which gives to each individual according to his abilities, his wealth, or his birth).

Isocrates and, above all, on the author of the *Laws*, who, he reckons, 'would have the most part of his Magistrates [...] to be designed yearly by lot'. Then he proceeds to thoroughly analyse the constitution of the Magnesian State that Plato developed in the sixth book of the *Laws* — a constitution which is in fact quite different from the system of government established in the *Republic*, especially regarding the importance it grants to lottery. It is worth noting here that, for the purposes of his demonstration, Gataker greatly overemphasizes the role — in reality very limited — that Plato grants to selection by lot, relative to the electoral system and tax qualification-based voting criteria (Demont, 2014). Moreover, the legitimate motivation that he provides to justify the pre-eminence of selection by lot, a motivation that was put forward by Plato himself, is not the quest for equality, but an attempt 'to prevent and meet with the peevishness and waywardness of the multitude' (Gataker, p. 74).[9]

After theory, time for practice: focusing on Athens, Gataker aptly describes the most important aspects of its government — insofar as one could do before the discovery of the *Constitution of the Athenians* at the end of the 19th century. However, this time, he does not comment on the significance of those procedures.[10] Drawing by lots similarly existed in Rome, and Gataker describes this tradition in great detail as well, albeit without any reference to the issue of democracy. As his last major example, Gataker remarks that sortition still exists in contemporary Italy. The first case to be mentioned is Venice, this 'Mirror of policy, [that] some suppose, to be a model of Plato's old platform' (p. 80), then Gataker quickly turns to Florence. Afterwards, he moves on to the other ordinary civil uses of sortition, in a way that hardly engages with political thought. It seems that his objective is mainly to demonstrate that even a well-governed state may derive great benefit from selection by lot, although this is particularly true for popular states, so long as

---

9   Cf. the *Laws* VI, 757e2–758a2, where Plato opposes the two kinds of equality, the arithmetical one and the geometrical one.

10 Boyle (2013, pp. 73–76). Boyle laments this in his preface: 'It is one of the great treasures of this book to realise just how much was already known about the use of lottery as a democratic device at those times. There have been many modern attempts to do something about the malaise of democracy by introducing some element of random selection.' Boyle then presents a detailed bibliography and adds that 'Gataker himself did not have much to say about this' (p. 18). Indeed, Gataker doesn't have the slightest thing to say about this, for the notion of the malaise of democracy was utterly unknown to him: democracy was, in his opinion, similar to anarchy.

the process is not used to establish a pernicious lack of distinction among otherwise unequal citizens.

The next chapter makes this point clear, justifying the ordinary use of lots by quoting from the Bible: 'Casting the lot settles disputes and keeps strong opponents apart' (*Proverbs*, 18.18). This quote reveals the different equality systems that the use of sortition may establish in any kind of social configuration, and of the variable awareness people may have of these different possibilities. Another condition is required: that the drawing of lots applies only to 'indifferent things'. Then follows a highly critical judgment of its use in politics, a judgment clearly marked by Ancient Greek philosophers and Plato and Aristotle in particular (pp. 110–111):

> The Lot makes no difference of good or bad; nor takes any notice of the fitness or unfitness, of the worth or unworthiness of those that be put together upon it. In which regard though many worthily condemn such promiscuous Lotteries, and prefer for the most part, and that justly, other courses of election before that Lot.

Gataker sees Greek history as completing this judgment: selection by lots, he argues, is in most cases supplemented and mitigated by a thorough examination of the abilities of those chosen by lot (what the Greeks called 'docimasy'). Moreover, as Plato declared in the first part of *Protagoras*, when a specific ability is required, it is better to call upon specialists. The logical consequences of this line of reasoning (quite far, at this time, from the text of *Protagoras*, which never explicitly mentions selection by lot) is to restrict the use of sortition for 'indifferent things': 'the less weighty the matter is wherein a Lot is used, the lawfuller the Lot is' (p. 119). This sets up the rest of the book quite nicely, whereby Gataker adopts a very tolerant position regarding games of chance. All things considered, his analysis is quite revealing of his reluctance towards popular systems of government and the motives that some-times justify the use of lot in political matters — most of the time, these have nothing to do with democratic theory. On the other hand, as far as Athens is concerned, Gataker overlooks the historical and literary accounts that emphasize the connections between sortition and religion, especially in the political field.

It is in this context, on the road to secularization, that the theory of representative government emerged during the 18th century. This theory developed by supplying new arguments against the use of random selection in Athenian democracy, then by arguing in favour of election and the need to take into account of the notion of 'consent', which leads to 'legitimacy' (Manin, 2012, pp. 74–124). The exaltation of the 'liberty of individuals' (or, in the works of Rousseau or Hegel, its condemnation as the liberty of the merchant and the bourgeois) marks the birth of modernity, in absolute contrast to the citizen's integration – or what was called 'enslavement' – into the Ancient State (Benjamin Constant). The British Radicals were in fact the first to genuinely attempt to restore the direct democracy practised in Athens. Of course, it remained 'unpalatable' to 'most modern readers', as the banker, politician, and historian George Grote noted, though this did not prevent him from earnestly speaking in favour of such attempts in his important *History of Greece* (1846–1856, vol. 4, p. 179), albeit without thinking that the use of sortition was vital for the Ancient Athenian democracy. According to Grote, the introduction of selection by lot to designate the archons (the chief magistrates in Ancient Athens) necessarily corresponds with the elimination of their responsibilities: 'So that there remained to these archons only a routine of police and administration, important indeed to the state, yet such as could be executed by anay citizen of average probity, diligence, and capacity' (p. 144). In agreement with Greek theoreticians, he argues that this reform was motivated by the desire to overcome the gap between the rich and the poor – although, according to Grote, selection by lot does not necessarily accomplish this task any better. It appears that Grote still maintains the perspective that there exists an ordinary and almost 'indifferent' use of random selection, to use Gataker's expression. At any rate, religion as well as the role supposed to be attributed to God entirely disappear from Benjamin Constant and George Grote's analyses of the institutions of Athenian democracy, just as they disappear from the descriptions penned by the great 19th-century historians.

It is Fustel de Coulanges who successfully reintroduced these two concepts: first in 1864 with *The Ancient City*, which grants a fundamental role to the religious foundations of Greek and Roman societies, and then in 1878, by looking more specifically at selection by lot in Greece in an article entitled 'Nouvelles recherches sur le tirage au sort appliqué à la nomination des archontes athéniens'.[11] After Fustel de Coulanges' death, this article was republished and annotated by his disciple Camille Jullian in 1891, following the discovery of the *Constitution of the Athenians* (whose first edition dates back to 1891).[12] Gustave Glotz, whose *Greek City and its Institutions* followed in the footsteps of

---

[11] In English: 'New research on the use of lots for designating Athenian archons.'
[12] For the rest of the present article, I am borrowing some elements from Demont (2001 and 2014).

Fustel de Coulanges' *Ancient City*, acknowledges his influence (Glotz 1907):

> Seul, Fustel de Coulanges osait, confiant en ses convictions sur la genèse religieuse des institutions antiques et en sa minutieuse étude des textes, relever une hypothèse abandonnée depuis l'époque lointaine de Meursius (*De archontibus Atheniensium, Lugd. Bat. 1621; cf. Gronovius, Thes. antiquitatum*, vol. IV, p. 1164 sq.) et soutenir que le tirage au sort remontait aux origines mêmes de la constitution athénienne.[13]

Fustel de Coulanges believed that it was 'only our modern ideas' that made selection by lot appear to be 'synonymous with equality' (1891, p. 157 and p. 166):

> Le tirage au sort n'était ni un procédé égalitaire, ni un procédé essentiellement oligarchique. Il a pris l'un ou l'autre caractère suivant les temps et suivant la façon dont il a été appliqué. Il a été aristocratique quand la société athénienne l'était; il est devenu relativement démocratique lorsque la société l'est devenue.[14]

In reality, sortition should primarily be interpreted as a selection mode of a religious nature, allowing a given deity to designate the individual s/he wants, with the result that the selection process in question is independent from any specific system of government. Thus, originally, 'for them, the lot was not chance; it was the revelation of the divine will' (Fustel de Coulanges, 1901, p. 243). Selecting a magistrate by lot therefore indicated the 'sacerdotal character belonging to the magistrate' (*idem.*, p. 242) — which implied that magistrates were priests in the first place, just as the *Bouleutai* must have originally been the guardians of fire (p. 390). From there, Fustel de Coulanges inferred that the appointment of magistrates by lot was a practice that dated back to the archaic era.

In chapter 8 of the *Constitution of the Athenians*, Aristotle attributes to Solon, and consequently to a very early period of the Athenian government (594–593 BCE), the introduction of choosing magistrates by lot 'between candidates appointed beforehand' from among the richest

---

[13] 'Fustel de Coulanges alone, confident in his beliefs regarding the religious foundation of ancient institutions and in his meticulous study of the texts, dared to revive a hypothesis which had been abandoned since Meursius's distant era (*De archontibus Atheniensium*, Lugd. Bat. 1621; cf. Gronovius, *Thes. antiquitatum*, vol. IV, pp. 1164 *sq.*) and to uphold that selection by lot dated back to the very origins of the Athenian constitution.'

[14] 'The use of lot was neither an egalitarian process, nor an essentially oligarchic one. Depending on the era and the way it was implemented, it has assumed either character. It was aristocratic when Athenian society was aristocratic; it became relatively democratic when society did.'

citizens. Camille Jullian was able to make a conclusive argument using this chapter, along with other excerpts, when the papyrus containing almost the whole text of the *Constitution*, which had hitherto only been known through a few fragments, was published in 1891. It has been suggested that this excerpt awkwardly projects a much later practice onto an ancient era. I do not agree, although it is impossible to have any certainty in the matter. However, Fustel de Coulanges' theory regarding the archons-priests, or the *Bouleutai* guardians of the civic hearth, remains very poorly documented, and has therefore been largely abandoned. J.W. Headlam discusses it in the beginning of his *Election by Lot at Athens*, published in 1891 and also written before the full publication of the *Constitution of the Athenians* (which had therefore only been taken into account in a partial fashion). In his preface, Headlam declares that Fustel de Coulanges 'has paid special attention to one part of the subject', which is 'certainly an important part of the truth' (p. XI): namely, the ancient practice of casting lots, especially in religious matters. Headlam partially acknowledges the validity of this practice, albeit only regarding the selection of the archons. Then he quotes the same aforementioned page from *The Ancient City*, adding the following commentary:

> I believe the only passages which expressly refer to the lot as giving religious sanction to an appointment are two which occur in the *Laws* of Plato; and it will be sufficient to point out that the constitution of the ideal state which the philosopher is describing is essentially different from that of Athens, and that he is in the second of the two passages expressly showing how different is his ideal from the 'equality' of a democracy. He is gravely reminding his readers of what the lot ought to be. Everyone will agree that the lot could be regarded as a religious institution, and that it had been such in old times, but nevertheless after the beginning of the fifth century it does not appear to have been so regarded at Athens. (p. 8)

While Headlam (1891) attaches great importance to Fustel de Coulanges' arguments, particularly in the appendices he added after the publication of the *Constitution of the Athenians*, he does not quote the two passages from Plato in question; he is content with alluding to them. In fact, the principal thesis of Headlam's book is that an intrinsic link exists between Athenian democracy and the use of selection by lot, primarily because Athenian democracy was an 'aristocratic' system which left citizens with enough free time 'not only [for] the discussion of political questions but also [for] the management of public business'. This situation was permitted by the concurrent existence of slavery and could consequently only be reproduced in modern times after significant industrialization and the reorganization of society, Headlam concludes.

In one of today's primary reference books on Ancient Athenian government, *The Athenian Democracy in the Age of Demosthenes* by Mogens H. Hansen, the two aforementioned passages from Plato are entirely eliminated: 'There is not a single good source that straight-forwardly testifies to the selection of magistrates by lot as having a religious character or origin' (p. 51, this idea is also addressed by Manin, 2012, p. 43; Manin also looks closely at the second of these passages from Plato, pp. 54–55). This oversight deserves a closer look.

The first passage from Plato contains a number of details which are difficult to understand:

> Heaven's favour and good-luck surely mark a seventh kind of rule (θεοφιλῆ… γε καὶ εὐτυχῆ τινα… ἀρχήν), where a man is called forward for a kind of drawing by lots (εἰς κλῆρόν τινα). If he gains (λαχόντα) the lot he shall rule, but if he fails (δυσκληροῦντα) he shall take his place among the ruled: here is what seems the rightest to us. (3, 690c5–8, transl. Bury modified)

In broad strokes, Plato establishes here the seven titles unanimously acknowledged as conferring the right to exercise power: in other words, of commanding (*arche*, 689c4–690c9). The progression between the seven titles, described as a 'succession', is simultaneously logical and genealogical. The three first titles rest upon the precedence of birth: the *arche* exerted by parents on their children, by noblemen on people of lower birth, and by elders on younger people. A change in per-spective appears when Plato switches over to the fourth and the fifth modes of commanding, which rest upon the necessity inherent to strength: the power of masters over their slaves, and the power of the strong over the weak. Plato implicitly refers to a famous quotation by Pindar regarding the *nomos*-king (the royalty of law), that Herodotus, the Sophists, and Callicles in Plato's *Gorgias* interpreted in different ways. The sixth category opposes the previous one by means of an ironic—and now explicit—apostrophe to Pindar: the sixth title in a position to exert authority, the possession of wisdom, also conforms to nature. That title, says the Athenian of the *Laws*, does not rest upon violence; it is a title naturally conferring the right of exercising power, a title which also corresponds to the 'power of law over the people who accept it' (690c1). Plato draws parallels between the philosopher-king of the *Republic* and the *Laws*, in a remarkable way which seems to resolve the problem set out in the *Politics*, as well as the problem of the relation between the three dialogues, simply by suppressing it: competence and the power of law over the people who accept it are interchangeable. Finally, and somewhat surprisingly, Plato comes to the last and seventh mode of commanding (a number which has special value): selection by lot.

The original Greek sentence is somewhat convoluted, but it undeniably comes at the end of a progression in intensity and significance. The fifth title sees the intervention of necessity and universality, while 'the greatest reputation' is associated with the sixth title, and then finally the power 'which the Gods love' is linked to the procedure of random selection. The lottery, which is explicitly presented as a characteristic of democracy in the *Republic*, is praised here as well as the choice of the gods, even if both of the indefinite adjectives suggest that the Athenian experiences a certain reticence with regard to his own words. It is impossible, in my opinion, to contest that we have here a genuine text from the end of the classical era attesting to the belief in divine intervention during the designation by lot of magistrates. While registering those beliefs in due form, Plato expresses his reservations, which does not prevent him from later observing (in an often neglected statement, pessimistic regarding for the possibility of making good laws, but consistent with the aforementioned classification) that since god and lots are associated, 'it is the divinity, and with the divinity, fortune and chance (καὶ μετὰ θεοῦ τύχη καὶ καιρός), that rules throughout all human things' (4.709b7–8).

The second passage is even thornier, appearing in connection with the construction of the Magnesian city, which is closer to a real city than to the ideal city described in the *Republic*. In this passage, Plato defines both of the modes of equality (geometric and arithmetic), before shockingly rejecting the use of sortition on both rational and religious grounds.

> For there are two kinds of equality which, though identical by name, are often almost opposites in their practical results. The one of these any State or lawgiver is competent to apply in the assignment of honors, – namely, the equality determined by measure, weight and number–, by simply employing the lot to give even results in the distributions; but the truest and best form of equality is not an easy thing for everyone to discern. (6, 757b1–6, transl. Bury)

The juxtaposition of those two texts confirms that the first may have been somewhat ironic in tone and that, in reality, the seventh mode of commanding described by Plato and attributed to lottery was not worth much in his opinion. Victor Ehrenberg (1927) even argues that in the second excerpt Plato opposes selection by lot to Zeus's divine will (which corresponds to remarkable mathematic knowledge), a statement which is correct (and thus rectifies an earlier mistake committed by

Fustel de Coulanges). However, if we continue reading, it appears that Plato reintroduces the position he had adopted in Book 3. Plato admits that a certain implementation of random selection procedures is absolutely necessary to avoid garnering the people's hostility and therefore recommends imploring the deity to ensure that the selection by lot will be a successful means to allocate offices.

> For the same reason it is necessary to make use also of the equality of the lot, on account of the discontent of the masses, and in doing so to pray, calling upon God and Good Luck to guide for them the lot aright towards the highest justice. Thus it is that necessity compels us to employ both forms of equality; but that form, which needs good luck, we should employ as seldom as possible. (6, 757e2–758a2, transl. Bury)

Here again, Plato expresses reservations about the efficacy of divine intervention in selection by lot, but he nonetheless mentions the use of prayers to accompany lottery systems in political affairs.[15]

It should be noted that no similar passage can be found in Aristotle's extant works. The outline and the text of the *Constitution of the Athenians* (whether we accept it as being written by Aristotle himself, or as a product of his philosophical school) do show that the widespread acceptance of lottery procedures without any associated religious connotations comes to characterize radical democracy in the 4th century BCE (Sève, 2006), both historically and institutionally. This period significantly comes to an end with the thorough description of the 'lot-drawing machine' used to designate the jurors in Athenian courts (Demont, 2003). In a similar vein, the *Politics* collects descriptions of the different uses of sortition and the debates concerning the practice, without making any references to religion. Aristotle was also apparently the first to propose a thorough, rational analysis of chance (in the second book of the *Physics*). In Aristotle, although the subordination of chance to religious explanations — which may, according

---

15 As far as religion is concerned, even Hansen (1991, p. 76) is forced to admit that, according to the *Laws* (759b c), 'priests were selected by lot so to let the Gods choose', which does not rule out the advent of a rigid docimasy, that Hansen (rightly) uses to downplay the religious nature of selection by lot. He leans on Morrow (1960, p. 163) to oppose the designation of the magistrates to that of the priests: 'These are the only offices that he appoints by the exclusive use of lot; in other instances, where the drawing by lots adds up to the election, it is not for a religious reason, but in order "to preserve friendship" that he vindicates the use of a combination of "democratic and non-democratic" procedures.' Although this statement is true, it does not take into account the possibility explicitly (albeit reluctantly) mentioned by Plato, of influencing the result of these procedures with the help of prayers.

to the Neo-Platonist Simplicius, allude to the excerpt from the *Laws* quoted above (4. 709b)—only appears in an incidental clause ('There are those who think luck (τύχη) is a cause that the human thought cannot distinguish, for it would be something divine (θεῖόν τι) and rather extraordinary (δαιμονιώτερον—*Physics* 2, 4, 196b), it is nevertheless present.

Thus, in two worlds that are completely different but connected to each another by a strong shared tradition, the Ancient Greek world and the modern Western world, we observe the gradual secularization and politicization of the use of random selection over the centuries. Both of these processes, stemming from the development of democratic (in the ancient sense of the word) ideals and systems of government, as well as ancient and modern challenges, were complex and remain ongoing. Perhaps it is modern secularization, much more thorough and widespread than its ancient counterpart, that has led us to underestimate the permanence of certain religious features in the political use of sortition in classical Athens.

References

Aquinas, Thomas (1976) *Liber De Sortibus ad Dominicum Jacobum de Tonengo, in Sancti Thomae de Aquino Opera omnia iussu Leonis XIII P.M. edita, t.* XLIII, Rome, pp. 203–241.

Boyle, C. (ed.) (2013) *Thomas Gataker, The Nature and Uses of Lotteries: A Historical and Theological Treatise*, electronic modernized version of Gataker (1627) with introduction and notes by C.B. (1st ed. 2008), Exeter: Imprint Academic.

Céard, J. (1996) *La Nature et les prodiges, L'insolite au XVIe siècle*, 2nd ed. revised and expanded, Geneva: Droz (1st ed. 1977).

Constant, B. (1819) De la liberté des Anciens comparée à celle des Modernes, in *De la liberté chez les Modernes*, Paris: Textes choisis, 1980.

Demont, P. (2000) Lots héroïques: remarques sur le tirage au sort de l'*Iliade* aux *Sept contre Thèbes, Revue des Études Grecques*, 113, pp. 299–325. Paper freely available on the website 'Persée'.

Demont, P. (2001) Le tirage au sort des magistrats à Athènes: un problème historique et historiographique, in Cordano, F. & Grottanelli, C. (eds.) *Pubblico sorteggio e cleromanzia: alcuni esempi*, Milan: Università degli Studi di Milano, pp. 63–81.

Demont, P. (2003) Le *Klèrôtérion* ('machine' à tirer au sort) et la démocratie athénienne, *Bulletin Association G. Budé*, pp. 26–52. Paper freely available on the website 'Persée'.

Demont, P. (2010) Tirage au sort et démocratie en Grèce ancienne, *La Vie des idées*, [Online], http://www.laviedesidees.fr/Tirage-au-sort-et-democratie-en.html.

Demont, P. (2013) Note sur un jeu enfantin avec tirage au sort chez Platon (*Phèdre*, 241B4 et *République*, V, 521C5), in Minos Pino Campos, L. & Santana Henriquez, G. (eds.) *Homenaje al Profesor Juan Antonio Lopez Ferez*, Madrid: Ediciones clásicas, pp. 237–240.

Demont, P. (2014) Platon et le tirage au sort, in Fumaroli, M., Jouanna, J., Trédé, M. & Jouanna, J. (eds.) *Hommage à Jacqueline de Romilly*, Paris: Académie des Inscriptions et Belles-Lettres, pp. 141–159. Paper freely available on the website 'Persée'.

Duxbury, N. (1999) *Random Justice: On Lotteries and Legal Decision-Making*, Oxford: Oxford University Press (reprint 2008).

Ehrenberg, V. (1927) *Real-Encyclopädie für Altertumswissenschaft*, vol. XIII, 2, col. 1451–1504, s.v. *Losung*.

Fustel de Coulanges, N.D. (1864) *La cité antique*, Paris: Librairie Hachette.

Fustel de Coulanges, N.D. (1891) Recherches sur le tirage au sort appliqué à la nomination des archontes athéniens, *Nouvelles recherches sur quelques problèmes d'histoire*, revised with notes by Camille Jullian, Paris: Hachette, pp. 145–179.

Fustel de Coulanges, N.D. (1901) *The Ancient City; A Study on the Religion, Laws, and Institutions of Greece and Rome*, Small, W. (trans.), Boston, MA: Lee and Shepherd.

Gataker, T. (1627) *Of the Nature and Use of Lots: A Treatise Historical and Theological* (1619, 2nd ed. revised in 1627).

Glotz, G. (1907) s.v. *Sortitio*, in Daremberg, C., Saglio, E. & Pottier, E. (eds.) *Dictionnaire des Antiquités grecques et romaines*, IV, Paris, pp. 1401–1417.

Grote, G. (1857) *History of Greece*, vol. 4, New York: Harper.

Hansen, M.H. (1991) *The Athenian Democracy in the Age of Demosthenes*, Norman, OK: University of Oklahoma Press.

Headlam, J.W. (1891) *Election by Lot at Athens*, Cambridge: Cambridge University Press (re-edition D.C. MacGregor, Cambridge, 1933).

Manin, B. (2012) *Principes du gouvernement représentatif*, Paris: Champs Essais (1st ed. 1995).

Morrow, G.R. (1960) *Plato's Cretan City*, Princeton, NJ: Princeton University Press (reprint 1993).

Porro, P. (2012) *Lex necessitatis vel contingentiae*. Necessità, contingenza e provvidenza nell'universo di Tommaso d'Aquino, *Revue des Sciences Philosophiques et Théologiques*, 96, pp. 401–450.

Saïd, S. (1978) *La Faute tragique*, Paris: Maspero.

Sève, M. (2006) *Aristote, La Constitution d'Athènes. Le régime politique des Athéniens,* new translation, introduction, notes and index by M.S., Paris: Le Livre de Poche.

Sintomer, Y. (2020) *Between Radical and Deliberative Democracy: Random Selection in Politics from Athens to Contemporary Experiments,* Cambridge: Cambridge University Press.

Virginie Hollard

Elections and Sortition in Ancient Rome
Was There Such a Thing as a Roman Democracy?

Translated by Romain Meltz, revised by Sarah-Louise Raillard

In Book VI of his *Histories,* the Greek historian Polybius (mid-2nd century BCE) praised the Roman political system for its perfect balance between three political forces: the Senate, the magistrates (with the consuls at the top), and the people. According to Claude Nicolet (1973, pp. 209–58), we should not jump to the conclusion that for Polybius the best constitution — a mixed one — 'should be made up of all the others'.[1] In terms of powers, any city or state (*politeia, politeuma*) was seen as being composed of parts or parties (*meros*). Thus, the three components of the Roman State were not abstractions such as the monarchy or the oligarchy, but concrete bodies: the consuls, the Senate, the people, each one of these possessing a measure of power and an area of competence. The word used at the time was *meris*. We cannot, therefore, say that a mixed constitution is composed of three 'powers': aristocratic, democratic, and monarchic. According to Polybius, simple constitutions (*suntaxeis*) can be qualified as 'democracies' or 'monarchies'. But in mixed constitutions, the political bodies or parties share power and competences. It is only according to the degree of power held by the various parties that a constitution can be labelled as 'more or less' aristocratic or democratic. This constitutional configuration, Polybius explains, delegates a very important share of power to the people:

> But nevertheless, there is a part — and it is a very important part — of power left to the people. For it is the people who alone has the right to

[1]   Polybius, VI, 11,11: the three ruling bodies of the State, quoted in Nicolet (1973, p. 225).

confer honours and inflict punishment, the only bonds by which kingdoms and states and in a word human society in general are held together [...] Again it is the people who bestows office on the deserving, the noblest reward of virtue in a state; the people have the power of approving or rejecting laws.[2]

Polybius's description of the powers invested in the people through their vote in legislative assemblies — the *comitia populi romani* — allows us to identify the democratic dimension of the Roman Republic.

Voting was one of the indispensable duties of Ancient Roman citizens.[3] Whether it was for legislative or electoral purposes (although popular voting on judicial cases gradually disappeared during the Republican era), voting was always seen as a political act embodying the power of the *iussum populi* to legitimize the final phase of the decision-making process (Hollard, 2010).[4] The almost sacred importance attached to regularly convening the people to act as a political force of legitimization was not fundamentally altered by the transition from the Republic to the Principate.

Even if it represented the democratic vestiges of the *res publica romana*, electoral voting in Rome has always been seen as the perfect illustration of the oligarchic dimension of this *res publica*. Two national assemblies allowed citizens to exercise their voting rights in Ancient Rome. The Tribal Assembly (*comitia tributa*) allowed for the election of lower-level Roman magistrates (those without *imperium*, or executive power, such as quaestors and aediles) and for voting on most laws. On the other hand, the role of the Centuriate Assembly (*comitia centuriata*) was to elect magistrates with *imperium* (higher offices such as consuls, praetors, and censors), and to vote on laws with containing military provisions (declarations of war and treaty ratifications). Depending on which assembly they were summoned to, the Roman people were organized in a different manner. In the Tribal Assembly, the people were gathered according to their tribes, with the geographic distribution occurring based on place of birth. After 241 BCE, Rome was comprised of 35 tribes — 4 urban and 31 rural. The tribes would remain territorially defined but would end up acquiring hereditary aspects.

---

2   Polybius, *The Histories*, VI, 14. Translated by W.R. Paton, revised by Frank W. Walbank and Christian Habicht, Cambridge, MA: Harvard University Press (2011, pp. 335–337).

3   Nicolet (1976): 'The people were convened at least seven times a year in all. Elections could last a fortnight altogether.' That situation leads Nicolet to conclude, after tallying up the number of legislative votes, that 'being a citizen was a full-time job' (p. 320).

4   On the sacred nature of the *iussum populi*, please see Magdelain (1978, pp. 74 *sq.*).

Citizens could not easily change the tribe they belonged to, as it was a stable part of one's identity, much like one's *tria nomina* (the combination of the three elements of official names in the Roman world, i.e. *praenomen*, first name, *nomen*, hereditary name, and *cognomen*, family name). In the Centuriate Assembly, Roman citizens were divided into census-based classes and centuries, whose formation dated back to the mid-4th century BCE, having possibly been established by the second Etruscan king Servius Tullius. The five census classes divided Romans according to their wealth, property, and the military equipment they were able to provide. Each class was divided into centuries (the units of the Roman army), *iuniores* (the youngest citizens), and *seniores* (the oldest), which translated into a distinction between active and reserve army members. Consequently, the centuries were military units and voting units at the same time. As a military organization, the assembly convened on the Field of Mars, outside of the *pomerieum* (the sacred area of the city inside of which weapons were prohibited). Based on the notion of geometric equality, the Centuries Assembly was designed to restrict political power and voting rights to the very wealthiest of citizens. All votes in the Centuriate Assembly were cast in a descending order, from the wealthiest down. The voting process stopped as soon as a majority (of 96 centuries) was reached. However, the first class (including the *equites*) accounted for 98 centuries out of the total 193, which meant it was capable of reaching an absolute majority on its own. The remaining lower classes, which included fewer centuries despite representing a greater proportion of the population, were therefore only seldom summoned to vote.[5] In the eyes of the Roman aristocracy, the nobility of the centuriate process stemmed precisely from the fact that the right to vote was reserved for the city's elites. In the Tribal Assembly, the role played by the lower classes appears to have been more significant. However, the socio-economic differences between the two assemblies should not be overstated. The Centuriate Assembly might have been compelled to let the lower classes vote when strong political divisions occurred within the elite classes. And in the Tribal Assembly, where rural tribes represented the majority, the balance of power effectively remained in the hands of rich Roman citizens, due to the overrepresentation of wealthy landowners in those tribes. However, our intention is not to reopen the long-running

---

[5]   The 18 *equites* plus the 80 centuries in the first census class (a reform adopted during the 3rd century BCE allegedly cut the first census class down to 70 centuries, thus forcing the assembly to turn to the second census class centuries to reach an absolute majority).

scholarly debate regarding the extent of Roman political participation in voting.[6] Whether or not it was conducted almost exclusively by the wealthiest citizens or included more popular swathes of the population, the act of voting has always been understood as embodying the political expression of the *populous Romanus* as a whole.

In this chapter, we shall investigate the significance behind the use of sortition procedures (drawing lots) in Roman elections. Although drawing lots, an Ancient Athenian legacy from the 5th century BCE, was traditionally perceived as the pinnacle of democracy, is it possible that, in fact, in the case of the Republic of Rome, random selection practices in fact had the opposite effect? Unlike in Ancient Athens, in the Roman Republic, citizens were not all viewed as peers who could exercise equal rights through sortition; random selection procedures were only conducted on a limited circle of elites. These two different conceptions of equality lead to two different uses of sortition by the Ancient Athenian democracy and the Roman Republic respectively. While Athenians trusted the drawing of lots to select the best rulers, Romans used the same tool to illustrate the link that existed between divine will and the elites. Shedding light on the meaning ascribed to the use of sortition in Roman elections shall, on the one hand, help us to describe the various political regimes adopted in ancient Rome and, on the other hand, to examine the profound changes that affected the political role of the people from the beginning of the Republic to the Principate. We shall first look at how traditionally, and in the early days of the Republic, the process of drawing lots was used to operate selections between peers whose ability to govern had been previously acknowledged. Then we shall examine how, in the late Republic, random selection became a controversial political and even ideological issue. To conclude, we shall consider the importance awarded to sortition in the development of voting procedures under the Augustan Principate. As I have no intention of covering every type of random selection used in an electoral context, I shall focus on those which appear to have had specific political implications, in accordance with evolutions in process of selecting city officials.

---

[6] Millar (2002) and Yakobson (1999) have proposed a more democratic vision of Roman elections than the historiographic tradition usually allows for; see Hollard (2010) for a lengthy discussion of the subject. Discussions on this topic are in general strongly influenced by the specific elections being examined.

At the Core of the Roman Republic: Drawing Lots as a Means of Establishing a Hierarchy amongst Magistrates and to Select between Peers

During the early years of the Roman Republic and while institutions were still being developed, sortition was a political tool used to establish a hierarchy amongst the first magistrates (Humm, 2012). The institutions created at the beginning of the 5th century BCE constituted a total break from the monarchy; in that sense, we can talk about a 'plebeian revolt'.

Sortition as a mean of organizing magistracies in the early Republic

What we refer to as the 'plebeian revolt' (the Conflict of the Orders) produced two major changes: the introduction of universal suffrage to elect magistrates and the adoption of the principle of collegiality for magistracies. The monarchical *imperium* could not be divided between two magistrates (this would remain the case throughout the Republic for *dictatores*). That non-division was confirmed by 'the rotation of the fasces'[7] (whereby the two elected magistrates alternately shared the *imperium domi* on a monthly basis). Although the first magistrates of the Republic were called praetors rather than consuls, only the *praetor maximus*[8] could carry the fasces, contrary to the plebeian tribunes, who were all created equal from the outset. During the first half of the 5th century BCE, following the drafting of the Laws of the Twelve Tables,[9] the collegium of the *praetores* who shared the *imperium* consecutively was said to have been replaced (from 444 to 367 BCE) by military tribunes with consular powers. These tribunes were of equal rank, although two of them were selected by lots to guide military affairs, while a third was primarily assigned to civil administration and the defence of the city. This sortition procedure thus introduced the distinction between *imperium militae* and *imperium domi*. The expression *consulari potestate* linked to the title of 'military tribune' alludes to the collegiality of the position and 'could derive, etymologically, from the verb *consulere* which refers to the consultative powers of these tribunes who were compelled by chance, so to speak, to divide up their duties

---

[7] The fasces carried by the *lictors* while escorting the magistrates possessing *imperium* were a symbolical representation of two different instruments used to punish wrongdoers.

[8] Liv., VII, 3, 5–8.

[9] First corpus of Roman laws, drafted by a decemvirate (board of ten magistrates) between 451 and 449 BCE. The emergence of written laws marked a break with the oral *ius* that had been traditional until that point.

by mutual agreement (*comparatio*)' (Humm, 2012, p. 122). In 367 BCE, the Licinan Rogations[10] allowed plebeians to access the highest political offices (Stewart, 2010, pp. 95–136). The collegium of three praetors was then divided (likely by drawing lots after their election) between two high magistrates transformed into consuls, and one praetor, still a member of the same collegium. While plebeians could become consuls, only patricians could be appointed praetors. Originally, these three magistrates, elected by the Centuriate Assembly under the same auspices, possessed equal rights. However, the power of the consuls was distinguished by the fact that their military command was always exercised in the collegial format. Hierarchical distinctions between consuls and praetors emerged in the mid-3rd century BCE when the number of praetors increased. By 242 BCE, the collegial structure of the three praetors was definitively transformed when a new praetorship, the *praetor peregrinus*, was created to deal with peregrine cases,[11] while the *praetor urbanus* presided in urban civil cases between Roman citizens. The praetorship was extended again when new provinces outside Italy had to be administered. Sortition was thus first used to decide between two consuls and a praetor (from 367 to 242 BCE), then between two consuls and two praetors (*urbanus* and *peregrinus*, from 242 to 227 BCE), and finally amongst the different praetors. The creation of additional provincial praetorships after 227 BCE defined a specific praetorian position, ranked below the consular level. Roberta Stewart (2010, p. 51) shows how the first magistrates (military tribunes with consulship power, as well as consuls and praetors) acquired their authority through sortition. The public ritual of drawing lots took place immediately after the corresponding election, adding divine legitimacy to popular validity. In fact, sortition was the incarnation of Jupiter's patronage of the city of Rome. It recalled the religious nature of all power in Rome, embodied in the auspices which were the source of *imperium*. Taking the auspices in order to decipher the divine will was a procedure with Etruscan origins: upon acceding to the throne, kings (and, later, higher magistrates entering office) were required to obtain the 'Jovian blessing' by first taking the auspices during a ceremony (*inauguratio*) that took place inside the *auguraculum* of the citadel (*arx*), a

---

[10] Roman laws adopted in 367 BCE, sometimes also called the Licinio-Sextian laws in honour of both of their authors, the plebeian tribunes Caius Licinius Stolon and Lucius Sextius Lateranus. They definitively restored the consulship, with the obligation that one of the two consuls must be a plebeian.

[11] Peregrines were free men who lived in the provinces conquered by Rome, but who did not enjoy the status of Roman citizens or the special status of the Latin tribe.

ceremony which granted them *imperium* (Magdelain, 1969–70). The ceremony allowed for the real 'creation' of kings and magistrates. According to Stewart, the sortition procedures implemented for the sake of the first higher Republican magistracies must be understood in connection with the divine dimension of elections and the procedure of taking the auspices.

Sortition therefore allowed for distinctions to be established between the various magistrates possessing *imperium*, individuals who were otherwise equals, in order to attribute specific and differing political duties. Subsequently, the implementation of the *cursus honorum* led to elections largely replacing random selection in this process of attributing different functions.

Sortition as a part of the process to elect magistrates during the Republic

Although, as the hierarchy of public officials was gradually established, sortition as a means to mark distinctions between positions was largely abandoned, random selection nonetheless remained an integral part of the electoral process to select magistrates presented below. After briefly discussing the structure of this electoral process, we shall examine the meaning attached to the use of sortition procedures embedded within it.

Every Roman election process began with a *professio* (a candidacy declaration) made by the candidate before the appropriate magistrate (this was the *nominatio* phase). As in the legislative assemblies, the auspices were taken and citizens were convoked on the election day. Then a *contio* (a preparatory voting assembly) was organized. But unlike in legislative voting procedures, there were no preliminary *contiones*. With regard to electoral *contiones* in the Republic, Dominique Hiebel argues that they were neither a place for *professiones* nor a time for canvassing, but rather an opportunity to address the *contio* 'in order to correct initially unfavourable situations' (Hiebel, 2004, p. 261). Once the *contio* was dissolved, and after citizens were sorted to their voting units and the prayer (*carmen*) preceding all assembly proceedings was intoned, the election, properly speaking, would start. Claude Nicolet describes a typical election in detail (Nicolet, 1976, pp. 345 *sq.*; Hall, 1964). The Tribal Assemblies would cast their vote all as a single entity, *uno uocatu*, at least after the *Lex Gabinia* was passed, which introduced the secret ballot[12] (before that date, votes must have been cast successively). We have less clarity regarding the precise voting order for the

---

12   Cic., *Pro Plancio*, 49.

electoral Centuriate Assembly. It appears that votes may have been cast class by class.[13] The Centuriate Assembly had, in fact, a clearer hierarchy than Tribal Assembly. Within each class, the centuries were called to vote separately. In both assemblies, random selection was used to determine which class (the *principium* in the Tribal Assemblies, the *praerogativa,* or prerogative, century in the Centuriate Assembly) would vote first. However, these rules were probably amended when the secret ballot was introduced: centuries within the same class could then probably vote simultaneously, although sortition was still used to choose the prerogative century. One can therefore assume that, until the beginning of the 3rd century BCE, the first *equites* of the 18 centuries would have been called first. With the reform of the century system in 241 BCE, the first century called to vote — the *praerogativa* — came to be randomly selected among the *iuniores* of the first class. The *Equilina* and *Suburana* tribes which represented the poorest neighbourhoods of Rome were probably excluded from this sortition procedure.

The vote of the *praerogativa* was considered to be highly significant, as many references indicate (Jehne, 2000). In 214 BCE, during a consular election, the prerogative century's vote was contrary to the one desired by the presiding magistrate, who consequently decided to interrupt the election.[14] In 211 BCE, the prerogative century elected a consul who turned down the position and asked him to vote again. The prerogative century's second vote was followed by all the other centuries.[15] This explains why Cicero sometimes described the vote of the *praerogativa* as an omen.[16] Let us skip over the detailed process of voting within the Centuriate Assembly (see Nicolet, 1976, pp. 357 *sq.*), as what matters was the core principle of this assembly: namely, that classes were called to vote successively. Once the voting was over, the counting of votes led to the *renuntiatio* (the proclamation) of the results, and finally the *designatio* (the designation) of the candidates.[17] In the Centuriate Assembly, the results had to be disclosed as soon as each class had voted, in order to determine whether to call the following class or not. In the Tribal Assembly where the tribes voted *uno uocatu*, the vote counting must have taken longer. The presiding magistrate would gather the results for all the tribes and, after counting the votes, would announce the results.

---

13   Liv., I, 43, 11.
14   Liv., XXIV, 7–9.
15   Liv., XXVI, 22.
16   Cic., *Diu.*, I, 103; *Mur.*, 38.
17   On the proceedings of the *renuntiatio* in the Tribal Assembly, see Nicolet (1970).

In the electoral process, therefore, sortition did not go beyond designating the first unit called to vote, which only concerned (especially in the Centuriate Assembly) citizens of the first class (i.e. the wealthiest). The premonitory value attached to this first step reminds us of the association between random selection and the divine legitimization of voting that would later be developed in Roman political life.

In conclusion, sortition in the Roman Republic was traditionally used prior to voting or immediately after voting to select from among a pool of citizens who were all members of the city's governing elite — the only individuals who were deemed worthy of leadership positions. Sortition was used to confer a sense of divine legitimacy to elected officials, in addition to the political validity awarded by the *iussum populi*. Such acts of sortition were, at least for the selection of the prerogative century and in the Centuriate Assembly more broadly, a question of choosing amongst a variety of peers. Random selection thus acquired a religious value and was portrayed as a kind of omen, a factor which would play an important role in the subsequent development of voting processes.

The Politicization of Sortition in Political Debates at the End of the Republic

While it is difficult to deny the oligarchic nature of the Roman Republic that prevailed until the 1st century BCE, the political turmoil that marked the end of this period can be interpreted as prompting the politicization of voting assemblies, which has led some historians like Millar to wonder whether a genuine democracy might have existed at that time. Were the electoral conflicts that occurred between the *optimates* and the *populares* in the assemblies the sign of massive popular engagement in politics, or merely the reflection of the political manipulation of both assemblies by their respective elites? And in either (or both) cases, what segments of the population were truly involved? It seems that, even for elections to the higher positions (those which implicated the Centuriate Assembly), a large swath of the population was involved. This is what allows Metataxi-Mitrou (1985) to argue that the urban-dwelling plebeians of the four tribes participated in the political violence. One should, however, distinguish between plebeian participation in the assemblies and plebeian interventions in the *contiones* before voting. Combined with the frequently corrupt practices of the time, these events suggest that the centuriate system did not exclude the citizens who belonged to the lowest census classes.

Amidst this context of political unrest and greater popular participation in electoral debates and elections, a number of electoral reforms were proposed which reflected the cleavage between *populares* and *optimates*. A legislative bill (*rogatio*) sought to dramatically alter the spirit — if not the letter — of voting procedures in the Centuriate Assembly. This modification would have given an altogether more prominent position to sortition within the electoral procedure, and a completely different meaning than it had possessed at the beginning of the Republic. A proposal put forward by Gaius Gracchus while he was a tribune suggested completely reforming the functioning of the Centuriate Assembly and giving a different significance to the random selection procedures employed therein:

> *Sed magistratibus creandis haud mihi quidem apsurde placet lex quam C. Gracchus in tribunatu promulgaret, ut ex confusis quinque classibus sorte centuriae uocarentur. Ita coaequata dignitate pecunia, uirtute anteire alius alium properabit.*

> [As regards the election of magistrates, I for my part very naturally approve of the law which Gaius Gracchus proposed during his mandate, that the centuries should be selected by lot from the five classes without distinction. In this way, dignity and wealth shall be valued equally and each man shall strive to outdo his peers in virtue.][18]

In this context, random selection was not solely used to designate the prerogative century; instead, an entire system of sortition grew to encompass the entirety of the voting process in the Centuriate Assembly. The excerpt below, from a letter written by Pseudo-Sallust to Caesar, is just one element in a series of general political recommendations:

> First of all then, deprive money of its importance. Let no one be given greater or less opportunity according to his wealth to serve as a juror in cases involving the life or honour of others; just as no consul or praetor should be chosen because of his riches, but because of his worth. In terms of magistrates, the decision can be left to the people; but for jurors to be selected by an oligarchy is tyranny, and for them to be chosen on the basis of money is shameful. (II, 7, 10–11)

The proposal of adopting *confusio suffragiorum* (the mixture of votes, not based on the centuriate system) outlined by this letter's author was perhaps an attempt to implement an old Gracchian law (or rather draft law) that sought to enable citizens belonging to the lowest classes to participate in the centuriate voting process. Suarez Pineiro (1998) has

---

[18] *The Letter to Caesar* by Pseudo-Sallust, Loeb Classical Library, 1921 (revised 1931).

pointed out that there is a certain continuity in the political action of the *populares* here, given that they had always pushed for a more open voting system. Two questions remain unanswered, however: is this letter authentic? And, if so, why is it the only document that mentions this law? Nicolet argues that the letter is indeed authentic (Nicolet, 1959; Virlouvet, 1984), comparing it to a passage of the *Pro Murena* in which Cicero alludes to an idea proposed by Servius Sulpicius Rufus and which would also lead, if implemented, to the resurrection of the Gracchian law.[19] This reform was seen as the sole means of re-establishing virtue as the decisive factor in elections (Dupla and Pina, 1994, p. 199).[20]

Many questions are raised by this letter, aside from the issue of identifying its author: how might the generalization of sortition have revolutionized the spirit of Roman elections, especially those taking place in the Centuriate Assembly? Can we argue that sortition, as proposed in this letter, was representative of a *populares* ideology inspiring attempts at electoral reform? Did this effectively mark the introduction of a democratic use of sortition in Roman politics?

The author of the letter to Caesar presents the virtues of this reform by emphasizing the fact that it would remove money from the competition: 'in this way, dignity and wealth shall be valued equally and each man shall strive to outdo his peers in merit.' Candidates would no longer see their political power justified solely by their wealth; in fact, the only remaining criterion to distinguish amongst candidates would be their individual virtue. Regardless of the practical success of this reform, does it theoretically posit the existence of a democratic ideology put forward by the *populares* 'party'? We cannot revisit the entirety of the historiographic debate regarding the existence of a political cleavage between the *populares* the *optimates*.[21] The expression 'ideology' can have several meanings. Whether one accepts the existence of a democratic ideology espoused by the Gracchus brothers and their successors among the *populares*, we must concede that their proposal to reform voting procedures in the Centuriate Assembly reflected an organic conception of the city, quite contrary to the notions that had underpinned the city's creation. From a certain perspective, this revolutionary reform of the Centuriate Assembly represented a new

---

[19] Cic., *Pro Mur.*, 47.
[20] But Moreau (2003) recalls that no *populares* ever tried to reduce the distance between the *contiones* and the *comitias*.
[21] On this broad question, see Ferrary (1997, pp. 228 *sq.*). More recently, see Robb (2010) and Le Doze (2010).

civic *weltanschauung* that refuted the organization's original principles. This new political vision was espoused by a social group that was united by a common culture, despite its fragmented social composition (Courrier, 2014). However, can this new vision of the political organization of the city be termed democratic? The expansion of sortition to all centuries would have given every citizen — regardless of the census class they belonged to and consequently their wealth — the same voting rights. The five census classes would therefore have been able to vote in the elections for higher offices. It seems difficult to *not* qualify such a proposal as democratic, given that it would have granted political responsibility to the whole *populous romanus*, and not merely to its wealthiest representatives. In fact, Diodorus Sicilius and Plutarch did not hesitate to label Caius Gracchus's endeavour as democratic (Botteri and Raskolnikoff, 1983).[22] However, Caius Gracchius's programme also had an important limitation: it posed no real challenge to the fundamental principle of geometrical equality, as the centuries remained unchanged in terms of their composition. In fact, Gracchius did not intend to challenge the fundamentally unequal system, in terms of arithmetic equality, of Roman voting units (as the lowest census classes continued to have much less weight, electorally speaking). The Roman voting system cannot, therefore, be viewed as a common good, equally shared in by the whole population.

Sortition and the Development of Voting Under the Augustan Principate

The transition between the Republic and the Principate has long been viewed as a political turning point, the moment when the citizens, which had traditionally gathered in *comitia* to elect magistrates and vote laws, were suddenly stripped of their power. Since the beginning of the 2000s, this interpretation of the political role of Roman citizens has been subject to a broad historiographical reassessment, an endeavour to which I have tried to contribute. This is apparent if we look at the evolution of magistrate elections and the role played by sortition in the new voting assembly created by Augustus, the *destinatio magistratuum* which served to pre-screen candidates for elections (Nicolet, 2000; Hollard, 2018). The *Lex Valeria Cornelia* (5 CE), put forward by the two consuls in charge that year, modified the procedure for the election of ordinary praetors and consuls. A limited assembly,

---

[22] Diodore, 34/35, 25, 1: Ὁ Ὑράκχος δημηγορήσας περὶ τοῦ καταλῦσαι ἀριστοκρτίαν, δημοκρατίαν δὲ συστῆσαι'; Plutarch, *C. Gracchus*, 5, 4.

composed of senators and *equites* belonging to the judicial *decuriones*, had to *destinare,* or 'pre-select', the candidates for praetorship and consulships. The election of these officials was a three-step process: first, the *nominatio* phase (when candidacies were received and accepted), then *destinatio* and *designatio* phases (when the candidates were pre-selected and then announced by the Centuriate Assembly). The centuries comprising the *destinatio* assembly were established in honour and memory of deceased princes of the imperial family (Domus Augusta): 10 centuries were created for Caius and Lucius Cesar, Augustus's late grandsons who would have succeeded their grandfather if not for their premature deaths in 5 CE; five centuries were created in honour of Germanicus (19 CE) and five more in honour of Drusus Julius Caesar (23 CE). The common trait shared by all these young members of the Domus Augusta was that they had been destined to succeed Augustus and Tiberius. The creation of this pre-selection assembly and the gradual increase in the number of centuries composing it were part of the honorific measures adopted after the death of these members of the imperial family. We know about these honours thanks to two major epigraphic sources: the *Tabula Hebana* and the *Tabula Siarensis.*[23]

Let us now examine how the *destinatio* assembly operated. Seston deserves credit for providing the first clear description of how the voting process unfolded in the *destinatio* assembly (Seston, 1955, pp. 39–41). Senators and *equites* enrolled in the judicial *decuriones* gathered in a primary assembly[24] to 'designate' the candidates for the praetorships and consulships. As Demougin points out, the area where the *destinatio* assembly was held had to be consecrated, as this assembly was called on to express the will of the late princes. In this respect, the power of the imperial family had to be highly visible on the premises chosen for the assembly. In fact, the assembly was held on the Palatine Hill where, as Demougin observes, 'the Augustan zone was a huge monumental

---

[23] *Tabula Hebana*: AE, 1949, 215 = 1992, 585. The *Tabula Hebana* was first edited by Coli (1947) in *Notizie delle Scavi*, pp. 49–68. *Tabula Siarensis*: CILA, II-3, 927 = AE, 2008, 651. The *Tabula Siarensis* was edited and published by Gonzalez and Fernandez (1981) in *Iura*, 32, pp. 1–36. I provide an extensive bibliography on the subject of these two inscriptions in Hollard (2010, pp. 187 *sq.*). The recent discovery of a new fragment of *Tabula Siarensis* does not provide any further details on our subject. However, one can find information about it in Cipollone and Bonamore (2011, pp. 3–19; 2012). The same can be said regarding the inscription discovered in 2000 in Italy and published by Buonopane (2010, pp. 401–404).
[24] The word is Seston's. He describes the *destinatio* as a forum for candidacy designation.

complex' which included 'not only the prince's residence but also the Temple of Apollo located at the centre of a large square, flanked by the Portico of the Danaids leading to two libraries of Latin and Greek texts respectively, situated on the south side' (p. 312). The Palatine complex became the centre of imperial political life. The senate met in the library of the Temple of Apollo; this was also where the *album iudicum* (official list of judges) was updated. Hence, this was likely where the *destinatio* assembly met as well.[25]

First, sortition took place amongst the members of 33 of the 35 total tribes (the poorest two tribes were excluded), which divided the senators and *equites* belonging to the judicial decurions who belonged to those tribes into the 15 *destinatio* centuries that would be called to vote (L. 6–13); then the *custodes* were randomly selected (L. 13–16). Next the *destinatio* centuries voted (L. 17–33). The *cistae* (urns) which contained the ballots were handed over to the *praetors qui aerario praesunt* (praetors in charge of the treasury) while awaiting the vote count (L. 34). Every voter in the assembly cast a ballot, within its century, for a candidate. This first stage produced the overall result of each century vote, which was written on a *tabella* (tablet). The ceremony then moved to the *Saepta Julia* (voting area on the Field of Mars) (L. 35). A lot was drawn from amongst the 15 *tabellae* (one *tabella* per each destination century) and the name written upon it was read aloud. This stage was interrupted as soon as a candidate obtained a majority of votes. The other 'destined' candidates were ranked according to the number of votes they obtained. The *pronuntiatio* (official declaration of the results) of the *destinati* was delivered by a *praeco* (a herald, town crier) (L. 46). The magistrate presiding over the *creatio* (election in the Centuriate Assembly) was required to guide the votes of the Centuriate Assembly (L. 48) towards the *candidati destinati* that had been pre-selected by the *destinatio* assembly. The sortition of the centuries ultimately produced a list of elected officials. On the whole, this interpretation affects how we understand lines L.46–48 of the *Tabula Hebana*: the number of Germanicus and Caesar centuries must always, according to Seston, *cedere in nu*[*merum centuriarum sorte ductarum*], that is, not be counted in addition to the number of the centuries of the Centuriate Assembly, but rather be included within the number of the pre-selected centuries which were drawn by lots during the *destinatio* procedure. This final figure was seen as expressing the will of Germanicus and the Caesars. In other words, a simple majority reached by a candidate was

---

[25] Demougin (1987) revisited the question of where the *destinatio* assembly met.

transformed into a unanimous vote by the 15 destining centuries. This step marked the end of the *destinatio* procedure (Hollard, 2010, p. 189). Let us add that although another round of sortition must have taken place, in order to determine which destining century would vote first, Seston does not mention any such process.[26]

Let us now quickly review the political objectives behind an electoral reform like the creation of the *destinatio* assembly. First of all, this measure sought to control the elections of higher public officials while maintaining the public assemblies which visibly embodied the ideology of the *res publica restituta*. Secondly, it sought to promote the Augustan ideal of *concordia ordinum* (harmony and agreement between the different units of Roman society) by bringing together ordinary people, senators, and *equites* in the context of electing praetors and consuls. Thirdly, this reform wished to highlight the relationship between the *princeps* and his followers in the name of whom consensus was reached and the foundations of the *res publica* were restored. And, finally, the reform embodied the linkages that Augustan Principate would always try to maintain between *auctoritas principis* (the authority of the *princeps*), dynastic politics, political control, and the preservation of the political institutions of the former Republic. The sum of these linkages and various attempts at achieving equilibrium between opposing forces represented the solidity of this new regime, which was nonetheless sometimes later labelled as ambiguous or hypocritical.

However, these are only superficial objectives that only regard the definition of the institutional functioning of the Augustan regime. There were others, with deeper significance for the Principate, which was more than just the sum of its visible institutions. How did the Principate understand the preservation of formal elections for praetors and consuls? In 23 BCE, Augustus abandoned the traditional consulship structure to create two new positions: *consular imperium* and *tribunicia potestas* (the power of plebeian tribunes), henceforth establishing the legal basis of the powers wielded by the *princeps* and his co-regents. In the years that followed this legal shift, the *princeps* was forced to intervene on two occasions when elections gave way to civic disorder—the consular elections of 21 and of 19 BCE.[27] While Augustus did attempt to re-establish a kind of aristocratic competition, especially in the political race for consular positions, candidates could not run

---

[26]   For further remarks about the *destinatio* procedure, see Demougin (1988, pp. 393–441).

[27]   About these two electoral incidents, see Hollard (2010, pp. 216–225) and finally Courrier (2014).

without the *princeps'* consent, consent which had historically been provided during the *suffragatio* and *commendatio* phases of the electoral process. By establishing a preliminary voting procedure in a memorial context honouring the members of the Domus Augustus, Augustus reinforced the connection between himself and the people, thus avoiding the potentially dangerous consequences of aristocratic competition (the latter, which had underpinned elections during the Republic, had nonetheless also been responsible for its ruin). Who could choose *not* to vote for those who had been 'destined' to the magistracies by senators and *equites* voting in the name of members of the imperial family, hence in the name of Augustus himself?

Once we have understood the implications of the *destinatio* reform, how should we understand the new role played by sortition in the *destinatio* process? Let us recall that sortition was first used to divide the tribes into the *destinatio* centuries ('the urn which will allow for the names of the tribes to be drawn at random to form new centuries shall be a spinning urn. There are two extant illustrations of this machine, one in a Carthaginian mosaic and one in a Roman painting, which depict a round object spinning around a horizontal axis anchored to two uprights'; Nicolet, 1976, pp. 348–349). The senators and the juror-*equites* of the same tribe were gathered in the same *destinatio* century. This division was made to create 10, then 15, and finally 20 centuries. Secondly, random selection was used to choose the *custodes* (the guardians of the urns). A third act of sortition determined the voting order. Finally, a fourth act of sortition in the *Saepta* indicated the names written on the *tabellae*.

Random selection thus seems to have played important role at all stages of the *destinatio* process. Sortition was not only used to choose the first citizen or unit to vote, but was at the core of the whole process: forming the *destinatio* centuries (distribution of the tribes into the centuries), designating those who guarded the urns until they reached the *Saepta*,[28] establishing the voting order and, finally, announcing the results. The question, then, is the following: was it because sortition played such an important role in the *destinatio* process that the latter was seen as an honorary memorial measure? Or, on the contrary, was it precisely because the *destinatio* was considered to be both a political and honorary measure that it included such a high degree of random selection? Sortition was seen as socially cohesive. Here, we find the

---

[28] The *custodes* in the Centuriate and Tribal Assemblies were not chosen by lots, but in part by the presiding magistrate and in part by the other candidates. On this point, see Nicolet (1976, p. 374).

political signification of the *destinatio* emphasized above: sortition was used to achieve total consensus, centred around the Domus Augusta, between the *princeps,* the senators, the *equites,* and ordinary citizens represented inside the assembly. This consensus was even stronger since it claimed to stem from the *pietas* owed to deceased members of the Domus Augusta. Senators, *equites,* and citizens alike were united in political decisions taken not only in the name of respecting the *auctoritas principis,* but also in the name of the deceased members of the imperial family, who posthumously intervened in an electoral competition rooted in the Republican tradition, thus establishing a direct link between the divine, the emperor, and the electorate. Sortition thus adopted a very clear significance and concretely expressed a specific relationship. Embedded within a set of memorial honours which had already been subject to a vote and thus embodied an institutional consensus, the use of sortition mechanisms symbolized all of the relationships at play: the relationship between citizens and the *princeps,* between men and gods, between the Republican electoral tradition and the *auctoritas principis* which henceforth governed aristocratic competition. The value of sortition resided in its ability to suspend conflicts and rivalries by instead focusing attention on the shared memory of the deceased princes. And finally, sortition also represented the relationship between the co-regent, destined to become an emperor, and the candidates, destined to become magistrates possessing *imperium.* The use of random selection also hinted at the possibility of divine predetermination with regard to elected officials. Claude Nicolet emphasizes this link between the deceased princes and the choice of magistrates, henceforth placed under an imperial and divine aegis:

> We shall see that this kind of pretext [the religious roots of the *comitiae* previously mentioned by the author, and confirmed by the existence of the prerogative century chosen by lot] was used during the reigns of Augustus and Tiberius to place the voting procedures of a limited assembly comprised of only senators and *equites* and in charge of 'destining' candidates to praetor and consul positions, under the patronage of princes of the imperial family who had died prematurely and to whom was conferred the honour, among other quasi-divine honours, of giving a name to, and hence of inspiring the ten, then fifteen centuries of this new assembly. (Nicolet, 1976, p. 357)

Once again, the similarity between the prerogative century and the *destinatio* assembly is stressed — not so much in the quantitative terms of their electoral weight in the total number of the votes, but rather in qualitative terms, on account of their religious impact. Both the prerogative century and the *destinatio* assembly were omens, and the strong connection between these two preliminary votes and the practice of drawing lots played an important role in ensuring the efficacy of a procedure that 'pre-selected' future magistrates. Given that the imperial cult was still in the early stages of its development, the religious impact of a pre-selection vote could only be guaranteed by invoking the name of a deceased prince, rather than the living representative of the imperial family. As a result, the common feature shared by the deceased members of the Domus Augusta was that they were all co-regents who had died prematurely while they were destined to become the successors of the reigning *princeps*. During the Principate, the legitimacy of the new imperial power could only be fully realized by linking Republican institutions with the quasi-sacred predetermination of a *princeps* endowed with *auctoritas*. The commemoration of potentially predestined princes, thus in connection with the divine, very naturally found its application in an electoral process of pre-destination, albeit in an institutional rather than religious sense, but still connected to the divine thanks to the widespread use of sortition. This process of random selection affected both those who were going to vote (when the tribes were divided into *destinatio* centuries, when the voting order was determined) and those who would be 'destined' (when the results were proclaimed). The names of the deceased princes were invoked at both ends of the process and in relation to both parties involved in the process, voters as well as elected magistrates.

Conclusion

This chapter focused on a few milestones in Roman political history, in particular the complicated relationship between elections and sortition. We can conclude that sortition was consistently a part of the Roman electoral process; it was used, on the one hand, to confer religious legitimacy to voting and, on the other hand, to select magistrates from amongst a pool of equal citizens. Notably, the political experiment led by the *populares* at a very troubled moment in the history of the Roman Republic is the only attempt documented where the use of sortition was politicized in an attempt to reform and democratize voting procedures (even if this expansion of democratic voting must be heavily contextualized, given the time period). In all other cases, sortition was used to provide a divine endorsement for Roman political power, exclusively in the hands of the city's social elites. Granting the Roman elites a monopoly over government and enshrining this power with divine consent allowed for social cohesion; it was an indispensable mechanism to ensure the proper functioning of the city and the *concordia ordinum* touted as the wellspring of Roman hegemony. Must we therefore conclude that Rome was never truly a democracy? As a component of voting procedures, random selection must take place among equals. The practice of random selection inserts a controlled element of chance within a predetermined group that has agreed to use sortition. Consequently, Romans never conceived of sortition as a democratic tool. Nevertheless, Roman voting procedures — whether for legislative or electoral purposes — enshrined the *iussum populi* (the order of the people) at the core of the Roman political process. The order of the people was granted an almost sacred dimension, which even Caesar and the emperors that followed him would not dare to attack. If democracy did in fact exist in Ancient Rome, it is to be found in this ritual and symbolic convocation of the *populous*, however limited the relevant segment of the population involved in selecting future public officials might have been. As a result, the *iussum populi* illustrates the great degree of political continuity that existed between the Republic and the Empire.

References

Except when explicitly noted, references to Greek literary texts are those of the Serie Collection des Universités de France (CUF), Paris: Les Belles Lettres.

Bonnafous, S., Chiron, P., Ducard, D., *et al.* (eds.) (2003) *Argumentation et discours politique. Antiquité grecque et latine, Révolution française, Monde contemporain*, Rennes: PU Rennes.

Botteri, P. & Raskolnikoff, M. (1983) « Diodore, Caius Gracchus et la Démocratie », in Nicolet, C. (ed.) *Demokratia et Aristokratia*, pp. 59–101.

Brunhs, H., David, J.-M. & Nippel W. (eds.) (1997) *Die Späte Römische Republik. La fin de la République romaine. Un débat franco-allemand d'histoire et d'historiographie*, Rome: École française de Rome.

Buonopane, E. (2010) « Germanico e Druso in una nuova iscrizione di Vicetia (*Regio X*) », in *Le tribu romane. Atti della XVIè rencontre d'épigraphie*, Bari: Edipuglia.

Cipollone, M. & Bonamore, S. (2011) *Boll. Arch. on line*, 2, 2011, pp. 3–19.

Cipollone, M. & Bonnamore, S. (2012) *Epigraphica*, 74, 2012, pp. 83–107.

Courrier, C. (2014) *La plèbe de Rome et sa culture (fin du IIe siècle av. J.-C.– fin du Ier siècle ap. J.-C.)*, Rome; École française de Rome.

Demougin, S. (1987) Quo descendat in campo petitor. Élections et électeurs à la fin de la République et au début de l'Empire, in *L'Urbs. Espace urbain et histoire. Ier siècle av.J.C.-IIIe siècle ap. J.C., Actes du colloque international, Rome, 8–12 mai 1985*, Rome: École française de Rome, Paris: De Boccard, pp. 305–317.

Demougin, S. (1988) *L'Ordre équestre sous les Julio-Claudiens*, Rome, coll. de l'EFR, Paris: De Boccard.

Dupla, A., Fatas, G. & Pina, F. (1994) *Rem Publicam Restituere. Una repuesta popularis para la crisis republicana : las Epistulae ad Caesarem de Salustio*, Zaragoza: Univ. de Zaragoza.

Ferrary, J.-L. (1997) *Optimates* et *Populares*. Le problème du rôle de l'idéologie dans la politique, in Bruhns, H., David, J.-H. & Nippel, W. (eds.) *Die Späte Römische Republik. La fin de la République romaine. Un débat franco-allemand d'histoire et d'historiographie*, Rome: École française de Rome, pp. 221–231.

Hall, U. (1964) Voting procedures in Roman assemblies, *Historia*, 13, pp. 267–305.

Hiebel, D. (2004) *Rôles institutionnel et politique de la* contio *sous la République romaine (237–49 a.C.)*, Doctoral Thesis, Univ. Panthéon-Assas, p. 261 (published in 2009, Paris: De Boccard).

Hollard, V. (2010) *Le rituel du vote*, Paris: CNRS.

Hollard, V. (2018) La mort de Germanicus et l'augmentation du nombre de centuries destinatrices. Une mise au point sur les liens entre *destinatio* et mémoire des membres défunts de la *Domus Augusta*, in *Mélanges offerts au Professeur Yves Roman*, vol. 2, Lyon: Société des amis de Jacob Spon.

Humm, M. (2012) Hiérarchie de pouvoirs et hiérarchie de magistratures dans la Rome républicaine, in Bérenger, A. & Lachaud, F. (eds.) *Hiérarchie des pouvoirs, délégation de pouvoir et responsabilité des administrateurs dans l'Antiquité et au Moyen-Age*, *Actes du colloque de Metz, 16–18 juin 2011*, Metz: Centre de recherche universitaire lorrain d'histoire, pp. 105–134.

Jehne, M. (2000) Wirkungsweise und Bedeutung der centuriae praerogatiuae, *Chiron*, 30, pp. 661–678.

Le Doze, P.H. (2010/2) Les idéologies à Rome: les modalités du discours politique de Cicéron à Auguste, *Revue Historique*, 654, pp. 259–289.

Magdelain, A. (1969–70) L'*auguraculum* de l'*arx* à Rome et dans d'autres villes, *Revue des Études Latines*, 47, pp. 253–269 (= *Ius Imperium Auctoritas. Études de droit romain*, Rome, 1990, pp. 193–207).

Magdelain, A. (1978) especially in *La loi à Rome. Histoire d'un concept*, Paris: Les Belles Lettres.

Metaxi-Mitron, F. (1985) Violence in the contio during the ciceronian age, *AC*, 54, pp. 180–187.

Millar, F. (2002), *The Roman Republic and the Augustan Revolution*, Cotton, M. & Rogers, G.M. (eds.), Chapel Hill, NC: Univ. of North Carolina Press.

Moreau, P.H. (2003) Donner la parole au peuple? Rhétorique et manipulation des *contiones* à la fin de la République, in Bonnefou, S., Chiron, P., Ducard, D., *et al.* (eds.) *Argumentation et discours politique. Antiquité grecque et latine, Révolution française, Monde contemporain*, Rennes: Presses universitaires de Rennes, pp. 175–189.

Nicolet, C. (1959) *Confusio Suffragiorum*: à propos d'une réforme électorale de Caius Gracchus, *Mélanges d'Archéologie et d'Histoire*, pp. 145–210.

Nicolet, C. (1970) Le livre III des *Res Rusticae* de Varron et les allusions au déroulement des comices tributes, *REA*, 72, pp. 113–137.

Nicolet, C. (1973) Polybe et les institutions romaines, in Gabba, E. (ed.) *Polybe*, Genève: Entretiens de la fondation Hardt, pp. 209–258.

Nicolet, C. (1976) *Le métier de citoyen dans la Rome républicaine*, Paris: Seuil.

Nicolet, C. (ed.) (1983) *Demokratia et Aristokratia*, Paris: Publications de la Sorbonne.

Nicolet, C. (2000) La *destinatio* à la lumière de la Tabula Siarensis et de Dion, in Fraschetti, A. (ed.) *La commemorazione di Germanico nella documentazione epigrafica. Tabula Hebana e Tabula Siarensis, Actes du congès international, Cassino, 21–24 October 1991*, Rome: L'Erma di Bretschneider, pp. 221–263.

Robb, M.-A. (2010) *Beyond Populares and Optimates: Political Language in the late Republic*, Stuttgart: Franz Steinerg.

Seston, W. (1950) La Table de bronze de Magliano et la réforme électorale d'Auguste, *CRAI*, pp. 105–111.

Seston, W. (1955) La procédure de la *pronuntiatio* des consuls et des préteurs d'après la *Tabula Hebana*, *Revue des Etudes Latines*, 33, pp. 39–41.

Stewart, S. (2010) *Public Office in Early Rome: Ritual Procedure and Political Practice*, Ann Arbor, MI: Univ. of Michigan Press.

Suarez Pineiro, A.M. (1998) La reforma del sistema electoral romano durante el ultimo siglo de la Republica, *Gallaecia*, 17, pp. 425–446.

Virlouvet, C. (1984) Le sénat dans la seconde lettre de Salluste à César, in Nicolet, C. (ed.) *Des Ordres à Rome*, Paris: Université de Paris 1, Publications de la Sorbonne, pp. 101–141.

Yakobson, A. (1999) *Elections and Electioneering in Rome: A Study in the Political System of the Late Republic*, Stuttgart: Franz Steiner.

Julie Bothorel

Civic Sortition in Republican and Imperial Rome
Physical Instruments and Technical Logistics

Translated by Sarah-Louise Raillard

Called *sors* or *sortitio* in Latin, the technique of sortition (the casting of lots) was frequently used in Republican and Imperial Rome. While *sortitio* was commonly called upon for everyday purposes (in games of chance or magic rituals, for instance), and played an important role in oracular prophesies, the procedure was also used by Roman magistrates in an official context to allocate public offices and civic goods, as well as to establish voting orders.

Despite its fundamental role in Roman history, the details of civic sortition and its attendant instruments remain largely unknown (Hurlet, 2006, p. 80). Literature on this subject is scarce, as random selection has never been comprehensively examined, unlike voting as a decision-making mechanism. The 19th-century German historian Theodor Mommsen (who is notably the author of *Roman Public Law*) and the scholars who followed in his footsteps studying the history of Roman institutions, as well as the handful of authors who examined the practice of *sortitio* in Ancient Rome (Lécrivain, 1911; Ehrenberg, 1927), only analysed the legal and political aspects of sortition, completely overlooking its material and logistical elements. Although Lily Ross Taylor (1966), Eastland Stuart Staveley (1972), Claude Nicolet (1976; 1991), and Roberta Stewart (1998a,b) have devoted some pages to the physical instruments and technical logistics associated with *sortitio*, the conclusions reached by these authors vary significantly; consequently, they do not allow us to accurately date the instruments and procedures described, nor to understand how these practices evolved over time. This lack of information on the physical equipment used in Rome to draw lots in civic procedures has often elicited negative comparisons with regard to its classical Athenian counterpart, the *kleroterion*, regarding which we have ample information. Nonetheless, the public use of random selection procedures remains poorly documented if we look at the Greek world as a whole. This obvious gap is also often compared with studies on the practice of *sortitio* in Italian oracular sanctuaries (Champeaux, 1982) and, more broadly, on divinatory and private uses of sortition. The existing research reveals that there are only a handful of sources available that focus on the issue of civic sortition. However, a number of interesting facts regarding the physical instruments and technical logistics of sortition can be gleaned from non-scholarly sources, in particular several parodic pieces by Plautus (*Casina*) and a number of inscriptions, such as the *Tabula Hebana*, the *lex Malacitana*, and the Augustan Edicts from Cyrene, in particular Edicts I and V.

This chapter shall investigate the 'receptacle' and the 'lots' used to conduct civil sortition procedures in Republican and Imperial Rome, seeking to demonstrate that the transition between 100 BCE to 70 CE from manual sortition conducted by means of a *sitella*, to mechanical sortition using a rotating sortition vessel (*urna versatilis*), corresponds to a number of significant changes in the aristocratic and political regime during the 1st century BCE.

Random Selection in Republican and Imperial Rome

There were numerous public uses of random selection in Republican Rome (509 BCE to 27 BCE). First and foremost, sortition was used to allocate specific tasks and duties among senators (e.g. selecting ambassadors and messengers) and magistrates (e.g. attributing provinces to consuls, praetors, and quaestors; choosing one of the censors to perform the ceremony marking the end of the census, the *lustrum*, or to appoint the first senator to be listed on the *album senatorium* (the *princeps senatus*); choosing one of the consuls to preside over the People's Assembly; or nominating, in the case of a military or political crisis, an extraordinary magistrate called a dictator; etc.). Assistants were occasionally attributed to support magistrates using random selection, much like the scribes who drew lots to select the magistrates who would be in charge of the public finances (quaestors) and who they would serve. In addition, before the various elective and legislative popular assemblies could proceed to a vote, sortition was used to select the *centuria praerogativa* and the first voting tribe, as well as the tribe in which the Latins would vote. Random selection similarly helped to determine in which of the four urban tribes and freed slaves would vote. After the popular assemblies voted, *sortitio* also determined the order in which the results were announced; in cases where results were too close to call, the procedure was used to choose the winner. In addition, random selection was frequently used in judicial procedures to designate jurors and their potential substitutes; in such cases, the method was referred to as *subsortitio*, or supplementary random selection. The *judicium recuperatorium*, or the 'arbiters' in charge of settling private disputes between Roman citizens, as well as between Roman citizens and *peregrine*, were selected by lot, as were the judges for criminal courts in the provinces. When jury members orally delivered their verdicts, random selection determined the order in which these declarations were made. Plots of land were distributed to settlers using sortition. Random selection also served to update the list of those who benefited from public wheat distribution. Finally, sortition was employed to appoint certain religious offices: for instance, the 17 tribes responsible for electing the priest in charge public worship (the chief pontiff) were selected by lot, as were the vestal virgins and members of certain religious colleges.

During the Imperial period (from 27 BCE to 476 CE), the use of sortition, far from decreasing, only expanded: most of the Republican uses of sortition persisted and new functions, the creation of the Empire and/or in the service of the emperor, began to be drawn by lot as well. For example, random selection was now used to attribute new duties to the *equites* (knights) and the senators serving the Empire (choosing the two praetors responsible for managing the public treasury, the *aerarium*; selecting senators to form commissions; etc.). The use of random selection allowed these new functions to resemble traditional public magistracies, even though the practice of direct nomination by the emperor was in fact becoming more prevalent. *Sortitio* was also used to select the *sodales*, or religious officials of the deified imperial cult, as well as the *quindecemviri*, or priests who distributed purification materials during the celebration of the Secular Games, which had marked the beginning of each new century since Rome was founded. In the Century Assembly as it was refashioned following the reign of Augustus, sortition was also used to determine the order in which voting proceeded and to choose the *custodes* in charge of supervising the procedure.

The political and social advantages of *sortitio* were numerous for public authorities: by excluding any rational or human interference, the use of random selection guaranteed equality among the candidates included in the sortition process. Random selection likewise helped to fight against corruption and machinations while simplifying and speeding up the political decision-making process. However, not all citizens could participate in official sortition procedures. In Rome, sortition candidates were always elected beforehand by the people, or selected by magistrates using examinations and other criteria and then placed on the list of eligible participants.

The Receptacle

The sitella

Several documents mention that towards the end of the 3rd century BCE and until the 1st century BCE, magistrates used a *sitella* to draw lots in civic sortition procedures. The *situla* or *sitella* is a type of container resembling a large bucket or pail, generally with a handle, whose contents could vary (Hilgers, 1969); the use of the diminutive *sitella* is only attested to in the context of sortition.

Livy (*History of Rome*, 41, 18, 9) recalls that the irregular consular sortition performed by the consuls in 176 BCE was conducted using a *sitella*. The same word can be found in descriptions of random selection procedures in various legislative assemblies as well as in a judicial context. To describe an act of sortition that took place in 212 BCE in the legislative assembly, Livy (*History of Rome*, 25, 3, 16) stipulates that a *sitella* was used to designate the tribe in which the Latins would vote. Referring to the conflict in 133 BCE that pitted the two plebeian tribunes Tiberius Gracchus and Marcus Octavius against each other on the subject of an agrarian aw, Cicero (*De Natura Deorum*, 1, 38, 106) also used the expression *deferentem sitellam*, which strictly speaking means 'to bring the *sitella*'. The procurement of the *sitella* in fact marked the opening of the electoral process, which began immediately after the first tribe called to vote was chosen by random selection (the *tribus principium*). Regarding the vote on another law, this one proposed by Lucius Appuleius Saturninus in 103 or 100 BCE, the anonymous author of *Rhetorica ad Herennium* (1, 12, 21) emphasizes that, after the tribunes vetoed the law, Saturninus had the *sitella* brought into the chamber (*sitellam detulit*) to randomly select the order in which the tribunes and centuries would vote, as well as the group to which new citizens would be attributed. Following this, a number of senators broke down the *pontes*, or the compartments separating the voting chambers, and spilled the baskets (*cistae*) containing the votes out onto the floor to prevent the law from being adopted. The use of a *sitella* is likewise confirmed in the context of designating jury members at random. Fragments of the *lex Acilia de repetundis* survive in the *Tabula Bembina* and describe the procedure followed to vote and announce voting results during the trials of governors being prosecuted for corruption (*repetundis*). The law stipulates that a randomly selected judge must in turn draws lots to select the jury ballots to announce the voting results. This law provides us with the official vocabulary of *sortitio* during the Republican era: the lots are called *sortes* or *sorticolae*, and the instrument used to draw them is called a *sitella* (*CIL* I², 583). Asconius's commentary on Cicero likewise mentions the use of a *sitella* and standardized *sortes* (*aequantur sortes*) to randomly selected judges (*Pro Cornelio*, p. 71, Stangl). We also find the term *sitella* under the pen of Symmachus (*Orations*, 4, 7), when the latter discusses the random selection of jurors and references the numerous electoral frauds committed under the Republic: 'Let us understand the benefits of our era: the unseemly wax tablet is no longer, nor the sorting falsified by troops of clients, the voting urn which could be bought (*sitella venalis*)...' The *sitella* thus appears as the pail or basket by means of which lots were drawn during the Republican era, where sortition was practised in a wide variety of contexts including assemblies and juries, and was also used to assign provinces and other official responsibilities.

Although there are no surviving figurative representations of sortition scenes that depict the use of a *sitella*, we can nonetheless refer to a number of Republican theatrical works to understand how this instrument was wielded. In the second act of *Casina*, to parody the use of sortition to attribute provinces to Roman consuls and praetors, Plautus depicts two slaves (who represent the two consuls) using a *sitella* to randomly select which of the two of them will be the master of the slave Casina (which represents the province to be attributed). This scene suggests that the *sitella*, as well as the water and the lots used, are brought from outside (v. 296, 363), that this equipment is checked (v. 380-399), that the lots are introduced (*conicere*, v. 342), and finally drawn by hand (*tenere*, v. 415) (cf. Stewart, 1998b, pp. 13–22). The *sitella* is thus associated with a manual practice of random selection and perhaps even, given that the receptacle is filled with water, to a form of hydromancy — hydromancy being a divinatory art practised using water. With somewhat less precision, we also find a description of the *sitella*'s use in the *lex Acilia*: to select jury members, lots are introduced (*coniectant*), thoroughly mixed up by hand (*manum demittito*), drawn, and then revealed to the public (*ostendito*). This time, no water is mentioned as being present in the *sitella* (*CIL* I², 583).

Another water receptacle, the *hydria* (ὑδρία, water jug) is mentioned by Plutarch and Cicero as an instrument used to conduct official

Roman sortition practices. Plutarch (*Tiberius Gracchus*, 11, 1) is the only one to mention the use of a *hydria* for randomly selecting the first unit that would vote in the legislative assembly in 133 BCE. This reference is especially striking since legislative *sortitio* is the official sortition procedure about which we have the most information and, in the number of accounts of legislative *sortitiones* that we possess, nowhere else is a *hydria* mentioned. It is therefore likely that the Greek author simply used this term to translate the Latin word *sitella*. Cicero also used the word *hydria* (often translated as an 'urn') to describe the receptacle used by the praetor Verres when the latter proceeds to select the priest of Jupiter at Syracuse, amidst a climate of rampant corruption. As Verres cannot directly appoint his 'intimate friend' Theomnastus to the priesthood, he throws three lots into the *hydria*, 'on all of which was written the name of Theomnastus' (*In Verrem*, 2, 2, 51, 127). Cicero is explicit that by drawing lots using a *hydria*, Verres is not following the traditional Roman procedure, but rather an ancient religious law with Greek origins. Despite Cicero and Plutarch's texts, therefore, we can conclude that the *hydria* was not used during official Roman sortition procedures; its use is in fact only attested to in traditionally Greek cities, and for primarily domestic and religious purposes (though in some cases the word merely appears as a Greek translation of the Latin term *sitella*). In the second act of *Casina*, Plautus likewise translates the Greek word ὑδρία (*hydria*) used by Diphilus as *sitella* (or *situla*), which shows that Romans did not use water jugs (*hydriae*) but water pails (*sitellae*) to draw lots for civic purposes.

The urna versatilis

The descriptions of official sortition practices as conducted after the 1st century BCE generally mention the use of an *urna*; no further mentions of a *sitella* occur. The word *urna* has several meanings: it can refer to a unit of measurement, a receptacle for water or wine, a ballot box, an instrument for drawing lots, or a funeral urn (Hilgers, 1969). More generally, the expression is used to describe a container, whose size and contents vary, and does not seem to have corresponded to a single item that can be identified by ceramics specialists.

The word *urna* is frequently used by Cicero (*In Verrem*, 2, 2, 42; *Against Vatinius*, 34; *Letters to his brother Quintus*, 2, 4a, 4; *De Divinatione*, 2, 69) and his commentators to describe the object used during sortition procedures in legislative and judicial contexts after 70 BCE. Other authors — Tacitus (*Histories*, 4, 6, 6; 4, 7) and Pliny the Younger (*Letters*, 10, 3a, 2; *Panegyricus*, 36) in particular — used the term to describe the equipment used in official *sortitiones* during the Imperial period. These two authors often associated the word *sors* (chance in the abstract sense, or fate) with the word *urna* (the instrument for drawing lots). During the Imperial period, moreover, many poets described allegorical or mythical processes of random selection conducted using an *urna*, such as Horace (*Odes*, 2, 3, 25–27; 3, 1, 14–16), Propertius (*Elegies*, 4, 11, 19–20), Apuleius (*Metamorphoses*, 10, 8, 2), Ovid (*Metamorphoses*, 15, 43), and Virgil (*Aeneid*, 6, 20–22). Under the Empire, the *urna* was used to draw lots and was an essential element of the ritual spectacle, determining the place that the different groups and factions were supposed to occupy within the amphitheatre (Sidonius Apollinaris, *Carmina*, 23, 315–325; Cassiodorus, *Orations*, 1, 4; Symmachus, *Relationes*, 9, 6). Lastly, a fragment from the Acts of the Secular Games mentions an *urna* being used to nominate the priests that would distribute to the people the perfumes to be burned during the Games (*CIL* VI, 32327, 1.11 = *ILS*, 5050a and *AE*, 1932, 70).

As it has come down to us through the *Tabula Hebana*, the *lex Valeria Aurelia* (*AE*, 1949, 215f) on honours to Germanicus (20 CE) was the first document to unambiguously outline the functioning of the *urna*, associating it with the adjective *versatilis* (*AE*, 1949, 215f), which Claude Nicolet (1991) translated as 'a revolving urn', an instrument used to draw lots at random. The first Augustan Edict from Cyrene, which we know through a Greek inscription (the Latin text did not survive into modern times, and we cannot therefore compare the original Latin terms with their Greek translation), likewise attests to the use of a *kleroterion* (in Greek, a randomization device) to select mixed juries (i.e. containing both Greek and Roman citizens) (de Visscher, 1940).

Several literary sources describe how the *urna* worked and confirm that it was indeed used as an instrument to draw lots at random. Recounting the fiasco that was the consular election conducted by Caesar in 48 BCE, Lucan (*Pharsalia*, 5, 392–394) depicts an empty *urna* spitting out (*versare*) the names of the tribes. The use of the verb *versare* to describe the *urna* can also be found in Horace (*Odes*, 2, 3, 25–27; 3, 1, 14–16) and Seneca (*Troades*, 974; *Controversiae*, 1, 2, 7). The *urna* is also combined with verbs of movement in Virgil (*movere*) (*Aeneid*, 6, 432), the pseudo-Vopiscus (*agitari*) (*Life of Probus*, 8, 6), and Cassiodorus (*vertiginem*) (*Orations*, 1, 4). These verbs all suggest that the urn is revolving on itself to jumble up the lots inside. Tertullian (*De spectaculis*, 16, 21) compares the motion of the lots inside the *urna* to eyeballs rolling around in their sockets. Constantine VII Porphyrogenitus (*The Book of Ceremonies*, I, 78) would later describe the *urna*'s mode of operation much more precisely, when depicting the sortition procedure used to determine race starting positions: 'as soon as he takes the balls from the bowl, he tosses them into the urn and turns the latter three times (to crank out a ball).' It therefore seems that the urn (*urna, kylistra*), taken out of storage from the Grand Palace and brought to the drawing location, is fixed on an axis around which it can rotate between two upright pieces of wood. The action of forcing the urn to rotate on its axis, completing a half turn so that its opening is now facing the bottom, was expressed in Greek by the word *kyliein*, which specifically means that the urn is turned upside-down, and not merely 'shaken'. This text therefore describes an elaborate instrument to draw lots. These various uses of the word *urna* thus allow us to determine what procedure was followed during civic *sortitiones*, as well as the official terminology: the lots, which had been previously checked, are inserted into an urn (*conicere, mittere* in Latin; *ballein* in Greek), then the rotating urn is spun (*versare* in Latin; *kyliein* in Greek), most likely using a hand crank to mix up the lots (*volure, dispergere, dissupare*); the lots then come out of the urn (*ducere, exire*) and are identified (*ostendere*).

Our understanding of how the *urna versatilis* worked can be further completed by studying iconographic, archaeological, and epigraphic sources. The first Republican representation of a random selection machine that we know of is a control mark on a coin minted by Lucius Roscius Fabatus, which Michael Crawford has dated back to 64 BCE (1975, I, no. 412.1, pp. 439–440). Most depictions of the sortition machine date from the 4th and 5th centuries CE and are difficult to interpret, however. Claude Nicolet (1991) has compiled the known depictions of the *urna versatilis*, to which he has added the illustration found on a mosaic at Carthage ('it was a sphere revolving on a horizontal axis fixed to two uprights, like the contrivance used for drawing numbers in a lottery', p. 257). The image of the *urna versatilis* can be found on coins, frescos, manuscript miniatures, and medallions, but it was primarily associated with either a legal context or circus games.

In a recent article, Marie-Thérèse Raepsaet-Charlier (2010) re-examined the discovery of a small bronze plaque from 237 CE, unearthed in the sanctuary of Bourbonne-les-Bains (France), and which mentions the dedication of an *urna cum sortibus*.[1] Raepsaet-Charlier compares this inscription with other dedications on random selection vessels found throughout the Western world and dating back to the

---

[1]   I would like to thank Marie-Thérèse Raepsaet-Charlier for sharing with me the invaluable documents consulted for this chapter.

Imperial era, such as a Martigny bronze plaque (*Forum Claudii Vallensium*) discovered in 2000, and an Eisenberg bronze plaque from 221 CE. She underscores that these dedications show the signs of having been affixed somewhere: these bronze plaques were likely attached to wooden credence tables, now lost, on top of which were placed two uprights and a horizontal bar. A metal vase, or *urna*, with a small opening for the lots (*sortibus*) to drop out of, would then revolve around that horizontal axis.

Figure 1: Fresco painting of the *Via Latina* in Rome, 5th century CE, before its deterioration. This scene perhaps represents soldiers casting lots for Christ's garments. It clearly depicts an *urna versatilis* (reprinted in Raepsaet-Charlier, 2010, p. 108—based on Ferrua, 1960, pl. LXXIII).

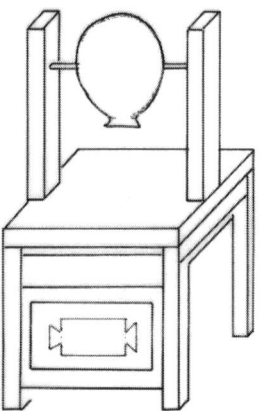

Figure 2: Sketch proposed by Raepsaet-Charlier, 2010, p. 110 for the Bourbonne, Martigny and (most likely) Eisenberg *urnae*.

This author examines one more inscription mentioning an *urna cum sortibus* that was found in Bioggio (formerly part of *Comum*). This inscription is particularly useful to understand how the Roman random selection machine operated. The engraving is found on a marble base with a pedestal; on the mortise at the top, traces can be seen of where the *urna* would have been attached. Unlike the dedications on the Bourbonne and Martigny plaques, here we see an entirely more monumental vessel for drawing lots: the marble base likely supported the wooden credence table allowing the *urna* to revolve.

Figure 3: Sketch of the Bioggio base and *urna* (Raepsaet-Charlier, 2010, p. 110).

The existing documentation appears to point to a change in the instruments used for official sortition purposes, a transition which occurred between the end of the 2nd century BCE (the accounts concerning public *sortitiones* conducted until ca. 100 BCE frequently mention the use of a *sitella* and *sortes*) and around 70 BCE (the *sitella* is no longer mentioned after this date, and the only term used to describe official acts of sortition from thereon out is *urna*). This evolution of random selection instruments was also reflected in contemporary poetry: while Plautus refers to a *sitella*, poets from the Augustan era, such as Horace, Ovid, and Virgil, all use the word *urna*. This transformation in the physical instruments used in public acts of sortition during the 1st century BCE is also corroborated by the creation and spread of the adjective *versatilis* (which incidentally remains rather difficult to translate) around 60 BCE. Between around 100 BCE and 70 BCE, a new instrument was thus developed for public sortition procedures. The manually operated *sitella*, whose undertones of hydromancy harked back to religious and divinatory *sortitio*, was replaced by a tool specifically designed for civic sortition procedures, the *urna versatilis*, which functioned much like the machines used for National Lottery drawings today (Nicolet, 1976). During the Augustan era, use of the device was regulated by the *lex Valeria Aurelia* explicitly referring to the *urna versatilis*, thus revealing that the use of a random selection machine to draw lots in a civic procedure was in fact a legal obligation.

The Lots

Sors

Sors was the term most frequently used to refer to the lots placed inside the *sitella* and, more generally, to the lots drawn in public sortition procedures, regardless of the receptacle from which they were drawn. However, it remains difficult to determine when sources refer to *sortes* in the literal sense as instruments used in random selection procedures, and when they refer to them figuratively as symbols of fate or fortune. When *sors* describes the object used to operate a random selection procedure, the expression can be used in the plural (*sortes*) and is often found in conjunction with verbs of manipulation (*conicere, educere, trahere*). In Plautus's play *Casina*, the lots used to randomly attribute Casina (the 'province' belonging to the slaves) are also explicitly referred to as *sortes* (v. 300, 359, 363, 374, 377, 384, 386, 389, 396, 413, 414). Moreover, *sortes* are also used for sortition among magistrates (Cicero, *In Verrem*, 2, 4, 64; *Pro Ligario*, 7). *Sortes* could also refer to judicial lots: the *lex Acilia* mentions the use of *sortes* (or *sorticulae*) to randomly select judges (*CIL* I², 583). They were also used to appoint the *recuperatores*, according to the *lex Irnitana* (*AE*, 1986, 333). Finally, the word *sors* could also refer to the lots establishing voting orders, as Livy described in the *History of Rome* (45, 15; 24, 7) or as stipulated by the *lex Malacitana* (*CIL* II, 1964 = *ILS*, 6089, chapter 53). The term *sorticula*, a diminutive of *sors*, could also be employed to refer to the specific lot that one had drawn (e.g. Suetonius, *Life of Nero*, 21, 1).

In the absence of any archaeological sources, literary and epigraphic documentation can provide information about the shape and size of the *sortes* used in civic sortition procedures. The *sorticolae*, as mentioned by the *lex Acilia* (*CIL* I², 583) were small wooden tablets four fingers long on which the judges' sentences were contained. These tablets were then jumbled up and drawn at random to be read in a correspondingly desultory order. Examining the use of divinatory *sortes* at the end of the Republican era also confirms the rectangular shape of the tablets. While the *sortes* used in private divination practices and discovered by archaeologists exhibit a wide variety of shapes and materials (rocks, discs, etc.), it seems that the lots used throughout Latium for private divination purposes were generally flat and rectangular (Champeaux, 1990a,b). When summarizing the history behind the discovery of the *sortes* in Praeneste, Cicero thus highlights that the lots used in this sanctuary resembled tablets (*De Divinatione*, 2 85–86; see also Crawford, 1975, I, p. 414, no. 405.2).

Our sources also provide some information regarding the materials out of which lots were made. In *Casina*, Plautus tells us that *sortes* are generally fashioned out of poplar or pine, and are notched or painted (v. 378, 384). The use of poplar or pine wood explains why we have not been able to uncover lots used in civic sortition practices in Ancient Rome — even though this argument from silence remains subject to new discoveries, including the fact that lots may sometimes have been manufactured out of metal. Lots were perhaps notched as Plautus suggests, but they were most likely covered in wax, which made it easier to write down names on top (lots thus resembled ballots, for which they are often mistaken). The lots used in civic sortition procedures were of equal weight and size (or at least relatively uniform in size). In *Casina* again, Olympic and Chalinus are concerned about the composition of their *sortes*: the pine or poplar wood lots could rise more quickly to the top of the water and thus destabilize the whole process. The word *aequus* and its derivative forms are used three separate times to describe the *sortitio* (v. 387, 375–379), thus illustrating that much attention is paid to the uniformity of the lots.

The pila

Starting in the 1st century BCE, *pilae* (balls) were used to conduct civic sortition procedure. These balls were better suited than *sortes* to the mechanical operation of the *urna versatilis*. *Pilae* only seem to have been used to draw lots in civic contexts, unlike *sortes*, which were also used for private and divinatory sortition purposes. The word *pila* is used in the *Tabula Hebana* to refer to the official lots used to randomly select the ex-ante designated centuries. It was also employed to describe the lots used to select jurors from official lists or 'albums'; for instance, in Pompey's judicial law passed in 52 BCE, the lots used to select jurors are called *pilae* (*CIL* I², 208; Asconius Pedianus, *Pro Milone* p. 39 Clark).

Most importantly, we find a reference to spherical lots (*sphairai*, 1. 25) in the first Edict from Cyrene dating from 7 or 6 BCE, which established the procedure for mixed juries. The close association between the *urna* and *pilae* is confirmed by a number of poetic sources, such as Propertius's *Elegies* (4, 11, 19; 4, 11, 27–28; 4, 11, 49–50), as well as by numismatic sources: the control mark on the obverse 'heads' side of the coins minted by Lucius Roscius Fabatus, which depicts a random selection machine, is matched by a *pila* on the reverse 'tails' side of the coins.

Archaeological discoveries in several Ancient Greek settlements in modern-day Sicily and its environs have provided further information about the physical aspect of the *pilae*. In Rhegion (today, Reggio Calabria), perfectly round balls of terracotta (*sphairai*) were found, dating from the 3rd to the 2nd century BCE and which may have been used to randomly select judges or distribute plots of land (Cordano, 2000), or even perhaps to allocate magistracies and civic duties. Round balls that are somewhat caved in on either side from the 5th to the 3rd century BCE were likewise discovered in Naxos. These balls are of a similar size (approximately 3 cm in diameter) and have engraved on them the *tria nomina* that made up the full name of all Roman citizens. While these *pilae* were made of terracotta, it is possible to envision that wooden balls were also used in Rome, much like the Republican *sortes*, or even perhaps balls of wax. Like their predecessors, the *pilae* were standardized in size and weight before every sortition. The first Edict from Cyrene stipulates that 'after the balls (*sphairai*) are weighed (*sekotheisai*) and the names of the judges are engraved upon them, the names of Roman citizens shall be drawn from one urn, and the names of Greeks from another…' (based off of the French translation by de Visscher, pp. 18–19). The *Tabula Hebana* further stipulates that the *pilae*, or balls, must be made as equal as possible: 'the president must randomly insert into a random selection machine (*urna versatilis*) thirty-three identical balls (*pilas quam maxime aequatas*), each one with the name of a tribe upon it, announce the sortition, and thus designate the senators and the *equites*.' The standardization of the *pilae* was also mentioned by Asconius Pedianus in his commentary on Cicero's argument in favour of Milon. We can therefore assume that, since the lots were equal in size and had to be inserted into a machine with specific measurements (i.e. the *pila* had to be small enough to be able to drop out of the *urna*'s opening), it is likely that they were publicly commissioned from local artisans, much like the Greek *pinakia*.

While *pilae* were generally used in random selection machines, we still come across instances of rectangular *sortes* or *sorticulae* being used in conjunction with an *urna*. Nothing therefore prevents us from supposing that rectangular *sortes* and spherical *pilae* were both used with the *urna versatilis*, especially since the Greek *kleroterion* similarly combined tablets and dice. The word *kleroterion* was moreover used to translate the expression *urna* in the first Edict from Cyrene. But although this hypothesis is tempting, we must reject it: the few representations of the *urna versatilis* that we have do not correspond to the actual *kleroteria* that have been preserved. Instead, we must accept the simpler explanation that, during the Imperial period, the word *pila* designates a specific type of *sors*, i.e. a spherical *sors*. Nonetheless, if the *sitella* and the *urna* only permitted the drawing of one kind of lot at a time (namely, *sortes* from the *sitella* and *pilae* from the *urna*), unlike the *kleroterion* which allowed for a combination of tablets, dice, and other instruments, this does not signify that the sortition procedures conducted in Rome were less elaborate. While the majority of Roman *sortitiones* were 'single-level' acts of random selection, meaning that a single drawing was conducted to designate a senator or magistrate, for example, Romans were naturally also capable of conducting more complicated, 'multi-level' sortition procedures by using several *sitellae* or *urnae* at the same time, or by holding several successive drawings using the same instrument—the distribution of colonial plots or provinces required several such successive drawings, for example.

One final question remains unanswered, however. Although the Greek text of the Edicts from Cyrene clearly mentions a random selection machine of the *urna versatilis* type, which worked using *pilae*, and not a more complex *kleroterion* like those that have been unearthed in Athens, we do not know in practice what kind of random selection machine was used in Cyrene on a more regular basis, the Roman *urna versatilis* or the Athenian *kleroterion*. The translation of the Latin word *urna* (presumably in the original text) by *kleroterion* in the inscription at Cyrene may suggest that Greeks continued to use the Athenian *kleroterion*—with the translation then merely being a notional correspondence; or on the contrary, it could suggest a material correspondence, meaning that use of the *urna versatilis* spread throughout the Greek world, ultimately replacing the traditional *kleroterion*. Further archaeological missions would be necessary to determine which kind of machine was in fact used for random selection procedures in Cyrene.

Conclusion

Between 100 BCE and 70 BCE, the invention of the *urna versatilis*, or random selection machine, gradually associated with *pilae* or spherical lots, can be explained by the political and civic evolutions at the end of the Republican era. The number of civic sortition procedures was constantly increasing (for the selection of jurors in permanent courts, to allocate colonial plots, to conduct legislative voting procedures, etc.), on account of demographic and territorial expansion, as well as institutional transformations (increases in the number of magistracies and priesthoods, for example). Changes in the physical instruments used to draw lots are not merely anecdotal, but reflect a desire to accelerate the sortition process (largely presided over by consuls and praetors during their mandates) and to make the process more random and harder to manipulate. The ritual's evolution was thus influenced by important political issues, in particular mounting acts of public violence and the deterioration of aristocratic competition. It likewise reflected efforts to eradicate corruption (*ambitus*) with regard to the selection of tribes, jurors, and provinces, since the increased numbers of praetors entailed augmented competition for consular positions and praetorian provinces, which helped to offset the costs associated with these expensive political careers.

It is possible that we owe the introduction of new random selection instruments to Sulla. Several reforms undertaken by the Roman dictator to restore the *res publica* helped, during the years 81–82 BCE, to augment the number of civic sortition procedures conducted each year. For example, Sulla's judicial law passed in 81 BCE, of which only fragments survive today, established a number of permanent courts (*quaestiones*) whose judges were appointed by random selection following the recusal of each party. The same year, two other laws passed by Sulla increased the number of praetors and quaestors drawing their provinces by lot. This kind of machine could therefore have simplified and accelerated the process of civic sortition, especially in a judicial context. Finally, it is important to remember the influence that the great Greek legislators and Aristotelian political philosophy had on the dictator: let us not forget that Sulla had the library belonging to Theophrastus, a disciple of Aristotle's who had inherited his works, transferred to Rome. At any rate, use of the random selection machine began to spread around 52 BCE. Pompey's judicial law passed that same year, also known to us in fragments, stipulated the use of *pilae* to limit corruption and thus made the use of the *urna versatilis* mandatory. The law moreover required two successive *sortitiones* to select jury members. In this context, we can easily understand why a random selection machine was used, given that it would allow the judicial procedure to unfold more smoothly and would ensure greater randomness of jury composition. Similar stipulations regarding the type of machine and lots to be used can be found in Augustan legislation. The *urna versatilis* became more popular during the Imperial era in Western cities where the Roman model was directly imposed as part of Latin and Roman law, notably in *municipia* and *coloniae*, and indirectly in foreign cities, where the desire to imitate Rome was manifest. It was perhaps also used throughout the Greek world during the Imperial period, as the first Edict from Cyrene seems to indicate. The *urna versatilis* has, at any rate, gone on to have a rich legacy, as we can see in the modern French National Lottery machines (and others), which are indirect heirs of the Roman *urna*.

While the practice of sortition extended past the end of the Republic era and became even more widespread during the Imperial era, as evidenced by the proliferation of activities requiring random selection, reaching a higher degree of complexity and sophistication (largely due to the invention of the random selection machine), the role played by chance in civic sortition procedures became in fact increasingly limited. Although the machine certainly prevented rigging from occurring, and ensured equality among the candidates that participated in the drawing, in practice, random selection fell more and more under the control of the emperor, who could withdraw a province or an attribution from sortition at any time, choosing instead to assign it directly to a person of his choosing (*nominatio extra sortem*), to recommend a new candidate, to grant one candidate the privilege of drawing before others, or even to eliminate certain candidates from the process altogether (Hurlet, 2006). Much like voting, therefore, sortition slowly became an increasingly theatrical and ritual performance under the Principate, rather than a truly random procedure; as a result, it came to be associated with the emperor's largesse, he who was the embodiment of *Fortuna* and the bestower of honours and privileges.

Sources

Apuleius, *Metamorphoses* 10, 8, 2.
Asconius Pedianus, *Pro Milone* p. 39 Clark.
Cassiodorus, *Orationes* 1, 4.
Cicero,   *Against Vatinius* 34.
            De Divinatione 2, 69; 2, 85–86.
            De Natura Deorum 1, 38, 106.
            In Verrem 2, 2, 42; 2, 2, 47; 2, 2, 51; 2, 4, 64.
            Letters to his brother Quintus 2, 4a, 4.
            Pro Cornelio p. 71 Stangl.
            Pro Ligario 7.
Constantine VII Porphyrogenitus, *The Book of Ceremonies* I, 78.
Horace, *Odes* 2, 3, 25–27; 3, 1, 14–16.

Livy, *History of Rome* 24, 7; 25, 3, 16; 41, 18, 9; 45, 15.
Lucan, *Pharsalia* 5, 392–394.
Ovid, *Metamorphoses* 15, 43.
Plautus, *Casina* v. 296, 300, 342, 359, 363, 374–399, 413–415.
Pliny the Younger, *Letters* 10, 3a, 2
                  Panegyricus 36.
Plutarch, *Tiberius Gracchus* 11, 1.
Propertius, *Elegies* 4, 11, 19–20; 4, 11, 27–28; 4, 11, 49–50.
Pseudo-Vopiscus, *Life of Probus* 8, 6.
Anonymous, *Rhetorica ad Herennium* 1, 12, 21.
Seneca,   *Controversiae* 1, 2, 7.
         Troades 974.
Sidonius Apollinaris, *Carmina* 23, 315–325.
Suetonius, *Life of Nero* 21, 1.
Symmachus,   *Orations* 4, 7.
              Relationes 9, 6.
Tacitus, *Histories* 4, 6, 6; 4, 7.
Tertullian, *De Spectaculis* 16, 21.
Virgil, *Aeneid* 6, 20-22; 6, 432.
AE, 1949, 215f (*Lex Valeria Aurelia* = *Tabula Hebana*).
AE, 1986, 333 (*Lex Irnitana*).
CIL I², 583 (*Lex Acilia*).
CIL I², 208 (*Pompey's judicial law*).
CIL VI, 32327, 1.11 = *ILS*, 5050a and *AE*, 1932, 70 (*Acts of the Secular Games*).
CIL II, 1964 = *ILS*, 6089 (*Lex Malacitana*).

References

Champeaux, J. (1982) *Fortuna. Recherche sur le culte de la fortune à Rome et dans le monde romain des origines à la mort de Cicéron*, I and II, Rome: École française de Rome.

Champeaux, J. (1990a) *Sors oraculi*: les oracles en Italie sous la République et l'Empire, *MEFRA*, 102, Rome, pp. 271–302.

Champeaux, J. (1990b) 'Sorts' et divination inspirée: pour une préhistoire des Oracles Italiques, *MEFRA*, 102, Rome, pp. 801–828.

Cordano, F. (2000) Strumenti di sorteggio e schedatura dei cittadini nella Sicilia greca, in Cordano, F. & Grottanelli, C. (eds.) *Sorteggio pubblico e cleromanzia dall'Antichita all'Eta moderna, Atti della Tavola Rotonda*, Milan: Università degli studi di Milano, pp. 83–93.

Crawford, M.H. (1975) *Roman Republican Coinage*, Cambridge and New York: Cambridge University Press, I and II.

De Visscher, Ch. (1940) *Les édits d'Auguste découverts à Cyrène*, Leuven: Recueil de Travaux d'Histoire et de Philologie.

Ehrenberg, V. (1927) *s. v. Losung, Realencyclopädie der classischen Altertumswissenschaft*, XIII, 2, pp. 1451–1504.

Ferrua, A. (1960) *Le Pitture della nuova catacomba di via Latina*, Rome: Pontificio Istituto di Archeologia Cristiana.

Hilgers, W. (1969) *Lateinische Gefässnamen: Bezeichnungen, Funktion und Form römischer Gefässe nach den antiken Schriftquellen*, Dusseldorf: Rheinland.

Hurlet, Fr. (2006) *Le proconsul et le prince d'Auguste à Dioclétien*, Bordeaux: Ausonius.

Lécrivain, Ch. (1911) *s. v. sortitio, Dictionnaire des antiquités grecques et romaines*, IV, 2, pp. 1417–1418.

Nicolet, Cl. (1976) *Le métier de citoyen dans la Rome républicaine*, Paris: Gallimard.

Nicolet, Cl. & Beschaouch, A. (1991) Nouvelles observations sur la « Mosaïque des chevaux » et son édifice à Carthage, *Comptes rendus de l'Académie des inscriptions et belles-lettres*, 3, Paris, pp. 471–507.

Raepsaet-Charlier, M.-Th. (2010) 'L'*urna cum sortibus* de Bourbonne dans le contexte des pratiques religieuses des *collegia* en Germanie supérieure', Signa *et* Tituli. Corpora *et* scholae: *lieux, pratiques et commémoration de la vie associative en Gaule méridionale et dans les régions voisines*, Bulletin de l'École antique de Nîmes, 31, Nimes, pp. 97–114.

Staveley, E.S. (1972) *Greek and Roman Voting and Elections*, London: Thames and Hudson.

Stewart, R. (1998a) 'Publicity and the lot: The politics of sortition', in *The Shapes of City Life in Rome and Pompeii: Essays in Honor of Lawrence Richardson Jr.*, New Rochelle: Caractzas, pp. 9–26.

Stewart, R. (1998b) *Public Office in Early Rome: Ritual Procedure and Political Practice*, Ann Arbor, MI: University of Michigan Press.

Taylor, L.R. (1966) *Roman Voting Assemblies from the Hannibalic War to the Dictatorship of Caesar*, Ann Arbor, MI: University of Michigan Press.

Wolfgang Blösel

The Sortition of Consular and Praetorian Provinces in the Roman Republic

Translation revised by Sarah-Louise Raillard

Before I began analysing the use of lot to distribute provinces to Republican consuls and praetors, I was not primarily focused on sortition, but rather on the extraordinary commands of Roman commanders such as Marius, Lucullus, Pompey, and Caesar. Since those extraordinary commands are one of the most conspicuous features of the Late Republic, I was interested in elaborating a precise definition which might help to explain their enormous historical relevance (Blösel, 2009). In his seminal book on Roman public law, German historian Theodor Mommsen (1887, II, pp. 651–657) defined extraordinary commanders as 'irregular military stop-gap magistrates', for whom the central principles of control were suspended. According to Mommsen, such commanders were not bound by the annual nature of regular magistracies. Moreover, several provinces were grouped under their control. Third, these commanders could govern their different provinces in absentia and through appointed legates. Unfortunately, none of these characteristics were ever mentioned by ancient sources when referring to an imperium *extraordinarium* or *extra ordinem (datum)*, meaning that military command was granted in an extraordinary fashion.

The most informative uses of the expressions *imperium extraordinarium* and *imperium extra ordinem (datum)* come from two speeches by Cicero. In '*De domo sua*' (24) from 57 BC, Cicero uses this expression to refer to the imperium granted to Pompey to combat first a band of pirates and then Mithridates in 67 and 66 BC, respectively. More surprisingly, he also uses this expression to refer to the imperia granted to the consuls A. Gabinius in Syria and L. Calpurnius Piso Caesoninus in Macedonia in 58 BC. The synonyms juxtaposed with *extra ordinem* ('extraordinarily'), namely *sine sortem* and *nominatim* ('without sortition and by name'), reveal the anomalous procedure: both consuls received their provinces not by lot, but through direct attribution, thanks to laws proposed by Cicero's archenemy Clodius, the Tribune of the Plebs. In his eleventh Philippic (17) from 43 BC, Cicero rails against the extraordinary commission granted to a man without any office (*privatus*), to fight against the rebellious Proconsul Cornelius Dolabella. So he demands that not just one senator, but all senators should be eligible to receive such a commission, arguing that there should be an actual election campaign with ballots in the Senate. Otherwise the other, less privileged senators would feel mistreated. Obviously, here again the direct award of a command without using any procedure of sortition or election was seen as an anomaly.

This is confirmed by Livy who uses the expressions *imperium extraordinarium* and *extra ordinem (datum)* to refer to consuls (3.2.2; 7.23.2; 10.24.3), consular tribunes (6.22.2; 6.30.6), and praetors (24.9.5). Six of those instances concern the circumvention of sortition when awarding provinces to consuls, consular tribunes, or praetors. Most revealing are again the synonyms for *extra ordinem* in the case of the assignment of the command in the war against the Volscians, a neighbouring people, to two of the six consular tribunes in the year 379 BC: *sine sorte* and *sine comparatione* ('without sortition and without arrangement'). Here, an alternative to the use of the lot is named, the *comparatio*, a joint agreement about the provinces among magistrates.

Since on no fewer than five occasions in our sources the expressions *extra ordinem* or *extraordinarium* occur alongside the words *extra sortem* or *nominatim*, it is quite astonishing that Mommsen missed this obvious connection. This is all the more surprising because two 16th-century scholars — Nicholas de Grouchy in his treatise *De comitiis Romanorum libri tres* (1558, 179D–180F) and Carlo Sigonio in his work *De antiquo iure populi Romano libri undecim* (1574, p. 335; also pp. 337, 352, 392, 423) — had already recognized the assignment of a province *extra sortem* ('without sortition') as the decisive criterion for an *imperium extraordinarium*. On the other hand, the great temporal and spatial dimension of many *imperia extraordinaria* and the private status of their holders were merely accidental, and, consequently, irrelevant to call them that.

Sortition and the Provinces, Before and After 367 BC

If this was the case, one cannot help asking why this deviation from the normal procedure for distribution was so serious that it was termed 'extraordinary', given the word's obvious connotations of irregularity. This is all the more striking because this deviation did not enhance or otherwise alter the actual nature of the consular or praetorian imperium. Even the status of a command's holder – whether he was a consul, a praetor, another kind of magistrate, or merely a private individual – had no bearing on the qualification as extraordinary. Only the geographical sphere of activity was affected by the direct attribution of a *provincia*. But it was the actual distribution process of these spheres of activity which was of utmost importance for the Romans. This importance stemmed from the opposition between collegiality with strict legal equality on the one hand, and the omnipresent hierarchy that existed amongst nobles on the other.

The rank of every Roman senator compared to his peers was determined on the basis of the magistracies he had previously held. Seniority in office gave an individual precedence over any other senator who had held the same office. Nevertheless, although the status of every senator was perfectly clear in the Senate's official list, the Romans ignored this ranking when distributing tasks between the senators and used selection by lot instead. So pervasive was the principle of collegiality that every office (with the sole exception of the dictatorship) was filled by at least two officials who not only had the same prerogatives but also the right to intercede against actions of their counterparts. The Romans were so fixated on collegiality that they created two positions even for tasks which could easily be accomplished by only one official.

This was particularly notable in the case of the two joint magistrates for building a temple (*duoviri aedi dedicandae*). Determining which of these two magistrates would dedicate the temple and which one would merely be awarded the office as an honour was a decision usually taken on the basis of precedence. In fact, it was often the case that one of the sacral officials had formerly consecrated the temple so that his colleague was expected to voluntarily relinquish the right to do it. But there were also some cases in which it was quite likely that procedures of sortition were used.[1]

Particularly interesting are the earliest instances where the Romans were said to have used the lot for allocating civic tasks. Examples can be found in the first years of the Roman Republic. According to Livy (2.8.6–8), the two consuls in 509–8 BC cast lots to see which one of them

---

[1]   Likely uses of sortition attested to in Livy (34.53.5–7; 35.41.8; 36.36.5). Cf. Orlin (1997, pp. 172–176).

should consecrate the temple of Jupiter Optimus Maximus on the Capitol, and the tribunes of the plebs in 449 BC were said to do the same for overseeing the election of their successors (Livy, 3.64.4–6). Finally, the consuls in 431 BC drew lots to see which of them would appoint the dictator (Livy, 4.26.11). But it is revealing that none of these three instances revealed a standard procedure. Their results were controversial and had an argumentative function in the context: either the official who was lucky enough to have drawn the lot was fighting for the right cause or sortition was an expression of his colleagues' deep discord. These accounts were therefore probably just products of annalistic historiographers and as such annalistic projections of a routine procedure from the middle Republic onto the early period with the intention of discussing the principal problems of Roman nobility.

The same holds true for the earliest mention of sortition being used to attribute a military task. The consul in 423 BC, C. Sempronius Atratinus, received the command against the invading Volscians by random selection, but was so negligent and careless in preparing his army for war that he would in the end be heavily fined for the Romans' defeat. In contrast, Livy (4.37.4–6) stresses the Volscians' diligence in selecting their own military leaders.

Livy's early accounts of extraordinary commands — those granted without the use of sortition — also have strong albeit opposite tendencies. The command against the Volscians was awarded directly to the famous victor against the Celts, M. Furius Camillus, as one of the six 'military tribunes with consular power' in 381 BC (*tribuni militum consulari potestate* — a board of officials which appears to have substituted the two consuls during two-thirds of the years between 444 and 367 BC). But Camillus was unable to win the battle until the foolhardy L. Furius, who was appointed by random selection to be colleagues with Camillus with equal rights (*par imperium*), lost and thus took on the subordinate role (Livy, 6.22–3). Whereas here privileged competence triumphed over indiscriminate and confused daring, the following instance shows the other side of the coin; i.e. the fatal consequences for the Roman army when the Senate favoured the incompetent brothers P. and C. Manlius Capitolinus, consular tribunes in 379 BC, by awarding them the command against the Volscians 'without sortition, without arrangement, beyond the rule' (Livy, 6.30.6: *sine sorte, sine comparatione, extra ordinem*), solely on account of patrician arrogance.

As with the earliest mentions of sortition, the seven examples of early extraordinary commands in Livy's first decade[2] resemble the actual *raison d'être* for the polemical narratives about competence, bravery, political arrogance, and military failure that ensue. This fact casts heavy doubt on their credibility and historicity.

The strongest argument against the use of sortition before the so-called Licinio-Sextian laws of 367 BC was the absence of collegiality in the magistracies. The *praetor maximus* obviously had no colleagues with equal rights. It is doubtful that the double consulship existed until the so-called consulate constitution was installed through the afore-mentioned Licinio-Sextian reform.[3] Before the plebeians managed to win admission to the consulship, there was no need for collegiality. Presumably the patricians had created this mechanism in order to enable the patrician consul to block the measures proposed by his plebeian colleagues that he disliked. At any rate, the ambiguous early mentions of sortition and its alleged circumvention as well as the general development of the Roman constitution suggest that random selection was not used for allocating public tasks before 367 BC.

After that date, sortition becomes much more probable, even if Livy's accounts of sortition and extraordinary commands for this period remain controversial. Thus the patricians are said to have used the death in battle of the plebeian consul in 362 BC, L. Genucius, as a form of propaganda to criticize the first use of sortition in 367–6 BC (and by means of which Genucius had won the command against the Hernicians) (7.6.8–10). In fact, several decades would pass before the patricians conceded full equality to the plebeians, including for example the right to be election supervisors. Nevertheless, it is certain that after the double consulship was established in in 367–6 BC, the Romans quickly became accustomed to distributing the different spheres of responsibility (the *provinciae*) by means of random selection from amongst both the patrician and plebeian consuls.

The Significance of Allotting the Provinces

As noted above, the use of sortition in such a deeply hierarchical society was astonishing. Within the small group of the *nobiles*, the assignment of a provincial command was of cardinal importance, since

---

[2] In addition to the two aforementioned cases cf. Livy (3.2.2; 4.46.2ff; 7.23–26; 8.16) (for this last case, see below).

[3] For the *praetor maximus* as highest office, see Bleicken (1980, pp. 280–287) and Bunse (1998, pp. 44–61; 213f.). For a new and slightly different picture of the highest magistrates of the early Republic, see Drogula (2015, pp. 46–181).

it afforded an individual *nobilis* the chance to earn both enormous glory and great riches in war, thus also gaining an advantage over his peers. The use of random selection in that context therefore requires a certain explanation, since the former was a means of distributing tasks and honours that was ostensibly not influenced by the *nobiles*.

Divine judgment?

In her detailed discussion of allotment in early Rome, Roberta Stewart (1998, pp. 38–51) construes allotment in general as a form of auspicetion which 'could forewarn of danger if there were an unfavourable sign or faulty ritual' (*ibid.*, p. 41). However, I believe this is a gross overestimation of the role of allotment procedures, as the Romans could in fact completely overlook or even avoid the process (see the critique by Lintott, 2001, p. 189).

Scholars like Jerzy Linderski (1986, p. 2175) and Robert Bunse (2002, pp. 421f.) have gone even further, interpreting the result of allotment procedures as a sign by means of which the gods demonstrated which of the magistrates would be victorious in the province in question. But two passages from Livy clearly refute this hypothesis. In the tenth book (10.24), Livy reports that the Senate as well as the People's Assembly awarded the supreme command for the imminent war against the Samnites, Celts, Umbrians, and Etruscans to Q. Fabius Maximus Rullianus, the consul in 295 BC (who had already been a consul four times prior), without having recourse to sortition. Thereupon, Fabius's colleague, P. Decius Mus, himself thrice a consul, vehemently demanded an allotment for this war and prayed that the gods would grant him the same chance as his colleague, provided that they were willing to bestow upon him the same bravery and the same favourable luck in war (10.24.16: *Iovem Optimum Maximum deosque immortales se precari, ut ita sortem aequam sibi cum collega dent, si eandem virtutem felicitatemque in bello administrando daturi sint*). Let us clarify: P. Decius Mus did not ask the gods to manipulate the sortition, but he called on them to guarantee that the sortition would be genuinely random. A second passage from Livy (8.16.5) further stresses this point. In 335 BC, the senators asked both consuls to let the famous M. Valerius Corvus obtain the command against the Ausones without having recourse to sortition (*extra sortem*), 'in order to prevent that through chance and luck a mistake may be made' (*ne forte casu erraretur*) (Johnston, 2003, pp. 152f.). In an argument with his colleague regarding which senator should be declared 'the first man of the Senate', P. Sempronius Tuditanus, the so-called *princeps senatus* and the censor in 209 BC, emphasized that the gods had given him free choice by means of drawing lots (*ius liberum*, Livy, 27.11.11). Cicero likewise used *sors*, the word for 'lot', as a synonym for *fors* ('chance') and *casus* ('accident').[4]

In order for there to be no loser in an act of sortition, the magistrate who did *not* receive the sought-after *provincia* must not feel neglected by the gods, compared to his luckier colleague. Otherwise, interpreting the result of random selection as the judgment of the gods would have produced an inferiority complex in nearly every second consul, as the 'loser' would have been driven to find defects in his own character or in his military or religious performance. Such an inferiority complex would have caused massive problems for the necessary cooperation between consular colleagues.

The pacifying effect of sortition

The same outcome — that is, the intensification of rivalries between colleagues — would have been produced if the Romans used another voting procedure in the Senate or the People's Assembly to decide separately which of the consuls should be awarded the more lucrative *provincia*. That would have provoked another election campaign with further expenses. The second contest between two consuls would make one consul a loser, even though both were winners of an initial election. Furthermore, a second vote, especially in the Senate, would create unnecessary polarization amongst the nobility. If every year the prestige of the clan, wealth, and political connections of the elected consul had become the decisive factors in another election for distributing the provinces, it would have been possible for the whole senatorial aristocracy to come under the permanent control of few superior consuls.

The story of the arrogant triple consul L. Postumius Megellus, who in 291 BC allegedly exerted pressure on his colleague to cede the allotted command against the Samnites and was ultimately fined by the Senate, demonstrates the awareness of the *nobiles* in that regard.[5] In order to avoid the peril of overly ambitious senators, Cicero suggests the use of secret voting tablets to decide which of the senators should receive an *imperium extraordinarium* against the rebellious proconsul Dolabella (in the aforementioned passage of his eleventh Philippic). Cicero moreover presupposes that, in principle, all senators possessed the necessary competencies for this job.

---

[4] *Sors* as synonym for *fors* and *casus*: see Livy (3.64.4) and Cicero (*Pro Murena* 18).
[5] Dionysius of Halicarnassus, *Antiquitates Romanae* 17/18, 4, 1f. Kiessling & Jacoby = 18 A Caire — Pittia — Robert. See Bravo and Griffin (1988).

One Imperial (rather than Republican) source demonstrates the pacifying function of sortition. Tacitus (*Histories* 4, 6–8; see Seelentag 2009, pp. 364–371) reports an argument between two senators about how to select the senatorial envoys to be sent to the new Princeps Vespasian. The praetorian Helvidius Priscus, an open critic of the Principate in general, proposed an election by sworn magistrates, whereas the consular Eprius Marcellus favoured sortition. Tacitus reveals Eprius's motive to be the fear of feeling rejected if others were elected. Therefore Eprius stressed that sortition would prevent competition and political enmity amongst the senators. Furthermore all senators were equally capable of doing the job (*Histories* 4.8.1: '...*secundum vetera exempla, quae sortem legationibus posuissent, ne ambitioni aut inimicitiis locus foret. nihil evenisse, cur antiquitus instituta exolescerent aut principis honor in cuiusquam contumeliam verteretur; sufficere omnes obsequio*'). Ultimately, Tacitus suggested that the most influential peers preferred sortition because they were afraid of incurring envy should they get elected (4.8.5: '...*et splendidissimus quisque eodem inclinabat metu invidiae, si ipsi eligerentur*').

A mechanism of uncertainty?

These discussions illustrate that the Romans primarily used sortition out of consideration for the unlucky magistrate who did not obtain the desired province, rather than for his fortunate colleague. This contradicts the argument put forth by Hubert Buchstein in his book on the history of sortition from Antiquity to the European Union (2009, p. 131). According to Buchstein, Roman sortition functioned as a 'mechanism of uncertainty': the recently elected consuls should not have the opportunity to establish close links with the legions destined for the province or to influence people there before the distribution of provinces by lot, so that they could not escape the senatorial control. But if this had been the intention of the Senate, there would be no explanation for the fact that every year the senators granted the two consuls the right to have a *comparatio*, a mutual agreement about the provinces without Senate interference or the exchange of already attributed provinces. The exchange of the provinces already drawn was certain for the consuls in 210 BC, among them M. Claudius Marcellus, and for those in 63 BC, M. Tullius Cicero and C. Antonius Hybrida.[6] Although only four instances of a *comparatio* that was actually put into practice can be found, there is no doubt that the Senate regularly

---

6   Livy (26.29.1) and Cicero (*In Pisonem* 5), respectively.

offered this means of distributing the provinces to the consuls.[7] For the praetors, however, a *comparatio* does not seem to have been allowed (Levi, 1926, pp. 74f. = 1978, pp. 29f.). In any case, the ancient sources do not imply that the *comparatio* was ever a standard practice; on the contrary, it appears to have remained a rare exception.[8] In reality, ambition was too pervasive among Roman nobles for them to willingly cede a more prestigious province to their colleagues. It is revealing, in that regard, that both Livy and Cicero use the word *sors* ('lot') as a synonym for *provincia*.[9]

Now we should briefly examine the final alternative to sortition. If the Senate had transferred decisions regarding the distribution of consular and praetorian provinces to a vote by the People's Assembly, it would have relinquished its power over foreign policy. Moreover, even in that case the unavoidable election campaign between the consuls or the praetors would have exacerbated existing tensions among colleagues.

We saw that using sortition to allocate provinces helped the Romans avoid many significant political risks. In short, it appears that the primary goal of sortition was to depoliticize the distribution of provinces and to eliminate the cost of negotiations.

Coping with the Results of Random Selection: Aristocratic Equality and Military Efficiency

Although the Romans avoided the negative consequences that might have come from other methods of allocating public tasks, they still had to deal with the results of random selection. For the competence of a Roman supreme commander determined a campaign's success, as well as the fate of thousands of soldiers. Therefore it was imperative for Roman leaders to be certain that all consuls and praetors were capable of leading their army to victory. The Romans evidently believed that all the noble men who had reached the highest magistracies possessed the

---

[7] So the wording of the Senate's offer: 'The senators decided that the consuls should either make terms about the provinces or draw lots' (*decreverunt patres, ut provincias ...consules compararent inter se sortirenturve*, Livy, 30.1.1; 32.8.2; 33.43.2; 38.35.9; 42.32.1–5; 43.12.1; 45.17.5f.).

[8] Livy (8.20.3 (329 BC)) – Livy (8.22.9 (327 BC)) – Sallust (*Historiae* 2,98 D 3-7 Maurenbrecher (75 BC)) – Cicero (*Ad familiares* 1.9.25 (54 BC). Thus already Heisterbergk (1890, p. 641); Rosenstein (1995, pp. 52f.; 67), against the opinions of Mommsen (1887, I p. 51; II pp. 199f.); Stewart (1998, pp. 137–181) and Bunse (2002, pp. 419f., 427f.).

[9] Livy (9.42.1), especially for the praetorian provinces: Livy (22.35.5; 23.30.18; 26.29.8); Cicero (*In Verrem* 1.34; *Pro Murena* 41; *Pro Ligario* 23).

same abilities as a military commander. Heisterbergk (1890, p. 641) was the first to explain this belief: 'In general, one was of the opinion that every consul had to be capable of managing a consular province, and every praetor a praetorian one, lest sortition run counter to the State's best interest' (see also Rosenstein, 1995, p. 46). Moreover, the statements contained in Cicero's eleventh Philippic and those made by Eprius Marcellus regarding the fact that all senators were equally appropriate for all jobs illustrate that this claim of aristocratic equality was generally valid across all public offices and tasks.

The most probable period of time for this claim of aristocratic equality to come into being was the 4th century BC, when the plebeian magistrates demanded to receive the same degree of honour and respect as their patrician counterparts. This also corroborates the approximate date provided in this chapter for the introduction of sortition.

The crucial role played by the principle of equality with regard to the Roman aristocracy's self-perception was obvious from the fact that even the first Emperor, Augustus, reintroduced sortition to attribute the provinces to be governed by former consuls or praetors—what Tiberius in his obituary of Augustus allegedly praised as the first benefaction to the senators.[10] Consequently, the ten imperial inscriptions containing the term *sortitus* used in conjunction with the title *proconsul* should be interpreted as follows, according to Hurlet (2006, p. 22): 'as a way of accentuating the prestige of a governor who had not been directly appointed by the Prince, but who owed his position to the traditional process of sortition.' But during the early Principate, the emperors intervened a number of times in the sortition processes used to allocate the senatorial provinces, often because the senators asked them to do so during military crises. Nevertheless, after the end of the first century AD, the senatorial provinces increasingly dwindled in military importance, to the extent that such forms of intervention became superfluous. Eventually, Diocletian abolished the use of random selection to attribute senatorial provinces, choosing to directly appoint their leaders instead (Hurlet, 2006, pp. 101–104; 125f.).

In Republican times, the claim of aristocratic equality within the military sphere was extremely important. When Decius Mus, the consul in 295 BC, complained about the certainly fictitious *imperium extraordinarium* awarded to his colleague, Fabius Maximus Rullianus,

---

[10]   Dio (56.40.3). Cf. Hurlet (2006, pp. 22–35) and Talbert (1984, pp. 350–353). *Proconsul sortitus* in CIL II² 14, 330; CIL IX 5533; AE 1940, 99; Inscr. It. IV 1² 126; CIL VI 1361 = CIL VI 8,3 4686 ad nr. 1361; AE 1990, 863; CIL X 5061; CIL IX 4119.

Livy has him say that it is naturally fair and useful as an example that those people were consuls each of whom is good at conducting the war in Etruria (10.24.17: *'Certe id et natura aequum et exemplo utile … eos consules esse, quorum utrolibet duce bellum Etruscum geri recte possit'*). This statement could ring true in the 4th and 3rd centuries BC because of the ordered nature of Roman warfare. Commanders then were primarily expected to go into the battle first and to fight bravely on the front lines, to serve as an example of courage, fortitude, and steadfastness (*virtus, fortitudo, constantia*) for the rank and file (Rosenstein, 1990; Goldsworthy, 1996, pp. 167–170; Roth, 2007, p. 374). Not until the end of the 3rd century were Roman commanders confronted with the stratagems and tactical ruses of Hellenistic generals; it was only then that Roman commanders began to deploy more strategic and tactical skills, rather than mere bravery.

Perspectives: The *Imperia Extraordinaria* as Cause for the Decline of the Late Republic

It is not by chance that during the second half of the 2nd century BC, the random selection process used to attribute consular provinces was increasingly circumvented, with extraordinary commands becoming more frequent. For example, it was through extraordinary commands that the consul Scipio Aemilianus waged war against Carthage in 147 BC and against Numantia in 134 BC. Similarly, the consul Marius was granted an extraordinary command for his wars against Jugurtha in 107 BC and the Cimbri and Teutones from 104–102 BC. During the Social War (91–88 BC), such commands for the *privati* Marius and Sulla were indispensable for the eventual Roman victory. The *nobiles* who had come to the consulship in this age were no longer equal in terms of military capability. Consequently, the basic condition of equality that underpinned the sortition process to allocate military commands no longer existed. This was the result of the increasing demilitarization of the Roman *nobiles*, who since the beginning of the 2nd century BC had become more interested in the rhetorical and judicial instruction of the *forum Romanum* than in the military training that took place in camps far away from the metropolis (Blösel, 2011; 2016). Moreover, Pompey and Caesar in particular were so overwhelmingly superior as military leaders that the Roman aristocracy could not withstand their demands, when they claimed direct assignment of many legions for several years at once. On the other hand, even a 'normal' command of one or two legions was too much competition for the two great generals to leave their assignment to the ordinary consuls to be drawn by lot.

References

Bleicken, J. (1981) Zum Begriff der römischen Amtsgewalt: *auspicium – potestas – imperium*, *Nachrichten der Akademie der Wissenschaften zu Göttingen*, 9, pp. 257–300.

Blösel, W. (forthcoming) *Imperia extraordinaria liberae rei publicae*, Studien zur Demilitarisierung der römischen Nobilität (Habilitation University of Cologne, 2009).

Blösel, W. (2011) Die Demilitarisierung der römischen Nobilität zwischen Sulla und Caesar, in Blösel, W. & Hölkeskamp, K.-J. (eds.) *Von der militia equestris zur militia urbana. Prominenzrollen und Karrierefelder im antiken Rom*, pp. 55–80, Stuttgart: Steiner.

Blösel, W. (2016) Provincial commands and money in the Late Republic, in Beck, H., Jehne, M. & Serrati, J. (eds.) *Money and Power in the Roman Republic (Coll. Latomus 355)*, pp. 68–81, Brussels: Peeters.

Bravo, B. & Griffin, M.T. (1988) Un frammento del libro XI di Tito Livio?, *Athenaeum*, 66, pp. 447–521.

Buchstein, H. (2009) *Demokratie und Lotterie. Das Los als politisches Entscheidungsinstrument von der Antike bis zur EU*, Frankfurt/M.: Campus.

Bunse, R. (1998) *Das römische Oberamt in der frühen Republik und das Problem der 'Konsulartribunen'*, Trier: WVT Wissenschaftlicher.

Bunse,R. (2002) Entstehung und Funktion der Losung (*Sortitio*) unter den *magistratus maiores* der römischen Republik, *Hermes*, 130, pp. 416–432.

de Grouchy, N. (1558) *De comitiis Romanorum libri tres*, Venice.

Drogula, F.K. (2015) *Commanders & Command in the Roman Republic and the Early Empire*, Chapel Hill, NC: University of North Carolina Press.

Goldsworthy, A.K. (1996) *The Roman Army at War 100 BC–AD 200*, Oxford: Oxford University Press.

Heisterbergk, B. (1890) *Provincia*, *Philologus*, 49, pp. 629–644.

Hurlet, F. (2006) *Le proconsul et le prince d'Auguste à Dioclétien*, Bordeaux: Ausonius

Johnston, S.I. (2003) Lost in the shuffle: Roman sortition and its discontents, *Archiv für Religionsgeschichte*, 5, pp. 146–156.

Levi, M.A. (1926) *Adsignatio provinciarum*, *Rivista di Filologia e di Istruzione Classica*, 4, pp. 74–86. Reprinted in: Levi, M.A. (1978) *Il tribunato della plebe e altri scritti su istituzioni pubbliche romane*, pp. 29–40, Milan: Cisalpino-La Goliardica.

Linderski, J. (1986) The Augural Law, in Haase, W. & Temporini, H. (eds.) *Aufstieg und Niedergang der römischen Welt*, II 16, 3, pp. 2146–2312, Berlin: De Gruyter.

Lintott, A. (2001) Review of Stewart 1998, *Classical Philology*, 96, pp. 188–192.

Mommsen, Th. (1887) *Römisches Staatsrecht*, 3ʳᵈ ed., Leipzig: S. Hirzel.

Orlin, E.M. (1997) *Temples, Religion and Politics in the Roman Republic*, (Mnemosyne Suppl. 164), Leiden: Brill.

Rosenstein, N. (1990) *Imperatores victi: Military Defeat and Aristocratic Competition in the Middle and Late Republic*, Berkeley, CA: University of California Press.

Rosenstein, N. (1995) Sorting out the lot in Republican Rome, *American Journal of Philology*, 116, pp. 43–75.

Roth, J.P. (2007) War, in Sabin, Ph., van Wees, H. & Whitby, M. (eds.) *The Cambridge History of Greek and Roman Warfare*, vol. 1, pp. 368–398, Cambridge: Cambridge University Press.

Seelentag, G. (2009) *'Dem Staate zum Nutzen, dem Herrscher zur Ehre'*, Senatsgesandtschaften im Principat, Teil 2, *Hermes*, 137, pp. 356–376.

Sigonio, C. (1574) *De antiquo iure populi Romano libri undecim*, Bologna.

Stewart, R. (1998) *Public Office in Early Rome: Ritual Procedure and Political Practice*, Ann Arbor, MI: University of Michigan Press.

Talbert, R.J.A. (1984) *The Senate of Imperial Rome*, Princeton, NJ: Princeton University Press.

Romain Loriol

Sortition and Divination in Ancient Rome
Were the Gods Involved in Casting Lots?

Translation revised by Sarah-Louise Raillard

Sortition was one of the numerous methods used by Ancient Romans to decipher the will of the gods or to glean information about the past, present, and future. The procedure was also regularly used during the days of the Roman Republic to assign public offices and responsibilities in an egalitarian fashion.

However simple it may seem, even this brief description immediately raises two issues. In Ancient Rome, our modern separation between religion and politics did not exist. In fact, the Roman religion was a civic one and religious law was part of public law (neither dogma nor an independent clergy existed). Before making any public decisions, magistrates were instructed to consult the gods by means of different sorts of mantic rites and techniques. With the help of priests, magistrates scrutinized the sky, measured the appetite of sacred chickens, or examined the entrails of sacrificial victims; they paid attention to the omens and prodigies that occurred, and occasionally referred to oracles. From this perspective, the status of sortition appears ambivalent: although the use of cleromancy was well attested to in private acts of divination, does this entail that the use of random selection to select individuals for civic duties was in fact a kind of divine consultation? To what extent were the Roman gods involved in ritual sortition? And did magistrates claim, or at least benefit from, the special legitimacy that was presumably associated with *sortitio divina* (divinatory sortition)?

The second issue regards the place of sortition in the broader realm of ancient divination. One of the main concerns of modern historians has been to establish different categories of signs and rites, either by creating new classifications or by following ancient ones. For example, historians now usually distinguish between prodigies—spectacular signs of divine wrath that required public ritual expiations—and omens—strange premonitory events destined for a specific individual. Distinctions are also generally made between inspired (or prophetical) divination, and technical divination, based on the conjectures of an expert; between 'impetrative' signs delivered by the gods when answering a ritual request, and 'oblative' signs emitted spontaneously by the gods. Without discussing each of these categories in depth, it should be noted that the main issue with making such differences is that it appears to negate the true homogeneity of all divine signs. Whatever techniques or rites they may have used, Ancient Romans were confronted with the same two questions: how could they be sure that a given event was a divine sign (the recognition phase)? And what did the sign mean (the interpretation phase)? Even if ancient sources provide less information about sortition than about other mantic practices, sortition was not an exception to the norm: in order to understand how the gods were implicated in the casting of lots, we must consider sortition as just one practice amongst others and examine it accordingly.

We shall discuss these two issues, first arguing that the extent of divine involvement was as much an actual question in sortition as in any other divination rite, and then focusing on the controversial issue of divine participation in civic sortition.

Recognizing Divine Signs: A Serious Problem

With all uses of divination, the first and most important problem is determining whether an event expresses the divine will, that is to say whether it operates as a sign or not. In traditional studies of Roman divination, this question has not yet been analysed as a central concern, for several reasons that we will summarize below.

In the ancient 'hysterical' interpretation of Roman divination, prodigies were thought to be mere hallucinations produced by human fears. According to the 'cynical' interpretation, it was believed that Roman politicians and authorities invented prodigies to manipulate and dominate the credulous population. From this perspective, the idea that the recognition of signs was a rational and well-regulated process, based on a public (or private) debate about the credibility of each prodigy, was unthinkable. Without denying the role of superstition or manipulation in Roman prodigies, we can nonetheless assume that the opposition between the naïve masses and the cynical (or at least sceptical) elites was largely exaggerated. More importantly, it leads us to underestimate the rational component involved in establishing belief in prodigies (MacBain, 1982, p. 7; Rasmussen, 2005, pp. 25–30).

In recent years, a sociological approach has examined public divination as a system of socio-political regulation used to prevent and resolve actual or potential conflicts by third-party arbitration calling on the gods (Vernant, 1974, p. 10). This concept harks back to the traditional advantages associated with drawing lots in a public context (the fact that the process was considered to be an egalitarian means of selection, entailing no individual responsibility). Nevertheless, considering divination practices as 'solutions' or 'resolutions' would mean overlooking the fact that not only were signs and rites frequently sources of conflict and controversy themselves, but also that Roman public belief—albeit variable and difficult to measure—was an important factor in decision-making processes. In reality, it seems evident that civic life in Rome was influenced by the way that Romans understood the form and the extent of divine participation in such ritual processes.

Finally, Roman religion has generally been described as focusing heavily on rites, the scrupulous respect of which was an essential component of piety. Within this perspective, public divination was sometimes described as a purely formal procedure: the simple fact that an individual provided with an official *auctoritas* or a specialist in the mantic arts announced that a sign had occurred would have been enough to have the public acknowledge it as a sign. But we can hardly imagine a system of belief—and *a fortiori* a consensus—based entirely on such blind obedience to the magistrates and priests of the state. Similarly, it would be an exaggeration to suggest that Roman magistrates were free to accept or deny the divine value of an incident that occurred before their eyes, depending on what was convenient for them. In reality, even if recognizing an act divine intervention could be and was often a subjective process, it was not meant to be arbitrary.

Religious authority, however influential it may have been in Roman public life, took a different form than that with which we are familiar. In present-day monotheism, the given religious authority, which is or has been embodied by prophets, priests, and interpreters of the word of God, comes in large part from revealed and sacred texts (Scheid, 2007, pp. 41–63). Since a religious orthodoxy of this sort did not exist in Roman public religion, speculation about the existence and the meaning of a prodigy was not limited, even after the official recognition of a sign. On the other hand, in ancient sources the reliability of a sign appears as a very important matter that was discussed in both public and private contexts (in the senate, or with priests, clients, or family, for example) and by the ancient authors themselves. The Ancient Romans were perfectly aware of the risks and dangers associated with divination practices, including conflicts of interest, which existed even at the largest oracular sanctuaries (hence the presumed collusion of the Delphi oracle with the most powerful leaders in the Greek and Roman worlds), and charlatanism, illustrated by the diviners and fortune-tellers who proliferated on the streets of Rome (on public suspicion towards diviners by lots, Cicero, *De diuinatione*, 1, 132; Santangelo, 2013, pp. 76–80).

The recognition of a divine sign was therefore a real problem, whose solution was determined by several criteria. The study of narrative sources illustrates three main conditions for recognizing divine signs, which we shall briefly present here (Loriol, 2016, pp. 27–170, with bibliography).

1) The spontaneity of the event: to identify a sign, the Romans paid careful attention to any hints that might indicate that someone had intentionally forged a sign. Animals, children, insane or drunken men, and slips of the tongue were some of the various forms of unconsciousness that served as a guarantee of divine spontaneity. 2) The abnormality of the event: a sign must by its very nature stand out in the continuum of events. The scale of abnormality ranged from the slightly unusual (a mistake or a coincidence) to events that were *contra naturam*, such as a speaking ox, or other such events that would seem entirely unbelievable to us today. 3) The 'familiarity' of an event, which had two different meanings. Several circumstances surrounding an event could be construed by Ancient Romans as being naturally conducive to divine manifestations (e.g. sacred spaces and artefacts or liminal moments). Secondly, a prodigy sometimes resembled other prodigies that had been officially recognized in the past: it is likely that the more convincing the precedents, the more credible the new prodigy became.

Given this framework, we shall look at a few examples of private sortition that took place in oracular sanctuaries during the Roman Republican period.

Sortition and Prodigy, from Association to Conflation

Let us begin with a passage by Cicero, from the second book of *De diuinatione*:

> According to the annals of Praeneste Numerius Suffustius, who was a distinguished man of noble birth, was admonished by dreams, often repeated, and finally even by threats, to split open a flint rock which was lying in a designated place. Frightened by the visions and disregarding the jeers of his fellow-townsmen he set about doing as he had been directed. And so when he had broken open the stone, the lots

sprang forth carved on oak (*perfracto saxo sortis erupisse*), in ancient characters. [...] There is a tradition that, concurrently with the finding of the lots and in the spot where the temple of Fortune now stands, honey flowed from an olive-tree. Now the soothsayers, who had declared that those lots would enjoy an unrivalled reputation, gave orders that a chest should be made from the tree and lots placed in the chest. At the present time the lots are taken from their receptacle if Fortune directs. What reliance, pray, can you put in these lots, which at Fortune's nod are shuffled and drawn by the hand of a child (*pueri manu*)? (Cicero, *De diuinatione*, 2, 85–86. All translations are from the Loeb edition)

Marcus Cicero, the character in charge of criticizing divination in the second book of the Ciceronian treatise, first describes the foundational prodigies that augmented the prestige of the Fortuna sanctuary in Praeneste, not far from Rome; then, with obvious irony, he explains how sortition took place in that sanctuary.

The association between sortitio *and prodigies*

The association between *sortitio* and prodigies can initially be glimpsed from the natural order of narrative, from the origins of sortition to the form taken by present-day sortition rituals; but it can also be interpreted as a meaningful link between two cumulative answers to the problem of the divine value of *sortitio*.

A young child casting lots: this was a very common procedural choice for random selection processes across many different eras. For the Ancient Romans, children up to the age of about seven were characterized by their *innocentia consilii*, which denoted a lack of real intentionality and rationality (Néraudau, 2008, pp. 92–93 and 221). This innocence ensured that they would not try to cheat when casting lots, as they had no reason to cheat, and moreover that they were too pure or lacked the intellectual capacity to be corrupted (Champeaux, 1982, p. 63; Grottanelli, 1993; Johnston, 2003, pp. 106–108). It seems that the Ancient Romans were largely unconcerned about the reverse argument: that young children were precisely quite easy to influence or manipulate on account of their innocence. It is in any case interesting to observe that children embodied spontaneity in many such narratives. We can thus infer that the Romans saw them as being closely linked, in a special and essential fashion, to divinity — Apuleius even mentions an 'inspired child' or a 'foreseeing child' (*puer prouidus*) in the *Apologia* (43, 3–4).

In the *Diuinatione,* an aetiological story is added to the ritual guarantee of a spontaneous act of sortition. The goddess Fortuna chose the place of the sanctuary herself, after enumerating a series of extra-ordinary and unsolicited prodigies: dreams, the prodigy of the *sortes* springing out from the split rock, which seems to indicate the ritual procedure to be used in the sanctuary, and the sign of the olive tree exuding honey. Here a functional complementarity clearly appears: the ritual procedure of the Fortuna lots lacks concrete signs indicating that the divinity is taking part in the rite, such as the wind blowing through the dodonian oak (a sign of Zeus), or the Apollonian fever of the Pythia at Delphi. The prodigy story compensated for that lack by illustrating how clearly the deity manifested itself when the sanctuary was founded, thus granting divine authority across the ages to the present-day rite (Cicero, *De diuinatione*, 1, 34).

This hypothesis is supported by the iconography of a relief from Ostia originally consecrated to Hercules. The relief was discovered in 1938 and dates back to the 1st century BC:

Fig. 1: Bas-relief of C. Fuluius Saluis (moulding). Photograph by R. Loriol.

At the centre of the relief, a child and the god Hercules (or a statue of him) are standing face-to-face on either side of a box. Hercules has a lot in his hand, which he has perhaps received from the child's hand. The letters 'ORT H', which stand for (s)ort(es/is) H(erculis), are inscribed on the lot. The right side of the relief shows two groups of men fishing the statue of Hercules out of the sea. On the left side, one can see what was likely the relief's dedicant, and above that, a winged personification of Victory. This relief was dedicated to the divinity by Caius Fuluius Saluis, a haruspex, perhaps to express his gratitude for a favourable prediction related to a 'victory'. From the dedicant's status as a diviner of a relatively high social rank, we can infer that the representational details of the ritual were accurate and, most importantly, that they were significant, as the dedicant was a religious expert who was familiar with the symbolic connotations of the scene (Champeaux, 1982, pp. 63–65, and note 278; Klingshirn, 2006, p. 145).

Jacqueline Champeaux has noticed the 'strange and interesting parallel' between the origin story of Praeneste and the depiction of Hercules being carried out of the water (Champeaux, 1982, p. 65). This parallel can be extended to the whole of the two narratives: here the child played the same role as in Praeneste. It is not clear whether Hercules gives him the lot, a situation that we could interpret as a transposition of the religious-symbolic facet of the rite (the child is casting the lot, but he is receiving it from Hercules); or whether the child has given it to Hercules for validation or verification. In any case, it illustrates the link between the innocent hand of a child and the effectiveness of the divine presence. The scene on the right depicts another form of authority: the oracular sanctuary was not founded by a human decision, not even a divinely inspired one, but on account of the prodigious discovery of a statue of Hercules that was immersed in the sea and subsequently extracted by men (fishermen?), whose large number suggests not only the statue's significant weight, but more importantly the great number of witnesses to the prodigy. More than just a prestigious memory coming to complement the representation of the rite, this scene of discovery reminds viewers of the active participation of the god Hercules in the establishment of the sanctuary, and consequently of his *actual* presence during every sortition ritual.

The passage of the *De diuinatione* and this relief use therefore the same rhetoric of persuasion, combining the three main criteria of sign recognition: the child was a guarantee of integrity when casting lots (the child's sympathetic relation with the divinity remains more hypothetical). The prodigy narratives surrounding the ritual gave it a level of credibility that unsolicited signs usually lacked: that is to say the supernatural and extraordinary mark of the divine. In both examples, the oracular sanctuaries preserved a material vestige of these prodigies: the box in which the lots are kept in Praeneste, the statue of the god in Ostia. These are artefacts favourable to the special manifestation of the gods, as confirmed by a miracle regarding the *arca* of Praeneste, which occurred during the reign of Tiberius and was recounted by Suetonius (63, 2). This functional association between ritual symbols and spontaneous signs, with the latter corroborating the former, was in fact a key feature of Roman divination, largely documented in the sources.

The conflation of sortitio with prodigies

The second way to increase the credibility of an act of *sortitio* entailed transforming the rite itself, so that it would acquire the features of a prodigy. Such a transformation appears clearly in three stories, two from Livy's *History* (respectively in 218 and 217 BC) and the third from Cicero's *De diuinatione*:

> In Lanuvium a slain victim had stirred, and a raven had flown down into Juno's temple and alighted on her very couch; in the district of Amiternum, in many places, apparitions of men in shining raiment had appeared in the distance, but had not drawn near to anyone; in the Picentian country there had been a shower of pebbles; at Caere the lots had shrunk (*Caere sortes extenuatas*); in Gaul a wolf had snatched a sentry's sword from its scabbard and run off with it. (Livy, 21, 62)

> At Falerii the sky had seemed to be rent as it were with a great fissure; and through the opening a bright light had shone; and lots had shrunk and one had fallen out without being touched (*sortes sua sponte attenuatas unamque excidisse*), on which was written: 'Mavors brandishes his spear.' (Livy, 22, 1, 11)

> But the most significant warning received by the Spartans was this: they sent to consult the oracle of Jupiter at Dodona as to the chances of victory. After their messengers had duly set up the vessel in which were the lots, an ape, kept by the king of Molossia for his amusement, disarranged the lots and everything else used in consulting the oracle, and scattered them in all directions (*et sortes ipsas et cetera quae erant ad sortem parata disturbauit et aliud alio dissipauit*). Then, so we are told, the priestess who had charge of the oracle said that the Spartans must think of safety and not of victory. (Cicero, *De diuinatione*, 1, 76)

In these three examples, the act of sortition, which was inserted in a series of various prodigies, was not, as we could expect, mentioned because it was a negative result obtained following the casting lots (and thus an unfavourable prediction), but because it gave rise to prodigies.

In the two first texts, the *sortes* 'shrank' by themselves. According to Jacqueline Champeaux, the *sortes* resembled narrow metal strips which were pierced at the tip and fastened together by a wire, so that they formed a bundle. The lots were likely stored in such bundles, which were sometimes used as material for the rite itself (with a lot being ritually cast from the bundle). It seems that in this case the *sortes* had shrunk, and one lot was ejected from the bundle, thus conducting a spontaneous act of sortition (as suggested by the word *excidere*) (Champeaux, 1989, pp. 63–72). We could also consider, in a more general way, that the sudden shrinking of the lots was itself a sign of the wrath of the local divinity, particularly if an oracular message was written in the *sortes*, since the shrinking would likely damage any message inscribed. Independently of the precise meaning of the verb *extenuare* (or *attenuare*), a prodigious incident took place in both stories. In Caere, the prodigy appeared separately from the rite; whereas in Faleries, which was perhaps an extended and better informed version of the first incident, an act of *sortitio* was triggered in a spontaneous and supernatural manner.

Cicero provides a more detailed example with a Greek prodigy, an example that would still have been quite relevant for a Roman audience (for a similar prodigy, without mention of sortition, see Cassius Dio, 50, 8, 1). As either the priest or the Spartans (the text is unclear on this point) were about to cast the lots, a monkey suddenly scattered the lots. The scene depicts a chaotic imitation of the blending of the lots or even of the disordered tossing of the lots out of the box. The monkey, an animal without intentionality, was an appropriate medium for divine will. In this story, the monkey performs exactly the same function as the child mentioned in various examples above: both the monkey and the child are tasked with proving the spontaneous nature of the prodigy. This comparison was explicitly drawn in the oniromantic treatise of Artemidorus (*Oneirocriticon*, 2, 69). The prodigy spectacularly introduced the divine initiative in the regular procedure of sortition.

In these examples, the direct, concrete manifestation of the divinity was substituted for an implicit form of participation, otherwise common in the ritual context. This substitution did not proceed from mere rhetorical amplification, but stemmed in fact from the great importance that the Ancient Romans placed on observing the correct ritual procedures, and consequently from their high degree of sensitivity to anything that could disturb a ritual sequence. Ancient sources recount how a great number of consultations were interrupted by an incident that 'vitiated' the entire rite, forcing the individuals involved to repeat it from the start. Such incidents were above all seen as unfavourable omens by the historians that recounted them. A paradoxical situation would thus emerge: although the divine sign was not produced following the consultation, it was in fact delivered, in expected fashion, by an incident that disturbed the normal unfolding of the ritual sequence. But if we adopt the perspective of the Romans, who constantly worried about the reliability of the signs they observed, we can easily explain this strange expectation. The prodigy circumvents the consultation—conducted through sacrifice or sortition—only to achieve it by another means, one that makes the special participation of the divinity even more intense and more obvious.

In conclusion, *sortitiones* were frequently associated or conflated with prodigies, since prodigies expressed a higher degree of the gods' involvement during the casting of lots, and increased the credibility of sortition as a divine rite. From this perspective, it is interesting to note that Roman sortition had no particular features that distinguished it from the other mantic rites in use at the time: ancient sources do not mention the element of chance that was unique to sortition and which was usually said to correspond to a divine manifestation. Divine participation in the casting of lots was not viewed as inherent to the rite. On the contrary, as for the other divination practices, the divine presence could be more or less noticeable, along a variable continuum. And the more clearly that presence manifested itself, the more it was worthy of interest and mention in the eyes of the Romans. Furthermore, ancient historians were apparently focused on the problem of recognition, and rather surprisingly overlooked what pertained to how the result was produced and what the prediction meant (the shape and number of the lots; the oral or written definition and formulation of the stakes involved with the given act of sortition; the content of the oracular message inscribed on the lots, and the interpretation of its meaning). We could of course explain this oversight by referring to the usual narrative trait of *breuitas*, which led authors to neglect minor details, but the 'prodigialization' of sortition seems to mirror the central Roman concern about divination: the need to be as certain as possible regarding the existence of divine involvement, which in turn determined the reliability of a divine sign.

Was Civic Sortition a Rite of Divination?

We can now return to our first question: was civic sortition, a technique used to appoint magistrates and attribute public offices, considered to be a divinatory rite (Rosenstein, 1995, p. 43)? Our purpose here is not to re-examine in depth this very thorny question, but merely to emphasize, in light of what we have said about private acts of divinatory sortition, that the participation of the gods in sortition was not considered by the Ancient Romans from a binary perspective of belief or non-belief, but along a rational continuum of believability—thus confirming that the our modern distinction between sacred and civic acts of sortition was not a readily accepted one in Ancient Rome.

The religious context of the rite

Civic sortition was not used to honour deities, and Roman law did not apparently regard sortition as falling under the *auspicatio*, the official right (and duty) for public magistrates to take the *auspicia*, i.e. to consult the gods before any official act (on this controversial issue, Linderski, 1986, pp. 2173–175 and 2193–94; Berthelet, 2015, pp. 234–235, note 98; Bothorel, forthcoming). However, civic sortition was usually performed in conditions that shared similarities with acts seeking to consult the gods. As Roberta Stewart has shown (1998, pp. 30–34 and

38–51), *sortitio* probably took place in an 'inaugurated' space, to which a certain degree of sacrality had been officially assigned (the temple of Jupiter Optimus Maximus or a military camp, for example). It seems that the material used for *sortitio* was itself seen as sacred, being defined as divine propriety or at least as having a special connection with the divine power. The *augures*, a kind of priests, exerted legal control over the process of selection by lots. Moreover, before casting the lots, the gods were invited, by means of a ritual prayer, to pay attention to the sortition (Livy, 10, 24, 16). Other rites of consultation, both before and after the casting of lots, could perform a similar function; namely, obtaining the prior consent of the gods, or an *a posteriori* confirmation of the legitimacy of the procedure's results (with the *litatio*, an agreement to a sacrifice, for example). Finally, the *religio*, or the religious scruple or obligation towards the gods, was required with respect to the result of the *sortitio*. In one of his accusatory speeches, Cicero protested: 'We shall fill life with danger and resentment and hostility at every turn, if the decisions of the lot are to lose all their sanctity' (*totam uitam periculosam, inuidiosam, infestamque reddemus si nullam religionem sors habebit*) (*Or. in Verrem*, 2, 1, 38). While there was obviously some rhetorical exaggeration in such a declaration (Rosenstein, 1995, pp. 62–63), for the Romans, the argument would have been ineffective if the act of sortition had not been associated with an actual *religio* or element of piety (Johnston, 2003, p. 151).

Therefore, sortition took place before the eyes of the gods. It is important to stress that in acts of sortition, as in sacrifices, the absence of explicit disagreement was sufficient to mark divine consent for a public act. If there was no sign of divine disfavour and no disruption of the ritual procedure, divine consent was seen as having been obtained by default. The Ancient Romans did not expect the gods to send spectacular prodigies in a systematic fashion; on the contrary, it sometimes happened that the gods remained silent, even after a ritual solicitation. This is why, even if ancient sources sometimes mention sortition without referring to any form of divine sanction, this cannot be an argument against the idea that *sortitio* was used to consult the gods. Similarly, mentions of the negotiations and disputes regarding sortition procedures and results (for example, the *comparatio*, which attributed public offices after mutual consent) were not at odds with the belief that the act of *sortitio* expressed the divine will: for Ancient Romans, the divine will was not expressed through dogmatic revelations sent down by an omnipotent and ubiquitous God, but a broader sense of goodwill that they could preserve by respecting religious law (*ius diuinum*) and ritual obligations.

The involvement of the gods in casting lots

The involvement of the gods in the actual casting of the lots was a second modality of divine participation. Did a deity directly make the act of sortition conform to his or her will, by setting up the lots in the box so that a specific lot was cast, or by guiding the hand of the individual(s) performing the consultation? Or did the deity perhaps merely ensure the fairness of the random selection process, by preventing any possible cheating, as has been suggested by Sarah Johnston (2003, pp. 152–153)?

It is likely that some Romans believed in the direct intervention of the gods, as a temporary suspension of the rules of nature (Cicero, *De diuinatione*, 1, 34). This interpretation presents two difficulties, however. First, it concerns the theological and philosophical understanding that the Romans had of their gods and of fate. However, ancient ritual practices were not contingent upon sacred revelations and to their interpretation by a religious authority. There was no strict official doctrine about the nature of the gods and how they were supposed to intervene in the human world, and the learned Romans who speculated on this matter in philosophical treatises were not expressing any kind of religious orthodoxy. It is therefore difficult to draw any conclusions regarding how the Ancient Romans may have imagined the concrete participation of the gods in acts of sortition. Secondly, the ancient sources which refer to this issue are extremely ambivalent and often lack precision (Caesar, *De Bello Gallico*, 1, 50, 4 and 53, 6–7; Cicero, *Philippicae*, 3, 26; Livy, 27, 11, 11). Similarly, the depiction of Hercules on the Ostian relief could be interpreted as either an allegorical representation of the deity, or as testimony of the dedicant's genuine belief in the active involvement of the divine in every act of sortition.

Roberta Stewart (1998, pp. 38 *sq.*) observed that the vocabulary of sortition and the augural terms used to describe divine signs were similar: for example, the verbs *euenire* or *obuenire* ('to occur') were used to refer to a lot springing out of the box and to a sign spontaneously sent by the gods. However, these words were not specific to augural terminology; they were in fact frequently used by Roman historians in a variety of contexts. Although they were used in reference to spontaneously occurring events, they did not mean that such events were necessarily signs sent by the gods. In short, by using this vocabulary, ancient authors merely suggested divine involvement rather than confirming it.

Divine manifestations

The third modality of divine participation was the direct intervention of the gods by means of unsolicited signs, manifesting themselves either as incidents disturbing ritual procedures (and thus seen as bad omens), or as signs following an act of sortition and providing some kind of commentary about it. Such signs made the gods' involvement in sortition more obvious. Valerius Maximus, following Cicero, provides a well-known example:

> It had fallen to him by lot (*sorte euenisset*) to conduct the war against king Perseus (*rege Perse*). Returning home from the senate house, he noticed that his little daughter called Tertia, a very small child at the time (*quae tum erat admodum paruula*), seemed sad when he gave her a kiss. To this question, why she looked like that, she answered that Persa had perished. Now a puppy called Persa (*nomine Persa*), the child's favourite, had died. So Paullus seized (*arripuit*) upon the omen and from a chance saying (*fortuito dictu*) conceived a pretty sure hope of a splendid triumph. (Valerius Maximus, *Facta et dicta memorabilia*, 1, 5, 3)

As modern scholars have noticed, Valerius Maximus explicitly identifies the link between the rite and the omen. But we can add that this link was strengthened by the mimetic duplication of the rite: here, the child plays precisely the role a child is supposed to play in sortition; the term 'fortuitous' (*fortuito*) reminds the audience of the verb *euenire* that opens this exemplary narrative; and the way that Paullus, himself an augur, accepts the omen by grasping it, could echo the formal acceptance of the result in the sortition rite (*suscipere*). This omen, which both repeats and clarifies the rite, is moreover described as a highly reliable sign — by insisting on the youth of Tertia, the author suggests that she is absolutely innocent. In addition, it contains a very clear premonition, thanks to the obvious play on the words Perseus/Persa. This is another example of the phenomenon of association/conflation that we have observed with regard to divinatory sortition.

Similarly, the ritual mistake that the consul Petilius made in 176 BC during the *sortitio* preceding a battle was itself a bad sign (*omen dirum*), but it is important to note that it took place amidst a series of unfavourable signs that happened to Petilius from the time he became consul to his death in front of the enemy. The series of prodigies surrounding sortition in Livy's narrative must therefore be taken as a confirmation of its divine value (Livy, 41, 15, 1–4 to 41, 18, 9–11).

To conclude, the Ancient Romans could believe in all these different modalities of divine involvement, or they could choose to believe in only some of them. The more obvious the incident of divine involvement, the more faith could be placed in sortition results, and the greater legitimacy was conferred by the gods onto the selected individuals. First, by taking place in a religious context, the result of a sortition ritual benefited from a common, generic divine legitimacy, like other public acts and rites. Second, the potential and probably variable belief in a direct involvement of the gods in sortition could confer an additional divine authority to the result of an act of sortition. Third, only the special intervention of a deity through more or less spectacular signs gave an outstanding divine value to an act of sortition, consequently denying or confirming its results. The prodigy generally delivered an additional message that commented on the result: for Paullus, the sign not only validated the sortition results but foreshadowed the Roman victory; for Petilius, conversely, the ritual error was an omen of death.

From a socio-political point of view, given the Roman religious conception of sortition, it seems apparent that two ideas could co-exist in the Roman mind without any contradiction (Johnston, 2003, p. 156). On the one hand, sortition was an egalitarian procedure, as it implied that all Roman aristocrats were able to fulfil the same functions with the same level of effectiveness; on the other hand, the extraordinary intervention of the gods could confer special legitimacy upon an individual and elevate him above his peers.

Conclusion

The problem of the gods' involvement in lots was more complex and concrete than certain modern approaches to religion and politics may seem to suggest. There was no real distinction between divinatory or sacral sortition and civic sortition in the Roman world, as the gods' involvement in both contexts was not an unconditional and *a priori* belief, but could develop gradually. As shown by the numerous examples where sortition was associated or conflated with prodigies — which often duplicated it in a manner that rendered the divine presence more tangible — the Ancient Romans did not primarily emphasize the randomness of sortition, as its dimension of chance did not necessarily imply divine involvement. The degree of divine participation in sortition rites was not stipulated by any theological doctrine, but rationally measured on a case-by-case basis depending on the circumstances of the rite, and could be subject to discussion and objection. For these reasons, the example of Roman sortition is an interesting point of comparison for studies of the links between religion, politics, and sortition in the context of modern monotheisms and secularized societies.

References

Berthelet, Y. (2015) *Gouverner avec les dieux. Autorité, auspices et pouvoir, sous la République romaine et sous Auguste*, Paris: Les Belles Lettres.

Bothorel, J. (forthcoming) *Le tirage au sort des gouverneurs sous la République romaine et au début du Principat (227 av. J.-C. - 14 ap. J.-C.)*, PhD Thesis, University Paris X — Nanterre.

Champeaux, J. (1982) Fortuna, *Recherches sur le culte de la Fortune à Rome et dans le monde romain des origines à la mort de César. I. Fortuna dans la religion archaïque*, CEFR, 64, Rome.

Champeaux, J. (1989) Sur trois passages de Tite-Live (21, 62, 5 and 8; 22, 1, 11). Les 'sorts' de Caere et de Faléries, *Philologus*, 133 (1), pp. 63–74.

Grottanelli, C. (1993) Bambini e divinazione, in Niccoli, O. (ed.) *Infanzie. Funzioni di un gruppo liminale dal mondo classico all'Età moderna*, pp. 23–72, Florence: Ponte alle Grazie.

Johnston, S.I. (2003) Lost in the shuffle: Roman sortition and its discontents, *ARG*, 5 (1), pp. 146–156.

Klingshirn, W.E. (2006) Inventing the *sortilegus*: Lot divination and cultural identity in Italy, Rome, and the provinces, in Schultz, C.E. & Harvey, P.B. (eds.) *Religion in Republican Italy*, Yale Classical Studies, 33, pp. 137–161, Cambridge: Cambridge University Press.

Linderski, J. (1986) The Augural Law, *ANRW*, 2, 16, 3, pp. 2146–2312, Berlin: De Gruyter.

Loriol, R. (2016) *Lire et écrire les signes divins. Recherches sur la divination romaine à travers l'historiographie impériale*, PhD Thesis, University Lyon 3 — Jean Moulin, 2 April 2016.

MacBain, B. (1982) *Prodigy and Expiation: a Study in Religion and Politics in Republican Rome*, Brussels: Latomus.

Néraudau, J.-P. (2008) *Être enfant à Rome*, Paris: Les Belles Lettres.

Rasmussen, S.W. (2003) *Public Portents in Republican Rome*, Rome: L'Erma di Bretschneider.

Rosenstein, N. (1995) Sorting out the lot in Republican Rome, *AJPh*, 116, pp. 43–75.

Santangelo, F. (2013) *Divination, Prediction and the End of the Roman Republic*, Cambridge: Cambridge University Press.

Scheid, J. (2007) Les sens des rites. L'exemple romain, in *Rites et croyances dans les religions du monde romain*, Entretiens sur l'Antiquité classique, 53, Vandoeuvre-Geneva: Fondation Hardt.

Stewart, R. (1998) *Public Office in Early Rome: Ritual Procedure and Political Practice*, Ann Arbor, MI: University of Michigan Press.

Vernant, J.-P. (1974) Paroles et signes muets, in Vernant, J.-P., *et al.* (eds.) *Divination et rationalité*, pp. 9–25, Paris: Le Seuil.

Sources

Apuleius, *Apologia*.
Artemidorus from Daldis, *Oneirocriticon*.
Caesar, *De Bello Gallico*.
Cicero, *De diuinatione*.
Cicero, *Orationes in Verrem*.
Cicero, *Orationes Philippicae*.
Cassius Dio, *Romaikè istoria*.
Suetonius, *De uita Caesarum*.
Livy, *History*.
Valerius Maximus, *Facta et dicta memorabilia*.

Part II:
Medieval and Early
Modern Words

Lorenzo Tanzini

The Practices and Rhetoric of Sortition in Medieval Public Life (13th–14th Centuries)

Translated by Sarah-Louise Raillard

Medieval history—and the medieval history of Italian communes in particular—poses a unique set of challenges for the study of electoral systems, and requires a different kind of language than that used in classical studies. Moreover, the study of electoral processes in medieval Italian cities calls for significant caution with regard to the use of various terms. When we talk about elections in the Middle Ages, this term encompasses many different means of selection, amongst which we find random selection as well as our modern election process, properly speaking (Théry, 2001). It is therefore necessary to understand the meaning behind these different processes and why they were used in any given context. Likewise, when examining the institutional mechanisms of medieval communes, we must always explain the different political roles that offices could play, roles that were often concealed by the use of a single appellation. The election of the *podestà*, the high-ranking foreign magistrate who lived in a city to steer its judicial and military affairs for one year, had a very different function than the election of the *Anziani*, who constituted the city's government and the expression of its political leadership (Maire Vigueur and Faini, 2010; Keller, 2014). And these two elections were in turn not strictly analogous to the election of the city's great councils, in which most citizens had the possibility to participate at several points during their lives, thus ensuring mass participation without requiring political initiative (Tanzini, 2014). Nevertheless, contemporary urban statutes and institutional practices always mentioned elections: we must therefore distinguish ordinary or extraordinary political practices from what was merely the norm.

Let us begin with the famous discussion on random selection that unfolded in 14th-century Florence: the long-distance conversation (in time albeit not in space) conducted between the chronicler Giovanni Villani, writing around 1340, and the humanist Leonardo Bruni, who published his *History of Florence* at the turn of the following century. Both men wrote about the pioneering institutional event that took place in 1328, when Florentine authorities introduced the *tratta* system of recruitment for high-ranking posts (Guidi, 1972): namely, a process of random selection conducted from a pre-established list of selected citizens.

The Florentine merchant and writer Villani described this new system of designation with great satisfaction, arguing that it would ensure 'a good and equitable order [of election]' (*'bello ordine e comune'*), as it represented a technical solution that allowed the commune 'to function smoothly and peacefully' (*'tranquillo e pacefico stato'*); it offered 'a true example for the generations that would follow' (Villani, 2001, p. 661). Villani's opinion was echoed by Stefani, Marchionne di Coppo (also known as Baldassarre Bonaiuti), who likewise felt that the new system was a very good way to ensure that the city's government was 'good, transparent, clear and free of factions' (*'buono e franco e schietto e non settaiuolo'*), with a view to avoiding all sectarian divisions (Stefani, Marchionne di Coppo, 1903–1905, §366). On the contrary, however, Bruni lamented the decision made in 1328, which he said was inspired by *'quadam popularitate'*, what we might call a 'kind of democracy' today. The effect of random selection was viewed as highly negative, since 'the majority of those designated for public offices were incapable' of fulfilling the tasks assigned to them (*'indigni plerumque ad magistratum ex sortitione sumuntur'*, Bruni, 2001–2004).

At first glance, this might appear to be just another expression of the traditional opposition, described in quite strong words by Guicciardini (Manin, 1995), between the 'popular' and participatory value of random selection, and the elitist consequences of electoral processes — an elitism for which Leonardo Bruni is often seen as the mouthpiece in 15th-century Florence (Sintomer, 2009). However, this discussion introduces a number of more complex elements: it goes beyond mere rhetoric, and involves the practical operation of random selection in long-standing communal traditions.

Random Selection, from Origins to Maturity

By the 14th century, random selection was already a well-known mechanism in Italian communal life; it is therefore worthwhile for us to spend some time on its origins before moving to more theoretical discussions on the topic. At the beginning of the communal history, and then all throughout the 12th century, there is no evidence to suggest that *ad sortem* electoral systems were used. As its standard procedure, the small council of consuls appears to have used a combination of election and co-optation to designate magistrates, often using the (typically episcopal) 'compromise' variant (*'per compromissum'*): i.e. by the direct election of one or several electors who in turn chose other colleagues with whom they conducted an electoral process to fill the office in question (Keller, 2014a).

In Cremona, for example, we know that in 1186, the consuls were elected 'by compromise' (*'per viam compromissionis'*) (Keller, 2014b). In Pistoia, an old statute regulating the elections of consuls (*Breve dei Consoli*, 1140–1180) stipulated that consul should select two citizens from the people's assembly (*'in aringo'*) who would be tasked with electing the 14 councillors (*Statuti di pistoiesi/Breve dei console, 1140–1180*, 1996, pp. 173–175). In 1224, in Volterra, the grand elector chosen by the consuls collaborated with two other grand electors that he selected to form a sort of electoral college responsible for designating all the individuals who would be appointed to offices (*Statuti di Volterra*, 1951, p. 113). This multi-round selection mechanism was primarily designed to depoliticize elections by entrusting the actual designation of individuals to a limited circle of elites who enjoyed the trust of the whole urban community. Moreover, such elites could not exploit this privilege for their own interests, as grand electors were not eligible for the offices that they were tasked with filling.

Dating back to 1224, the aforementioned example from Volterra is in fact a very late one, since random selection had become the norm almost everywhere during the 13th century. In Reggio Emilia, a chapter on the use of random selection was the first to be included in the collected volume of municipal law (the *Consuetudines*) compiled in 1242: 'Neither *podestà* nor *consul* shall be elected but rather randomly selected' (*'Quod nullus eligatur in potestatem vel consulem nisi ad sortem'*) (*Consuetudini e statuti reggiani*, 1933, pp. 3–4). In Novara in 1281, the local statutes stipulated that 'offices both ordinary and extraordinary shall be selected by lot' (*'dentur et eligantur ad brevia ipsi officiales omnes tam ordinarii quam extraordinarii'*) (*Statuta communitatis Novariae*, 1876, coll. 541–44). The statutes of Verona included very similar provisions in 1276 (*Gli Statuti veronesi del 1276*, pp. 72–73).

Edoardo Ruffini, the most important historian of electoral systems in the Italian communes, declared in 1927 that random selection was 'as old as the world itself' (Ruffini, 1977). However, if we look at its genealogy in those same communes, it is hard to reconstruct the precise evolution of electoral systems. It is no longer a viable argument, as many believed in Ruffini's time, that the medieval communes were consciously imitating the practices of Ancient Roman municipalities (*municipia*). Research conducted by Hagen Keller and his students has instead focused on the linkages between the communes' electoral practices and the tradition of episcopal elections or those of the Germanic Holy Roman Empire (Keller, 2014a). Moreover, the long-standing existence of electoral systems in the monastic world may have provided several models for towns and cities to emulate (Moulin, 1953). Nonetheless, the religious and episcopal examples cited generally refer to the *per compromissionem* voting model, whereas random selection and lotteries were expressly forbidden by the Church (save for a very small number of exceptions). In fact, a bill issued by Honorius III in 1225 had definitively prohibited the use of sortition in a religious context (Gaudemet, 1979, pp. 328–331; Moulin, 1958). At any rate, the emergence of sortition did not reveal a direct line of descent with any of its ancient or medieval precedents. Its widespread diffusion was doubtless related to the socio-political complexity of the communes at the beginning of the 13th century: since the councils were beginning to include citizens from various social classes, it was necessary to pay greater attention to selection mechanisms in order to avoid conflicts.

This moment in history also illustrates the central role played by representative mechanisms in the communal system. The municipal institutions of the Middle Ages were not 'representative' in the modern sense of the word, but the need to obtain a 'descriptive' reproduction of society in its institutions was clearly understood (Costa, 1999; Hayat and Sintomer, 2013). As a result of this need to depict the social tapestry, urban statutes often contained regulations on how different communal functions were to be allocated across a city's different neighbourhoods, categories of people, and social classes (Tanzini, 2017).

Here we can begin to understand the reason for the marked difference that existed between the use of electoral systems in Italian cities and their use in European cities north of the Alps, where sortition was rarely documented. During that period, the 'bourgeois' homogeneity of the French municipal elites did not require such a system, as co-optation was a much simpler mechanism that fulfilled the governing group's representation requirement (Rigaudière, 2002). The plurality of social groups that came onto the urban political stage in 14th-century Germany due to the rise of corporations (*Zünften*) sometimes justified the use of random selection, but such cases remained very rare (Isenmann, 1997; Richard, 2008, p. 200).

The specific modalities of *ad sortem* appointment and the use of random selection did not share any veritable historical connection with examples from the Ancient World, or Greek Antiquity in particular. Nonetheless, the first commentaries made on Aristotle's *Politics*, and in particular the commentary penned by Albertus Magnus (shortly after 1260), described the system of selection using the *kleroterion* as 'the reason of chance' ('*ratio sortialis*') (Fioravanti, 1979; Cambiano, 2000, p. 372). It is no coincidence that Albertus's commentary appears to be the most 'contemporary' and full of references to the institutional reality of Italian cities at the time. In addition, the expression *sortialis* clearly referred to the use of *ad sortem* designation in many cities during the same period. Examples from Antiquity were therefore not at the root of the communal systems of appointment; nonetheless, the technical affinity the latter shared with classical cities helped to consolidate the effectiveness of such systems and legitimize them by means of traditional precedents. A century later, the Chancellor of Florence, Coluccio Salutati, drawing on a much vaster knowledge of ancient texts, was therefore able to speak about the electoral systems of Ancient Rome (Baggioni, 2016, pp. 302–306).

Be that as it may, in the 13th century the growing practical need to develop new systems of official selection throughout Italian cities almost certainly won out over any desire to imitate the Ancient Romans and Greeks. Lexical analysis confirms this hypothesis: the traditional expression '*electio ad sortem*' was frequently used in sources during the period but remained ambiguous and non-technical. The word '*sors*' could even mean something like 'the expression of desire or choice in the council'. In Reggio, for example, the statutes from 1265 state that 'with regard to the choice to be made in the council using black and white fava beans' ('*De sorte danda in conscilio per fabas nigras et albas*'); in this text, '*dare sortem*' simply meant 'to vote', without any reference to random selection (Archivio di Stato di Reggio Emilia, Comune, Statuti 1, c. 67v–68r). When it was necessary to clearly define the practice of sortition, local legislators were more likely to use more phrases with references to material objects, such as *ad brevia, ad apodixas, ad polizzas, per rodolum* (*brevia* or *apodixe* both referred to the small scrolls used to randomly draw the names of those who would fill certain offices).

This reference to scrolls also had the advantage of eliminating the image of chance. In fact, chance not was explicitly considered to be an asset in the political discourse of the Italian communes. This can clearly be deduced from the communal statutes of the 13th century, where the practices for the random selection of officers displayed a sort of indirect and partially corrected form of chance. These corrections occurred at multiple levels:

1. First of all, even during the golden age of sortition, cities used various corrective measures that they borrowed from the '*per compromissum*' election method. For example, in Viterbo in 1251, two names were randomly drawn from among the members of the council, and those two grand electors in turn selected four other 'intermediaries' ('*mediani*') with whom they would then elect the members of the new council, in collaboration with the current officeholders (*Statuti della provincia romana*, II, 1930, pp. 99–100). This practice of selection thus recalls the principles of compromise voting, but with an initial stage of random selection. One of the most complex versions of the multi-round system of selection was later developed in Venice for the election of the Doge (Judde de Larivière, 2020).

2. Secondly—though not in significance, as this was the most important trait of medieval uses of voting mechanisms—the *ad brevia* system was used in most cities to choose electors and not officers. The practice was rather uniform almost everywhere. In a large assembly, each individual took a sealed scroll: a small number of those scrolls were inscribed with the word *elector* or similar, and those who found this inscription when opening their scroll would become the electors. Chance then ceased to operate in the final election process, as each elector had to declare his choice. In Bologna, even after 1264 (though this is likely a unique case) fragments of lists of electors were preserved, with each elector indicating the name of his preferred candidate. While it is true that sometimes—in Bologna and Lucca for instance (Tamba, 1982; *Statutum Lucani communis*, 1991)—electors could nominate themselves, most of the time the electors and the elected could not be one and the same. The random chance involved in sortition was thus strictly monitored and corrected: since the *ad brevia* procedure was applied to groups, and often according to urban neighbourhoods, electors were exposed to pressure from their socio-political and familial environment. As a result, sortition did not break the personal ties that informed the electors' choices.

3. Thirdly, another factor came into play to limit the role of chance: in general, not all citizens were allowed to draw the small scroll ('*qui possunt ire ad brevia*'). A version with much greater levels of participation could sometimes be found, such as in Padua in 1271, where section XXI of the city's statutes ('*De electione offitialium ordinariorum*') granted all citizens registered on the fiscal rolls the possibility of being randomly drawn for election to office (*Statuti del comune di Padova*, 1873). A similar situation existed in Piacenza, where the 1323 statutes foresaw a

general council (*'consilium generalissimum'*) open to all citizens who asked to participate (*Lo Statuto di Piacenza del 1323*, 2012, p. 13). Most of the time, however, sortition took place *in consilio*, that is, only the members of the council were allowed to draw the *brevia*. In Perugia in 1279, the names of all those who would become officeholders had to be selected in the council at the beginning of the *podestà* or *capitano*'s term: 'every officer of the commune of Perugia shall be elected by the major council by sortition at the beginning of the term of the *podestà* or the *capitano*' ('*omnes et singuli officiales communis Perusii per maius consilium civitatis et populi sorte brevium eligantur in principio regiminis potestatis et capitanei*') (*Statuto di Perugia del 1279*, 1996, pp. 104–106). As a result, one of the first tasks that each new *podestà* or 'captain of the people' had to undertake was convening the council to conduct the drawing. The members of communal councils were very numerous in the 13th century — several hundred individuals even in medium-sized towns), but admission to the council nonetheless had a certain number of prerequisites with regard to assets, legal status, and occupation: the random selection thus unfolded based on a list of pre-selected individuals.

4. Fourth limitation: although sometimes grand electors could directly make their selections for the individual(s) to be appointed, most of the time (and especially for high-ranking offices) there was an intermediate stage that impeded a direct relationship between grand electors and the councillors elected. For example, in Pistoia in 1284, 12 grand electors were randomly selected for each major position, and they were required to choose the councillor that received two-thirds of the vote (*Breve et ordinamenta populi Pistorii*, 2003, p. 86). In Padua in 1277, seven grand electors were randomly selected, and had in turn to choose two citizens who were 'the best of their neighbourhoods' ('*de melioribus sui quarterii*'), only one of whom would be randomly drawn. In that context, sortition and direct selection alternated two separate times in the same election (*Statuti del comune di Padova*, 1873). In passing, it should be noted that an example of this procedure can be found in the Bible, in a passage of *Acts* (1, 25) where the twelfth apostle was selected after Judas's death: the community chose two faithful disciples, Matthias and Joseph Barabbas, and then 'they cast lots' to determine who would take over the apostolic ministry ('ἔδωκαν κλήρους αὐτοῖς').

The intermediate stage between random selection and election sometimes also took place in the council. One very clear example of the precarious seesaw between chance and choice can be found in the statutes for the city of Parma in 1266, which used a hybrid *ad sortem–ad brevia* system. When a councillor's name was selected according to the procedure in place (*'si vocatus per illam cedulam sortem habuerit, veniat ad faciendum electionem'*): that is, 'he will be responsible for making the choice as elector if his name obtains the vote of those present' (*Statuta communis Parmae ab anno MCCLXVI*, 1857, pp. 39–40). In this case, *'habere sortem'* simultaneously meant 'being fortunate enough' to be randomly selected and 'obtaining the votes' of one's council colleagues.

A first conclusion can be drawn from this presentation of different cases. In the 13th century, sortition was evidently viewed as the ultimate system for appointing individuals to office. At the same time, however, and despite the central role it played, sortition was almost never used to ensure that chance helped to select the individuals that would occupy public office. In an excellent study of political recruitment in Bologna between the 13th and 14th centuries, Sarah Blanshei shows that the use of different sortition mechanisms to elect members of the communal council did not prevent the council from ultimately reproducing the political composition of the government: that is, the College of the *Anziani* (Blanshei, 2010; Vallerani, 2011). This representativity was a structural mechanism rather than a statistical accident.

The true function of sortition was in fact to ensure that the selection of councillors sufficiently accounted for representation from the different groups that composed the city's political society. To that extent, *ad brevia* selection seemed to be the most natural choice. It should be recalled, following the suggestions made by Hagen Keller and his students, that elections in the Middle Ages were first and foremost designed to safeguard peace and establish consensus (*'konsensorientiert'*), rather than to pit different political choices against each other (Dartmann, 2012; Keller, 2014a). That observation can perhaps also be applied to the *Ancien Régime* as a whole (Christin, 2014). In his history of sortition throughout the ages, Yves Sintomer highlights that in the major medieval republics, random selection operated primarily to achieve consensus and resolve conflicts, rather than to ensure participation as it had in Greek democracies (Sintomer, 2020). Dartmann was perhaps exaggerating somewhat when he spoke of a '[political] culture of defeat', namely because the elective system was first and foremost designed to ensure that the defeated party accepted its defeat without resorting to violence. The involvement of random selection, even when conducted in a purely ritual fashion, must therefore be understood in that context (Dartmann, 2010). The exaggeration lies no doubt in the fact that Dartmann seems to overlook the ferocious conflicts that erupted even when this system was used, as well as the fact that the party opposed to the city's ruling government was simply eliminated from participation in politics (Milani, 2003). We should therefore focus on the socio-political profile of the limited number of individuals who could genuinely participate in the ritual of random selection. Nonetheless, it is evident that sortition first and foremost satisfied the need to nuance the brutal reproduction of a given party's political hegemony in the city's various bodies: the ritual of random selection concealed the direct expression of public will behind what might be called the veil of chance.

For that reason, electoral practices in the Italian communes exhibited a level of ritual complexity that was almost religious in nature. Their ritual dimension was not a formal accessory: it represented and preserved the symbolic power behind acts of selection. The chronicler Baldassarre Bonaiuti explains that after voting was used to draw up the lists of citizens to serve in the subsequent random selection process, the boxes used were opened in a location that those who had voted were prohibited from entering. Six priests chose the location: two representatives each from the Dominican, Franciscan, and Augustinian orders, all six of whom were foreign (i.e. not from Florence). After the boxes were opened, the purses (*borse*) containing the names to be randomly drawn had to be kept in the Sainte Croix chapter in a triple-lock cabinet; the first key was entrusted to the *custos* of the Franciscans, the second to the prior of the Cistercian monastery of Settimo, and the last to the captain of the people (Stefani, Marchionne di Coppo Stefani, 1903–1905, §366). Moreover, the sacralization of electoral procedures was tied to the use of terms with obvious religious connotations: *votum, electio, suffragium*. It is worthwhile here to note that, in Italian, *votum* signifies a 'wish' as well as a 'vote': the ultimate '*electio*' was the divine choice of its people, and suffrage normally dictated Mass intentions. Those who participated in the procedure were fully aware of the religious connotations of the institutional lexicon: in Siena in 1262, for example, the 'signed' scrolls with which the councillor became the elector of officers in charge of amending the city's statutes (*emendatores constituti*) were marked with the inscription 'A and Ω' (*Il constituto del comune di Siena dell'anno 1262*, 1896, pp. 56–57), and thus entailed a very strong association between the elector's task and a divine vocation ('I am the Alpha and the Omega', *Revelation*, 1:8). Even if the ritual did not envision the presence of religious symbols, the electoral process was often presented in urban statues with exceptional solemnity: in Foligno in 1350, the council's notary, in charge of counting votes, used a copper box so that the sound of each ball falling into the box could be heard by all those in attendance (*Statuta communis Fulginei*, 1969, II, pp. 30–32). We can imagine the tense, expectant silence as the vote count took place.

Changes During the 14th Century

The hybrid systems of random selection used in the 13th century that we have seen so far were obviously flawed. They required frequent council meetings for the *brevia,* that is, for the random selection using scrolls of officers at the beginning of each new *podestà*'s mandate; this required a complex procedure that disturbed the council's ordinary activities. More importantly, the *brevia* did not completely eliminate the expression of the elector's individual choice, thus weakening the consensus function of the 'scroll' election (*ad brevia*).

At the end of the 13th century, and especially at the beginning of the 14th century, Italian communes began to introduce new corrective measures and sometimes even radical changes to the system. In Bologna in 1288, the city's statutes changed how the *Anziani* (the city's highest-ranking officers) were selected (*Statuti di Bologna dell'anno 1288,* 1937, pp. 297–298). Up until that point, they had been appointed by the city's corporations, each one according to a randomly selected electoral college. Wary of the wisdom exercised by the corporations, the statutes imposed a second step: the corporations now had to propose six elected officials, and the council was responsible for selecting which of those individuals would be recruited as *Anziani.* The random selection was thus constrained by a choice; this choice was made by the Assembly rather than by the grand electors. The concept of directly electing officeholders spread throughout Italy during the beginning of the 14th century. According to Pisa's statutes, the members of the city's council were chosen by the *Anziani* when '*quando et sicut eis videbitur*', that is, 'when and as they like' (*Brevi del comune e del popolo,* 1998, §I, 55), whereas in Florence the choice was entrusted to the Priors (the city's leading magistrates) with 40 'wise men' (*sapientes*) (*Statuti della Repubblica fiorentina,* 1999, I, pp. 32–33). In a certain way, this can be seen as a refurbishing of the ancient system used to elect consuls in the 12th century; here, however, the council of the *Anziani* or the Priors — the leaders of the popular regime — were the ones in charge of making this highly 'politicized' choice. The system's meaning thus stemmed from the idea that popular colleges like the *Anziani* or the councils offered a kind of 'symbolic representation' of the urban community, and thus that their choice was equivalent in value to election by the urban community as a whole.

One alternative sometimes adopted was the creation of a council with the exclusive task of filling other positions. The *ad brevia* system of random selection was preserved in such cases, but the number of individuals who could participate in the drawing was fixed by an *ad hoc* assembly. This system was likewise introduced in Bologna, this time for more minor offices: the Councils of the 2,000 and the 4,000 were not true councils, but they were used to designate the number of individuals who could 'participate in random selection' (*'ire ad brevia'*) (Tamba, 1982).

In 1306 in Modena, after a period where the city was controlled by the House of Este, the commune recovered its freedom. One of its first actions was establishing the Council of the 1,600 (Modena at the time had about 20,000 inhabitants), which would serve not for ordinary deliberations, but 'to designate the officers of the commune of Modena who are elected by sortition, and to hand down convictions and sentences' (*'ad faciendum ellectiones officialium comunis Mutine que fient ad brevia, et ad audiendum condempnationes et sententias'*) (*Respublica mutinensis*, 1929–1932). This was therefore a truly 'Greek-style' council used for public judgments and the random distribution of offices.

At any rate, the role of these giant councils did not ordinarily concern the election of major offices such as the *Anziani*, a task usually entrusted to communal governments. In Italian cities during the 13th and 14th century, hundreds of minor offices existed, linked to daily administration and the governing of neighbouring rural communities under communal control. An appointment to one of these minor offices was a sign of social recognition and prestige for the individuals who were randomly selected; it fell short, however, of conferring real political power. Moreover, the gap separating the multitude of minor offices from the full political responsibility of the inner circle of government means that we cannot see the communal regimes as forms of direct democracy: even in their most participatory incarnations, communal governments made choices that preserved a relationship with forms of selection that were more complex—and doubtless less 'blind' in nature.

In that regard, the most remarkable innovation of the 14th century came from cities in Tuscany, in particular Siena and Florence, where changes to the electoral system led to the birth of an entirely new process called the *tratta*. The word *tratta* came from a Florentine tradition and simply meant selection by lot. But, by the 14th century, the meaning of the word had significantly changed. The *tratta* process involved first creating a list of citizens who had been publicly deemed worthy of holding office. The composition of this list was ensured by several colleges, each working independently on lists that were later added together (the *recata*, or 'presentation' phase). The next step was decisive: the *recata*, i.e. the compiled list, was put to a vote, name by name, in the great council (in Siena) or in an *ad hoc* council of one hundred citizens selected by the government (in Florence). The names that were approved by the majority were then inserted into electoral purses and entrusted to the various urban religious communities. Sortition would subsequently be conducted at the end of each office's mandate by drawing a new name from the purse, until the purse was emptied within a few years (Najemy, 1982). It is evident that, in such a process, chance was almost entirely eliminated: it only played a role with regard to the order in which all the names placed in the purse were to be drawn for an office. When a citizen's name was placed in the purse, that individual merely had to wait for his turn to come up (unless he lost the right to hold office on account of absence, death, or unpaid taxes). And yet, thanks to an irony of history, by the end of the Middle Ages this system would have become, in terms of both political practices and discussions, the image *par excellence* of random selection (the discussion between Villani and Bruni referred to this model, for example). The irony stems from the fact that this was the least 'blind' version of sortition practices introduced in the communes.

It is important to fully understand the changes wrought by the introduction of the *tratta* model, which was a complete innovation with regard to electoral technologies and provided an effective solution to the shortcomings of existing systems. However, the *tratta* model did not fundamentally change how the communes viewed the role of random selection in politics. First of all, it preserved the full lexical and ritual apparatus of chance (which, as we saw above, was almost exclusively ritual in nature): the secret ballot, the interdiction of expressing a choice (for or against) the names on the *recata*, the fact that the purses were hidden away — in short, the exclusion of any direct control or influence over the outcome. As evidenced by the Giovanni Villani citation contained at the beginning of this chapter, politics at the beginning of the 14th century tended to view the *tratta* model as a means to perfect the classical systems of sortition, even if this new mechanism in reality eliminated all element of chance. Once again, communal political culture did not see the element of chance at the heart of random selection procedures: the true centre of the system was, on the contrary, the rotation of offices between the individuals that society had deemed to be politically qualified citizens (Vallerani, 1994). In the 13th century, this recognition would come from participation in one of the councils (where the *ad brevia* selection processes took place), whereas in major cities in the 14th century it would instead come from electoral qualification by means of the *recata*. This did not, however, change the core principles: every individual who became part of the qualified group, whether through participation in a popular council in the 13th century or through recognition thanks to the *recata*, would then be called upon to play their active role as a citizen and an office-holder. This did not mean, however, that random selection was a useless fiction. The need to depoliticize choices, to demonstrate that officers somehow 'naturally' reproduced the urban society from which they came, gave the sortition ritual a very real role. This was not a complete innovation: the history of voting in Antiquity, and in Rome especially, illustrates the central role played by the ritual dimension of elections, even when the expression of choice remains almost entirely absent (Hollard, 2010, pp. 231–233). Moreover, electoral systems during the Middle Ages usually had as their primary function staging the unity and identity of the community (Peneau, 2008, p. 27).

Theoretical Considerations

We should therefore revisit the aforementioned long-distance discussion between Villani and Bruni. When the latter said that the *tratta* was not a good system, that was not just because it was likely to confer responsibilities to citizens who did not possess the necessary political abilities. His argument was as follows: 'people are not likely to expect responsibilities that they can picture today in the same fashion as those that will materialize later on: on the contrary, people see the former very clearly and with enthusiasm, whereas the latter seem far-away' (*'Neque enim pari diligentia providetur praesenti officio et multis secuturis; sed remota quidem illa, et an futura sint minime certa, hebetiori intuemur oculo'*). For that reason, being chosen on a list of names from which one might be selected at a later date did not foster attention with regard to the responsibilities in question, but in fact weakened such attention, 'extinguishing in particular the quest for political virtue' (*'extinguit praeterea virtutis studium'*). On the contrary, in the competition to be elected, public figures are involved in a positive fashion (*'si suffragiis certandum foret… multo magis sese homines circumspicerent'*).

Bruni's criticism attacked the system at its core: the principle according to which individuals were qualified once and then benefited from this qualification in all successive acts of random selection. According to Bruni, the fact that individuals were qualified once and for all weakened enthusiasm and quest for (political) virtue, since individuals who knew they would eventually be attributed an office no longer exerted themselves to demonstrate their virtue. Consequently, it would have been better to follow the Roman example, and proceed to a true selection of candidates each and every time.

This was a very profound observation, which perhaps even surpassed the understanding of the Florentine elites who read and officially celebrated Bruni and his work. In fact, this observation illustrates the opposition between two institutional and cultural models of election. In the communal tradition, the mechanism of sortition was a necessary system, albeit a complex one that was difficult to manage and which often did not achieve what we consider to be the essential aim of elections. The communal governments were aware of the system's flaws, but preserved it because the ritual dimensions of sortition highlighted the role of assemblies and councils, which were so many expressions of the citizens' collective identity. In that kind of political culture, individuals did not exist. What did exist, on the other hand, were groups — urban collectives — where the 'public' identify of individuals was recognized and submitted for representation: hence the councils, corporations, societies, and colleges that made up the *recata*. This was a system that was highly participatory and yet very closed, since it did not envision the possibility of expression for those individuals that groups shunned and did not include in their inner circle.

On the contrary, Bruni's work presents the idea that individuals must be pitted against each other in order to determine which are the best and the most competent candidates. This system was primarily beneficial for the elites, since it was almost exclusively members of the elite who could demonstrate their competencies in terms of experience, knowledge, and social relations. At the same time, however, this system was more open than its communal incarnation, since it was theoretically possible for any individual to join the inner circle of the best individuals, regardless of his origins.

In my opinion, it is not a coincidence that Bruni refers to the Ancients in his argument. His discourse relies on a specific image of election, the *suffragia* of Ancient Rome, to elaborate a new conception of political identity, in opposition to recent communal traditions. This is not the only subject with regard to which 15th-century political culture turned to the lexicon of Antiquity in order to justify a radical change in its political values.

Primary Sources

Archivio di Stato di Reggio Emilia, *Comune, Statuti* 1.

Brevi del comune e del popolo di Pisa del 1287 (1998), Ghignoli, A. (ed.) Rome: ISIME.

Breve et ordinamenta populi Pistorii, a. 1284 (2003), Nelli, R. di & Pinto, G. (eds.) Pistoia: Società storica pistoiese.

Bruni, L. (2001–2004) *Historiae Florentini populi*, 3 vols., Hankins, J. (ed.), Cambridge, MA: Harvard University Press.

Consuetudini e statuti reggiani del secolo XIII (1933), Cerlini, A. (ed.), Milan: Hoepli.

Il constituto del comune di Siena dell'anno 1262 (1896), Zdekauer, L. (ed.), Milan: Hoepli.

Gli statuti veronesi del 1276 colle correzioni e le aggiunte fino al 1313 (cod. Campostrini, Bibl. Civica di Verona), I (1940), Sandri, G. (ed.) Venice: Deputazione di storia patria per le Venezie.

Lo statuto di Piacenza del 1323 (2012), Fugazza, E. (ed.), Pavia: Pavia University Press.

Respublica Mutinensis (1306–1307) (1929–1932), Vicini, II, E.P. (ed.) Milan: Hoepli.

Statuta communis Fulginei (1969) Messini, A., Baldaccini, F., *et al.* (eds.), Perugia: Deputazione di storia patria per l'Umbria.

Statuta communis Parmae ab anno MCCLXVI ad annum circiter MCCCIX (1857), Ronchini, A. (ed.), Parma: Fiaccadori.

Statuta communitatis Novariae (1876), Ceruti, A. (ed.), Turin: Bocca (*HPM* XVI, *Leges Municipales*, II).

Statuti del Comune di Padova dal secolo XII all'anno 1285 (1873), Gloria, A. (ed.), Padua.

Statuti della provincia romana, II (1930), Tomassetti, F., Federici, V. & Egidi, P. (eds.), Rome: ISIME.

Statuti della Repubblica fiorentina editi a c. di Romolo Caggese – Nuova edizione (1999), Pinto, G., Salvestrini, F. & Zorzi, A. (eds.), Florence: Olschki.

Statuti di Bologna dell'anno 1288 (1237), Fasoli, G. & Sella, P. (eds.), Vatican City: Biblioteca Apostolica Vaticana.

Statuti di Volterra, I (1210–1224) (1251), Fiumi, E. (ed.), Florence: Deputazione di storia patria per la Toscana.

Statuti pistoiesi del secolo XII (1996), *Breve dei console, 1140–1180, Statuto del Podestà, 1162–1180*, Rauty, N. (ed.), Pistoia: Comune/ Società pistoiese di storia patria.

Statuto del comune di Perugia del 1279 (1996), 2 vols., Caprioli, S. (ed.) with the collaboration of Bartoli Langeli, A., Cardinali, C., Maiarelli, A., Merli, S., Perugia.

Statutum Lucani communis: anno 1308 (1991), Tirelli, V. (ed.) Lucca: Pacini Fazzi.

Stefani, Marchionne di Coppo (1903–1905) *Cronaca fiorentina*, Rodolico, N. (ed.) Bologna: Zanichelli.

Villani, G. (1991) *Nuova Cronica*, Porta, G. (ed.), Parma: Guanda.

References

Baggioni, L. (2016) *La fortresse de la raison: lectures de l'humanisme politique florentin d'après l'oeuvre de Coluccio Salutati*, Geneva: Droz.

Blanshei, S.R. (2010) *Politics and Justice in Late Medieval Bologna*, Leiden-Boston: Brill.

Cambiano, G. (2000) *Polis. Un modello per la cultura europea*, Rome-Bari: Laterza.

Christin, O. (2014) *Vox populi. Une histoire du vote avant le suffrage universel*, Paris: Seuil.

Costa, P. (1999) *Civitas. Storia della cittadinanza in Europa. Vol I. Dalla civiltà comunale al Settecento*, Rome-Bari: Laterza.

Dartmann, Ch. (2010) Eine Kultur der Niederlage? Wahlen in der italianischen Stadt des Hoch- un Spätmittelalters, in Ders. Wassilowsky, G. & Weller, Th. (eds.) *'Technik und Symbolik vormoderner Wahlfahren', Historische Zeitschrift*, 52, pp. 53–70, Berlin: De Gruyter.

Dartmann, Ch. (2012) *Politische Interaktion in der italienischen Stadtkommune (11–14–Jahrundert)*, Ostfildern: Jan Thorbecke Verlag.

Fioravanti, G. (1979) Politiae Orientalium et Aegyptiorum. Alberto Magno e la Politica aristotelica, *Annali della Scuola normale superiore di Pisa — Classe di Lettere e Filosofia*, Series III, No. IX/1, pp. 195–246, Pisa: Scuola normale superiore.

Gaudemet, J. with the collaboration of Dubois, J., Duval, A., Champagne, J. (1979) *Les élections dans l'Église latine des origines au XVle siècle*, Paris: Lanore.

Guidi, G. (1972) I sistemi elettorali agli uffici del Comune di Firenze nel primo Trecento: Il sorgere della elezione per squittinio (1300–1328), *Archivio Storico Italiano*, 130, pp. 373–424, Florence: Olschki.

Ianziti, G. (2012) *Writing history in Renaissance Italy. Leonardo Bruni and the Uses of the Past*, Cambridge, MA: Harvard University Press.

Isenmann, E. (1997), *Wahl, II. Ratswahl, in Lexikon des Mittelalters*, VIII/9, Munich: Lexma, coll. 1911–1912.

Hayat, S. & Sintomer, Y. (eds.) (2013) *La représentation politique*, monographic issue of *Raisons politiques*, 50, Paris: Presses de Science Po.

Hollard, V. (2010) *Le rituel du vote. Les assemblées romaines du peuple*, Paris: CNRS.

Keller, H. (2014a) *Il laboratorio politico del comune medievale*, Naples: Liguori.

Keller, H. (2014b) Formes électorales et conception de la communauté dans les communes italiennes (12e–14e siècle), *Revue française de Science politique*, LXIV (6), pp. 1083–1107.

Judde de Larivière, C. (2020) Ducal Elections, Institutional Usages, and Popular Practices: Drawing Lots in the Republic of Venice, in *Sortition and Democracy: Practices, Instruments, Theories*, Exeter: Imprint Academic.

Maire Vigueur, J.C. & Faini, E. (2010) *Il sistema politico dei comuni Italiani (secoli XII–XIV)*, Milan: Bruno Mondadori.

Manin, B. (1995) *Principes du gouvernement représentatif*, Paris: Calmann-Lévy.

Milani, G. (2003) *L'esclusione dal comune. Conflitti e bandi politici a Bologna e in altre città italiane tra XII e XIV secolo*, Rome: Istituto storico italiano per il Medioevo.

Moulin, L. (1953) Les origines religieuses des techniques électorales et délibératives modernes, *Revue internationale d'histoire politique et constitutionnelle*, new series, 10, pp. 106–148.

Moulin, L. (1958) Sanior et maior pars. Note sur l'évolution des techniques électorales dans les Ordres religieux du VIe au XIIIe siècle, *Revue historique de Droit français et étranger*, series IV, XXXVI, pp. 348–397 and 491–529.

Najemy, J. (1982) *Corporatism and consensus in Florentine electoral politics, 1280–1400*, Chapel Hill, NC: University of North Carolina Press.

Peneau, C. (2008) Élections et pouvoirs politiques. Une introduction, in Peneau, C. (ed.) *Élections et pouvoirs politiques du VIIe au XVIIe siècle*, Actes du colloque réuni à Paris 12 du 30 novembre au 2 décembre 2006, pp. 13–40, Paris: Bière.

Richard, O. (2008) *Élire pour contraindre: L'élection du conseil de Ratisbonne à la fin du Moyen Âge, dans Élections et pouvoirs politiques du VIIe au XVIIe siècle*, Actes du colloque réuni à Paris 12 du 30 novembre au 2 décembre 2006, Peneau, C. (ed.), pp. 197–212, Paris: Bière.

Rigaudière, A. (2002) Les procureurs urbains en Auvergne, Velay et Lyonnais aux XIVe et XVe siècle, in 'La représentation dans la tradition du *Ius civile* en Occident, Mélanges de l'École française de Rome — Moyen Age', 114 (1), pp. 121–149, Rome: École française de Rome.

Ruffini, E. (1977) *La ragione dei più: ricerche sulla storia del principio maggioritario*, Bologna: Il Mulino.

Sintomer, Y. (2009) De Leonardo Bruni à Francesco Guicciardini: actualité de l'humanisme civique?, *Raisons Politiques*, 36, pp. 5–24, Paris: Presses de Sciences Po.

Sintomer, Y. (2020) *Between Radical and Deliberative Democracy. Random Selection in Politics from Athens to Contemporary Experiments*, Cambridge: Cambridge University Press (forthcoming).

Tamba, G. (1982) Consigli elettorali degli ufficiali del comune bolognese alla fine del secolo XIII, *Rassegna degli archivi di stato*, XLII, pp. 34–95, Rome: Ufficio centrale per i beni archivistici.

Tanzini, L. (2014) *A consiglio. La vita politica nell'Italia dei comuni*, Rome-Bari: Laterza.

Tanzini, L. (2017) *Il fantasma della rappresentanza: sorteggio e rotazione delle cariche nelle città comunali (secc. XIII-XV)*, in Menzinger, S. (ed.) *Cittadinanze medievali. Dinamiche di appartenenza a un corpo comunitario*, pp. 145–174, Rome: Viella.

Théry, J. (2001) Moyen Age, in Perrineau, P. & Reynié , D. (eds.) *Dictionnaire du vote*, pp. 667–678, Paris: PUF.

Vallerani, M. (1994) La città e le sue istituzioni. Ceti dirigenti, oligarchia e politica nella medievistica italiana del Novecento, *Annali dell'istituto storico italo-germanico di Trento*, 20, pp. 165–230, Bologna: Il Mulino.

Vallerani, M. (2011) Comune e comuni: una dialettica non risolta, in *Sperimentazioni di governo nell'Italia centro-settentrionale nel processo storico dal primo comune alla signoria*, pp. 9–34, Bologna: Bologna University Press.

Claire Judde de Larivière

Ducal Elections, Institutional Usages, and Popular Practices

Drawing Lots in the Republic of Venice

Translated by Cynthia J. Johnson

The Republic of Venice occupies a privileged place in the history of the political uses of the lottery. The procedure for electing the doge, who ruled the city's institutions for life, combined voting with drawing lots, which was thought to prevent electoral corruption and the influence of factions. The complexity of this process has long been subject to a multitude of analyses and interpretations, and has made Venice one of the emblematic political regimes when considering the lottery in the period before political 'modernity'. Yet, there were many other uses of the lottery throughout late Medieval and Early Modern Venetian society. Whether selecting the electors of young nobles for early entry to the Great Council, the carpenters who could work at the Arsenal, or the parishes who would organize important religious rituals, the drawing of lots was widely used throughout Venetian society from the Middle Ages to the end of the Republic. It was part of larger culture of voting (Judde de Larivière, 2018b).

The prevalence of this practice raises questions about the meaning that the actors of the time attributed to this process and what it reveals about their conception of society. Keeping these complex and long procedures over centuries reveals a deep attachment to chance and to the values that it was supposed to guarantee. In Venice, the principles of fairness and equality framed the horizons of expectation and political theory shared among patricians. These principles were the foundations of an ideology that considered drawing lots an effective way to put into practice the values that framed the political culture of the rulers as well as the inhabitants.

The purpose of this chapter is to show the diversity of the lottery by considering the various areas in which this practice was used. Rather than analysing medieval thinkers' and humanists' theoretical discourses and justifications, this study focuses on practices and actions. In examining the moral economy of the lottery, we shall see how it embodied the ideals of justice, equality, and impartiality. Its widespread and generalized use reveals the foundations of the Republic's political culture, which dictated the sharing of resources and duties: the power and government of the city among patricians, work and armed service for the inhabitants, as well as, more generally, a multitude of other means and tasks whose distribution called for random attribution.

The examples here refer mainly to practices whose precise origins are rather difficult to date, but began sometime between the 12th and 14th centuries. Electoral procedures, decision-making processes, political practices, and methods of appointment within guilds and confraternities date back to the early days of the medieval city. At that time, the rulers and the inhabitants created procedures that would later be adapted and adjusted to political and social changes. Consequently, although the institutional and demographic configuration of Venice changed profoundly over time, the ways of doing things were still often inspired by practices established in the communal period. These practices were taken up again during the Renaissance by thinkers and humanists who wanted to theorize and explain Venetian political uses. However, this chapter does not seek to unravel the successive chronological layers and changes to the lottery, but rather to show the ubiquity of this practice and what it reveals about Venetian political ideals.

Sharing and Distributing Power

In the middle of the 12th century, Venice became a commune like many other Italian cities. This step enabled the city to negotiate its definitive independence from the Byzantine Empire, which up until then had claimed political authority over the lagoon. Communal institutions were gradually established, headed by a group of richer and more influential inhabitants such as wealthy merchants, who succeeded in seizing power. These leaders became part of an assembly, the Great Council (*Maggior Consiglio*), which quickly became the city's main political institution. Through a well-known political process — the *Serrata* (closure) of the Great Council — which took place between the end of the 13th century and the first decades of 14th, the members of the Great Council asserted that they formed an hereditary nobility. They also claimed that only this nobility was allowed to join the assembly and to run the city-state's institutions (Chojnacki, 1997; Rösch, 2000). The contours of the Venetian institutional apparatus were increasingly specified over time. The jurisdictions and functions of the magistracies were defined at the same time as the election procedures for the hundreds of government and administrative offices (over 700 posts in the early 16th century), most of which were organized by the Great Council (Maranini, 1927–31; Finlay, 1980).

Venice was thus an oligarchic republic. The city, and the territorial state in the Mediterranean and in Italy of which it was the capital, were collectively run by the noble (or patrician) group. The Venetian 'constitution', composed of a disparate set of texts and laws, established the collegial sharing of power. It was necessary to prevent certain families from seizing power for themselves as had been the case elsewhere in Italy, such as Milan where the Visconti took over from the end of the 13th century, or Florence with the Medici in the 15th century. The assemblies as well as the magistracies were composed of nobles who shared power: between forty and sixty members for the assemblies and three to five for the offices and magistracies. This multiplication of institutions and the rapid rotation of posts also meant the absence of specialization; the patricians ruled without favouring a certain type of office or jurisdiction. This prevented factions or family groups from seizing certain institutions or considering a specific area as their own specialty. The potential influence of pressure groups was thus limited by the fragmentation of offices and duties.

The only magistracy occupied by a single person was that of the doge, who was also elected for life (Da Mosto, 1960; Benzoni, 1982). It was the only office that was not subject to a division of power or a mandate limited in time. As we shall see, this explains in part the recourse to drawing lots to elect him. Originally, in the 8th century, the doge's power was military. Then, as Venice became a commune in the 12th century, the doge was seen not as the ruler of the city but as the incarnation of the city-state's sovereignty, which the elites shared as a group, like a collective figure of a prince. The doge did not rule the patriciate; he was more like its emanation and represented the power that the group possessed collectively. The doge, therefore, could not defend the particular interest of any one clan or belong to any faction or party: he served the patriciate as a whole and defended the common good of the entire city. The ducal office was reserved for patricians who had demonstrated their abilities over their long careers. The doge was generally chosen from among the nine procurators of San Marco, the wisest and richest magistrates of the city (Mueller, 1977). Their advanced age at the time of their election also prevented them from confiscating power. The system worked well, as noble conspiracies were virtually non-existent in Venice; only Doge Marin Falier in 1354 was stripped of his office and sentenced to death after attempting a *coup d'etat*.

The Election of the Doge

It is therefore the specific nature of the office of the doge, as it was bound up with the institutional principles organizing the regime, that enables us to understand the reasons behind this complex electoral procedure. Established in 1268, this process remained fairly constant over time and at the end of the Middle Ages began to be commented on and analysed (Sanudo, 1980, pp. 85–90, pp. 145 *sq.*; Contarini, 2003, pp. 86–92). Since then, the system's complexity has continued to inspire a great number of interpretations (Da Mosto, 1960; Finlay 1978; Muir, 1981, pp. 275 *sq.*; Tucci, 1982).

First, let us briefly summarize this procedure, which began after the funeral of the previous doge. The election began in the Great Council, where thirty members over the age of thirty were drawn by lot and were then isolated in a room. A new drawing of lots was held among them so as to select only nine out of the thirty. These nine patricians then elected forty other patricians (seven votes out of nine were required to be elected). Then, the nine returned to the Great Council Hall with the list of the forty candidates they had elected. Their names were publicly announced to verify that they belonged to different families, since it was forbidden for two members of the same family — brothers, fathers, cousins, uncles — to be part of the same electoral committee. After this first phase of the election, there were seven similar phases in succession combining a lottery and voting. The forty patricians met in turn and twelve of them were drawn by lot. That twelve then elected twenty-five patricians, of whom nine were drawn by lot. These nine patricians elected forty-five patricians, among whom eleven were drawn by lot. The latter, in turn, elected forty-one patricians. It was this group of forty-one who formed the committee charged with electing the doge.

1,500/2,500 members of the Great Council => lottery => 30
30 => lottery => 9
9 => vote => 40
40 => lottery => 12
12 => vote => 25
25 => lottery => 9
9 => vote => 45
45 => lottery => 11
11 => vote 41
41 = election committee

Fig. 1: The stages of ducal election.

The stated goal was to form an electoral committee made up of forty-one patricians who were considered able to make an appropriate political choice. In other words, the committee was composed in such a way that no interest group or faction was represented more than any other. It then met to elect the doge (with at least twenty-five positive votes needed out of forty-one voters), a procedure that could last several days or even weeks. In general, the elected doge was one of these forty-one electors and was chosen because he was experienced and trustworthy. Whatever their disagreements and divergent interests, the electors were considered apt to make the 'right' choice.

This long and complex procedure for establishing the electoral committee had an essential ritual dimension, which transposed the impartiality of the procedure into action. On the Sunday following the funeral of the previous doge, the bells of the Church of San Marco rang out to call the patricians to assemble at the Doge's Palace. The vacancy of the ducal throne was a special moment in the Venetian political calendar, as in Rome between two pontificates. In the capital of Christendom, the election of the pope was longer and required the involvement of civil authorities during a period often marked by disturbances and riots. In Venice, while excesses were rare, the power vacancy could make the political situation more tense, especially since there was no authority to substitute for the doge. The population knew the importance of what was playing out behind the closed doors of the Doge's Palace and awaited the result of the election to approve the patricians' choice (Van Gelder, 2018). At the end of the election, the bells of San Marco resounded once again to call the people to gather. Shops and workshops in the city closed and bonfires were lit while the inhabitants organized parades and celebrations. Traditionally, the inhabitants gathered at Piazza San Marco to cheer the new doge, who then displayed largesse and gifts, throwing coins down to the people. This highly ritualized ceremony ended several days of political tension, whose secrets were hidden within the walls of the Doge's Palace.

Despite its complexity, this electoral process would last for centuries, even though it was sometimes criticized. In 1475, for example, after the election of Pietro Mocenigo, chronicler Domenico Malipiero recounted the scandal that several important senators had not been chosen among the forty-one (Finlay, 1980, p. 144). In 1521, a proposal was made for the forty-one to be directly elected by the Great Council, primarily to limit the length and the cost of the process. Debates on this suggestion would continue throughout the Early Modern period, although the original method was never abandoned (Muir, 1981, p. 280).

Political Fiction?

Alternating drawing lots and votes sought to avoid corruption and prevent clans from imposing their influence. Even the most powerful patricians, despite their best efforts, could not possibly control the voters' choices at all stages of the proceedings. Moreover, by isolating the electoral committees in separate parts of the Doge's Palace, contact between the members of the Great Council and the electors was avoided and the latter could not be pressured by the former.

Drawing lots also seemed the most fair, since it gave the members of the Great Council the impression that they were involved in choosing the doge and were part of the process. The successive steps meant that a great many patricians were consulted (as many as 180 of them), which 'diluted' the decision-making process and allowed everyone to believe that he had or could have had a part in selecting the doge. Even though all voices were not heard, each person could potentially be drawn or designated. This also prevented criticism: since everyone may have helped choose the new doge, it was difficult to challenge the final result.

This Venetian system has long intrigued and even fascinated historians, in particular North American scholars who viewed *La Serenissima* as one of the precursors of capitalism and republican democracy. But the complexity of the doge's election has also raised doubts as to its effectiveness. A recent study subjected the procedure to probability testing and showed that there was in fact some logic to the procedure and that it was not entirely random, although that logic was more empirical than theoretical (Mowbray and Gollmann, 2007). The number of rounds and electors was optimal to limit the effects of corruption and the power of factions while ensuring that minority groups could participate. While this may have worked in theory, whether that result was achieved in practice is hard to prove, since it is difficult to precisely map the influence groups within the Great Council as well as to determine whether there were attempts at electoral corruption. Doing so would require reconstructing the composition of the Great Council during a specific ducal election to measure the actual effects of drawing lots. The difficulty lies not only in the large number of patricians involved (up to 2,500 in the 16th century), but above all in the complexity of reconstituting interest groups in Venice. Several attempts have been made to sketch out the contours of the various 'parties': young against old, old noble houses against newcomers, maritime wealth against landed fortunes, and so on. It is precisely because the Venetian system worked well that it is not easy to identify the members of these groups, their composition, their political influence, and whether they lasted over time. Yet without this information, our understanding of the doge's election remains theoretical. Certainly, repeating the steps of the process limited the power of factions and ensured that the wisest and most competent patricians were among the forty-one electors. However, those same results could have been attained by another means as well and may not have been due to the election process.

Thus, the actual effects of this process can be questioned. The first nine electors had to choose from the pool of the Great Council, which was the same pool from which the last forty-one voters were chosen. Does this mean that the successive steps sought to give merely the illusion of justice, rather than truly guaranteeing the absence of corruption? Whatever the complexity of the process leading to the final stage, this complexity was decisive. One might argue that the election process was merely staging and ritual, making a show of the fight against corruption. Yet even if that were the case, it does not in any way detract from its importance: whether its effects were due to the laws of probability or the illusion of impartiality, the procedure did limit attempts at corruption and had the effect of asserting that corruption was not tolerated in the system. The ducal election functioned because it imposed a discourse of equality that the patricians adhered to and believed in. The ritual existed to make that discourse of equality manifest to all—the fact that it lasted for so long is proof of its effectiveness.

The ducal election was thus partly fiction, but it was a fiction that succeeded in producing the appearance of consensus. The election was based on a convention that patricians were equals, which corresponded precisely to the principles informing the city's institutions. Drawing lots also reaffirmed the refusal of tyranny and of personal power, which the constitution tacitly founding the Republic and the agreement connecting the governing group had been elaborated specifically against. That is why, beyond the rather particular election of the doge, the drawing of lots was widely employed in Venice. Leaving the decision between candidates or electors to chance was part of the discourse of impartiality that was necessary for the cohesion of the noble group.

Institutional Uses

The ducal election, although emblematic, was far from being the only election to rely on drawing lots; many elections used it at one point or another in the process. Although an exhaustive inventory of uses is beyond the scope of this chapter, I would insist here on the diversity of those uses, for example designating the heads (*capi*) of certain assemblies such as the judicial magistracy of the Council of Forty (*Quarantia Criminale*) (Sanudo, 1879–1903, VIII–2). Many other elections to offices also had recourse to lotteries, always with the idea of avoiding electoral fraud and pressure from factions. Beginning in 1482, the Great Council took new steps to organize the elections which took place within that body every Sunday. In general, nine elections were held at the beginning of each session. For each election, four electoral committees (*mani*) of nine members were constituted. Therefore, thirty-six committees needed to be constituted, which was done using a lottery.

Three large bronze urns, covered inside with red velvet, were placed in front of the tribune of the *Signoria* (a group of sixteen patricians, including the doge, who headed the institutions), and each was monitored by one of the doge's counsellors. Placing them high on platforms was done to make sure that no one could look inside. To constitute the four electoral committees, about 800 balls of silver and thirty golden balls were placed in the two side urns. The middle one contained twenty-four balls of silver and thirty-six golden ones. The sources describe these balls as small, round or oval discs, the size of a cherry or slightly larger. They were originally made of wax and then cloth to prevent them from sticking to the sides of the urn (Mueller, 2013). The first random drawing, done according to the benches on which the patricians were seated, decided the order of their passage to draw from the urns. The benches were placed on four sides of the room, in four directions symbolized by well-known spaces in Venice: Piazza San Marco (north), the island of San Giorgio (south), the Arsenal quarter of Castello (east), and the Broglio, a space located in front of the Doge's Palace on the Piazzetta (west). The patricians each rose in turn and proceeded to the side urns. If they drew a ball of silver, they would return to sit down. If they drew a golden ball, they would then draw again in the central urn: if that ball were silver, they would also return to sit down; if it was golden, they were then on the electoral committee. A notary cried out the person's name and another in the middle of the room repeated it to ensure that the large number of patricians present heard it. This was done to verify that two members of the same family had not been appointed to the same electoral committee. The candidates who had drawn two successive golden balls then had to sit on a special bench near the doge, turning their backs on the other members of the Great Council to avoid receiving instructions by signs on how to vote.

Once the electoral committee was composed, members had to swear before the Grand Chancellor (the head of the Chancery) to carry out their task impartially. Two secretaries came to escort the committee members to small rooms where the election would be held (four separate rooms therefore for the four committees). The members were seated in order of their age. The youngest of the nine electors was given a list of the nine posts to be filled, arranged in hierarchical order and preceded by a number. A secretary read out the current electoral laws, recalling in particular those against fraud. He then placed nine balls in an urn with the numbers corresponding to the positions to be filled. Each person drew a number and this established which patrician would be in charge of the election for which office.

For the first post, the patrician who had been appointed had to suggest the name of a candidate, who could be a member of his family, or even himself. Then the committee proceeded to vote. With six 'yes' votes, the candidate was elected; otherwise, another name has to be suggested and then voted on. The election continued until nine patricians were proposed for the nine positions. Once the election was over, the electoral committees did not return to the Great Council—the two secretaries communicated the results to the Grand Chancellor by giving him a note with the candidates proposed by each committee. The Chancery then verified that all the candidates were eligible for the office for which they had been elected, by consulting the registers of magistrate lists (in Venice, there was the *contumacia*, a period during which one could not fill the same post again). For each post, the Great Council was finally presented with four potential candidates, and the assembly voted after the members of the candidate's close family had left the room. The person who received the most approval votes was elected.

The Grand Chancellor ran the institution responsible for verifying the legitimacy of the patricians and for drafting and archiving the documents produced by Venetian institutions (Zannini, 1993). He was also designated by a procedure involving the drawing of lots. Selected among the *cittadini* — the bourgeois of Venice — he was elected for life. He was often considered the equivalent of the doge for the non-noble inhabitants, hence the importance accorded to his election. For example, in 1523, six citizens presented themselves before the Great Council, which on that day was composed of 1,673 voters. Lots were drawn for the order of passage of the candidates, and then a vote was organized in turn for the six candidates (Sanudo, 1879–1903, XXXIV–377).

This practice of drawing lots for the order of the candidates' passage was also done in Murano, a neighbouring island of Venice with relatively autonomous status (Judde de Larivière, 2018a, pp. 39–45). While it was subject to Venice, the island had its own institutions, in particular a limited deliberative assembly termed the Council of Thirty, which governed in collaboration with the *podestà*, the Venetian representative elected by the Great Council to govern the island. Murano also had a Chancellor, responsible for producing and archiving official documents. For his election, various candidates were invited to present themselves and to justify their candidature to the Council of Thirty ('Statuto', p. 245; Judde de Larivière, 2018a, p. 83). Each wrote his name on a piece of paper (*bollettino*) and then lots were drawn for the order of presenting the candidates. A mixed lottery/voting procedure was also used for renewing the Council of Thirty. The *podestà* and members of the outgoing council nominated fifty people of Murano who were eligible for office and wrote their names on pieces of paper. The order of voting was then randomly drawn and votes (yes or no) were cast successively for each of the fifty candidates. The sophistication of the electoral process shows that the legislators knew that the election procedure could influence the results, and so even the order of candidates had to be entrusted to chance.

Finally, there was another political use of the lottery that was especially important for Venetian patricians: the *Balla d'oro*, a ritual that marked the entry of young noblemen into politics (Chojnacki, 2000). The ceremony, whose first mentions date to 1319, guaranteed early entry to the Great Council for a small number of these young nobles (before age 25, the age of political majority). The choice was made by drawing lots, which took place every year on December 4, the day of St.

Barbara, hence the ceremony's name, Barbarella. The patricians who wished to participate had to register their sons, who had to be at least 18 years of age and legitimate. The name of each candidate was written on a piece of paper and then placed in an urn (*capello*). There was a second urn containing a number of balls equivalent to the number of candidates, one fifth of which were golden balls. The doge would pull out a name at the same time that a young boy (*ballottino*) drew a ball: if it was golden, the candidate was guaranteed early entry into the council. The ceremonial was obviously of great importance to all the patricians present, the young candidates as well as their families, and the doge had to be present. The public and ritual character of the lottery was essential, as it was for all the other uses mentioned thus far.

In the end, it was perhaps the image of impartiality that counted most: whether lots were drawn to decide the order of candidates' passage in the chancellery or to choose the head of an assembly, the procedure was intended to show the distributed nature of power. Government offices were numerous in Venice and the drawing of lots had the appearance of impartiality and equality. The sophistication of the various procedures in these political institutions also reveal a real awareness of the role of the state, and the confidence patricians had in their ability to defend the principle of equality. The multiplication of gestures and rituals, as well as their public character, made the procedures acceptable and reinforced belief in the justice of the institutional system.

Beyond Patrician Practices

Patrician institutions did not have the monopoly on drawing lots. The process was used for many other kinds of selection at different levels of Venetian society, starting in the communal period. For example, the lottery was used to select the inhabitants who had to defend the city with arms. Venice, like most medieval Italian city-states, did not have a permanent army. If necessary, it had recourse to the *condottieri* and their companies of mercenaries (Hale and Mallett, 1984). But in military situations that demanded larger contingents, mobilizing the inhabitants of Venice or subjects of the Stato was also needed. From the end of the 13th century, the procedure for designating conscripts was elaborated: Venice was divided into six large administrative districts, the *sestieri*, and within each of them lots were drawn for mobilization (Settia, 1995, p. 464). Some years later, conscripts were chosen through each *contrada* (the administrative equivalent of the parish). The procedure was public and highly ritualized. The inhabitants were summoned to certain places in the city: at the Lido, where training operations were generally held, or in Sant'Elena, east of the city near the Arsenal (Zug Tucci, 1997, pp. 254–255). The administrative districts were chosen in turn by lottery and then the inhabitants were chosen, designating who would be mobilized first, then second, and so on. Chance meant that each person had the same probability of being selected: while with political elections the practice guaranteed equal chances, here it was a matter of equitably distributing military duty. To draw lots for military conscripts was clearly a means of selecting among the inhabitants, the majority of whom sought to avoid the dangers of war.

This is what happened in the first half of the 16th century when Venice changed the way it recruited its sailors (Lo Basso, 2004). Prior to that time, they were paid volunteers chosen for their experience at sea. But faced with the lack of men for the galleys, from the 1530s Venice decided to have recourse to condemned criminals and to the subjects of the Terra ferma (the mainland). Yet neither of these groups proved to be up to the task and other ways had to be found to mobilize the population. In 1539, it was decided that the guilds and the major confraternities (*Scuole Grandi*) would designate the contingents of galley sailors (Trebbi, 1994, p. 189). The system was gradually modified until, in 1595, a new method was established: lists of guild members were used and the people who had to serve were drawn by lot. Very rapidly, the wealthiest artisans circumvented the system by paying their less well-off peers to serve in their stead, and thus changes to the law were again necessary.

The guilds, or professional associations, were indeed familiar with the drawing of lots. Their heads, the *gastaldi* and *soprastanti*, were chosen among the members of the trade through a procedure combining lottery and peer designation established at the end of the 13th century. In the glass-makers' guild, for example, the *gastaldo* had to choose twenty men among whom five were drawn by lot, and these five were to elect the new *gastaldo*. In the caulkers' guild, nine electors were drawn by lot among members over 25 years of age and residing in Venice for at least 10 years, and those nine elected the guild's representatives. The shoemakers' and blacksmiths' guilds also used the lottery in similar ways to designate the electors of their representatives (Bonfiglio Dosio, 1995, p. 599).

Moreover, the guilds used the procedure for other decisions. For example, *ternieri* (sellers of edible oil, honey, and cheese) attributed market stalls by drawing lots (Bonfiglio Dosio, 1995, p. 611). The gondoliers working at the *traghetti* (the ferry system connecting several places in the city, the lagoon, and the neighbouring cities) resorted to the lottery in 1535, after the death of the gondolier who worked the passage in the Ghetto Nuovo (Biblioteca del Museo Correr, Mariegole, 187, Barcaruoli al traghetto, 13–13v°). His replacement was left to the choice of one of the three *provveditori di Comun* (magistrates in charge of supervising commercial activities), who had to be designated by lottery. In the 17th century, the booksellers decided to use the lottery to divide up production (Zorzi, 1997, p. 935). In a period of intense competition, lots were drawn to decide which of the small printers would produce study books, which was a large share of the book market. The various booksellers and printers could thus hope to obtain these profitable contracts to keep their business afloat.

Chance was also used in the public shipyard of the Arsenal, where the organization of work was controlled by the government. Workers at the Arsenal were generally employed in the many private shipyards in Venice, but regularly came to work in the public shipyard for pay. From the middle of the 15th century, several laws were written to ensure a fair distribution of labour between the various candidates. In the 1460s, a rotation system was set up for carpenters (Caniato, 1996, p. 665). Those who wanted to work at the Arsenal had their names inscribed on slips of paper or tokens (*tessere nominative*) kept in a bag by the guild's *gastaldo*. The leaders of the shipyard had to seek out the *gastaldo* when they needed to draw lots for the names of those who would work at the Arsenal.

Finally, the lay confraternities (*scuole*) also used the procedure to establish the distribution of alms. For example, a lottery was used when deciding which poor girls would have their dowry paid by the *scuola* (Fortini Brown, 1996, p. 344). After an examination of the candidates to verify their morality, lots were drawn to decide which would benefit from the *scuola*'s help. In addition to charity, these confraternities played an essential role in the religious and political rituals that punctuated the Venetian calendar and they also used the lottery in them. For example, lots were drawn for one of the most popular medieval Venetian rituals, the Twelve Marys, which appeared in the middle of the 12th century (Muir, 1981, p. 143). Organized between the end of January and Candlemas, twelve statues of the Virgin were placed in two of the city's parishes. The parishes were chosen by drawing lots as were the six noble houses in which the statues were exhibited.

Finally, it should be noted that the *lotto*, invented in Italy in the 15th century, became very popular in Venice in the following century (Welch, 2008). The chronicler Marino Sanudo reported the huge success of the game in 1522: 'Rialto has been invaded by the lottery', he lamented, and 'nobody cares about anything else' (Sanudo, 1879–1903,

XXXIII 47–8). The state was in charge of organizing the lottery through specialized officers, the *sensali*, who supervised the sale of tickets and the drawing in exchange for a share of the profits. Drawing the winning tickets was done during a large public ceremony, to which the population was invited in order to ensure that there had been no fraud. Inhabitants themselves were even drawn by lots to assist the officers conducting the proceedings. The drawing generally happened inside or in front of one of the city's large churches, especially those of the mendicant orders such as Santa Maria Gloriosa dei Frari or Santi Giovanni e Paolo, or near the Rialto in the San Polo area. These vast squares allowed large crowds to attend this performance of Chance, with trumpets and bells ringing when the winning tickets were drawn.

Conclusion

In the Doge's Palace on the walls of the Sala dell'Anticollegio, four Tintoretto paintings from the 1570s represent the allegory of Concord, the founding value of the Republic. In one of them, *Mercury and the Three Graces*, a young woman lays her hand on a die, a symbol of the chance that governed the selection of city's rulers. Chance was of inestimable value in a republic that considered impartiality, distribution of power, and equality as the founding values of concord and as guaranteeing the stability of patricians' rule over the city.

The drawing of lots was considered to protect the common good, a discursive justification omnipresent in Venetian political discourse. Beyond mere rhetoric, the common good also served to justify actions and the horizon of expectation shared by the inhabitants of the lagoon. In the Republic, it was necessary to defend what belonged to all. This shared interest was not the same for patricians and for ordinary people, but nevertheless referred to a reality that everyone could name and call on. Defending the common good and distributing resources ensured equality, which the drawing of lots also allowed. The supposed or actual impartiality of the procedure, as well as its public and ritual dimension, made equality permissible. Whether patrician or *popolano*, a member of a trade or a *lotto* player, living in Venice meant familiarity with drawing lots. In a society where justice remained one of the main drivers of political discourse, recourse to chance was a highly respected practice.

References

Benzoni, G. (ed.) (1982) *I dogi*, Milan: Electa.

Bonfiglio Dosio, G. (1995) Le arti cittadine, *Storia di Venezia. Dalle origini alla caduta della Serenissima*, vol. II, pp. 577–625, Rome: Istituto della Enciclopedia italiana.

Caniato, G. (1996) L'Arsenale: maestranze e organizzazione del lavoro, *Storia di Venezia. Dalle origini alla caduta della Serenissima*, vol. V, pp. 641–677, Rome: Istituto della Enciclopedia italiana, Rome.

Chojnacki, S. (1997) La formazione della nobiltà dopo la Serrata, *Storia di Venezia. Dalle origini alla caduta della Serenissima*, vol. III, pp. 641–725, Rome: Istituto della Enciclopedia italiana.

Chojnacki, S. (2000) Political Adulthood, *Women and Men in Renaissance Venice*, pp. 227–243, Baltimore, MD: The Johns Hopkins University Press.

Contarini, G. (2003) *La Repubblica e i Magistrati di Vinegia* (Venice, 1544), Florence: V. Conti ed.

Da Mosto, A. (1960) *I dogi di Venezia nella vita pubblica e privata*, Milan: Aldo Martello Editore.

Finlay, R. (1978) Politics and the family in Renaissance Venice: the election of Doge Andrea Gritti, *Studi Veneziani*, pp. 97–117.

Finlay, R. (1980) *Politics in Renaissance Venice*, London: Benn.

Fortini Brown, P. (1996) Le Scuole, *Storia di Venezia. Dalle origini alla caduta della Serenissima*, vol. V, pp. 307–354, Rome: Istituto della Enciclopedia italiana.

Hale, J.R. & Mallett, M. (1984) *The Military Organization of a Renaissance State*, Cambridge: Cambridge University Press.

Judde de Lariviere, C. (2018a) *The Revolt of Snowballs: Murano Confronts Venice, 1511*, Cohen, T.V. (trans.), London: Routledge.

Judde de Lariviere, C. (2018b) 'Il fait bon voir de tout leur sénat ballotter': The ubiquity of voting in late medieval and Renaissance Venice, in Ferente, S., Kunčević, L. & Pattenden, M. (eds.) *Cultures of Voting in Pre-modern Europe*, pp. 242–256, London: Routledge.

Lo Basso, L. (2004) *Uomini da remo: galee e galeotti del Mediterraneo in età moderna*, Milan: Selene edizioni.

Maranini, G. (1927–31) *La costituzione di Venezia*, 2 vol., Venice.

Mowbray, M. & Gollmann, D. (2007) Electing the Doge of Venice: Analysis of a 13th Century Protocol, *HPL-2007-28R1*, online.

Mueller, R.C. (1977) *The Procuratori di San Marco and the Venetian Credit Market*, New York: Arno.

Mueller, R.C. (2013) Nel segreto dell'urna. La riforma della procedura elettorale adottata nel 1492 dal Consiglio dei dieci di Venezia, *Quaderni Veneti*, 2 (1–2).

Muir, E. (1981) *Civic Ritual in Renaissance Venice*, Princeton, NJ: Princeton University Press.

Rösch, G. (2000) The Serrata of the Great Council and Venetian Society, 1286–1323, in Martin, J. & Romano, D. (eds.) *Venice Reconsidered: The History and Civilization of an Italian City-State, 1297–1797*, pp. 67–88, Baltimore, MD: The Johns Hopkins University Press.

Sanudo, M. (1879–1903), *I Diarii*, Venice.

Sanudo, M. (1980) *De origine, situ et magistratibus urbis Venetae ovvero La città di Venetia (1493–1530)*, Caracciolo Aricò, A. (ed.), Milan: Centro Studi Medioevali e Rinascimentali.

Settia, A.A. (1995) L'apparato militare, *Storia di Venezia. Dalle origini alla caduta della Serenissima*, vol. II, pp. 461–505, Rome: Istituto della Enciclopedia italiana.

'Statuto de Muran del 1502', Pasqualetto, M. (ed.) (1989) in *Statuti della laguna veneta dei secoli XIV-XVI*, pp. 207–287, Rome: Jouvence.

Trebbi, G. (1994) La società veneziana, *Storia di Venezia. Dalle origini alla caduta della Serenissima*, vol. VI, pp. 129–213, Rome: Istituto della Enciclopedia italiana.

Tucci, U. (1982) I meccanismi dell'elezione dogale, in Benzoni, G. (ed.) *I dogi*, pp. 107–124, Milan: Electa.

Van Gelder, M. (2018) The People's Prince: Popular Politics in Early Modern Venice, *Journal of Modern History*, 90.2, June, pp. 249–291.

Welch, E. (2008) Lotteries in Early Modern Italy, *Past and Present*, 199 (1), pp. 71–112.

Zannini, A. (1993) *Burocrazia e burocrati a Venezia in età moderna: i cittadini originari (sec. XVI–XVIII)*, Venice: Istituto veneto di scienze, lettere ed arti.

Zorzi, M. (1997) La produzione e la circolazione del libro, *Storia di Venezia. Dalle origini alla caduta della Serenissima*, vol. VI, pp. 921–985, Rome: Istituto della Enciclopedia italiana.

Zug Tucci, H. (1997) Le milizie terrestri, *Storia di Venezia. Dalle origini alla caduta della Serenissima*, vol. III, pp. 251–296, Rome: Istituto della Enciclopedia italiana.

Yann Lignereux

The Drawing of Lots versus the State

Fate, Divine Inspiration, and the Vocation of Town Magistrates in 17th-Century France

Translated by Cynthia J. Johnson

In 1654, the day after Oliver Cromwell was appointed as Lord Protector of the Commonwealth of England, Scotland, and Ireland, James Harrington began writing *Oceana*. This magnum opus of political philosophy describes a utopian egalitarian republic in which the union of arms and wisdom reigns (Harrington, 1995). The regime's perfection stems from agrarian laws which prevent inequalities with regard to landholding and from a complex electoral system that involves drawing lots to constitute elected bodies and select town magistrates. This system reveals that the author drew inspiration from the model used in Venice—that 'incomparable' city Harrington had visited 23 years earlier. Likewise in 1654, but on the other side of the English Channel, *Le reglement du sort* was published, which detailed electoral reforms undertaken in Marseilles to designate the city's councillors and described a system which allocated a significant role to sortition (the drawing of lots).

This chronological coincidence does not mean that these two works were identical, of course—there were great differences between Cromwell's republican Commonwealth following the execution of Charles I, the ideal model described by Harrington, the French monarchy in the process of absolutist social and political royalization after the Fronde, and the local arrangements used in Marseille to regulate access to municipal offices. However, the similarities between both countries and the reform impulses they witnessed can help to shed light on a number of issues regarding town magistracies, in particular the procedures used to designate officeholders. Providing an exhaustive history of political relations between the French monarchy and cities throughout the realm or thoroughly describing the social, ideological, and regulatory transformations of the *corps de ville* (the municipal governing bodies) in the first half of 17th-century France are both ambitions beyond the scope of this chapter. Instead, we shall build on Olivier Christin's work concerning elections in the Early Modern period by analysing some of the issues involved in sortition that were discussed in the context of projects to reform municipal electoral practices, particularly in Lyons and Marseilles (Christin, 2014).

The impetus for reform should first and foremost be considered in light of the considerable dysfunctions that existed within the *corps de ville*. The royal state's role with regard to the origin and nature of the most salient of these dysfunctions will guide our analysis of the introduction of chance in elections. The use of lottery systems was viewed as a means of resistance against forms of 'statization' and new attempts to legitimize absolutism during the period surrounding the Edict of Nantes (1598–1685). Our investigation draws on James Collins' recent study of the transition from a republican monarchy to a monarchical state during the first half of the 17th century (Collins, 2016) and is largely in agreement with contemporary reassessments of the political theories of the *dévots*, a political movement aligned with a Catholic policy of opposition to Protestants within France, and to alliance with the Hapsburg monarchy internationally (Maillet-Rao, 2015). In this chapter, we shall focus on the theatrical performance of power, which made the drawing of lots resemble the providential interference of a deity, implicitly harking back to a mythical age of popular magistracies. Behind politics as a source of wonder and mystery, however, we can also recognize a paradoxical and Machiavellian form of 'the political domestication of chance', employed by an oligarchy seeking to maintain the social and political status quo throughout its territory (Sintomer, 2020).

'The Old Order is Lost, Everything has Fallen into Decadence; There is Trouble in the Cities which Grows Day by Day'[1]

Presented in such a way, French municipal life during the first third of the 17th century could be seen as merely the bemoaning of an old man who misses the olden times of perfection, destroyed by the new century's growing corruption. The dysfunctions and clashes observed in most cities' *corps de ville* were described by many contemporaries as disrupting municipal customs that had previously ensured relative order in the succession of elected officials. One of the common tropes of political literature at the time was the denunciation of cabals and intrigues which allegedly disrupted municipal order by manipulating electoral liberty and the common good — thereby sublimating that common good to unbridled personal ambitions and the dominance of private interests. The Marquis de St. Chamond, in his fight against Charles de Neufville, the governor of Lyons, felt it an honour to reveal the governor's violation of consular electoral practices: whenever possible, the governor eliminated the right to vote and instead imposed 'elected' officials who were beholden to him. At the turn of the decade in both 1610 and 1620, the rivalry between de Neufville and the Marquis turned municipal elections in Lyons into a spectacle of political perversion on one side and an image of virtuous adherence to municipal practices on the other. The *Saint-Chamontists* repeatedly denounced the governor's deviation from electoral customs: he used the annual election of town magistrates as a source of incidental income and prostituted the honour of the People's Magistracy for venal interests and sordid machinations, in exchange for a diamond, a tapestry, or even a satin gown for his wife (Lignereux, 2003).

These intrigues, fuelled by the great regional nobles' appetite for power, chiefly stemmed from the modifications made by the royal state to the very nature of the town magistrates' function, however: a change whose effects were as great as the disorder they also caused with regard to the process of being selected for these offices. The increasing rivalry and disorder each time the the the *corps de ville* had to be renewed through election was the most visible consequence of the crown's interference, which reduced the number of town councillors as part of a

---

[1] 'L'ordre ancien est perdu, tout est en decadance; / C'est un mal aux Citez qui va tousjours croissant.' *La Velleyade ou délicieuses merveilles de l'église Nostre Dame du Puy et païs de Velay, par Noble Hugues Davignon, Seigneur de Monteilz, Docteur és Droicts, et Advocat en la Seneschaussée du Puy,* Lyon, chez Louis Muguet, rüe de la Grenette, 1630, in-8°, pp. 158–159.

broad attempt to restore royal order at the end of the Wars of Religion, making it harder to accede to these offices as there were increasingly fewer of them. At the end of a century of royal intervention in civic matters, the edict issued in August 1694 transformed the municipal functions of mayors into hereditary and venal offices (before proceeding to do the same for councillors, *jurats*, consuls, and *capitouls* in January 1704). The arguments in this decree portray the monarchy's attempts at reform as fighting against abuses, corporate privileges, and machinations. This reform was viewed as a matter of necessity and virtue, in the sense that mayors

> no longer being indebted for their offices to the suffrage of private individuals, and no longer having to deal with successors, will exercise their functions without passion and with all the liberty required to preserve equality in the distribution of public offices. Moreover, being permanent, they will be able to acquire a perfect knowledge of the affairs of their community and will be able, through long experience, to satisfy all the duties and obligations attached to their ministry. (Cornette, 1997, pp. 393–394)

It was by claiming to struggle against such intrigues that the crown legitimized its reforms during the consecutive reigns of Henry IV and Louis XIII, as evidenced by the monarchy's numerous interventions in urban election processes. It interfered by designating the electoral body as a whole as well as the multiple offices that made up the *corps de ville* and by the means that it chose to express its choice of 'elected' representatives (Coste, 2012). As recent urban historiography has shown, although this shift was both authoritarian and intrusive, it was less a polemical matter of the monarchy systematically trying to destroy urban privileges, and more the expression of a certain pragmatism on the part of the royal state which sought to end recurrent political disorder. It was less a manifestation of deliberate hostility by a genetically absolutist monarchy than an *ad hoc* response to local leaders' inability to re-establish a *modus vivendi* in the aftermath of civil war. In other words, the monarchy's intervention was an attempt to ensure political pacification at the level of municipal institutions, as proposed by Reinhart Koselleck (Koselleck, 1979; Cassan, 1996, p. 302). In the case of Lyons, for example, the crown took control through the various means mentioned above. Henri IV's 1595 reform transformed Lyons' *corps de ville* by changing it from a collegial group of twenty-four councillors to the Parisian model, which named a *prévôt des marchands* and four councillors. Amid tensions with the country's neighbours and major financial problems owing to the discharging of the public debt — which led to the city's rejection of Catholic League divisions — modifications to the town council were intended to strengthen royal authority over a city that had only returned to monarchical obedience eighteen months prior. Later, in 1603, during the difficult restoration of civil peace, the monarch imposed the compilation of a list of three candidates for the election of the *prévôt des marchands*. The king then chose from that list the person who would hold the aforementioned office for two years. For a time, the increasing oligarchization of the *corps de ville* sharpened rivalries in electoral competition; then gradually, as a result of intendants and governors managing their clients more efficiently, electoral competitions stabilized and relative calm was restored.

While the venality of municipal offices occurred somewhat later in this timeline, it should be noted that the ambition to end open electoral competition embodied by Louis XIV's reform had been expressed by his predecessors. It was not until July 1681 that the first attempt was made by the king of France to sell Parisian municipal offices, before expanding this policy more widely in 1690 and again in 1692. But the first hints of these reforms can be found under Richelieu, in 1633 and in 1636 in particular (Descimon, 2012). Even earlier in Lyons, in 1607–1608, there was opposition to giving municipal officers life mandates — that is, associating the *corps de ville* (reformed in 1595) with a city council composed of a certain number of permanent members. This attests to the resistance provoked by an attempt to politically and socially neutralize the importance of elections and illustrates the desire that existed to preserve the regular expression of a civic community, even at the cost of occasional problems and reprehensible practices (Bibliothèque nationale de France, fds frçs 16661, ff. 436–37). The principle of election to public office was defended against the monarchy's desire to make public offices hereditary. Later, the monarchy's financial problems, which had only multiplied since the 1630s, were an opportunity for the crown to try to introduce new kinds of permanent city councillors. Lyons fought against such measures just as vehemently as it had when attempting to limit the length of mandates and to preserve the freedom to choose its own magistrates, even though this meant paying the price of increased liability to taxation by the administrative monarchy and increased dependence on the monarchy's patron-client network, which was ministerial as well as provincial.

With the intendant's growing control over the city and the governor's office taken over and inherited by the Villeroy family, town magistrate elections in Lyons were gradually reduced to mere ventriloquism, according to commentators who viewed this spectacle of ceremonial seriousness and the rhetorical fervour in praise of rigged 'elections' as a sort of political farce. Near the end of Louis XIV's reign, René Lehoreau, Cathedral Chaplain of Angers, described the city's elections as just this kind of spectacle, as electors were given a note bearing a single name previously selected by the governor and asked to consider the process as an election (Lehoreau, 1967):

> The mayor of the city, who was formerly elected only by the votes and free will of all the *corps de ville* and the deputies of each parish, was elected by Mr d'Armagnac [Louis de Lorraine, Count d'Armagnac and de Brionne, 1641–1718, Grand Squire of France, governor of the province since 1666], the governor of Anjou, without any consent from the *corps de ville*. Anyone wanting to become mayor makes sure to have friends near Mr d'Armagnac in Paris, where he ordinarily resides, and never in this town of Angers. The person, I say, who is agreeable to him, is thus received as mayor of the city, and for this purpose [the governor] gives notice to Mr d'Autichamp, his lieutenant, and to some of the most important corporate bodies in the town, that he has chosen a certain person … as mayor of the city of Angers and so requests them to welcome him. You may pass judgement, my dear reader, on these pretend votes and what follows the reception of the new mayor. With the parishes thus present, two of the mayors' guards pass their hats around both sides of the council chamber, filled with little notepapers for all present, both the city magistrates and those witnessing the ceremony. I speak of this as an eyewitness since I was given one. On these pieces of paper, persons foreign [to the proceedings] had written these words: Mr Robert, Professor of Law. The pieces of paper for the town councillors were the same as those for private individuals. All of us having these notes, which we were given simply as a formality, without saying anything, the Deputy Mayor [then] … said to the whole assembly: Gentlemen, I see that by common consent you approve the election of Mr Robert.

This ironic testimony about electoral 'consent' highlights the pure farce that municipal elections had become under the combined impact of three major changes: the exclusion of the bourgeoisie from royal offices, who then transferred all their hopes for honour and reputation onto the urban magistracies, since the sale of royal offices resulted in an increasingly impenetrable financial market; the increasing influence of the king, the governor, and the intendant on the nomination of the senior officers of the *corps de ville*, thus roping communal institutions into the machinery of monarchical administration; and the reduction in number and the increasingly oligarchical nature of elected offices, which transformed what was supposed to be for the common good into the object of private greed.

If we stopped here, we would be limiting ourself to recounting the history of the unrestrained statization of *Ancien Régime* society. But with the disgusted consent described by Lehoreau, we glimpse a counter-history of Early Modern civic elections. In this, we see contemporaries who are not *able* to consent to the results of the vote, and who unwaveringly defend the principle of liberty, even though the latter had been reduced to acquiescence to servitude (as paradoxical as that may seem). In fact, some elements continued to resist the change. There was a shift in Lyons in 1630–1640 from a republican rhetoric that saw intrigues as damaging the Roman model of the *res publica*, to a religious discourse that denounced these same machinations as a kind of sacrilege perpetrated against the purity of a sanctified city. While both forms praised the disinterestedness of candidates for municipal offices, that does not mean they were merely two sides of the same rhetorical coin. Rather, this shift in discourse reveals the seductive power of a model of political vocation wherein the elected person is called to serve by Providence; it is a model that mobilizes its own register of discourse when engaging in the traditional condemnation of intrigues (Lignereux, 2006). While elections had become a comedic farce by the end of the 17th century, during 1630–1660, urban elites actually aspired to the theatre of political sacredness.

From the Comedy of Electoral Vanities to the Theatre of Providence

Olivier Christin calls for us to distance ourselves from the idea that Early Modern municipal elections were solely an inexorable dissipation of civic life, reduced to 'so many useless spectacles, ridiculous or cynical masquerades' (Christin, 2014, p. 20). Yet it is precisely this language that offers us the magic words to pave the way for a different reading of these mechanisms affecting age-old communal practices. Denouncing municipal elections as the mere theatricalization of urban politics, in which the spectacle was no longer that of debate and free decision but the *mise en scène* of the vanity of the few and the comforting sublimation of the subordination of all, tells us that something else was at play in this performative construction. We could read the ceremonialization of these elections as political vacuity camouflaged by comforting *decorum*; yet it is precisely the ceremonial aspect of these civic rituals that reveals a political world which was less dull and lifeless than the one apparently suggested by the royalization of urban institutions and the exclusion of ordinary townspeople. In light of Christin's adjective 'enchanted', used to describe the discourse on the city's origins that legitimized its privileges, this political theatre must be examined more closely and considered as something more than rhetorical trickery or a deceptive veil that historians must tear away to reach the truth.

It is easy to say that the discourse of historians, in qualifying the vigour of electoral competition as intrigue, discounts royal order. Yet should we not recall Richelieu's judgment that 'disorder, not without usefulness, forms part of the order of the State' when we examine what these performative theatres of vanity tell us about a world that refuses to be an actor in someone else's play (Richelieu, 2012, p. 157; Christin, 2014, p. 39)? Christin explains the oligarchical discourse on the elective nature of the offices that were co-opted by the elites: their republican rhetoric referring back to Ancient Rome was not chosen unthinkingly, out of habit or mere eloquence, but rather because the elites adhered to a conception of the *res publicae* that differed from the sovereign's. When the king made these town magistracies venal, thus achieving the process of exclusion, we find the oligarchs fighting for the freedom to hold elections. Logically, these elected positions-turned-offices 'should have sealed the triumph of the local elites, the consecration of the oligarchies, [now] authorised to appropriate and manage as a patrimony the powers and responsibilities henceforth separated from all electoral uncertainty and perhaps from any republican reference' (Christin, 2014, p. 22). However, in buying the offices 'venalized' by Louis XIV and transferring them back into the elective system, these urban elites seem to have made an aberrant decision, based on a short-sighted interpretation of social and political dynamics that ultimately confined the urban political game to the sole model of patrician oligarchization and the calculated strategies of hereditary interests. Herein lies a contradiction, however: the oligarchs should have been content that offices were now sold, as this granted them a permanent source of income. And yet, they seemed to act against their own interests in stating that they wanted elections for the general good. This leads us to re-examine what may have motivated these municipal actors and to rethink their involvement in elections. In other words, they combined politically, socially, and economically *useful* strategies with the idea of the *disinterested* vocation of urban magistrates and an autonomous form of political representation. This representation was not viewed as a reflection of worldly powers, but instead as a vocation to participate in an enchanted universe in which politics were providential and the drawing of lots was an instrument of revelation.

By observing that lotteries were employed to prevent 'the intrigues and strategies of the great lineages', Christin established a pertinent connection between the actual practice of drawing lots and its intended purpose. But in so doing, does he not limit the scope of this practice, since it was also used to mitigate the extreme oligarchization of the *corps de ville* and to stave off their complete subordination to the king and the statization of the town magistracies? The qualities inherent to sortition meant that the process could not be assimilated to other practices established to prevent electoral machinations, such as secret ballots, even though they might have shared the same end goal. In order to take stock of the uniqueness of drawing lots, it is necessary to return to the notion of political theatre mentioned above.

Stage actors and town councillors had a common experience, in that they were both subject to a certain *mise en scène* of their person and required to recognize the audience in front of which they played a role. This analogy is evident and contemporaries even seemed to endorse it, though they may also seem to distort the comparison if we do not pay enough attention to the historical regime of political representation specific to the Early Modern period. Indeed, the fundamental element of political vocation in the *Ancien Régime* was the theatre of political office, rather than the person involved (as is predominantly the case today, whether it takes the form of spin doctors, storytelling, or the cannibalistic consumption of politicians as stars) (Salmon, 2007; 2013).

In proposing a history of Western theatre that starts with the 'ruses of appearance' and substitutes the term 'reality' for that of 'image', Anne Surgers leads us through a trajectory that links representation in the 17th century and the political vocation of town magistrates (Surgers, 2012). One of the main points of her research is the 'particularly significant' phenomenon of 'the inversion, in the 17th century, of the system of reference points used to orient the staging space' (*ibid.*, p. XXII). The action by which an actor *comes on stage*, for us contemporary readers, was called an exit (*sortie*) during the Baroque period. In fact, at that time, space was not defined by the spectator's perspective, nor was the effectiveness of the acting understood solely from the audience's point of view. This inversion of terms helps us understand how representation was elaborated according to different terms: belief in the action represented came from the invisible realm offstage, and not from verisimilitude and the visible or from a contract of belief between the spectator and the actor (i.e. the perspectivist or illusionistic tradition familiar to us). In scenography up to the 1640s–1670s, representation stems not from the gaze of the viewer but from what is invisible.

In printed works, substituting *entry* for *exit* enables us to reconstruct a genealogy of Early Modern representation and helps to clarify the competition between sortition and nomination with regard to the selection of civic leaders in early 17th-century elections. When connected with the fact that theatre now 'renounces manifesting the invisible' (*ibid.*), the basis of this new system of political representation of town magistracies becomes perhaps more comprehensible. Politics was thus no longer managed by the divine; it was not a secular goal in opposition to a religious conception of politics, but became a sacred goal in itself, a paradoxical form of horizontal transcendence.

This form of secularization, observable during the middle of the century, rejected the legitimacy of any supernatural origins. On the one hand, this new approach grounded the source and effects of belief in human beings, and, on the other hand, it changed the relationship between stage actors and the backstage, with a new contract of belief between actors and the audience. A relationship of hierarchical immanence replaced transcendent and communitarian continuity. The very notion of the stage, as part of the 'stage house', only became apparent in the late 1660s with Racine, especially in his plays written between 1689 and 1691. Racine was the first playwright to have his characters 'enter' on stage. The Italian model of representation was thus superimposed on its Baroque predecessor (Surgers, 2012, p. 122). If, therefore, 'exit' still signified metamorphosis and appearance until the 1660s, the councillor elected by sortition was seen as becoming a different person during his mandate. Could we perhaps argue that the drawing of lots revealed an actor within the political theatre? The play of assonances and an immediate etymological proximity suggest that we should examine these two universes of representation jointly. One of the meanings Surgers identifies in the verb *to exit* is 'the manifestation of something that until then had been invisible', and she explicitly refers to the drawing of lots, arguing that 'in Baroque thought, an actor does not *enter* the place of fiction—the stage house—but manifests in front of the audience' (*ibid.*, p. 84).

What Olivier Dowlen (2011, p. 137) terms the *blind* break in drawing lots—the break in the chain of reasoned selection that separates sortition from planned decision-making—was the means through which these changes in theatrical representation were transposed into the political scene. The non-rational moment of chance breaks with the economic rationality of venality, as well as with the social mechanisms of clientelism; it introduces another from of 'rationality' that has nothing to do with calculation and private interests. To return to the example of Lyons, we can see the extent to which the argument for drawing by lots was prevalent during the first half of the 17th century, both in regard to choosing individual councillors—mainly in 1623 and 1637—as well as in regard to selecting the entire *corps de ville*. This is evidenced by the evolution during the 1640s and 1650s of speeches eulogizing the election of civic magistrates on the Feast Day of St. Thomas, when political ceremonies were held for the publication of 'election' results. Designating new town councillors did not so much publicize a social hierarchy that was already visible as it revealed a hidden elite. While the masters of the trades and the *terriers* (the two outgoing magistrates who could not be re-elected) still selected the new magistrates, it is clear that from that point on something more than the simple expression of power relations was at stake, regardless of whether these forms of dominance were political, economic, cultural, or social, and whether they were termed intrigues, cabals, and clientelism by those who had lost the political game. In the 1630s, what the losers had depicted as a betrayal of the civic republic was replaced by the idea that intrigues were a sort of violence against the Christian community and a form of sacrilege against the selection of city councillors, which should be governed by vocation.

More so than the collective exaltation of the magistracy itself as evidenced by the construction of the magnificent Hôtel de Ville in 1646, the incredible *mise en scène* of the magistrate's personhood illustrates a break in the political imaginary of Lyons. This break was fostered by (1) the influence of writings on heavenly and human hierarchies of the 5th–6th-century mystic known as Pseudo-Denys (Le Gall, 2007; Durand, 2001); and (2) by the confraternity of the Blessed Sacrament and its fight for the sacralization of Christian society among town councillors (Martin, 2000; Guigue, 1922). Let us look at one example of this spiritual rhetoric in a speech eulogizing magistrates during post-election ceremonies given by Melchior Lagrive on 21 December 1643. At the heart of this speech was the idea of revelation, of the councillor's legitimacy coming from an invisible power. Men were not elected by their peers, but chosen by God who revealed their qualities, which then justified the fact that these individuals were in turn selected by their peers. Innate qualities were not *why* individuals were elected, but they were revealed to all *by* the election. A selected councillor exited from the common, ordinary world not so much thanks to the drawing of lots, but as a result of Providence re-enchanting the entire political body which then casts its votes:

> Gentlemen, your responsibilities being most necessary for the maintenance of society and civil life, you have been drawn out from the night of a private and solitary life to be revealed in the theatre of honour; you have been unveiled, your virtues, which were hidden from us, have been brought to light. You have rendered those virtues more brilliant and more elevated. (Lyons municipal archives, BB 197, fol. 206)

In the imaginary of drawing lots, we see the gratifying subordination of the *corps de ville* to Providence, which impugns and keeps at bay the elites' subservience to the financial logic of the offices market, as well as their subjection to the client-patron games of the administrative monarchy. Contrary to an Early Modern conception of sovereignty based on the idea that 'politics is a human affair and, as such, translates a human project' (Mairet, 1996, p. 19), the councillor model deployed in Lyons was a declaration of faith in political transcendence and its providential inspiration, with the result that authority can be therefore based on something other than self-interest, self-love, and the desire for power (*ibid.*).

To return to the changes in the theatre mentioned above, the mid-17th century witnessed 'the transition from one system of representation to another', shifting between two human attitudes towards the visible and the invisible. In the older system, 'the invisible is that which cannot be directly apprehended by the eyes and the consciousness of man, [and] does not have to be hidden, since it is invisible' (Surgers, 2012, p. 199). Yet in the new system, in particular according to the rules laid down by the Abbot of Aubignac (*La pratique du théâtre*, 1657) and the Italian-style illusionistic theatre, the invisible 'must not be seen, otherwise the illusion would be spoiled; it is "outside the frame" and would be contrary to verisimilitude if it were seen' (Surgers, 2012, p. 199). Election by lot was less a strategy deployed to conceal the vulgar reality of councillor authority, which was controlled by money and power, and more an attempt to render manifest the invisible legitimacy of an earthly government guaranteed by the divine order and the mysteries of its Providence. However, this conception needs to be tested in light of Machiavellianism, according to which private interests may have had a greater role to play than merit.

Elect 'in Such a Way that the Artifices and the Machinations of Men Can Play No Part'[2]

While the attempts to establish the practice of sortition in Lyon in 1623 and 1637 did not work (Lyons municipal archives, BB 162, ff. 301–02 and BB 191, fol. 218), on account of customary practices that it was considered wiser to preserve, Marseilles availed itself of its long familiarity with this form of designation, and in the early 1650s

---

[2] *Le reglement du sort. Contenant la forme et la maniere de proceder à l'eslection des Officiers de la Ville de Marseille. Revu et augmenté de nouveau de plusieurs autres Reglemens et Ordonnances de Police*, à Marseille, chez Claude Garcin, Imprimeur ordinaire du Roy, du Clergé et de la Ville, M.DC.LIV, in-4°, article I, p. 31.

established a mixed procedure that combined voting with sortition (Ruffi, 1696, chap. XII). The preface to the book *Le reglement du sort*, published in 1654, states that among the five electoral regimes that had historically followed one another in designating Marseilles' town councillors, four involved the drawing of lots. In this context, the lottery was associated with an explicit manifestation of divine will and benevolence, in which 'votes' and the 'balote' were a means to overcome the darkest of human passions, 'factions, which create disorder and confusion, that ... have so often shaken the Estate of this city, and have overwhelmed it with such great debts, that it almost succumbed under so heavy a burden' (*Le reglement du sort*, 1654, p. 6). Recourse to the lottery in Marseilles occurred in a context of extreme division provoked by the governor's desire, following the death of Richelieu in 1643, to overthrow the Valbelle clan. This bourgeois family had been ennobled during the Wars of Religion and had held sway over the city since 1617. The municipal life of Marseilles, and more generally of the whole of Provence, was mired in incessant rivalries until the king recalled the governor in 1650. Antoine de Valbelle immediately endeavoured to consolidate his victory over the governor by rallying political forces to his advantage. To do so, he had the town councillors propose new legislation in 1651. He entrusted its writing to his ally and cousin Antoine de Felix, who in 1653 was in fact the person who had been designated by the lottery as first councillor. The regulatory text of 1654 stated, without irony, that 'the drawing of lots, depicted as blind, seems to have had the eyes to fall upon him and to begin with its own creator [of the system]' (*Le reglement du sort*, 1654, p. 11). Historian Raoul Busquet speaks of this electoral system as a 'masterpiece of subtlety, complexity, mysticism and humour' (Busquet, 1998, p. 223).

According to the decision made in December 1651 by the General Assembly, composed up of eight hundred inhabitants, all the elections were held amongst a fixed, permanent Council of three hundred members to fill public offices: the *viguier* (the city's main magistrate), the three councillors, and the assessor, as well as a number of subordinate posts. The voting rules, drawn up at the beginning of 1652, were submitted for approval to the king, who ordered the full implementation of this electoral process according to a series of letters from October 1652. For the first time, he reserved the right to appoint councillors and other main officers. A new version of these rules was drafted in April 1653 and was broadly approved by the king. Generally speaking, there was a reasonable split between sortition and election being used to designate new magistrates. It was also stipulated that, out of the three hundred councillors, one hundred of them would be drawn by lot annually in order to constitute the town Council, and would be responsible for 'deliberating and resolving ordinary and incidental affairs during the year'.

In addition to the repetitive aspect of the elections, in which informal designation, nomination, and secret suffrage alternated, it is interesting to note that, while sortition played a large role, the random nature of that process was greatly undermined by the composition of the group from which the lots were drawn. Indeed, in the group of the three hundred councillors responsible for all elections, two-thirds of members were chosen by the outgoing consuls, namely the Valbelle clan, while the remaining one hundred councillors were chosen by a commission of six members evenly divided among the men of the Valbelle clan and those of the opposing party. Alphonse Cremieux (1917) drew attention to the subtle art, in that pre-statistical age, of 'the political domestication of chance'. He demonstrated how the allegedly objective nature of drawing lots was corrupted at the outset, by establishing a permanent council whose rules of composition ensured that 'fate' or chance was fully mastered. In addition, among the three hundred councillors, one hundred were chosen by lot to constitute the town Council, which then played a key role in countering any unfavourable chance that might have designated the Valbelles' opponents as councillors. In reality, the town magistrates lost their power to designate the city's officers, as that selection was now operated by the Council of Three Hundred. Moreover, the Council of Three Hundred controlled the magistrates' action through the town Council, which co-opted the magistrates' authority. 'Although the rules provided means for correction', with two hundred and fifty councillors chosen by the Valbelles, '...fate would have had to have been truly blind for this personage [Antoine de Valbelle] not to have directed the government of Marseilles at will' (Crémieux, 1917, p. 444).

Despite the azure cross of the city's coat-of-arms referring to medieval crusaders and their sacred vocation, and despite Antoine de Felix's stated pleasure that he and the other leaders of the city had been elected 'in a religious house', that they were 'the first who God made councillors without the intervention of men', and that 'that their greatest desire was to conform to the happiness and innocence of their election', it must be said that if fate did indeed preside over the renewal of public offices it still observed a handful of rules (*Le reglement du sort*, 1654, pp. 26–27). These rules were not so much those of *blind* chance, but rather those of a *clairvoyant* understanding of the logic of probability.

There is perhaps a lesson to be learned from the fact that one of the clearest arguments made in defence of drawing lots can be found in a book that suspected a Machiavellian influence on the apparent neutrality of introducing a 'demarchic' regime. After arguing for the need to open the *corps de ville* to foreigners, Laurent Melliet then states that 'it is better to elect magistrates by plurality of votes than to choose them by lot', and in so doing overcomes the indecision marked by Tacitus (Melliet, *Discours politiques et militaires*, 1628, p. 779). For Lyons, he argues that drawing lots would be preferable to the tumultuous campaigns and scandalous emotions generated by electoral competitions. In that way, the dignity of the people's magistracy would be safe from any disturbers of the public peace – the 'partisans of democracy' denounced in the previous discourse – as well as from the governor's hegemonic machinations and ambitions. Echoing the debates of the Estates General in 1614, Melliet starts with the municipal offices and mentions the need to extend the lottery to other functions, such as 'offices, charges, and authorities that depend on the monarch', to remove the taint of venality from these public functions. As such, his discourse exalts a monarchical regime based on the sacrality of the king and the defence of the Catholic religion, which was threatened by the 'wily republican Protestants of La Rochelle'. Between the lines of Melliet's text, we can hear the voice of its real author, the Italian Scipione Ammirato. In 1594 in Florence, Ammirato published the *Discorsi sopra Cornelio Tacito*, which Melliet translated into French in 1619 (Senellart, 1997). Ammirato was one of the main figures of Tacitism, which he tried to frame within the bounds of Christianity. But although Ammirato firmly condemns Machiavelli, he often 'seems to appropriate [Machiavelli's] most scandalous maxims' (Thuau, 2000, p. 119). With regard to his preference for the lottery, Melliet praises sortition not as the expression of a benevolent Providence but rather as a rational and pragmatic pacification strategy:

> The elected person would then not boast as much as if he had been chosen by men and preferred to his competitors: he who loses would not be so afflicted, and would conceive no hatred or desire for vengeance against anyone, seeing that it is not judgment, but *an event of fate*, which is the cause of his acceptance or of his rejection. (Melliet, *Discours politiques et militaires*, 1628, p. 782; emphasis mine)

In Melliet's work, the Old and New Testaments are quoted alongside Roman history and reference is made to St. Matthias's vocation by chance; Melliet also knew the work of St. Thomas Aquinas. Melliet strives to distance those men ordinarily 'elected' to town magistracies from providential sacrality, which must remain solely for the Christian king. For the king, the Holy Ampulla and the miracles of the 'religion of Reims' (E. Renan); for the rest, mere *occurrences of fate*. Going against the mystical enthusiasm of providential exceptionality, this meant that divinity was left to express itself through its own discrete means of action, without being obliged to an annual pronunciation or mandatory plebiscite, which would perhaps have been equally scandalous to the Catholic Melliet as to the fervently democratic Protestants.

Although it was seen as a pragmatic solution to the crisis ravaging a number of towns across the realm provoked by the administrative manoeuvres of the absolutist monarchy, for Early Modern French town councillors the technique of sortition was ideologically in conflict with its political regime: the lottery system contradicted the monarchy's essential providentialist principles by widely expanding the mysteries of divine selection to encompass the election of town magistrates. Even when the election of the *corps de ville* was inspired by the divine, random selection remained suspicious to the absolutist monarchy, which did not intend to grant others the power of revelation or supreme political legitimacy. The invisible made visible to the public by the theatre actor through his speech and gestures would come to be erased by the new rules of illusion that emerged in the second half of the 17th century. Civic magistrates likewise had to renounce this irruption of transcendence in the earthly realm—except when drawing lots was not decided beforehand, as in Marseilles. It was thus necessary for magistrates to abandon the idea of having a vocation, and instead reconcile themselves with a more banal fate, that of notables whose turn would come one day.

In 1669, in the Jesuit Ménestrier's eulogy for the councillors of Lyons, he expressed this renunciation of the absolute, which councillors had briefly drawn closer to through the drawing of lots. From that point on, public officials had to embrace a new process in which their money and their good name once again became the very reason—and the sole reason—for their good fortune and election to office (Ménestrier, *Eloge historique de la Ville de Lyon...*, 1669, letter).

References

Busquet, R. (1998) *Histoire de Marseille*, Paris: Robert Laffont.

Cassan, M. (1996) *Le temps des guerres de religion. Le cas du Limousin (vers 1530-vers 1630)*, Paris: Publisud.

Christin, O. (2014) *Vox populi. Une histoire du vote avant le suffrage universel*, Paris: Seuil.

Collins, J.B. (2016) *La monarchie républicaine. État et société dans la France moderne*, Paris: Odile Jacob.

Cornette, J. (1997) *Chronique du règne de Louis XIV*, Paris: SEDES.

Coste, L. (2012) Etre candidat aux élections municipales dans la France d'Ancien Régime, in Hamon, P. & Laurent, C. (eds.) *Le pouvoir municipal. De la fin du Moyen Age à 1789*, pp. 209–219, Rennes: Presses universitaire de Rennes.

Crémieux, A. (1917) *Marseille et la royauté pendant la minorité de Louis XIV (1643-1660)*, Paris: Librairie Hachette et Cie.

Descimon, R. (2012) La vénalité des offices politiques et perpétuels de la municipalité de Paris (procureur du roi, greffier et receveur de la Ville, XVIe siècle-années 1750), in Hamon, P. & Laurent, C. (eds.) *Le pouvoir municipal. De la fin du Moyen Age à 1789*, pp. 59–79, Rennes: Presses universitaires de Rennes.

Dowlen, O. (2011) Le tirage au sort en politique, *Esprit*, 377, pp. 136–143.

Durand, Y. (2001) *L'ordre du monde. Idéal politique et valeurs sociales en France du XVIe au XVIIIe siècle*, Paris: SEDES.

Guigue, G. (1922) *Les Papiers des dévots de Lyon. Recueil de textes sur la Compagnie secrète du Saint-Sacrement, ses statuts, ses annales, la liste de ses membres, 1630-1731*, Lyon: Librairie ancienne Veuve Blot.

Harrington, J. (1995) *Océana*, Paris: Belin.

Koselleck, R. (1979) *Le règne de la critique*, Paris: Éditions de Minuit.

Le Gall, L. (2017) *A voté: une histoire de l'élection*, Paris: Anamosa.

Lehoreau, R. (1967) *Cérémonial de l'Eglise d'Angers (1692–1721)*, Lebrun, F. (ed.), Paris: Klincksieck.

Le reglement du sort. Contenant la forme et la maniere de proceder à l'eslection des Officiers de la Ville de Marseille. Revu et augmenté de nouveau de plusieurs autres Reglemens et Ordonnances de Police (1654), à Marseille, chez Claude Garcin, Imprimeur ordinaire du Roy, du Clergé et de la Ville, M.DC.LIV, in-4°.

Lignereux, Y. (2003) *Lyon et le roi. De la « bonne ville » à l'absolutisme municipal (1594-1654)*, Seyssel: Champ Vallon.

Lignereux, Y. (2006) *Vox populi, Vox dei?* Les élections consulaires lyonnaises dans la première moitié du xviie siècle, in Castagnetti, P. (ed.) *Images et pratiques de la ville (xvie–xixe siècles)*, 2, pp. 103–132, Saint-Etienne: Publications de l'Université de Saint-Etienne.

Maillet-Rao, C. (2015) *La pensée politique des dévots. Mathieu de Morgues et Michel de Marillac. Une opposition au ministériat du cardinal Richelieu*, Paris: Honoré Champion.

Mairet, G. (1996) *Le principe de souveraineté. Histoires et fondements du pouvoir moderne*, Paris: Gallimard.

Martin, C. (2000) *Les compagnies de la propagation de la foi (1632–1685). Paris, Grenoble, Aix, Lyon, Montpellier. Etude d'un réseau d'associations fondé en France au temps de Louis XIII pour lutter contre l'hérésie des origines à la Révocation de l'Edit de Nantes*, Genève: Droz.

Melliet, L. (1628) *Discours politiques et militaires sur Corneille Tacite, Excellent Historien, et grand homme d'Estat. Contenans les fleurs des plus belles Histoires du Monde. Et des notables advetissemens concernans la conduitte des Armées. Oeuvre utile et necessaire aux Roys, Princes, Generaux d'armée, Conseiller d'Estat, Capitaines particuliers, Gentilshommes et tous Magistrats Ecclesisatiques et seculiers, ayans le maniement de la chose publique, Traduit, paraphrasez et augmentez par Laurens Melliet, sieur de Montessuy en Bresse*, à Lyon, chez Antoine Chard, M.DC.XXVIII. in-4°, livre XI, 8ᵉ discours.

Ménestrier, C.-F. (1669) *Eloge historique de la Ville de Lyon, et sa Grandeur Consulaire sous les Romains, et sous nos Rois, par le P. Claude François Menestrier de la Compagnie de Jesus*, à Lyon, chez Benoist Coral, M.DC.LXIX., in-fol.

Richelieu (2012) *Testament politique*, Hildesheimer, F. (ed.), Paris: Honoré Champion.

Ruffi, A. de (1696) *Histoire de la ville de Marseille… par feu M. Antoine de Ruffi, seconde édition, reveuë, corrigée, augmentée… par M. Loüis-Antoine de Ruffi son fils*, à Marseille, par Henri Martel, Imprimeur-Libraire, 1696, t. II, in-fol.

Salmon, C. (2007) *Storytelling. La machine à fabriquer des histoires et à formater les esprits*, Paris: La Découverte.

Salmon, C. (2013) *La cérémonie cannibale et la performance politique*, Paris: Fayard.

Senellart, M. (1997) La traduction des *Discorsi* d'Ammirato par L. Melliet (1628): déplacements, additions, reconstruction, in Dottoli, G. (ed.) *Politique et littérature en France aux xviᵉ et xviiᵉ siècles*, pp. 273–290, Bari: Adriatica — Paris: Didier.

Sintomer, Y. (2020) *Between Radical and Deliberative Democracy: Random Selection in Politics from Athens to Contemporary Experiments*, Cambridge: Cambridge University Press (forthcoming).

Surgers, A. (2012) *L'automne de l'imagination. Splendeurs et misères de la représentation (xviᵉ-xxiᵉ siècles)*, Berne: Peter Lang.

Thuau, E. (2000) *Raison d'État et pensée politique à l'époque de Richelieu*, Paris: Albin Michel.

Raphaël Barat

The Introduction of Sortition in Elections in the Republic of Geneva (1691)

Translation revised by Sarah-Louise Raillard

In 1691, sortition was introduced in the Republic of Geneva in the election of magistrates, notably for the election of auditors. After a brief description of the Republic's electoral system and the role of sortition within it, we shall see that the available documentation makes it difficult to assess the impact of sortition on electoral results. More information is available, however, on how the introduction of sortition was justified by the government of the Republic in 1691, and on the problems it raised for the various actors involved. Three guiding ideas shall structure our analysis. First, sortition was introduced with the explicit goal of reducing the formation of cabals (in French, '*brigues*', a word which referred to all the forbidden electoral practices in the context of Genevan law; namely, recommendations, libel, and the offering of money or free meals in exchange for votes—Barat, 2015). But sortition was in no way adopted as a democratic means to broaden the recruitment base for offices. Sortition on the contrary provided a response to the growing criticism of oaths for their lack of effectiveness as a bulwark against the formation of cabals. Finally, the staging of sortition was itself an issue, as some critics argued that it should not be performed 'in the people's sight'.

The Election of Auditors and
the Introduction of Sortition

At the end of the 17th century, the Republic of Geneva was governed by the Small Council, or Council of the Twenty-Five, which was dominated by the so-called great families. Its antechamber was the Council of the Two Hundred, where young aristocrats sat. Nevertheless, the small Republic had kept its popular assembly, which was inherited from the medieval commune, the General Council. This was quite peculiar, as patrician regimes were dominant throughout European and Swiss city-states in the late 17th century. The assembly was composed of all the burgesses and citizens of the city — accounting for about one third of the adult male population — and it was theoretically the sovereign power of the Republic. Geneva was therefore a *de jure* democracy — even the most conservative contemporary thinkers acknowledged that fact — but a *de facto* aristocracy. The General Council had for a long time been deprived of the true basis of its sovereignty, which resided in its extra-electoral functions: voting on laws and taxes, as well as declarations of war and peace. The Council had not met in that capacity for over a hundred years — since 1584, to be exact. The only power left to the assembly was therefore to choose the Republic's main magistrates from a list drawn up beforehand by the Small Council, and subsequently confirmed by the Council of the Two Hundred. In January, the General Council chose the four syndics from a list of eight candidates selected by the Small Council. In November, it chose the lieutenant, the magistrate responsible for the police and operations of justice in the city, and two of the six auditors who helped him with that task. Every three years, it also elected the treasurer (*trésorier général*) and the attorney-general (*procureur general*), who were selected from among the Two Hundred, as were the auditors.

Sortition was introduced to the electoral process in 1691 at two different levels. When the Small Council nominated candidates for the elections of the auditors, attorney-general, and treasurer, one third of the ballots were randomly 'withdrawn' and then burnt before the votes were counted (Rivoire, 1935, p. 569). The first election attesting to this practice took place in November 1691, and concerned the nomination of six candidates for the office of auditor (Registers of the Small Council [from now on, R.C.], 191, 11/01/1691, pp. 316–320). Each member of the Small Council went 'between the two doors' to fill out his ballot, and placed it in a round box (*boîte*). Then, the boxes were brought to the First Syndic in a big bag, all mixed up, and one third of them were randomly withdrawn (they were 'selected indifferently and without affectation from the said bag'). They were immediately burnt, without ever having been seen. Then the remaining boxes were opened and the votes were counted (Rivoire, 1935, p. 569).

In the elections of the auditors, sortition was used a second time, when the General Council was responsible for making the final choice from amongst the nominated candidates. Before citizens voted, two out of the six candidates were 'excluded by [means of] the black ball' (*ibid.*, pp. 569–570). Though the subtraction (*retranchement*) of ballots was abandoned in 1700 (*ibid.*, p. 673), the use of black balls was preserved until the Act of Mediation in 1738.[1] We shall focus more specifically on the use of sortition to elect auditors, a process which was better documented than the subtraction of ballots, though this very surprising practice is also worth noting.

Auditors were city officials who served in the lieutenant's court. In collaboration with the latter, they adjudicated civil cases in the first instance, and investigated criminal cases under the direction of one of the syndics. One third of the auditors were replaced every year (each year, two of the six auditors were elected for three-year terms, thus replacing those who had been elected three years prior and who were then leaving office — Edicts on the offices, p. 21). Auditors served only once in this capacity. The auditors came from a relatively restricted social background (Cicchini, p. 124). One third were young aristocrats for whom the office was the first step of their *cursus honorum*, and who would rise politically to obtain a position in the Small Council (this applied to 22 of the 59 auditors elected between 1679 and 1707, or 37 per cent). Eighteen of these auditors, or 30 per cent, ultimately reached the syndicate, which was the most prestigious magistracy.[2] 37 other auditors, or 63 per cent, never entered the Small Council. But, as Marco Cicchini writes about the 18th century, 'the impossibility of guaranteeing chances of success to all auditors was largely structural', the Small Council (and, all the more so, the syndicate), representing 'bottlenecks' in the political ascension of auditors (*ibid.*, p. 121). Some of them were aristocrats who were not allowed to enter the Small Council because

---

[1] During the 1707 crisis, the proposal of having the Council of the Two Hundred elect itself, which included some degree of sortition, was submitted to the First Syndic, Jean de Normandie, by twelve citizens on 17 February. It was immediately rejected as an overly radical project, the Small Council seeing in it 'the end of the Edicts' and the 'overthrowing of the government' (R.C., 207, 18/02/1707, p. 111). The proposal, which seems to have been elaborated by Pierre Gallatin, suggested that all citizens could register in the chancellery, with the Small Council and the Council of the Two Hundred having the right to reject candidates that they did not deem worthy. During the first year, the necessary numbers to fill vacancies in the Council of the Two Hundred (which had to include 215 members) were chosen by lot among the candidates, to which were added forty honorary councillors who were allowed to attend debates without being permitted to vote. Every year, new vacancies were to be filled out by randomly selecting among the honorary councillors. New honorary councillors would be chosen when their number was reduced by half (Fatio, 2007, p. 106).

[2] This proportion is quite similar, albeit slightly smaller, to that observed by Barbara Roth-Lochner across a longer period, from 1650 to 1794. According to her calculations, nearly half of the auditors entered the Small Council (132 out of 291, or 45 per cent), most of whom also became syndics (Roth-Lochner, 1992, p. 86).

one of their parents was present in the assembly (their older brother, father, or father-in-law). They sometimes successively held the offices of auditor and attorney-general during this waiting period. Some others came from families which were not yet powerful enough to have a member elected to the Small Council (Favet, 1998, pp. 66–67), or, like Pierre Fatio or Pierre Gallatin, who were among the leaders of the 'popular party' during the 1707 crisis, were barred from advancing their political careers on account of their radical ideas.

It is difficult to assess the impact of sortition on election results. What we do know is that the same members of the Two Hundred were very often nominated to be auditors, and that they almost always ended up being elected after a few years. While there was theoretically a maximum of 150 different candidates that could have been nominated between 1679 and 1707, in practice only 73 were nominated, and only 63 of whom (or 86 per cent) would end up being elected.[3] The main effect of sortition was making the waiting period a bit longer. Before 1691, a candidate often had to fail once before being elected; sometimes twice. After 1691, some candidates failed three or four times before being elected, because they were repeatedly 'excluded by the black ball'. Most auditors serving between 1692 and 1707 were excluded by lot at least once before they were finally elected: most often once (this was the case for 15 auditors), more rarely twice (4 auditors), and up to three times for the unluckiest (2 auditors).

It must be asked if sortition actually deterred the formation of cabals, as was the stated goal of this reform. Unfortunately, the primary sources do not present sufficient data to make a quantitative analysis possible. We cannot take for granted the numerous condemnations of cabal formation in the Registers of the Small Council, or in the Registers of the Company of Pastors. These remain very vague, and do not provide much information about the scope of cabals, or about the actors and the practices involved. They likely reveal much more about how these institutions believed that the Republic should ideally function, rather than about the reality of electoral practices. When there appears

---

[3]   The maximum number of different candidates eligible for nomination between 1679 and 1707 was theoretically 150 (4 candidates times 12 equals 48, between the years 1679 and 1690 included, plus 6 candidates times 17 equals 102, between the years 1691 and 1707 inclusively). In practice, there were only 73 candidates: the 59 auditors who had been elected between 1679 and 1707, 4 candidates who were nominated between 1679 and 1707 but became auditors later (Jean Tronchin and Paul Mallet, who were elected in 1708, Théodore de Saussure, elected in 1709, Jacob Du Pan the younger, who was elected in 1710), and 10 candidates who were nominated between 1679 and 1707, but never became auditors.

to have been a surprise in the result of an election, we cannot distinguish what might have been due to cabals, and what might have stemmed from other factors (the extreme popularity or unpopularity of a candidate, for instance), since we do not know the number of votes that were cast for each candidate prior to 1728.

Though it is very difficult to measure the impact of sortition on election results, we have a much better understanding of how its introduction was justified by the government in 1691, and of the problems that this practice raised for the various actors involved (the Small Council, the pastors, the citizens, etc.).

Fighting Cabals by 'Making Nominations Uncertain'

In his opening speech during the election of 1 November 1691, the first where sortition was used, the First Syndic clearly stated the reasons for the introduction of this mechanism. The goal of this reform was 'to prevent the cabals which in the end can only have disastrous effects, and lead to the ruin of the State, as was the case in several flourishing republics' (R.C., 191, 01/11/1691, p. 318). The solution was therefore to 'make nominations uncertain'.

Though it was a quite arduous and ungrateful task, the office of auditor was much coveted, because it enabled young aristocrats to start their progression in the *cursus honorum*. Until 1691, auditors could automatically enter the Council of the Sixty when they left office, which gave them precedence over the other members of the Two Hundred. In September 1691, this privilege was revoked in order to discourage the formation of cabals: when leaving office, auditors now kept the rank that they had previously in the Two Hundred. It was for the same purpose that sortition was introduced to those elections the same year. The Small Council would nominate six candidates instead of four, two of whom would be excluded by lot before the General Council on election day (Rivoire, 1935, p. 569; Edicts on the offices, p. 21 [note N]).

This use of sortition was quite widespread at the time. It was used to discourage the formation of cabals, either as a deterrent, or as one of the steps in an election, following the Venetian model (Manin, 1996, pp. 88–93). As Yann Lignereux observes regarding the proposal to introduce sortition to the election of Lyon's city councillors in the first half of the 17th century, this was often closer to 'an aristocratic and conservative Venetian model' than to an Athenian model, where lottery formed the basis of popular government (Lignereux, 2006, p. 122).

Several Swiss cantons introduced sortition to their electoral process for similar motives, almost always amidst a context of increasingly oligarchic tendencies, sometime between the mid-17th century and the early 18th century. It was introduced in Basel in 1718 to discourage the formation of cabals (Braun, 1988, pp. 173 and 210): if a cabal was uncovered, it was decreed that the election in question would be conducted by lot. In the patrician canton of Bern, 'the election of the Small Council follow[ed] a very complex process, with elements of co-optation by the Small Council, election by the Grand Council, and complementary sortition'. In some rural cantons where the *Landsgemeinde*, the assembly of citizens, was the sovereign authority, lottery became the last stage of the election of magistrates after the mid-17th century (in Schwyz sometime between 1692 and 1706, and in Glaris in 1640 among Evangelical Protestants and 1649 among Catholics). To take part in this last stage, candidates in the lottery were first required to pay a fixed sum of money and be chosen by a show of hands. As in other cantons, the aim was to prevent political intrigues and rivalry between the great families (*ibid.*, pp. 174–175).

Oaths or Lottery?

The introduction of sortition was also part of a broader reflection on the various means to fight the formation of cabals. It was most notably an answer to growing criticism of oaths and their lack of effectiveness (Spurr, 2001, pp. 37–63), as illustrated by the debates held by the commissions that were established between 1689 and September 1691 to discuss the prevention of cabal formation, particularly for the election of auditors.

After the pastor's exhortation and the speech of the Lieutenant (for the November elections), one of the two Secretaries of State read the passage on elections of the Edicts, and the 'oath for the election'. Citizens were required to swear the oath just before voting, by placing their hand on the open Bible before them when they walked past the table of syndics (Rivoire, 1935, p. 534). This oath contained a double measure of protection. On the one hand, citizens swore to elect 'those who [were] fit' — and after 1705, 'the fittest' (R.C., 205, 04/01/1705, p. 1) — and to vote 'according to the public good and not to any particular affection of hate or favour' (Edicts on the offices, p. 2). On the other hand, they also swore that they had not 'taken part in any cabal, or had somebody form a cabal, nor had recommended somebody, or had somebody recommend someone else' since 1674, when this clause was added after the words 'of hate or favour' (Rivoire, 1935, p. 416).

On 2 December 1689, Ami Le Fort suggested that, 'to address the disorder of cabals, we should reinstate the oath in all its strength, as it used to be a few years ago'. Le Fort seemed well aware, however, that reinforcing the oath was not sufficient, as he also suggested that 'in order to avoid the formation of cabals, especially for the election of auditors', the General Council should choose not between four candidates, but amongst eight, nine, ten, or more, four of whom would be chosen in the temple by lottery, and then submitted to a vote by the people (R.C., 189, 02/12/1689, pp. 455–456). Likewise, the councillor Franconis argued that resorting to sortition was necessary in order to find an effective remedy against cabals, even proposing that a commission be set up on the subject. Others voiced their concerns about the effectiveness of oaths even more explicitly. The attorney-general Jean-Pierre Trembley asked for a commission to be set up 'to strive to reform the way we conduct our elections, and to avoid fake oaths'. The councillor Jean-Louis Mestrezat suggested that 'we abolish the use of oaths in elections entirely' (*ibid.*) – one month earlier, he had already suggested that 'one should eliminate from elections the oaths which so clearly bring many people to commit perjury', while Jacob de Normandie of the Two Hundred asked that 'other remedies than oaths should be considered to prevent cabals' (R.C., 189, 04/12/1689, p. 425). One year later, such scepticism was still persistent, as evidenced by Daniel Le Clerc suggesting to the Two Hundred in November 1690 that 'one should subtract from the oath what goes beyond the formation of cabals', i.e. the part concerning recommendations. In December 1690, the Small Council set up another commission to examine ways of avoiding the formation of cabals; its activities were revived by the Syndic Franconis in August 1691. The commission's report was handed over to the Small Council on 26 August 1691, and then submitted to the Two Hundred, which discussed the subject on 28 August, 7, 9, and 14 September (regarding the introduction of lot for the election of auditors), and 28 October of that year (regarding the practical details of exclusion by lot) (Rivoire, 1935, pp. 569–570). It was also decided that auditors leaving office would no longer enter the Council of the Sixty, but would keep the rank that they used to have in the Two Hundred. This was meant to discourage those who coveted the office for reasons of precedence (Edicts on the offices, p. 21 [note O]).

The introduction of sortition in 1691 was part of a process that began as early as 1683, in response to the complaints of pastors on the declining effectiveness of oaths, with the fear of God no longer appearing to be a sufficient deterrent against the formation of cabals. Between 1683 and 1687, it was first argued in the governmental commissions that citizens should be restrained 'by the fear of the sentence rather than the fear of the oath', and that 'rigourous sentences' should be instituted, which a chamber of cabals (*chambre des brigues*) would enforce 'in a manly way' (R.C., 184, 03/12/1684, fol. 181 v°-182). This led to the creation of the chamber of cabals in 1687, though with fewer powers than initially proposed, since it could neither pass judgment nor impose sentences, but could only investigate and collect information—notably thanks to denunciations (R.C., 187, 28/11/1687, fol. 229). The nomination by the Small Council and the confirmation by the Two Hundred—held on a Tuesday and a Friday respectively—were also both moved in 1687 to the eve of the election by the General Council, on a Saturday, thus making it more difficult to buy votes, as a candidate would have to buy votes during the week without even knowing if he would be presented to the suffrage of the General Council (Rivoire, 1935, p. 531).

The introduction of sortition in 1691, as well as the elimination the same year of automatic entry into the Council of the Sixty for auditors leaving office, contributed to the search for profane remedies to cabals.

How to Stage Sortition?

The staging of lottery procedures was also a problem. It reflected, more generally, the ambiguity of Genevan elections, where everything was done to channel the popular vote (prior nomination of the candidates; organization of space according to precedence; the process of auricular voting, i.e. in the ear of secretaries, which placed pressure on voters), while some aspects of the electoral ceremony still seemed to suggest that the Republic theoretically remained a democracy. Thus, the Lieutenant in November (or the First Syndic in January) always addressed the citizens as 'Sovereign Lords' ('*Souverains Seigneurs*') in his opening speech, where he never failed to emphasize magistrates accept such a heavy burden only to serve the people.

Should the exclusion of two of the six candidates be done in the Small Council, in the town hall, or in the Temple of Saint-Peter, 'in the people's sight'? And according to which procedure? In the November 1691 election, the exclusion of two of the six candidates by lottery appears to have followed a precise order. Six 'balls' or 'boxes' of the same size and colour were displayed before the syndics (in the people's sight), two of which were black inside. A child between six and seven years old, in this case Leonard, son of the attorney-general Jean-Pierre Trembley, drew them one by one from a bag, giving each one to each of the six candidates according to their rank. Each of the candidates then opened up his box: the first and the fourth boxes were black inside, and Jacob De la Rive and Jean Sales were therefore excluded from the election. After the vote took place between the four remaining candidates, André Dunant and Pierre Lect were finally elected (R.C., 191, 01/11/1691, pp. 316–320).

In 1692, the Small Council suggested that the process of exclusion should take place at the town hall just before the election, rather than in the General Council 'in the people's sight'. This idea was submitted to the Two Hundred, which rejected it. The process of exclusion continued to be conducted in the people's sight (R.C., 192, 06/11/1692, pp. 301–304), but such proposals reflected a general tension in the organization of sortition between elements which emphasized the democratic nature of Genevan government—the exclusion of candidates by lot should be done before the eyes of the sovereign people—and other elements which just as clearly revealed the reality of aristocratic power—as evidenced by the desire to have exclusion conducted in the town hall, where the lieutenant and the auditors were also sworn into office after the vote (Edicts on the offices, p. 22).

Conclusion

If we limited ourselves to a quantitative analysis, the existing data would only allow us to say that the introduction of sortition in the election of auditors in 1691 slightly extended the waiting period the young councillors of the Two Hundred had to go through before being elected as auditors. But if we examine the reasons put forward by the Small Council and the Two Hundred to justify its introduction, however, we can see that it was presented as a remedy against the cabals which were said to be so frequent in those elections. This remedy appeared more effective than the swearing of oaths, which were less and less feared from a religious point of view. How sortition was performed also reflected the fundamental ambiguity of Genevan government, which was democratic *de jure* but aristocratic *de facto*. But its introduction can also be understood in the context of the Republic's self-representation, which was characteristic of governmental discourse. The Republic was in theory a community of equals, where nobody attempted, through cabals, to put their own personal interests above the public interest (Walter, 1993, p. 4).

Lottery was used for more than forty years in the elections of auditors, until the 'Illustrious Mediation' of 1738 (Sautier, 1979, p. 837; Illustrious Mediation, 1738, p. 150). The process of being excluded by receiving a black ball and the elimination of the right to automatic entry into the Council of the Sixty when leaving office had entailed a lack of interest in the office of auditor, which was already quite an ungrateful task. At times, exclusion by lot had meant falling back on candidates with little talent (Sautier, 1979, p. 838). In 1738, the Small Council asked the mediators *in extremis* to abolish this rule, and the former procedure was restored: four candidates would be submitted to a vote by the General Council, which would elect two of them. However, this measure did not solve the problems associated with this office, since the Small Council would complain again in 1751 about 'the repugnance shown for the office of auditor by almost all those who should naturally aspire to it' (*ibid.*).

References

Primary sources

Edicts on the offices: *Édits faits et revus en Conseil général sur les offices de la ville le 29 de janvier 1568 (1707)*, Geneva: Société des libraires.

Illustrious Mediation of 1738: booklet published on the 'Règlement de l'Illustre Médiation pour la pacification des troubles de la République de Genève' (1738), Geneva: by the De Tournes brothers, publishers of the Republic (booklet inserted in the Registers of the Small Council, R.C., 238, 07/05/1738, p. 150).

Registers of the Small Council: Registres du Petit Conseil de la République de Genève (in the State Archives of Geneva).

Rivoire, E. (1935) *Les sources du droit du canton de Genève*, vol. 4 1621–1700, Aarau: H.R. Sauerlander and Cie.

Secondary sources

Barat, R. (2015) Qu'est-ce qu'une brigue? Pratiques et acteurs des brigues électorales dans la République de Genève à la fin du XVIIᵉ siècle, *Revue Suisse d'Histoire*, no. 3, pp. 379–393.

Braun, R. (1988) *Le déclin de l'Ancien régime en Suisse. Un tableau de l'histoire économique et sociale au XVIIIᵉ siècle* (translated from German 1984), Lausanne & Paris: Éditions d'en bas, Éditions de la maison des sciences de l'homme.

Cicchini, M. (2012) *La police de la République. L'ordre public à Genève au XVIIIᵉ siècle*, Rennes: Presses universitaires de Rennes.

Fatio, N. & Fatio, O. (2007) *Pierre Fatio et la crise de 1707*, Geneva: Labor et Fides.

Favet, G. (1998) *Les syndics de Genève au XVIIIᵉ siècle, Étude du personnel politique de la République*, Geneva: Société d'histoire et d'archéologie de Genève.

Lignereux, Y. (2006) Vox populi, vox dei? Les élections consulaires lyonnaises dans la première moitié du XVIIᵉ siècle, in *Images et pratiques de la ville (XVIᵉ–XIXᵉ)*, no. 2, pp. 103–132, Saint-Étienne.

Manin, B. (1996) Venice, in *Principes du gouvernement représentatif,* pp. 88–93, Paris: Flammarion.

Roth-Lochner, B. (1992) *Messieurs de la Justice et leur greffe: aspects de la législation, de l'administration de la justice civile genevoise et du monde de la pratique sous l'Ancien-Régime,* Geneva & Paris: Droz, Champion.

Sautier, J. (1979) *La Médiation de 1737–1738. Contribution à l'histoire des institutions politiques de Genève,* Doctoral dissertation, Paris II.

Spurr, J. (2001) A profane history of early modern oaths, *Transactions of the Royal Historical Society,* 6th series, vol. 11, pp. 37–63.

Walter, F. (1993) *Felicitas Reipublicae*: Leurs Excellences, le pouvoir et l'argent XVIIe–XVIIIe siècles, *Revue suisse d'art et d'archéologie,* 50, pp. 1–12.

Antoine Chollet and
Aurèle Dupuis

Kübellos *in the*
Canton of Glarus
A Unique Experience
of Sortition in Politics

Translated by Kate Davis

In all of the analyses done by specialists in sortition, or drawing lots, Switzerland, or more correctly the communities that would later make up Switzerland, is strangely absent.[1] Neither Bernard Manin, Oliver Dowlen, nor Hubertus Buchstein mention it, to take just a few important overviews of the subject (Manin, 1995; Dowlen, 2008;[2] Buchstein, 2009). Yet drawing lots was used extensively beginning in the 17th and up until the 19th century. There are of course some exceptions. Engelstad (1989), for example, describes some uses of drawing lots in the old Swiss confederacy. We can imagine that Lyn Carson and Brian Martin got their information from this text, although they do not specifically mention it (Carson and Martin, 1999, p. 33). Yves Sintomer dedicated a paragraph to Glarus in his *Petite histoire de l'expérimentation démocratique* (Sintomer, 2011, p. 96). With the exception of these few examples, there is no mention of Swiss cases in research on drawing lots in politics, even when the subject is examined from a historical angle.

---

[1]   This text stems from research currently underway on the Swiss experiences in sortition financed by the Swiss national research fund (fund no. 10001A_163126). We would like to thank Alexandre Fontaine for his valuable comments.

[2]   In his book, Oliver Dowlen mentions Switzerland once, without going into any detail as he is in fact referring to the examples given by Elinor Ostrom whom we will mention later, according to the information provided by the author (Dowlen, 2008, p. 216).

Several different regions used sortition in '*Ancien Régime*' Switzerland. The historical context was one of numerous social and political uprisings that Swiss cantons and cities experienced at the end of the 17th century. These movements drew their impetus from certain factions in society that wanted to force local elites to share the most important, and sometimes most lucrative, positions, which up until then had remained the preserve of a few families, and which for the most part would remain in their hands (Braun, 1988; Church and Head, 2013, pp. 104–131; Walter, 2009, pp. 9–17).

The first of these regions, certainly the most important, were the oligarchic city-states. These were cities dominated by a local patrician class, such as Bern or Fribourg, and also cities governed by guilds. Near the turn of the 18th century, we see significant use of sortition. As indicated by Rudolf Braun, 'election by drawing lots was a particularity of urban cantons' (Braun, 1988, p. 174). In Bern it was used after the uprisings of 1691, and it was formally introduced in a regulation (*Losordnung*) in 1710, and used in particular to select bailiffs. This method of selecting a candidate, which combined elections with a draw, was practised throughout the entire 18th century but did not survive the revolutionary period (Weber, 2014; von Steiger, 1954, pp. 86–109). In Basel, the ordinance of 1718 provided for the use of a draw to designate people for a number of important judgeships, and even university professors (Engelstad, 1989, pp. 26, 32, and 35; Braun, 1988, pp. 210–211; Burkhardt, 1916). We also see it used in Geneva, although at the time the city was not part of the Confederation strictly speaking (Barat, 2018) and in Shaffhausen (Hofer, 2012, pp. 148–149), with a variety of specific methods. In all of these towns, the method was being used primarily to limit corruption among the elite and the venal practices of officeholders, with only limited success given that the true role of luck in the draw seems to have often been bypassed.

Subsequently, sortition was also used during the Helvetic Republic (1789–1803) and under the Act of Mediation (1803–1813), when the former confederation was under French control. It was, however, for quite different reasons and in a very different historical context from the previous examples that sortition was introduced in these cases. The political institutions of the Helvetic Republic were inspired by those of the French Directoire, where draws were used as a tool for 'deselection' (Dowlen, 2008, pp. 206–211). Every two years, a portion of each of the two houses of parliament was replaced by draw. The exercise, however, was carried out only once, in 1799 for the Senate and in 1800 for the Grand Council, as the political strife in the following years gradually rendered the Helvetic institutions less and less powerful. The executive functioned on a similar model and every year one of the five directors was designated by a draw and had to step down (Kölz, 2006, p. 128). Under the Helvetic Republic and the Act of Mediation governments, other procedures that combined election and sortition were also used, for example for the nomination of parliamentarians. It is, however, not possible to positively equate these uses of chance in politics with the ideas of the French Revolution, as the most conservative members of the Geneva patrician class who recovered power in the city in 1813–14 would later also draft a constitution that would include the use of a draw in some of its procedures, however residual that presence was (Ruchon, 1941).

The third context for random draws, of which we find examples throughout Europe, concerns their use to allocate goods, particularly land or land usage rights, notably in rural communities in the Alps. This aspect is covered by Robert Netting in two ethnographic works dedicated to the village of Törbel (in Visp, Valais) and used later by Elinor Ostrom in her book on the commons (Netting, 1972; Ostrom, 1990, pp. 61–65). There are many examples of allocating rare goods by draw in regions where farming or grazing were particularly difficult and where misuse of land, water, or sun exposure could have catastrophic consequences (Weiss, 1941). In the case of Switzerland, these practices developed in villages where the influence of external authorities was weak and where, consequently, the residents were nearly completely self-governing. In mountainous regions, the distance from higher authorities (church or state) often fostered the development of democratic forms not merely limited to the use of sortition (Mouthon, 2011; Barber, 1974).

It was in any case in the cantons referred to as 'democratic' that use of a draw dates back the farthest in the old Confederation. Fredrick Engelstad mentions these Swiss examples and relies on Eugène Rambert's text from the end of the 19th century (Engelstad, 1989, pp. 26 and 42). In a series titled *Les Alpes Suisses*, Rambert (1830–1886) examines *Landsgemeinden,* the open-air assemblies held once a year where all free men (those having the right to bear arms) would gather in some cantons in central Switzerland.[3] He dug up some old sortition practices, mentioning as an example the case of Schwytz. He stressed that the *Landsgemeinde* in this canton introduced the practice in 1692 for certain magistrates in order to 'put a stop to the deeply rooted abuses

---

[3]   There is very little work on *Landsgemeinden* in French, what does exist is very old or of poor quality. We refer rather to Silvano Möckli (1987) or Hans-Peter Schaub (2016).

of elected positions and corruption' (Rambert, 1889, p. 226). The assembly almost as quickly gave up this system and by 1718 had declared it illegal to even propose a return to drawing lots. In the Grisons, draws seem to have been used at a local level for a long period (Barber, 1974, p. 176), although it should be noted that neither Randolf Head nor Florian Hitz mention these practices in their studies of the political structures in the Grison Valley (Head, 1995; Hitz, 2012).[4] However, it is a very particular case, that of Glarus, that will retain our interest here.

Balls of Silver, Balls of Gold

The canton of Glarus[5] is located south-east of Zurich, in the Alpine Linth River valley. It joined the Confederation in 1352, at that time made up of the cantons of central Switzerland, Zurich, and Lucerne, although for some time it had a secondary status. Sparsely populated (22,000 residents at the end of the 18th century), it differed from other cantons in two principal ways. It was a mixed denomination canton from the 16th century, although the majority of residents were Protestant. Secondly, industrialization occurred much earlier there than in other *Landsgemeinde* cantons in Switzerland, with numerous factories setting up along the Linth River from the 18th century to make use of its hydraulic energy. It was in the early part of the century that the first Zurich-owned spinning businesses, still artisanal-scale, set up in Glarus in search of labour (Braun, 1988, p. 99; Bergier, 1984, pp. 157–160). While Switzerland quickly became one of the most industrialized regions of Europe, this transformation affected mainly the plains areas around Zurich and Geneva. Industrializsation in Glarus made it stand out from other cantons that used *Landsgemeinde* whose economies were based essentially on agriculture.

It seems that in 1640 Glarus was the first canton in the old Confederation to begin using a system of lots (Braun, 1988, p. 174). This is supported by the *Dictionnaire historique de la Suisse*, which does not include any earlier mention of the practice. The canton of Glarus therefore played an innovative role in this sense and likely influenced other Swiss towns of the *Ancien Régime* (Mathieu and Stauffacher, 1986, p. 343). We do not know what inspired those people who decided to

---

4   Head (1995, p. 83) does, however, note the use of a draw for use of common goods.
5   In German it is common to refer to *Ort* or *Stand* to indicate political communities under the old confederation. The term *canton*, much older in French, was only introduced into the German political vocabulary, as *Kanton*, much later (Oechsli, 1916, pp. 74–88).

draw lots for some of the magistrate positions in Glarus. Ancient Greece seems improbable, even if the learned people of the time did know something of Athenian and Roman customs, as demonstrated by the book by Thomas Gataker, first published in 1619 (Gataker, 2008, pp. 37–45). The Italian examples from the late Middle Ages must have been known north of the Alps, but we find no references to it in the context of Glarus. A third possible source of inspiration could be the many examples of lots drawn in the Old Testament of the Bible. Lastly, surely the most plausible explanation draws a connection between this practice and the practices of distributing rare goods in Alpine communities, which predates it and in which chance frequently played a role.

The political system in the canton of Glarus became more complex in 1623, when the institution of the *Landsgemeinde* was divided in two following the conflicts between Reformation supporters and the communities that remained faithful to the Catholic church. At this time, an agreement between Catholics (minority) and Protestants (majority) determined the distribution of power between the denominations. Below are a few of the principal elements:

> Since the third agreement (1623), each denomination held a separate *Landsgemeinde* eight days before the general *Landsgemeinde* (the Protestant in Schwanden, the Catholic in Näfels) and these assemblies were responsible for approving military capitulations with foreign countries[6] and filling public positions. Elected officials then had to be presented to the general *Landsgemeinde*; despite the denominational division, they governed jointly. A Catholic would be *Landamman* for two years, followed by a Protestant in the position for three years. The denominations alternately elected the banneret, a position for life, the newly-created position of flag-bearer being given to the other party. The treasurer, the master builder and the judicial officer were selected from among the Protestants for six years, then from the Catholics for three years. The Protestants supplied two secretaries and two messengers, the Catholics one. The shared bailiwicks[7] falling to Glarus to be filled were attributed twice to a Protestant then once to a Catholic. Each party chose a representative to the Diet and for diplomatic missions. [...] The denominational division spread to the Council in 1625 and later to the courts. (Marti-Weissenbach, 2006, p. 609)

---

[6]   'Capitulations' here refers to foreign service, or the hiring out of mercenary companies to foreign sovereigns, a particularly lucrative practice in Glarus up until the 18th century.

[7]   In the old Confederation, many regions were controlled by another canton and under the administration of a bailiff. In some cases, particularly modern-day Ticino, Argovia, Thurgovia, and in the Rhine Valley, lands would be under the control of several cantons, and these we refer to as shared bailiwicks. They played a significant role in consolidating ties between sovereign cantons under the old Confederation.

In this context, the Protestant and Catholic *Landsgemeinden* each separately introduced the use of drawing lots. The Protestant one took this decision in 1638, and first put it into practice in 1640, while its Catholic counterpart made use of it beginning in 1649. Like elsewhere, the main idea was to stem the tide of corruption, known as *Gauzen und Trölen* or *Praktizierend*, which was deeply rooted in the political mores of Switzerland at the time. Seen as a form of redistribution of earnings from the position held, the practice consisted of buying participants' votes by organizing celebrations with liberal wine and dinners (Stauffacher, 1989, p. 64; Head, 1997). It was not uncommon for candidates to host banquets on the eve of an election, a practice which puts us in mind of Evergetism in Ancient Greece.

Since most of the measures taken to combat this corruption, such as making candidates swear an oath or fines in case of repeat offences, had very little effect, the two sides of the canton sought to institutionalize this informal purchasing of positions (Stauffacher, 1989, pp. 64–65). And so at the beginning of the 17th century a 'system of obligations' was introduced that consisted of setting a fixed price for each position, with the money collected being then redistributed to voters and the cantonal coffers. The official elected by the majority then had to spend a set amount to access a given position. To become guardian of the arsenal (*Zeugherr*) in 1744 cost 92 florins while the position of vice-*Landamman* (*Landesstatthalter*, second-most important public position) cost 337 florins (Mathieu and Stauffacher, 1986, p. 341). These amounts were equivalent to 400 and 1,500 days of work, respectively, at an average salary (Stauffacher, 1989, p. 284), and obviously limited access to the positions to only the wealthiest families in the canton. Such sums of money, however, did not curb corruption, and in order to more effectively combat it, drawing lots was instituted in the mid-17th century in the canton of Glarus.

There is another reason that explains the introduction of sortition for certain positions in the canton. The agreement of 1623 suddenly created more positions to fill. The denominational division had ended up multiplying the number of magistrates in order to satisfy both religions, and drawing lots was also introduced as a way to deal with the low number of candidates (*ibid.*, p. 66).

In Glarus, the system was initially a combination of election by majority by a show of hands and drawing lots. Within the Protestant *Landsgemeinde*, magistrates were drawn after election (by a show of hands) of eight candidates. The Catholic *Landsgemeinde* put in place an identical procedure in 1649, but with only five or six candidates. A regional distribution was guaranteed at election in the case of the

Protestant *Landsgemeinde* with two people from the *Hinterland* (southern part of the canton), four from the *Mittelland* (the region around the county town), and two from the *Unterland* (the north of the canton). Once the election by show of hands took place, a boy was chosen to give an egg-shaped box to each of the eight candidates all gathered in the centre of the assembly. The eight boxes each contained either one of seven silver balls or the single golden ball. The candidates then opened their box and the person with the golden ball won the position (Winteler, 1952, p. 416; Stauffacher, 1989, pp. 65–66).

This system, known as *Mehr und Los* (Majority and Chance) was used for the positions of judges, emissaries (*Gesandschaft*), and all cantonal positions with the exception of the *Landamman* (head of government and most important position in the canton), the *Landesstatthalter* (vice-*Landamman*), and certain bailiff positions, in particular Werdenberg, a bailiwick located in the Rhine Valley and purchased by Glarus in 1517.

Let us hear directly from an eye-witness who describes how the process played out. Louis Ramond (1755–1827), a French botanist, attended the Protestant *Landsgemeinde* in Schwanden (a village located a few kilometres to the south of the town of Glarus) in 1777. Here is how he describes it in his travel account:

> They then proceeded to nominate various officers of the regency; the election was done thus: the Chairman having named the position to be filled, the Clerk went around the entire circle taking down the names dictated to him as persons proposed. Any citizen was free to put forward a name, but as the names of those who had some right to hold office was always very limited, the same names were on everyone's lips and the number of persons put forward did not reach past a certain point; the list was then given to the Chairman who put forward the candidates one by one for a vote of the Assembly. As he called them out, the number of votes was counted by raised hands, and all the names with the least number of hands were rejected; sortition or the votes taken decided among those who were left. One might guess that this process was very slow, and the session which had begun at 10 o'clock in the morning went on until seven in the evening. (Quoted in Gehring, 1943, pp. 74–75)

Our research shows that it was a desire to decrease the amount spent on electoral corruption that led to the adoption of this method. By decreasing the chance of acceding to the position sought, the role of chance tempered individuals' enthusiasm and reduced the sums spent on banquets and drink, practices which were incidentally frequently criticized for moral reasons in contemporary accounts. In concrete terms, Hans Rudolf Stauffacher affirms that access to those positions that were attributed by sortition grew during the 18th century. He went so far as to qualify it as a 'surprising success', counting the number of persons who acceded to new positions during this period and noting the large number of new names among them (Stauffacher, 1989, p. 66). To give just one example, between 1733 and 1798, 16 candidates stood for election for the bailiwick of Werdenberg, which had instituted drawing lots during this period; of these 16 people, only three acceded to no position. The use of lots seems then to have offered a possibility to newly wealthy, less important families to enter into competition with the traditional cantonal elites (*ibid.*, p. 66).

However, the introduction of draws did not truly curb corruption. On the one hand, the *Landsgemeinde* was still responsible for electing the eight persons to whom the golden and silver balls would be distributed, determining who would receive the position, which meant that buying votes was not entirely useless, although the final result was not guaranteed. More importantly, the distribution of the balls seems to have suffered from some irregularities. In his history of the canton of Glarus, Jakob Winteler mentions the fraud during the random draws, which he jokingly referred to as resulting in a 'miraculous chance of luck' (*wunderbaren Zufall des Loses*) (Winteler, 1954, p. 128). It seems that some candidates were allowed to exchange their ball until they got the right one. And lastly, we see confirmation of this cheating in the decision of the Protestant *Landsgemeinde* in 1764, which threatened to withdraw the honour of a position from anyone drawing multiple balls. Exchange of balls also occurred, doubtless for a fee. Another similar incident occurred during the vote for an important military rank (*Landesfähnrich*) in 1769. The golden ball went to the only candidate who did not belong to the dominant elite. The chosen person then declined the position, and the following year for nominations for the same position, only representatives of the canton's major families took part in the draw (Mathieu and Stauffacher, 1986, p. 345).

Finally, we should note that, similar to the oligarchical city-states, the introduction of drawing lots in the democratic cantons went together with the more or less complete closing off of access to the bourgeoisie, and therefore to citizenship (we know that here bourgeois, *Burger* in German, means the inhabitant of a town who enjoys full rights and only indirectly has any economic meaning, quite different from the meaning it would take on in the 19th century). Rudolf Braun notes this closing off of access in the case of Schwytz, but the phenomenon spread throughout the Swiss regions in the 18th century (Braun, 1988, p. 221). This shows that once again the expansion of rights, liberties, and privileges for citizens almost necessarily goes together with an increasingly exclusive citizenship.

The modest success of introducing sortition in Glarus, continued corruption and citizens' desire to enjoy the revenue generated by the canton would lead to a significant change in the procedure in Glarus by the end of the 18th century.

The *Kübellos*: A Double
Draw Involving All Citizens

It was at the end of the 18th century that an unprecedented reform was introduced in Glarus. On 27 April 1791, the *Landsgemeinde* decided that the positions of chancellor (*Landschreiber*), messenger (*Läufer*), and boat master (*Schiffmeister*), as well as the emissaries (*Gesandten*) to the baili-wicks of Laui (a shared Italian bailiwick over which the canton of Glarus shared control with other confederacy cantons) and Gaster (a bailiwick located at the north of the Linth Valley and shared with the canton of Schwytz) would be drawn from a pool of all the citizens, using a double draw system (Stauffacher, 1989, p. 278). The initial election by majority by show of hands was done away with for these public positions. Two years later, this system, referred to as *Kübellos*, was extended to include the judicial officer (*Landweibel*), and also the bailiwicks of Werdenberg and Mendrisio (another Italian bailiwick). The only groups excluded from the draw were members of the clergy and the citizens who had held a position the previous year. Conversely, citizens living outside of the canton but who paid taxes there were allowed to participate.[8] It should be noted that the most important positions, first and foremost the *Landamman,* remained outside of this system (Winteler, 1954, p. 228; Braun, 1988, p. 175).

All citizens then could potentially accede to important positions. Unlike in Athens, the selection was not based on volunteers, but rather drew from the entire body of citizens, which at that time included roughly 5,400 people. The procedure included two subsequent draws and was particularly slow and complex; the first time it was used, the election lasted three days. Here is a description of this double draw given in 1795 by Othmar Heer, son of former *Landamman* Cosmus Heer, in a letter titled *Briefe, auf einer kleinen Schweizerreise*:

---

8   We have chosen the term 'citizen' here while the original German is *Landeleute*, meaning 'people of the land'. The status of *Bürger* is more often found in urban contexts, although it is also used in texts dealing with Glarus.

> The names of all eligible citizens, meaning those aged sixteen or older, are written on sealed papers and placed in a rotating cylinder, and in another similar cylinder are placed the same number of tickets as in the first cylinder, all blank except for eight ballots numbered from one to eight with the name of the position also written on it. Once all of this is ready, *in pleno senatu* [in the council room], the cylinders are given to two magistrates, who simultaneously draw names from the first one and ballots from the other. Once a name is drawn at the same time as a winning ballot, it is included in the draw. The lucky ones who will take part in this drawing must number eight, and only then can the one who will occupy the position be selected from among them. (Quoted in Winteler, 1954, p. 229, our translation)

Subsequently, another draw decided among these eight people selected. These 'rotating cylinders' do put one in mind of the revolving urn (*urna versatilis*) used in Rome for draws (Bothorel, 2020), although it is impossible to establish a clear link between the two things. In the case of Glarus, the tools used for the draw were in fact simple butter churns, a common household object in this Alpine canton.

There are several reasons this practice was extended to include all citizens, something absolutely unheard of in modern European history, which remain unclear, all the more so because the practice of drawing lots in other cantons within *Landsgemeinde* was abandoned, as we saw in the case of Schwytz, a canton neighbouring Glarus. Jakob Winteler and Hans Rudolf Stauffacher seem to agree in their assessment that it was an application of the egalitarian ideals of the French Revolution. Stauffacher qualifies the *Kübellos* as a 'precursor to widespread equality' (Stauffacher, 1989, p. 67). In the first decision of the council governing the functioning of the *Kübellos*, we see a direct reference to the French context:

> On 7 May 1791, the Protestant Council decided on the procedure for the *Kübellos* that the *Landsgemeinde* had adopted in the spring of 1791 [...]. By doing so, they were inspired by the 'way in which French (school) bursaries had formerly been distributed by draw'. (*ibid.*, p. 278, our translation)

Reference to the French revolutionary context to explain the institution of the *Kübellos* is not new. In his *History of Glarus* published in 1836, the pastor Melchior Schuler (1779–1859), a native of the canton, also mentions the 'influence of the revolutionary spirit' and adds that, by instituting this system, the canton was going too far (Schuler, 1836, p. 353).

While the system involving the double draw put in place by the *Landsgemeinde* in 1791 may seem unnecessary, it was not unheard of in history. As Engelstad notes, 'At first sight, this practice appears meaningless. Why not select one candidate at once?' (Engelstad, 1989, p. 38). His hypothesis, specifically addressing the Glarus system, is that the double draw can be substituted for other procedures used in the past which involved an election. The adoption of a two-phase draw is then a way to preserve something of the old system, given that the second step remains the same.

We might also wonder why the drawing of lots involved two separate urns, rather than directly selecting the eight names needed in the second draw, a procedure which would have had the advantage of being infinitely faster. It should first be noted that this system granted more effective protection against fraud because two separate officers are drawing at the same time, the name of the person on the one side and the winning or losing tickets on the other. Next, we must also consider that this endless drawing of thousands of names would become a sort of civic ritual, creating a public event with a particular quality (an element that we also see in some ways during the *Landsgemeinde* assembly days).

We see this illustrated in a letter from French archaeologist Raoul-Rochette (1789-1854) written on 15 August 1820 in which he describes the electric atmosphere in Glarus on the day of the draw:

> From the early morning, I noticed in all of the population a movement, an agitation that seemed to announce some extraordinary event. A crowd of people of all ages took to the avenues, flooding the vestibule and the steps of the town hall; and for such hard-working men it certainly would have taken a very clear interest, or a cause for powerful curiosity to get them to leave aside their labour. [...] At the time of this writing, the evening of this stormy day, calm has returned to everything around me. All the chances of fortune have been exhausted, and all legitimate claims satisfied. (Raoul-Rochette, 1823, pp. 159 and 163)

The *Kübellos* system led to a particular practice: in most cases, the citizens chosen by draw did not have the financial means for the position they were to accede to, and they chose to sell it. Positions received within this system were the subject of some speculation (Blumer, 1858, p. 129). In his work, Eugène Rambert mentions this aspect of the system:

> The inhabitants of Glarus [...] moved boldly forward. They ended up establishing a sort of absolute drawing of lots, involving all citizens, first for some minor positions, which did however include the secretary of state, and then for higher positions and important missions. The bailiwicks were drawn for. The chosen person, if he were a poor devil, bartered his luck; he would sell the job that had fallen to him to the person offering the largest sum. This was *Practisiren*, the unavoidable *Practisiren* reaffirming its hold. To top this accumulation of impossible

chances and contradictions, the Council reserved the right to examine whether this highest bidder, the replacement for a man whose lot was drawn, offered sufficient guarantees of skill and character. (Rambert, 1889, pp. 217–218)

However widespread this practice of selling off one's position was, it should be remembered that, unlike other historic cases for which we have evidence in medieval and modern Europe, the canton of Glarus is the only one, along with Schwytz, in which the drawing of lots was imposed by an assembly of theoretically sovereign citizens, and it was that body itself which imposed the switch to the *Kübellos* system.

The question of using lots in fact remained a burning one in the first decades of the 19th century. In 1804, a special *Landsgemeinde* session decided to extend the *Kübellos* to honorific positions (*Ehrenämter*). In 1813, the paid positions of lesser importance were also attributed this way, drawing the criticism of the *Landamman* who maintained that this procedure was a stain on the honour of the country (Winteler, 1954, p. 346).

The introduction of this double draw system is already in and of itself surprising; even more surprising is the fact that it continued after the revolutionary period (Glarus had new constitutions in 1803 and again in 1814) and was maintained in one form or another up until the constitution of 1836 put an end to it. This makes Glarus one of the last examples in Europe of a sovereign political community using the drawing of lots to decide its principal magistracies.

Finally, the use of sortition was expressly prohibited in the 1836 constitution of the canton of Glarus: 'Auctioning and drawing lots for magistracy are hereby abolished' (*'Die Versteigerung und die allgemeine Verloosung von Landesbedienstungen ist abgeschafft'*, Glarus Constitution, 1836, chap. 3, §29). Along with eliminating positions held for life, clearly separating powers and guaranteeing certain fundamental liberties, this 1836 constitution, described by Alfred Kölz as 'one of the best of the Regeneration,[9] both in its form and in its content' (Kölz, 2006, p. 245), put an end to a two hundred year-old practice of drawing lots in the canton.

---

[9] The period known as the 'Regeneration' was an important time of transformation of political institutions at the beginning of the 1830s, when the liberal movement was taking off in Switzerland. It would later, in 1848, lead to the founding of the Federal state, the birth of Switzerland as a unified political entity.

An Incomplete and Laconic History

Compared to other historical examples, we cannot fail to be surprised by historians' silence on the use of sortition in Glarus. We have already noted that those specializing in sortition hardly speak of the use of draws in Swiss cantonal politics, and even less of the case of Glarus. The few mentions of Swiss cases are merely factual in nature and most often are limited to the dates when the practice of drawing lots started and when it ended, as we have seen above.

Among the Swiss historians focusing on the *Ancien Régime*, other than the few monographs mentioned above (von Steiger, 1954; Burkhardt, 1916), we can mention Rudolf Braun, who examines in greater detail than his colleagues the practice of drawing lots. For the specific case of Glarus, he relies on the work of Hans Rudolf Stauffacher, whose thesis he directed. The few histories of the canton of Glarus, however, take no specific interest in this issue (Brunner, 2004; Winteler, 1952).

This relative silence seems to be, more than ignorance, the result of the harsh judgment on sortition in politics. Winteler writes for example that, at the end of 18th century, the words 'liberty and equality' made people 'lose their heads', making the *Kübellos* a game of chance allowing the winner to earn money easily (Winteler, 1954, pp. 229–230). Remarks on the problems encountered in the use of draws are always included in the passages dealing with the practice, and they insist on the supposedly unrealistic or impractical nature of such a mechanism in political institutions.

This judgment in fact seems to be a very old one. The account by Eugène Rambert of the use of lots in democratic cantons is edifying in this respect. He sees in it the last example of the corruption and 'rottenness' of the old democracies, which would lead to their defeat at the hands of the French troops in 1798 (Rambert, 1889, p. 228). We have already mentioned the 'accumulation of impossible chances and contradictions' that he sees as part of the institution of *Kübellos*, while he takes a generally positive view of the equally surprising institution of the *Landsgemeinde* in the second half of the 19th century. These views led him to pronounce this final judgment: 'more than one landsgemeinde had recourse to the desperate measure of beleaguered democracies, the draw' (*ibid.*, pp. 225–226).

According to almost unanimous general opinion, the failure of the community was at work as much in the causes as in the consequences of sortition. On one side there is the extreme corruption of the elites buying the various public positions and, on the other side, the weakness of the political body that together would have brought about the selection of magistrates by a draw. As it concerns an institution used for two centuries in a society that was undergoing profound economic and social transformations, the judgment does seem somewhat harsh.

Hans Rudolf Stauffacher stands out in that he goes on slightly more at length about the drawing mechanism in Glarus, and also in that he provides a more nuanced evaluation. He is interested in the egalitarian, progressive dimension of the *Kübellos*. He notes that, unlike in other cases of sortition in politics at the end of the 18th or beginning of the 19th centuries, whether considering the Bern patricians or the constitution of Geneva of 1814, the rules decided by the *Landsgemeinde* in Glarus were turned definitively toward the future rather than the past.

Conclusion

The limited number of works that directly address sortition in Glarus highlights how insufficient research into the question is. And yet, this small, bi-denominational canton constituted a veritable laboratory of political experimentation from the 17th to the beginning of the 19th century, which was not merely limited to drawing lots.

Not only did this experiment continue over a long period of time, it was also characterized by very original voting procedures in a conservative context where political positions were considered private property passed down within families (Mathieu and Stauffacher, 1986, p. 346). Introduced initially to reduce electoral corruption, random selection, firstly combined with elections and then opened up to all citizens, failed to effectively address the problem, which persisted until the Helvetic Republic. It should also be recalled that the truly important positions, such as the *Landamman*, were never included in a draw.

While the use of a draw seems to have allowed a few, less influential but nonetheless still well-off families in Glarus to access political positions and compete with the traditional elite, Stauffacher and Mathieu also affirm that "the introduction of the draw to determine cantonal functions led to a decrease in political competition and strong social cohesion among the leading families" (Mathieu and Stauffacher, 1986, p. 353). Draws thus served to pacify the population as can be recognized in a number of historic cases (Delannoi, 2011, p. 157). It is also intriguing to note that, in terms of techniques, there are a number of similarities between towns in the north of Italy in the late Middle Ages and in the Swiss context (the use of balls, a child being included, and a combination of drawing lot with elections).

The establishment of this technique in a political entity where the entire body of citizens exercised sovereignty and where power was viewed as belonging to every part of the citizenry is particular to the canton of Glarus in this decisive period on the brink between the 18th and 19th centuries. The experiment with sortition in politics there is thus both exciting and very original, and it deserves, in our opinion, to be added to the tradition of political lotteries in classical history.

References

Barat, R. (2018) *Les élections que fait le peuple (République de Genève, 1680–1707)*, Geneva: Droz.

Barber, B. (1974) *The Death of Communal Liberty: A History of Freedom in a Swiss Mountain Canton*, Princeton, NJ: Princeton University Press.

Bergier, J.-F. (1984) *Histoire économique de la Suisse*, Lausanne: Payot.

Blumer, J.-J. (1858) *Staats- und Rechtsgeschichte der schweizerischen Demokratien (Uri, Schwytz, Unterwald, Glarus, Zug, Appenzell)*, vol. 2, St-Gall: Scheitlin und Zollikofer.

Bothorel, J. (2020) Civic sortition in Republican and Imperial Rome: Physical instruments and technical logistics, in Lopez-Rabatel, L. & Sintomer Y. (eds.) *Sortition and Democracy: Practices, Instruments, Theories*, Exeter: Imprint Academic.

Braun, R. (1988 [1984]) *Le déclin de l'Ancien Régime en Suisse*, Lausanne: Éditions d'en bas; Paris: Éditions de la Maison des sciences de l'homme.

Brunner, C. (2004) *Glarner Geschichte in Geschichten*, Glaris: Baeschlin.

Buchstein, H. (2009) *Demokratie und Lotterie. Das Los als politisches Entscheidungsinstrument von der Antike bis zur EU*, Frankfurt: Campus.

Burkhardt, A. (1916) Ueber die Wahlart der Basler Professoren, besonders im 18. Jahrhundert, *Basler Zeitschrift für Geschichte und Altertumskunde*, vol. 15, pp. 28–46.

Carson, L. & Martin, B. (1999) *Random Selection in Politics*, Westport, CT: Praeger.

Church, C. & Head, R. (2013) *A Concise History of Switzerland*, Cambridge: Cambridge University Press.

Delannoi, G. (2011) Le tirage au sort: une approche démocratique, *Esprit*, n° 377, pp. 153–161, Paris: Esprit Presse.

Dowlen, O. (2008) *The Political Potential of Sortition*, Exeter: Imprint Academic.

Engelstad, F. (1989) The Assignment of Political Office by Lot, *Social Science Information*, 28 (1), pp. 23–50, London: Sage.

Gataker, T. (2008 [1627]) *Of the Nature and Use of Lots. A Treatise Historicall and Theologicall*, 2nd ed., Exeter: Imprint Academic.

Gehring, J. (1943) Das Glarnerland in den Reiseberichten des 17.-19. Jahrhundert, in Collectif, *Jahrbuch des Historischen Vereins des Kantons Glarus*, Glaris: Kommissionsverlag J. Baeschlin.

Head, R. (1995) *Early Modern Democracy in the Grisons: Social Order and Political Language in a Swiss Mountain Canton, 1470-1620*, Cambridge: Cambridge University Press.

Head, R. (1997) Shared Lordship, Authority, and Administration: The Exercise of Dominion in the Gemeine Herrschaften of the Swiss Confederation, 1417-1600, *Central European History*, 30 (4), pp. 489-512, Cambridge: Cambridge University Press.

Heer, O. (1795) *Briefe auf einer kleiner Schweizerreise geschrieben, über die Amter Verküblung in Glaris*, Glaris: Landesbibliothek.

Hitz, F. (2012) *Fürsten, Vögte und Gemeinden. Politische Kultur zwischen Habsburg und Graubünden im 15. bis 17. Jahrhundert*, Baden: Hier und Jetzt.

Hofer, R., *et al.* (2012) Schaffhouse, in Collectif, *Dictionnaire historique de la Suisse*, vol. 11, pp. 142-163, Hauterive: Éditions Gilles Attinger.

Kölz, A. (2006) *Histoire constitutionnelle de la Suisse moderne, ses fondements idéologiques et son évolution institutionnelle dans le contexte européen, de la fin de l'Ancien Régime à 1848*, Berne: Stämpfli.

Manin, B. (1995) *Principes du gouvernement représentatif*, Paris: Calmann-Lévy.

Marti-Weissenbach, K. (2006) L'État, le gouvernement et l'administration sous l'Ancien Régime, in Laupper, H., *et al.*, « Glaris », *Dictionnaire historique de la Suisse*, vol. 5, pp. 608-611, Hauterive: Éditions Gilles Attinger.

Mathieu, J. & Stauffacher, H.R. (1986) Alpine Gemeindedemokratie oder aristokratische Herrschaft? Eine Gegenüberstellung zweier schweizerischer Regionen im Ancien Régime, *Itinera*, n° 5/6, pp. 320-360, Bâle: Schwabe.

Möckli, S. (1987) *Die schweizerische Landsgemeinde-Demokratien*, Berne: Haupt.

Mouthon, F. (2011) *Histoire des anciennes populations de montagne*, Paris: L'Harmattan.

Netting, R. (1972) Of Men and Meadows: Strategies of Alpine Land Use, *Anthropological Quarterly*, 45 (3), pp. 132-144, Washington, DC: The Catholic University of America Press.

Oechsli, W. (1916) Die Benennungen der alten Eidgenossenschaft und ihrer Glieder. Erster Teil, *Jahrbuch für schweizerische Geschichte*, 41, pp. 51-230.

Ostrom, E. (1990) *Governing the Commons*, Cambridge: Cambridge University Press.

Rambert, E. (1889) *Études historiques et nationales. Les Alpes et la liberté, notre forteresse, de l'art national dans la Suisse centrale, les Landsgemeindes de la Suisse*, Lausanne: Librairie F. Rouge.

Raoul-Rochette, D. (1823) *Lettres sur la Suisse, écrites en 1819, 1820 et 1821*, vol. 2, Paris: Nepveu.

Ruchon, F. (1941) *De la restauration de la République à la retraite du Syndic Joseph des Arts (31 décembre 1813–7 décembre 1818)*, Geneva: Imprimerie centrale.

Schaub, H.-P. (2016) *Landsgemeinde oder Urne – was ist demokratischer? Urnen- und Versammlungsdemokratie in der Schweiz*, Baden-Baden: Nomos.

Schuler, M. (1836) *Geschichte des Landes Glarus*, Zurich: Friedrich Schulthess.

Sintomer, Y. (2011) *Petite histoire de l'expérimentation démocratique. Tirage au sort et politique d'Athènes à nos jours*, Paris: La Découverte. (English translation: *Between Radical and Deliberative Democracy: Random Selection in Politics from Athens to Contemporary Experiments*, Cambridge: Cambridge University Press, forthcoming.)

Stauffacher, H.R. (1989) *Herrschaft und Landsgemeinde. Die Machtelite in Evangelisch-Glarus vor und nach der Helvetischen Revolution*, Glaris: Tschudi.

von Steiger, C. (1954) *Innere Probleme des bernischen Patriziates an der Wende zum 18. Jahrhundert*, Berne: Stämpfli.

Walter, F. (2009) *Histoire de la Suisse. L'Âge classique (1600–1750)*, Neuchâtel: Alphil.

Weber, N. (2014) Gott würfelt nicht. Losverfahren und Kontingenzbewältigung bei Ratswahlen in der frühneuzeitlichen Republik Bern, Historikertag, Göttingen, 26 septembre (texte inédit).

Weiss, R. (1941) *Das Alpwesen Graubündens. Wirtschaft, Sachkultur, Recht, Älplerarbeit une Älplerleben*, Erlenbach: Rentsch.

Winteler, J. (1952) *Geschichte des Landes Glarus. Band I: Von den Anfängen bis 1638*, Glaris: Kommissionsverlag E. Baeschlin.

Winteler, J. (1954) *Geschichte des Landes Glarus. Band II: Von 1638 bis zur Gegenwart*, Glaris: Kommissionsverlag E. Baeschlin.

Maxime Mellina

The Use of Sortition in the Helvetic Republic

The Decline of Chance

Translated by Sarah-Louise Raillard

The use of random selection as a method to designate political representatives raises a number of interesting historical and socio-political
questions.[1] In particular, the disappearance of sortition practices at the
end of the 18th and the beginning of the 19th century remains an enigma.
Before the 18th century, the most famous examples of drawing lots
came to us from the 6th and 5th centuries BCE in Ancient Athens
(Headlam, 1891; Hansen, 2009 [1993]; Manin, 2012 [1995]; Dowlen,
2008, pp. 31–66; Sintomer, 2020, pp. 19–61), as well as from the Italian
city-states of the late Middle Ages and the early Renaissance, in
particular Florence and Venice (Wolfson, 1899; Rubinstein, 1966;
Najemy, 1982; Manin, 2012 [1995], pp. 74–93; Dowlen, 2008, pp. 67–136;
Sintomer, 2020, pp. 54–79). But even though there appear to have been
a few arguments made for the preservation of random selection
mechanisms during the French and American Revolutions, the idea of
using sortition for political purposes completely disappeared over the
course of the 19th century (Manin, 2012 [1995]; Sintomer, 2020, pp. 118–
131; Dupuis-Déri, 2013, pp. 87–158).

In that regard, Swiss experiments with sortition can shed new light
on the mechanism's progressive disappearance, as they are in fact late
examples of the use of random selection in Europe—perhaps among
the last for sovereign political communities. The town of Glarus used
sortition until 1836, for instance (Chollet and Dupuis, 2020). As was the

[1] This article was published thanks to funding provided by the Swiss National
Science Foundation (project No. 163126 titled 'Expériences du tirage au sort en
Suisse' [Random selection experiments in Switzerland], as well as SNSF Scientific
Exchange No. 10CO17_175429).

case in most European countries, starting in the 16th century, many Swiss cantons and their allied territories adopted various forms of random selection; these institutions then practically disappeared during the 19th century (Carson and Martin, 1999, p. 33). This change appears to have been rather abrupt, prompting many debates and controversies among contemporaries which are useful to understand the logic at work behind longer-term developments.

More specifically, the end of the 18th century and the short-lived Helvetic Republic were a particularly ebullient period, marked by the intellectual effervescence of the Enlightenment and the rapid transformation of the *Ancien Régime* at the dawn of the 19th century. As such, this period provides new elements for reflection on the disappearance of chance in politics — on the one hand, because this period gave rise to a vast body of writing, whether political, literary, scientific, or journalistic, that discussed the issues of political freedom, equality, sovereignty, representation, and the separation of powers (Kölz, 2006 [1992], pp. 65–68). And on the other hand, because this period was rife with institutional and intellectual innovation, sometimes combining traditional aristocratic (patriotic and corporatist) elements with new democratic (constitutional and egalitarian) components (Weeber, 2015, p. 62). Following the drafting of the Helvetic Constitution on 12 April 1798 and until the Act of Mediation establishing the Swiss Confederation in 1803, the political elites of the Helvetic Republic engaged in intense discussions regarding political structures. In the wake of the government coups that began to multiply after 1800, the constitutional question became the main subject of domestic policy, inciting all parties to propose potential solutions.

According to historian Andreas Fankhauser, 'as seen from Paris, the [Helvetic Republic] was both a satellite State among others and a kind of constitutional laboratory' (Fankhauser, 2013). For example, the prefectural system was only introduced in France in 1800, after having been 'tested out' in Switzerland. The idea of Switzerland as a laboratory was likewise espoused by the historian of constitutional law Alfred Kölz in his work *Histoire constitutionnelle de la Suisse moderne*, when he wrote that 'Switzerland has been a living laboratory to test out new theories of State and society inspired by rationalism and the Enlightenment. It has experienced a constant struggle around the constitutional issue' (Kölz, 2006 [1992], p. 65). The period of the Helvetic Republic therefore represents a key moment in the conceptual, institutional, and political transformation that occurred between the pre-revolutionary period and the creation of Swiss federalism in 1848, a moment during which the country began to lay the foundations of our contemporary systems of representative democracy (Holenstein, 2015, pp. 129 *sq.*).

Nonetheless, the numerous studies on the history of sortition have largely overlooked this political chapter (Dowlen, 2008, p. 216; Carson and Martin, 1999, p. 33).[2] Studies on random selection in Switzerland are few and far between, even though many of the country's communities adopted various forms of sortition throughout the years, generally to fight against the concentration of power in the hands of a few overly powerful families or corporations, or to limit the corruption of political elites. As for historical studies that examine the Helvetic Republic specifically (Andrey, 1986); Simon and Schulchter, 1995–2000; Fankhauser, 1993; Delvaux, 2004; Holenstein, 2009; Oddens, Rutjes and Jacobs, 2015),[3] while they sometimes mention chance as an element of the new state's institutional structures, to our knowledge none of them have examined in depth the use of chance by Helvetic institutions.

In this chapter, we shall examine the various chance-based mechanisms employed in the Helvetic Republic Constitution. It is essential for us to understand the political practices of random selection during this transitional period in order to comprehend the changes that disrupted contemporary political imaginaries, and to illustrate how the institutional complex of the Helvetic Republic combined elements from the *Ancien Régime* with components from the revolutionary period. By looking at sortition as a means of devolving power, we shall demonstrate that the Helvetic period represented a turning point in a longer socio-historical evolution by analysing the uses of random selection at the end of the 18th century and, in particular, the uses of sortition at court in the Helvetic Republic. Given that we do not believe that chance has an inherent theoretical meaning, but rather that any meaning developed is the result of complex dynamics, this chapter shall also examine a letter written by Peter Ochs, a resident of Basel who in 1798 penned the first draft of the Helvetic Constitution – later modified by the French Directory – in which he outlined his position on the political use of sortition.

---

[2] For example, Olivier Dowlen alludes to it but without providing any further details. Carson and Martin likewise mention Switzerland and the random selection procedures that persisted until the 19th century in passing, but do not give any specific references.

[3] No work of general history devoted to the Helvetic Republic presents an in-depth analysis of sortition, although some mention it briefly.

A Wealth of Experiments and Uses

The first lesson we can glean from the turbulent period of the Helvetic Republic concerns the uses of random selection at the end of the 18th century. Chance was massively used in the former Confederation (Chollet and Dupuis, 2020) at the city and canton level alike, and also by the central authorities of the Republic, a few decades before the Federal Constitution was proclaimed in 1848 (a document in which no mention of chance is made). Random selection was employed in a number of well-established practices and represented an integral part of the Swiss political landscape.

The *Ancien Régime* was the period that saw the most widespread dissemination and proliferation of sortition practices, particularly during the 18th century. Random selection was used in oligarchic city-states such as Bern, Basel, and Schaffhausen (Kölz, 2006 [1992], pp. 7–64), but also in the so-called 'democratic' cantons, Glarus (Dupuis, 2018) and Schwyz (Braun, 1988 [1984]; Stauffacher, 1989) in particular, primarily to fight against the corruption of governing elites. Ten years after the French Revolution, sortition continued to be widely practised in various bodies of the Helvetic Republic, which over the course of a few years established an embryonic centralized Swiss State following the arrival of Napoleonic troops on the territory in 1798. The Constitution of the Helvetic Republic has often been described as a constitution imposed by France and based on the model of that country's 1795 Constitution of the Year III. While the influence exerted by the French Directory is undeniable, Swiss political elites were also highly involved in this project, most notably Basel resident Peter Ochs. If we look more closely at these two constitutional texts (French and Swiss), we can in fact see several important differences that shall be pointed out below.

Chance was therefore particularly present in the Constitution sworn into law on 12 April 1798[4] and in the Bulletins des Loix des Conseils législatifs (Official Anthology of the Laws of the Legislative Councils)[5] that expounded upon the initial constitutional text. In the 12 April 1798 Constitution, random selection was incorporated in a unique way into the political, legal, and military spheres to fulfil two different objectives. On the one hand, sortition was used to select representatives and magistrates, but it was always combined with elections and the possibility of elimination. It was also envisioned as a means to renew

---

[4]   Constitution of the Helvetic Republic of 12 April 1798 (Kölz, 2006 [1992], pp. 126–151).

[5]   Bulletin des Loix et Décrets du Corps Législatif de la République helvétique (1798).

the membership of government assemblies and deployed as a method of eliminating representatives who were already elected somewhere else, including members of the two main legislative chambers (the Grand Council and the Senate), as well as members of the executive Directory.

Selection Procedures for Magistrates

In the context of selecting legislative representatives and members of the Directory, popular sovereignty was an important principle enshrined in the 1798 Constitution, especially since citizens' assemblies, called 'primary assemblies' (art. 28 to 35) represented the institutional underpinning of the new state. These popular assemblies, composed of active citizens (art. 19) — the definition of a citizen being somewhat limited[6] — were called to meet once a year to elect the members of the cantonal electoral body, the grand electors who were tasked in turn with nominating members of the central legislative authorities (the Grand Council and the Senate). These primary assemblies used proportional voting, relative to the size of their population, to select the members of cantonal electoral assemblies. But all elected representatives did not become grand electors: half of them were in turn eliminated by random selection.

Just as in the majority of constitutional texts, many matters were left unaddressed by the Helvetic Constitution. The legislative councils were therefore in charge of elaborating clarifications through legislation. The elimination at random of members of the electoral assembly was thus outlined in the Law of 3 September 1799 on the Elimination of Half of the Electors Nominated by the Primary Assemblies:

> 1. Ten days after the primary assemblies are held, the national prefect shall gather together all the presidents of the administrative chamber, the cantonal court and the district court; these individuals shall be summoned to appear accompanied by the secretaries of the aforementioned competent authorities.
> 2. The doors to the hearing shall remain open, and as many individuals shall be allowed inside to listen as can be suitably accommodated.

---

[6] The Constitution of 1798 temporarily eliminated property qualifications for voting. In fact, former inhabitants who lacked real estate obtained the right to vote. Nonetheless, since elections were indirect and went through an electoral college, the eligibility requirements for voting, including the need to have established residence in the commune at least five years earlier, illustrate that political rights largely continued to be the purview of the property-owning bourgeoisie.

3. The secretaries of the competent authorities shall sit at a table, on which two empty leather purses shall be placed, each one trimmed with fringes inside the opening at the top.

[...]

5. The secretaries shall count and place upon the table as many white ballots of equal size as there are names of electors.

6. On these ballots, the names of the electors shall be clearly written down.

7. When it has been verified that the names of all the electors presented by the national prefect are indeed written down on these ballots and that the latter have been counted, they shall all be folded separately and in an equal fashion.

[...]

11. The ballots shall then be divided into two equal groups, on which the phrases 'remaining elector' and 'outgoing elector' shall be written, respectively.

[...]

16. The municipality of the capital city shall make arrangements beforehand so that two intelligent children shall enter the room, neither of which shall be older than six years of age.

17. These children shall open the ballots. One shall be placed in front of the national prefect and the other in front of the president of the administrative chamber.

18. After drawing the ballots on which the names are written down, one after another from one of the purses, the first child shall hand over the ballots drawn to the president of the cantonal court, who shall open them and read them aloud.

19. The secretaries shall then write down each name on a register, which shall again be read out loud immediately after being written down.

20. The other child, drawing the ballots designating whether the electors shall remain or be eliminated, shall immediately after hearing the name read by the first child, likewise draw a ballot from the second purse, and hand it over still closed to the president of the cantonal court, who shall immediately open it and read it aloud.

[...]

22. This process shall continue uninterrupted until all of the ballots have been drawn from both purses.[7]

The primary assemblies therefore represented the basis of the new state's political organization, since they legally established municipalities as the foundational level of the Helvetic Republic (Kölz, 2006 [1992], pp. 122–124). The precision and complexity of the random

---

[7] Loi du 3 septembre 1799 sur la Sortie de la moitié des Électeurs nommés par les Assemblées Primaires (Law of 3 September 1799 on the Elimination of Half of the Electors Nominated by the Primary Assemblies). In *Bulletin des Loix et Décrets du Corps Législatif de la République helvétique*, Cahier III, pp. 239–242.

selection and elimination procedures are immediately apparent, as is the fact that sortition was perceived as means to legitimize the new legal order (more on this below). Primary assemblies had been established as the institutional basis of sovereignty in the Constitution of Year III (1795), text on which the Helvetic institutions were modelled, thus enshrining the principles of natural law, individualism, and rationalism and basing the state on the individual – the Swiss citizen being seen as the 'driving force of the process of shaping popular political will' (*ibid.*, p. 124). However, this new model clashed with the interests of local cantonal elites, who were afraid of losing their privileges as more individuals gained political rights (*ibid.*, p. 122). This is likely why the procedure was limited in two important ways. On the one hand, the Constitution limited the definition and expansion of the civic body; the conditions for acquiring citizenship were stricter than in the French system, given that it was necessary to be a second-generation citizen and to fulfil residency and property requirements (art. 19 to 25). On the other hand, the Constitution also introduced the notion of a representative democratic system (starting in article 2) which, while it ensured the regular participation of citizens in the selection process, inherently circumscribed the possibility of direct democracy, which otherwise still survived in a number of cantons. This transformation of the concept of sovereignty can be at least partially explained by societal changes, and more specifically by the rivalries that existed between the elites, who now came to see the citizens that they claimed to represent as the source of their political legitimacy (Dupuis-Déri, 2013, p. 98).

The procedure used to select the Directors was uniquely Swiss, however, as it included a process that had no predecessor in the French Constitution of 1795. In fact, Peter Ochs drafted the Helvetic Constitution in 1798 following the orders of the French Directory, which would in turn modify his work. In Switzerland as in France, the Directory was composed of five members and enjoyed broad political reach: it had the greatest concentration of power in the Republic. The main difference between the French and Helvetic Constitutions was that in Switzerland sortition was used in a more complicated process to elect the Directory. In France, the Council of Five Hundred compiled a list in secret with the names of the Directory members that were to be nominated, and then presented this list to the Council of Elders, which in turn elected one representative from the list by secret ballot. In the Helvetic Constitution, the procedure described was more complicated: 'the first year, chance shall determine before voting, which of the two councils shall compose the list of candidates. The other council shall then vote on the names' (art. 73). The second year, as the Constitution also stipulated, the procedure would be even 'more complicated':

> The second year and subsequently, the mode of election will be more complicated: first, chance will exclude from the election half of the members of each Council, and that excluded half will previously decide, whether the election meant to be held, will take place, this time, with the greatest intervention of chance, or not. If it decides no, the non-excluded half will fulfill the functions of electors in the manner indicated above. If, on the contrary, it decides the affirmative, it will be begun by drawing of lots, which one of the two Councils, each one reduced as said to the half, will form the list of candidates. Afterwards the Council so designated will appoint, by an absolute majority of the voices, six candidates; from these six, chance will exclude three, and the other Council will choose the new Director between the three remaining, (art. 74)

This electoral procedure, already described in Peter Ochs' text, was not modified by the French Directory. It was therefore almost certainly a Swiss invention, tailored to the specific circumstances on the ground. At this point, it is difficult to explain with certainty why this addition was made, but we may advance the hypothesis that chance was called upon to mitigate denominational and partisan fragmentation and other cleavages related to birth place and social class and thus prevent one social group from accumulating too much power. In any case, while we must not underestimate the daunting French influence on the elaboration of these procedures, neither should we forget that the French government gave quite broad leeway to the Helvetic elites in terms of political choice, which resulted in political structures that were a mixture between traditional elements and new components, a juxtaposition of concepts both foreign and domestic (Weeber, 2015, p. 62). These selection procedures were nonetheless reflective of a slow and gradual evolution towards our modern conception of sovereignty and representativeness.

At the cantonal and municipal level, moreover, random selection was also used to designate the members of the municipal and cantonal administrative chambers using the same modalities, which we shall discuss further below.

Renewing Membership by Sortition

The second rationale for using sortition in the Helvetic Republic regards the renewal of membership in the legislative chambers and the Directory. In fact, while each canton sent four representatives to the Senate and eight to the Grand Council, it was not yet broadly accepted that an entire assembly could be renewed every four years via election, as we are familiar with in our representative systems today. The Helvetic Republic did, however, envision the partial renewal of legislative chambers via sortition, most likely to ensure greater continuity among political staff within the assembly.

According to the Constitution, the renewal of Senate membership was scheduled to take place every odd year and affect one-fourth of its membership (art. 41), whereas one-third of the Grand Council was to be renewed every even year (art. 43). In reality, these renewals only took place one time each, the first on 16 September 1799 and the second on 1 August 1800. Swiss federal archives contain the transcripts[8] of these random selection procedures, where we can read that the selection took place canton by canton and in alphabetical order, and that the representatives drew balls from a purse by order of age. A yellow ball indicated that a representative could remain, while a white ball indicated that the representative had been eliminated. The transcript then noted the results of the procedure: the names of the remaining and eliminated representatives are listed in cantonal alphabetical order.

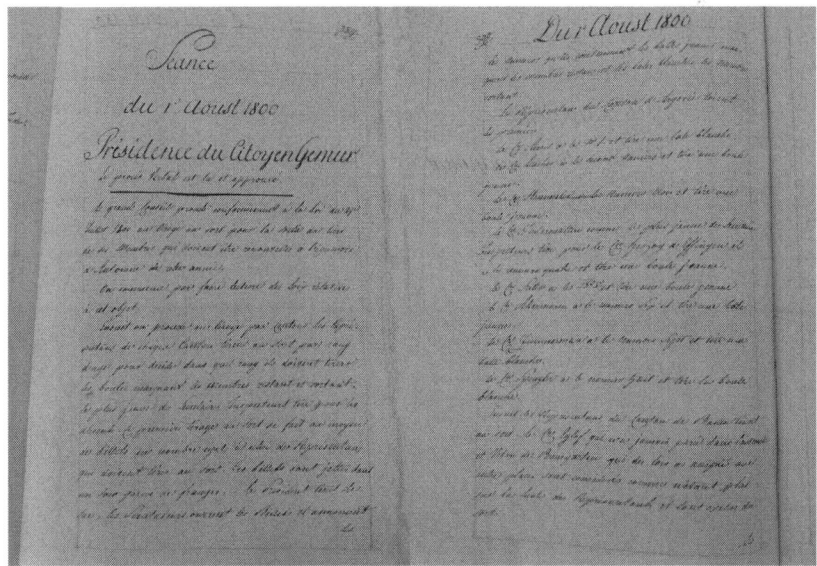

Fig. 1: *'Séance du 1er août 1800'*, Swiss federal archives, B0#1000/1483#18

---

8   Swiss federal archives, B0#A.1, Das Archiv der helvetischen Legislative (Parlamentsarchiv). Gesetzgebung und Verfassungsberatungen.

Even if this procedure was only used twice during the Helvetic Republic, it occupied an important role in the institution and was imbued with genuine legitimacy – as attested to by the degree of detail contained the different transcripts describing this procedure.[9] The use of chance was therefore also part of the political practice of representatives: the latter knew that they had to head towards the prefect and draw a ball, accepting that a white ball would mean their elimination and conversely that a yellow ball ensured they could remain.

It is also important to highlight the numerous *ad hoc* measures and other institutional arrangements that in reality transformed this practice into a means of delegating power under the Helvetic Republic. In fact, several kinds of arrangements existed between political actors to ensure that outgoing representatives who had been eliminated by sortition could in fact continue to wield power. There were at least two reconversion procedures used. On the one hand, we can observe that several representatives who had drawn a white ball on 1 August 1800 reappeared a few months later in Senate proceedings. This was the case for Johann Wernhard Huber from Basel[10] and Charles Thorin from Freiburg,[11] for example. Moreover, certain eliminated representatives were offered a plum administrative position or a post in cantonal political institutions. This was the case for Louis Secretan,[12] on behalf of whom his friend Frédéric de la Harpe[13] wrote to the Lehman cantonal

---

[9] See, for instance: Swiss federal archives, BO#1000/1483/18*, 'Séance du 1 août 1800' (1 August 1800 session). In *Manuel du Grand Conseil*, January 1800 to August 1800.

[10] Johann Wernhard Huber (1753–1818) was a Protestant pharmacist from Basel. In 1787, he joined the Helvetic Society and sympathized with the French Revolution, which led him to support the revolution in Basel in 1798. He became the president of the National Assembly of Basel and would later be a member of the Grand Council and the Senate of the Helvetic Republic from 1800 to 1801 (Source: DHS).

[11] Charles Thorin (1744–1830) was a member of the Grand Council in 1798, then of the Senate in 1801. He later became a member of the administrative chamber of Freiburg canton and a tax collector (Source: DHS).

[12] Louis Secrétan (1758–1839) was a jurist in Lausanne who actively participated in the political life of his canton. He was a member of the Provisional Assembly in 1798, then of the Grand Council from 1798–1800. After being randomly eliminated in 1800, he occupied a variety of positions in the Vaud canton (Source: DHS).

[13] Frédéric de la Harpe (1754–1838) was from a Protestant family in Vaud and studied the law. He expressed interest in the French Revolution and later became one of the main actors calling on the French Directory to intervene in Switzerland. He became a member of the Helvetic Directory and then, ousted by a coup in 1800, fled to France where he lived in exile until the end of the Helvetic Republic (Source: Kölz (2006 [1992], p. 111)).

prefect, informing the latter that his friend had recently been eliminated and thus needed a good local post.[14]

The re-election or elimination of Directors was similar to the procedure used to renew membership in the legislative chambers. Each year, random selection was employed to exclude one of the five Directors, using white and yellow balls. Unlike in the procedure used for the councils, the Law of 10 June 1799 on the Manner of drawing lots to exclude members of the Executive Directory stipulated that the Directors must 'draw the balls themselves using leather gloves' and that the drawing must 'take place in public'.[15]

Finally, it should be noted that sortition was not only the purview of legislative and governmental bodies. White and yellow balls were also used, according to the same modalities as described above, to select which members would be eliminated from the Supreme Court and the cantonal courts.[16] Random selection was also used in the military, in particular to determine officer hierarchy if servicemen were of the same age and rank, or to complete military contingents with soldiers selected in the following manner: 'in a family where there are two or three brothers, the inspector shall select one at random, and if the contingents are still not sufficient, he shall draw lots at random among unwed citizens.'[17]

The numerous and frequent uses of random selection in all different aspects of public life are thus especially significant regarding the historical scope of sortition at the end of the 18th and beginning of the 19th century. The nomination of members of parliament, which combined election and sortition in complex, detailed procedures, also illustrates the historical importance wielded by the combination of these two practices.

---

[14] Correspondence of Frédéric-César de la Harpe during the Helvetic Republic, Volume IV, August 1800.

[15] Loi du 10 juin 1799 sur la Manière de tirer au sort pour la sortie des membres du Directoire Exécutif (Law of 10 June 1799 on the Manner of drawing lots to exclude members of the Executive Directory). In *Bulletin des Loix et Décrets du Corps Législatif de la République helvétique*, Cahier III, pp. 79–81.

[16] Décret du 29 août 1799 sur la Sortie des membres du Tribunal Suprême (Decree of 29 August 1799 on the Exclusion of members of the Supreme Court). In *ibid.*, pp. 205–208.

[17] Loi du 13 décembre 1798 sur l'Organisation de la milice sédentaire (Law of 13 December 1798 on the Organization of a sedentary militia). In *ibid.*, Cahier II, pp. 153–167.

Complexity and Legitimacy of Selection and Elimination Procedures

Describing these practices allows us to highlight their complexity. While the 12 April 1798 Constitution already contained a fair number of details (as seen in article 73), the chambers were the ones to flesh out the procedure legislatively. These laws, as well as the highly detailed proceedings of meetings illustrate the great efforts authorities exerted to justify the validity of operations which consisted in eliminating citizens or candidates by random selection.

In the Law of 3 September 1799 on the Elimination of Half of the Electors Nominated by the Primary Assemblies, the procedures of random selection and elimination are described as highly complex operations. These practices were in fact codified rituals, whose many details stand out: the 'national prefect', representing the highest authority in the cantons and the central administration, presides over the session, which takes place 'in public', thus revealing the desire to limit manipulation and confer legitimacy upon on the procedure. The random selection is conducted using 'two leather purses trimmed with fringes', almost certainly so that the participants could see inside them. One of the purses is filled with 'white ballots of equal size on which the names of the electors are written'.

The Law of 10 June 1799 on the Manner of drawing lots to exclude members of the Executive Directory, adopted by the federal chambers one year after the 1798 Constitution was ratified, reveals that the chambers also paid close attention to the details of random selection procedures. The legislative assemblies stipulated that the selection process would take place 'using five metal balls of the same size' and that the 'Directors must draw these balls wearing leather gloves' in order to prevent them from feeling any kind of irregularities or details on the balls using their fingertips. The session also took place in public. These details are interesting because, in France, the process used to exclude Directory members (and on which the Helvetic procedure was based) was particularly vulnerable to rigging. In his memoires, Antoine Claire de Thibaudeau[18] describes this procedure, during the course of which the members of the French Directory would randomly select the member to be eliminated behind closed doors, reaching an agreement so that the member who wished to resign would be that randomly

---

[18] I would like to thank Biancamaria Fontana for having drawn my attention to this text (see Antoine Claire de Thibaudeau, *Mémoires sur la Convention et le Directoire*, 1824).

selected Director. In the Helvetic Republic, the procedure adopted reflects the desire to limit the ways that random selection might be subverted — with the legislation indicating various elements such as the gloves and the public session — and to ensure that it remains impartial and thus legitimate.

One other important procedural detail is mentioned: 'two intelligent children, neither one of which shall be older than six years of age'[19] are called upon to conduct the drawing. Yves Sintomer has shown how the figure of the child drawing lots recurs in many different historical situations, with these numerous examples all symbolizing the innocence and purity of the process and thus granting it legitimacy: 'in this light, impartiality could be seen as a consequence of purity' (Sintomer, 2018, p. 247). But this element, inherited from ancient models, was now accompanied by a new component outlined in article 34 of the Constitution of 1798, which indicated the exclusion of half of the elected electoral body. In fact, the Constitution stipulated that 'the day of this drawing of lots will be the occasion of a third civic festival and of a speech in which the national prefect will develop the principles that must guide the electoral body, when it will be convoked to make the appointments that are of its competence'. Imbued with quasi-religious traits (Kölz, 2006 [1992], p. 122), this civic celebration symbolically instituted the procedure of drawing lots as a properly political implement used by the new state and infused the political sphere with the rhetoric of civic virtue, thus reflecting the contemporary transformation of republicanism which Switzerland was experiencing at the time (Dupuis-Déri, 2013, p. 78; Weeber, 2015, pp. 57–59).

These elements were already contained in the text that Peter Ochs proposed to the French Directory and which the latter did not modify. The complexity of the procedure was therefore almost certainly a Swiss invention. We hypothesize that this complexity in fact stemmed from denominational and partisan fragmentation and other cleavages related to birth place and social class that existed in the country, and therefore that this procedure was introduced to avoid the Directory being dominated by a single segment of the population. The Diet of the Old Swiss Confederation was already designed to achieve the peaceful resolution of conflicts between cantons and to manage the administrative network of *baillages* (bailiwicks) that were often caught in the crossfires of

---

[19] Loi du 3 septembre 1799 sur la Sortie de la moitié des Électeurs nommés par les Assemblées Primaires (Law of 3 September 1799 on the Elimination of Half of the Electors Nominated by the Primary Assemblies). In *Bulletin des Loix et Décrets du Corps Législatif de la République helvétique*, Cahier III, pp. 239–242.

denominational clashes (Kölz, 2006 [1992], p. 9). The precision used in describing these selection operations likewise recalls the great complexity of the legislative procedure used to designate the doge in the oligarchic Republic of Venice until 1797. In fact, this 'masterpiece of electoral technique' (Sintomer, 2020; and for more details on this procedure, Lane, 1973, p. 111) — which unfolded in nine stages, combined election and random selection, and similarly included children — was likewise designed to limit positions being monopolized by a handful of individuals from the same families or factions; instead, it sought to ensure the neutral and impartial distribution of posts. The political logic of chance reflected in the procedure's complexity tends to confirm this hypothesis.

The Political Logic of Sortition
in the Helvetic Republic

The third lesson we can glean stems from the first two, given that it revisits the theoretical meanings behind the different uses of sortition. It should be noted at the outset that the legal and political process that led to the creation of the Constitution of 1798, in which the aforementioned procedures were described, did not include its drafting by a constituent assembly, for a number of political reasons. The most influential elites are the ones who penned texts explaining why sortition was used, in particular Peter Ochs. In fact, the French Directory asked Peter Ochs to draft the Constitution; Ochs had many relationships with individuals at the highest levels of government, both in Switzerland and in France, and continued to draw on those relationships throughout the duration of the Helvetic Republic. In 1802, as this Republic was falling, the constitutional question became a particularly urgent topic in domestic policy. Through a number of letters sent back and forth with the members of the French Directory, Peter Ochs suggested new institutional structures for Switzerland. In his *Note sur l'intervention du sort* (Note on the intervention of chance)[20] that Ochs sent to Charles-Maurice de Talleyrand, he defended his vision for the use of sortition in Swiss institutions. Ochs justifies his defence of

---

[20] This letter was written by Peter Ochs in 1802, while the Helvetic Republic was falling and the constitutional question became the dominant topic of domestic policy. Peter Ochs was always trying to develop new institutional structures for Switzerland and he proposed a new constitutional draft to Talleyrand in which he said that there were three points he was very attached to, including the intervention of chance.

sortition in the following introduction, and elaborates upon seven points later in his letter:

> The intervention of chance in elections is highly necessary in Switzerland. It is the only process that can ensure the equality of rights, bring people together, appease party agitation, and reassure peaceful citizens.[21]

Three fundamental points must be highlighted in this letter. First of all, in presenting his primary reason for using chance, Ochs repeats the classical argument of conflict reduction. The impartiality and neutrality of chance is seen as fighting against the formation—and later dominance—of factions. This conception was in fact confirmed by article 70 of the Constitution of 1798, which stipulates that 'neither one nor the other Council may create from within a permanent committee'. These arguments emphasize the fear that legislative power might be monopolized by factions. Olivier Dowlen has likewise shown how Sieyès and Lanthenas also recognized that sortition could be used to fight against factions, which embodied the notion of political conflict at the time (Dowlen, 2008, pp. 189–214).

The terms used by Peter Ochs in the rest of the letter are rather eloquent: sortition can 'appease party agitation', it is 'less blind than the spirit of factionalism or nepotism', it 'cuts down pride', 'appeases without inciting resentment against the electors', and 'reassures peaceful citizens'. Although this logic consistently reappears throughout the history of random selection (Sintomer, 2020, p. 194), Ochs stresses the idea that, because of its impartiality, the use of chance justifies the merit of random selection procedures. The need to legitimize sortition is also revealed by this strong statement: random selection 'produces submission and even trust among the people'. This is a rather unique take on the logic of the impartiality of randomness, based on a typically medieval and early Renaissance conception of sortition and a perspective that would have been absolutely central in the Italian Republics and the Crown of Aragon in the Middle Ages and the Renaissance (Dowlen, 2008, pp. 67–136; Sintomer, 2020, pp. 54–79).

The idea of providence is referred to a second time, albeit with less importance. Peter Ochs declares that 'for want of other means, and with the public good in mind, Providence does not leave fate up to chance'. He attributes to randomness a degree of predestination that humans are not in a position to comprehend and which here at least appears to be viewed in a positive light, given that it must guide the

---

[21] *Korrespondenz des Peter Ochs (1752–1821)*, Band III, December 1802.

public good. This idea was relatively marginal in medieval times but likely had great significance in Ancient Rome (Sintomer, 2020); this interpretation no longer exists today.

Let us return to the idea of the equality of chance, also briefly alluded to in Peter Ochs' text. According to Ochs, chance 'gives real merit more opportunities than merely apparent merit'. This statement appears to be in slight contradiction with the reality of the Helvetic Republic, since the selection procedure was not explicitly designed to maximize the participation of all citizens, but rather to limit the monopolization of power. In reality, even though the egalitarian dimension was ensured by the regular participation of citizens in the processes to select representatives, the definition of citizenship remained extremely circumscribed, given that it continued to depend on residency and social status requirements (articles 19 and 20 of the Constitution) (Arlettaz, 2015). Moreover, the conditions for acquiring citizenship in Switzerland were, as we have seen, much stricter than those imposed by the French system. The Helvetic regime was therefore situated at the inflection point between a restrictive conception of the people and a more egalitarian and universal notion of citizenship: 'The universality of the citizens is sovereign', the second article of the Constitution proclaims. But a second paragraph imposes direct limits on this notion of sovereignty with regard to broader democratic participation, as it adds that 'the form of government [...] will always be a representative democracy', thus limiting popular rights to elections.

Finally, it should be noted that Peter Ochs could not anachronistically have intended to achieve the descriptive representation of citizens — that is, a form of representation that would mathematically reproduce all segments of the population in a more egalitarian fashion. Ochs proposed random selection for the purposes of elimination and was therefore not seeking to create a randomly selected representative sample of the population (Sintomer, 2020). In reality, the political concept of chance goes far beyond the statistical understanding that Ochs and his contemporaries had of sortition as a technical tool and its potential uses.

The Rise of 'Representative Democracy'

Now that we have presented the different uses of random selection in the Helvetic Republic, as well as the political logic driving such uses, we shall return to our first observation regarding the gradual disappearance of the idea of chance at the end of the 18th century, and, on the contrary, the socio-historical rise of representative government and democracy. Bernard Manin was the first to identify the disappearance of random selection from politics in the wake of modern revolutions (Manin, 2012 [1995], pp. 19–124), as well as the appearance of representative government. He argued that the 'founding fathers' of the French and American Revolutions did not wish to establish a democracy, in the sense of a political regime where the people governed itself, but rather a representative regime wherein voting was certainly free, but access to power was significantly limited.

While, in general, the disappearance of chance in Swiss institutions can be explained using the same reasons as those for other European political contexts, the Swiss context does display one particularity that merits further attention: this shift took place extremely quickly. In fact, many Swiss communities were still using sortition when the Helvetic Republic was established and continued to do so for a few years thereafter. Fifty years later, however, all mentions of chance had disappeared in the negotiations that led to the adoption of the Swiss Constitution of 1848.[22] This institutional change therefore occurred very rapidly and was particularly illustrative of the conceptual evolution of political regimes during this period (also seen in France, Italy, and Holland). Nonetheless, while the new elements were the result of numerous discussions that took place during the Swiss Enlightenment, in particular during the revolutionary period, they only crystallized thanks to the forced impetus provided by the new Constitution, which acted as a decisive turning point (Weeber, 2015, p. 64).

The constitutional and political framework of the Helvetic Republic was therefore an inflection point in the development of political imaginaries, combining ancient elements—the complexity of procedures inherited from the oligarchic city-states of the Renaissance, which juxtaposed elections and random selection, the figure of the child drawing lots, and the typically medieval–early Renaissance logic of the impartiality of chance, such as defended by Peter Ochs—with new components such as the relative expansion of citizenship (since the 1798 Constitution at least temporarily eliminated certain voting requirements) and the egalitarianism alluded to in passing by Peter Ochs, which resembled the notion of universal citizenship. Intellectual historians have moreover confirmed this transition from a conceptual perspective, highlighting the evolution of the imaginary of republican-

---

[22] See Protocoles des délibérations de la commission chargée le 16 août 1847 par la Haute Diète fédérale de la révision du pacte fédéral du 7 août 1815 (Deliberation protocols of the committee entrusted on 16 August 1847 by the Federal Diet to revise the Federal Treaty of 7 August 1815).

ism during the 18th century and the Helvetic Republic in particular (Dupuis-Déri, 2013, pp. 87–158; Weeber, 2015, pp. 60–64): new ideas (the Constitution, which guaranteed freedom, representative elections, and equality before the law) were incorporated into traditional frameworks, such as the idea of the political virtue of each citizen.

A number of other elements confirm this shift in political imaginaries, at the end of which random selection was no longer seen as an inherently democratic procedure, and which likewise translated into the advent of representative government. Although the French constitutions adopted between 1789 and 1795 recognized the importance of representativeness, an expression that can be found under the pen of several others, the Swiss text contains, to our knowledge, the first use of the term 'representative democracy' in a constitutional context (article two).[23] This idea marks the obvious shift from the political system bequeathed by the French and American Revolutions, an attempt to establish a representative government based on the indirect exercise of sovereignty by citizens.

This objective was only strengthened on 12 April 1798 when the Republic was officially proclaimed by the chambers, as the first article of the new Constitution declared that 'the Helvetic Republic is one and indivisible' and the Senate later reinforced this statement.[24] On 12 April 1798 in Aarau, the Senate in fact adopted a decree which proclaimed 'the independence of the Helvetic Republic, one, indivisible, democratic and representative'.[25] This development is entirely compatible with Bernard Manin's theory, which argues that at the turn of the century there was a tendency to call representative republican systems, established on popular grounds and with power exerted by elected authorities, 'democratic', as the word was now imbued with a positive connotation. The clarity of this proposal, in the context of the Helvetic Republic, is nonetheless particularly noteworthy.

Nevertheless, it does not seem that the question of democracy was ever posed directly in relation to election and sortition procedures. Debates on the issue of democracy tended to focus on the question of

---

23 I would like to thank Biancamaria Fontana for having drawn my attention to this point.
24 I would like to thank Georges Andrey for having made this observation.
25 Décret du 12 avril 1798 sur la Proclamation de l'indépendance de la République Helvétique, une, indivisible, démocratique, représentative, et lecture publique de l'acte constitutionnel (Decree of 12 April 1798 on the Proclamation of the independence of the Helvetic Republic, one indivisible, democratic and representative, and the public reading of the constitutional decree). In *Bulletin des Loix et Décrets du Corps Législatif de la République helvétique*, Cahier I, p. 3.

popular sovereignty. In this regard, the Constitution imposed by France ushered in a genuinely representative republic. And yet, as Danièle Tosato-Rigo has observed, we should not forget that this new system did not unite together all of the Confederate entities in Switzerland (Tosato-Rigo, 2011). In fact, questions of sovereignty and democracy were viewed in a very different light by the city cantons and by the Catholic cantons governed by *Landsgemeinde*. The cantons of Uri, Schwytz, Unterwalden, and Zug, in which democratic political practices were already well-established, expressed strong opposition to the new Constitution, which also represented a threat to local clergy. Ultimately, cantonal elites wondered what the most democratic system would be (and which system would best defend their interests): 'a unified constitution based on a representative republic or the "pure" democracy of popular assemblies like the *Landgemeinde*? […] In a certain way [in fact], France brought a republican constitution to a number of old republicans. That being said, the progress that the latter made in just a few weeks, from Basel to Schwytz, towards egalitarian political structures that had been hitherto unknown in the Swiss republics can largely be attributed to the catalysing effect of the French model' (*ibid.*, pp. 25 *sq.*). Therefore, while the speed with which chance disappeared as a means to delegate power remains a mystery, the beginnings of an explanation may perhaps be found in the evolution of republican and democratic concepts and regimes, an evolution that began well before 1798.

References

Unpublished sources

Swiss Federal Archives BO*, Zentralarchiv der Helvetischen Republik (1798–1803), 1712–1857 (Bestand).

Published sources

Bulletin des Loix et Décrets du Corps Législatif de la République helvétique (1798–1801), Lausanne: l'Imprimerie d'Henri Emanuel Vincent.
Constitution de la République helvétique du 12 avril 1798 (1992), in Kölz, A., *Quellenbuch zur neueren schweizerischen Verfassungsgeschichte*, Bern: Verlag Stämpfli & Cie AG.
Correspondance de Frédéric-César de la Harpe sous la République helvétique, *Volume IV, January 1800–February 1803* (2004), Bastide, P., Kastl, E. & Hofmann, E. (eds.), Geneva: Éditions Slaktine.

Korrespondenz des Peter Ochs (1752–1821), Band III, Ausgang der Helvetik Mediation und Restauration, 1800–1821 (1937), von Steiner, G. (ed.), Basel: Verlag von Emil Birkhäuser & Cie.

Thibaudeau, A.C. (1824) *Mémoires sur la Convention et le Directoire, Volume II*, Paris: Baudouin Frères Libraires.

Bibliography

Andrey, G. (1986) La quête d'un État national, in *Nouvelle histoire de la Suisse et des Suisses*, Lausanne: Payot.

Arlettaz, S. (2015) From rights to citizenship to the Helvetian *indigénat*. Political integration of citizens under the Helvetic Republic, in Oddens, J., Rutjes, M. & Jacobs, E. (eds.) *The Political Culture of the Sister Republics, 1794–1806: France, the Netherlands, Switzerland, and Italy*, pp. 85–96, Amsterdam: Amsterdam University Press.

Braun, R. (1988 [1984]) *Le déclin de l'Ancien Régime en Suisse*, Lausanne: Éditions d'en bas; Paris: Éditions de la Maison des sciences de l'homme.

Carson, L. & Martin, B. (1999) *Random Selection in Politics*, Westport, CT: Praeger.

Chollet, A. & Dupuis, A. (2020) *Kübellos* in the canton of Glarus: A unique experience of sortition in politics', in Lopez-Rabatel, L. & Sintomer, Y. (eds.) *Sortition and Democracy: Practices, Instruments, Theories*, Exeter: Imprint Academic.

Delvaux, P. (2004) *La République en papier. Circonstances d'impression et pratiques de dissémination des lois sous la République helvétique (1798–1803)*, 2 vols., Geneva: Presses d'histoire Suisse.

Dowlen, O. (2008) *The Political Potential of Sortition: A Study of the Random Selection of Citizens for Public Office*, Exeter: Imprint Academic.

Dupuis, A. (2018) Tirage au sort et lutte contre la corruption à Glaris, in Fontaine, A. & Chollet, A. (eds.) *Actes du colloque « Tirage au sort : état des lieux »*, pp. 69–87, Bern: Bibliothek am Guisanplatz, Schriftenreihe der Bibliothek am Guisanplatz (BiG).

Dupuis-Déri, F. (2013) *Démocratie. Histoire politique d'un mot Aux États-Unis et en France*, Montréal: Lux.

Fankhauser, A. (1993) Die Zentralbehörden des helvetischen Einheitsstaates, *Itinera*, 15, pp. 35–49.

Fankhauser, A. (2009) Die « Staats-Maschine » der Helvetischen Republik. Institutionelle und personelle Kontinuität innerhalb eines revolutionären Verwaltungsapparats, in Schläppi, D. (ed.) *Umbruch und Beständigkeit. Kontinuität in der Helvetischen Revolution von 1798*, pp. 65–82, Basel: Schwabe.

Fankhauser, A. (2013) République helvétique, in *Dictionnaire historique de la Suisse,* version 09/24/2013, [Online] http://www.hls-dhs-dss.ch/textes/f/F9797.php [01/10/2018].

Hansen, M.H. (2009 [1993]) *La démocratie athénienne à l'époque de Démosthène,* Paris: Tallandier.

Headlam, J. (1891) *Elections by Lot at Athens,* Cambridge: Cambridge University Press.

Holenstein, A. (2009) Die Helvetik als reformabsolutistische Republik, in Schläppi, D. (ed.) *Umbruch und Beständigkeit. Kontinuität in der Helvetischen Revolution von 1798,* pp. 683–704, Basel: Schwabe.

Holenstein, A. (2015) The invention of democratic parliamentary practices in the Helvetic Republic: Some remarks, in Oddens, J., Rutjes, M. & Jacobs, E. (eds.) *The Political Culture of the Sister Republics, 1794–1806: France, the Netherlands, Switzerland, and Italy. Intellectual and Political History,* Amsterdam: Amsterdam University Press.

Kölz, A. (2006 [1992]) *Histoire constitutionnelle de la Suisse moderne,* Bern: Stämpfli Verlag.

Lane, F.C. (1973) *Venice: A Maritime Republic,* Baltimore, MD: Johns Hopkins University Press.

Lerner, M.H. (2004) The Helvetic Republic: An Ambivalent Reception of French Revolutionary Liberty, *French History,* 18, pp. 50–75.

Manin, B. (2012 [1995]) *Principes du gouvernement représentatif,* Paris: Flammarion.

Najemy, J.M. (1982) *Corporatism and Consensus in Florentine Electoral Politics, 1280–1400,* Chapel Hill, NC: The University of North Carolina Press.

Oddens, J., Rutjes, M. & Jacobs, E. (eds.) (2015) *The Political Culture of the Sister Republics, 1794–1806: France, the Netherlands, Switzerland, and Italy,* Amsterdam: Amsterdam University Press.

Rubinstein, N. (1996) *The Government of Florence under the Medici, 1434–1494,* Oxford: Clarendon Press.

Simon, C. & Schulchter, A. (eds.) (1995–2000) *Dossier Helvetik,* 6 vols., Basel: Helbing & Lichtenhahn.

Sintomer, Y. (2018) A child drawing lots: The 'pathos formula' of political sortition?, in Fontaine, A. & Chollet, A. (eds.) *Actes du colloque « Tirage au sort : état des lieux »,* Bern: Bibliothek am Guisanplatz, Schriftenreihe der Bibliothek am Guisanplatz (BiG).

Sintomer, Y. (2020) *Between Radical and Deliberative Democracy: Random Selection in Politics from Athens to Contemporary Experiments,* Cambridge: Cambridge University Press.

Stauffacher, H.-R. (1989) *Herrschaft und Landsgemeinde: die Machtelite in Evangelisch-Glarus vor und nach der Helvetischen Revolution*, Glarus: Tschudi.

Tosato-Rigo, D. (2011) « Constitution parisienne » et Suisse républicaine: attraction, rejet et malentendus à l'ère des révolutions, in Heger-Étienvre, M.-J. & Poisson, G. (eds.) *Entre attraction et rejet: deux siècles de contacts franco-suisses (XVIIIe–XIXe s.)*, pp. 15–40, Paris: Michel Houdiard Éditeur.

Weeber, U. (2015) New wine in old wineskins. Republicanism in the Helvetic Republic, in Oddens, J., Rutjes, M. & Jacobs, E. (eds.) *The Political Culture of the Sister Republics, 1794–1806: France, the Netherlands, Switzerland, and Italy. Intellectual and Political History*, Amsterdam: Amsterdam University Press.

Wolfson, A.M. (1899) The Ballot and Other Forms of Voting in the Italian Communes, *The American Historical Review*, 5, pp. 1–21.

Part III:
Chinese World

Pierre-Étienne Will

Appointing Officials by Drawing Lots in Late Imperial China (1594–1911)

As they have been rarely been the subject of scholarly attention, the origins and history of the Chinese system of drawing lots to select individuals for official appointments may seem like an insignificant detail of institutional history.[1] Nothing could be farther from the truth, however, as the process of 'appointment and selection' (*quanxuan* 銓選) – in other words, of finding the right men to administer the empire (*de ren* 得人) – was always considered to be the most crucial task of the Central Government's most important ministry, the Ministry of Personnel (*libu* 吏部). As the eminent Southern Song scholar and politician, Ye Shi 葉適 (1150–1223), once explained: 'The Ministry of Personnel is where the throat and tongue of the Court are!' These words were quoted by Gu Yanwu (1613–1682) in a section of his famous *Knowledge acquired day by day* (*Rizhi lu*) entitled 'What is wrong with appointment and selection' (*Quanxuan zhi hai* 銓選之害), a passage in which he discusses issues to which I shall return later in this essay (Gu, 1834, 8: 32a).[2]

Nothing about the selection and appointment procedure, including the drawing of lots as soon as the latter became an established mechanism, would have seemed trivial to anyone in late Imperial times. As we shall see below, the drawing of lots was adopted in 1594 amidst much political furore and was subject to harsh criticism almost from the outset. Yet it survived the violent political confrontations of the final half-century of the Ming dynasty (1368–1644), and was preserved

---

[1]   This is the slightly abridged and revised version of an article published in Chinese in *Zhongguo xueshu*, 2 (3) (2001), and in English in *Ming Qing yanjiu*, 2002 (printed in 2004).

[2]   The phrase 'throat and tongue', found in ancient texts, meant that the prime minister transmitted the words of the sovereign to the country and informed the sovereign of what was being said in the country.

by the Manchu Qing dynasty (1644–1911) despite further criticism in its early decades. Indeed, the consolidation, routinization and, ultimately, universal acceptance of this procedure provide an interesting case study of the institutional and political changes that unfolded during the Ming–Qing transition.

The Invention of Drawing Lots
During the Late Ming Period

The decision to make candidates who were eligible for a local official position[3] draw lots (*cheqian* 掣籤) publicly and in person in order to determine the post where they would be appointed was reportedly made by Sun Peiyang 孫丕揚 (1532–1614) shortly after he was appointed President of the Ministry of Personnel (all of the sources save one give this date as 1594).[4] The standard account, as found in Sun's biography in the dynastic history of the Ming (*Mingshi*, 1974, 224: 5901), reads as follows:

> Since Peiyang was rigid and inflexible, ordinary officials never dared interfere in order to advance their private interests. He was only

---

[3] That is, mainly, as 'magistrate' of a county (*xian* 縣) or a department (*zhou* 州) — *xian* and *zhou* are sometimes collectively termed 'districts'. District magistrates were called *zhixian* 知縣 or *zhizhou* 知州 depending on the case. There were about 1,500 districts in late Imperial China. As we shall see below, other sorts of positions were gradually added to the list of appointments subject to random selection. The candidates eligible were individuals who had passed the palace examination in the capital (or 'doctors', *jinshi* 進士), or under certain conditions, individuals who had passed the provincial examination (or 'licentiates', *juren* 舉人), or local students who had been ranked 'selected prefectural examination graduates' (the so-called 'presented students', *gongsheng* 貢生). As I will note, under certain circumstances and during certain periods — principally during the Qing period — such academic qualifications could be dispensed with through the acquisition of a rank, or even a position, in exchange for a contribution paid to the state (see note 35 below).

[4] For example, the *Wanli dichao* (see below for this source), which one would tend to trust first of all for chronological accuracy, states that this decision took place during the eighth lunar month of 1591, almost immediately after Sun's appointment as president of the Ministry at the end of the seventh month. The sole dissenting source is Tan Qian's *Guoque* (77: 4745), which places it during the fifth month of 1595; the *Guoque*'s chronology of the entire episode is in fact somewhat muddled. Another discrepancy occurs in the 'Treatise on examinations' of the Ming dynastic history (*Mingshi*, 1974, 71: 1716). According to that text, the random selection procedure was proposed not by Sun Peiyang in 1594, but by one Ni Sihui 倪斯蕙, then head of the Department of Appointments (*Wenxuan qinglisi*), in 1601, and then approved by the President of the Ministry of Personnel, Li Dai 李戴, with the result that Sun Peiyang only 'followed in his footsteps'. This is plainly an error by those who compiled the *Mingshi*; see also Zhang (1978, pp. 11–12).

annoyed by the demands of powerful courtiers. Therefore he instituted the method of drawing lots. Both in 'general selections' and 'priority selections',[5] candidates were allowed to draw a lot in person; it was forbidden to ask to be replaced. For a while the selection of officials enjoyed an admirable reputation for impartiality; but from this point the management of appointments changed considerably.[6]

Creation and conflict

To what extent was the use of random selection (the drawing of lots) actually an innovation? The concept was unlikely to have shocked Sun's contemporaries. In addition to the fact that drawing lots for a variety of purposes had always been an element of popular culture in China, historical sources mention several instances of administrative posts being attributed through random selection. As early as the Mongol Yuan dynasty (1271–1368), we hear that local officials in Zhejiang province were appointed by drawing lots (*nianjiu* 拈闈, a term more or less synonymous with *cheqian*) in order to avoid corruption by the administrative clerks. The text describes how soldiers would use bamboo chopsticks to pick up the 'wads of paper' on which candidates' names had been written, then show them to the clerk as the latter read out the list of vacant posts (Kong, 1987, pp. 123–124). Likewise, it is reported that, in 1371, Zhu Yuanzhang 朱元璋, the founder of the Ming dynasty (r. 1368–1398), subjected the winners of the first palace examination of the new Ming dynasty to a similar process of drawing lots (here called *wan* 丸), pieces of paper on which the names of the unfilled offices had been inscribed (Pan, 2001, pp. 97–98, and 2002, pp. 289–291; *idem* for the following examples).

On two occasions, in 1556 and 1628 respectively, the Ming emperor is said to have resorted to drawing lots to select the members of his grand secretariat, with the explicit intent of relying on the will of Heaven to make an otherwise difficult choice. More importantly, however—especially because we are dealing with a regular bureaucratic

---

5 Respectively *daxuan* 大選 and *jixuan* 急選. The former took place in the even months and mostly concerned first candidacies as well as promotions; the latter, held during the odd months, were reserved for candidates who re-entered their careers after a leave of absence, or for other categories entitled to a priority appointment. On these institutions during the Ming dynasty, see for instance *Mingshi* (1974, 71: 1716), or *Ming Huiyao* (1963, p. 894); and Pan (2001, pp. 77–85). The even/odd month system continued under the Qing: see, for example, the very clear description provided in Kondō (1958, pp. 36–39). During the course of the Qing dynasty there were some changes made to the categories (*ban* 班) eligible for either the *daxuan* or the *jixuan*.

6 See also Sun's biography in Goodrich and Fang (1976, pp. 1219–220). For the text of Sun Peiyang's original memorial proposing the reform, see Zhang (1978, p. 11).

process documented in administrative sources, not *ad hoc* measures mentioned in secondary, non-official works — random selection appears to have been adopted at one point during the Ming dynasty to attribute internships to the students of the Imperial University in the various metropolitan administrations, until those with better grades became eligible for regular appointment. Likewise, the same method of 'drawing lots' in public (*nianjiu*) appears to have been used to select and promote clerks in various ministries.

In other words, relying on chance to allocate positions among equally qualified candidates was not altogether foreign to the bureaucratic culture of the Ming dynasty. However, Sun Peiyang's decision to systematically appoint ranking magistrates by random selection, first during the 'priority selections' and later during the 'general selections',[7] was a momentous decision in the history of the Chinese civil service, and indeed it was regarded as such by his contemporaries.

Most historical sources concur with Sun's *Mingshi* biography that 'for a while' everyone welcomed the new procedure as a means of reintroducing fairness into the selection of provincial officials. At the same time, however, most sources also mention that the procedure was soon subject to criticism. The *Guoque* (Discussions on the dynasty), for example, observed that 'for a while [this procedure] was commended as fair (*yishi chenggong* 一時稱公); [but] experienced people did not agree (*shizhe buwei ran ye* 識者不謂然也)' (Tan, n.d., 77: 4745). One assumes that when they spoke of 'some pedants' who criticized the reform as 'failing to observe the tradition of selecting the right man for the right post according to talent and merit', Sun's biographers in the *Dictionary of Ming Biography* were referring to the same 'experienced people' (Goodrich and Fang, 1976, p. 1220). One of these experienced individuals might have been the influential statesman Yu Shenxing 于慎行 (1545–1608), who wrote: 'At once everybody in the palace talked about the reform as being extremely fair, while down in the villages people were unanimous in praising it. But they were not aware of the fact that it was contrary to principle.'[8] Indeed, Yu Shenxing, as

---

[7] Sun Peiyang's original memorial from 1594 implies that he had 'recently'—and successfully—instituted the procedure of drawing lots for the 'priority' selections held within the Ministry of Officials: it was for the 'general selections', which were held within the imperial palace, that he needed to secure the approval of the emperor (Zhang, 1978, p. 11).

[8] Gu (1834, 8: 22b–23a), quoting from the *Gushan bizhu*, Yu's collection of notes printed in 1613; for the original text, see Yu (1984, 5: 54–55). Yu Shenxing was not in office when the reform was implemented; he had been dismissed in 1591, one of the numerous casualties of the controversy that raged during those years over the

well as many others, deplored the fact that the new system did not select men according to their talents and to the special conditions of the posts to which they would be assigned. For example, at one point in the lengthy development following the words of Yu quoted above, Gu Yanwu writes:

> The way men are selected today, the Ministry of Rites pastes their names [on their examination essays] to select them, which means putting forward people one doesn't know; the Ministry of Personnel draws lots to appoint them, which means appointing people one doesn't know. As a result, the ministers are bad at knowing men, but good at avoiding problems.

The problem of corruption

We will come back to this sort of consideration. Another type of criticism emerged very early on the corruption and manipulation that were reportedly affecting the random selection procedure. After mentioning the disagreement expressed by 'experienced people' in its entry on Sun Peiyang's reform, the *Guoque* adds: 'Then unscrupulous clerks selected the best posts to be filled and interfered in the process [for a profit]. It became impossible to denounce them. At the time [the Ministry of Personnel] was nicknamed "the Ministry of Lots".'

What was the exact nature of this manipulation? Here we can only turn to that most damning and yet most entertaining of commentators on political mores during the Wanli period, Shen Defu (1578–1642). In the entry on 'Appointments by drawing lots' in his *Wanli yehuo bian* [Information collected in the wilderness on the Wanli era], Shen offers the following narrative:

> The method of drawing lots at the Ministry of Personnel was started recently by President Sun Fuping [Sun Peiyang was a native of Fuping county, in Shaanxi province]. It did not exist either in ancient or modern times. Sun had come to power thanks to his enduring prestige; he and recently appointed Premier Zhang [Wei] were looking for a pretext to pick a quarrel with each other. He was concerned about those 'mouse-holes' in the appointment system which were difficult to close up due to Zhang's control. Thereupon he made this proposal, leaving the entire responsibility [of appointing officials] to pieces of dry bamboo. When this method was first implemented, the officials in charge, being

---

Wanli emperor's designation of his heir apparent (i.e. the so-called controversy on the 'foundation of the state' [*guoben* 國本]). Yu Shenxing was called back to court in 1607 and became a grand secretary, but died shortly thereafter (Goodrich and Fang, 1976, pp. 1614–615). His criticism of the random selection system is quoted in several other sources.

exempted from the responsibility of evaluating [the candidates], were happy not to have to ponder [the appointments]; and the new appointees, accepting the results as a decree of Heaven, were at peace with themselves. The frustration and resentment diminished somewhat. This was altogether a good plan.

Now at that time there was an old presented student from Shaanxi who was selected by lot to be prefectural judge of Hangzhou. He was terrified and asked to be relieved. Mr. Fuping flew into a rage, saying: 'You dare disturb my system on account of native-place personal feelings [as we hail from the same province]!', and in a loud voice ordered him to be handed over to the judicial authorities for punishment. The man wiped away his tears and went [to his post]. When he arrived, the many demands heaped up on the judicial official of the capital prefecture [of Zhejiang were such] that he proved unable to perform his duties. The grand coordinator and the provincial administrator asked in a memorial that his posting be exchanged with that of a metropolitan graduate [located] in Eastern Zhejiang. In his heart, Fuping knew the reason [for this situation], but he pretended not to know and [simply] gave his approval.

From then on the position markings were differentiated. In the open, distinctions were made between north and south, or according to distance, or depending on the place where [the candidates' families] were registered, with different boxes [for the lots corresponding] to each situation. When a candidate did not have a special connection, he was left to take [his lot] himself; but the best positions were secretly kept hidden, being reserved for candidates who would come later. Those who drew a post in a remote region or a malarial district cried and cursed, but the box had already been assigned for the use of other candidates. In the beginning [the officials] were still involving the clerks in trickery. But later, two or three days before each great selection the Department of Appointments officials would shut themselves up in a heated room and paste on the names of the localities with their own hands, secretly marking their ranking, so that the length, size and thickness of the lots always concealed a riddle. Even the clerks were not in the know. This was called 'fabricating the lots'. They talked about it openly and did not consider the subject to be taboo. Thus, paradoxically, it was not the subalterns who plotted and transgressed the law. If the candidate who had entered into a preliminary arrangement happened to draw the wrong lot, they were allowed to draw again one, two, or even three more times until they got what they wanted. When others expressed their wishes, they were showered with insults and shown to the door. When people talk about uniformity and fairness, this is what it means! (Shen, 1997, 11: 288-9, with a few ambiguities with regard to the translation)

There are two main points made by Shen in this passage. The first concerns the need to introduce some degree of regionalization in the system used to appoint officials by drawing lots. Sun Peiyang was apprised of this situation thanks to the aforementioned unfortunate episode of a modest Shaanxi graduate who was plunged into the merci-less environment of a major south-eastern prefecture and found that he was not up to the challenge (we will discuss this problem later). Secondly, according to Shen Defu corruption became rife as soon as the drawing procedure became more complicated, as there were con-sequently more opportunities for rigging. What is unique in Shen's account is that he had no qualms about identifying the ranking officials of the Ministry as the main culprits, instead of accusing (as was customary) the reviled clerks for everything that went wrong. What-ever the case, the unanimous praise that welcomed Sun's reform may not have lasted very long, since the manipulation of the system was denounced almost immediately, in terms that closely anticipated those that would be used by Shen Defu just a few years later.

Political conflict

Such condemnations were not innocent, however. A closer look at the sources reveals that the corruption which allegedly defeated Sun Peiyang's attempt to ensure fairness in the appointment procedure was in fact used as a weapon in one of the period's typically acrimonious and noisy political conflicts that so enraged the Wanli emperor. This conflict, in reality, was only partially concerned with the selection of officials.

It was apparently not accidental that Sun Peiyang's reform of the appointment system took place at the end of 1594, shortly after he became president of the Ministry of Personnel. In that capacity, he would be required just a few months later to preside over the triennial 'great reckoning' (*daji* 大計) of 1595, which affected all the officials holding positions outside of the capital. This was an event that usually produced a large number of promotions, demotions, appointments, and dismissals. Like the sexennial 'capital evaluations' (*jingcha* 京察), the great reckonings were the occasion of intense political activity and the cause of much trafficking in influence. The president of the Ministry of Personnel naturally played a central role in the whole process: he submitted to the emperor the list of the evaluated officials drawn up with the aid of a few highly placed colleagues in the Ministry and the Censorate. Sun's dramatic innovation in 1594 may well have been one means of liberating himself, or rather the Ministry, from the influence of highly placed people at court, beginning with his enemy Grand Secretary Zhang Wei 張位.

In any case, the conflict between Sun Peiyang and his opponents, of which the attacks against random selection were only a part, started soon after the 'great reckoning' of 1595. One of Sun's most bitter enemies was Censor Shen Sixiao 沈思孝, a protégé of Zhang Wei, who was in fact stewing in frustration after having been barred by Sun from becoming the head of the Department of Civil Appointments, despite his best efforts at scheming and manipulation.[9] In other words, Sun started making enemies as soon as he took charge of the Ministry. He was attacked indirectly through the man who had been given the position coveted by Shen Sixiao, a certain Jiang Shixing 蔣時馨. Another censor, Zhao Wenbing 趙文炳, was entrusted with writing a memorial denouncing Jiang for allowing the most terrible corruption to reign with regard to promotions and appointments — that is, for 'selling positions and ranks'. He even went so far as to mention the monetary amount of the bribes that Jiang was said to have received for promoting or appointing various officials, designating the people who acted as intermediaries, and so forth.[10] Interestingly enough, Zhao's memorial claims that the idea of using random selection did not originally come from Sun Peiyang himself, but from the Department of Appointments. At the head of that Department was Jiang Shixing, who hoped to conceal his deeds from the public by claiming to ensure a fair process. Zhao argued, not without hypocrisy, that Sun Peiyang — who he implicitly described as gullible and unable to choose the right men for such important positions — was an eminent statesman who had to be protected from his collaborators.[11]

Jiang Shixing fought vehemently to defend himself, claiming that Shen Sixiao and his henchmen were behind the attack. He even asked to be examined at the imperial court by the equivalent of a panel of judges, a request that was refused after the censors had countered it by claiming it would be inappropriate. For his part, Sun Peiyang stood up for his appointee, but to no avail: the emperor angrily denounced Jiang Shixing's corruption and downgraded him to commoner status. It was a definitive setback for Sun Peiyang.

But this by all accounts respectable official had other conflicts on his hands. During the 'great reckoning' that took place in early 1595 — just before the Jiang Shixing affair, which seems to have been a

---

[9] On this episode, and others recounted below, see among others the biography of Sun Peiyang contained in Chen Ding (1711, 15: 13a), which gives a coherent account of Sun's 1594 reform, the conflict with Shen Sixiao (called Sidao 道 in that source), the 1595 great reckoning (where, it says, 'people submitted to its fairness'), and the attacks subsequently launched by Shen Sixiao's friends.

[10] It seems that Zhao Wenbing would later change his mind: see his memorial in *Wanli dichao*, vol. 2, pp. 915–919.

[11] Zhao Wenbing's full memorial, dated from the seventh month of 1595, is found *ibid.*, pp. 901–904.

consequence of it—Sun had requested the dismissal of another censor, Ding Cilü 丁此呂, denounced for exceptionally serious corruption during an earlier special assignment in Shanxi. As Ding's friends, Shen Sixiao the first among them, were trying to rescue him, claiming that he was unjustly accused by his political enemies, and despite the pressure exerted on Sun Peiyang, Sun felt compelled to transmit the 'investigation slip' (*fangdan* 訪單) on which he had based his censure of Ding to the emperor. In this case the slip was a fourteen-page document enumerating all sorts of misdeeds.[12] The Wanli emperor flew into a rage and ordered that Ding be stripped of all his titles and sent to the border to serve as a soldier (*Wanli dichao*, 1969, vol. 2, pp. 905ff.). As is explained in his *Mingshi* biography, Sun Peiyang made many enemies with this affair: all the metropolitan officials hailing from Jiangxi, like Ding Cilü, turned against him, including Zhang Wei, the Grand Secretary, who came from the same county as Ding. To these were added officials hailing from Zhejiang, since Shen Sixiao, the censor to whom Sun had denied an appointment in the Ministry of Personnel, was a Zhejiang native.

In the end, Sun chose to attack Zhang Wei personally, accusing him of manipulating power and 'forming a faction'. The emperor, however, supported Zhang, and Sun asked to be discharged from his duties on account of ill health. After several such requests, the emperor reluctantly allowed him to retire, though he valued Sun's attempts to restore a modicum of integrity in bureaucratic life.

Why dwell on this imbroglio? For one thing, it seems interesting that an administrative procedure related to the important task of selecting men for offices—a procedure which would moreover be preserved until the empire's final days—should have been devised amidst such lousy politics and vicious political infighting. In a long memorial addressed to the throne at the end of 1595, a certain Yue Yuansheng 岳元聲 (then a vice-director in the Ministry of Public Works) painted a horrendous picture of the corruption and infighting in official circles: censors attacking censors, ministers attacking ministers, a war of all against all, resulting in the disappearance of any semblance of

---

[12] Investigation slips were confidential documents compiled at the time of the great reckonings and based on investigations of 'public opinion' (that is, among officials) on the quality of the individuals subjected to evaluation (*Mingshi*, 1974, 229: 6006, biography of Shen Sixiao). Communicating this sort of information to the emperor was an unprecedented move; in his *Gushan bizhu*, Yu Shenxing cites this action as one of the two instances in which Sun Peiyang—a highly respectable statesman in every other respect—'gravely flouted the great principles'; the other instance was of course the adoption of random selection to appoint officials (Yu, 1984).

propriety at court and in the government (*Wanli dichao*, 1969, vol. 2, pp. 907–915). Large sections of the text detail Jiang Shixing's corruption and viciousness, deploring that Sun Peiyang could have allowed himself to be deceived by such an individual. Ultimately, the text concluded that everyone 'must go', including Sun Peiyang. Here again we find mention of random selection:

> Sun Peiyang is self-conscious of his own value and takes the purification of the empire to be his own responsibility. He claims that with his procedure of drawing lots, he can carry out his duty toward the court. But all sorts of abuses have come to light, like making big lots and small lots, or using recognizable tickets with secret marks to make a difference. In every case, this is fooling Your Majesty under the pretence of being fair and transparent to the utmost. As I see it, if Peiyang is so completely honest and fair, why does not he allow the nominees to draw the lots from the boxes themselves for both the candidates and the positions,[13] so that every move can be subject to Heaven's decree, and people who walk away do not criticize him behind his back? I am perfectly aware that Peiyang's tricks go this far. Even though at present [Jiang] Shixing has been dismissed, Peiyang is unable to overcome his private feelings of blind affection and support. He urges all the officials of the Censorate to follow him in a swarm. Even those he recommends betray his reputation, like Vice Censor-in-Chief Zhang Yangmeng, who as soon as he had entered the capital shouted at [Zhao] Wenbing to defile and curb him so that he could not extend his opinion, blocked him so that he could not follow his purpose, enjoined him to wait at home pretexting illness so as to get rid of him. This is destroying the speaking officials' spirit of loyal remonstrance, and encouraging the crooks' habits of sycophancy, the rules are upside down, loyalty and viciousness are confused. Knowledgeable gentlemen have their blood running cold. Can one call this a minister who cares for the State? I am thinking of the State, therefore I believe that Peiyang must go.

At the very least, in this memorial Sun Peiyang was accused of allowing practices that undermined the very reform for which he had advocated. If we are to believe this text, about one year after the reform was enacted, these practices were already in full swing. First and foremost, the passage cited above serves as an illustration of the style and tone of the memorials, edicts, attacks, and counterattacks that circulated everywhere in the empire through the medium of the *Peking Gazette*, and which can be found in abundance throughout the extracts

---

[13] This seems to be alluding to a system described by one sole author, Huang Liuhong in the late 17th century (see below): there was one box containing the candidates' names (the Ministry officials drew the lots), and one containing the names of the positions to be filled (the candidates themselves drew the lots).

copied into the *Wanli dichao*.[14] Such writings offer a striking contrast with what politicians would allow themselves under the Manchu regime just a few decades later.

The problem of regionalization

Let us now turn to the other issue addressed in the *Yehuo bian* entry quoted above: namely, the problems raised by a system that often sent officials to faraway posts in completely unfamiliar environments. Shen Defu remains vague about the system of multiple 'boxes' that, according to him, Sun Peiyang instituted after the unfortunate episode of the Shaanxi man who left for Hangzhou as if he were facing execution. However, Sun Peiyang's biography in the *Donglin liezhuan* (Biographies of Donglin personalities) is much more detailed. It explains how Sun distributed the lots between four regions—namely, north-east, south-east, north-west, and south-west—each consisting of two or more provinces, plus groups of neighbouring prefectures, and each reserved for candidates who hailed from the same region, with the possibility of compensating between neighbouring regions if suitable candidates were lacking within one system.[15]

It is unclear how long this regional pattern for appointing local officials lasted. In a programmatic memorial dated seventh month 1602, the recently appointed president of the Ministry of Personnel, Li Dai 李戴, cited it among many subjects on which he was requesting an imperial decision; and what he criticized was not the possibility for manipulation that such a system afforded, but the fact that its extreme complexity made people *suspect* that it was inherently unfair. This passage is worth quoting in full because it illustrates the numerous adjustments and bargaining that were apparently required when carrying out the monthly appointments:

---

14 The author of these handwritten excerpts from the *Peking Gazette* may have been one Qian Yiben 錢一本, a former censor who was dismissed from the bureaucracy in 1592 because of his position in the *guoben* controversy; Qian would later become a member of the fundamentalist Confucian opposition known as the Donglin Party, the political sensitivities of which are indeed illustrated in the selection of documents contained in the work (Ono, 1980).

15 Quoted in a note by Huang Rucheng (Gu, 1834, 8: 23a). According to this and other sources, this system was instituted from the start. Sun Peiyang's memorial to the throne speaks of three regional groups, composed of northern, central, and southern provinces, respectively (Zhang, 1978, p. 12). It may be that four groups were created shortly afterward. It seems that a fifth 'box' was added in 1626 for positions located in the frontier regions, but that the original three-group pattern was restored in 1628 (Liu, 1996, pp. 32–33).

Previously, posts were attributed on the basis of [the qualifications of]
men, and this unfolded entirely through the process of selection and
appointment conducted by our Ministry. Then it was decided to draw
the places [where people would be appointed] by lot. This method is
perfectly just, but when its clauses are examined in detail, there are
some that are not publicly known, and this is what makes people
harbour doubts about its fairness. They completely ignore that the
territory is divided between north and south, that in the south there is
the southeast and the southwest, and that in the north there is the
northeast and the northwest, which is why one divides up [the drawing
of lots]; and that if the positions open in the southeast are too few, then
one will borrow from [those available in] the northeast, while if the
positions open in the northeast are too few one will borrow from the
northwest — meaning further splitting up [of the random selection pro-
cess]. As for the qualifications, they are different: for the position of a
magistrate or prefectural judge, for example, it makes a difference
[whether the candidate is] a doctor, a licentiate, or a presented student.
The lots left by the doctors are kept for the provincial graduates, and the
lots left by the provincial graduates are kept for the presented students
— and this again makes a difference. As a result, all these small details
combine with each other: it always works like that.

If there is [only] one candidate [eligible] for a position, he will automatically have his lot reserved. If there are two candidates [eligible for]
two positions, the differentiation will occur by province. Then there are
cases with many positions and few candidates, or many candidates and
few positions, or candidates who must avoid their native province, or
candidates who are not suitable for the region [to which they are to be
dispatched], but who are willing to exchange with each other. For all of
this, people have to be moved around, regions have to be correctly
balanced, and this is also a pain. [...] Wouldn't it be better to publicize
one day in advance the list of all the candidates and posts available,
stipulating that there are not enough positions in such-and-such region
and that they will be borrowed from such-and-such region, and the next
day to draw lots from the [corresponding] boxes? [That way,] one
would first exhaust the regions that need to be filled by random
selection, then one would proceed to the borrowed posts; and in the case
where there is just one man for one position, or the post is isolated and
lonely [i.e. a post for which there is no competition], there is no problem
in reserving them openly, and these cases would not be included in the
drawing of lots. Thus the utmost clarity would reign, and people would
know that the drawing of lots does not permit the involvement of
private interests! (*Wanli shuchao*, 1609, 21: 34a–35a)

Whether or not the measures requested by Li Dai were accepted is
unclear. At any rate, it seems that in 1628, at the beginning of the
Chongzhen reign, a simpler regional pattern was adopted (Liu, 1996,
p. 33). By the time of the Qing dynasty, it appears certain that the 'four
corners' system was no longer in use.

Fairness against efficiency

More interesting, perhaps, is the fact that the problem of distance and unfamiliarity with new surroundings—hence the desire to regionalize appointments—was part of a wider debate provoked by the use of sortition to select local officials. This debate revolved around the opposition between 'fairness' (*gong* 公)—meaning the elimination of influence-trafficking and backdoor interference, precisely what Sun Peiyang had tried to abolish—and efficiency, meaning making an informed selection of the right man for the right position; such an informed choice was *a priori* contradictory with the process of random selection.

Yu Shenxing, a contemporary of Sun Peiyang cited above, criticized the new procedure on such grounds, arguing that the candidates were not interchangeable and could not therefore be thrown together into a basket from which they would be drawn at random:

> As far as the greater or lesser talents of men are concerned, there is in each case an appropriate [posting]. When one considers their status, there is in each case [a position] that suits them. When one considers the difficulty of a place, there exists in each case the right man. When one considers the distance [between native place and posting], there are in each case criteria to follow. But now all of this is left to chance: if one covers a mirror, is it possible to get a reflection from it? If one breaks a scale, is it possible to weigh something with it? Since Antiquity I have not heard of such a method. (Gu, 1834, 8: 23a)

This quote from Yu Shenxing was inserted by Gu Yanwu in his entry on 'selection and appointment' (*xuanbu* 選補) in the *Rizhi lu*, which starts by contrasting the flexibility that existed under the hallowed Han dynasty (206 BC–AD 220) when it was necessary to appoint magistrates to difficult regions, with the sorry situation that exists 'today':

> Today one always entrusts [magistracies] to students who have just left their commoner clothes. Among them, less than one or two out of ten possess a sound knowledge of administrative matters, while eight or nine are weak and incompetent men. Besides, people are not selected according to their talents: the method of selection and appointment consists in drawing a chip or casting a hook.[16] This is how the government of districts a hundred *li* wide [the equivalent of a county] is entrusted to mediocre and talentless persons. Not only does it harm the people, in the end it also harms the officials. As a result, places that are burdensome and difficult to govern become traps for their officials; and

---

16   These phrases, which come from a passage in the *Xunzi* (a philosophical treatise dating to pre-imperial times), are roughly equivalent to 'drawing lots'.

while they succeed each other year after year, the resulting abuses grow more and more serious, to the point where it becomes impossible to correct them.

This is typical of Gu Yanwu: almost by definition, 'today' everything is going wrong—though in such cases, one is never sure whether Gu is contrasting the present with the late Ming period, which he had known in his youth, or with the early Qing dynasty, contemporaneous with his writing. For Gu, the dysfunctional effects of this (albeit no longer new) procedure of appointment merely compounded the impact of mediocre learning and insufficient training.

This passage from Gu's *Rizhi lu* is followed, as we have seen, by an extract from Yu Shenxing's *Gushan bizhu*, from which we have already quoted a few passages. Among other reflections, Yu mentions the need to take distance into account when attributing posts. After this quotation, Huang Rucheng (the editor of the most popular edition of the *Rizhi lu*) inserted a lengthy note based on Sun Peiyang's *Donglin liezhuan* biography and which explained the aforementioned 'four-corners' system. At this point Gu Yanwu's original text resumes, with the author lamenting the lack of regionalization of appointments—a probable consequence of the suppression at some point of the four-corners system:

> Selecting southerners for the South and northerners for the North, this has been the ancient rule of past years. In 1116 under the Song, it was ordered that when appointing magistrates, even those sent the farthest [from their native places] should not have to travel more than thirty postal stations. Thirty postal stations, this is 900 *li* (ca. 450 km). In today's selection system, people sometimes have to go several thousand *li* away: they do not know the local customs, they do not understand the language, and the expenses incurred in getting to their post and travelling back home are incalculable. This is treating the empire as a single province. If one wants to eradicate the abuses in the appointment system, why must it be necessary to preserve such modalities to achieve complete fairness?

Further on, Gu Yanwu elaborates upon the same points at great length. Officials were sometimes required to journey several thousand *li* to reach their posts, thus incurring debts to pay for their travel expenses. Once they arrived, they did not know the local customs and found it hard to understand the local dialects. More often than not, the result was that the crafty clerks came to wield the real political power. And that was the case 'ever since Southerners have been appointed in the North and vice versa'. Once again, the chronology is uncertain. It does not appear that appointing northerners to the South and vice versa was the rule during the Ming dynasty, except perhaps under its founder

(*Ming huiyao*, 1963, p. 895).[17] According to the author of a compendium on government institutions compiled at the very end of the Ming dynasty, the opposite appears to have in fact prevailed: 'Localities are divided into North and South, large and small, frontier and interior. Southerners mostly go to the South, northerners mostly go to the North; it also happens that North and South are exchanged in the appointments, but there is no fixed rule' (Lu, 1746, 1st part, 1: 4a).[18] In any case, Gu Yanwu concludes this section with more criticism of the system of drawing lots:

> Before the system of drawing lots was instituted, the Department of Appointments could still form an opinion to decide on the attribution of posts. Even though in most cases the place was selected for the sake of the man, it was still possible to select the man for the sake of the place. But since the new system has been enforced, everything is left to fate and is [therefore] unpredictable. As a result, in certain busy and difficult localities, appointment after appointment it is impossible to get a worthy magistrate, each one having to be dismissed after the other. The way of the gentleman relies on fairness, he does not want to give cause for suspicion; as a result, local officials are employed in a tentative way. (Gu, 1834, 8: 26a)

Late Ming developments

As a matter of fact, in the end the Qing rulers opted for the non-regionalization of appointments, possibly to discourage the development of local cliques; and they maintained and further developed the system of appointment by random selection invented by Sun Peiyang. I will shortly introduce some elements of the debate that the introduction of sortition continued to provoke during the early years of the Qing dynasty (interestingly, it no longer seems to have been an issue after the turn of the 18th century). Staying with the Ming period for a moment, it should be noted that despite numerous criticisms of the use of sortition to appoint officials, not only was random selection *not* eliminated, on the contrary, its scope of application was enlarged. While in the late 1590s sortition was already used for some transfers and promotions, there is evidence that by 1611 (when Sun Peiyang was

---

[17] The decision was reportedly made in 1380. The text provides the list of the provinces from which officials were chosen and those where they were appointed.

[18] The passage quoted occurs in a section describing the random selection method. The author does not specify whether special 'boxes' corresponding to the different categories he mentions were used. He suggests selection by rank instead: the more desirable posts—in the interior rather than on the frontier, large rather than small—tended to go to doctors, while the rest went to licentiates and presented students.

again appointed Minister of Personnel), educational officials were also drawn by lots, and that the procedure was subsequently extended to yet other categories. Furthermore, in the final years of the Ming dynasty, the Ministry of War also adopted the random selection to appoint military officers (for these late-Ming developments, see Pan, 2001, pp. 98–101, and 2002, pp. 292–295).

The only reported move against the random selection of officials was attributed to Zhao Nanxing 趙南星 (1550–1628), a prestigious Donglin Party fellow traveller who was made Minister of Personnel in 1623, after a thirty-year absence from government.[19] Here is the only account of this known to me:

> At the beginning of the reign of Xizong (i.e. the Tianqi era, 1621–1627), Zhao Nanxing was in charge of the Ministry of Personnel. He sent a memorial saying: 'The method of drawing lots has not been in existence since Antiquity. It was resorted to during the Wanli era in order to proclaim fairness. From the start it could not be [properly] implemented; then there was the abuse of "fabricating lots". Whoever was fishing for a post could get it. Censor Zhai Xuecheng's memorial finds the system perfectly ridiculous; but there truly is nothing strange that it should be so. When Xun Qing (author of the *Xunzi*) says that "drawing chips and casting a line is how to be fair", it is just a hypothesis to illustrate that implementing a system depends upon [the quality of] men; by no means does he imply that such a thing should actually exist in the empire! It seems that the procedure must be changed in order to restore the original laws of the dynastic ancestors.' Thereupon the procedure of drawing lots was suspended. But it was again enforced at the end of the Tianqi period, and until the end the Ming did not change it any further. As a result, people made fun of the Ministry of Personnel, calling it the Ministry of Lots. (*Xu Tongdian*, 1935, 22: 1255; *Xu Wenxian tongkao*, 1936, 36: 3169)

There is no mention of this event in Zhao Nanxing's biography or elsewhere in the Ming dynastic history or other contemporary chronicles. However, it may well have been one of the drastic actions Zhao is known to have taken during his tenure in order to restore a modicum of order and integrity in the operation of the Ministry of Personnel (Goodrich and Fang, 1976, pp. 128–132).

---

[19] On Zhao Nanxing's political problems, see Goodrich and Fang (1976, pp. 128–129). He reportedly made enemies of powerful individuals by demonstrating unyielding uprightness during the 1593 evaluation of capital officials. The so-called Donglin Party (Donglin dang 東林黨), whose members strove to return to power advocating an uncompromising brand of Confucianism, was named after an academy founded in Wuxi in 1604 by Jiangnan literati who had been dismissed from the bureaucracy during the conflicts in the early 1590s (see note 8 above).

Incidentally, it does not seem that the intellectual and political orientation of those who criticized Sun Peiyang's initiative was particularly decisive. As we know, Zhao Nanxing was very close to Gu Xiancheng 顧憲成 (1550-1612) — whose examiner he had been when he passed the metropolitan examination, and who was his associate during the 1593 sexennial evaluation — and to his comrades in the Donglin Party, who brought him back to the government in the early Tianqi era in spite of his reluctance. But Sun Peiyang also had close ties with the Donglin scholar-politicians, with whom he was actively involved in the years following his resignation in 1596 and whose fortunes he tried to promote when he returned to power. (As we saw, he was included in the *Donglin biographies* compiled by Chen Ding in 1711.) We also know that Jiang Shixing, his subordinate as chief of the Department of Appointments, who was bitterly attacked for his alleged corruption in 1595, was an intellectual associate of another of the future Donglin leaders, Zou Yuanbiao 鄒元標 (1551-1624), and of his friends. For his part, Yu Shenxing, one of the most vocal opponents of Sun Peiyang's reform, does not seem to have had particularly close intellectual ties with the milieu which was to coalesce in the Donglin Party; yet his disgrace in 1591 was largely a result of the emperor's displeasure with his position in the *guoben* controversy, an experience he shared with a number of the 'good elements' later associated with the Donglin and other such groups.

Whatever the case, the authors I have cited in the debate surrounding the use of random selection are too few in number to allow for any kind of broad generalizations. Beyond constituting a facile argument during the 1595 political row, the corruption and manipulation that were denounced almost from the beginning were certainly a factor in determining the attitude of those who were sincerely concerned with preserving (or restoring) the reliability and objectivity of the appointment procedure. Despite claims to the contrary, sincerity and a concern for 'purity' in governmental operations were not the sole purview of the Confucian revivalists usually associated with a Donglin sensibility. As we saw, the real debate seems rather to have revolved around issues of fairness and efficiency, about which diverging opinions existed. Insofar as efficiency meant making an informed choice regarding the men who would be sent to postings of variable importance and difficulty, not everyone was equally confident that it was possible to be at the same time fair and efficient. Given the circumstances of late Ming political culture, it required a certain degree of idealism to believe that objectivity could be maintained within the workings of the Ministry of Personnel machinery; or in other words, to believe that wise men impervious to influence and partisanship could be found who would also be able to impose discipline and impartiality (thus rendering a technique like drawing lots pointless). Zhao Nanxing and his political friends certainly considered themselves to be such men, but as is well known, they were unable to stay in power for very long. Indeed, it is not certain that the outcome would have been significantly different, had they not been ousted in the mid-1620s by the eunuch Wei Zhongxian, then the most powerful man in the empire.[20]

Routinization and Further Debates during the Qing Dynasty

As we shall see, the same issues of efficiency and fairness were raised in the early years of the Qing regime by individuals trying to determine the best method to appoint officials. The extracts from Gu Yanwu quoted above have already introduced us to such discussions. During the Qing dynasty, however, the debate took on a somewhat different tone. There were several reasons for this, some of which were rather complex; we shall focus on only a few here.

First of all, the nature of imperial power changed completely with the arrival of the Manchus in Beijing in 1644, and the replacement of the Ming dynasty with the Qing dynasty that had been founded in Manchuria a few years earlier. It was clearly impossible for the Manchus to administer the empire without the help of the Chinese scholarly elite. Yet under the circumstances of their conquest, and due to the urgent necessity of strengthening their dominion, Qing emperors (and regents, during certain periods) were not willing to allow Chinese politicians to control the central organs of the new regime, let alone paralyse them with their factional infighting and networks of influence. In this respect, together with the imposition of a Manchu-Chinese diarchy within the central administration, coupled with the exercise of more direct control by the throne regarding daily government operations, the procedure of drawing lots may have been seen as a means of reducing the impact of factional politics on proper personnel management.

---

[20] Eunuchs were sometimes entrusted with important responsibilities within the palace and acted as an interface between the emperor (with whom they were in daily contact) and high officials in the capital. During the Ming dynasty, some eunuchs were able to prevail over young, weak, or frivolous emperors, and dominate the government by forming alliances with various factions amidst the bureaucracy.

At the same time, in the context of the early Qing regime, where its security was still at stake in many regions, the governors and governors-general appear to have wielded significantly greater power in the provinces than their Ming counterparts. Even in the 18th century, under emperors who claimed that they were able to keep an eye on everything, the governors acted indisputably as 'viceroys' (as they used to be called by Europeans). For instance, the evaluation of local officials was largely their responsibility, as the hallowed Ming institution of regional inspectors being regularly sent to the provinces by the Censorate (the *xun'an yushi* 巡按御史) had come to an end by 1661, and the Ming practice of magistrates paying triennial visits to the capital and presenting their 'government records' (*zhengshu* 政書) for direct evaluation by the central government had also been discontinued. As far as the actual appointment of local officials was concerned, in time the governors came to hold considerable sway with regard to placing the men of their choice in the more important and/or rewarding positions within their province. There is not much evidence on this practice in the early decades of the Qing dynasty; but as we shall see it was already a topic of debate in the 17th century, with more than one author admitting that the comparative importance of the Ministry of Personnel organs of appointment and evaluation was diminished as a result. Returning to the procedure of drawing lots, it seems that, after an initial period of hesitation, better controls drastically limited the opportunities for corruption and rigging. In other words, the opponents of the system were deprived of one of their main arguments.

Technical changes

This leads us to say a few words about the technical changes that the procedure of drawing lots appears to have undergone, despite the persistence of a number of uncertainties. The sources cited earlier are rather vague on the details.[21] For example, we do not know exactly when the 'four-corners' system of drawing lots was abandoned. In 1655, at the beginning of the Qing dynasty, an imperial edict ordered that, as a first step, the candidates had to be evaluated on their appearance (*shen* 身), their speech (*yan* 言), and their ability to write judgments (*shupan* 書判). Candidates were then graded into three categories, while the prefectures and counties would also be divided into three categories according to their importance. Then the candidates from the

---

21 The Ming 'Collected Statutes' (*Huidian*) is of no help since the last edition was published in 1587, before Sun Peiyang's reform.

first category would be appointed to first-category offices 'by equitably drawing lots' (*conggong cheqian* 從公掣籤), and the same for the other categories (*Qingchao wenxian tongkao*, 1936, 55: 5367; *Da Qing huidian shili*, 1909, 44: 5a). But after this edict, this system of three categories disappears from the sources. On the other hand, several 18th-century edicts show that, at least theoretically, a thorough check of the physical condition and abilities of the candidates was conducted by the Nine Ministers and the Censorate, but only *after* they had drawn lots and received assignments. Candidates were then required to present their *curriculum vitae* (*lüli* 履歷) and encouraged to expose their views on government in writing before being introduced to the emperor. A man appointed to be a magistrate could be downgraded to an educational official if the check proved unsatisfactory. It is unclear, however, how thoroughly these controls were applied.[22]

The physical details of the random selection ceremony during the Qing dynasty vary depending on the source being consulted, as can be seen, for example, when comparing the descriptions provided in three different 17th-century magistrate handbooks we will mention in a moment. However, all of the sources, both Ming and Qing, stress one crucial aspect, namely, that the drawing was done *publicly*—'in full view of all the candidates' (*gongtong kanche* 公同看掣), as the Qing *Collected Statutes and Precedents* says when describing the procedure as it was established at the beginning of the dynasty (*Da Qing huidian shili*, 1909, 43: 4a). Qing sources also stipulate (unlike the Ming texts I have encountered) that the drawing took place 'in front of the Gate of Heavenly Peace', some of them even describing the route that the candidates who had been shortlisted for the bi-monthly sessions followed inside the government compound to arrive at that location.

Another question is when (whether during the Ming or the Qing dynasties) the drawing of lots began to also be used to appoint personnel in the metropolitan administration offices. Initially it appears to have been reserved exclusively for the first-time appointments (*xinshou* 新授) of provincial officials (*waiguan* 外官). Subsequently—at the end of the Ming or the beginning of the Qing, depending on the source—promotions and re-appointments after a period of leave (*shengbu* 升補) were also included in the procedure. Likewise, all the descriptions we know of, including those in official regulations (such as the Qing *Collected Statutes and Precedents*) and in official handbooks, deal

<hr/>

22 See *Da Qing huidian shili* (1909, 44: 4b–5b) (section on 'verification of the officials appointed at the monthly selections'), edicts of 1726, 1735, and 1752—the last one deploring that the Nine Ministers 'do not care to take the examination seriously'.

exclusively with the appointment of provincial officials. Yet there is no lack of evidence that during the Qing dynasty at least, though from an unspecified date, the same system was used to appoint middle- and lower-ranking personnel in the ministries and other capital administrations. However, it does not seem that the selection of capital personnel took place during the ceremony alluded to above.[23]

There are also uncertainties regarding the levels of appointments that were involved at first. In the mature Qing system, all levels from provincial intendant (*dao* 道) and ministry department director (*langzhong* 郎中) down were concerned — in other words, everyone except the provincial administration chiefs, and the ministers and deputy ministers in the central government. The only exceptions were the posts subject to a special imperial decision, in which case the emperor himself would choose from a list submitted by the Ministry of Personnel.[24] Ming sources, on the other hand, seem to suggest that random selection was only used for county and department magistrates, their deputies, and prefectural deputies.[25] We do know, however, that in 1640 the Ministry of War was authorized to use the procedure of drawing lots to appoint officers to the positions of vice-general (*canjiang* 參將), colonel (*youji* 游擊), commander (*shoubei* 守備), and captain (*yingzong* 營總), wherever they needed to be filled in the provinces.[26]

The only type of institutional innovation that was relatively well documented during the early years of the Qing dynasty concerns

---

[23] As for the Ming dynasty, the only source that says that the procedure of drawing lots was also applied to the 'high and low officials attached to the Nine Ministers in the capital' (在內大小九卿之屬員) is the 'Treatise on examinations' of the *Mingshi* (71: 1716), which we have already seen (see note 3 above) was erroneous concerning the date and initiator of the 1594 reform.

[24] The emperor had other means of directly intervening, however. Sun Hong, writing at the beginning of the 18th century, spoke of intendants or prefects selected by lot who had the unpleasant surprise of being replaced at the last moment by people who had been seen by the emperor in an audience or had been recommended to him by influential people. Even when one was selected by lot for a magistrature, according to Sun, it was advisable to wait until receiving the imperial appointment decree in hand to celebrate with one's friends (Sun, 1702, 1: 5a–b).

[25] See the sources quoted in Pan (2001 and 2002); prefectural judges (*tuiguan* 推官) must probably be counted among the 'prefectural deputies': this would correspond to the *Wanli yehuo bian* anecdote translated above.

[26] One memorial sent to the throne by a certain Zhang Ruoqi 張若麒, dated 9 September 1640 and preserved in the No. 1 Historical Archives in Beijing, describes in some detail the sortition ceremony that took place at the Ministry of War. There were two 'boxes', one for the North and one for the South.

security. As will be seen in more detail below, even though opportunities for rigging the procedure did not completely disappear, the new regime was apparently successful in making corruption much more difficult. Several authors imply that the reliability thus ensured endowed the procedure with a new legitimacy. Cai Fangbing 蔡方炳 (1626-1709), a contemporary of Gu Yanwu who hailed from the same county, commented that, from the outset, the Qing divided the supervision of the drawing of lots between Chinese and Manchu officials of ministerial rank, thus preventing the process from being entirely controlled by the Department of Appointments; as this appeared not to be enough, starting in 1661 supervision by two censors (one Manchu and one Chinese) was added to the procedure (*Huangchao jingshi wenbian*, 1873, 17: 10b; *Qingchao wenxian tongkao*, 1936, 55: 5369). The gist of Cai's text is that as a result the procedure became 'pure' and impartial, as the candidates could no longer resort to trickery in order to outdo their rivals, and that the selection of officials was protected from the animosity that was the result of influence-trafficking and factional alignments. Therefore, Cai concluded, the drawing of lots must be maintained, even though it did not guarantee the *quality* of the appointees once they are operating in the field.

In any event, from that point on, the procedure of drawing lots was largely unchallenged. As far as we can tell, after the turn of the 18th century it was no longer a subject of discussion at all, having evidently become routine in the selection and appointment process. Although the procedure was occasionally subject to new regulations, these were nothing that elicited passionate comments and criticism such as before.

The comments that we do find during the second half of the 17th century deal with two issues that were already discussed by Ming authors: firstly, that drawing lots was by definition incompatible with selecting the right candidate for the right post; secondly, that corruption was always a risk. Let us look at corruption first.

Discouraging corruption

We have just seen that, according to some, the rampant trafficking lamented by all at the end of the Ming dynasty was successfully curbed by the new Qing regime. Other sources suggest that corruption remained at least a possibility. As it happens, our interest in the system of drawing lots was originally sparked by a satirical description of the selection ceremony and its associated corruption, penned by the Jesuit missionary Gabriel de Magalhães in reference to an incident that allegedly took place in 1669. It reads as follows:

Now it is the custom to write as many names of Cities as there are *Mandarins* that stand for employments, upon little thin Ministrys, which are thrown into a Vessel, and every one is Governour of that City of which he draws the Name. Nevertheless when a man has agreed with the Tribunal, the Tablets are so order'd that the Person draws the City which he desires. However this Artifice fail'd a *Mandarin* in the year 1669, who had given a good Sum to a Prothonotary, who had promis'd him the ready draught of a City of great Trade, and not far distant. For he drew a miserable City in the Province of *Quei cheu*, the most remote and the poorest in the whole Empire. Thereupon the wretched and unfortunate *Mandarin* quite out of his wits at his ill Success, without any respect for the Tribunal, or the presence of above three hundred *Mandarins*, rose up all in a rage (for they draw upon their knees) crying out with a loud voice he was undone, and throwing off his Robe and his Cap, fell upon the Prothonotary, threw him upon the ground, and with his Foot and Fist belabouring the poor Officer, cry'd out, Knave and Impostor as thou art, where is the mony that I gave thee? where is the City of which thou gav'st me a promise, with many other reproaches of the same Nature? Thereupon the Tribunal broke up, and the *Mandarin* and the prothonotary were both committed to the Prison of the Criminal Tribunal, where they were both in great hazard of being condemn'd to death. For such sort of merchandizing is death by the Laws, besides that the scandalous Circumstances of the Action render'd the Crime much more enormous. (Magaillans, 1688, pp. 246–247)[27]

Despite purporting to describe the 'marvels' of the vast Chinese empire (as was the manuscript's original title), Magalhães's account of China is astonishingly and systematically harsh about its *Mandarins*, everywhere characterized (Chinese-style) as 'ravenous wolves' and utterly corrupt (Will, 2015). Much rosier in its depiction of Chinese institutions is Father Du Halde's *Description de la Chine*, published in 1735 in Paris, in 1736 in The Hague, and the same year in London in an English translation. Du Halde — who, it may be noted, had not travelled to China — drew his information from twenty-seven Jesuit missionaries, including Magalhães, whose texts he had a clear tendency to edit so as to smooth out comments that he deemed overly critical (Landry-Deron, 2002, chap. 4). Still, after a brief description of the ceremony of drawing lots, Du Halde added:

[...] and it is said, when [the candidate] has Friends, or Money to bestow, the *Chinese* are not wanting in Stratagems to cause the best Governments to fall to the Lot of those they design to favour. (Du Halde, 1736, vol. 2, p. 46)

---

[27] This is an English translation of the first French edition of the book, published in Paris the same year. The latter was itself a translation of the original Portuguese manuscript, now lost.

Thus, even the greatest Sinophile among the Jesuit authors admits the possibility of trafficking. What did contemporary Chinese authors have to say on the subject? Interestingly, the three early Qing sources known to us which expressed the fear that corruption might mar the procedure were roughly contemporaneous with Magalhães's anecdote. All three are magistrate handbooks: the first is Pan Biaocan's *Weixin bian* (*An Unreliable Treatise*, 1684, preface), the second is Huang Liuhong's *Fuhui quanshu* (*The Complete Book of Happiness and Benevolence*, 1694, preface), and the third is Sun Hong's *Weizheng diyi bian* (*Manual of Government, First Installment*, 1702, preface). Chronologically speaking, the first two were even closer to Magalhães's story than the dates of their prefaces suggest, since Pan Biaocan's work was composed in 1675 and drew upon his experience of earlier years, while Huang's career as a magistrate also took place during the 1670s.

These three authors did not dispute the legitimacy and appropriateness of drawing lots to appoint magistrates: after all, their perspective was that of the candidate who had to follow a prescribed ritual to obtain a post, not that of the statesman or commentator who deplored that this was not a good system to obtain the right candidate. First, they describe the appointment procedure, including the drawing lots ceremony, in more or less detail; and then they warn their readers that when they are in the capital awaiting the day their fate will be decided, they will no doubt be approached by suspicious people who will assure them that in return for a fee they can be guaranteed a 'handsome post' (*meique* 美缺). Such con men who claim to have the right connections to sway the outcome are, the authors insist, most probably crooks, and the rumours one hears in Beijing about opportunities for rigging the procedure of drawing lots should not be so quickly believed. And lastly, Pan Biaocan and Huang Liuhong remind their readers that cheating is neither a respectable nor an auspicious way of embarking on a career. Let us take a look at what the three authors had exactly to say about the procedure of drawing lots. First, Pan Biaocan in his *Weixin bian*:

> Even though abuses such as 'sealed lots' and 'sitting lots' do exist, the 'box' is deep and the lots are short, and [such counterfeited lots] are extremely difficult to make. It is best to allow things to just run their course. Besides, drawing lots marks the start of a career. Of course one ought to be upright and refuse duplicity; opportunism is not admissible here. (Pan, 1684, 5: 2b)[28]

---

[28]   The precise meaning of what we translate as 'sealed lots' (*fengqian* 封籤) and 'sitting lots' (*zuoqian* 坐籤) is not altogether clear. In some administrative sources the former

Then Huang Liuhong in the *Fuhui quanshu*:

> The rumour in the capital has it that there is a fraud called 'sitting lots'. However, scoundrels who seek their fortune should not be foolishly trusted. Whenever 'sitting lots' [are arranged] they will necessarily designate a fixed number of posts as 'beautiful', and more than one man will have reserved such posts in order to widen his path to success. If it works, [these people] will prevail upon their service to extract a reward; if it does not, [their victims] will close their mouths and not dare say anything. It is clear that [those who deal with them] will fall for their tricks. Now, to be the people's father-and-mother [a conventional way of calling magistrates] and insist on having a fat post, what kind of attitude is that? When one embarks on one's career, one must be determined to be righteous. The advantages and disadvantages of being an official lie with the man: it would not seem that they are entirely dependent on whether the place is 'handsome' or 'terrible'. (Huang, 1694, 1: 3b–4a)[29]

And lastly Sun Hong, who was adamant that 'the method of appointment is perfectly fair' and that 'there is not the slightest abuse':

> For first appointments and re-appointments, each candidate draws his lot himself. For promotions, the officials of the Department draw on behalf of the candidates. Before the draw, the officials take the lots they have sealed and shuffle them inside the box. At the moment of the drawing, the clerks take the lot that has been drawn and publicly tear up the piece of paper [bearing the name of the post that has been selected]. The President in person writes down in the register which candidate has drawn which lot. The method of appointment is perfectly fair and there is not the slightest abuse. As for [the claim] that it may be possible to 'examine' the lots inside the box, just think for a minute: a tall box is placed on a very high table; then, the lots inside the box are shorter than it by several inches; even standing on tiptoes and dropping one's hand, one can barely reach the lots inside the box: how could this permit fraudulently picking up [the coveted lot]? Besides, the minister and deputy minister preside sternly from above, and the personnel of the Department are standing beside you, watching. When the names are called and the lots are drawn, the slightest hesitation is immediately greeted with angry shouts. That is why all this talk about bribing and plotting is totally useless. (Sun, 1702, 1: 4b–5a)

---

simply refers to lots prepared and sealed by the Ministry officials. The latter possibly means 'reserved', 'waiting for a specific person'. Regarding the exact nature of the 'box' (literally, a tube, *tong* 筒), the only description I know of, dating to the late 19th century, compares it to a brush holder (*bitong* 筆筒), i.e. a cylindrical container. Some late-Ming texts speak of a vase (*ping* 瓶).

29 'Handsome' and 'terrible' were common professional jargon to describe the profitability of a given position.

A far cry indeed from the seedy atmosphere of corruption which, according to Shen Defu, pervaded the offices of the Ministry of Personnel during the Wanli era. Indeed, Sun Hong's enthusiasm about the fairness of the procedure—so long as it was implemented with the required guarantees of honesty—is rather remarkable. Earlier in the text, he recalled that the proportion of eight first appointments against two promotions (that is, out of every ten posts to be filled) was scrupulously observed even though it could raise technical difficulties when the number of candidates shortlisted in one session could not be split accordingly. Once again, he exclaims: 'This shows even better just how fair the appointment system is!'[30] (*ibid.*, 1: 4a).

Whatever the case may have been, the only point where the three authors just quoted differ is that, while admitting that the possibility of corruption exists, Pan Biaocan and Huang Liuhong warn that taking such a risk is inadvisable and dishonourable, whereas Sun Hong, writing somewhat later, simply says that rigging the selection process is not possible. Sun seems to inaugurate a new era in the sense that, from then on, there was apparently no more point in discussing which mistakes to avoid or the risks that were involved in a procedure through which everybody had to pass and which had become so routinized that the candidate about to get his post did not even need to be told what to do and what not to do. Strikingly enough, after 1702 (the date of the *Weizheng diyi bian* preface), no magistrate handbook seems to discuss the issue: most treatises written in the 18th or 19th century begin, as before, with a description of the first steps of a magistrate's career, from appointment at the capital to assuming one's new post; but none contain so much as a brief description of the ritual of drawing lots.

Selecting the right candidate

As noted above, the few Qing texts that overtly criticize the procedure of drawing lots date back to the early decades of the regime. Moreover, instead of condemning the procedure as an open invitation to corruption, like Ming texts did, they focus on its lack of effectiveness for finding the right candidate for the right post. This was, as we have seen, a long-standing debate. Chapter 17 of the *Huangchao jingshi wenbian*—a famous anthology of essays on government by Qing

---

[30]   The promotions discussed here are promotions to a magistrate position from a local subaltern official position. Subaltern officials, who already had some administrative experience, competed with the doctors and licentiates awaiting their first post.

authors published in 1826 — abounds in essays regarding the problem of who to appoint where, following what criteria and for how long, and how to remedy issues such as forcing candidates awaiting their first appointment to spend too much time in the capital and incur debts while paying for their accommodation and travel expenses. Gu Yanwu figures prominently here, as he does in the *Jingshi wenbian* in general, where he is the absolute best-seller. Besides him, however, only two authors, both part of the same generation, discussed the procedure of drawing lots.

One is Ren Yuanxiang 任源祥 and the other is Cai Fangbing, already mentioned. Like Cai Fangbing and Gu Yanwu, Ren Yuanxiang (a native of Yixing 宜興 county in Jiangnan) had earned his bachelor degree under the Ming dynasty, had no official career, and was primarily known as a man of letters. Yet he is said to have been deeply interested in administrative matters, and apparently worked for a time as a private adviser to a relative who was a local official.[31] Interestingly enough, the first of the two texts of his that open the chapter on 'electing officials' in the *Huangchao jingshi wenbian* insists on the need to take the right decisions at the beginning of a new regime 'in order to establish the system of a whole dynasty on a firm footing' (*yi ding yidai zhi zhi* 以定一代之制). In other words, whatever his feelings about the new dynasty may have been, he believed in the future of the Qing. Ren mentions with approval a number of recent measures he read about in the *Peking Gazette* concerning the appointment and promotion of officials,[32] and gives his opinion on other proposals not yet implemented. One of these proposals, which he says was made by several provincial chiefs 'who had not conferred with each other', regards the desirability of being allowed greater leeway to move magistrates around in order to take account of their different abilities and of the various requirements of different posts. This is where Ren condemns the system of drawing lots, which he says has now become an 'established rule' (*dianyao* 典要) applied not only for first appointments, but also for posting expectant officials (*houbu* 候補) and for promotions (*tuisheng* 推升).

---

[31] He has one biography in *Qingshi liezhuan* (1928, 70: 20b), and two in *Beizhuan ji bu* (1923, 44: 16b).

[32] One of these measures was the abolition of the 'great reckonings' (*daji*) which, according to Ren, encouraged rivalries at the expense of substantive accomplishments. (I mentioned earlier the bitter enmities that arose from the 1595 great reckoning.) It seems, however, that the great reckonings were only briefly cancelled between 1662 and 1665: this would date the text to the early years of the Oboi regency during the Kangxi emperor's (r. 1662–1722) childhood.

Like Cai Fangbing, Ren acknowledges that the system is now shielded from corruption. This, however, remains a purely negative quality: 'The officials of the Department supervise the drawing of lots, the censors supervise the drawing of lots, all of this is simply to allay suspicion and be able to proclaim the absence of any fault!' His request is that the candidates and locations should at least be divided into two categories ('outstanding' and 'ordinary', and 'busy' and 'remote', respectively) before the selection process. The thrust of his text, which derides a method that 'blindly leaves things to chance', is that, in an age that is 'striving for carefulness and prudence', the people in charge —here, the Ministry of Personnel—'do not take personal considerations into account', so that there is no need to 'allay suspicion': their sole ambition is that 'officials serve the sovereign' (*Huangchao jingshi wenbian*, 1873, 17: 1a–b).

Ren's other text in the *Jingshi wenbian* reiterates the same criticism of resorting exclusively to chance. The procedure of drawing lots was instituted to combat corruption and restore fairness. Now, 'regarding fairness, we have it; but if we leave it all to a blind method, is it possible not to stumble?' There is, however, no point in spelling out his arguments here, which again revolve around the need to find ways of using officials where they can do their best (*ibid.*, 17: 1b–2b).

The governors and the Ministry

As we saw, in his text included in the *Huangchao jingshi wenbian* anthology Cai Fangbing mentioned various reforms during the first decades of the Qing dynasty that he saw as ultimately ensuring the reliability and honesty of the procedure of drawing lots. But he then added that the age-old problem of getting people attuned to the peculiar conditions of their postings remained unsolved. His main argument, espoused by other authors at the time, is that once an official had been dispatched to a province using this perfectly fair method, sufficient leeway should be left to the governor and governor-general to evaluate his performance and propose, if necessary, to transfer him to a different post:

> I think that once the governors-general and governors have lucidly tested the officials [under them], their opinion [of their abilities] is necessarily just. When they send memorials to transfer them, it is entirely appropriate to respond with an authorization. Some will say that the requests of the governors-general and governors cannot be trusted. This can only mean that *certain individuals* cannot be relied on; and if they cannot be relied on, then they must be replaced. Otherwise, [men] who have been entrusted with the affairs of a region but are not allowed to modify the distribution of talents in that region will have

nobody around to whom they can distribute the tasks at hand, and their orders won't be answered: then how will they be able to promote their policies? Presently the Court considers that if one wants to improve things, one must first eradicate the abuses; which is why energy has been focused on supervising the drawing of lots. Now that we see that the abuses in appointing officials have been discontinued, we must deal with the benefits of evaluating those who have been appointed. (*Huangchao jingshi wenbian*, 1873, 17: 10b)

The issue continued to be debated: how much latitude should be allowed to the provincial chiefs in managing, or even appointing, the local officials in their jurisdiction? Corruption once again appears to be a central issue. Inasmuch as the positions available in a province were of varying attractiveness in the eyes of the officials selected to fill them, there was always intense competition to obtain those deemed the most desirable—what, in bureaucratic jargon, was called a 'handsome post' (美缺) or, more cynically, a 'fat post' (*feique* 肥缺). In the same way as candidates in the capital were tempted to pay bribes and to cheat in order to obtain a good assignment, similarly governors empowered to redistribute posts in their provinces were subject to all sorts of flattery and requests. Faced with such demands, could powerful provincial officials, even the most committed and competent among them, be trusted to systematically discourage practices that amounted to buying positions? This raised, once again, the issue of efficiency versus fairness.

In his entry on 'selection and appointment' cited above, Gu Yanwu discussed the alternative between a centralized system of appointment controlled by the Ministry, on the one hand, and entrusting provincial chiefs with the power to evaluate local officials and move them to posts more suited to their capabilities, on the other. (In Cai Fangbing's argument, the two methods were seen as complementary rather than mutually exclusive.) Taking examples from the Tang (618–907), Song, and Yuan periods, Gu clearly leaned toward the latter practice; and, significantly, he dismissed the argument that it necessarily led to corruption:

Commentators today always say that if one proceeds this way, in most cases it will be an invitation to ask for favours and pave the way for bribery. But why should men during the Tang period have been totally upright and why should all of our contemporaries be avaricious and vicious? (Gu, 1834, 8: 24a)

As a matter of fact, one important reason why drawing lots to appoint local officials became a non-issue during the 18th century may well have been that the power to decide who would ultimately obtain a 'handsome post' — and the potential power of influence and bribe-taking that went along with it — was increasingly transferred to the provinces themselves: in other words, to the governors. By the mid-18th century, about one-quarter of the magistrate positions in the empire — those that were simultaneously the most strategic and the most economically significant — were marked as 'priority posts' (*tique* 提缺) or 'transfer posts' (*diaoque* 調缺); that is, posts to which the governors were allowed to transfer deserving officials who had proved their worth in the province for at least three years. The Ministry would simply endorse the moves retroactively after it had been informed. The rest were 'selection posts' (*xuanque* 選缺); that is, positions filled by the Ministry of Personnel using the procedures outlined above (Watt, 1972, pp. 46–47). There is plenty of evidence that over the course of the 18th century governors tended to use every available pretext to increase their discretionary powers in every area, and especially to strengthen their control over local appointments. Moreover, it is an established fact that in the first half of the 19th century, during the Jiaqing and Daoguang periods, magistrates were constantly shuffled around by governors, and more often than not counties normally controlled by the Ministry were administered by 'acting' (*shu* 署) officials chosen by the provincial government. As a result, the orderly succession of officials appointed by the Ministry, each one carefully checking the accounts of his predecessor through the so-called 'transfer process' (*jiaodai* 交代), was in fact the exception rather than the rule.[33] Indeed, during the 19th century at least, part of the eligible candidates selected by the Ministry appear to have drawn lots indicating not a particular post, but a province; they would then be sent to the capital of that province as 'expectant' officials (*houbu*). Once they had arrived, it was up to the governors to select them to fill acting positions, usually for short periods of time, until they finally received a substantive appointment. In reality, however, many never received such an appointment.

Thus, provincial governors during the Qing dynasty had considerable leeway in deciding where local officials would be posted; and this evidently encouraged bribery and flattery on the part of local officials. Following Gu Yanwu's above-mentioned criticism of leaving

---

[33] Weiss (1980) insists on the constant moving around of magistrates and short-term replacements with 'delegates' (*weiyuan* 委員) in Hunan during the first half of the 19th century (see esp. pp. 6–17). See also Suzuki (1958, pp. 262–263). Whereas Weiss saw this as a sign of flexibility and efficiency, in Suzuki's emphatically dark vision of the late-imperial Chinese officialdom, it was merely an illustration of pervasive influence-trafficking and corruption.

things to chance rather than carefully choosing appointees in accordance with the requirements of the job, his editor Huang Rucheng inserted the following comment by the famous scholar and historian, Qian Daxin 錢大昕 (1728–1804):

> Today magistracies are divided into two categories, 'selection posts' and 'transfer posts'. But in addition, the governors-general and governors ask that the men selected for appointment be used as probationary officials when they arrive at the provincial capitals. As a result, the positions to be filled by the Ministry are retained [by the governors] in a proportion of eight or nine out of ten. The power of selection and appointment has been entirely devolved to the governors, and corrupt officials grow more numerous by the day. Such is the evil that results from not trusting the Ministry of Appointment and trusting the governors instead. The more powerful governors grow, the more difficult it becomes to forbid magistrates to offer gifts. Whenever a post falls vacant, those who scheme to obtain it feel no qualms about paying bribes in the amount of thousands and tens of thousands. How could one expect that there be upright officials among them? Gu Yanwu only sees that the drawing of lots does not allow for the appropriate men to be selected; he does not see that in the provinces the selling of posts is ruinous for the State and harmful to the people. This abuse is even deeper and more poisonous [than what he denounces]. Therefore, Sun Peiyang's method of drawing lots should not be over-criticized. The governors-general and governors already have the power to recommend and to censure; it is unadvisable to allow them to select and appoint officials as well. Belittling the power of the central government and increasing the power of the provinces is not, I am afraid, the best way to prevent bad practices from developing! (Gu, 1834, 8: 26b)

The Japanese view and the general organization of the system

As we saw, from the beginning of the 18th century the use of random selection to appoint officials seems to have disappeared from public debate: as evidenced by Qian Daxin's comments on Gu Yanwu's criticism, the drawing of lots was no longer seen as the primary issue. Interestingly, not until the beginning of the 20th century do we encounter a similar attack on the procedure of drawing lots; this time, however, it comes from a Japanese rather than Chinese source. The great compendium on Chinese institutions commissioned by the Japanese authorities on Taiwan and published between 1905 and 1913 as *Administrative Law of the Qing State* includes a very clear, detailed account of the various procedures used for selecting civilian officials (*Shinkoku gyōsei hō*, 1972, vol. 1b, pp. 229ff.). It contains a description of the sortition process, followed by the reflection that 'deciding the appointment of officials by drawing lots is only good for children — truly ridiculous! Moreover, it will easily give rise to corruption. This is because those who are aiming for a [particular] post will offer bribes to the officials of the Ministry of Personnel and to the clerks beforehand and scheme to be selected. It's everywhere like this'.

The text goes on to quote from some of the authors I have presented in this chapter, Gu Yanwu and Cai Fangbing in particular. It adds that 'even if it were possible to eliminate bribery and manipulation from this procedure, how could a system which merely uses drawing lots to fill positions and does not concern itself with whether or not the post and the candidate fit each other be a good system? Moreover, even if one cares about fairness, the procedure of drawing lots is precisely what causes corruption'. Proof of this is found in the passage from Huang Liuhong's *Fuhui quanshu* quoted above. In conclusion, the authors lament: 'Alas! If such abuses already existed during the heyday of the Qing, how much worse it must be nowadays, when this heyday is over!' (*ibid.*, p. 233).

As I have suggested in the second part of this chapter, this does not properly portray the history of the procedure of drawing lots during the Qing dynasty. What is interesting is that a method used to select officials that had become completely routine and was considered unproblematic, even by the time of the late-Qing reforms, should be considered with such disdain by the Japanese — in other words, by people who saw themselves as the vanguard of political modernization in Asia, and indeed were also seen as models and a source of political inspiration in China during these years. At the same time, it is revealing that they had to look for evidence that was over two centuries old to support their views.[34]

The notion of 'heyday' (*longsheng* 隆盛) is also worth noting. The author of a recent carefully researched study on the selection of officials during the Ming dynasty marvels that a system which could only be a stopgap measure in an age of decadence (as he considers and as many Ming authors also believed) was nonetheless maintained and systematized during the so-called heyday (*shengshi* 盛世) of the Qing regime. His explanation is that the Manchu regime was only interested in maintaining its ethnic prerogatives and that as a result it chose to ignore the principle of the 'separation of powers', as well as the 'democratic spirit', inherent (or gradually developing) in the domestic Han-Chinese tradition (Pan, 2002, p. 297).

---

[34] It should be remembered that the *Shinkoku gyōsei hō* compilers lived in an isolated fashion in recently Japanese-occupied Taiwan and worked from a limited number of printed sources.

Despite the fact that this interpretation is congruent with the ideas espoused by several generations of nationalist Chinese historians in the Republican era, for whom the Manchu dynasty could only have been an improbable and regrettable episode interrupting the natural historical development of the Chinese nation, I have great reservations about its validity. While it is true that the Qing founders were anxious to limit the Chinese academic elite's means of controlling access to public office and to curb its tendency to disrupt the orderly pursuit of an authoritarian style of governance with its factional politics (whether or not we think of these as 'democratic'), it remains far from evident that the preservation and expansion of the random selection procedure was simply part of a concerted plan with such an objective in mind. For one thing, we should not allow ourselves to be blinded by the idealized notion of a body of impartial and virtuous officials at the Ministry of Personnel, who would be impervious to pressure and always manage to combine fairness and efficiency in a perfectly objective way, at least before the Ming entered a period of decay. The selection of officials has always been an integral part of politics, and clientelism was as rife during the high Ming era as it was under the Manchu regime.

Furthermore, it is important to remember that the general organization of the system used to appoint officials to provincial posts changed considerably during the transition from the Ming to the Qing. Partly due to their foreign origin and the fact that they operated as a 'conquest dynasty', the Qing were much more open-minded than their predecessors about recruiting talents that had developed outside of the examination system.[35] No serious Qing historian would dispute the positive effects of such flexibility with regard to recruitment. In fact, it demanded as much objectivity and evaluative ability from those who were in a position to determine careers as it did in the more academically regulated system that had prevailed in the Ming era. In other words, the risk of favouritism and influence-trafficking was

---

[35] In this respect, one should recall the importance of selling official ranks and positions by the government during the Qing dynasty (the so-called 'contributions', or *juanna* 捐納, system). This practice was much criticized at various times, though in reality it acted as an important means to promote non-academic candidates whose professional qualifications might be equal or superior to those of candidates with doctoral degrees. For example, a sizable number of former private secretaries (*muyou* 幕友) with significant administrative experience made their way into officialdom by purchasing the necessary status. In addition, many prominent administrators coming from the Manchu or Chinese militarized 'banner' system took advantage of the same mechanism to start their bureaucratic careers, especially during the first half of the dynasty.

equally great in both cases, and could only be controlled by exercising the same kind of professional and moral authority.

Above all, focusing on the system of drawing lots probably overlooks a number of more important issues. By itself, drawing lots to allocate relatively similar posts to people whose formal qualifications are more or less identical is in no way a shocking proposition: after all, Ancient Athenian democracy used sortition to attribute a large number of functions. Many other examples from a wide variety of political and administrative cultures could also be adduced here. In fact, the serious work of promoting people who had proved their worth and could be evaluated on the basis of their achievements only came later. As we have seen, during the Qing dynasty provincial governors increasingly became in charge of evaluating and appointing local officials, both for 'transfer posts' and when vacant positions had to be temporarily filled with acting officials. Whether such practices were more conducive to corruption than others, or whether, on the contrary, they allowed for a more flexible and informed use of administrative talent, remains an open question. As we have seen, this question was hotly debated by contemporary authors. In fact, everything points to a highly fluctuating combination of both situations, with a trend toward more influence-trafficking on the part of the governors seeming likely during the 19th century.

At court, too, the practical limitations of a procedure based on chance (otherwise widely accepted as fair) were to a large extent compensated for — in the case of prefects and intendants — by the existence of positions deemed important enough to be filled by special imperial decree. As indicated above, in such cases the emperor would choose from a list of names submitted by the Ministry of Personnel, itself based on a careful examination of the records of the best candidates eligible for a promotion. Moreover, the emperor had the possibility of picking officials who had impressed him with their character and competence during an audience, subsequently putting them on the fast track to a position: many examples of this can be seen throughout the Qing dynasty.

While it might certainly be argued that this was only one manifestation among others of the generally increased involvement in government of Manchu autocrats, and in personnel management in particular, especially compared to the more hands-off stance adopted by Ming monarchs who were more inclined to trust the judgment of their high officials (or their eunuchs), it is in fact possible to view this simply in terms of a different distribution of competence among the higher rungs of the Central Government under the Qing. Though under both regimes the emperor was the ultimate authority with regard to official appointments — no selection was valid unless it was sanctioned by an imperial rescript — what made the difference was the much greater involvement of all the Qing rulers in the daily routine of evaluation and recruitment. In any event, the existence of direct appointments made by special rescript only confirms that the generalization of the lot-drawing procedure for routine appointments in the Qing period did not in any way preclude the possibility of an 'intelligent' selection of officials based on their proven competence to serve in posts with special needs or addressing particular issues.

References

Beizhuan ji bu 碑傳集補 (1923), Beijing: Yanjing daxue guoxie yanjiusuo.

Chen Ding 陳鼎 (1711) *Donglin liezhuan* 東林列傳, reproduction in *Siku quanshu*.

Da Qing huidian shili 大清會典事例 (1909 [1899]), Shanghai: Shangwu yinshuguan.

Du Halde, J.B. (1736) *The General History of China: Containing a Geographical, Historical, Chronological, Political and Physical Description of the Empire of China... Done from the French of P. Du Halde*, London: John Watts.

Goodrich, L.C. & Fang Chaoying (1976) *Dictionary of Ming Biography 1368–1644*, New York: Columbia University Press.

Gu Yanwu 顧炎武 (1834 [1670]) *Rizhi lu jishi* 日知錄集釋, edited by Huang Rucheng 黃汝成, reproduction in *Sibu beiyao*.

Huangchao jingshi wenbian 皇朝經世文編 (1873 [1827]), reprint, Taipei: Shijie shuju, 1964.

Huang Liuhong 黃六鴻 (1694) *Fuhui quanshu* 福惠全書, reprint, Tokyo: Kyūko shoin, 1972.

Kondō Hideki 近藤秀樹 (1958) Shindai no senzen: gaifusei no seiritsu 清代の銓選——外補制の成立, *Tōyōshi kenkyū*, XVII, 2, pp. 34–55.

Kong Qi 孔齊 (1987 [Yuan period]), *Zhizheng zhiji* 至正直記, Shanghai: Shanghai guji chubanshe.

Landry-Deron, I. (2002) *La preuve par la Chine. La "Description" de J.-B. Du Halde, jésuite, 1735*, Paris: Éditions de l'École des Hautes Études en Sciences Sociales.

Liu Yulong 劉渝龍 (1996) Ming houqi cheqian fa shulun 明後期掣籤法述論, *Jiangxi shehui kexue*, 10, pp. 31–34.

Lu Lun 魯論 (1746 [1643]) *Shixue quanshu* 仕學全書.

Magaillans, G. de (1688) *A New History of China, Containing a Description of the Most Considerable Particulars of that Vast Empire*, London: Thomas Newborough.

Ming huiyao 明會要 (1963 [1887]), Taipei: Shijie shuju.

Mingshi 明史 (1974 [1739]), Beijing: Zhonghua shuju.

Ono Kazuko 小野和子 (1980) 'Banreki teishō' to 'Banreki sosho' 萬曆邸鈔と萬曆疏鈔, *Tōyōshi kenkyū*, XXXIX, 4, pp. 33–52.

Pan Biaocan 潘杓燦 (1684) *Weixin bian* 未信編.

Pan Xinghui 潘星輝 (2001) Mingdai wenguan quanxuan zhidu yanjiu 明代文官銓選制度研究, PhD dissertation, Beijing University.

Pan Xinghui 潘星輝 (2002) Chengxi beihou de geduan: cong 'cheqian fa' kan Ming Qing zhidu de shanbian 承襲背後的割斷——從 '掣籤法' 看明、清制度的嬗變, *Zhongguo xueshu*, III, 2, pp. 288–299.

Qingchao wenxian tongkao 清朝文獻通考 (1936), Shanghai: Shangwu yinshuguan.

Qingshi liezhuan 清史列傳 (1928), Shanghai: Zhonghua shuju.

Shen Defu 沈德符 (1997 [1606]) *Wanli yehuo bian* 萬曆野獲編, Beijing: Zhonghua shuju.

Shinkoku gyōsei hō 清國行政法 (1972 [1905–1913]), Tokyo: Kyūko shoin.

Sun Hong 孫鉽, *Weizheng diyi bian* 為政第一編 (1702), reproduction in *Siku quanshu cunmu congshu*.

Suzuki Chūsei 鈴木中正 (1958) Shinmatsu no zaisei to kanryō no seikaku 清末の財政と官僚の性格, *Kindai Chūgoku kenkyū*, 2, pp. 189–282.

Tan Qian 談遷 (s.d. [1640s]) *Guoque* 國榷, Taipei: Dingwen shuju.

Wanli dichao 萬曆邸鈔 (1969 [Wanli era]), Taipei: Guoli zhongyang tushuguan.

Wanli shuchao 萬曆疏鈔 (1609), reproduction in *Siku jinhui shu congkan*.

Watt, J.R. (1972) *The District Magistrate in Late Imperial China*, New York: Columbia University Press.

Weiss, R. (1980) Flexibility in Provincial Government on the Eve of the Taiping Rebellion, *Ch'ing-shih wen-t'i*, IV, 3, pp. 1–42.

Will, P.-É. (2015) Le mandarinat entre admiration et détestation: De Ricci à Magalhães à Du Halde, in Shenwen Li, Laugrand, F. & Nansheng Peng (eds.) *Rencontres et médiations entre la Chine, l'Occident et les Amériques: missionnaires, chamanes et intermédiaires culturels*, pp. 153–178, Quebec: Presses de l'Université Laval.

Xu Tongdian 續通典 (1935), Shanghai: Shangwu yinshuguan.

Xu Wenxian tongkao 續文獻通考 (1936), Shanghai: Shangwu yinshuguan.

Yu Shenxing 于慎行 (1984 [1613]) *Gushan bizhu* 穀山筆塵, Beijing: Zhonghua shuju.

Zhang Ronglin 張榮林 (1978) 'Cheqian fa' kao 「掣籤法」考, *Dalu zazhi*, LVII, 5, pp. 11–15.

Part IV:
Contemporary World

Dimitri Courant

From Kleroterion *to Cryptology*

The Act of Sortition in the 21ˢᵗ Century, Instruments and Practices

Translation revised by Sarah-Louise Raillard

At the end of the 20th century, as representative government appears to face a growing 'crisis', sortition, the 'forgotten child of democratic history', has returned to politics through a series of academic studies, practical experiments, and activist demands linking together participation and deliberation (Sintomer, 2020; Courant and Sintomer, 2019).[1] The random selection of representatives, an ancient procedure which had almost entirely vanished from current use, could only be found in two situations prior to the 1970s: to designate jurors and thus ensure the principle of *impartiality*, and in opinion polls, to ensure the principle of *representativeness* (Courant, 2019a).

The political return of sortition was accomplished through three channels: theoretical research, concrete deliberative experiments, and democratic activism. Since the 1970s, Anglo-American thinkers, such as Dahl (1990), Burnheim (1985), and Barber (1984), have put forth sortition as a means to achieve a *strong democracy*. This academic channel has only grown with the proliferation of studies on this topic (Vergne, 2010).

Random selection was implemented in 1969 for the selection of members of the *Conseil Supérieur de la Fonction Militaire* (High Council of Military Services, CSFM) in France (Courant, 2014; 2019b). Sortition was also used for citizens' juries, *Planungzellen,* in Germany (Vergne,

---

[1]   This chapter was presented at two symposia, in Athens (October 2015) and in Lausanne (June 2016). I would like to express my gratitude to all participants for their comments, and especially to Yves Sintomer, Yves Déloye, Antoine Chollet, and Liliane Lopez-Rabatel.

2011) at the time, and has moreover been employed since 1987 for the citizens' conferences on techno-scientific risks created by the Danish Board of Technology (Boy and Bourg, 2005). Hundreds of democratic innovations based on sortition have emerged all around the globe, such as the deliberative polls invented by Fishkin (1991) and the Citizens' Assemblies in British Columbia (2004), Ontario (2006), and Iceland (2010) (Sintomer, 2020). The most recent examples have been the Irish Convention on the Constitution in 2012–2013 and Citizens' Assembly in 2016–2018, which respectively led to the legalization of same-sex marriage and of abortion (Courant, 2018a).

Interestingly, sortition has become integral to the various political demands issued by several activist groups asking for direct, 'true democracy' or a deeper democracy. Citizens' groups continue to grow in France, Mexico, Australia, the United Kingdom, the United States, and Switzerland, among others (Courant, 2013; 2018b). Belgium even saw the creation of a grassroots minipublic, the G1000; one of its creators, the journalist David Van Reybrouck (2016), moreover wrote the successful essay 'Against Election', a plea for democracy by random selection.

Regardless of whether we are discussing thinkers, experimenters, or activists, the concrete question regarding how to actually perform the act of sortition is all too often overlooked. Confronted with this blind spot, we may ask: what are the various instruments and practices used for sortition in the 21st century, and what are their social and political implications? What are the ruptures and continuities between the different goals, eras, social fields, political contexts, and groups involved? What is the impact of the digitalization of random selection, of the transition from the ancient *kleroterion* to cryptology? What is the logic embodied by such practices, and do the latter in fact reveal a 'new spirit of sortition'?[2]

With the objective of contributing to a 'material history of democracy' (Déloye and Ihl, 2008) beyond the act of voting, we shall focus on the relationship to instruments in order to provide an overview of contemporary methods of sortition. I draw my inspiration from analyses devoted to materiality, on the one hand by historians of sortition such as Hansen (1991), Manin (1997), and Sintomer (2020), and on the other hand by historians of voting and elections such as Christin

---

[2] This concept is currently being developed in my doctoral dissertation, *Le nouvel esprit du tirage au sort. Principes démocratiques et représentation au sein de dispositifs délibératifs contemporains*, Doctoral dissertation in political science, Université de Lausanne et Université Paris 8.

(2014), Garrigou (1992; 2002; 2008), Offerlé (2001; 2002), and Déloye and Ihl (2008). I shall concentrate exclusively on the uses of sortition aimed at ensuring representation and selecting participants for deliberation, leaving aside other uses with aims such as distributive justice, divination, or gambling.

Beyond being of merely academic interest, the question of which tools to use for random selection is also an important democratic issue. Sortition technologies determine in part the technical reliability and the psychological credibility granted to this procedure. Taking part in the current debate on the potential and limits of random selection to renew democracy in the 21st century, this study offers a qualitative analysis of random selection techniques and instruments. In order to give tools their due, I have chosen to first analyse the instruments in continuity with traditional practices, and secondly to examine contemporary digital processes, highlighting the difficulties that increasing technical sophistication will present for actors; given that sortition claims to be inclusive and anti-elitist, complex practices would stand in sharp contradiction with those democratic goals. While depicting this mosaic of technologies and uses, it seems important not to neglect sortition 'at the margins' (Graeber, 2014), without nonetheless claiming to be exhaustive.

Manual Instruments and Collective Rituals

Coin flipping

Choosing heads or tails by means of flipping a coin is probably the simplest and most common random selection practice in the world. The procedure is often publicized during sporting competitions of various kinds. However, its current political use is less well known. Nevertheless, sortition is the official tie-breaking procedure in many English-speaking countries, for example when two candidates in an election receive the exact same number of votes.

In the United Kingdom, for instance: 'Where there is a tie between two or more candidates receiving the same number of votes the Acting Returning Officer will decide the result by lot. It is a matter for the Acting Returning Officer to determine the method to be used.'[3] During the May 2000 local elections in the United Kingdom, a seat in Nottinghamshire was attributed by flipping a coin. Both the Tory and

---

[3] *General Election 5 May 2005 Briefing Information*, Electoral Policy Division Constitution Directorate, Department for Constitutional Affairs, DCA, April 2005, p. 33.

the Labour candidates obtained exactly 572 votes and three recounts failed to break the tie. According to the BBC, 'There are two methods to decide the outcome in the event of a draw—either a coin is flipped or the parties draw straws.'[4] The Tory candidate being absent, a coin toss was performed and the seat went to the Labour candidate. Given that the official document does not actually specify the tools to be used, it is the standard practice that informed the choice between flipping a coin and drawing straws in this case.

The use of chance is also common in the United States of America, where the laws of 35 states are written to resolve electoral situations where candidates have an equal number of votes by sortition, usually by flipping a coin for heads or tails. In Idaho, the law explicitly requires this procedure.[5] In New Mexico, a committee composed of party leaders and a judge must decide on the method of sortition to be used.[6] In 2014, there was a case where two candidates for a judge's seat obtained 2,879 votes each. To solve this impasse, lawmakers chose to toss a 50-cent coin; this was the third time random selection had been used to break a tie in that state since 1980.[7] A similar situation occurred in San Diego, California, in 2000, where the procedure is regulated by a text describing 'the coin (a minted quarter chosen at random from a pool of coins), how far it had to be tossed (at least six feet) and its required path to the floor (unimpeded by, say, the drapes, walls or any people who happened to be around)'. During a drawing in 2010, the former registrar of voters admitted: 'It was almost laughable in how you actually flipped the damned coin and got it done.'[8]

Drawing straws

Mississippi recently saw two ties broken by drawing straws. In 2014, in Poplarville, the losing candidate, Stephanie Bounds, having drawn the short straw from 'what looked like an empty bleach bottle, [...] decorated to look like a hat', stated her intention to lobby to change the law, on the grounds that the random method was 'archaic and disenfranchises voters', and that 'maybe we should have just arm-wrestled

---

4   BBC, 'Hague savours local victories', *BBC News*, 05/05/2000.

5   Idaho Statutes, Title 34, Elections, Chapter 12, Canvass of Votes, 34–1210. *Tie Votes in County Elections*, added 1970, ch. 140, sec. 194, p. 351.

6   2013 New Mexico Statutes, Chapter 1 — Elections, Article 13 — Post-Election Duties, Section 1–13–11 — *Post-election duties; tie vote* (1969), NM Stat §1–13–11 (2013).

7   Schwarz H., 'In most states, tied elections can be decided by a coin toss', *The Washington Post*, 07/14/2014.

8   Donohue A., 'What Happens if the Election Ends in a Tie?', *Voice of San Diego*, 06/25/2010.

for [the seat]'. The Secretary of State defended the use of sortition and refused her request, as a new election 'delays governance and is expensive and cumbersome to the taxpayer'.[9]

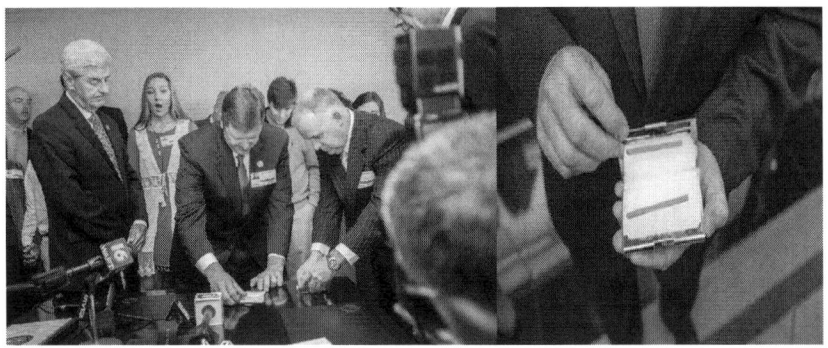

Fig 1: Gov. Phil Bryant supervising the drawing of straws between the two candidates in a dead heat, Blaine Eaton II and Mark Tullos. © William Widmer, *The New York Times*, 11/20/2015.

In 2015, in Jackson, the stakes of the tie-breaking procedure were much higher, as the candidates were competing for the Mississippi House of Representatives; each candidate had received 4,589 votes. The Governor and the Secretary of State decided to use two small silver boxes, to place a long green straw in one of them, to put the boxes in a bag, and to make the candidates draw one box each. The idea of a coin toss was rejected: 'I think they thought that was just too informal, and then what happens if the coin were to drop out of someone's hand, or do you let it land in someone's hand, or let it fall on the ground', wondered Mark Tullos, the Republican candidate;[10] while Bo Eaton, the Democratic candidate, stated: 'It's wrong—philosophically, morally. It's archaic, it's medieval, and it's wrong. We need a new election.' Eaton, who swore to respect the outcome of the sortition, drew first as his name came first on the ballot and got the green straw, but claimed to hope that the law would be changed to prevent future acts of sortition. His opponent had sworn in advance that he would accept the result if it was favourable to himself, but that he would file a challenge if he lost the draw, seeking for the 'elected representative' to be

---

9   Pender G., 'Candidate who drew short straw wants tie-vote law change', *The Clarion-Ledger*, 10/12/2014.

10   Pender, G., 'A "long green straw" will decide winner of House race', *The Clarion-Ledger*, 11/18/2015.

nominated by the state legislature, which was controlled by the Republicans at the time.[11]

In the United Kingdom, during a May 2017 local election, the drawing of straws broke a tie in Northumberland, awarding the seat to the Liberal Democrat candidate and denying Conservatives overall control of the County Council. 'It was very traumatic and I certainly would have preferred it to be a majority, but the way our system works, after a couple of recounts, we had no choice', the wining candidate admitted.[12]

These acts of random selection, which are only a few examples among many others, are always conducted by officials in a public, ceremonial context, in front of the press. While coin-flipping has the advantage of being simple and straightforward, it only allows for a decision to be made between two options. As soon as there are more options, the number of coin flips would have to increase, thus risking becoming tedious: drawing straws then becomes preferable. In France, however, it is age (in favour of the older candidate) that breaks a tie, rather than chance. The choice of a given method is never a neutral one: deference to the eldest is rooted in *gerontocratic* logic, while nomination by other elected officials stems from *oligarchic* logic, calling for a new election reflects *competitive aristocratic* logic, while sortition embodies *egalitarian* and *impartial* logic (Courant, 2019a).

Cards, sheets of paper, and books

Other cases from the United States reveal the creativity of practices and the diversity of instruments, including several hybrid forms. In Borrego Springs in 1944, rather than drawing straws, the two candidates drew envelopes from a box, one envelope containing a white sheet of paper and the other a sheet with the word 'elector' on it. The problem was deciding which candidate should draw first: that was settled by another act of random selection using a coin, the incumbent getting to choose whether to bet on heads or tails. In 1992, two rivals had to write their names down on five cards and the interim general manager drew one to determine who would call the toss. Similarly, an electoral deadlock in Nevada was solved by a game of five-card stud.[13]

---

[11] Fausset, R., 'Democrat Wins Mississippi House Race after Drawing Straw', *The New York Times*, 11/20/2015.

[12] Elgot, J., 'Lib Dem and Tory Candidates Draw Straws in Northumberland Vote', *The Guardian*, 05/05/2017.

[13] Donohue A., 'What Happens if the Election Ends in a Tie?', *art. cit.*

Sheets of paper are also used in the biblical process of 'casting of lots' to select ministers in the Amish communities of the United States. Whenever a new minister must be designated after the death of his predecessor, on a Sunday, two deacons go into a room and one of them puts a slip of paper that has a Bible verse or proverb on it inside of a hymnbook and shuffles a number of identical hymnbooks on a table while the other deacon has his back turned. The second deacon then turns around and shuffles the books again while the first deacon has his back turned. No one knows which book holds the slip of paper. The candidates are then called into the room and asked to pick up a book. All candidates then open their respective books and the candidate with the book containing the slip of paper becomes the new minister. According to Professor Donald Kraybill (2001, pp. 128–131), this unknown traditional practice works remarkably well, as no one complains or feels offended by the outcome.[14]

Books are also used to randomly select jurors in Belgium, as the researcher Vincent Jacquet explains: 'There is a provincial list from which we randomly draw citizens for various jury trials. Before, we used to put every name in a book and open it up to page at random. A magistrate told me that as time went by, the book tended to fall open to the same page, so some people were selected more often than others. This issue has disappeared with digitalisation.'[15]

The urn: Ballots, balls, sticks, and tokens

Sortition is also used to designate the spiritual leaders of certain religious groups, in addition to the Amish. According to the official procedures of the Coptic Orthodox Church of Egypt, the largest Christian community in the Middle East, each new Pope of Alexandria must be randomly selected from among the few candidates who received the greatest number of votes in a prior election. The last sortition of this sort took place on Sunday, 4 November 2012, in Saint Mark's Cathedral in Cairo. The Bishop Pachomius, acting patriarch since the death of the Pope Shenouda III, blindfolded a young boy and cut the ribbons sealing the lid of a glass urn containing three transparent balls, each one with a folded piece of paper inside. The bishop then shuffled the balls using his fingertips, but without taking them out, and then guided the child's hand into the urn. The boy took out one ball and handed it to Pachomius, amidst applause from the crowd,

---

[14] Kraybill, D. (2012) *On Amish Use of Sortition*, David Grant, Vimeo.
[15] Interview by correspondence, November 2016.

which turned into clamour when the Bishop unfolded the piece of paper with 'Bishop Tawadros' written upon it and proclaimed that name out loud. 'The two other slips of paper, with the names of the other candidates on them, were then shown to the crowd and the television cameras [...] Several hundreds of people could not access the overcrowded cathedral and were following the event on giant screens outside.' This several-hour long ritual, which includes prayers, chants, and incense, is certainly impressive; but surprisingly enough, 'none of the three candidates were present at the ceremony'.[16]

In the Buddhist tradition, certain Dalai Lamas and Panchen Lamas have been randomly drawn from a golden urn. A symbol of the power of the Qing dynasty in Tibet, the golden urn was given to the 8th Dalai Lama in 1781 by the Emperor. Despite being the subject of several controversies, the urn's functioning remains relatively simple. The name and date of birth of the children who are potential reincarnations of the Dalai Lama are written down on sticks of ivory. After prayers and a religious ceremony in the Jokhang temple in Lhasa, the sticks are inserted in the golden urn and an imperial representative draws one at random. In reality, however, the results of the random selection often ratified the choice made by the monks, especially in the case of the 10th, 11th, and 12th Dalai Lamas; it was consequently declared useless in certain cases, such as for the selection of the 13th Dalai Lama (Wang-Toutain, 2007; Chayet, 2002). In 1995, the Chinese government used the golden urn to designate a rival Panchen Lama, defying the one recognized by the Tibetan government in exile (Goldstein, 1997).

While sortition can be used by a dominant power to limit the legitimacy of a dominated actor, specific cases of this kind are quite rare; in the vast majority of experiments, the opposite can in fact be observed. In 2010, in the local Metz chapter of the French Green Party, militants decided to draw their candidates for the cantonal elections at random from among a dozen volunteers, despite the protests of some elected party officials. According to one of the initiators, 'sortition is a soothing method that diminishes or suppresses the wounds caused by narcissism. Collective work—which is necessary for political activism—is facilitated by the conviction that we are not competing with our rivals for positions of power, but working amongst our peers, any one of whom one could be chosen at random to represent his or her fellow citizens.'[17] In 2010, the method used involved an urn and slips of paper

---

16   LeMonde.fr, 'L'évêque Tawadros II désigné nouveau patriarche des Coptes orthodoxes d'Égypte', *Le Monde*, 11/04/2012.

17   Achour, P.-A., 'Au sort citoyens!', *Blog Médiapart*, 05/05/2013.

bearing the names of the candidates. The act of sortition was carried out in public and filmed, but its ceremonial aspect was not as visible as in religious cases. The 'urns' were simply three hats placed on a table covered by the Green Party flag. A young woman drew the constituency from the first hat, followed by the name of the female candidate from the second, and finally the name of the male candidate from the last hat, in order to form parity tickets. A similar procedure was used for the random selection amongst volunteers of the Parisian Youth Council, which was created in 2003 and is composed of 50 girls and 50 boys. In 2014, one could see a bailiff randomly extracting the names of candidates written on paper slips from transparent voting urns, transformed into sortition urns for the occasion: one bore a female symbol and the other a male one. A similar process took place publicly on 6 May 2017 in Paris, when a notary working for the political collective MAVOIX ('My Voice') randomly drew 'citizen candidates' for the parliamentary election using two urns, for men and women respectively (Courant, 2018b).

Fig. 2: Urn and tokens for sortition in the last step to compose a jury. © Stéphanie Para, *Le Berry Républicain*, 05/17/2013.

For trial juries, in general, only one urn is used; parity is not strictly enforced, but chance ensures a good level of diversity. The French Code of Criminal Procedure stipulates that 'drawing by lot' is a required process, but does not specify its modalities. Four successive drawings, whose methods may vary, are in fact required to select jurors. The first step, executed each year in May by elected municipal officials using regional electoral lists, is the most variable. While more and more cities are turning to digital tools, others continue to conduct the sortition manually using different kinds of urns. In Castres, on 19 May 2016, in the city council chambers, a municipal councillor designated 93 citizens by drawing rectangular tokens out of cardboard box: 'The first token gives a page number in the electoral list and a second one gives the line number on that page. A random selection is conducted canton by canton in ascending order of the number of registered voters.'[18] In the Hérault region, in the city of Lunel, the urn is a small transparent box containing numbered balls. First, some of the canton's municipalities are randomly eliminated, then potential jurors are selected from the remaining cities: 'each number matches a person on the electoral list.' For the city of Lunel itself, however, computing has replaced manual sortition, which was a 'never-ending' process. 'In a few clicks and much less time than it takes to write it down, the computer delivers 60 random names that fit the criteria, 35 men and 25 women.'[19] In some small towns, the 'urns' are paper envelopes, like in Picardy, where the deputy mayor 'draws numbers from an envelope and, in front of her, municipal representatives scan their electoral lists for the names corresponding to those numbers [...]. Previously, one used to first randomly draw one of the 6 municipalities, and the 12 persons selected were all from that town. Nowadays, we draw the municipality each time, then the number for the page of the electoral list and finally the line on that page.'[20]

The lists of the randomly selected citizens are handed over by the municipalities to the courts and tribunals, which proceed to a second sortition to compose the annual list; this round of sortition is conducted by a commission chaired by the president of relevant tribunal (art. 262 *sq.*, French *Code of Criminal Procedure*). A court clerk confirmed that the names (written on slips of paper) were shuffled inside several drawers and then picked at random.[21] The third sortition takes place at least 30 days before the opening of the trials: during a public hearing, the president draws 'from the annual list, the names of the 40 jurors that will compose the session list. He draws, furthermore, the names of the 12 substitute jurors from the special list' (Art 266). The fourth round of sortition is the most familiar to us. Before each session, all of the jurors, including the substitutes, are summoned into the courtroom, where they stand up and answer as their names are called by the clerk. As each name is called, the corresponding paper bearing the juror's name, or, most often, the wooden token covered by a piece of paper bearing that name, is inserted into a wooden or terracotta urn. The president

18   N.A., 'Tirage au sort de futurs jurés', *La Dépêche du Midi*, 05/20/2016.
19   Prades, F., 'Des jurés d'assises Lunellois à l'heure du tirage au sort', *Midi Libre*, 05/04/2016.
20   Verkest, C., 'Et les jurés d'assises de 2014 seront...', *Le courrier picard*, 06/14/2013.
21   I am grateful to Célia Gissinger-Bosse for this information.

then mixes up the tokens in the urns and draws them out one by one, placing them on a wooden board with numbered lines and/or columns, with 'acting jurors' written on top and 'substitute jurors' written on the bottom (see picture Fig. 2). The president then calls the name of the selected juror, who stands up and can possibly be disqualified by the prosecutor or the defence attorney. Jurors then swear an oath. Thanks to this 'democratic conversion ritual', sortition 'inducts jurors into a new role, different from the one they play in their ordinary lives' (Gissinger-Bosse, 2012, p. 307).

A regular urn is also used for tie-breaking in the United States. In Oklahoma, legislation details the procedure to be followed, stipulating the colour, size, and manner of folding of the papers bearing the names of the candidates.[22] This method was used in 2015 in San Gabriel, California, the mayor explaining that he felt it was 'the fairest and most transparent decision. I feel it gives the random process a little bit more legitimacy and credibility than what seems very casual, like the tossing of a coin'.[23]

The lottery machine: A playful tool with political utility

To avoid the manual mixing of the lots and to increase the credibility of sortition, some actors use lottery machines, which recall the *urna versatilis* used in Ancient Rome (Bothorel, 2020). For the space of a day, this playful tool is transformed into an instrument for political selection. In France, a lottery machine was thus used for the sortition of the Budgetary Advisory Committee of the small town of Pont-de-Claix, as well as for the second round of random selection of the candidates of the Green Party in Metz during the 2012 legislative election. The sortition equipment was even depicted on a campaign poster which emphasized the Party's 'randomly selected candidates' and portrayed the two candidates, one holding the numbered cards and the other turning the crank of the lottery machine to shuffle the balls. Below this image, a short text presented the initiative as a way to combat the professionalisation of politics.

---

[22] 2006 Oklahoma Code — Title 26 — Elections, §268104.
[23] Tompkins, C., 'Officials select "lot" method to break tie between two San Gabriel City Council candidates', *The Pasadena Star-News*, 03/18/2015.

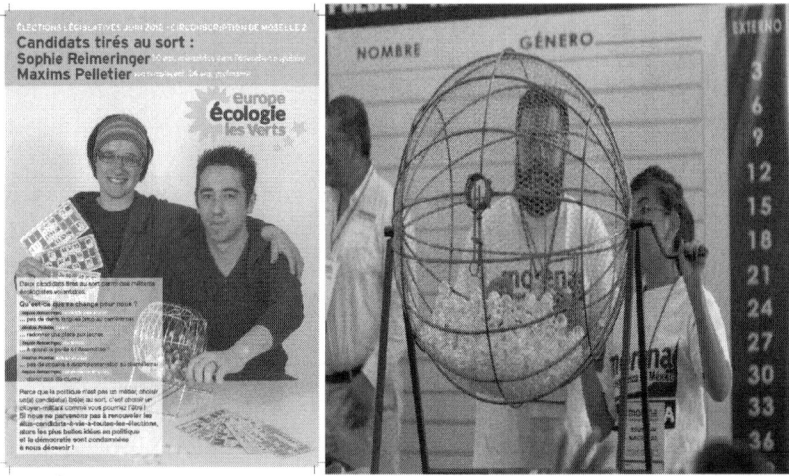

Fig. 3: Poster for the June 2012 legislative election in Moselle © EELV Lorraine
(Left)—Sortition for Morena in February 2015 © *Sinembargo* (Right).

In Mexico, a similar process received much broader media coverage. On Sunday, 1 February 2015, the left-wing party Morena randomly selected two-thirds of its candidates for the Mexican legislative election from amongst 3,000 activists that had been elected to the 300 local assemblies (five men and five women per constituency). The procedure took place in a noisy venue usually reserved for sporting events. In front of a large audience, six tables were set up bearing two massive lottery machines each, one for men and one for women, to achieve parity. At each table, a representative from the party's electoral commission read the names of the pre-candidates written on pieces of paper and handed to them by an assistant. The representative then folded each slip and put it in a transparent plastic ball, all of which s/he then inserted into the *urna versatilis*. Then, amidst general cheering, a party activist turned the crank to shuffle the balls. Each time he stopped turning the crank for a moment, a ball fell down into the small hatch below the machine. A female party activist, also wearing the party's t-shirt, took the ball, opened it under the public's gaze and in front of the cameras, to which she presented the unfolded piece of paper, raising her hands and walking from left to right so that everyone could see the name of the selected candidate.[24] The names were announced on the microphone, but almost none of these were well-

---

[24] Rosagel, S., 'La suerte, con tamales y atole, elige a dos terceras partes de los pluris de Morena', *Sinembargo*, 02/24/2015.

known individuals. The 200 official party candidates were thus selected quite rapidly, each lottery machine designating about sixteen people during this collective ritual. The 100 other candidates — academics, human rights activists, and rural leaders — were designated by Morena's national assembly. 'We successfully incorporated sortition into the process of selecting candidates. It is unprecedented, never seen before in the history of our country', said Manuel López Obrador, a two-time left-wing candidate for the country's presidency, turned party leader then President of Mexico since 2018. According to Obrador, the decision to use sortition breaks with political correctness and seeks to innovate.[25] The use of random selection ensured a great diversity of candidates, 'housewives, students, professionals, retirees, academics, indigenous people and farmers'.[26] The party has therefore pledged to use sortition to select at least part of its candidates for municipal elections. Founded as a movement in 2012, Morena became a party in 2014 and won 35 seats in the Mexican Chamber of Deputies after its first campaign, and is since 2018 the ruling party in Mexico.

Another use of the lottery machine has been seen in China since 2005, in the Zeguo district of the city of Wenling (120,000 inhabitants), where members of the committee in charge of establishing budgetary priorities are selected at random. As in other cases, notably in Pont-de-Claix in France, sortition is coupled with participatory budgeting (Sintomer, Herzberg and Röcke, 2016). Here again, the procedure is conducted in public and its supporters justify the use of a lottery machine with numbered balls on account of the public's familiarity with these tools, which they deem reliable and trustworthy enough to be used for betting important amounts of money. Conducting the sortition with a lottery machine with full visibility was preferred to using software, in order to avoid suspicions of manipulation, a concern which seems legitimate in an authoritarian context.[27] Practices such as these are experimental and repurpose a gambling instrument, rather than creating a new tool specifically designed for political use. We can see the opposite in the world of improv games, a competitive theatrical form invented in Canada. Since the 1990s, these games have used a transparent rotating cylinder called 'the barrel', specially designed for referees to draw sheets of paper indicating the themes and

---

[25] Gat, Y., 'Morena allots its candidacies for the multi-member congressional districts', *Equality by Lot*, 02/03/2015.

[26] Gat, Y., 'Morena has selected its pool for sortition of congressional candidates', *Equality by Lot*, 02/03/2015.

[27] I would like to thank Yves Sintomer for this information.

requirements for each scene, while showing the audience the random and unrehearsed aspect of the show—this tool is somewhat reminiscent of the 'drum' used for military conscription.

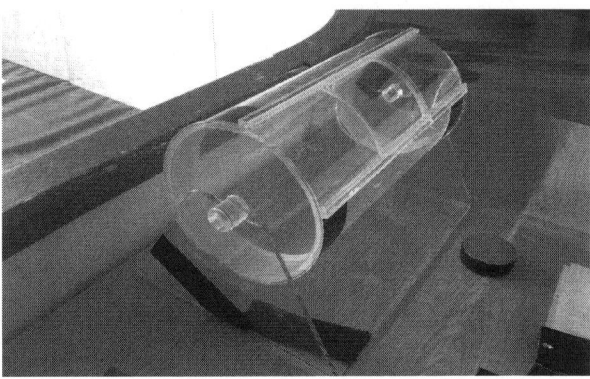

Fig. 4: Barrel and heads/tail token used for improvisation matches, Lausanne, June 2016. © Dimitri Courant.

This overview allows us to make a preliminary assessment. The techniques and procedures described above present a number of obvious continuities with past uses of political sortition, but also with games of chance. Relatively simple procedures are carried out in public and thus limit the risk of fraud. In fact, the main difference lies not in the diversity of methods used—though some tools are seen as more inherently ceremonial than others—but in each procedure's degree of ritualization. It is by being associated with a specific ritual that each procedure derives its meaning. Various political logics may be highlighted using the same procedure. Drawing lots to break a tie between candidates refers to the democratic principle of equality. Meanwhile, the principle of impartiality behind juries is part of the civic duty imposed on citizens, as was also true for the Chinese case described above. On the contrary, however, religious uses also entail a ritual that asserts group unity as well as a form of divination. This dimension of unity can also be seen for Morena and the French Green Party, which seek more social diversity amongst candidates in order to achieve better representativeness (Courant, 2014; 2019a).

Digital Sortition: Field-Dependent Questions

Do distinctions based on the instruments used become more important with the advent of digitalization, towards which political sortition has massively shifted since the 1980s? Does digitalization lead to substantial changes compared to manual sortition? As we will see, computing is not 'neutral' and its uses are not as uniform or immaterial as one might think.

The High Council of Military Services: An intermediary case

The armed forces form an institution known throughout history for its use of sortition for conscription; an *urna versatilis* called a 'drum' was used in France and Belgium. However, the contemporary use of sortition in the *Conseil supérieur de la fonction militaire* (French High Council of Military Services, CSFM), a body created in 1969, remains largely unknown. This deliberative assembly seeks to defend and promote the military services as well as the working conditions of military servicemen and women; it meets twice a year for one week, at the end of which it delivers an official statement to the Minister of Defence.[28] This legal note, which discusses all laws impacting military status and conditions, is then studied by the Council of State. The assembly must also provide an account of troop morale from the bottom-up, and disseminate information to soldiers from the top-down, from the administration and the chief of staff (Courant, 2019b). The High Council of Military Services is composed of 79 members randomly selected from each branch of the forces (army, navy, air force, etc.) and of every rank (officer, private, etc.), to achieve proportional representation based on actual staff distribution. A former secretary general of the CSFM explains the reasons for choosing sortition:

> The advantages of sortition are the opposite to those for elections. The process eliminates electoral campaigns, one-upmanship, demagogy, and polarization. The Army seeks to prevent factions, which is why it also bans unions. Impartiality is produced by sortition, but also by the collective gaze which prevents all kinds of favouritism. (Courant, 2014, p. 96)

An official text from 1970 shows that decision-makers had envisioned calling on the National Lottery to conduct the sortition procedure, before rejecting this idea for psychological reasons: it did not look serious enough—the opposite conclusion reached by the Chinese in the aforementioned case, where use of the lottery machine was chosen precisely to enhance trust. Lawmakers then decided to call on the *Institut national de la statistique et des études économiques* (French National Institute for Statistics and Economic Research, INSEE) and the Rand

---

28 I am citing from Courant, D. (2014) *Tirage au sort et concertation dans l'Armée française: Le cas du Conseil Supérieur de la Fonction Militaire (1969–2014)*, Master's thesis in political science, EHESS, Paris.

Corporation. The sortition was carried out manually over the course of a whole day and required a lot of manpower to handle the numerous balls and 20,000 horizontal lines (Courant, 2014, pp. 28–31).

Since 1990, this manual procedure has been replaced by computers. Throughout history, whenever humans have used random selection for political aims, it has been crucial to publicly exhibit the complete *impartiality* of the process, and the total absence of manipulation, in order to ensure the system's credibility and therefore legitimacy. In the 21st century, it seems logical that the act of sortition would be adapted to contemporary techniques. However, even if digital software is now part and parcel of our everyday lives, it nonetheless remains potentially dangerous. A military computer scientist explains that most programmes generate the same sequences of pseudo-random numbers, which can therefore become predictable:

> In computing, one cannot generate pure randomness, it is impossible, at least for now [...] Computers produce 'pseudo-random' numbers, this process is very important in cryptology, which is an important field of computer programming. To create randomness, you take non-repeating elements and combine them with mathematical formulas. In this case, for the CSFM, we generated randomness thanks to the date and time. 'Brownian motion' is even more random, as it is based on the vibrations of the thermal motion of the electron in the atom which are totally unpredictable, and not too difficult to implement electronically. (Courant, 2014, pp. 46–47)

Regarding the program used by the CSFM, the application was developed internally by the Army. Although sortition began to be digitalized in 1990, it is only since 1999 that a proper software program has been designed, later revised and rewritten in 2010: 'The source code (basic visual) is open, therefore easily verifiable and accessible on demand, but this type of suspicion never happened. Computing is more reliable and convenient but people tend to mistrust it because they believe they do not master the tool' (*ibid.*).

Once every two years, under the scrutiny of a supervisory committee during a formal ritualized procedure, a member of the general secretariat of the CSFM presses the button 'random selection' on an Excel file. The random operation is twofold: the software randomly assigns 8-digit numerical values to each candidate, then selects the ascending values after having randomly determined a start value. For each seat, there is a holder (the one with the lowest value) and three alternates, in ascending order of their numbers. Contrasting the CSFM with the aforementioned Mexican case, a question arises: why does Morena use a lottery machine, while the CSFM uses digital software? Beyond the fact that there are numerically many more servicemen and women than party members, the explanation can be found in the fact that Morena first and foremost wants to establish the act of sortition as a *public ritual of unity*, thus choosing to have a performance in front of large audience. Impartiality is therefore only a secondary concern for Morena. On the contrary, the CSFM primarily seeks to conduct an efficient *ritual of impartiality*: a limited supervisory body is therefore sufficient.

Statistics and opinion polls: Digital selection inside a black box

Are these questions, both technical and political, also applicable to other uses of sortition based on pseudo-random numbers? The comparison between the military case, statistics, and politics offers an enlightening contrast. In Switzerland, for instance, 'quantitative' researchers in fact conduct few sortition procedures themselves: 'For the big recurring FNS (*Fonds National Suisse* — Swiss Research Institution) surveys, the Federal Office of Statistics gives us the samples already prepared. For surveys of lesser importance, we buy the samples from private companies, such as AZdirect.'[29] In the rare cases where researchers must conduct the random selection themselves, they rely on random number generators using programmes like Excel, R, or SPSS. 'We can use the random number generator for the names on a list, the frequency of selection in a randomly shuffled list, the numbers in phone numbers, geographic coordinates, the building number, and the apartment number.'[30] In the case of questionnaires, statisticians are not overly concerned that the randomness simulated is not 'real'; the fact that the selection is based on pseudo-random numbers is not a problem, so long as the sample is representative and every member of the 'sample frame' has an equal chance of being selected. This lack of interest in how machines generate pseudo-random numbers seems logical, given that there are no suspicions that a poll is being manipulated to include specific people on the list. Samples aiming for representativeness would at any rate be congruent with the demographic weight of the different population categories, thanks to the algorithms and software which are the focus of particular attention (Tillé, 2001), but also thanks to corrective measures implemented at various stages throughout the selection procedure (Fourniau, 2020).

---

[29] Interviews with social science researchers from the University of Lausanne, December 2016.
[30] *Ibid.*

The situation does not seem to be very different for opinion polls. Significantly, while studies generally insist on using random samples, little attention is paid to generating randomness (Meynaud and Duclos, 2007). The majority of the techniques are the same as those used by statisticians and involve software programmes. Rolland Cayrol (2001, pp. 47–48) explains that 'you can use a random number table (i.e., numbers that are not connected by any statistical link), you can use a specific spreadsheet, you can draw a person every x'. Then, once the pollster has a person on the phone, s/he can ask 'which family member has the next upcoming birthday?', in order to avoid skewing the survey by only interrogating those individuals more likely to answer the phone in the first place. Random number tables can be found 'in most books dealing with statistics', explains Yves Fournis (2004, pp. 64–65), according to whom poll organizers can also 'reshuffle the file (the sampling frame market research) like a deck of cards' or 'let a number of pins matching the size of the sample fall onto the (geographical) map, and include in the sample the homes closest to the pinheads'. The two authors also mention the 'road of chance', where poll organizers can 'draw the points of departure and arrival at random' and ask pollsters to follow a predetermined itinerary (e.g. third building on the right, second floor on the left, etc.) (*ibid.*, p. 67; Cayrol, 2000, p. 51).

According to Loïc Blondiaux, 'very early on, there were machines to perform [the sortition], first Hollerith machines then IBMs. The former were impressive electromechanical machines that operated (before the invention of the computer) with punched cards'.[31] In France, however, survey samples are not probability based, but compiled according to quotas, in contrast to the standard practice in the United States. 'Sometimes, polling companies ask for a "step" to be followed: by phone, to take one number out of every ten; while canvassing, to take one street number out of every three [...] By phone, it is possible to conduct the sortition by randomly dialling numbers then eliminating them if the call fails', explains the researcher Rémy Caveng.[32] In contrast with the case of the CSFM, here the act of sortition is neither ritualized nor performed in public out of concern for transparency; it is a technical operation conducted by professionals behind closed doors, using proprietary software, a black box, without true supervision, but on the basis of a relationship of trust between the polling organization and sponsor. Opinion polls ultimately succeeded in acquiring legitimacy by

---

[31] Interview by correspondence, November 2016. See also Didier (2009).
[32] *Idem.*

combining public and scientific legitimacy with technical capacity (Blondiaux, 1998). It is significant that the numerous critiques waged against polls challenge how public opinion is 'formed', 'constructed', and how questions are framed, but do not question the generally accepted guidelines regarding random samples; probably due to the methodological proximity with questionnaire surveys (Bourdieu, 1980; Garrigou and Brousse, 2011; Lehingue, Caveng and Garrigou, 2011).

Digital sortition in politics: Issues of democratic control

The reason sortition procedures for minipublics—which represent the majority of contemporary political experiments in sortition today—are so understudied is that, most of the time, these procedures are delegated to polling organizations which conduct random selections digitally without an audience or public present. Vincent Jacquet explains that 'for the G1000, we use random digit dialling (RDD), therefore it is a computer which automatically generates numbers, as is often the case in Fishkin's deliberative polling. For the G100 and G32, everything was also done through computers. I think that we just used Excel.'[33] This was also the case for minipublics in the French region of Poitou-Charentes:

> For citizens' juries, the polling company gave us a list of randomly selected individuals, their names and addresses, but we contacted them ourselves. For the participatory evaluation workshops, we used Excel to randomly select individuals from a list of users. There was no advantage to doing it in public. We wanted to gather information based on user expertise, so there was no point in not conducting a real sortition.[34]

Nowadays, almost all minipublics in the realm of democratic innovation are randomly selected using digital instruments, or more accurately, by combining computing and 'manual' corrections as illustrated by Fourniau (2020); in the overwhelming majority of cases, there is no public supervision of the way the minipublics are formed (Gastil and Levine, 2005).

However, in the official and traditional political field, the use of proprietary software, or a 'black box', with no open source code—and therefore unverifiable and potentially susceptible to manipulation—can be a problem, especially if competition is tough and the stakes are high. In Ticino canton, Switzerland, during the elections for the National Council (Parliament) in autumn 2011, a random selection operated by

---

[33] *Idem.*
[34] Phone interview with Marion Ben-Hammo, December 2016.

computer and aiming to break the tie between two candidates was invalidated by the Federal Court, which required that a new selection had to be carried out manually and in accordance with federal legislation and the by-laws of the concerned body. The first sortition handed the victory to the candidate Monica Duca Widmer, eliciting anger from her competitor Marco Romano, who declared: 'We are engaged in politics, not playing a game of chance. My result was very good. I do not want to put my political career in the hands of chance.'[35] Nevertheless, he expressed great pleasure when the odds turned in his favour during the second sortition. The manual drawing took place in the Gran Consiglio in Bellinzona in the presence of councillors of state, the press, and the public. Printed on small sheets of paper, the names of the candidates were placed inside two little spherical boxes then put in a white bag, from which the Government Vice-President drew one.

It appears that, in less competitive political contexts, the use of pseudo-random numbers is less of an issue. In France, the small party *Nouvelle Donne* used sortition several times: to select some of its candidates on electoral lists, to appoint the representatives of the Campus group (who rotated every six month) by manually drawing papers out of a black hat (while ensuring gender parity), and finally to constitute its Ethics Comity in March 2015 using software but during a procedure that was filmed and live-streamed on YouTube. The grassroots educational organization *Les Citoyens Constituants*, which promotes the political use of sortition, has also used this method to randomly and publicly designate its administrative officials using an Excel spreadsheet during its general assembly; previously, papers in a hat had been used, but that method of sortition took longer (Courant, 2018b).

---

[35] ATS, 'Fédérales 2011/TI: recomptage des voix demandé entre deux PDC', *Romandie*, 10/24/2011.

Fig. 5: Campaign posters. © DemoRun, 2015.

However, even for marginal parties and movements, some situations seem to require more precautions. Some 'sortition activists' are also mindful of ensuring that the element of chance is 'pure' and verifiable. Founded in 2015, the DemoRun Project randomly selected citizens from the electoral lists of La Réunion, a French overseas region, then offering them the chance to be candidates in the regional elections. The movement's campaign posters showed the randomly selected citizens holding their electoral card in front of their faces, as if to say 'no matter who I am, I am just a citizen like you', as well as three, ten-sided dice on an electoral card. The generation of random numbers, then combined using an algorithm, was performed in public using the decimal dice 'that I use for my role-playing games', one of the movement's leaders explained.[36] This list obtained 3,895 votes, or 1.47 per cent.

The anti-austerity movement *Démocratie Réelle*, founded by a few 'outraged citizens' in the wake of Occupy, in time for the 2012 French parliamentary election (Courant, 2013, p. 39), proposed lists of randomly selected candidates for the 2014 European elections and the 2015 departmental elections (Courant, 2018b). This 'anti-party' organizing 'counter-elections' first considered using the free software Hasard designed by the company PMEtool, but rejected it because it was an unverifiable black box. After also considering Blockchain, the group ultimately decided, via its online forum, to use the stock market index of the CAC40 (the French equivalent of the Dow Jones):

[36] Phone interview, August 2015.

You assign a number to each person starting from 0, the day of the sortition, you collect the closing value of the CAC40 for the 5 previous days. For each value, you only keep the 2 decimal points that you put end-to-end in anti-chronological order, which gives you a 10-digit number. You divide this number by 1000000000 and multiply it by the number of candidates. The integer part of the result gives the number of the winning candidate. If they refuse, you take the following number [...] You keep the decimal after the winning number which corresponds to the unused random part.[37]

This technique was also recommended in a note by the Internet Engineering Task Force (IETF), *3797 – Publicly Verifiable Nominations Committee (NomCom) Random Selection. 1997, revision 2004*. This programmer collective, 'the international, informal and open group that produces most of the technical standards of the Internet' (Cardon, 2010, p. 78), recommends using external random numbers such as national lotteries, sports results, stock market indices, etc., then mixing those numbers in the algorithm: 'The exact algorithm to be used, as well as the public future sources of randomness, is made public in advance.' The moderators of the Slashcom forum software are also randomly selected, although through a lottery weighted by 'karma', the points that users give to moderators they find efficient.

However, the most cutting-edge fields in terms of randomness studies are cryptology and quantum physics. The sources of randomness used are the movement (or polarization axis) of photons captured by an optical laser, the Brownian motion of electrons, atmospheric noise, and white noise. The work of cryptologist David Chaum (2001) on online voting security led him to propose *random-sample voting* as 'more democratic, better quality and far lower cost'. The aim would be to 'select a random sample of eligible voters in a verifiably valid manner and empower them to study and make a decision on a matter of public policy. This can be done in a highly transparent manner which allows anyone to verify the integrity of the election, while optionally preserving the anonymity of the voters'.[38] Will cryptology and quantum physics be perceived as being suspiciously invisible, or on the contrary as indisputable, with scientism replacing religion? Will the public be more inclined to trust cryptology rather than polling organizations? That will probably depend on the issue at stake. I make the hypothesis that when a selection involves a collegial body, rather than a candidate, when there is no competition, and when politicization

---

[37] N.A., 'Outils de tirage au sort', *Wiki Gentils Virus*, 12/06/2015.

[38] https://en.wikipedia.org/wiki/Sortition#Methods.

is weak, then it will be possible to use software without risk of tension. In cases where the opposite is true, the traditional procedures and instruments combined with public scrutiny will prevail; if digital tools are used, they shall be accompanied with efforts to ensure maximum transparency.

A New Spirit of Sortition?

What are the rituals, instruments, and performances of political sortition in the 21st century? Acts of sortition are often performed in a formal ceremony before the media and the public. This formality is quite obvious in religious cases, but can also be seen in legal or tie-breaking situations. In the case of political movements, the moment of sortition can become a collective ritual displaying the group's unity, a sort of 'identity affirmation ritual' (Déloye and Ihl, 2008, pp. 44–50). Sortition can also become a campaign element, potentially stronger than the act of voting which, even though ritualized, is accomplished individually in the loneliness of the polling both (Garrigou, 2008). Sortition is more similar to the collective and public phase of ballot counting and the announcement of the results.

What significance do these practices embody? Simply layering technical categories (either manual or digital) onto political principles seems untenable. A number of trends can be identified, however. The 21st century has seen the persistence of manual instruments for sortition —the emergence of computing has not eliminated them. 1) In some cases, the traditional practice remains strictly manual, including in religious uses or to break ties. 2) In others, computing has replaced physical instruments for the sake of efficiency but without changing the institution, as for the CSFM and Les Citoyens Constituants. 3) There are situations where the digital and the manual co-exist: for the party Nouvelle Donne, as well as for juries (although big cities draw lots digitally, sortition in the courtroom is still performed using an urn). 4) Certain new procedures choose to rely solely on physical instruments, as is the case for Morena, the Chinese participatory budget, the Parisian Youth Council, and MAVOIX. 5) Finally, some new mechanisms have opted exclusively for computing, as did Démocratie Réelle and the Internet Engineering Task Force. Therefore, despite the emergence of digital technologies, the old and the new clearly continue to co-exist. There has been no break or systematic change in the underlying logic of random selection provoked by a change in sortition instruments.

Political parties like the French Green Party or Morena seem to prove that if *unity* is the main goal, sortition tends to be performed manually, so it can be more spectacular, public, and ritualized. If *representativeness* is the primary objective, sortition is performed digitally, without publicity or ritual. Another important cleavage regards the size of the selection pool, the source population, relative to which the lottery is done. If the pool is substantial, computing tends to be chosen: large cities have adopted software to select jurors, while small towns continue to draw lots in the traditional way using manual tools. The hypothesis can be made that manual instruments are very often associated with the 'ancient spirit of sortition', whose objectives are primarily *impartiality* and *equality*, and is thus accompanied by an important degree of ritualization. Of course, new digital tools can be used to achieve this same ancient practice, as for juries and the CSFM. However, the emergence of computing has coincided with the rise of the representative sample and of polling companies in general (Sintomer, 2020), which raises issues regarding a potential 'new spirit of sortition' focused on *representativeness*, as the advent of minipublics has revealed.[39] If there is indeed a 'new spirit', it is not a systematic one, and it is not strictly correlated with computing, as software can be used even when representativeness is not the goal (e.g. Nouvelle Donne, DemoRun, Démocratie Réelle, Les Citoyens Constituants). The emergence of digital instruments has not itself led to changes, as the uses of digital technology are what truly modify things—in our case, the creation of representative samples from massive populations. This raises a challenge: in a democracy, can sortition be conducted by experts using proprietary black box software in a non-transparent manner, without losing the public's trust?

Historians endeavour to understand the ancient procedures and instruments used in the past, but most sociologists continue to overlook those that they can observe today, whilst democratic innovators and activists only pay them marginal attention for purely instrumental aims. How can we make sense of this paradox? Our first argument regards the focus on an overwhelmingly theoretical justification of sortition, rather than its practical implementation. Academics and actors are primarily interested in the question of 'why' sortition should be conducted and much less by 'how' to do so. Our second hypothesis is that the institutions performing sortition in a routinized fashion, such as courts or polling companies, have acquired legitimacy by building

---

[39] This concept will be further analysed in my doctoral dissertation, *Le nouvel esprit du tirage au sort. Représentation et principes démocratiques au sein de dispositifs délibératifs contemporains*, Doctoral dissertation in political science, Université de Lausanne et Université Paris 8.

their reputation and insuring their position through long-lasting efforts (Blondiaux, 1998). Our third conclusion is that sortition remains marginal. Drawing lots does not have the importance nor the scale of elections; its uses are activist-driven and experimental and the goal is not (yet) to standardize a procedure that would be repeated identically across the whole territory and whose task would crystallize political sentiment (Déloye and Ihl, 2008, pp. 58, 67). However, things are changing. Sortition appears to be inexorably on the rise, which leads to questions regarding its operation. Thus, in Ireland, activist groups have criticized the Citizens' Assembly and its deliberations regarding the potential legalization of abortion: 'Those citizens [...] we do not really know how they were randomly selected. Even if RedC is a very respectable polling company [...] It raises questions.'[40] The polling company's refusal to disclose the details of its protocol has not put minds at ease. That being said, this is the standard procedure for demo-cratic innovations based on a minipublic (Courant, 2018a). Moreover, according to liberal logic, the task of ensuring a truly random selection is entrusted to a non-state third party, here a polling company, which increases the legitimacy of sortition as it remains outside state control. Our final hypothesis is that a 'new spirit of sortition' in politics is possible, at least regarding minipublics, that is to say, the series of experiments that have attracted the most attention to this mechanism. Unlike elections, which focus attention on campaigns and voting as the source of the victor's legitimacy, the moment of sortition elicits little interest, as the selection process is not a trial conferring legitimacy onto those selected. The most important moment is that of collective deliberation, in which all the randomly selected persons are equal to each other, all equally the results of an impartial process.

Voting entails as many operations as there are voters, whereas sortition can be conducted in a single, centralized operation. Questions regarding technical feasibility, psychological credibility, efficiency, and verifiability remain relevant, however. Digitalization poses the risk of establishing a technocratic hierarchy between experts, who master the instruments, and lay citizens, who are either gullible or suspicious (Cardon, 2010). That situation would be in contradiction to the equali-tarian demands of those preaching the democratic virtues of sortition (even if there always remains a distinction between *performance*, the capacity to create and understand tools, and *competence*, the capacity to

---

[40] Interview with a representative of the Repeal the 8th Coalition, Malahide, January 2017.

use tools). Statisticians and polling companies creating samples and minipublics are the only case of simultaneously non-public and non-verifiable sortition procedures. As soon as uses of sortition begin to concern primary political functions, black box software and the opacity of polling companies may no longer seem suitable, as suspicions of electronic voting demonstrate (Déloye and Ihl, 2008). It is likely that we will soon witness debates on how to equip sortition for it to be carried out, not experimentally, but in a homogeneous, reiterated, ritualized, and standardized manner — echoing the lively debates regarding the urn, the envelope, and the polling booth (*ibid.*; Garrigou, 1992; 2002; 2008; and Offerlé, 2002). What shall become the new *kleroterion* of the 21st century remains to be seen.

Looking forward, it is likely that one aspect of this upcoming debate and its implications for the future of democracy will be a confrontation between two clashing ideal-types. On the one hand, we can delegate to experts, relying blindly on 'the professionals of sortition' without demanding transparency of their opaque software. On the other hand, we can express the democratic desire to associate sortition with inclusion even in its practice, making sure that all can understand and judge the tangible processes of random selection. This dichotomy can be reflected in the choice of the instruments, between, on one hand, purely digital methods which are difficult to verify (i.e. black box software designed by polling companies or truly random quantum cryptology), and, on the other hand, verifiable methods, whether entirely manual, combined with algorithms (as in the case of DemoRun and its dice), or using publicly verifiable sources (such as national lotteries or stock market indices). The issue is not so much publicizing a ritual, but ensuring that the public has the ability to check the results. Sortition instruments are imbued with their own socio-political logic. Some are inherently unverifiable, which reflects an expert technocratic logic, while others can be verified by anyone and are therefore inclusive and controllable, which reflects a more democratic logic. This tension between the type of instruments, similar to the cleavage between proprietary software and open-source software (Cardon, 2010, pp. 18–20), might also reveal tensions regarding the elective affinity between a 'new spirit of sortition' and a 'model of democracy'. Will the return of sortition to politics become a mere supplement to representative government or usher in the dawn of a radical democracy? Will sortition be used to legitimize current power structures by enhancing elected institutions with a sample of carefully selected 'enlightened' citizens, therefore justifying the non-consultation of the vast majority of the population, with deliberative democracy thus abandoning mass democracy (Chambers, 2009)? Or on the contrary, will sortition be used to establish a more direct, radical, and inclusive democracy (Courant, 2019a)? Whether the instruments of random selection chosen are opaque and in the hands of experts, or on the contrary public and accessible to all, shall be an indication of the future of sortition in politics.

References

Barber, B. (1984) *Strong Democracy*, Berkeley, CA: University of California Press.

Burnheim, J. (1985) *Is Democracy Possible? The Alternative to Electoral Politics*, Cambridge: Polity Press.

Blondiaux, L. (1998) *La fabrique de l'opinion. Une histoire sociale des sondages*, Paris: Seuil.

Bothorel, J. (2020) Civic sortition in Republican and Imperial Rome: Physical instruments and technical logistics, in Sintomer, Y. & Lopez-Rabatel, L. (eds) *Sortition and Democracy*, Exeter: Imprint Academic.

Bourdieu, P. (1980) L'opinion publique n'existe pas, in *Questions de sociologie*, Paris: Minuit.

Boy, D. & Bourg, D. (2005) *Conférences de citoyens, mode d'emploi*, Paris: Descartes et Cie.

Cardon, D. (2010) *La démocratie Internet. Promesses et limites*, Paris: Seuil, La république des idées.

Chayet, A. (2002) Chapitres 6 et 7, in Blondeau, A.-M. & Buffetrille, K. (eds.) *Le Tibet est-il chinois?*, Paris: Albin Michel.

Cayrol, R. (2000) *Sondages: Mode d'emploi*, Paris: Presses de Sciences Po.

Chambers, S. (2009) Rhetoric and the public sphere: Has deliberative democracy abandoned mass democracy?, *Political Theory*, 37 (3), June 2009, pp. 323–350.

Chaum, D. (2011) Random-sample voting: Far lower cost, better quality and more democratic, *rs-elections.com*.

Christin, O. (2014) *Vox populi. Une histoire du vote avant le suffrage universel*, Paris: Seuil, Liber collection.

Courant, D. (2013) *Militer pour le tirage au sort: Crises du gouvernement représentatif et expérimentations démocratiques*, Master's thesis, Sciences Po Rennes, Rennes.

Courant, D. (2014) *Tirage au sort et concertation dans l'Armée française: Le cas du Conseil Supérieur de la Fonction Militaire (1969–2014)*, Master's thesis in political studies, EHESS, Paris.

Courant, D. (2018a) The Curious Institutionalisation of Deliberative Democracy: The Irish Citizens' Assemblies and the Future of Democratic Innovation, *Les Cahiers de l'IEPHI*, no. 72, pp. 8–23.

Courant, D. (2018b) The sortition activists: Sociology of new democratic claims, paper presented at *CLAIMS workshop*, Paris, 02/02/2018.

Courant, D. (2019a) Sortition and democratic principles: A comparative analysis, in Olin Wright, E. & Gastil, J. (eds.) *Legislature by Lot*, pp. 229–248, London: Verso.

Courant, D. (2019b) Délibération et tirage au sort au sein d'une institution permanente. Le Conseil Supérieur de la Fonction Militaire (1968–2016), *Participations*, 23 (1), pp. 69–92.

Courant, D. & Sintomer, Y. (eds.) (2019) 'Le tirage au sort au xxie siècle. Actualité de l'expérimentation démocratique', *Participations*, 23 (1).

Dahl, R.A. (1990 [1970]) *After the Revolution? Authority in a Good Society*, New Haven, CT: Yale University Press.

Déloye, Y. & Ihl, O. (2008) *L'acte de vote*, Paris: Presses de Sciences Po.

Didier, E. (2009) *En quoi consiste l'Amérique ?*, Paris: La Découverte.

Fishkin, J. (1991) *Democracy and Deliberation*, New Haven, CT: Yale University Press.

Fourniau, J.-M. (2020) The selection of deliberative minipublics: Sortition, motivation and availability, in Sintomer, Y. & Lopez-Rabatel, L. (eds.) *Sortition and Democracy*, Exeter: Imprint Academic.

Fournis, Y. (2004) *Les études de marchés. Techniques d'enquête, sondages, interprétation des résultats*, 3rd ed., Paris: Dunod.

Garrigou, A. (1992) *Le vote et la vertu, comment les Français sont devenus électeurs*, Paris: Presses De Sciences Po.

Garrigou, A. (2002) *Histoire sociale du suffrage universel en France, 1848–2000*, Paris: Seuil.

Garrigou, A. (2008) *Les secrets de l'isoloir*, Paris: Le bord de l'eau.

Garrigou, A. & Brousse, R. (2011) *Manuel anti-sondages. La démocratie n'est pas à vendre!*, Paris: L'observatoire des sondages, La ville brûle.

Gastil, J. & Levine, P. (2005) *The Deliberative Democracy Handbook*, San Francisco, CA: Jossey-Bass.

Gissinger-Bosse, C. (2012) *Vers une conversion démocratique: Analyse du dispositif de parole de la Cour d'Assises*, Doctoral dissertation in information and communications science, Université de Strasbourg.

Goldstein, M. (1997) *The Snow Lion and the Dragon: China, Tibet, and the Dalai Lama*, Berkeley, CA: University of California Press.

Graeber, D. (2014) *La démocratie aux marges*, Paris: Le bord de l'eau.

Hansen, M. (1991) *The Athenian Democracy in the Age of Demosthenes*, Oxford: Blackwell.

Kraybill, D. (2001) *The Riddle of Amish Culture*, Baltimore, MD: Johns Hopkins University Press.

Lehingue, P., Caveng, R. & Garrigou, A. (2011) *Sondages. Souriez, vous êtes manipulés*, Paris: Bruno Leprince.

Manin, B. (1997) *The Principles of Representative Government*, Cambridge: Cambridge University Press.

Meynaud, H.-Y. & Duclos, D. (2007) *Les sondages d'opinion*, 4th ed., Paris: La Découverte.

Offerlé, M. (2001) Les figures du vote. Pour une iconographie du suffrage universel, *Sociétés et Représentations*, 2001-2, 12, September 2001, pp. 108–130.

Offerlé, M. (2002) *Un homme, une voix? Histoire du suffrage universel*, 2nd ed., Paris: Gallimard.

Sintomer, Y. (2020) *Between Radical and Deliberative Democracy: Random Selection in Politics from Athens to Contemporary Experiments*, Cambridge: Cambridge University Press (forthcoming).

Sintomer, Y., Herzberg, C. & Röcke, A. (2016) *Participatory Budgeting in Europe: Democracy and Public Governance*, London: Routledge.

Tillé, Y. (2001) *Théorie des sondages*, Paris: Dunod.

Van Reybrouck, D. (2016) *Against Elections: The Case for Democracy*, London: Bodley Head.

Vergne, A. (2010) A brief survey of the literature on sortition: Is the age of sortition upon us?, in Delannoi, G. & Dowlen, O. (eds.) *Sortition: Theory and Practice*, Exeter: Imprint Academic.

Vergne, A. (2011) *Kleros et Demos : la théorie du tirage au sort en politique au banc d'essai de la pratique de la Planungszelle et du jury citoyen*, Doctoral dissertation in political science, IEP de Paris and Freie Universität Berlin.

Wang-Toutain, F. (2007) *Le Dalaï-Lama*, Paris: Médicis-Entrelacs.

Jean-Michel Fourniau

The Selection of Deliberative Minipublics
Sortition, Motivation, and Availability

The international literature on participation differentiates the mechanisms of democratic deliberation by the ways in which the public is selected: whether there is no specific procedure, as in the case of public debate prior to major projects in France (Fourniau, 2014), or whether there is, as in the case of citizens' assemblies (Warren and Pearse, 2008), deliberative polls (Fishkin, 2009), juries (Coote and Lenaghan, 1997; Dienel, 1997; Crosby, 2003), or consensus conferences (Joss and Durant, 1995), all of which depend on sortition. In the latter case, the specific sortition procedure through which randomly selected subjects effectively join a 'minipublic' is rarely described, the simple mention of sortition seems itself to suffice. Yet, in volunteer situations (i.e. as opposed to jury service, participation in minipublics is not obligatory), the recruitment process is always the result of a combination of chance and the motivation and availability of participants. Minipublics thus blend different logics, making them difficult to qualify in terms of the categories of representation theories and the properties expected from sortition. This chapter aims to shed light on this combination of chance, motivation, and availability of participants, based on the detailed observation of a consensus conference in France, from the recruitment of participants to the group's deliberation. The first section reviews the concept of sortition and its current use in forming inclusive and deliberative minipublics. The second section describes how the combination of chance, motivation, and availability operates during the observed recruitment process and the ways it prevents us from considering the final composition of the minipublic as the result of a simple sortition of participants. The third section argues that the selection process of volunteers can never be considered impartial, and examines various selection biases that can influence deliberation. The chapter concludes with the hypothesis that the combination of chance, motivation, and availability favours the selection of individuals with more deliberative dispositions than those that don't participate.

Minipublic Sortion Properties

Originally a method of political appointment characteristic of Athenian democracy, sortition is today the technique generally used to recruit citizens so as to maximize the inclusive nature of the minipublic; that is, to ensure that participants are ordinary citizens. In other words, 'the selection of a specific group of people for a clearly defined task [...] the process is impartial because the competence of all the participants has been recognized (or equalized), the playing field is level, and the result, being unpredictable, eludes any undue influence or pressure' (Delannoi, 2013). This definition highlights three properties that have been associated with sortition since Antiquity: equality, impartiality, and unpredictability. Sortition today is expected to ensure the inclusiveness of deliberative minipublics and, moreover, offer better representativeness than other selection mechanisms. The work of Yves Sintomer (2020) describes changes in the concept of sortition in politics since Antiquity, particularly since the end of 19th century with the spread of representative sampling. His work can be summarized with the following table:

	Antiquity	Since the end of the 19th century	Since the end of the 20th century
Type of representation provided by the sortition	'everyone'	'anyone'	'anybody *and* everybody'
Type of associated legitimacy	**Similarity** (Individuals occupying public offices **in turn**)	**Statistical Representativeness** (*mini-populus*)	**Inclusiveness** (equality of no matter who with no matter who)
Today, mechanisms mobilizing this type of representation	**Grand juries** (judgment on particular situations among like people)	**Opinion polls** (public opinion as an aggregation of individual opinions)	**Minipublics** (the construction of a collective recommendation through deliberation)

Table 1: Changes in Conceptions of Sortition in Politics.

This table does not include uses of sortition in politics observed in the Italian Republics of Venice and Florence from the 13th to 15th centuries. Yves Sintomer instead ties the latter to conflict resolution, whereby properties of impartiality enabled victories in battles between the reigning oligarchies of the Middle Ages, as well as in the towns of the Crown of Aragon during the Spanish Golden Age (mid-14th to early 16th centuries). During the age of communes in Italy, sortition functionally realized the idea of self-government of the people in that it was associated with the rapid rotation of offices (even if this applied only to the — relatively large in Florence — fraction of politically active citizens). However, contrary to its current use, sortition was not associated with any deliberative dynamic. With the Renaissance, sortition in politics disappeared, and was then systematically rejected during the revolutionary era due to the larger scale of modern societies, making it impossible to bring together all citizens within a same collective deliberation. On the contrary, this era saw the origination of representative government founded on the election of representatives, as opposed to direct democracy (Manin, 1996).

Inclusive and deliberative minipublics

Sortition in politics did not reappear until the end of the 20th century, again because it functionally fulfilled the normative ideal of self-government of the people. However, the democratic ideal of freedom of the people as self-legislation had itself profoundly changed; now deliberation of all was seen as the foundation of democratic legitimacy: 'the legitimate decision is not the *will* of everyone, but that which results from the *deliberation of everyone*' (Manin, 1985, p. 82). While the inclusion of everyone in political deliberation can be considered in different ways — based on substantive criteria of social justice or on solely procedural criteria relative to the quality of the discussion — it nevertheless forms the basis of the legitimacy of decisions. Sortition thus seems to be the functional instrument for inclusion, as it is meant to eliminate the self-selection of only those already involved in political life and, on the contrary, ensure that participants will not have particular political expertise. As such, today the functional role of sortition is to allow, as expressed by Jacques Rancière (2003, p. 82), 'the unconditional equality of anybody and everybody' as the basis of the exercise of political rights.

Sortition itself has, however, profoundly changed with the development of calculating probabilities and social statistics. Since the end of the 19th century, sortition has been closely linked to the notion of representative samples, and its routine use in the sciences, statistical surveys, and polls has generalized its perception as a microcosm of the city. 'Citizen participation is no longer thought of as enabling government by all. The idea, rather, is to construct representation of the people in miniature, a "micropopulus", to use the term coined by Robert Dahl (1989, p. 340). This "minipublic", as it is more frequently called today, is composed of selected individuals that think, discuss, and give their views as the people itself would do if it were suitably informed and had the right conditions in which to deliberate' (Sintomer, 2011, p. 149).

Contrary, however, to that which opinion polls achieve, or the aggregation of given preferences, the sortition of minipublics seeks to make them mechanisms of 'democratic deliberation'. This normative ideal contrasts with polls, where most respondents do not have an opinion or defined political preference relative to the majority of the questions or problems, until they are actually asked to have one (e.g. spontaneous reactions to questions for which the implicit expectation is that one should 'normally' have an opinion). And yet opinions and preferences are always formed in communication and dialogue with others as opposed to in exclusively internal or monological processes. Preferences are thus never strictly 'individual', rather their free formation requires open and egalitarian communication so as to rationally be able to consider, know, and weigh that which others hold to be true and desirable, the beliefs and preferences they choose to form and adopt, and why (Manin, 1985; Offe, 2015). Hélène Landemore (2013) similarly emphasizes inclusive deliberation, as opposed to the aggregative logic of the law of large numbers, underlining the links between inclusiveness and cognitive diversity, and advancing the idea that collective intelligence is one of the factors that makes democracy desirable. Because they are inclusive, deliberative democratic assemblies maximize the diversity of ways of thinking about and approaching a problem, considered by theorists of deliberative democracy as an essential component of a group's ability to solve shared problems.

The attainment of this ideal of democratic deliberation thus rests on strong procedural requirements—open-mindedness and diversity (Barabas, 2004)—so as to allow for a discursive dialogue, distinguishable from ordinary discussion (Urfalino, 2005) and other opinion-changing processes by its egalitarian, inclusive, and contradictory nature, as well as by its inclusion in an effective decision or resolution process of shared problems (Girard, 2013). These requirements are potentially contrary to one another: a broad inclusion of citizens versus maintaining the quality of debate; an old adage would see the latter as inversely proportional to the size of the group.[1] Their implementation

---

[1] Deliberative polls or citizens' assemblies overcome this obstacle by bringing together hundreds or even thousands of citizens in the same place of deliberation, but randomly distributing them to discussion tables of about 10 people each, with

gives rise to different types of minipublics, depending on whether the emphasis is placed on representativeness (which means sufficiently large groups), or on cognitive diversity within small groups, thanks to a mixture of 'stakeholders' and 'lay people' (Rip *et al.*, 1995; Klüver *et al.*, 2000), or rather due to an emphasis placed on learning, collective work, and the contradictory nature of deliberation among ordinary citizens (Hermitte, 2014).

Consensus conferences: A collective intelligence mechanism

Consensus conferences are a reflection of the latter type of minipublic in that they aim to resolve disputes on complex and contentious issues by going beyond expert controversy and giving voice to ordinary citizens in the form of a group of 15 to 25 individuals, selected through sortition and devoid of any specific interest in the issue under discussion. After a period of training on the subject matter, participants question experts in a series of round tables, deliberate amongst themselves, and then deliver a recommendation. In order to further situate consensus conferences within the range of democratic deliberation mechanisms and differing understandings of inclusion, we might ask the following question: what does it mean to represent by inclusion within a minipublic?

Is it a matter of representing the preferences of citizens potentially affected by the decision? If so, only the statistical representativeness of the minipublic would seem to guarantee that all voices are equally heard in the discussion.[2] The minipublic must be selected randomly such that the evolution of participant preferences in the deliberation is reflective of the process of forming a collective will that expresses that of the whole population under the same information and discussion conditions. This approach lies at the heart of the deliberative polling proposed by James Fishkin (2009), whose function is precisely that of showing that the opinions of informed citizens who participated in a discussion are different from the raw opinions gathered from classic polls.[3]

---

participants changing tables multiple times over the course of the day. The exercise also includes some plenary moments.

[2]   Minorities, however, may not be sufficiently represented in selection by sortition. See, for example, native under-representation in the citizens' assembly on the electoral system in British Columbia (Warren and Pearse, 2008), or that of cyclists on the citizens' jury on urban traffic in Turin (Bobbio and Ravazzi, 2006).

[3]   Individual opinion trends observed in deliberative polls also contradict laboratory experiments in social psychology showing mechanisms of polarization and

Or is it rather a question of representing the arguments or speeches by which citizens express how they are or could be affected by the decision? The good diversity of a minipublic, guaranteeing a real deliberative dynamic among its members, will then suffice for examining the issues at a given moment within a population potentially affected by the decision to be made. A good diversity will also allow for exploring their formation, their circulation, and their resistance to critique, all of which form part of long-term processes (Chateauraynaud, 2011). Indeed, the arguments and speeches to be examined form an inevitably limited (Dryzek and Niemeyer, 2008; Rennes, 2011) and relatively stable repertoire over time (Hirschman, 1991; Angenot, 2008). Deliberation on the part of a sufficiently diverse group allows for their equal consideration.[4]

On complex issues, where uncertainties relative to the causes persist, where scientific controversy over the consequences of the decisions to be made remain, and where ethics and moral values are strongly engaged, the consensus conference specifically allows for just such exploration of arguments and speeches. The group must accordingly update and recombine the latter, depending on the issue under examination. They must also indicate what they retain from the different answers provided by the protagonists, and not resolve a question that is, by nature, controversial. Group work allows to link, on the basis of shared societal values, themes that are separated by experts. It also allows to identify through discussion a balanced synthesis of all the information acquired and to prioritize the acceptability of the different potential consequences (Hermitte, 2013a).

The Recruitment of a Minipublic:
A Mixed Process Rather than Mere Sortition

The consensus conference on radioactive waste and the Cigéo project, the industrial centre for the deep, reversible storage of high-level and long-lived radioactive waste in the Departments of Meuse and Haute-

---

reinforcement of individuals' primary opinions (Sunstein, 2002) produced through collective discussion. Bernard Manin (2002) provides a good summary of this issue.

4   Dryzek and Niemeyer (2008) suggest that this is because the number of speeches that it is necessary to examine on any issue subject to decision is much lower than the number of people that would need to be elected so as to guarantee the representation of all citizens affected by the decision. The deliberation must thus first guarantee a good representation of the speeches. To this end, they envisage the formation of a 'House of speeches'. Its establishment would involve a targeted selection of speeches to be represented, and a non-random choice of participants able to represent their diversity.

Marne, carried out by the French National Radioactive Waste Management Agency, took place between December 2013 and February 2014 and was organized by the National Commission for Public Debate (CNDP, 2014). Public debate on this project, initiated by the CNDP beginning in May of 2013, was considerably disrupted by vocal local associations expressing concern that the two rural departments had been on the road to becoming a 'nuclear waste bin' since the creation, in 2000, of an underground laboratory tasked with preparing the industrial project. Strong opposition manifested during assemblies, the first of which had to be rapidly discontinued, led the CNDP to propose, in early July 2013, alternative forms of debate to the public meetings. To this end, a steering committee was formed in September of 2013. Close observation[5] of this minipublic allows for a description of the recruitment methods of the 17 citizens who participated (Fourniau and Bobbio, 2014). From this particular case, it is possible make more general observations on the combination of chance, motivation, and availability of the participants that characterizes the selection of all minipublics and to question the relationship between such selection processes and sortition.

Recruitment procedures for the consensus conference on radioactive waste and the Cigéo project

Specifications for the consensus conference on radioactive waste and the Cigéo project defined by the CNDP stipulated the recruitment of 15 to 20 people 'whose main socio-demographic characteristics will be similar to those of the general population affected by the debate (i.e., sex, age distribution, cultural level, occupation; without crossing these criteria)'. The primary recruitment method used by the polling organization chosen to manage the selection of the minipublic was based on 'an opinion survey/national recruitment' of a random sample drawn from a base of 600,000 panellists in France, which the organization regularly interviewed via the internet (access panel)[6]. From this

---

[5] The organization of the consensus conference included an Evaluation Committee whose members included Cécile Blatrix (AgroParisTech), Luigi Bobbio (University of Turin), and Jean-Michel Fourniau (Ifsttar), who were able to closely observe the entire process, including the recruitment of the group of participants. This chapter is based on the evaluation report submitted to the CNDP on the 13th of June 2014, on the part of Luigi Bobbio and Jean-Michel Fourniau (2014).

[6] Qualified panel (respecting the representative quotas of the general population) of voluntary internet users created by the organization in order to respond quickly to requests for political polls or from commercial advertisers through a questioning of a sample drawn from the panel.

opinion survey of a sample of 400 internet users, the recruitment was then carried out under a tight deadline, in the three weeks preceding the first meeting of the minipublic. Participation in the conference on the part of several of the 17 citizens was confirmed only just before the training weekend, as a number of withdrawals had been submitted a few days beforehand. The recruitment proved particularly difficult for the polling organization and necessitated supplementary recruitments in the ten days leading up to the first weekend.

Table 2 shows the different phases of recruitment. This process is quite common in the selection of minipublics, whether for groups of a few hundred people for deliberative polls (Hansen and Andersen, 2004), or for groups of about 20 for juries or consensus conferences.

In the case of Cigéo, the sample met the established quotas in terms of sex, age, socio-professional categories (CSP), type of agglomeration, and place of residence: 400 people, half of whom were living in the two departments home to the underground laboratory and where the Cigéo underground storage industrial centre was to be established, and the other half in six large French agglomerations. In the first phase of recruitment, the polling organization sent an email to the sample, asking them to respond to a self-administered online interview on 'Nuclear energy and the issue of nuclear waste in France' and on the usefulness of public debate on the Cigéo project. The online form explained that in addition to public debate on Cigéo, '...a consensus conference is being prepared. The conference is intended to enable 20 non-specialist citizens to formulate and provide a collective recommendation to the government, the parliament, and the Cigéo leadership on the issue of radioactive waste.'

Respondents were asked if they would agree '*a priori*' to participate, and in the affirmative, if the polling organization could contact them by telephone. 71 of the 400 online respondents agreed at this step, and provided their phone numbers. Then began what is often described as the recruitment stage of the minipublic (Baker *et al.*, 2010). The telephone contact questionnaire specified the dates of the consensus conference and the participation rules (notably the absence of remuneration). The interview allowed the polling organization to check motivation and availability for the planned dates of those who had in principle agreed to participate, as well as to identify any conflicts of interest, particularly among those who reported having 'participated in the debate', checking the extent of their engagement in nuclear energy issues. Following the end of this wave of personalized calls, by the 2nd of December only 16 firm agreements to participate in the three

		1st stage of recruitment		2nd stage		3rd stage
Phase	Preliminary Phase t_0	1st phase t_1	2nd phase t_2	3rd phase t_3	4th phase t_4	5th phase t_5
Action	Creation of a sampling frame (access panel or other)	**Random or non-random sampling and specific survey of this sample.**	Request for expressions of interest in participating and contact information so as to confirm their motivation to participate and their availability	Direct contact with those who gave their contact information and additional recruitment if needed, with differing procedures **Enrolment process of the minipublic**	Further participants to ensure their participation in the minipublic	Direct contact with participants to ensure their participation in the minipublic
Panel Size	Several hundred thousand people (or even millions in the USA)	Several hundred or thousands of people	**Participation Rate** Ratio between the number of actual participants and the sample size originally queried: t_s/t_i, generally varying from 1 to 15%			150 to 450 people for a deliberative poll; 15 to 25 for a jury or consensus conference
Cigéo Case	600,000 individuals	400 individuals	71 individuals	10 individuals (participation rate = 2.5%)	7 individuals among the 459 poll; 15 to 25 contacts in the additional recruitment	17 individuals (participation rate = 1.9%)
Quality	**Statistical Representativeness** relative to general population			**Diversity** in terms of the initial sampling criteria and **Motivation** and **Availability**		
Duration	3 to 8 weeks before the minipublic					

Table 2. The process of recruiting a minipublic (process commonly referred to as the recruitment stage)

weekend sessions had been obtained, coupled with an imbalance between the 'local' and national recruitment, as well as a strong distortion in the age distribution. Additional recruitment became necessary in order to redress these imbalances and counter any eventual withdrawals. In fact, there were five cancellations in the week leading up to the first weekend of the consensus conference. The first stage of recruitment (phases 1 to 3 in Table 2), combining random selection and personalized enrolment, is comparable to that observed for all minipublics. It ultimately provided just 10 participants for the Cigéo consensus conference.

The second stage (phase t_4), more specific to smaller-sized minipublics, saw additional recruitment so as to achieve the established objectives in terms of the size and socio-demographic composition of the group. The first approach aimed to reinforce the local participant component through telephone contacts with a random sample of about 100 people taken from the phone directories of the two departments and several geographically relevant cities. This method resulted in just one additional recruit. Another approach aimed to balance the age distribution through almost 350 telephone numbers obtained from a roster of qualified candidates (i.e. in terms of sex, age, socio-professional category, agglomeration type, place of residence) likely to participate in surveys. This method resulted in five additional recruits. Lastly, direct contact with a group of young people with whom the facilitators of the consensus conference had already worked resulted in one last recruit. Overall, these additional recruitment methods resulted in a total of seven more participants for the minipublic. The final group of 17 individuals was officially completed the day before the opening of the consensus conference (phase t_5).

Difficulties in recruitment are reflected in the ratio between the number of citizens who effectively participate in a minipublic and the total number of people contacted (the 'participation rate'). While this ratio can surpass 10% and even go as high as 15% in less challenging situations, in the case of Cigéo it was less than 2%.[1] According to the polling organization, this can be explained by both the high level of commitment asked of the participants — three entire weekends, from

---

[1] Rates generally reported in the literature (although this rarely done). For example, the EuroPolis project in 2009 had a group of 348 participants from a starting sample of 3,000 people invited to participate, or a participation rate of 11.6% (Isernia *et al.*, 2013, p. 83). In the case of a citizens' jury on federalism in 2010 in Italy, the participation rate for a commitment of two unpaid weekends was 1.7% (Bobbio, 2013, p. 38).

Friday afternoon to late Sunday evening—and, especially, contrary to common practice the absence of any remuneration.

The socio-demographic characteristics of the conference's 17 participants: Significant differences from the structure originally envisioned

Recruitment difficulties can also lead to distortions in the composition of the group participating in the minipublic, compared to that originally planned. In the case of the conference on radioactive waste and the Cigéo project, the final group consisted of 6 men and 11 women. This demographic imbalance was even more pronounced when crossed with geographic origin, as 5 of the 6 men, as opposed to 3 of the 11 women, lived in Haute-Marne and Meuse, in local council communities (*communautés de communes*), or conurbation communities (*communautés d'agglomération*) of less than 100,000 inhabitants. Conversely, 7 of the 11 women lived in large urban centres. There was also a notable absence of rural inhabitants among the group of citizens, and only one labourer, also 'local'. The age structure was more balanced (average age within the group was 51.2 years of age—52.2 for men, 50.7 for women—compared to 49.5 years of age for the adult population in France). Although the data collected by the polling organization did not include information on educational attainment, interviews helped fill this gap. Almost all of the participants (15 out of 17) had a bachelor's degree or higher, much higher compared to that of the general population (about 40%; half of the group had a 'bac + 2' or higher, compared to 13% of the French population). Such bias is, however, commonly observed in minipublics and was accepted by the consensus conference's Steering Committee. The use of different complementary recruitment methods both increased some of these differences (e.g. sex distribution) and aimed to correct others (e.g. age distribution). Yet both national and European surveys show significant variations in opinions on nuclear power according to these socio-demographic variables (NEA, 2010). The minipublic recruitment process can thus distort opinions within the group, which an evaluation should assess.

Distortions in the socio-demographic structure during the minipublic selection process

In the case under observation, we can identify how discrepancies arose —made all the more inevitable due to the group's small size—between the desired composition and that obtained by the end of the recruitment process. Table 3 summarizes the differences between the initial sample (in t_1) and the final group (in t_5).

First, it should be stressed that distortions in the characteristics of the group were due to the use of complementary recruitment strategies and then to last-minute participant withdrawals. Supplemental recruitment phases were carried out quickly due to the need to obtain a final group of the desired size, where compliance with socio-demographic criteria posed less of a dilemma, and some of the gaps had been accepted by the steering committee.

	t_1: 400 interviews from *access panel*	t_5: 17 conference participants (6 M, 11 F)
Age		
From 18 to 34 years of age	20%	3 (17.6%)
From 35 to 44 years of age	20%	2 (11.8%)
From 45 to 59 years of age	30%	6 (35.3%)
60 and older	30%	6 (35.3%)
CSP (Active = 12; Unemployed = 1; Retired = 4)		
Farmers	5%	—
Artisans, merchants, entrepreneurs, liberal professions, senior executives	15%	3 (1 M, 2 F) (17.6%)
Intermediate occupations, employees	30%	8 (2 M, 6 F) (47.1%)
Workers	15%	1 (H) (5.9%)
Retired, non-working	25%	4 (1 H, 3 F) (23.5%)
Students, civil servants, stay at home mothers	10%	1 (H) (5.9%)
Agglomeration size		
Rural (less than 2,000 inhabitants): Haute-Marne and Meuse only	20%	—
From 2,000 to 19,999 inhabitants: Haute-Marne and Meuse only	16%	5 (3H, 2 F) (29.4%)
From 20,000 to 99,999 inhabitants	16%	4 (2H, 2F) (23.5%)
100,000 or more inhabitants	48%	8 (1 H, 7 F) (47.1%)

Table 3. Socio-demographic characteristics of the 17 consensus conference participants. Source: Fourniau and Bobbio (2014, p. 111)

Second, in the first phase of recruitment (t_1), the original rate of agreement for the inhabitants of Haute-Marne (10%), and to a lesser extent that for Meuse (18%), was lower than that for the individuals in the rest of the sample: 14% for these two departments compared to 22% for the rest, but with considerable variation relative to agglomeration (between 28 and 18%). However, a survey conducted in mid-June 2013 by the CNDP indicated that 88% of the inhabitants of these two departments were aware of the Cigéo project (three-quarters of those interviewed reported that they 'very well aware of it') and 61% had heard about the public debate, and thus undoubtedly also about the difficulties regarding the latter. Thus, knowledge of a decidedly contentious situation could have generated a high refusal rate among of the inhabitants of Haute-Marne and Meuse. These individuals may have viewed accepting to participate in the consensus conference as involving themselves in a conflict of which they had a certain familiarity.

Finally, the importance of 'biographical availability' (McAdam, 1986) in accepting to participate should be underlined. Reflecting this is the evolution of the age and occupation structure in the various phases of the first stage of recruitment. For example, three-quarters of those who had in principle agreed to participate in the consensus conference (phase t_1 in Table 2) were over the age of 45. The 10 individuals who resulted from this phase (t_3) were the oldest, with an average age of almost 59, and only half were employed compared to 12 of the 17 total participants. The presence in this subgroup of 10 individuals of 5 retirees or job-seekers suggests that having free time is a major determinant in responding affirmatively to a request for civic participation, beyond the stronger interest in politics often reported in the literature (Hansen and Andersen, 2004; Sanders, 2012). A lack of remuneration for participation accentuates this bias: the citizens more willing to participate are those with free time, ready to dedicate the latter to a civic activity concerning a matter of common concern.

A highly manufactured selection process

Like most opinion polls, minipublics are initially built using random selection (usually non-probability based, quotas being one of the most commonly used methods) from a sample in one of the large voluntary online panels maintained by polling agencies. These 'access panels' are themselves generally set up on a non-probabilistic basis.[2] In the French

---

[2] Deliberative polling selection, as practised by Fishkin and his team, differs in that the latter generally excludes stratification according to quotas (as this entails distortions), in favour of a purely random (probability-based) draw in a sample specifically constructed from telephone directories by the research team for each minipublic. In contrast, in the case of Europolis, the random draw was stratified according to quotas (Isernia and Fishkin, 2014). Fishkin and his team avoid any replacement and thus accept significant distortions in the socio-demographic structure of the final group in terms of variation in refusal rates. From the same initial sample size, the size of the group can also different significantly from one deliberative polling to another.

context, the sponsor of the minipublic typically draws up a set of specifications covering support for the organization, facilitation, and recruitment of the group of participants. The selected design office[3] then acts as the contractor, providing recruitment methods and association with a specialized institute able to carry out the recruitment and manage the minipublic enrolment contacts. Polling organizations regularly use online panels already at their disposal for opinion studies, so as to achieve higher participation rates than with other randomly selected bases. The use of online polls has, however, been strongly criticized because a panel of volunteers built through a non-random procedure does not necessarily fulfil the fundamental criteria of representativeness. This bias is amplified in the random selection from one of these panels — whether probabilistic or not — of a sample invited to respond to a survey or participate in a focus group or minipublic. Those who agree to respond or participate differ significantly from those who refuse (Baker *et al.*, 2010).

Distortions in the socio-demographic structure of the respondents during the selection process and notable differences from that originally envisaged are found to varying degrees in all minipublic selection processes. Indeed, rates of participation in the recruitment of volunteers are always much lower than those for the random selection of jury members.[4] Discrepancies between the final group and that of the structure initially foreseen are primarily the result of participant motivation and their availability, conditions that are not equally distributed throughout the population. Furthermore, enrolment contacts may reveal eventual conflicts of interest, leading those with overly strong views to withdraw (a case described by Isernia and Fishkin, 2014, p. 322) or to be excluded by the organizers (a case in the Cigéo consensus conference) so as to avoid polarization within debates and facilitate deliberation. It is thus necessary to compensate for the different ways that distortions occur during the selection process, so as to best ensure the desired socio-demographic diversity and structure of the minipublic.

In the recruitment of large groups, the participation rate determines the size of the initial sample necessary for obtaining a group of the desired size. As the participation rate is not controllable *a priori*, the size

---

3   This can itself be a polling institute, as Ifop does, which has organized a number of important consensus conferences in France.

4   Only 15% of citizens randomly selected in France for jury duty succeeded in exempting themselves from short trials, and only slightly more for longer trials. Source: Ministry of Justice website.

of the final group can differ substantially from that expected. Depending on the level of acceptance in phases t_2 and t_3, the samples may need to be recalibrated (e.g. by not contacting certain individuals in the following phase), so as to meet the socio-demographic representative criteria. In the recruitment of small groups, a very low participation rate can lead to conducting additional recruitment and replacing last-minute withdrawals using methods that differ from sortition, so as to increase the group's diversity. Either way, this means that the property of equality linked to random selection is not respected, due to distortions arising from the differential motivation and availability of individuals in the initial sample.

The process of recruiting a minipublic of volunteers cannot therefore generally be considered as resulting from a simple random selection. In the case of groups of several hundred people, with probability-based random selection in deliberative polls or where fixed socio-demographic quotas are respected, the final group preserves the desired criteria of inclusiveness and representativeness (Isernia *et al.*, 2013, p. 88). In small groups, such as juries or consensus conferences, it is diversity, both in socio-demographic and opinion terms, and not representativeness that is indicative of the sought-after inclusiveness. In any case, the group that ultimately participates in the minipublic is the product of a combination of the initial random selection (whether purely random or according to controlled variables), the motivation of contacted individuals, their availability on the dates set for the minipublic, and, where appropriate, their exclusion by the organizers. Despite being a highly manufactured process, the selection remains largely unpredictable, and the part played by each of the aforementioned components in the final composition of the group is not controllable *a priori*.

Finally, in equating the recruitment process with a random selection, factors such as motivation and availability are typically considered as not influencing the opinions represented in the final group, as long as its representativeness or socio-demographic diversity is ensured. One might, however, question the properties of impartiality of the recruitment process.

Selection Bias in Minipublics in Favour of Participants with an Appetence for Collective Discussion

The organization of minipublics and their subsequent evaluation seeks to verify that the selection process did not introduce any specific bias into the group's opinions, other than specification biases common to all randomly selected samples (e.g. over-representation among respondents of individuals who are socially better integrated, more educated, and with stronger political skills than the general population −Luskin *et al.*, 2002). Generally, questionnaires are distributed at the beginning of the group's work and then, following its deliberation, not only for monitoring purposes but also to analyse the evolution of individual opinions and document the collective intelligence produced by deliberation. For small groups, in the absence of sufficient statistical power, it is necessary to analyse the influence that distortions in the composition of the final group could have had on the recommendation produced by the minipublic. The evaluation report for the Cigéo case concluded that, overall, the recruitment process had functioned properly, enabling a sufficiently diverse group to be formed in terms of socio-demographic characteristics and opinions, and composed of people without strong views regarding the issues under discussion, who were thus open to shifting their opinions through collective discussion (Fourniau and Bobbio, 2014, p. 116).

Beyond this specific case, how might we better understand the effect of the combination of chance, motivation, and biographical availability produced by the recruitment of a minipublic on the opinions of the participants and on their willingness to deliberate? Three types of approaches can help shed light on the inclinations of individuals giving their agreement in principle, confirming the latter, then actually participating in the minipublic. More specifically, in what follows I address: appeals to motivations to participate typically employed in recruitment strategies, types of pre-deliberative positions, and the characteristics of the subject matter, all of which can influence the deliberation dynamic.

Motivations to participate

The recruitment process selects volunteers by appealing to a variety of motivations to participate. Analyses of large panels for opinion studies indicate that these motivations combine to various degrees depending on the recruitment conditions (e.g. type of random selection, recruitment scheme, etc.) and the proposed exercise. Motivations may include incentives to participate, curiosity, the entertainment value of taking surveys, the importance attached to expressing one's opinions and wanting to have them heard, the social value attributed to a collective exercise allowing for comparison with others, ease of joining and participating, etc. (Baker *et al.*, 2010, p. 720).

Compensation is the top reason given among the motives driving participation in an online survey. In the general practice of selecting minipublics, remuneration[5] is considered a mark of consideration that sponsors should extend to citizens, much like personalized contact during enrolment, or recognition relative to any publicity of their work. Such shows of consideration are essential for achieving better representation of youth, immigrant workers, or individuals with lower levels of education, especially in open systems that rely entirely on participant self-selection. Although this has generally proved to be true, the use of remuneration is not systematic and continues to be a subject of debate. In the Cigéo case, the Steering Committee considered the absence of remuneration as a condition of participants' sincere commitment to a demanding deliberative task. As described, however, this absence led to a much lower participation rate than might have been expected with remuneration, making it more difficult to control the socio-demographic composition of the group, and more likely to select individuals already willing to devote their free time to civic activities.

Methodological reflections on non-responses and ways of reducing the latter recommend a variety of incentive schemes (Comley, 2005; Koch *et al.*, 2012) to ensure that all the motivations to participate are solicited and to improve response rates, while taking into account cultural differences across countries in transnational polls. Practices which offer a choice among different forms of retribution—e.g. the expected sum can be received in the form of cash, a gift linked to the subject matter, or donated to a humanitarian association—are, however, also the subject of much literature reflecting on the ethics of compensating participants for research projects in biomedicine, psychology, or experimental economics.

In preferentially appealing to certain types of motivations, the recruitment process can influence the subsequent deliberation dynamic. To this regard, a study by Comley (2005) on the motivations of those who agree to participate in large online panels proposes a typology of four broad categories: *'opinionated'* (35%), or those 'who want to have their views heard and enjoy doing surveys'; *'professionals'* (30%), or those who do many surveys and 'generally will not respond unless there is an incentive'; *'incentivized'* (20%), or those who are primarily 'attracted by incentives but will sometimes respond when

---

5   Remuneration between 60 and 100 euros per day is the practice widely observed throughout the world, for juries and consensus conference, deliberative polls, or citizen assemblies (Sintomer, 2011, Chapter 4).

there isn't one'; and '*helpers*' (15%), who 'enjoy doing surveys and like being part of the online community' (Baker, 2010, p. 720). Solicitation of a sample of volunteers online to participate in a minipublic mobilizes these profiles in very unequal ways, likely attracting more 'opinionated' and 'helpers' than others due to the deliberative nature of the task.

Other factors further reinforce systematic biases resulting from the recruitment of minipublics from this population of voluntary internet users. Interest in the subject indubitably influences—more so than opinion polls—the decision to participate in a minipublic, given that the task is more demanding and requires greater time availability. Although some studies suggest that general online survey behaviour can have a greater influence on the decision to participate than attitudes towards the topic itself (Tourangeau *et al.*, 2009, cited by Baker *et al.*, 2010, p. 733). Interviews carried out in the Cigéo case highlight, on the one hand, the greater likelihood of selecting active panellists who join multiple panels and more frequently accept to respond to polls and, on the other hand, the specific biases of this population compared to those polled by the more traditional means of telephone interviews. Nevertheless, high online participation does not mean participants are exposed to political views contrary their own, rather we observe audience fragmentation (Dahlberg, 2007). Accepting to participate in a minipublic thus implies a certain appetence for collective discussion, contrary to a common fear of expressing political disagreement face to face (Eliasoph, 1998; Mutz, 2006).

Types of pre-deliberative positions

Bobbio (2010) proposes another approach, whereby the opinions that participants can adopt before entering a collective deliberation are classified, independent of their motivational profile. The classification draws on recommendations of the most suitable designs for the smooth functioning of the deliberation. More specifically, Bobbio organizes 'pre-deliberative opinions' into two dimensions, the degree of structure of the initial positions (firm conviction and definitive choice in favour of one of the alternatives under discussion *vs.* doubt, confusion, and unstable opinions) and the extent of reflection or lack thereof on the expressed positions (more or less well-informed of the consequences of the chosen option and more or less informed relative to the discussion and opposing arguments). The intersection of these two largely independent dimensions results in four broad types of positions (Table 4). For the reflective position: either a certainty of judgment when the position is well-defined, or a suspension of judgment if there are doubts that new discussions will help remove. For the unreflective position: an uncertainty of judgment when the position is ill-defined, or an expression of injustice (because the expressed opinion is not taken into account—Bobbio writes of an expression of 'prejudice'), if the position is well-defined. The nature of the participants' initial positions is not solely determined by psychological personality traits, but also by the characteristics of the context in which the deliberation takes place.

		Positions	
		Well-defined	Ill-defined
Positions	Reflective	**Certainty of judgment**	**Suspension of judgment**
	Unreflective	**Prejudice**	**Uncertainty of judgment**

Table 4. Four types of position upon entering a minipublic. Source: Bobbio (2010).

Since it is unlikely that participants who have neither reflective nor well-defined positions on a topic decide to meet to make collective decisions, minipublics are artificially constructed experiences of deliberation in situations of participant 'uncertainty of judgment'. The discussion on the part of an expert panel typically requires a suspension of judgment at the beginning of the deliberation. A parliamentary debate may instead illustrate a situation of certainty of judgment, where the initial positions expressed by elected representatives are more directly linked to their party affiliation than to their knowledge of the issue. An open public debate, like those organized by the CNDP in France, reflect instead a situation where primarily a sense of injustice is expressed (in particular, 'a declaration of a wrong against democracy'—Fourniau, 2007), but there is often an intertwinement of uncertainty of judgment.

While the aim of deliberation in situations of 'certainty of judgment' and 'suspension of judgment' is to bring the positions of participants closer together, in minipublics the objective is above all that of forming these positions, of allowing participants to make up their own minds. To my knowledge, however, there are no studies that allow us to infer differential motivations to frequently participate in polls, an inclination I believe to be overrepresented in minipublics, particularly when participants are recruited from online panels. There is similarly a lack of studies on the pre-deliberative opinions of participants in a minipublic compared to the general population.

Single-peaked preferences

A third approach is to measure how deliberation effectively transforms the initial, pre-deliberative opinions of participants and allows them to reach a collective opinion. To this end, List *et al.* (2013) endeavoured to measure the proximity of opinions before and after deliberation to a situation of 'single-peaked' preferences. That is, a situation of choice where there is a left–right ordering of alternatives such that each individual has a most preferred alternative and a decreasing preference for other alternatives as they get more distant in either direction from it. While it is known that majority voting among several alternatives may introduce Condorcet cycles, making it impossible to come to a stable decision, the appeal of single-peaked preferences is that they constitute a sufficient condition such that these cycles do not occur (Dryzek and List, 2003). Deliberation, through the learning and the reflection it develops, leads to better structured and more reflective positions, approaching 'single-peakedness': at the end of the debate all the participants agree 'not about the preference ordering of alternatives but about a dimension on which the alternatives can be arrayed' (List *et al.*, 2012, p. 80). It is this type of 'meta-agreement' (List, 2002) that generally expresses the recommendation produced by a jury or a consensus conference, specifying under what conditions and with what consequences this or that choice can be made.

List *et al.*'s (2013) empirical results highlight two characteristics of the issues under discussion differentiating the measured changes towards a single-peaked distribution of the expressed preferences: their salience in the public space and the ease of arraying the presented alternatives. The salience of the issues in the public space facilitates participants' formation of reflective positions by multiplying the possibilities of discussion in their daily environment, providing them with a better understanding of the topic and its related arguments even before the minipublic. The ease of arranging alternatives encourages well-defined positions on the issues. Thus, for the most important questions, which participants are likely to have discussed with their families or colleagues, preferences are relatively closer to single-peakedness, and knowledge gains such as the effect of more formal deliberation in the minipublic are weaker. In contrast, for questions less salient in the public space, which do not lead to the prior elaboration of reflective positions, discussion within a minipublic can produce substantial differences in opinions before and after the deliberation and movement towards single-peakedness, made all the greater when alternatives on the subject matter are simply arrayed.

These authors did not, however, consider that the characteristics of the debated issues could also influence motivations to participate in the minipublic. While the above-mentioned studies indicated that interest in the topic does not constitute a differential motivation to participate in a poll, List *et al.*'s (2013) results conversely showed that the recruitment process in deliberative polls makes it a variable that influences the evolution of preferences of participants during deliberation. We can thus conclude that interest in the subject of a minipublic influences individuals' motivations to participate beforehand as well. For example, greater knowledge of the different sides of a controversy over a salient issue might more strongly incite those who have a well-defined position on the issue to make their voices heard at the minipublic. We can accordingly make the following hypothesis: individuals who decide to participate due to better knowledge of the issue, or because they consider it important to voice their opinions, likely have pre-deliberative preferences closer to single-peakedness, explaining the smallest measured gains during the deliberation. List *et al.*'s (2013) results could thus be as much explained by the effect of the characteristics of the debated issue on the participants' self-selection process as by their influence on deliberation, the only measure found in the paper.

Conclusion: Deliberative Inclinations
for Participating in a Minipublic

The proliferation of minipublics as emblematic instruments of a more deliberative democracy relies on the method of sortition. The latter, since Antiquity, supposedly does away with self-selection, and instead guarantees equality, unpredictability, and impartiality of the selection. Moreover, from the contemporary point of view of deliberative theory, sortition ensures better inclusiveness. However, the process of recruiting a minipublic, generally described as 'random selection', is in fact the selection of individuals who are ultimately volunteers. The process combines an initial random sampling (often non-probability based) with self-selection of volunteers according to various motivations to participate and their availability. The recruitment of randomly selected individuals, in particular when the latter belong to an online panel, mobilizes them differently depending on their motivations to participate in a collective and deliberative exercise, their activity online where applicable, the topic itself, and the conditions of participation (especially remuneration). In the case examined here, as in the reviewed studies, the biases that motivation and differential biographical availability introduce in accepting to participate tend to select citizens, where 'there is no doubt that they strongly and non-negligibly differ from those who don't [participate]' (Baker *et al.*, 2010, p. 728). The minipublics recruitment process does not therefore equalize the chances of anybody and everybody to participate. Moreover, when it plays its functional role of forming a sufficiently diverse group, it does not respect (or poorly respects) the properties of equality and impartiality and, to a lesser degree, that of unpredictability associated with sortition.

That there are differences between participants and non-participants is widely agreed upon in studies of minipublics. Moving beyond this observation and the opposition between 'lay people' and experts which structures the legitimacy of minipublics, the focus here is on how the combination of random selection, motivation, and availability in the recruitment process distorts preferences of participants compared to those from the initial randomly selected sample. Particularly, which factors can move preferences towards or away from single-peakedness even before deliberation. Undoubtedly, on many topics, a simple random sampling of a population (probability or non-probability based) has a good chance of selecting an initial sample of uncertain judgment, far from single-peaked preferences. This is in accordance with the presuppositions of deliberative theories, which view most individuals as not having a well-defined political preference until they are asked to form one. Notably, profiles selected preferentially through the mixed process of random selection (often in a panel of volunteer internet users), motivation to participate in a minipublic, and bio-graphical availability to do so, influence the dynamics of subsequent deliberation, as similarly suggested by numerous studies on juries (Karpowitz and Mendelberg, 2007). In the Cigéo case, this combination resulted in an over-selection of individuals without clear preferences, willing to shift their opinions over the course of discussion. While it is not possible to generalize this specific observation, this case taken together with the studies mentioned above allow us to reasonably pro-pose the hypothesis that participants in minipublics have a greater inclination for deliberation compared to the rest of the population. More specifically, they place greater importance on expressing their opinion and participating in a collective exercise conducive to doing so, are less wary of expressing political disagreement face-to-face, and are more willing to shift their opinions given the social value they attribute to collective discussion.

The functional role of the minipublic recruitment process is thus, thanks to direct recruitment contacts, to select a sufficiently diverse group of open-minded individuals, portending their involvement in the deliberation. Yet the effects of the composition of the group on collective deliberation remain unclear (Barabas, 2004; Farrar *et al.*, 2009). They do not seem to constitute an explanatory variable for preference changes during the deliberation (Sanders, 2012). Notably, the influence of the recruitment on the subsequent deliberation depends on the extent to which this process plays its functional role; the selection of deliberative profiles appears as a necessary condition for the success of the deliberation. Failings of the deliberation are, conversely, related to the recruitment of a group composed primarily of other profiles, for example 'professional' panellists waiting passively for their remuneration (Hermitte, 2013b, p. 324).

These recruitment characteristics are often used to criticize the use of minipublics for controversial topics, where the actors are already well-defined: a minipublic privileging deliberative profiles would attempt to bypass the conflict between antagonistic stakeholders with preferences rooted in their ability to mobilize (Fung and Wright, 2005; Mutz, 2006). The characteristics of minipublics have also led some democracy theorists (Urbinati, 2014) to see in their frequent use for salient public policy issues a risk of confiscating political debate by 'reflective' intermediate layers, and to criticize a certain technocracy more favourable to the multiplication of these biased but controlled procedures of participative democracy than to the free development of critique within society.

To summarize, for small groups, juries, and consensus conferences, the recruitment process involves quite strong self-selection (due to very low participation rates) and enrolment aimed at ensuring the diversity of the minipublic. For larger groups, deliberative polls, or citizen assemblies, self-selection is equally strong, but it is the statistical representativeness of the enrolled group that guarantees inclusive deliberation. In both cases, however, the recruitment process does not automatically ensure the representation of minorities, despite that fact that the latter can be decisive for certain issues (e.g. those where ethical values strongly come into play). The quality of the recommendation produced by a minipublic thus depends in part on the cognitive diversity of the group (verified by representativeness in the case of large groups), which the recruitment process must control by preferentially selecting deliberative citizens. It also depends on the dynamics of the deliberation, which itself depends on organizational quality and the complete and contradictory nature of the information given to the participants. Yet as soon the as the cognitive diversity of the group is confirmed by a relatively inclusive composition of individuals with sufficiently deliberative profiles, the quality of the recommendation produced rests on the group's internal deliberation dynamic; on its ability to turn the discussion into a balanced synthesis of the information acquired. Studies on the mechanisms of preference changes resulting from collective deliberation confirm this conclusion, as they identify as explanatory variables of measured changes those relating to the deliberation dynamic and to an awareness of the importance of the issues, and not those relative to the composition of the minipublic (Farrar *et al.*, 2009; Sanders, 2012; Himmelroos and Christensen, 2014). This likely explains why the majority of studies on minipublics focus on the deliberative process itself as opposed to the selection process combining sortition, motivation, and availability of the participants.

References

Angenot, M. (2008) *Dialogues de sourds: Traité de rhétorique antilogique*, Paris: Mille et une nuits.

Baker, *et al.* (2010) Research synthesis: AAPOR Report on Online Panels, *Public Opinion Quarterly*, 74 (4), pp. 711–781.

Barabas, J. (2004) How deliberation affects policy opinions, *American Political Science Review*, 98 (4), pp. 687–701.

Bobbio, L. (2010) Types of deliberation, *Journal of Public Deliberation*, 6 (2).

Bobbio, L. (ed.) (2013) *La qualità della deliberazione*, Roma: Carocci.

Bobbio, L. and Ravazzi, S. (2006) Cittadini comuni e decisioni pubbliche. L'esperienza di una giuria di cittadini, *Studi organizzativi*, 2, pp. 89–112.

Chateauraynaud, F. (2011) *Argumenter dans un champ de forces. Essai de balistique sociologique*, Paris: Petra.

Comley, P. (2005) Understanding the online panelist, *Worldwide Panel Research: Developments and Progress*, Amsterdam: ESOMAR.

CNDP (Commission nationale du débat public), *Bilan du débat public. Projet de centre de stockage réversible profond de déchets radioactifs en Meuse / Haute-Marne (Cigéo)*, Paris: CNDP.

Coote, A. & Lenaghan, J. (1997) *Citizens' Juries: Theory into Practice*, London: IPPR.

Crosby, N. (2003) *Healthy Democracy: Empowering a Clear and Informed Voice of the People*, Edina: Beaver's Pond Press.

Dahl, R. (1989) *Democracy and its Critics*, New Haven, CT: Yale University Press.

Dahlberg, L. (2007) Rethinking the fragmentation of the cyberpublic: From consensus to contestation, *New Media & Society*, 9 (5), pp. 827–847.

Delannoi, G. (2013) Tirage au sort, in Casillo, I. *et al.* (eds.) *Dictionnaire critique et interdisciplinaire de la participation*, Paris: GIS Démocratie et Participation.

Delannoi, G. & Dowlen, O. (eds.) (2010) *Sortition: Theory and Practice*, Exeter: Imprint Academic.

Dienel, P. (1997) *Die Plannungzelle*, Wiesbaden: Westdeuscher.

Dryzek, J. & List, C. (2003) Social choice theory and deliberative democracy: A reconciliation, *British Journal of Political Science*, 33, pp. 1–28.

Dryzek, J. & Niemeyer, S. (2008) Discursive representation, *American Political Science Review*, 102 (4), pp. 481–493.

Eliasoph, N. (1998) *Avoiding Politics: How Americans Produce Apathy in Everyday Life*, Cambridge: Cambridge University Press.

Farrar, C., Green, D.P., Green, J.E., Nickerson, D.W. & Shewfelt, S. (2009) Does discussion group composition affect policy preferences? Results from three randomized experiments, *Political Psychology*, 30 (4), pp. 615–647.

Fishkin, J.S. (2009) *When the People Speak: Deliberative Democracy and Public Consultation*, Oxford: Oxford University Press.

Fourniau, J.-M. (2007) L'expérience démocratique des "citoyens en tant que riverains" dans les conflits d'aménagement, *Revue européenne des sciences sociales*, XLV (136), pp. 149–179.

Fourniau, J.-M. (2014) Débat public, in Casillo, I. *et al.* (eds.) *Dictionnaire critique et interdisciplinaire de la participation*, Paris: GIS Démocratie et Participation.

Fourniau, J.-M. & Bobbio, L. (2014) *Conférence de citoyens du débat public Cigéo. Rapport du Comité d'évaluation*, Paris: CNDP.

Fung, A. (2003) Recipes for public sphere: Eight institutional design choices and their consequences, *The Journal of Political Philosophy*, 11 (3), pp. 338–367.

Fung, A. & Wright, E.O. (2005) Le contre-pouvoir dans la démocratie participative et délibérative, in Bacqué, M.-H., Rey, H. & Sintomer, Y. (eds.) *Gestion de proximité et démocratie participative. Une perspective comparative*, Paris: La Découverte, pp. 49–80.

Girard, C. (2013) Démocratie délibérative, in Casillo, I. *et al.* (eds.) *Dictionnaire critique et interdisciplinaire de la participation*, Paris: GIS Démocratie et Participation.

Hansen, K.M. & Andersen, V.N. (2004) Deliberative democracy and the deliberative poll on the Euro, *Scandinavian Political Studies*, 27 (3), pp. 261–286.

Hermitte, M.-A. (2013a) Conférence de citoyens, in Casillo, I. *et al.* (eds.) *Dictionnaire critique et interdisciplinaire de la participation*, Paris: GIS Démocratie et Participation.

Hermitte, M.-A. (2013b) *Le droit saisi au vif. Sciences, technologies, formes de vie*, Paris: Petra.

Hermitte, M.-A. (2014) La Conférence de citoyens sur la gestion des déchets nucléaires dans le cadre du projet Cigéo, *Les cahiers de Global Chance*, 35, pp. 44–51.

Himmelroos, S. & Christensen, H.S. (2014) Deliberation and opinion change: Evidence from a deliberative mini-public in Finland, *Scandinavian Political Studies*, 37 (1), pp. 41–60.

Hirschman, A. (1991) *Deux siècles de rhétorique réactionnaire*, Paris: Fayard.

Isernia, P., Fishkin, J.S., Steiner, J. & Di Mauro, D. (2013) Toward a European public sphere: The EuroPolis project, in Kies, R. & Nanz, P. (eds.) *Is Europe Listening to Us? Successes and Failures of EU Citizen Consultations*, London: Routledge, pp. 79–124.

Isernia, P. & Fishkin J.S. (2014) The EuroPolis deliberative poll, *European Union Politics*, 15 (3), pp. 311–327.

Joss, S. & Durant, J. (eds.) (1995) *Public Participation in Science: The Role of Consensus Conferences in Europe*, London: Science Museum with the support of the European Commission Directorate General XII.

Karpowitz, C.F. & Mendelberg, T. (2007) Groups and deliberation, *Swiss Political Science Review*, 13 (4), pp. 645–662.

Klüver, L. *et al.* (2000) *EUROPTA. European Participatory Technology Assessment. Participatory Methods in Technology Assessment and Technology Decision-Making*, Copenhagen: Danish Board of Technology.

Koch, A., *et al.* (2012) *Field Procedures in the European Social Survey Round 6: Enhancing Response Rates*, London: ESS.

Landemore, H. (2013) *Democratic Reason: Politics, Collective Intelligence, and the Rule of the Many*, Princeton, NJ: Princeton University Press.

Lev-On, A. & Manin, B. (2006) Internet: la main invisible de la délibération, *Esprit*, 5, pp. 195–212.

List, C. (2002) Two concepts of agreement, *The Good Society*, 11 (1), pp. 72–79.

List, C., *et al.* (2013) Deliberation, single-peakedness, and the possibility of meaningful democracy: Evidence from deliberative polls, *The Journal of Politics*, 75 (1), pp. 80–95.

Luskin, R., Fishkin, J.S. & Jowell, R. (2002) Considered opinions, *British Journal of Political Science*, 32, pp. 455–487.

Luskin, R., *et al.* (2017) *Deliberative Distorsions? Homogenization, Polarization, and Domination in Small Group Deliberation*, working paper presented at Sciences Po Grenoble le 24/10/2017.

McAdam, D. (1986) Recruitment to high-risk activism: The case of freedom summer, *American Journal of Sociology*, 92, pp. 64–90.

Manin, B. (1985) Volonté générale ou délibération? Esquisse d'une théorie de la délibération politique, *Le Débat*, 33, pp. 72–93.

Manin, B. (1996) *Principes du gouvernement représentatif*, Paris: Flammarion, Champs.

Manin, B. (2002) L'idée de démocratie délibérative dans la science politique contemporaine. Introduction, généalogie et éléments critiques. Entretien avec Loïc Blondiaux, *Politix*, 15 (57), pp. 37–55.

Mutz, D. (2006) *Hearing the Other Side: Deliberative versus Participatory Democracy Hearing the Others*, Cambridge: Cambridge University Press.

Offe, C. (2015) Crisis and innovation of liberal democracy: Can deliberation be institutionalised?, in Coleman, S., Przybylska, A. & Sintomer, Y. (eds.) *Deliberation and Democracy: Innovative Processes and Institutions*, Frankfurt: Peter Lang, pp. 291–309.

Rancière, J. (2010) *Dissensus: On Politics and Aesthetics*, London: Continuum.

Rennes, J. (2011) Les formes de la contestation. Sociologie des mobilisations et théories de l'argumentation, *A contrario*, June, pp. 151–173.

Rip, A., Schot, J. & Misa, T. (1995) *Managing Technology in Society: The Approach of Constructive Technology Assessment*, London: Pinter Publishers.

Sanders, D. (2012) The effects of deliberative polling in an EU-wide experiment: Five mechanisms in search of an explanation, *British Journal of Political Science*, 42 (3), pp. 617–640.

Sintomer, Y. (2020) *Between Radical and Deliberative Democracy: Random Selection in Politics from Athens to Contemporary Experiments*, Cambridge: Cambridge University Press.

Sunstein, C.R. (2002) The law of group polarization, *Journal of Political Philosophy*, 10 (2), pp. 175–195.

Tourangeau, R., *et al.* (2009) The presentation of a web survey, non-response and measurement error among members of web panel, *Journal of Official Statistics*, 25, pp. 299–321.

Urbinati, N. (2014) *Democracy Disfigured*, New York: Harvard University Press.

Urfalino, P. (2005) La délibération n'est pas une conversation. Délibération, décision collective et négociation, *Négociations*, 2 (4), pp. 99–114.

Warren, M.E. & Pearse, H. (eds.) (2008) *Designing Deliberative Democracy: The British Columbia Citizens' Assembly*, New York: Cambridge University Press.

Oliver Dowlen

Random Recruitment as an Element in Constitutional and Institutional Design
A Dialogue between Means and Desired Outcomes

Introduction

It is worth reflecting on the fact that it was only in 1937 that the archaeologist Sterling Dow identified a number of slotted stone blocks found in the Athenian *agora* and elsewhere in the ancient *polis* as *Kleroteria* or lottery machines. What this indicates is that it is only relatively recently that the full extent and sophistication of the use of random recruitment in Ancient Athens has been really known.[1] By 1937 democracies had already been designed, discussed, set in place, championed, and defended without any real knowledge of (or interest in) what the random recruitment mechanism might or might not contribute to the democratic project. Indeed it would be true to say that throughout the various phases of twentieth-century democratic development this mechanism has been conspicuous by its absence from the design agenda.

A further difficulty is raised by the fact that there is no definitive theoretical account surviving from those in the past who supported the systematic use of random political recruitment as to exactly why it was used and what purposes it fulfilled. In the sources from the Ancient World, for instance, the written history of the mechanism is largely in

---

[1] Dow (1937); also note the contribution made by Traill (1975) in identifying the *demes* and recognizing the importance of the *deme* ratio. See also Whitehead (1986).

the hands of its detractors.[2] It is, of course, possible that those who advocated its use thought the reasons for doing so were so obvious that no further explanation was considered necessary. Whatever the reasons for this lacuna we are left in a position where a key element in the understanding of random recruitment—a precise knowledge of the desired outcome or outcomes of lottery use for selecting political officers—is absent.

This inherited context or political landscape poses considerable problems for anyone undertaking serious study of what benefits this mechanism might bring to the modern polity and what sort of institutional or constitutional arrangements might be used to achieve these. Constitutional and institutional design, like all other forms of design, consists of a series of dialogues: between means and ends, between desired outcomes and practical mechanisms, and between observation and innovation. The fact that random political recruitment is a largely discontinued practice and the fact that the ends it served in the past are, for the most part, hidden from us means that we cannot turn to direct experience as a source for our design thinking.

At the same time this lack of continuity in theory and practice raises two intriguing possibilities. First is the possibility that modern democracy might be structured and designed around a series of fundamental premises that differ considerably from those of the sortive-based regimes of the past. Second is the idea that our modern understanding of democracy and the political process might owe *something* to the lottery-based regimes of the past, but that the nature of this inheritance is far from clear.

One way of getting around these problems and probing these possibilities is to start from the beginning, that is, from the lottery process itself. From this approach we can formulate a number of key questions. The answers to these, or the process of exploration undertaken in pursuit of answers, might then begin to make up for the lack of the type of dialogue between theory and practice that would characterize a normal, more continuous, design process. These questions can be presented as follows:

---

[2] See especially Socrates' argument against lottery selection on the grounds of capability in Xenophon (1940, p. 7; [*Mem.* I. 29]) and the curious absence of any comprehensive explanation of the value of lottery selection in Aristotle. For this see Aristotle (1946) and Dowlen (2008) pp. 57–58.

1) How are we to understand the lottery process in a way that would distinguish it from other forms of decision-making that might be used for political recruitment?
2) What might be the advantages and what might be the disadvantages of using such a mechanism for political recruitment at the particular level of institutional design?
3) How are we to understand the broader democratic ends and desired outcomes that might be served by its systematic use in the future?

These three questions set out the basic ground for exploration in this chapter. The first two can be addressed largely through an analysis of the qualities of the lottery process aided by, but not reliant upon, past practice. Any attempt to answer the third question, however, requires reference to practical and historical examples and involves consideration of the changing nature of democratic endeavour. As we address these questions the key issue that confronts us concerns the nature of the desired outcomes of democratic politics. Unless we can identify and articulate these, I would argue, we can neither have a proper hold on the design process nor understand the potential of random recruitment within that process.

After a preliminary discussion about the nature of design thinking therefore, the chapter looks at the qualities of the lottery process and its role as an anti-power mechanism in politics. This is largely a response to questions one and two. The theoretical heart of the chapter follows and this consists of the presentation of a framework for addressing the question of desired outcomes at a general level. It is couched in terms of a sketch of a three-way conversation between the desired outcomes of the lottery-based regimes of the past, those of the largely election-based regimes of the modern period, and the possible desired outcomes of future democracies. This is followed by an attempt to define two major principles for democratic design using random recruitment that result from the creative combination of the qualities of the lottery process with a particular cluster of desired democratic outcomes.

Design Thinking:
The Mechanism and the Desired Outcome

Perhaps the most straightforward way of thinking about design is to make a distinction between the desired outcome for any project and the mechanism or mechanisms that might be utilized in order to achieve that outcome. This clarifies the design process: the desired outcome is articulated in advance and serves to guide the process of considering different ways or options that could be used to reach that end. It also sets up the success criteria by which the designer can begin to assess the potential value of the various options.

The first point that I need to make is that in this project (the consideration of how and in what manner random recruitment might be of value to modern politics) this relationship is reversed — at least to begin with. We have decided upon the mechanism that we wish to explore but (at this stage) we are unaware, or only partially aware, of the desired outcomes that prompted its use or might prompt its future use. This presents us with a different pattern and a different distribution of the known and unknown elements than that of traditional design project work.

In terms of design method, however, this reversal is only temporary. Once we have defined the qualities of the lottery process and isolated a number of specific problems that it was used to address, random recruitment can begin to take its place in the democratic toolbox alongside other mechanisms for choosing political office holders such as appointment and election. This bridging of the gap, this telling of the untold story, is an important and necessary task without which we cannot start to make a comprehensive and considered assessment of the value of this method of selection. It is, however, only one part of the overall picture. The other part, and the part that is, arguably, of greater long-term significance, concerns the ongoing nature of desired democratic outcomes — in short the future shape of democracy.

My second point concerning design is based on the observation that the relationship between mechanisms and desired outcomes is one that is potentially reciprocal or symbiotic. In other words it can be more than just a simple relationship between expressed aims and the possible means for achieving them. One way that this manifests itself in the political sphere is when a mechanism or institutional solution adopted for one reason, in respect to one particular desired outcome or in pursuit of one normative value, then brings another value or series of values into the frame of reference.[3] The mechanism then becomes less subservient to the ruling ideas or desired outcomes for which it was initially created or employed but begins to generate new ideas itself through its work on the ground and the new possibilities that this

---

[3] One example of this is the measure that introduced the random selection of jurors in Britain in 1730. Introduced to inhibit corruption by under-sheriffs in their choice of jury members, the fuller implications of this move were not realized until later. See especially Pettingal (1769) and Devlin (1966). See Dowlen (2008, pp. 176–177) for the 1730 act.

opens up. Perhaps the best example of this comes from the lengthy period of democratic development in Ancient Athens stretching from Solon in the mid-6th century through to the early 4th century BCE (Headlam, 1933; Hignett, 1952; Ehrenberg, 1968; Murray, 1990; Hansen, 1999). Throughout this period we can track a continuous ongoing dialogue between means and ends where the successful use of random recruitment in one area of the *polis* stimulated greater democratic innovation in other areas.

We see a similar reciprocal dialogue between means and ends in the drive for universal franchise in the emerging democracies of Europe during the 19th and 20th centuries where new forms of electoral political participation created new political ideas, new perspectives, and new values.[4] For the purposes of this study, what matters are the differences and similarities between the desirable outcomes or political goods generated by the Athenian and late medieval lot-based polities and those generated by the 19th- and 20th-century elective democracies. As we look towards the design possibilities for the old mechanism of random recruitment in the new modern political climate, the discourse and interchange between these two sets of ideas and political forms becomes increasingly pertinent.

The Qualities of the Lottery Process

In the context of this study there are two main reasons why it is important to investigate the qualities of the lottery process. The first is to provide a point of reference by which to evaluate the past use of political random recruitment. The second is that an understanding of the qualities of the lottery process is essential for any designers of future institutions who might consider using this mechanism.

By looking closely at the qualities of the lottery we can get closer to identifying the desired outcomes that prompted its use in the past. This is based on the assumption that those who used lotteries for political random recruitment consciously attempted to match the qualities of the lottery to their various desired outcomes when the original design choices were made. Here we use past practice as a source of knowledge, especially in terms of political context. Knowledge of the qualities of the lottery also provides us with a means of judging the past practice of political random recruitment. Not all past applications of random

---

4   It could be argued, for instance, that the social democratic policy of welfare-state provision in post-war Britain stemmed directly from the gradual extension of the franchise during the previous 80 years.

recruitment were successful[5] and it would be wrong to base future design choices solely on the *fact* of past practice without employing some positive means of evaluating that practice, particularly from a design point of view.

A lottery is a decision-making process of a particular type. It is a human invention that has a number of distinct functions, some social, some religious, and some recreational. It is, however, useful to distinguish the religious use of lotteries in divination and its recreational use in games of chance from its use as a means of making a decision for practical social or political purposes. It is this third use that most concerns us here.[6]

All lotteries involve the drawing up of a number of possible options and the making of a choice between them.[7] This choice is undertaken in a manner that specifically excludes the act of making a rational assessment of the value of each option in comparison to the others. In other words, it excludes those characteristics that pertain to a normal choice made by a human agent. The procedure by which this is done can involve various different means: the toss of a coin, the choice of beans from a bag, the choice of straws, and so on. This use of some external mechanism (i.e. external in comparison to the thought process of the individual decision-maker) is an important characteristic of lottery use.

We can illustrate the basic qualities of the lottery process as follows:

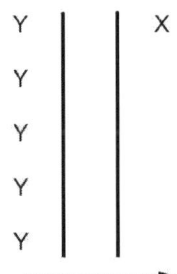

Figure 1.

---

[5] The most infamous example is the decision to de-select members of the French Directory of 1794 randomly. This led to uncertainty and instability at the very time when greater stability was needed. Sydenham (1974 p. 127); Dowlen (2008, pp. 206–211).

[6] This distinction is strongly made in Gataker (1627).

[7] A fuller version of the following can be found in Dowlen (2008, pp. 11–30).

This illustration is, in the first instance, a simple procedural diagram of a lottery. On the left are the options. These are different values but for the purpose of the lottery draw they have been converted into elements that are of equal appearance or arranged in such a way as to have an equal chance of being chosen without reference to their qualitative differences. On the right is the chosen option, the result of the lottery. What will happen to the chosen option (e.g. the terms of the office, the nature of the prize, the action that is to be taken) is usually determined in advance of the drawing or acting out of the lottery. When the act of choice is made in certain forms of lottery, such as a lottery draw, the chosen symbol is then "cashed out" and its nature as one particular option is revealed. In other forms, such as a coin toss, these values are known before the defining act of the lottery, such as the actual tossing of the coin, takes place.

In the centre of the diagram is the zone in the decision-making that I call the 'blind break'. This is where the act of choice is made. It is a break because it constitutes an interruption in the rational process of making a decision. It is 'blind' because it is unpredictable, unknowable in anything but the most general sense, and incapable of being ordered or controlled by anyone.

This is the defining feature of every lottery. If the blind break ceases to be blind and becomes subject to interference by any party, the process cannot be regarded as a proper lottery. Since the lottery is a human invention, we can presume that there is a level of intention, design, and purpose behind the development and application of a decision-making process of such a nature (i.e. one that excludes rational and purposeful differentiation between options).

The value of this representation is firstly that it shows how the lottery is a decision-making procedure that consists of a number of distinct elements.[8] The options in the pool from which the choice is to be made are decided upon rationally in advance of any particular draw. Likewise the general nature of the prize or outcome is also determined in advance. This is of specific importance for the design of lottery schemes because it defines a lottery as an arational decision-

---

[8] The status of this illustration of the lottery procedure is also important. It is empirical in the sense that it is based on the objective observation of lotteries; but it seeks to identify the common and essential properties of all the particular observations. Because it is in visual form it has a relationship with the invariably physical nature of all lottery processes that is closer to the observed phenomenon than a purely verbal description or mode of analysis.

making procedure subject (or potentially subject) to considerable rational, conscious control and focus.

The second value of this descriptive formulation is that it gives us access to the fundamental design question in any proposed, existing, or past lottery application. By isolating the blind break as the essential, defining feature of a lottery we can now ask of any application, 'What work is the blind break doing?' In short this question gives us a conscious, concrete, and practical way of linking the desired outcome of any application to the proposed mechanism for achieving that outcome. If this question cannot generate a positive answer in the case of any proposed application, if there is no clear advantage in using this type of decision-making process, then another form of decision-making should be considered. This process of questioning and evaluating also helps us to separate applications where the blind break is used to address real concerns from applications where lottery choice is used or advocated simply as a matter of presumed convenience. It also enables us to look at the design of constitutions and their respective institutions with a view to assessing where and how random recruitment might make the greatest positive contribution.

If we think of the procedural diagram as the first framework through which and by the aid of which we can explore the qualities of the lottery process, the second framework comes as a result of asking what happens in the blind break. We know that, by definition, a lottery is a mechanical decision-making process. This is an observable, objective quality of every lottery. The next analytical task, therefore, is to explore the further implications of this mechanical nature. In essence the mechanical nature of the lottery means that all attributes that relate to a person or human agency making a decision are absent from, or excluded from, a lottery decision. This can be illustrated by a kind of 'box of epithets' or an imaginary box of words that can be used to describe a lottery decision in respect to this mechanical/non-personal quality.

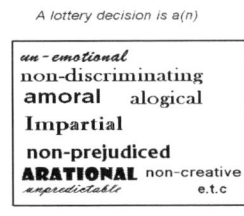

A lottery decision is a(n)

un-emotional
non-discriminating
amoral   alogical
Impartial
non-prejudiced
ARATIONAL non-creative
unpredictable   e.t.c

decision

Figure 2.

In addition to these qualities[9] we also have to add two general points. First the observation that a lottery is not just a decision that excludes the qualities of agency from its operation, it also excludes agency itself: a lottery decision is an anonymous decision. Second is the observation that a lottery is designed as a procedure that is not open to manipulation. This is a consequence of the lack of agency, but it is important to highlight how central this quality is to the structure of the lottery and its operation as a shared social procedure.

Clearly the number of epithets in the box is very large and very varied. From a design point of view and in respect to potential applications the most significant point is that, whenever a lottery is used, all these qualities will pertain to the decision that is made. We might be keen to use one or two specific qualities — perhaps impartiality or the lack of prejudice in a lottery decision — but when a lottery is used we get *all the qualities*, and we get them *all at the same time*.

Because we get both the desirable and the undesirable outcomes or qualities, the job of the constitutional or institutional designer considering the use of a lottery is to weigh up the positive attributes of the use of the mechanism against those that might be problematic in any given context. Another way around this dilemma is for the designer to counteract any unwanted effects of the lottery process by using other (rational) elements in the overall design of the institution or constitution in question. The use of challenges in the selection of jurors operates in this manner.[10]

The Lottery as an Anti-Power Mechanism

We can think of these two frameworks, the procedural diagram and the box of possible epithets, as design tools or formulations with which we can check out and explore the possible value of using lottery selection in any given context in advance. This goes a long way to answering the first question: how to make a conscious distinction between random recruitment and other possible means of choosing political officers. I

---

[9] Gil Delannoi (2011) speaks of the qualities of 'equality, impartiality and serenity' and Peter Stone (2011) isolates the 'sanitizing effect' of lottery selection. We should, however, note that in certain contexts or in badly designed schemes there is also a potential for a lottery choice to generate the more disruptive aspects of unpredictability.

[10] Note that before 1730 in Britain juries were not randomly selected but initially selected by magistrates and then subject to up to 36 challenges before being finally empanelled. See Green (1985).

now turn to the second question: what might be the advantages of using such a mechanism in a political context.

Given the range of values revealed by the box of possible epithets this could prove to be a lengthy and complex line of investigation. For the purposes of this chapter, however, I wish to concentrate on one particular aspect of the lottery, but one that promises to be particularly relevant to random recruitment for political office and one that corresponds with the historical practice of random recruitment. This is the use of the lottery as an anti-power mechanism.

Perhaps the best historical example that illustrates this in action comes from 1465–66 in Florence and involves a republican movement that emerged in opposition to the oppressive authoritarian Medici regime that had ruled the city since 1434 (Rubinstein, 1966; Kent, 1978). The Medici had maintained their rule by replacing the previous republican arrangement, which involved systematic use of lottery selection, with a range of limited franchise elections that they could control through their extensive patronage system. Although the movement was unsuccessful, its two main demands and the relationship between them are pivotal in our search for the political value of random recruitment. These demands were firstly for the freedom of political expression and secondly for the restoration of lottery selection for the holders of public offices.

Here we see random recruitment in the front line of the fight against the concentrations of arbitrary power that we associate with dictatorship or other forms of authoritarian or totalitarian rule. It shows a community in the act of demanding that the political system, the *res publica* or things of the public, should remain in public rather than in private hands. It indicates how random recruitment can be an important tool in establishing an inclusive political order based on clear, agreed procedures — particularly those governing appointment or the placing of people in positions of political authority. From this explicit example we can begin to see random recruitment as a preventative mechanism that has been traditionally called into use to counter despotism and factionalism: the twin dangers likely to arise from concentrations of unaccountable political power.

In design terms and in our analysis of the dialogue between means and ends we can also see in this example how random recruitment was clearly recognized as a primary means by which a primary desired outcome, the freedom of political expression, could be obtained and defended.

If we now combine this with our understanding of the lottery process, we can now see how, by the use of an anonymous, non-partisan, agreed mechanism, the power of appointment is taken away from all particular political actors. This then has the effect of protecting the shared political system against those who might wish to misuse that power of appointment for their own ends.

The Anonymous Mediator

To get a further idea of how lotteries can contribute to political order I now turn to another example, or series of examples.[11] This time they are taken from what I call proto-political contexts: contexts that either pre-date or operate independently of any centralized state decision-making apparatus. These particular examples come from Elinor Ostrom's work *Governing the Commons* and they deal with the distribution of commonly held resources.

These examples include: the distribution of log-piles among Swiss villagers who collect and stack wood in the forests (p. 65); allocation of fodder bundles in Japanese villages; water distribution in Spain (p. 77); and the allocation of fishing grounds to fishermen in Alanya (pp. 19–20) and Nova Scotia (p. 173). To this we can add the ubiquitous practice of distributing grazing rights for commonly-held pasture on a rotational system by lottery (Ostrom, 1990).[12]

The point about these examples is that they demonstrate the role of the lottery as a kind of anonymous mediator between potentially competitive or hostile parties. The use of the lottery and its anti-power capacity means that no member of the community who might have a stake in the outcome can make certain decisions concerning the distribution of the commonly-held resources.

The transition from what might otherwise be competitive or 'oppositional' relationships to those that follow the lines of an agreed 'mediative' solution also serves as an example in miniature of the principles of political consolidation. The key factor here is that the mediating element, whether a lottery held between members of a fishing village or a national parliament bringing potentially warring factions under the auspices of a single political system, is sufficiently impartial to engage the trust and cooperation of the parties involved. In this context the lottery examples are particularly important because they emphasize the distinction between the mediating body and the contending parties and draw attention to the need for agreed impartiality in the mediating process. Above all they give us a further

---

[11] This is explored in Dowlen (2016).
[12] See Gretton (1910) on allocation of meadow grazing at Yarnton near Oxford.

clear indication of the type of desired outcomes obtainable from lottery processes and lottery recruitment: long-term, inclusive, impartial mediative arrangements. These constitute the practical components of political order.

For our purposes perhaps the most instructive example is the Athenian democratic settlement of 507 BCE in which Kleisthenes made a deal with the *demos* in order to put an end to a period of rivalry between aristocratic factions that threatened the stability of the *polis*.[13] The origins of democracy therefore coincide with the need for political order. In the subsequent arrangements, which included the total reorganization of Athenian political society, the introduction of ostracism, and the selection of the *boule* or council of 500 by lottery, great emphasis was put on political structure and unity. Aristocrats were not excluded from the political sphere, but their power (especially over the *boule*) was severely restricted through the use of lottery selection. In this context we can read the *demos* as a force that maintained a fair and inclusive political order in a mediative (rather than an oppositional) sense.[14]

A Three-Part Conversation

These considerations immediately lead us into the idea of a three-part conversation or exploration that I believe to be central to the question of how random recruitment might be beneficial in modern conditions. This consists of a critical comparison between the desired outcomes or political goods of the lot-based polities of the past, the desired outcomes or political goods of modern democracy, and the desired outcomes that might prompt the use of random recruitment in the institutions and constitutions of the future. In this chapter I can only give an initial indication of how this conversation might play out. I would, however, suggest that a comparison of this nature is a primary requirement if we are to understand the more general or long-term implications of using random recruitment systematically in a modern context. I would also assert that it is an absolutely necessary preliminary to any design project that has the serious intention of using random recruitment to advance the cause of democracy. Without undertaking such an evaluation the relative advantages and disadvantages of the main democratic mechanisms or procedures (random recruitment, direct

---

[13] Herodotus (1998, p. 327 [*Hist.* V. 66]).

[14] See particularly Murray (1990, pp. 13–14) for an overall assessment of the value of these reforms.

democracy, and representative democracy) can only be assessed in terms of their short-term impact.

Perhaps the best way to illustrate this evaluative framework is by the following sketch:

A Democracies using a combination of Random Recruitment, Electoral and Direct Democracy.	**B** Modern Democracies with limited use of Random Recruitment and an emphasis on Electoral Representation.	**A+B** Future Democracies: Drawing from the mechanisms and desired outcomes of both.
Examples of Desired Outcomes:	**Examples of Desired Outcomes:**	**Examples of Desired Outcomes:**
Widespread citizen participation.	Government by consent via regular elections and a plurality of parties.	Citizens' rights linked to greater responsibilities and greater political participation.
Shared political order:		
Protection against tyranny and factionalism.	Accountability by elections.	Constraints on oligarchic and factional tendencies, especially within parties.
Citizen ownership of the political process.	Curbs on executive power via separation of powers and constitutional checks and balances.	Greater political accountability outside the electoral process.
Citizens involved in judicial process.	Independence of the judiciary.	A greater emphasis on the value of a shared political order.
	Citizens' rights as a defence against the state.	

Table 1.

The sketch sets out a *formal* or procedural structure for any design inquiry into possible desired outcomes, but it also contains a number of important proposals or options concerning the *substance* of the desired outcomes that might apply to future democracies.

From the formal side the sketch presents us with a process through which we can look at changing patterns of desired democratic outcomes. We can then relate these to the outward mechanisms and structures that might be used to achieve these. By attempting to identify and examine these desired outcomes in this way we can get an idea of how new designs and procedures are a response to experience and the evaluation of that experience. In this respect the key feature of this sketch is the lack of experience of random recruitment in the modern period and the sketch can be seen as an attempt to overcome this in design terms.

The presentation of these ideas in this fashion does not necessarily exclude the generation of new ideas that are *not* based on past practice or the acquired knowledge of that practice. Neither does it exclude the articulation of new desired outcomes that have not been part of earlier democratic endeavour. The implication behind this framework is, however, that new designs are the better pursued if accompanied by a knowledge of past practice. One clear reason for this is that political institutions develop slowly and new ideas invariably develop on the back of existing forms and inherited political outlooks. The sketch also opens the possibility of creating a similar parallel three-way conversation between mechanisms. This would enable us to track the reciprocal interplay between desired outcomes and mechanisms during their process of development and to assess their possible future value.

The desired outcomes listed in the columns are really only examples and would be the subject of considerable debate in the context of a real design project. Nonetheless they do serve to illustrate some of the major differences between the political priorities of the republican democratic regimes that made consistent use of random recruitment and those where the electoral form was (and is) the dominant procedure.

The major point that emerges from these examples is that the lot-based schemes of the past (particularly Ancient Athens, but also the more popular republican forms of the late medieval period) put considerable emphasis on the role of the citizenry in protecting the integrity of their respective political systems. In this way they differ from the later, predominantly electoral, systems. Within these earlier regimes there seems to have been a clearer idea of the dangers inherent in the concentration of political power in the hands of the few and the threat this posed to political order.[15] We can also see evidence, in the use of lotteries and other mechanisms, of a determined effort made to counteract those dangers. This intention is also present in the later systems, but here the role of the citizenry is limited to the act of voting and giving consent to those in power on an intermittent basis rather

---

[15] We can see this as a major concern of the late-medieval Italian city republics where factionalism was a major problem and lottery selection one of a number of means used to counter it (Waley, 1988; Dowlen, 2008, p. 72).

than achieving these ends through forms of more consistent engagement.

From the other side of the equation the sketch and the three-way conversation helps us to understand the political values of electoral politics from a wider, comparative perspective. From a democratic point of view government and governmental accountability by universal electoral consent can be characterized as a considerable democratic achievement. The same applies to the idea of using rights as a means of protecting individuals and minorities against potentially hostile centralized state power or from the dictatorship of the majority. The design of future democratic measures should, I suggest, be focused on how these gains can be retained and advanced through the use of random recruitment. This can help us to avoid a kind of binary 'either/or' perspective in which random recruitment is advocated as a replacement for electoral choice.

What I hope to have shown by these examples, therefore, is how the best of past and present systems can contribute to the formulation of the desired outcomes for future democratic design and planning. This approach goes some way towards addressing the third of my initial questions: how we might understand the broader democratic ends and desired outcomes served by its systematic use.

Formulating Design Principles
for Random Recruitment Schemes

Before I start to define the principles that I regard as necessary for the effective incorporation of random recruitment in democratic institutions and constitutions I need to give some consideration to the question of agency. In the formulation of any new constitution there are usually a number of forces, influences, and contingencies that frame the final outcome. Because many constitutions resemble a pact between rival forces seeking a political settlement, it is easy to relegate the role of the constitutional designer to that of a paid servant or technician brought in at the behest of these mighty opposites. From a democratic standpoint, however, the major consideration is that the design process should be a public process in which the desirable outcomes and the mechanisms proposed for achieving them are placed clearly on the table for all to see and all to debate.

Unfortunately it would seem that in both of these two models (the pact made behind closed doors and the open public process) the role of the individual designer or dedicated team of designers is somewhat diminished, curtailed, or made subject to prevailing power politics. My response to this, and the viewpoint taken in this chapter, is not to dismiss the pact or the public process but to envisage a role for design discourse at a high level as a general political good. Good design thinking can put well-researched options on the table at the time they might be needed. We can also think of political and constitutional design as stimulating the demand for innovation by making it clear how ideas and political goods could be achieved in practice.[16]

With these considerations in mind we can begin to look at the principles that could be valuable for the democratic designer or design team considering how random recruitment might be valuable for modern politics.

I start the discussion of design principles with three basic statements or premises about design in general. I then consider how further principles can be developed in respect to our particular topic: democratic government and the use of random recruitment.

The first basic design premise is that the desired outcomes should be fully explored and consciously articulated throughout the design process. The second is that any mechanism that might be considered as a means of achieving these outcomes should be assessed in respect to its particular qualities. The third premise is that any design project considers a broad range of desired options within the general framework of democratic development and likewise conducts a thorough exploration of the range of mechanisms likely to be used to realize the chosen outcomes.

These are essential aspects of any design process but it is important to anchor our further discussion on such basics. If, for instance, we begin to realize how a particular mechanism might bring something more than anticipated to the design process and thus change or otherwise temper the desired outcomes, then we can be fully aware of what is going on. Within the articulation of desired outcomes we also need to be aware of the distinction between and the interaction between longer- and shorter-term outcomes: between the discrete problem-solving capacity of any mechanism and the broader consequences arising from its more systematic application.

The next task is to consider how we might frame the desired outcomes if we are seeking to establish, defend, or extend democratic government. To do this we need first to separate the question: *who is to*

---

[16] Here my support for institutional design as a distinct, integrated, and intentional process differs from the view expressed by Goodin and others that we should be wary of thinking of institutional design as more purposeful than, '...lots of localized attempts at partial design cutting across one another...' (Goodin, 1996, p. 28).

govern? from the question: *how is government to be conducted?* From the answer to the first question we get the basic premise of democracy: government by the people. This can then be further defined in terms of meaningful participation and the idea of citizens as those who have certain entitlements and certain responsibilities in respect to the operations of government. This cluster of political goods constitutes our first batch of desirable outcomes.

The answers to the second question are more complex, but a similar cluster of political goods can be put forward in respect to the trajectory of our inquiry. If government is to work in the general interest (which is in itself a hidden implication of the first question) it must consist of an efficient process consisting of rational collective decision-making and the mechanisms by which decisions can be put into practice. Governmental procedures and institutions need to be stable, accessible, accountable, and fair. They need to be capable of change when necessary and there needs to be freedom of political expression. As a fundamental operational premise governmental procedures also need to be protected from misuse and from the operations of arbitrary, special interest, or self-seeking power.

If we now look at the possible combination of these two clusters of political goods, a number of dynamics begin to reveal themselves. The first is contained in the working hypothesis that active participation by the citizenry can be a major means by which good government in the general interest can be achieved, extended, and defended. Linked to this is its converse: that good, efficient government is needed to protect democracy and the interests of the many. Within this dialogue between means and ends we can also see how participation of itself might not necessarily produce good, inclusive, or fair government. Likewise efficient government in and for itself could act as a hindrance to the regular participation and thus the political development of the citizenry.

Perhaps the best way of expressing this total dialogue as a desired democratic outcome would be in terms of ownership. This is conveyed in the idea that the design of democratic institutions and constitutions should be aimed at securing the citizens' ownership of the political process and that this process, of necessity, involves active participation, inclusiveness, fairness, and efficiency. We can think of this ownership as potentially manifested in two distinct areas: first in citizen participation in the substance of political decision-making; second in citizen participation in the maintenance of the structures and procedures by which the political process is to operate.

We now turn our attention to the qualities of the process of random recruitment and its potential for delivering desirable outcomes from these (or similar) clusters of democratic goods. As we saw earlier, the overall design principle is that the choice to use any particular mechanism or procedure should be based on an understanding of the qualities of that procedure and an assessment of its suitability for the task in hand. In the case of random recruitment this takes two main forms: one involves assessing what value might be brought to the process of choice by the use of an arational decision-making mechanism. The second is a consideration of how the rational elements of lottery design can be used to support, complement, and control the random element in the lottery procedure. This, as we saw, could include decisions concerning the terms of office, the nature of the pool, rotation, training, etc. To these two approaches we can add a third, derived from the box of epithets. This is that if there was a quality of the lottery process that could be of overriding value in any given context, then that would constitute grounds for the considering the use of a lottery. By the same token, if there was a quality of the lottery process that could be distinctly harmful to the decision-making process and which could not be counteracted by any other design feature, then this would be a good reason for *not* using a lottery. The nature of decisions such as these would be determined by reference to the desired outcomes, preferably in respect to both their shorter and the longer-term implications.

If we now seek to combine our consideration of the desired democratic outcomes with the need to consider the qualities of the lottery process then we can begin to see the emergence of more guiding principles. The first, and perhaps the most important, is that random recruitment, as a fundamentally arational means of decision-making, *should only be used where it supports and enhances the existing provisions for collective rational decision-making.*[17] It should not be used when it might challenge or counteract that collective and rational process. Random selection from an elected pool, for example, if it has the effect of excluding those not selected rather than determining the order in which they might serve, would tend to undermine the rational choices made within the original election process.[18]

---

[17] See Dowlen (2017) for an example of how randomly selected citizen groups could be used in combination with representative democracy to defend the integrity of the political system.

[18] One of the best examples of this comes from William Penn's first draft for the constitution of Pennsylvania in which he suggests that one third of the elected Council

A second guiding principle is the suggestion, derived from the discussion of the mediative qualities of lottery selection, that random recruitment could be most valuably employed when the offices to which citizens are to be selected are themselves of a mediative character. In other words, where these are offices that help to maintain the fairness, inclusiveness, and integrity of the political system rather than those that contribute directly to substantive decisions within that system. In this respect the quality of impartiality inherent in random recruitment is commensurate with the role asked of those selected. This is not to say that randomly selected citizens should not be selected to bodies that make substantive decisions. In terms of the total package of desirable outcomes, however, the suggestion here is that attention should be given to the common ownership of the political system as a long-term aim. It then follows that the deployment of randomly recruited citizens in pursuit of this aim constitutes an appropriate and potent use of the mechanism.

Concluding Remarks

In this chapter I have only really made a start in what I hope will be a thorough and inclusive discourse about the design of institutions that involve random recruitment in the service of new forms of democracy. I have concentrated here on the theory of design—particularly on the relationship between desired outcomes and the mechanisms needed to achieve these outcomes. In this respect the lack of a first-hand experience of the systematic use of random recruitment is a problem—but in design terms this is not an insurmountable problem. We can bridge this gap by looking at the history of random recruitment for political office through the framework of a working knowledge of the lottery process and its potential.

From a design perspective the procedural diagram and the box of epithets can serve as useful tools to assess the qualities of the lottery process. In particular we can ask what work is done by the blind break in any proposed lottery application; differentiate between the rational and arational components in lottery design; and understand the relationship between valuable and problematic qualities of lottery

---

should be deselected by lottery each year in order to kickstart a rotational scheme. In the final draft this was changed to the election of members for different lengths of tenure (Penn, 1982, vol. 2, p. 145, VII, and p. 165; Dowlen, 2008, p. 160). The same can be said for using a lottery to decide a tied election. Dividing the period of office between the two tied candidates would be a better reflection of the electoral outcome.

choice. This helps us to address the first two questions raised in the introduction.

By applying these insights to the political sphere and with the help of historical examples from the periods when random recruitment was regularly used I was able to identify the major rationale for its political use: its capacity to act as an anti-power mechanism in respect to political appointment. An extension of this insight enabled me to put forward the mediative model for the establishment of political order. While revealed through the study of the lottery mechanism, we can identify political order on a mediative basis as a desirable political and democratic outcome.

Moving further into the realm of desired outcomes I then put forward my sketch of the three-way conversation. This provides us with a means of bridging the gap between the ideas of the lot-based polities of the past, the current forms of largely electoral democracy, and the democratic forms of the future. Combining this with the earlier discussion on the qualities of the lottery process then enabled me to advance two important principles for the modern application of random recruitment. First: that random recruitment should complement and support rational collective decision-making; and second: that random recruitment is particularly well suited to mediative roles such as establishing and defending shared, inclusive political systems. Of considerable importance in this respect is the notion of the citizens' ownership of the political process. I would put this forward as a fundamental tenet of democracy and therefore a highly desirable outcome for any future democratic system.

If we are to take anything away from this chapter, it would, I hope, be the understanding that for successful and meaningful design of democratic institutions and constitutions we need to explore a wide range of desired outcomes and make a thorough assessment of the mechanisms available to achieve them. Citizen participation is essential to democracy but participation cannot be the only desirable outcome.[19] We need to take a longer view of the establishment of fair and inclusive political systems and how these can be owned and defended by the citizens themselves. I would suggest that random recruitment is an ideal mechanism by which to achieve this.

References

Aristotle (1946) *Politics*, Barker, E. (trans.), Oxford: Clarendon Press.

---

[19] See also the call for multi-level governance in Sintomer (2010, p. 51).

Aristotle (1986) The Athenian Constitution, Moore, J.M. (trans.), in *Aristotle and Xenophon on Democracy and Oligarchy*, Berkeley, CA: University of California Press.

Delannoi, G. (2011) Le tirage au sort: une approche démocratique, *Esprit*, Août-septembre, pp. 153–161.

Devlin, P., Baron (1966) *Trial by Jury*, London: Methuen.

Dowlen, O. (2008) *The Political Potential of Sortition*, Exeter: Imprint Academic.

Dowlen, O. (2017) *Citizens' Parliamentary Groups, a proposal for democratic participation at constituency level*, A feasibility study funded by the New Democracy Foundation, [Online], https://www.newdemo cracy.com.au/docs/researchpapers/2017/Oliver%20Dowlen%20-%20Citizens'%20Parliamentary%20Groups.pdf.

Dowlen, O. & Delgano, J.C. (2016) *El sorteo en politica cómo pensarlo y cómo ponerlo en práctica*, Tradducción y notas de José Bellón Aguilera Doble J, Cadiz: Efialtes.

Dow, S. (1939) Aristotle, the kleroteria, and the courts, *Harvard Studies in Philology*, 50.

Ehrenberg, V. (1968) *From Solon to Socrates*, London: Methuen.

Gataker, T. (1627) *Of the Nature and Use of Lots: A Treatise Historicall and Theologicall*, London: John Haviland. First published 1619.

Goodin, R.E. (1996) Institutions and their design, in Goodin, R.E. (ed.) *The Theory of Institutional Design*, Cambridge: Cambridge University Press.

Green, T.A. (1985) *Verdict According to Conscience*, Chicago, IL: University of Chicago Press.

Gretton, R.H. (1910) Lot Meadow customs at Yarnton, Oxon, *Economic Journal*, 20 (77).

Hansen, M.H. (1999) *Athenian Democracy in the Age of Demosthenes*, Bristol: Bristol Classical. First edition 1991.

Headlam, J.W. (1933) *Election by Lot at Athens*, Cambridge: Cambridge University Press. First edition 1891.

Herodotus (1998) *The Histories*, Waterfield, R. (trans.), Oxford: Oxford World's Classics.

Hignett, C. (1952) *A History of the Athenian Constitution to the End of the Fifth Century B.C.*, Oxford: Clarendon Press.

Kent, D. (1978) *The Rise of the Medici Faction in Florence 1426–34*, Oxford: Oxford University Press.

Murray, O. (1990) Cities of reason, in Murray, O. & Price, S. (eds.) *The Greek City from Homer to Alexander*, Oxford: Oxford University Press.

Ostrom, E. (1990) *Governing the Commons: The Evolution of Institutions for Collective Action*, Cambridge: Cambridge University Press.

Pettingal, J. (1769) *An inquiry into the use and practice of juries among the Greeks and Romans, from whence the origin of the English jury may probably be deduced*, London.

Penn, W. (1982) *The Papers of William Penn*, Dunn, R. & Dunn, M.M. (eds.), Philadelphia, PA: University of Pennsylvania Press.

Rubinstein, N. (1966) *The Government of Florence under the Medici: 1434–1494*, Oxford: Clarendon Press.

Sintomer, Y. (2010) Random selection and deliberative democracy, in Delannoi, G. & Dowlen, O. (eds.) *Sortition Theory and Practice*, Exeter: Imprint Academic.

Stone, P. (2011) *The Luck of the Draw*, Oxford: Oxford University Press.

Sydenham, M.J. (1974) *The First French Republic 1792–1804*, London: B.T. Batsford.

Traill, J.S. (1975) *The Political Organisation of Attica*, Hisperia Supplement XIV, Princeton, NJ: Princeton University Press.

Waley, D. (1988) *The Italian City State Republics*, London: Longman.

Whitehead, D. (1986) *The Demes of Attica*, Princeton, NJ: Princeton University Press.

Xenophon (1940) *Memorabilia*, Watson, M.A. (trans.), in Plato and Xenophon (1940) *Socratic Discourses*, London: Everyman; Dent and Sons.

José Luis Moreno Pestaña

Castoriadis and Rancière
Contributions to
Philosophy of Sortition

Translated by Sarah-Louise Raillard

In this chapter, we shall present two interpretations of Athenian democracy, the first provided by the French thinker Jacques Rancière and the second by Cornelius Castoriadis, a philosopher of Greek origin whose intellectual career has largely flourished in France.[1] We shall ask three questions, the final one representing the crux of our inquiry. First of all, in what way does our interpretation of the Ancient World raise a number of questions regarding the economics of philosophical discourse? Secondly, why were Rancière and Castoriadis initially motivated to analyse Ancient Athenian democracy? (This question would lead us to investigate intellectual and personal circumstances as the source of specific philosophical positions, a matter which is outside the scope of this article.) The third and most important question we shall ask is what contributions Rancière and Castoriadis have made to a theory of the democratic uses of sortition. While neither of these thinkers offers a truly innovative theory of sortition, both make insightful contributions to the field. However, before beginning we shall say a few words about the first two questions raised by this investigation, in order to fully understand what a philosophical reading of Athenian democracy can bring to the table.

These analyses now allow us to understand, albeit in a highly specific context, the challenge that philosophical discourse constantly faces: how can it protect its identity, given that it is intimately bound

[1] This text has been written in the frame of the project I + D financed by the Spanish Ministry of Economy and Competitiveness 'The reception of the Greco-Roman philosophy in philosophy and human sciences in France and Spain from 1980 to the present. Comparative study in sociology of philosophy: a proposal' (FFI2014-53792-R). A former version of this chapter was published in *Imago Crítica*, 6, pp. 79–94.

up with history and politics? More exactly, what unique traits must an oral or written intervention exhibit in order to be identified as philosophical, rather than political, sociological, historical, or just the contribution of an informed citizen? This is a thorny question that requires a highly nuanced sociological perspective on knowledge. Without any pretensions to being exhaustive, we shall examine what kind of internal economy allows for a discourse to be identified as philosophical in nature.

First of all, we must look at the selection of sources, which is a crucial component in establishing a special space reserved only for philosophy. Out of the entire existing corpus that could inform us about Athenian democracy, what should we select to stake out a claim to the philosophical territory? By selecting their sources, authors reveal what they consider to be legitimate and/or indispensable references, philosophically speaking. And in that sense, each philosopher in general — as well as the two which we shall examine in particular — preserves, limits, or expands the referents that must be taken into account in order to avoid being scornfully labelled as a sociologist, a historian, or a mere intellectual who knows nothing about 'real' philosophy. Obviously, source selection is not the only element that matters: the 'style' with which these sources are treated also matters, as it is the means through which the trappings of 'philosophical belonging' are exhibited (this aspect is naturally the most difficult to describe objectively).

Secondly, should philosophers limit themselves to canonical authors, or should they on the contrary expand their field of study? Should they content themselves with Plato and Aristotle, and solely the most philosophical segments of their work, or should they also consider those with a more descriptive ambition? Should they examine only the 'philosophy' contained in Plato's *Laws*, or also take a look at the constitutional procedures analysed therein? Should we include, following an *ex ante* re-evaluation of their philosophical relevance, some of the tragic playwrights? The latter certainly play an important role for Castoriadis, who is careful to avoid anachronism, which would result from projecting what we consider to be philosophy today onto the Ancient World, where a different conception of academic disciplines most likely existed.

In addition to Castoriadis, Nicole Loraux (1981, p. 181) is one of the few authors to tackle the subject of politics and discourse modalities as a joint phenomenon: if writing on democracy tends to have a strong oligarchic streak, this is precisely because the use of speech is what sets democratic thinkers apart. Moreover, and still according to our sources, it is rare to find a philosopher who examines the political lessons that archaeology can teach us (with the exception, however, of historians like Josiah Ober and Mogens Hansen who draw extensively on archaeology in their noteworthy reconstructions of Athenian democracy). We must therefore analyse the relationships of competition and cooperation that philosophy maintains with other disciplines. What common ground can be found between the interpretations of Athenian democracy provided by Moses Finley or Pierre-Vidal Naquet, and that offered by Paul Veyne in his major sociological study *Bread and Circuses* (original French title: *Le pain et le cirque*)? Is the Athens imagined by Castoriadis and Rancière fundamentally different from the Athens envisioned by Foucault in the 1980s, thus replicating the opposition between Finley and Veyne?

We come now to our third question: how is it that source selection itself becomes the subject of academic and political controversy? Aristotle's oeuvre can allow for different interpretations of Athenian democracy. Cornelius Castoriadis exploits the latter's theory of mixed constitutions and his description of selection by lot to reveal latent democratic sympathies. Jacques Rancière, on the contrary, tends to show the Stagirite as rather critical of the *demos* and its power. To highlight the subversive dimension of random selection, Rancière draws on a highly unique reading of Plato's *Laws*. Even when agreement exists regarding the corpus, therefore, there can be as many different readings as there are authors. Ultimately, an analysis needs to operate on two levels in order to be successful: at the level of the interpretation (and its associated potential) and at the level of the interpreter.

Political and Intellectual
Trajectories towards Greece

Given what we propose to study, it is also important ask ourselves what elements of Rancière's and Castoriadis's biographical and intellectual trajectories may have driven them to focus on Athenian democracy. While answering this question comprehensively is outside the scope of this study, we can nonetheless offer a few general lines of analysis below.

Let us start with the most evident: philosophical legitimacy is almost always conferred to those scholars who study classical Antiquity. For example, Rancière has always struggled to be recognized as a veritable philosopher. His study of auto-didactic workers in the era of pre-Marxist socialism, *Proletarian Nights* (original French title: *La nuit des prolétaires*), placed him halfway between philosophy and history, with neither discipline ultimately considering him as one of theirs. Rancière's position at this difficult crossroads can perhaps help us to understand Foucault's quip from 22 February 1982, that 'as a professor of philosophy, you have to do a course on Socrates and Socrates' death at least once in your life' (2009, p. 14). Is the study of Antiquity a kind of toll that has to be paid in order to be granted entry into the world of philosophy? Such an explanation cannot be ruled out entirely.

We must also seriously consider another, more specifically historical effect: how did these thinkers see the philosophical crisis of Marxism that unfolded in the late 1970s and early 1980s reflected in the study of Ancient Athens? Foucault's and Castoriadis's seminars on Athenian democracy were given almost at the same time (Castoriadis, 2004; 2008; 2010; Foucault, 2008; 2009; 2012; Moreno, 2014). Rancière (2009a, p. 121) also talked about the political need to endorse a critical view of Hellenism in an attempt to counter the conclusions made popular by Arendt in *The Human Condition* (1958). The pressure exerted by Arendt in the philosophical sphere appears rather explicitly in Castoriadis's and Rancière's work, and implicitly in Foucault's. It seems that the classical legacy therefore also bequeathed a philosophically 'legitimate' way of considering post-Marxism. Other figures are also present in this intellectual landscape, including Léo Strauss and especially Jürgen Habermas and his theory of communicative action.

Nevertheless, Foucault's, Rancière's, and Castoriadis's trajectories oriented them towards subtly different centres of interest. During his leftist period, Foucault began by examining prisons; with *Œdipe-Roi*, he then turned to the subject of judicial truth. In contrast, Castoriadis, who was a legendary member of the group *Socialisme ou barbarie*, moved from the study of self-governance to the study of radical political democracy, including its procedures and cultural presuppositions. As for Rancière, he continued to focus on the same issue, whether looking at workers through the prism of Fourier or defending the uses of random selection. His 'scenes', whether considered individually or as a set, all illustrate situations of rebellion against the social distribution of posts and functions. Finally, Castoriadis and Rancière—the latter acknowledging his debt to the former—consistently criticize technocracy and evince a great degree of sympathy for sortition. It is also possible that the irony Rancière (2012, p. 31) exhibits towards the temple of knowledge where he received his education (the *École Normale Supérieure*), as well as Castoriadis's status as a statistical technician with the OECD for several years, gave both of these authors a certain amount of lucidity with regard to the scientific smokescreens that traditionally legitimize hierarchies.

Philosophical Achievements

By reading classical authors, Castoriadis and Rancière hit upon a number of fundamental problems and consequently developed a set of philosophical tools to help us understand the logic behind the use of sortition in politics. As is well known, random selection was one of the unique methods used to distribute responsibilities in the Ancient Greek world, a method that differs from our contemporary practices. We shall look at the most salient points in the work of these two philosophers while also comparing them to contemporary research on the use of sortition to highlight points of convergence, divergence, and perhaps even a number of proposed uses that go beyond their own intellectual projects. In Ancient Greece, Castoriadis finds the seed of autonomy, which he links to other emancipatory phenomena: liberal revolutions, the worker's movement, feminism. Rancière, on the other hand, selects historical episodes of democratic confrontation to shed light on how the natural order of domination can be interrupted.

Given that comprehensively exploring both of these authors is outside the scope of this chapter, we shall focus on the following: conceiving of radical democracy entails dealing with the question of popular assemblies, established according to census-based criteria (which designate those who are authorized to participate) and which can be composed by personally motivated action or the random selection of the citizens involved. Regarding popular assemblies, there are three main dimensions (beyond the formal census) which can be exploited to encourage citizens to participate (or not). We shall briefly present these three dimensions below.

The first is the dimension of knowledge. What epistemological qualifications do we attribute to those who participate in assemblies (Elster, 2013; Urfalino, 2015)? Is it sufficient to possess some oratory skills, do these need to be evaluated in any way (for Bentham, it was enough to be able to read Mass), or, on the contrary, must citizens be subject to electoral processes that ultimately select a talented elite?

The second axis concerns motivation. Aristotle preferred the kind of democracies where many peasants participated, and their presence became more difficult when political meetings exclusively took place in urban centres. Ephialtes established juror compensation, so that poor people could participate when randomly selected. During the French Revolution, many people complained that the meetings took place in spaces with such poor acoustics that they ultimately favoured 'a pulmonary aristocracy' (Heurtin, 2003). Consequently, various modalities of motivation can in fact limit the practical participation of individuals who theoretically enjoy full rights to said participation.

The third axis is that of moral qualities. The punishments inflicted on sycophants in Athens were designed to promote the participation of free and un-manipulated citizens. Similarly, Bentham suggested penalizing absentee representatives. Finally, managing political participation will always promote a specific ethos, qualities which define what political engagement is or is not valuable for a given community.

Sortition as a Means to Correct Inequality in the Assemblies

Ever since Thucydides first depicted Pericles as a *de facto* monarch, there have been many scholars who have expressed doubts regarding the true nature of Athenian democracy (Moreno, 2014). In his translation of *The Peloponnesian War*, Thomas Hobbes inserted a frontispiece with the portrait of Archidamus, King of Sparta, in negotiations with his peers, the Spartan *aristoi*. On the other hand, Pericles holds forth in front of a passive and already convinced assembly (Skinner, 2008, pp. 31–32). Foucault presents a relatively similar vision of things when he analysed Athenian democracy in his course from 1982–83 (Foucault, 2008), as well as in the conferences he gave in California in 1983 (Foucault, 2016). In those courses, Foucault argues that equality among citizens is affected by power relationships, though he finds no fault with a democratic system where Pericles enjoys enormous, quasi-royal power within the Assembly. He reminds us that all assemblies have their share of power struggles concerning the moral references that ensure their functioning, regarding how prestige is acquired, and what intellectual or cultural qualities those who speak must possess, qualities which delicately combine the courage to say what one thinks and the accountability to accept the consequences of one's acts. In that regard, Foucault seems to be describing what the North American scholar Bouricius (2013) calls 'self-selected assemblies', within which *de facto* aristocracies are perpetually recreated.

What can sortition accomplish, faced with such forms of inequality? First of all, random selection can doubtless mitigate the number and intensity of inequalities. Drawing on the work of Moses Finley (whose *Democracy Ancient and Modern* was translated into French in 1976), Castoriadis recalls that control did not depend on a constitutional text, but on the vigilance of citizens with regard to assemblies. In the 4th century BCE, *le graphe paranomon* allowed those who believed that a law had been illegally promulgated to convoke a tribunal, composed of randomly selected citizens, who could then impose heavy penalties on the law's author. Judicial control was similarly exercised over individuals who might attempt to propose a law using false statements.

Randomly selected tribunals hence played a crucial role in ensuring legality. Sortition could limit demagogic behaviour and attempts at manipulation that were characteristic of political factions and opportunists (Castoriadis, 2008, pp. 136–137).

We shall now take a look at the inequality surrounding prestige. Once again, it seems that the widespread use of random selection helped to limit the democratic assembly's aristocratic tendencies (or quasi-monarchical penchant, if we are to believe Thucydides, Hobbes, and Foucault). Thanks to random selection, ordinary citizens gained access to the central bodies of political deliberation and decision-making, such as the Council of the Five Hundred. It is obvious that this modality made access to the political sphere a possibility for entire social classes that would otherwise have had difficulty being heard on the Pnyx. Claire Taylor (2007) draws a number of salient conclusions, having studied the trajectories of 2,200 politically active Athenian citizens: during the 5th century BC, 19 per cent of these citizens were part of the 'liturgical class', that is, they were among the most powerful members of society (which accounted for about 4 per cent of the total population). Moreover, 58 per cent of them lived in the *demes*, or suburbs, that were the closest to the city (which accounted for 25 per cent of the total population). By the 4th century BCE, these numbers had shifted, and only 11 per cent still belonged to the 'liturgical class', and about 31 per cent to the suburbs. Taylor credits random selection, a process which was further implemented throughout the 4th century BCE, with adding a democratic component to elite recruitment. Random selection allowed Athenians to feel closer to their institutions, and at little cost to society: all they had to do as present their candidature as citizens of the People's Court, or as representatives of their own *deme* in the Council of the Five Hundred. Taking the floor in front of the Assembly was a distinctly less appealing option, as one had to face a series of professional orators and deploy significant resources to participate in the process, including the clout necessary to stand up to the squabbling factions in cahoots with the powerful leaders.

The Assembly was also the body where the rich and the ambitious invested all of their time and efforts (Sinclair, 1991). Continuing in the same vein as Thucydides and Hobbes, Foucault does not miss the opportunity to depict the Assembly as an aristocratic locus. Thanks to the use of sortition practices, however, Athens did not possess a *cursus honorum*, the relatively predictable trajectory that Roman Republicans were forced to follow to access political power (Taylor, 2007, p. 325). Once again we must agree with Castoriadis (2008, p. 90) who argues that Pericles was a leader controlled by his people. Prestige, sortition, and democracy thus all worked together to produce a kind of equilibrium that deserves to be further nuanced. The vision of Greek democracy as a constant competition to 'shine' has been highlighted by Jacob Burckhardt and observed by Hannah Arendt. As Castoriadis is right to note, we should not believe that the prestige for which Homeric heroes hungered was left unaffected by democracy. In fact, Athenian democracy prided itself on the fact that every individual could shine politically thanks to the training that they received simply by participating in public affairs (Castoriadis, 2010, p. 237).

Similarly, the question of knowledge — an obvious element of inequality — can also be applied to the difference between election and sortition. The use of electoral methods was reserved for magistracies that required specific skills and know-how. On the other hand, sortition was used to appoint magistrates where no special skills or training were required, or where said skills could be acquired on the job. As Castoriadis explains (2008, p. 93; 2010, p. 231), Plato's *Protagoras* presents an enlightening epistemology: in order to build, we need architects, but deciding what needs to be built is a political matter. And in that domain, there are no experts. In that regard, while one of the most important political and moral lessons of Foucault's *Œdipe Roi* is that anyone can have access to the truth, his reflections on how access to the different Athenian institutions was ensured (by election or sortition) sheds further light on why random selection was overwhelmingly used to select jurors. In fact, as the cornerstone of the participation of the lower classes, the selection of jurors could rely solely on the common sense shared by all citizens. As Yves Sintomer (2020) explains, even Hegel believed that understanding the facts of court cases was within the reach of all citizens.

In terms of courage, Foucault's observations are also essential. For Foucault, the concept of courage refers to the consubstantial risks and responsibilities associated with democracy, though it is difficult to see how random selection might come to affect the veracity and sincerity of citizens. However, Foucault seems to exaggerate the aristocratic aspect of this dimension, relying on pro-aristocratic sources and largely overlooking the democratic potential contained in Aristotle and Thucydides (Foucault, 2016, p. 180).

At any rate, a critical perspective like Foucault's remains valuable because it prevents us from excessively idealizing the democratic nature of participatory structures. Foucault surveys the assemblies structured by inequalities by and from the point of view of knowledge, bodies in which individuals seek to obtain prestige and where moral excellence amounts to the ability to remain truthful without ceding to flattery or demagogy. This description can help us to understand radical Greek democracy, but also to shed light on any of our contemporary democratic assemblies. The problem stems from the fact that Foucault reconstructs a world without sortition, without public indemnities, without liturgies for wealthy citizens, and where Pericles plays the role of a democratic monarch. As a result, Athenian democracy appears much more unequal under his pen that it was in practice.

Castoriadis and the Greek Imaginary

Although it is important to recall that Castoriadis and Foucault largely overlapped in giving their respective courses on the matter, Castoriadis's work in fact diverges in three significant places from the arguments put forth by Foucault. First of all, Castoriadis interprets several scenes recounted by Thucydides and a number of analytical passages in Aristotle as singing the praises of democracy. When Thucydides writes about Pericles' funeral oration or, even more importantly, about the Mytilenian Debate, Castoriadis (2010, pp. 190–193) sees a democracy threatened by a grave danger, but ultimately capable of self-governance and establishing the necessary limits. Secondly, even though Castoriadis shares with Foucault a certain tendency to mythologize the century of Pericles, the former's vision of democracy in the 4th century BCE is overall a more positive one, in large part due to his reliance on Aristotle. Finally, Castoriadis clearly examines the role of random selection in Athenian democracy, which does not, however, mean that he discusses in any great detail the potential expansion of sortition into the world of politics. When describing a certain political programme launched in Porto Alegre in 1991, for example, Castoriadis (2013, p. 464) limits sortition to the modest role of judicial organization.

This author nonetheless expresses great interest in the philosophical analysis of random selection procedures, with regard to both his historical interpretation of the Athenian experiment and his attempts to legitimize the use of sortition in contemporary contexts. While it is outside the scope of this chapter to comprehensively examine all of these contributions, it should be noted that Castoriadis, unlike Rancière or even Foucault, reconstructs a meticulous bibliography and an ambitious agenda that addresses every aspect ranging from slavery to the relationship between class warfare and the Empire in the large-scale conflict between Athens and Sparta. We shall present his main contributions according to the three dimensions mentioned above: Castoriadis's perspective allows us to understand the challenges facing randomly selected assemblies first and foremost with regard to question of knowledge, and then with regard to motivations and the promotion of moral righteousness.

First of all, knowledge. Let us look at the link between the Greek imaginary and sortition, which Castoriadis highlights by analysing the forms of inequality and discussions on religion and mythology. We shall first present the points of convergence in Rancière and Castoriadis with regard to this first element.

'Arithmetic' and 'Geometric' Equality in Castoriadis and Rancière

The issue is clearly addressed in one text devoted to a discussion of Marx's theory of value. Leaving aside the Marxist component, we shall concentrate on the reflections presented in this text on Aristotle. By taking as its fulcrum the difference between 'arithmetic' equality (among individuals deemed to be equals) and 'geometric' equality (among individuals judged according to their merit), Castoriadis investigates what becomes a society's primary value. This primary value distinguishes between what can be apportioned out and distributed, and what must remain a common good, exclusively open to participation without appropriation. What can be distributed will be allotted using specific criteria in every society, Castoriadis (1987, p. 372) adds while commenting Aristotle, because individuals do not have the same value in an oligarchy and in a democracy. In an oligarchy, some individuals have been excluded from power, which is concentrated in the hands of the 'best'. In a democracy, power cannot be appropriated, since all citizens must participate in the system. This essential division constitutes the primary value of any society and defines who is or is not a citizen, and who can or cannot hold public office (Castoriadis, 2008, p. 75). Once this geometrical difference is established, excluding certain citizens from power or not, justice—which claims to establish equality among individuals—can truly begin to operate. Social matters then come into play, which also depend on the primary value. For example, the use of public funds to remunerate political participation in Athenian democracy was contingent on the prior establishment of politics as something to which everyone—including poor citizens, but excluding women, children, slaves, and mixed-race individuals—must participate.

Rancière (1995) adopts a similar approach. Geometric equality determines what can and cannot be distributed to individuals. As a result, every society is defined by its pre-established system of accounting: what can and cannot be compared, what can and cannot be dispensed, which rights must be taken into consideration and which can be ignored. Rancière does not explicitly mention distribution or Castoriadis, but his point of view is similar: he describes a constituent form of accounting by virtue of which individuals are satisfied with (and thus do not challenge) the titles attributed to each individual. For example, person x is a citizen and person y is not; these resources must be distributed and those cannot be. Acts of resistance are the only thing that can unmask the total arbitrariness of any system of accounting. As a result, democratic politics contains the inertia of dominance and forces us to consider primary forms of geometric distribution. In that way, it opens up the possibility for other forms of accounting. Since every system contains some degree of randomness in its initial organization, traditional criticisms of democracy generally go down one of two different paths. On the one hand, Plato extols the 'government of the best', which assigns a function to each individual and ensures that this becomes a *habitus*. Aristotle, on the other hand, attempts to find a middle ground, so that a regime can avoid tipping over into either oligarchic despotism or democratic excess. Hence his incorporation of random selection in institutional mechanisms – though we must add that Plato likewise granted a role to sortition in the *Laws* (Demont, 2014).

Random Selection and Religious Imaginaries

The second main contribution made by Castoriadis concerns the Greek imaginary of causality. Like all religions, the Ancient Greek religion introduced order into chaos, but without the existence of an overall plan as contained in the Christian concept of Providence. This notion also included a kind of proto-value, which excludes the myth that a predetermined solution existed for every problem. Castoriadis (2004) provides several different examples, foremost among which we find the distribution of kingdoms among Zeus, Hades, and Poseidon using lots (*Iliad*, XV, 187). Other elements stand out in this imaginary, which does not ask whether chance should be eliminated or not: the Platonic demiurge must create the world by taking into account pre-existing materials, which cannot be entirely dominated by divine will. A cosmos stripped of any predetermined meaning forces men to produce their own meaning, without seeking for supernatural (or superhuman) guarantees. Democratic impulses are part and parcel of this religion, in which the gods are not always more trustworthy than the humans below them, who must consequently try to establish order on their own terms (Castoriadis, 2004).

This aspect of the Greek imaginary is just as fundamental as the relationships engendered by geometric equality in our vision of the world. Castoriadis emphasizes the importance of Greek religion and mythology in the experience of a democracy that reserves a place for chance. In this way, we can see the vast distance that separates this notion of democracy from its modern ideal as providing a purely technical solution to every problem (Castoriadis, 1975). Castoriadis shows us just how far we are from the Greek experience, but also helps us to understand what bridges we might be able to cross to transform sortition into an acceptable procedure today. While analysing the debate regarding sortition in 14th-century Florence, Olivier Dowlen (2008, p. 113) has demonstrated how Girolamo Savonarola ultimately defended elections for moral and religious reasons. He argued that our political elections must be the result of our moral judgment, a process in which God can intervene. This combination of religion, sortition, and election should be incorporated into a broader analysis of the role of chance in our worldview, as suggested by Yves Sintomer (2020). Such fundamental assumptions can strengthen — or diminish — the legitimacy of sortition practices. According to Sintomer, we are currently witnessing a crisis of the positivist imaginary in politics: there is no social science in existence that allows us to accurately predict when this imaginary will develop, or how to exploit it as engineers. Finally, all of this will help us to better comprehend how 'the rituals of reason' shape our view of politics (Elster, 1989, p. 37). Moreover, Elster maintains that we would rather perform rituals of reason based on the possibility of planning, rather than admit that uncertainty and indeterminacy exist. If we admit that uncertainty exists, we necessarily move away from the belief that we have the ability to organize our preferences in an adequate fashion and to select from among them using voting mechanisms. In addition to highlighting the mythological dimensions of voting systems, the argument in favour of sortition can also illustrate how, once the black box of political elections is pried open, reasoned decision-making is far from being the only component we find inside. We can moreover suggest other imaginaries that help to legitimize political action: the distribution of political offices as a form of participatory pedagogy, or the disappearance of factions from the public sphere. The crisis of the technocratic imaginary of politics and the ritual sacralization of voting present new opportunities for the use of random selection mechanisms. Castoriadis is an invaluable guide along this path, as he sheds light on what separates us from the classical world in terms of our perspective on random selection, while proposing new, contemporary uses for sortition.

Social Motivation and Integration

Over the years, Athenian democracy has been interpreted in a variety of different ways, especially with regard to the social conditions of its development. During the 18th century, Athenian democracy was still considered to be a system in which farmers and labourers participated, whether this supposed reality was used to praise or on the contrary denigrate the system's validity. While Montesquieu saw popular participation as an asset, James Harrington and Adam Ferguson lamented that such servile individuals could be involved in politics. In the 19th century, as epitomized by Hegel's interpretation, the tide began to shift: Athenian democracy was seen as resting on the backs of its slaves, an interpretation which would go on to inform Marxism. We now know that we were much closer to the truth in the 18th century: regardless of the importance that slavery may have had in Athens, the city did in fact involve working-class citizens in its political machinery (Meiksins Wood, 1988). Consequently, Marxist interpretations such as Hannah Arendt's, which separate Greek politics from social matters, are ultimately flawed. These erroneous readings were widespread when Castoriadis and Rancière were writing, however, and thus had a significant influence on their work; it is therefore noteworthy that these authors were able to move beyond such influences to assert their own interpretations.

In a book published in France in 1983, the same year as Foucault and Castoriadis were offering their seminars, Rancière studied how the Platonic critique of democracy investigated the possibility of reconciling professional occupations with political activity (Rancière, 2004). The democratic individual, capable of many different functions, is an illusion: only the elites who do not work and who, in the Platonic model, do not own property must be in charge of political matters. Democracy therefore becomes an impossible regime, as it presupposes that government is compatible with other activities. Plato's critique, which argues for the existence of a body of philosophers to be trained within the government, is therefore far removed from contemporary arguments for political specialization. The latter necessarily relies on the social division of labour. Both arguments, however, agree that lay people should be expelled from political affairs, claiming that democratic regimes which use sortition and rotating mandates are merely utopian fantasies.

It is therefore significant that Castoriadis (2008, pp. 50, 84, 82) highlights how Athens, once political equality was declared, took economic measures to implement said equality. In fact, thanks to public compensation measures, participation in the Assembly, the courts, and public spectacles became possible. Consequently, the material conditions of political participation were emphasized. On the one hand, sortition and compensation eliminated the need for individuals to plan out an entire political career just to participate in public activities, which dramatically reduced the economic costs and efforts necessary to penetrate into the circles of political power. On the other hand, these measures doubtless served to encourage the participation of citizens of more modest means, including the 6,000 candidates who presented themselves as potential jurors. It is not surprising that one of the first measures passed after the oligarchic coups in 400 and 411 BCE was to eliminate public compensation for political participation.

We now find ourselves examining a strange characteristic of the Athenian system. The fundamental key to sortition-based democracy with rotating public mandates was in fact the link between political participation and the distribution of wealth.[2] Our social system does not use political insertion as a condition to procure subsidies and today no one is even demanding for that to be the case. In our societies, social integration is the result of other mechanisms, such as professional training, and it only very rarely hinges on political participation in any way. We must therefore ask ourselves if we are not at risk of overlooking a crucial idea: that social insertion should perhaps be linked to responsible political participation. Is it possible to envision forms of socialization that are tied to democratic participation? Castoriadis (2010, pp. 100–102) asks this question and, if we have a mind to reflect upon the close relationship between public salaries and democracy in Athens, as well as the corresponding aversion expressed by the oligarchical elements of that society, we realize that we have before us a useful tool for politically motivating the most disenfranchised citizens.

Pericles' Funeral Oration
and the Moral Fabric of Society

Castoriadis (2008, pp. 160–161) suggests that the famous funeral oration attributed to Pericles by Thucydides contains the answer to a fundamental question: why participate in politics? The epitaph supposedly comes to counter the idea, popularized by Hannah Arendt, that politics is an arena where individuals can compete for notoriety, a situation which characterized the spirit of the Homeric heroes. At the same time, Castoriadis also explores the hypothesis put forth by Nicole Loraux, who sees Pericles' epitaph as presenting democracy through the prism

---

[2]   Perhaps this link could also be detected in the Florentine Republic.

of aristocratic values. Unlike Arendt, Castoriadis defends the idea that political competition goes hand-in-hand with a form of being; he argues moreover that Loraux is asking the wrong questions. While it is true that Pericles' oration is not a constitutional treatise and thus does not contain references to sortition or participatory incentives or rotating public mandates, it does nonetheless illustrate a certain shared culture that gave meaning to such activities (Castoriadis, 2010, p. 235).

What other interesting elements can we derive by reading Pericles' funeral oration with a view to developing a philosophy of sortition? The first corresponds to the possibility of reconciling private occupations with public responsibilities, which Pericles compares to the military devotion of Spartans to their city. The second element is the idea that poverty should not prevent individuals from serving their city. In addition, democracy requires inflections in the collective sensibility. Without necessarily being philosophers or artists, Athenian citizens love wisdom and beauty, which means that they develop varying skills and taste preferences (*ibid.*, pp. 164–166). The democratic city does not define all individual qualities once and for all. The culture of political de-professionalization, which is characteristic of sortition and rotating mandates, increases the ability of individuals to move from one social status to another, and to discover new opportunities for themselves. This theme is essential in Rancière's reflections on democracy.

Rancière and Random Selection as the Essence of Democracy

Rancière's relationship to random selection appears to be a paradoxical one. While we have already highlighted the value of many of Rancière's analyses, we must also add that this author justifies the use of random selection by relying on the association—traditional in Aristotle's work and further supported by Bernard Manin's magnum opus *Principles of Representative Government* (1997)—between random selection and democracy. However, Rancière's perspective raises a certain number of issues.

Democracy, Rancière tells us, dissolves the functions assigned to every individual. In that regard, every democratic scene entails the preliminary distribution of positions and establishment of merit. From that point of view, democratic competition reveals all of the hidden aspects of the model of geometric equality, which defined what needed to be taken into account. Democracy alters the established order and engenders new qualities, as well as mechanisms of oppression that they do not know how to measure.

This kind of vision aligns with Rancière's reading of a passage from Plato's Laws, one which he returns to on multiple occasions. According to Plato, there are several different ways to justify a system of government, one of which is chance. Chance breaks free from the fundamental structures of power, whether these are patriarchal or epistemological, and allows us to see the arbitrary nature of power. Any kind of democracy that encourages political professionalization and/or expertise thus functions like an oligarchy.

When we describe the democracy of Ancient Athens, it is not enough to ask whether Plato is the best reference to consult: even worse is the fact that many conclusions reached regarding Athenian democracy are somewhat lopsided. Random selection has never been linked to such an anarchic procedure, and not only because random selection depended on the census and a minimum age. Not all public offices could be attributed using random selection, even to those who were recognized as citizens; the only mandates for which sortition was used were those that did not require any specific skills. Concluding that democracy therefore depended on 'the absence of any right to govern' (Rancière, 2009b) leads to a historically inaccurate portrait of this political system.

Other expressions used by Rancière (2009b) while discussing Plato and the use of random selection mechanisms must be further nuanced —as, for example, when Rancière observes that random selection hands over the reins of the government to those who do not want it. This idea only makes sense if it refers to the fact that, with sortition, individuals cannot plan their political trajectories out ahead of time, with a view to accessing power. Historically, however, this idea is devoid of meaning, given that all the candidates who presented themselves for random selection in Athens did so voluntarily (Hansen, 1991). It is certain that the desire to participate in sortition lowered the costs associated with obtaining political power. At any rate, it is tricky to reconcile Rancière's reconstructions with a critical analysis of the existing sources. Rancière bases his argument on a juxtaposition of historical scenes—the Scythian slave revolt, the division of the citizen body into tribes by Cleisthenes, the retreat of the plebeians on the Aventine Hill—whose meanings are not elucidated by major contextual reconstructions. On this point, Rancière and Castoriadis are quite opposed, as the latter makes no arguments without first meticulously establishing the state of the question. Rancière, on the other hand, maintains that every instance of resistance against established power structures—among which he includes Cleisthenes but also the plebeians on the Aventine Hill in dialogue with the Roman ambassador—contains a similar temporality of resistance. This hypothesis is based on a powerful analysis of anachronism. Any given historical situation includes several different temporal lines, some of which travel through time by embedding themselves into far removed contexts (Rancière, 1996, pp. 67–68). In this manner, Rancière establishes a useful framework for reflecting on elective affinities in the historical uses of sortition (Sintomer, 2020).

It is also useful to analyse processes of political motivation by drawing on Rancière's ideas. Democracy is not ultimately a set of institutions, but a transformation of the spaces in which unexpected actors appear, suddenly becoming the authors of actions that had hitherto been inaccessible to them and traditionally unfolded in spheres occupied by the elites. Motivation is therefore born of activity, whether political or artistic (Rancière, 2012). This anthropological vision is perfectly aligned with the best uses of sortition, which impose responsibilities based on the hope that, in the exercise of the aforementioned responsibilities, individuals will become experts in their field. It is therefore unsurprising that what Rancière offers us is rebellion, albeit sometimes a very modest form of rebellion, against the attribution of established social functions and identities. Random selection undoubtedly makes this rebellion possible at the institutional level.

Conclusion

Through the prism of the three dimensions of democratic assemblies — i.e. knowledge, motivation, and moral control — we have examined the work of both Rancière and Castoriadis on the subject of random selection. Castoriadis has helped us to understand the imaginary roots that made random selection possible in the first place, and which make its contemporary uses more difficult: the imaginary on which our modern political knowledge is based appears to be largely overoptimistic. In this regard, we are seduced by what Jon Elster calls 'the sirens of reason', namely, the belief that electoral procedures can be designed to solve any political dilemma (Elster, 1989, p. 103). On the contrary, Rancière vigorously deconstructs the epistemocentric model of politics, while always assuming the democratic radicalness of sortition. Unfortunately, his arguments on this subject are somewhat sloppy and ultimately less useful than those developed by Castoriadis if we wish to reflect on the problems that we face today with regard to incorporating sortition into contemporary political practices.

Similarly, two characteristics of motivation with regard to democratic participation must be highlighted: the economic conditions, which were taken into account in Ancient Athens, are the subject of nuanced analysis in Castoriadis's work. As for Rancière, he emphasizes the ability of individuals to learn about government by exercising power directly. Ultimately, the question of why citizens choose to participate can be answered using the lessons learned by Castoriadis's reading of Thucydides. Random selection and radical participation not only prevented the emergence of moral dangers intrinsically linked to political factions, they moreover produced a specific model for citizens to gain civic prowess. This model should be used as a critical impetus for action today.

References

Arendt, H. (1958) *The Human Condition*, Chicago, IL: University of Chicago Press.

Bouricius, T.G. (2013) Democracy through multi-body sortition: Athenian lessons for the modern day, *Journal of Public Deliberation*, 9 (1), [Online], http://www.publicdeliberation.net/jpd/vol9/iss1/art11.

Castoriadis, C. (1975) *L'institution imaginaire de la société. Vol. 1. Marxisme et théorie révolutionnaire*, Paris: Seuil.

Castoriadis, C. (1978) Valeur, égalité, justice, politique, de Marx à Aristote et d'Aristote à nous, *Les carrefours du labyrinthe I*, Paris: Seuil.

Castoriadis, C. (2004) *Ce qui fait la Grèce. 1. D'Homère à Héraclite: Séminaires 1982–1983. La création humaine II*, Paris: Seuil.

Castoriadis, C. (2008) *Ce qui fait la Grèce. 2. La cité et les lois: Séminaires 1983–1984. La création humaine III*, Paris: Seuil.

Castoriadis, C. (2010) *Ce qui fait la Grèce. 3. Thucydide, la force et le droit: Séminaires 1984–1985. La Création humaine IV*, Paris: Seuil.

Castoriadis, C. (2013) *Quelle démocratie? Tome 2. Écrits politiques 1945–1997, IV*, Paris: Éditions du Sandre.

Demont, P. (2014) Platon et le tirage au sort, in Fumaroli, M., *et al.* (eds.) *Hommage à Jacqueline de Romilly: L'empreinte de son œuvre*, Paris: Académie des Inscriptions et Belles-Lettres.

Dowlen, O. (2008) *The Political Potencial of Sortition: A Study of the Random Selection of Citizens for Public Offices*, Exeter: Imprint Academic.

Elster, J. (1989) *Solomonic Judgements: Studies in the Limitation of Rationality*, Cambridge: Cambridge University Press.

Elster, J. (2013) A dialogue with Bentham, in *Securities Against Misrule. Juries, Assemblies, Elections*, New York: Cambridge University Press.

Foucault, M. (2008) *Le gouvernement de soi et des autres. Cours au Collège de France. 1982–1983*, Paris: Gallimard-Seuil.

Foucault, M. (2009) *Le gouvernement de soi et des autres II. Le courage de la vérité. Cours au Collège de France. 1984*, Paris: Gallimard-Seuil.

Foucault, M. (2012) *Du gouvernement des vivants. Cours au Collège de France. 1979–1980*, Paris: Gallimard-Seuil.

Foucault, M. (2016) *Discours et vérité précédé de La parrêsia*, Paris: Vrin.

Hansen, M. (1991) *Athenian Democracy in the Age of Demosthenes*, Oxford: Basil Blackwell.

Heurtin, J.-P. (2003) Architectures morales de l'Assemblée nationale, in Detienne, M. (ed.) *Qui veut prendre la parole?*, Paris: Seuil.

Loraux, N. (1981) *L'invention d'Athènes. Histoire de l'oraison funèbre dans la 'cité classique'*, Paris: Éditions de l'École des hautes études en sciences sociales.

Manin, B. (1997 [1995]) *Principles of Representative Government*, New York: Cambridge University Press.

Meiksins Wood, E. (1988) *Peasant-Citizen and Slave: The Foundations of Athenian Democracy*, London: Verso.

Moreno Pestaña, J.L. (2013) Isegoría y Parresia: Foucault lector de Ión, *Isegoría. Revista de Filosofía Moral y Política*, 49, pp. 509–532.

Moreno Pestaña, J.L. (2014) Pericles en París, *Pensamiento. Revista de Investigación e Información Filosófica*, 70 (262), pp. 99–119.

Rancière, J. (1995) *La mésentente. Politique et philosophie*, Paris: Galilée.

Rancière, J. (1996) Le concept d'anachronisme et la vérité de l'historien, *L'Inactuel*, 6, pp. 53–68.

Rancière, J. (2004) *The Philosopher and His Poor*, Parker, A. (ed.), Drury, J., Oster, C. & Parker, A. (trans.), Durham, NC: Duke University Press.

Rancière, J. (2009a) *Et tant pis pour les gens fatigués. Entretiens*, Paris: Éditions Amsterdam.

Rancière, J. (2009b) *Hatred of Democracy*, London: Verso.

Rancière, J. (2012) *La méthode de l'égalité. Entretien avec Laurent Jeanpierre et Dork Zabunyan*, Montrouge: Bayard.

Sinclair, R.K. (1991) *Democracy and Participation in Athens*, Cambridge: Cambridge University Press.

Sintomer, Y. (2020) *Between Radical and Deliberative Democracy: Random Selection in Politics from Athens to Contemporary Experiments*, Cambridge: Cambridge University Press.

Skinner, Q. (2008) *Hobbes and Republican Liberty*, Cambridge: Cambridge University Press.

Taylor, C. (2007) From the whole citizen body? The sociology of election and lot in the Athenian democracy, *Hesperia*, 76, pp. 323–345.

Urfalino, P. (2015) Décider en corps. Identité, réalité et mode d'être des corps délibérants, *Tracés*, 29, pp. 29-64.

Julien Talpin

Does Random Selection Make Democracies More Democratic?
How Deliberative Democracy has Depoliticized a Radical Proposal

Translation revised by Sarah-Louise Raillard

Random selection embodies the radical principle of absolute equality between all citizens. As several contributions to this book have shown, as well as a number of classical studies (Finley, 1976; Rancière, 2005; Sintomer, 2007), the use of random selection in politics presupposes that every individual possesses sufficient common sense and civic competence to participate in decision-making. Today, the appeal of this democratic mechanism is due in part to its radical nature, which breaks with the alleged naturalness of political delegation, disrupts the capacity-based conception of democracy, and underscores the key principle of equality.

Encouraged by a number of social, technical, and political factors, random selection has made an unexpected comeback in politics during the last forty years (Stone, 2009; Sintomer, 2020). Since the 1990s, the resurgence of random selection has been partly fuelled by theories of deliberative democracy, which view sortition mechanisms as central spaces for democratic deliberation. James Fishkin, a political theorist and the creator of a deliberative mechanism using random selection that enjoyed great success, the deliberative poll, is of crucial significance in this context. Fishkin's academic enterprise — in every sense of the word — has been highly successful. Ultimately, the deliberative poll became the new 'gold standard' — in the words of Jane Mansbridge (2010) — against which deliberation could be tested and random selection promoted. As we shall see, this adoption has not been without its share of challenges. It has been driven by the scientific trajectory of some of its advocates, as well as by other parallel developments within the political sphere. It has had a significant impact on contemporary uses of random selection mechanisms.

Despite bringing a fresh perspective to representative government, the scientific promotion of random selection by the champions of deliberative democracy has not necessarily translated into the democratization of democracy (Pateman, 2012). In fact, sortition mechanisms have often proven to be rather limited from a political perspective: while they have often revealed the deliberative capacities of ordinary citizens, they have not necessarily increased the latter's decision-making power. A number of theorists have therefore been highly critical of the emphasis placed on the analysis of deliberative dynamics within sortition mechanisms. These theorists call instead for a return to a Habermasian view, advocating the need for greater deliberation within the public sphere, rather than within minipublics (see in particular, Chambers, 2009). Taking into account these criticisms, deliberative theorists have recently adopted a 'systemic' turn to focus on the conditions of deliberation in different social spaces (Parkinson and Mansbridge, 2012). This theoretical shift has led to the recent marginalization of random selection mechanisms within deliberative democracy. We shall first review the intellectual trajectories followed by these theorists and then outline possible avenues for reflection on how random selection may help to rekindle the critical flame of deliberative theory, which has faltered somewhat in recent years.

Deliberative Democracy and Random Selection: A Contingent Encounter

Random selection has become an integral part of the operational toolkit used by the proponents of deliberative democracy. The deliberative variant of democracy is indeed strongly associated with the organization of so-called 'minipublics', in which randomly selected citizens debate a specific matter of public interest for a set period of time. However, the rise to prominence of random selection within theories of deliberative democracy was not a given: it was in fact linked to a set of both theoretical and practical circumstances, and most importantly to the fact that it succeeded in responding to some of the challenges encountered by deliberative theorists since the 1980s.

Random selection was not initially a key component of deliberative democracy's theoretical arsenal. The earliest philosophers of deliberative democracy, such as Jürgen Habermas (1981), Bernard Manin (1985), Jon Elster (1987), and Joshua Cohen (1989), never referred to sortition practices directly. Their historical references stemmed primarily from the world of 17th- and 18th-century salons and cafés, the debates held in the constituent assemblies created during the French and American revolutions, and New England town meetings (Cossart, Felicetti and Kloppenberg, 2016). Although Jon Elster (1987) mentions Ancient Athens indirectly by referring to the 'forum', he discusses the Ecclesia, which was a space for public deliberation open to all men, rather than analysing the other institutions drawn by lot which existed at the time. According to Elster and other pioneers of deliberative theory, what mattered most was the ability to discuss and debate in the public sphere, rather than ensuring the participation of ordinary citizens in decision-making processes through random selection. This omission is all the more surprising as Elster has made one of the greatest contributions to the renewed interest of the social sciences in the use of random selection mechanisms (see, for example, Goodwin, 2011).

In his 1989 book, *Solomonic Judgments*, Elster describes at great length the lot-drawing procedures in Athens, Florence, and Venice. However, his primary objective regarding the random selection of representatives was understanding how the limits of individual and collective rationality could be overcome. Drawing on debates with the proponents of rational choice theory, his defence of random selection, in politics and elsewhere, was primarily based on analysing the conditions under which 'good decisions' were made when logic failed. Random selection thus frequently makes 'pareto-optimal' decisions possible and avoids the creation of permanent minorities. Elster's reflections on the formation of individual preferences and the limits of vote aggregation (with regards to promoting the common good) played an important role in the subsequent development of deliberative theory (Elster, 1998). They emerged, however, on the fringes of a strictly democratic conceptualization of the role that random selection could play in the deliberative process—though others were also considering the properly democratic role of sortition at the time, however. For instance, in his book *Strong Democracy* (1984, pp. 290–293), Benjamin Barber mentions the use of random selection mechanisms in Ancient Athens. This practice is simply one institutional reform among others that he examines in his reflection on how to strengthen democracy, however. Most importantly, his theoretical project was somewhat removed from the deliberative conceptualization of democracy that was emerging at the time; Barber was ultimately seen as a proponent of participatory, rather than deliberative, democracy.[1]

Although reflections on the role of random selection in politics became more frequent at the end of the 1980s, the connection between deliberative democracy and random selection was initially promoted by James Fishkin. In his 1991 book, *Democracy and Deliberation*, Fishkin sought to reconcile the imperatives of political equality between citizens with the central role of deliberation in the development of legitimate collective choices. While deliberation and participation may appear to be contradictory—the quality of deliberation may entail limiting participation and, conversely, a large number of participants may make deliberation more difficult—Fishkin argued that random selection was a means through which it was possible to reconcile these two objectives: 'random selection can resolve our main issue of conciliation between deliberation and political equality' (Fishkin, 1991, p. 90).

The reference to random selection was borrowed directly from the Athenian experience,[2] as Fishkin's project sought to create a 'direct deliberative democracy' under the conditions of the large nation-states that existed at the end of the 20th century. Fishkin envisions his work as 'part of a 2,500-year quest to better adapt the democratic idea, originally suited to populations of several thousand in a Greek city-state, to populations of many millions in a modern megastate. It is about how we might bring some of the favourable characteristics of small-group, face-to-face democracy to the large-scale nation-state' (Fishkin, 1991, p. 1). Although Fishkin was primarily referring to the American founding fathers and the work of Robert Dahl (1989), rather than the theories of Jürgen Habermas, his theoretical ambition was to reconcile the virtues of deliberation with the democratic imperative of equality among citizens. Whether or not his intellectual trajectory has continued to develop in this direction is a matter of discussion. However, as we shall see later, Fishkin nonetheless played a central role by incorporating random selection mechanisms within the theoretical and practical arsenal of deliberative democracy, thus strongly orienting debates within this field of research. More specifically, since his 1991 publication, Fishkin has proposed the creation of an original device using random selection: the deliberative poll.

---

[1] For the differences and relationships between participatory democracy and deliberative democracy, see Hayat (2011) in particular.

[2] Even if it is marked by interpretation errors and anachronisms (Girard; 2011).

Fishkin's promotion of random selection was part of a broader movement that began in the 1970s with the proliferation of deliberative experiments such as planning cells in Germany, citizen juries in the United States, and consensus conferences in Denmark (Sintomer, 2007).[3] Fishkin helped this movement to spread by referring to some of these experiments in *Democracy and Deliberation*. Moreover, the procedural turn embodied by deliberative theory also engendered favourable conditions for rediscovering the value of random selection. In fact, deliberative theory deepens the Habermasian procedural approach (Cohen, 1989) by emphasizing the conditions that allow for good—i.e. informed, inclusive, and egalitarian—deliberation. This shift sought to respond to the criticisms levelled against Habermas; namely, that in the real world the social situation of speakers and existing power relations both influence deliberation, which cannot be reduced to the strength of the best argument alone (Bourdieu, 2000; Sintomer, 2010). Regulation of discursive interactions through specific procedures therefore attempts to neutralize the distortions produced by social inequalities.

Minipublics, to borrow the expression used by Archon Fung (2003) to characterize these different randomly selected mechanisms, thus appear to embody this procedural shift, as they seek to control the social and cultural inequalities that impact democratic communication. However, the academic and political success of minipublics went beyond merely theoretical considerations. These experimental approaches also resonated with the increasingly urgent appeal, from the 1990s onwards, to conduct empirical investigations of deliberative theories, either in terms of debate dynamics or the effects of learning on participants. In a seminal article, Jane Mansbridge (1999a, pp. 291 and 318) thus explained that:

> [P]articipating in democratic decisions makes many participants better citizens. I believe this claim because it fits my experience. But I cannot prove it. Neither, at this point, can anyone else… The kinds of subtle changes in character that come about, slowly, from active participation in democratic decisions cannot easily be measured with the blunt instruments of social science… More important, the studies in political science do not usually even reach the threshold for serious consideration in a field such as psychology, due to major failures in their internal validity, such as not having a control group and not measuring effects

---

[3] The founders of these democratic innovations such as Peter Dienel and Ned Crosby set their projects within a political and technocratic perspective—allowing citizens to participate in complex scientific and technical choices—without directly referring to a deliberative conception of democracy. This approach did not exist, strictly speaking, at the time when they began their experiments.

before and after treatment. One solution to these problems would be to design a study with randomised control large enough so that even small affects would be significantly different from zero.

This appeal was heard loud and clear, and the mechanisms utilizing random selection that emerged during this period had the advantage of acting as mini-laboratories for political scientists to test their hypotheses.

The Beauty of Minipublics

Fishkin (1991, 1995), initially a political theorist, gradually became the engineer-in-chief of deliberative democracy (Blondiaux, 2002). However, a number of other social scientists before him had paved the way by creating quasi-experimental deliberative devices. For instance, in the 1970s Peter Dienel experimented with planning cells in West Germany, and Ned Crosby created citizen juries in America. While these initiatives helped to disseminate minipublics and the use of random selection in politics (Sintomer, 2020), their creators had no theoretical ambitions as such. James Fishkin, on the other hand, already occupied a central role among deliberative theorists when he elaborated the deliberative poll.

Deliberative polling is based on the constitution of a random sample of approximately 400 people, representative of the larger population. Participants meet during one or two weekends and alternate between periods of training and collective discussion; they also pose questions to a diverse panel of experts and elected representatives. Using questionnaires distributed before and after the deliberative polling experience, Fishkin and his colleagues were able to show that deliberation fostered learning and changes in preferences (Luskin, Fishkin and Jowell, 2002). This mechanism — notably when compared against most other minipublics — draws its strength from the statistical representativeness of the sample of selected citizens, which allows its developers to extrapolate the results to the entire population. In other words, the rationale is that any group of citizens placed under similar conditions would adopt the same opinions as the participants in the deliberative poll.

Deliberative polls are experiments orchestrated by a team of scientists and are often funded by foundations and think tanks. Although the topics discussed are public interest issues (health insurance reform, national security, admittance to the Eurozone, etc.), deliberative polls do not primarily seek to inform public decision-making. Rather, their main objective is answering an important scientific question: is political competence an inherited and unchanging attribute, or can it be influenced by the institutional context in which citizens are situated? This question has divided political scientists for decades (Blondiaux, 1996). Philip Converse (1964) has observed that, far from meeting the expectations of the classic theories of democracy which perceive citizens as political beings interested in public affairs, most individuals in fact possess scant knowledge of political issues and have opinions that are, at the very least, unstable — what Converse calls 'nonattitudes'. In France, Pierre Bourdieu (1979) and Daniel Gaxie (1978) made similar observations, albeit from a more critical perspective. In that regard, empirical studies of deliberation thus immediately took centre stage in American political science, in large part because they responded to some of the discipline's canonical questions concerning the rationality of political choices, electoral choices in particular. As political science has spent thirty years underscoring the political incompetence of the masses, it has consequently paved the way for an elitist interpretation of democracy. Conversely, deliberative studies have demonstrated that it is possible to create institutional conditions which favour the formation of an enlightened citizenry. In this sense, deliberative theories were initially highly critical, attacking the elitist paradigm that assumed that the masses were inherently incompetent. Attempting to empirically prove that political competence is universal undeniably involves a subversive aspect, given the otherwise conservative bent of American political science.

In addition to embodying a genuine normative and political ambition on the part of deliberation theorists, such critical endeavours also echoed a number of recent developments in public opinion studies, which emphasized how context (the wording of questions, the importance of the interviewers' race and gender with regard to respondents' answers, priming and framing effects, etc.) influences responses to questionnaires and surveys (Zaller, 1992). The deliberative paradigm also considers seriously the role played by context, which is no longer viewed simply as the distribution questionnaires but more broadly encompasses the elements of institutional design in which political opinions are expressed. The focus on the transformative power of institutions also echoed the broader movement initiated by the neo-institutionalist paradigm within the social sciences, which underscored the role played by the rules of the game and institutional frameworks in the development of actors' preferences (March and Olsen, 1984; Powell and Di Maggio, 1991).

Although Fishkin's studies rapidly came under fire, notably in relation to the durability of the perceived preference changes (Merkle,

1996), they gained increasing popularity. In the early 2000s, empirical studies of deliberative devices using random selection proliferated (Gastil and Dillard, 1999; Hansen and Andersen, 2004; Grönlund *et al.*, 2010). Deliberative theory rapidly endorsed minipublics. According to Archon Fung (2003, p. 339), minipublics 'are among the most promising constructive efforts that promote deliberative democracy'. Although she also pointed out some limitations, Jane Mansbridge (2010) stressed that 'combining representativeness and balance, decision-making links, the protection of participants and inclusion makes deliberative polling the gold standard of institutional processes which attempt to create informed deliberations among a representative sample of citizens'. Some even went as far as to describe minipublics as the 'most advanced method for institutionalising deliberative democracy' (Estlub, 2014, p. 166). The rise of deliberation within randomly selected small groups over the last two decades has been so significant that one might be tempted to conclude that minipublics are synonymous with deliberative democracy (for a critical perspective, see Parkinson, 2006; Currato and Bocker, 2016).

Two elements characterize these early empirical studies of deliberation. First, they primarily focus on preference change, in particular by using pre- and post-deliberation analyses.[4] These analyses seek to determine whether participants' opinions are different after the experiment—better informed, more robust, more 'tolerant', or more 'altruistic'. Almost all of these studies have shown that deliberation results in enlightened preferences, confirming that it can make better citizens. In a study comparing 65 deliberative polls (in which a significant change in the opinions of participants was observed), John Gastil and his colleagues (2010) observed that participating in this type of experiment resulted in more open, 'cosmopolitan' viewpoints, without systematically orienting individuals towards progressive positions. The focus placed by deliberation theory on preference change is due both to the scientific framing of the question, linked to the issue of political competence, and to the essentially quantitative methods used. Moreover, deliberation is primarily analysed experimentally in artificial contexts, within frameworks designed by researchers rather than by public authorities. These quasi-experimental mechanisms have nonetheless helped to legitimize the parallel rise of randomly selected

---

[4] The evolution of preferences is generally analysed based on the responses given to questionnaires; it is then tested statistically. For a slightly different qualitative method based on the use of Q-methodology, both before and after the minipublic, see Niemeyer (2011).

minipublics promoted by institutional actors and civil society, albeit with contrasting results. Along the way, the critical potential of deliberative democracy has largely been eroded.

The Rise of the Random Selection Industry

The success of this scientific endeavour was reflected in the fact that 'thousands of well-moderated and well-organized deliberations may occur every year in a country like the United States' (Levine, 2014, p. 1), as well as in Europe and beyond. The successful return of random selection to politics led to, but was also reciprocally supported by, the emergence of a genuine 'public participation market' (Mazeaud and Nonjon, 2018). Local authorities in particular typically rely on external consultants to design and implement sortition mechanisms, while the random selection itself is usually performed by polling institutions with the necessary expertise. Sometimes, however, random selection procedures are conducted internally by institutions in a less scientific fashion (Flamand, 2011). Debates within this field became more and more technical (and thus less political), focusing on issues such as whether participants should be drawn from electoral lists (but this would exclude foreigners and those who were not registered to vote), administrative and commercial lists (electricity supplier lists, telephone lists, etc.), or whether only volunteers should participate. Another issue that arose was whether or not participants should be compensated. Depending on which choices were made, the random sample could thus vary significantly, and be more or less diversified in terms of gender, age, income, socio-professional status, etc. With the exception of the deliberative poll, most minipublics have given up on the ideal of composing a representative sample and have instead relied on the constitution of diversified groups taking into account socio-demographic factors. Nevertheless, overall, the citizen response rate remains very low. When participants are not remunerated, it averages approximately 2%, rising to 10% when compensation is offered (Jacquet, 2017). These figures raise questions regarding the actual representativeness of samples, as random selection only partially compensates for participant self-selection. In the absence of remuneration, the most educated and politicized participants are over-represented in the minipublics.

This is an important issue, as the resurgence of random selection in politics attempts in particular to involve participants other than the 'usual suspects', i.e. active citizens often engaged in local associations or party structures, in order to reach 'lay citizens'. While this may be understood as a desire for inclusion, it is also accompanied by more instrumental goals, namely the circumvention of both interest groups and more oppositional movements which could thwart institutional agendas. More prosaically, using random selection enables local authorities to engage a captive public, thus making it possible to address the 'empty-room' syndrome (Gourgues, 2012). Although sampling often poses a challenge with regard to the lack of interest displayed by most citizens once they are selected, random selection makes it possible to create a public and highlight the *demos* in action, which can make it an end in itself, rather than merely an element of a specific political project.

To what extent has the return of random selection in politics translated into the democratization of democracy, as envisioned by its champions? On the one hand, the ability to organize sortition mechanisms in a serious and effective manner has helped to legitimize the use of random selection in other political arenas. Thus, during the 2017 French presidential election, several left-wing candidates proposed the frequent use of minipublics, with some even going so far as to propose the creation of a third legislative chamber whose participants would be selected at random. Although such a proposal had long been recommended by academics (Dahl, 1989; Sintomer, 2007), it had, until then, attracted little interest in the political sphere, sometimes being met with outright contempt. The return to favour of random selection has also resulted in the emergence of new citizen collectives such as #mavoix, which is experimenting with the random selection of candidates for French legislative elections. The resurgence of random selection has thus helped to loosen the electoral monopoly on representation.

It must be highlighted, however, that institutional use of minipublics over the last twenty years has done little to strengthen democracy. The majority of these minipublics have no impact on public decision-making, and their recommendations are rarely implemented (Papadopoulos and Warin, 2007; Blondiaux, 2008). Although institutions may sometimes adopt some form of 'selective listening' (Sintomer and Talpin, 2011; Font, Pasadas del Almo and Smith, 2016) and choose the proposals they perceive to be the most relevant, they ultimately have the final word. Not only has power not been redistributed in any meaningful way, such experiments risk increasing citizens' mistrust of politics. Indeed, citizens often feel deceived or exploited (Funes, Talpin and Rull, 2014). Some innovative experiments—such as the British Columbia Citizens' Assembly in Canada—nevertheless seek to combine random selection and direct democracy. The legalization of same-sex marriage by referendum in Ireland was notably the result of a deliberative process whose participants had been selected at random

(Suiter, Farrell and Harris, 2016). While such exceptions attest to the potential radical contribution of random selection, most experiments to date have not had a lasting impact on public decisions. Worse, random selection sometimes appears to be a weapon deployed by elected officials to undermine associations or more radical social movements.[5] As Caroline Lee and Zachary Romano have pointed out in their analyses of American cases: 'What clients and donors particularly seek from deliberation is a conflict management strategy to address potential or tangible resistance to austerity policies that emerge from social reorganisation, cuts in state spending, and urban renewal' (Lee and Romano, 2013, p. 743). In other words, by choosing lay citizens who often belong neither to community organizations nor to any partisan groups, random selection procedures can ensure the constitution of a docile public (Blondiaux, 2008). The manner in which deliberative democrats and most political actors have addressed random selection has helped to depoliticize it, instead transforming sortition into an instrument and a transferable procedure, albeit at the cost of reduced political radicalism.

Drawing on a study about how consultants facilitate minipublics in the United States, Caroline Lee (2014) also comes to a number of harsh conclusions. In particular, she highlights the effects of the 'small is beautiful' ideology that is widespread in participatory culture. While the local nature of deliberative mechanisms allows citizens to experience the tangible effects of their participation, the large-scale major decisions made in parallel are undertaken by political and economic elites alone. The promotion of local action as a means of encouraging social change is thus undermined. Even when participatory mechanisms succeed, all the small victories do not automatically add up to social justice. Indeed, how these mechanisms are linked to other scales is fundamental: 'Unfortunately, all these little steps towards empowerment have not paved the way to social justice but, rather, have led to an oppressive spiral of resignation and withdrawal from public life' (p. 226). The criticism levelled against the local context of minipublics thus aligns with recent theoretical arguments denouncing a shift from deliberative democracy to democratic deliberation, as embodied by this focus on microscopic mechanisms.

---

[5] See, for instance, the study by Barbier, Bedu and Buclet (2009) about the instrumentalization of a citizen jury in Brittany, or Freschi and Mete's study (2009) about a 21st-century town hall meeting in Tuscany.

From Deliberative Democracy
to Democratic Deliberation

In a seminal article published in 2009, Simone Chambers points out that deliberative theorists have gradually shifted from an interest in deliberative democracy — i.e. how to make democracy more deliberative — to democratic deliberation and the study of the conditions that favour discussion, usually in small groups, while respecting a certain number of procedural criteria (inclusion, equal respect, information, etc.). Chambers argues that this focus on deliberation in restricted circles stems from the mistrust of many deliberative theorists of demagogic and populist discourse. Quality deliberation is seen as being simply impossible within the public sphere.[6] Deliberative theorists have thus 'abandoned mass democracy'.

This criticism has led a number of theorists to clarify the connection they envisage between randomly selected devices and mass democracy. Theorists such as Archon Fung (2007, p. 159) consider that minipublics fulfil a core function: 'Reforms in the wider public space may consist mainly in the multiplication of mini-publics rather than seek to improve the mass public (or public opinion)'. Insofar as he considers the opposition between deliberation and mass participation to be irreducible, James Fishkin (2009) sometimes goes so far as to argue that deliberative polls should have a decision-making role. This point of view, however, is rarely shared by his fellow theorists. Fishkin argues that the opinions voiced during deliberative polls are those that would have been voiced by the public at large had they been able to participate. Moreover, he considers that, given that the sample of citizens is statistically representative — an essential element on which the democratic legitimacy of Fishkin's mechanism is based, unlike citizen juries or consensus conferences for instance — it is legitimate that participants in a deliberative poll should be able to make decisions directly. Fishkin is nonetheless aware that the centrality of the notion of consent in traditional conceptions of democracy makes such a proposal quite unlikely to be adopted.

Beyond this pragmatic argument — namely, that people do not wish to delegate their power to a group of randomly selected citizens — this proposal has also been deemed elitist. For instance, Lafont (2015) argues that if the legitimacy of minipublics to make decisions stems from the quality of the judgments or opinions held by citizens after deliberation, that would amount to delegating decision-making power

---

6   Chambers (2009) contests this and defends large-scale forms of deliberative rhetoric.

to experts. Indeed, an epistemic conception of legitimacy (Estlund, 2008) cannot rely on the argument that random selection represents, both statistically and sociologically, the whole population, since deliberative experiments specifically transform participants into beings who are different from their ordinary peers. In this sense, minipublics embody a form of 'deliberative elitism' (Chambers, 2009; Pourtois, 2013).

Taking Fishkin's arguments to their logical extreme, Lafont (2015) counterfactually wonders whether, from a normative perspective, it would be desirable to delegate one's power to a randomly selected assembly. Even if this assembly was authorized to govern—by way of a referendum, for instance—such a scenario would still not be democratic and would result in the domination of the masses by informed beings who were initially close to them, but who now have nothing in common with the people and are hardly accountable to them. In such a system, citizens would 'blindly follow the views and preferences of their delegates, in a near yet inaccessible world. They would be dominated by their ideal self, but dominated nonetheless'. In keeping with the principle of non-tyranny, Lafont thus considers such a scenario to be democratically unsustainable.

Should random selection therefore be eliminated from the political system? Over the years, many theorists have attempted to answer this question and have called for a renewed focus on deliberation within the public sphere, rather than in artificial settings. One of the consequences of this 'systemic' turn has been the marginalization of random selection in deliberative theory.

The Marginalization of Random Selection:
The Systemic Turn of Deliberative Democracy

In light of the criticisms levelled against the key role played by minipublics in research on deliberation, many theorists now defend a systemic conception of deliberative democracy. The creation of perfect deliberative spaces that are isolated from social reality is no longer the issue at stake. Rather, the challenge now lies in instilling deliberation at all levels of democratic governance (Mansbridge, 1999b; Parkinson and Mansbridge, 2012).

Lafont (2015) therefore argues that just multiplying the number of minipublics does not entail the democratization of the public sphere. Indeed, even when these mechanisms can help to produce informed and reasonable proposals, their impact will remain insignificant if the rest of the public remains uninformed. This was precisely the pitfall encountered by the British Columbia Citizens' Assembly. Although the randomly selected participants gained much knowledge through their participation and even succeeded in formulating an original and sensible proposal to reform the voting system (Lang, 2007), they were nonetheless unable to influence public opinion at large. While citizens who were aware of the existence of the Citizens' Assembly over-whelmingly voted in favour of the referendum, the majority of the public was unaware of its existence, and the referendum thus failed to obtain the 60% approval necessary for ratification (Warren and Pearse, 2008). It therefore seems difficult to introduce deliberation in the public sphere without taking into account the influence of actors other than randomly selected minipublics. As a result, studies are now concentra-ting on reinforcing deliberation and information in electoral and referendum campaigns (Gastil and Richards, 2013; Talpin, 2016b), in political parties (Lefebvre and Roger, 2009), and in mass media (Parkinson, 2006; Girard, 2010). Random selection has therefore been marginalized in reflections on deliberative democracy.

This does not mean, however, that random selection has no role to play in the deliberative system. Sintomer (2020) argues that randomly selected minipublics can fulfil four types of democratic functions: they advise the *prince* by proposing recommendations; they evaluate public policies and decisions; they propose draft laws or referenda; and they inform public opinion.[7] Niemeyer (2011) and Curato and Böker (2016) identify two additional functions. First, minipublics can be 'brokers of knowledge', acting as a reliable intermediary between citizens and complex information. Second, they can act as 'schools of democracy', providing citizens with knowledge and know-how that they can reinvest in other spheres. Böker and Elstub (2015) have attempted to radicalize minipublics in order to reconnect with the critical elements of deliberative democratic theory. Specifically, they promote the idea of bottom-up mechanisms, self-organized by civil society and thus more autonomous from public authorities, both with regarding to setting agendas and conducting deliberations. While such experiments may be interesting, they do little to solve the question of their relationship with political decision-making and, more broadly, with the deliberative system. This situation has been clearly illustrated by the randomly selected devices organized by civil society in Iceland and Belgium in recent years and which have failed to have a significant impact (see

---

[7] As was the case with the *Citizen Initiative Reviews* in Oregon, where a randomly selected panel of citizens deliberates regarding ballot initiatives to provide balanced information to citizens before they make a decision on referendum proposals. See Gastil and Richards (2013).

Reuchamp and Suiter, 2016). Curato and Böker (2016, p. 185) ultimately acknowledge that the 'systemic approach requires that mini-publics play an auxiliary rather than a central role in deliberative democratisation'.

Can the Critical Dimension of Deliberative Theory Be Revived via Random Selection?

At a time when the trend towards plebiscites and authoritarian logic both seem to prevail in several liberal democracies, and 'post-truth politics' is rapidly gaining ground, the defence of public reason and an epistemic conception of democracy by the champions of deliberation represent an important political horizon. However, we must address the growing gap between the abstract considerations of deliberative theorists and the advent of a 'post-democratic' era (Crouch, 2004), in which major decisions are taken outside elected bodies and out of the public eye. While the systemic turn of deliberative theory supposedly embodied a shift in focus away from the microscopic gaze adopted in recent years, in order to take account of power relations when analysing democratic functioning, one cannot help but be struck by the short-sightedness of some of the literature in relation to the anti-deliberative dynamics that shape representative government today. What role can deliberation play when it encounters the influence of money in electoral campaigns, the pressure of credit rating agencies on governments, or lobbying practices in decision-making (Bartels, 2009; Lessig, 2012; Brown, 2015)? At this stage, these questions have not been addressed by most deliberative theorists. Random selection and all forms of political inclusion thus seem like distant horizons. Nevertheless, if the goal of deliberative theory is to stimulate greater discussion and reflexivity within the public sphere, can random selection play a greater role in the deliberative system and help to radicalize a deliberative theory that has become entirely too prudent?

One of the limitations of the existing theories of deliberation lies in their cooperative conception of collective decision making and social change. Even though there has been some progress in this direction (see Mansbridge *et al.*, 2010), a more agonistic use could be envisioned for random selection within the deliberative system. Over fifteen years ago, Archon Fung and Eric Olin Wright (2003) defended the virtues of a deliberative 'countervailing power', capable of challenging institutions and reminding them of their democratic and deliberative principles. This was not so much a matter of the system's equilibrium than a question of ensuring social progress and the emancipation of subaltern classes. Fifteen years later, Eric Olin Wright seeks to revive this project by making random selection one of the facets of his 'real utopias' project. This intuition has nevertheless been largely forgotten by deliberative theory and remains associated mostly with certain oppositional aspects of participatory democracy, distinct from deliberation (Pateman, 2012). A good illustration is the fact that the key text of the systemic approach to deliberation (Parkinson and Mansbridge, 2012, pp. 17–18) devotes only two pages to social movements to highlight their possible contribution to the epistemic and democratic dimensions of the system. Collective action thus remains largely marginal in their conceptualization of democracy. This absence is striking, especially at a time when democratic demands and deliberative practices in assemblies have been central to anti-globalization movements, and more recently to the protests launched by the Arab Spring and pursued by the 15M in Spain and Occupy Wall Street in the United States (Della Porta, 2009; Ancelovici, Doufour and Nez, 2016).

Random selection could thus act as both a weapon in the hands of social movements and as an instrument to radicalize the deliberative system. Deliberative countervailing powers do not necessarily have to emerge from a process of random selection. Their autonomy requires that actors organize themselves and freely determine the forms that participation must take (Cossart and Talpin, 2015; Talpin, 2016a). Nevertheless, random selection can play an important role. First, even though this possibility has received little attention to date, social movements and countervailing powers may use random selection to expand their social base and recruit new members, in a more or less sustainable manner. Much like the scheme initially envisioned by Marie-Hélène Bacqué and Mohamed Mechmache (2013) for *Tables de quartier* (Neighbourhood Tables) in France, one can imagine that such pluralistic countervailing powers might rely on random selection[8] — especially as this would allow them to address a criticism often levelled in an attempt to delegitimize them, namely, their lack of representativeness. Once established, these spaces could then promote the emergence of new voices and perspectives in the deliberative system, thus contributing to its epistemic dimension. Moreover, the random selection of delegates within these spaces could help counter the 'iron law of oligarchy' (Michels, 1910) and the perpetual dominance of a

---

[8] This raises other difficulties, however, insofar as there is evidence that the emancipation of subordinate groups may require the creation of hidden spaces for the latter to develop their discourses and interests (Scott, 1990; Talpin, 2017). This may provoke tension with the inclusive, pluralistic, and heterogeneous logic of random selection.

representative caste. As many contemporary social movements reject representation and the designation of spokespersons, random selection can be an effective means of expressing their horizontal aspirations and facilitating the rotation of leader positions. While the experience of *Nuit Debout* in France was weakened by the avant-garde tendencies of some of its leaders (Guichoux, 2016), random selection might have helped to reconcile the rejection of delegation with the need for organization. Social movements in Spain and Greece have occasionally used such mechanisms in recent years. Finally, various relationships between countervailing powers and institutionalized deliberation spaces wherein members are randomly selected could be envisioned. It is indeed surprising that, to date, deliberative theorists have shown little interest in mechanisms such as the random selection of representatives (however, see Parkinson, 2012). This omission merely reflects the overly conciliatory conception of collective decision-making and social regulation that underlies many of these theories, which have therefore overlooked the role of social movements in the deliberative system (Cervera-Marzal and Dubigeon, 2013). Conversely, and following some lines of thought opened by others (Fraser, 1992; Fung, 2011), it seems that a truly deliberative democracy cannot do without structured countervailing powers to fight against the plebiscitary and authoritarian tendencies of contemporary societies; within such countervailing powers, random selection can once again become politically radical.

References

Ancelovici, M., Dufour, P. & Nez, H. (eds.) (2016) *Street Politics in the Age of Austerity: From the Indignados to Occupy*, Amsterdam: Amsterdam University Press.

Bacqué, M.-H. & Mechmache, M. (2013) Pour une réforme radicale de la politique de la ville. Ça ne se fera plus sans nous. Citoyenneté et pouvoir d'agir dans les quartiers populaires, *Report to the Deputy Minister for Urban Affairs*, July 2013.

Barber, B. (1984) *Démocratie forte*, Paris: Desclée de Bouwer.

Barbier, R., Bedu, C. & Buclet, N. (2009) Portée et limites du dispositif 'jury citoyen', *Politix*, 2, pp. 189–207.

Bartels, L. (2009) *Unequal Democracy: The Political Economy of the New Gilded Age*, Princeton, NJ: Princeton University Press.

Blondiaux, L. (1996) Mort et résurrection de l'électeur rationnel. Les métamorphoses d'une problématique incertaine, *Revue française de science politique*, 46 (5), pp. 753–791.

Blondiaux, L. (2002) Sondage et délibération, *Politix*, 57, pp. 167–180.

Blondiaux, L (2008) *Le nouvel esprit de la démocratie. Actualité de la démocratie participative*, Paris: Seuil.

Bourdieu, P. (1979) *La distinction, critique sociale du jugement*, Paris: Minuit.

Bourdieu, P. (2000) *Pascalian Meditations*, Stanford, CA: Sanford University Press [1997].

Böker, M. & Elstub, S. (2015) The possibility of critical mini-publics: Realpolitik and normative cycles in democratic theory, *Representation*, 51 (1), pp. 125–144.

Brown, W. (2015) *Undoing the Demos: Neoliberalism's Stealth Revolution*, Boston, MA: MIT Press.

Cervera-Marzal, M & Dubigeon, Y. (2013) Démocratie radicale et tirage au sort, *Raisons politiques*, 2, pp. 157–176.

Chambers, S. (2009) Rhetoric and the public sphere: Has deliberative democracy abandoned mass democracy?, *Political Theory*, 37 (3), pp. 323–350.

Cohen, J. (1989) Deliberation and democratic legitimacy, in Hamlin, A. & Pettit, P. (eds.) *The Good Polity*, Oxford: Basil Blackwell.

Converse, P. (1964) The nature of belief systems in mass publics, in Apter, D. (ed.) *Ideology and Discontent*, New York: The Free Press.

Cossart, P. & Talpin, J. (2015) *Lutte urbaine. Participation et démocratie d'interpellation à l'Alma-Gare*, Vulaines-sur-Seine: Le Croquant.

Cossart, P., Felicetti, A. & Kloppenberg, J. (2016) Introduction. Les town meetings, mythe fondateur de la démocratie américaine, *Participations*, 2, pp. 5–47.

Crouch, C. (2004) *Post-Democracy*, Cambridge: Polity.

Curato, N. & Böker, M. (2016) Linking mini-publics to the deliberative system: A research agenda, *Policy Sciences*, 49 (2), pp. 173–190.

Dahl, R. (1989) *Democracy and its Critics*, New Haven, CT: Yale University Press.

Della Porta, D. (ed.) (2009) *Democracy in Social Movements*, Basingstoke: Palgrave Macmillan.

Elster, J. (1987) The market and the forum, in Bohman, J. & Rehg, W. (eds.) *Deliberative Democracy: Essays on Reason and Politics*, Cambridge, MA: MIT Press.

Elster, J. (1989) *Solomonic Judgements: Studies in the Limitation of Rationality*, Cambridge: Cambridge University Press.

Elster, J. (ed.) (1998) *Deliberative Democracy*, Cambridge: Cambridge University Press.

Elstub, S. (2014) Mini-publics: Issues and cases, in Elstub, S. & McLaverty, P. (eds.) *Deliberative Democracy: Issues and Cases*, pp. 166–197, Edinburgh: Edinburgh University Press.

Estlund, D. (2008) *Democratic Authority: A Philosophical Framework*, Princeton, NJ: Princeton University Press.

Finlay, M.I. (1976) *Democracy Ancient and Modern*, New Brunswick, NJ: Rutgers University Press.

Fishkin, J. (1991) *Democracy and Deliberation: New Directions for Democratic Reform*, New Haven, CT: Yale University Press.

Fishkin, J. (1995) *The Voice of the People*, New Haven, CT: Yale University Press.

Fishkin, J. (2009) *When the People Speak: Deliberative Democracy and Public Consultation*, Oxford: Oxford University Press.

Flamand, A. (2011) La fabrique d'un public régional. Observation participante du premier jury citoyen en Poitou-Charentes, in Sintomer, Y. & Talpin, J. (eds.) *La démocratie participative au-delà de la proximité: le Poitou-Charentes et l'échelle régionale*, Rennes: Presses Universitaires de Rennes.

Font, J., Pasadas del Amo, S. & Smith, G. (2016) Tracing the impact of proposals from participatory processes: Methodological challenges and substantive lessons, *Journal of Public Deliberation*, 12 (1).

Fraser, N. (1992) Rethinking the public sphere: A contribution to the critique of actually existing democracy, in Calhoun, C. (ed.) *Habermas and the Public Sphere*, Cambridge, MA: MIT Press.

Freschi, A.C. & Mete, V. (2009) The political meanings of institutional deliberative experiments: Findings on the Italian case, *Sociologica*, 3 (2–3).

Funes, M., Talpin, J. & Rull, M. (2014) The cultural consequences of engagement in participatory processes, in Font. J., Della Porta, D. & Sintomer, Y. (eds.) *Participatory Democracy in Southern Europe: Causes, Characteristics and Consequences*, pp. 151–189, London: Rowman & Littlefield.

Fung, A. (2003) Survey article: Recipes for public spheres: Eight institutional design choices and their consequences, *Journal of Political Philosophy*, 11 (3), pp. 338–367.

Fung, A. (2007) Minipublics: Deliberative designs and their consequences', in Rosenberg, S. (ed.) *Deliberation, Participation and Democracy: Can the People Govern?*, pp. 159–183, London: Palgrave Macmillan.

Fung, A. (2011 [2005]) Délibérer avant la révolution, *Participations*, 1, pp. 311–334.

Fung, A. & Wright, E.O. (2003) Countervailing power in empowered participatory governance, in Fung, A. & Wright, E.O. (eds.) *Deepening Democracy, Institutional Innovations in Empowered Participatory Governance*, pp. 259–289, London: Verso.

Gastil, J. & Dillard, J. (1999) Increasing political sophistication through public deliberation, *Political Communication*, 16, pp. 3–23.

Gastil, J., Bacci, C. & Dollinger, M. (2010) Is deliberation neutral? Patterns of attitude change during the deliberative polls, *Journal of Public Deliberation*, 6 (2), art. 3.

Gastil, J. & Richards, R. (2013) Making direct democracy deliberative through random assemblies, *Politics & Society*, 41 (2), pp. 251–283.

Gaxie, D. (1978) *Le cens caché. Inégalités culturelles et ségrégation politique*, Paris: Seuil.

Hansen, K. & Andersen, V. (2004) Deliberative democracy and the deliberative poll on the Euro, *Scandinavian Political Studies*, 27 (3), pp. 261–286.

Grönlund, K., Setälä, M. & Herne, K. (2010) Deliberation and civic virtue: Lessons from a citizen deliberation experiment, *European Political Science Review*, 2 (01), pp. 95–117.

Girard, C. (2010) *L'idéal délibératif à l'épreuve des démocraties représentatives de masse: autonomie, bien commun et légitimité dans les théories contemporaines de la démocratie*, PhD dissertation in Philosophy, Université Paris 1.

Girard, C. (2011) L'usage des références aux cités grecques dans les théories contemporaines de la délibération, in Werlings, M.-J. & Schulz, F. (eds.) *Débats antiques*, pp. 141–153, Paris: Maison d'Archéologie et d'Ethnologie René-Ginouvès.

Goodwin, B. (2011) Utiliser le hasard contre la confiscation du pouvoir, *Esprit*, 8, pp. 145–152.

Gourgues, G. (2012) Des dispositifs participatifs aux politiques de la participation. L'exemple des conseils régionaux français, *Participations*, 1, pp. 30–52.

Guichoux, A. (2016) Nuit debout et les 'mouvements des places' désenchantement et ensauvagement de la démocratie, *Les Temps Modernes*, 5, pp. 30–60.

Habermas, J. (1981) *Théorie de l'agir communicationnel*, 2 vols., Paris: Fayard.

Hayat, S. (2011) Démocratie participative et impératif délibératif: enjeux d'une confrontation, in Bacqué, M.-H. & Sintomer, Y. (eds.) *La démocratie participative. Histoire et généalogie*, Paris: La Découverte.

Jacquet, V. (2017) *Délibérer ou ne pas délibérer? La (non-)participation dans les dispositifs délibératifs tirés au sort*, PhD dissertation in Science, Université de Louvain-La-Neuve.

Lafont, C. (2015) Deliberation, participation, and democratic legitimacy: Should deliberative mini-publics shape public policy?, *Journal of Political Philosophy*, 23 (1), pp. 40–63.

Lang, A. (2007) But is it for real? The British Columbia Citizens' Assembly as a model of state-sponsored citizen empowerment, *Politics & Society*, 35 (1), pp. 35–69.

Lee, C. (2014) *Do it Yourself Democracy: The Rise of the Public Engagement Industry*, Oxford: Oxford University Press.

Lee, C. & Romano, Z. (2013) Democracy's new discipline: Public deliberation as organizational strategy, *Organization Studies*, 34 (5–6), pp. 733–753.

Lefebvre, R. & Roger, A. (2009) *Les partis politiques à l'épreuve des procédures délibératives*, Rennes: Presses Universitaires de Rennes.

Lessig, L. (2012) *Republic Lost: How Money Corrupts Congress. And a Plan to Stop it*, New York: Twelve.

Levine, P. (2014) Beyond deliberation: A strategy for civic renewal, *Journal of Public Deliberation*, 10 (1).

Luskin, R.C., Fishkin, J.S. & Jowell, R. (2002) Considered opinions: Deliberative polling in Britain, *British Journal of Political Science*, 32, pp. 455–487.

Manin, B. (1985) Volonté générale ou délibération? Esquisse d'une théorie générale de la délibération politique, *Le débat*, 33.

Mansbridge, J. (1999a) On the idea that participation makes better citizens, in Elkin, S. & Soltan, K. (eds.) *Citizen Competence and Democratic Institutions*, Philadelphia, PA: Pennsylvania University Press.

Mansbridge, J. (1999b) Everyday talk in the deliberative system, in Macedo, S. (ed.) *Deliberative Politics: Essays on Democracy and Disagreement*, Oxford: Oxford University Press.

Mansbridge, J. (2010) Deliberative polling as the gold standard, *The Good Society*, 19 (1), pp. 55–62.

Mansbridge, J., Bohman, J., Chambers, S., Estlund, D., Føllesdal, A., Fung, A. & Luismarti, J. (2011) The place of self-interest and the role of power in deliberative democracy, *Journal of Political Philosophy*, 18 (1), pp. 64–100.

March, J. & Olsen, J.P. (1984) The new institutionalism: Organizational factors in political life, *American Political Science Review*, 78, pp. 734–774.

Mazeaud, A. & Nonjon, M. (2015) De la cause au marché de la démocratie participative, *Agone*, 1, pp. 135–152.

Mazeaud, A. & Nonjon, M. (2018) *Le Marché de la démocratie participative*, Vulaines-sur-Seine: Le Croquant.

Merkle, D.M. (1996) The polls — review: The national issues convention deliberative poll, *Public Opinion Quarterly*, 60, pp. 588–619.

Michels, R. (1910) *Les partis politiques. Essai sur les tendances oligarchiques de la démocratie*, Paris: Payot.

Niemeyer, S. (2011) The emancipatory effect of deliberation: Empirical lessons from mini-publics, *Politics & Society*, 39 (1), pp. 103–140.

Papadopoulos, Y. & Warin, P. (2007) Are innovative, participatory and deliberative procedures in policy making democratic and effective?, *European Journal of Political Research*, 46 (4), pp. 445–472.

Parkinson, J. & Mansbridge, J. (eds.) (2012) *Deliberative Systems: Deliberative Democracy at the Large Scale*, Cambridge: Cambridge University Press.

Parkinson, J. (2006) Rickety bridges: Using the media in deliberative democracy, *British Journal of Political Science*, 36 (1), pp. 175–183.

Parkinson, J. (2012) Democratizing deliberative systems, in Parkinson, J. & Mansbridge, J. (eds.) *Deliberative Systems: Deliberative Democracy at the Large Scale*, pp. 153–171, Cambridge: Cambridge University Press.

Pateman, C. (2012) Participatory democracy revisited, *Perspectives on Politics*, 10 (1), pp. 7–19.

Pourtois, H. (2013) Mini-publics et démocratie délibérative, *Politique et sociétés*, 32 (1), pp. 21–41.

Powell, W. & DiMaggio, P. (1991) *The New Institutionalism in Organizational Analysis*, Cambridge: Cambridge University Press.

Rancière, J. (2005) *La haine de la démocratie*, Paris: La Fabrique.

Reuchamps, M. & Suiter, J. (eds.) (2016) *Constitutional Deliberative Democracy in Europe*, Colechester: ECPR Press.

Scott, J.C. (1990) *Domination and the Arts of Resistance: Hidden Transcripts*, New Haven, CT: Yale University Press.

Sintomer, Y. (2007) *Le pouvoir au peuple. Tirage au sort, jurys citoyens et démocratie participative*, Paris: La Découverte.

Sintomer, Y. (2010) Random selection, republican self-government, and deliberative democracy, *Constellations*, 17 (3), pp. 472–487.

Sintomer, Y. & Talpin, J. (eds.) (2011) *La démocratie participative au-delà de la proximité: Le Poitou-Charentes et l'échelle régionale*, Rennes: Presses Universitaires de Rennes.

Sintomer, Y. (2019) *Between Radical and Deliberative Democracy: Random Selection in Politics from Athens to Contemporary Experiments*, Cambridge: Cambridge University Press (forthcoming).

Stone, P. (2009) The logic of random selection, *Political Theory*, 37 (3), pp. 375–397.

Suiter, J, Farrell, D. & Harris, C. (2016) The Irish constitutional convention: A case of high legitimacy?, in Reuchamps, M. & Suiter, J. (eds.) *Constitutional Deliberative Democracy in Europe*, Colechester: ECPR Press.

Talpin, J. (2016a) *Community Organizing. De l'émeute à l'alliance des classes populaires aux États-Unis*, Paris: Raisons d'agir.

Talpin, J. (2016b) How can constitutional reforms be deliberative? The hybrid legitimacies of constitutional deliberative democracy, in Reuchamps, M. & Suiter, J. (eds.) *Constitutional Deliberative Democracy in Europe*, Colechester: ECPR Press.

Talpin, J. (2017) Emancipation et participation, Conference, *GIS Participation et démocratie*, Paris, 29 January 2017.

Warren, M. & Pearse, H. (eds.) (2008) *Designing Deliberative Democracy: The British Columbia Citizen Assembly*, Cambridge: Cambridge University Press.

Zaller, J. (1992) *The Nature and Origins of Mass Opinions*, Cambridge: Cambridge University Press.

Afterwords

Yves Sintomer

A Child Drawing Lots
The 'Pathos Formula' of Political Sortition?

Translated by Sarah-Louise Raillard

The drawing of lots is not imbued with an essential, trans-historical meaning that exists independently of the different contexts in which actors have wielded, justified, or criticized this instrument.[1] The same can be said of the various other procedures of selection and decision-making, in particular election (in the modern sense of the word) and majority voting. When Aristotle wrote that 'it is thought to be democratic for the offices to be assigned by lot, for them to be elected oligarchic' (Aristotle, 1944, IV, 9, 1294-b), he was accurately summarizing two centuries of radical Athenian democracy. He nevertheless nuanced this stark dichotomy by arguing that these procedures only gained political meaning depending on how they were used, and especially on the context within which selection by lot took place (Buchstein, 2015). In addition, Aristotle's assertion would have been meaningless in Republican or Imperial Rome, in China during the Ming and Qing dynasties, or even when applied to the election of the Venetian doges. A historical sociology of selection by lot in politics can, on the other hand, elaborate a number of ideal types that, thanks to a Weberian approach, allow us to reconstitute the abstract logical reasoning behind different uses of sortition and thus establish trans-historical comparisons. Naturally, analysis of such concrete cases will still require the combination of several ideal types: although the latter cannot exhaustively account for the wide diversity found in reality, they can provide cardinal points for reference. Using this approach, I thus distinguished five ideal types of logic mobilized when using selection by lot in politics in a previous work (Sintomer, 2020).

---

[1] A first version of this chapter was published with the same title in *Publications en série de la bibliothèque Am Guisanplatz*, Bern, 2018, pp. 222–253.

However, such an approach does not answer all of our questions, especially since it seems necessary to combine genealogical investigation with formal inquiry. Is it possible to identify some formal similarity between the various uses of random sortition in politics, which would help to better understand this practice? Historical research has shown that the instruments and rituals of sortition greatly differ from one case to the other. Is it, however, possible to find something in common when one looks at its iconography? Political theory is not frequently inclined to study images, but it can methodologically learn from the field of cultural studies and the history of representations. Selection by lot in politics deserves a treatment similar to that provided by Marc Bloch (2015) in *The Royal Touch* on the issue of the healing powers of monarchs, by Carlo Ginzburg (1991) in *Ecstasies* on witchcraft, and by Aby Warburg (1999) in *The Renewal of Pagan Antiquity*: on the issue of the survival of artistic forms from one civilization to another.

For these authors, the combination of two approaches corresponds to a methodological imperative: chronological reconstruction makes it possible to trace transfers and establish historical genealogies; morphological investigation can bring out formal similarities in contexts for which there is no *a priori* evidence of chronological lineage, if only because of the insufficiency of the sources. These two methods may be pursued independently, but they may also be combined: a morphological connection may, for example, lead researchers to look for transfers where they initially seemed unlikely. Beyond methodological considerations, these trailblazing historians sought to elaborate more complex, multi-layered explanations. Thus, Marc Bloch based himself on comparative anthropology to identify a mental predisposition to accept or promote the idea of a royal healing power. At the same time, he argued that the 'crystallization' of such beliefs in a specific practice — for example, the 'royal miracle-workers' in France and England who reputedly healed scrofula by their touch — is a contingent event whose emergence and evolution need to be identified and described (Bloch, 2015). Carlo Ginzburg, for his part, conducted a vast survey of shamanism in Eurasia, showing that the formal similarity of practices that seemed otherwise quite dissimilar pointed to the existence of a common cultural substratum. Without that substratum, and without the 'slow sedimentation' that it permitted in popular cultures and practices, the appearance of the witches' Sabbath in the Western Alps in the second half of the 14th century would not have been possible. At the same time, however, minutely detailed historical investigation was necessary to unravel why the image of the Sabbath emerged precisely at that time and place, and how it evolved and eventually died out in subsequent centuries (Ginzburg 1991). Similarly, Aby Warburg argued that the survival of certain practices, such as that of divination between Babylon and Rome, is explicable both by 'direct links' (that is, transfers through Etruria) and by almost innate 'primal needs' without which we would be unable to understand the persistence of the link for two thousand years (Warburg, 1999). Consequently, Warburg elaborated a conceptual tool that he called the *Pathosformel,* translated as the 'pathos formula'. This tool allowed him to combine two otherwise competing components: 'pathos' is a heightened physical reaction produced by an onslaught of emotions, but it flows into the stable 'formula', which can control emotions up to a certain point. Ethnographic observation of the serpent ritual among indigenous Pueblos in Mexico allowed Warburg to bring to light a ritual and artistic form that expressed fear in Ancient Greek statuary as well as in Renaissance art. And yet, while genealogical links could be found between the Ancient World and 15th-century Europe, the same could not be said of the Mexican Pueblos (cf. illustrations 1–3).

Illustrations 1–3. The serpentine form, a pathos formula according to Aby Warburg: *Serpent Ritual* (Aby Warburg with a Pueblo Indian, 1924, Washington, Library of Congress. Source: Warburg, 1979, p. 323, ill. 1.); *Laocoön and His Sons*

(Agesander, Athenodoros and Polydorus from Rhodes, 2nd or 1st century BC, Vatican Museum); *Battle of the Naked Men* (Antonio del Pollaiuolo, circa 1470, Washington, National Gallery—this is the first engraving signed by an old master).

The pathos formula is constantly updated by new combinations and is thus differentiated from the more fixed concepts of the *topos* or canon (Bredekamp, 2015, pp. 272 *sq.*). Because of this flexibility, it could be a well suited methodological tool when looking for a potential formal similarity between the various uses of random selection in politics. In addition, a pathos formula is not merely formal: it implies a tension between an artistic form and an emotional substance. Passing from the artistic field to the political one, could a potential pathos formula of sortition reveal something substantial to us about the practices relying on political sortition? Drawing on this method and seeing what a morphological approach can bring to the table, we shall especially examine whether it is possible to better account for the 'survival' of selection by lot in politics as it successively appeared, disappeared, and resurfaced throughout the ages.[2]

We must therefore find an equivalent to the formal homologies studied by Marc Bloch, Carlo Ginzburg, and Aby Warburg in relation to the royal touch for scrofula, the nocturnal travels of men and women with certain physical characteristics to take part in strange festivals, and the use of serpentine shapes to express the emotions felt during a serpent ritual (illustration 1) or combat (illustrations 2 and 3). At first glance, however, it does not seem easy to identify a pathos formula of sortition in politics amidst the abundant literature and iconography, as sortition was employed using a number of different techniques. The young boy drawing lots is, however, a figure that demands thorough investigation. We shall devote this chapter to the subject. First, we shall look at the various appearances made by the figure of the young boy drawing lots in the political realm, in order to determine if this figure can be assimilated with a pathos formula. Secondly, we shall broaden our scope to include non-political practices, attempting to identify the various borrowings and overlaps between the different situations in which the figure of the child drawing lots appears. In conclusion, we will try to understand whether this figure can teach us something about the role of sortition in politics.

---

2   I am grateful to Muriel Pic for initially having pointed me in this direction for my research.

Is the Child Drawing Lots a Pathos Formula?

The election of the doges in Venice offers a prime example of this procedure, which may echo the role of the serpent ritual for Warburg. The procedure was described many times throughout history and was already famous by the late Middle Ages. The canonical narrative of this procedure can be found below.

The Venetian ballottino

Venetian law stipulated that, when the office of the doge fell vacant, the Grand Council should meet in solemn session. The youngest councillor left the hall where it was gathered and came back with the first child aged between eight and ten years old that he had met in the street. A large bag was placed in the middle of the hall containing as many little wooden balls (or ballots, from the original Italian *ballotte*) as there were councillors. The word 'elector' was stamped on thirty of these. The *ballottino*, the boy chosen in the street, took the balls and gave one to each of the councillors as they processed in silence before the urn. The thirty who received a ball marked with the word 'elector' on it remained in the hall, while the others immediately left. The councillors who stayed were not allowed to belong to the same family or have blood ties with one another: if they did, they had to give up their role and be replaced through the same mechanism by another councillor.

The same system was next used to reduce the 30 remaining councillors to 9, and, in a third phase, the latter elected 40 individuals from the Grand Council by a qualified majority vote. In the fourth phase, those 40 electors were reduced by sortition to 12; in the fifth, these 12 elected 25 from the councillors; in the sixth, those 25 were reduced by lot to 9; these 9 then elected 45 councillors, who were reduced by lot in the seventh phase to 11. In the eighth phase, these 11 individuals elected (again by a qualified majority vote) the 41 councillors who, in a ninth and final phase, formed a conclave and elected the doge by a qualified majority of 25 votes (Sintomer, 2020; Judde de Larivière, 2020). The *ballottino* was present at every step of the process, since he was in charge of extracting the wooden balls every time chance played a part (cf. illustration 4).

Illustration 4. Ballottino, Venice, by Jan van Grevenbroeck (or Giovanni Grevembroch) (1731–1807), 'Gli Abiti dei Veneziani', engraving from an illustrated book (copyright GettyImages).

The use of the *ballottino* was not limited to the election of the doge: it was also called upon for the ritual of the *Ball d'Oro* (or Barbarella), which marked the political debut of certain young nobles (Chojnacki, 2000, quoted by Judde de Larivière, 2020, p. 228). First mentioned in 1319, this ceremony allowed a limited number of young nobles to enter the Great Council before the statutory age of 25. The lottery took place each year on the 4th of December, the day of Saint Barbara. 'The patricians who wished to take part had to register their legitimate sons under the age of 18. The name of each candidate was written down on a piece of paper, and then placed in an urn (*capello*). Another urn contained a number of balls that was equivalent to the number of candidates; one-fifth of the balls were covered in gold. The doge selected a name at the same time as a young boy (*ballottino*) extracted a ball: if the latter was golden, the candidate was guaranteed an early entrance to the Council' (Judde de Larivière, 2020, p. 229).

Established during the 13th century, this procedure for selecting the doge would last until the end of the Republic of Venice in 1797. Elsewhere during this time, moreover, numerous examples of the use of an 'innocent' child to operate random selection procedures could be observed in a wide variety of contexts. Without establishing an exhaustive inventory of such practices, we shall present several examples below.

Insaculación *in the kingdoms of Aragon and Castile*

As early as the 14th century, the use of random selection for public offices, generally combined with election or co-option, began to develop throughout the various communes of the Crown of Aragon; the practice would become widespread by the following century and would last until the beginning of the 18th century (Sintomer, 2020). The specific method used was called *insaculación*[3] and frequently involved the presence of a child, as seen in the case of the Aragonese city of Huesca. *Insaculación* occurred in a multi-stage fashion. Representatives from different neighbourhoods formed a sort of general assembly. Volunteers' names were written on pieces of parchment and then rolled in wax to form little balls called *redolinos* (bearing some semblance to the Venetian *ballotte*). When the *redolinos* were placed into purses, the candidates' names were read out loud. When it came time to randomly select candidates, the purses were emptied into a basin of water. 'Extraction was then conducted by a seven-year-old child who inserted his bare right arm into a bowl of water, covered by a towel. Once extracted, the *redolino* was placed on a shelf where all participants could see it' (Gracia, 2006, p. 311). The individuals selected were called the 'electors' and formed an electoral committee responsible for choosing those who would hold public office. In other communes, the procedure allowed for the direct appointment of magistrates using a list of pre-selected names.

Starting in 1446, sortition also became part of the process used to appoint representatives to the *Cortes*, or parliament, of the Kingdom of Aragon. The ceremony was even more complex than at the afore-mentioned municipal level. It began with a 'Mass of the Holy Spirit' in the chapel of the *Cortes*. A notary was then responsible for taking the chest where the ten purses were stored out of the archives. The chest's five locks were opened simultaneously by a representative from each of the Crown's four representative groups and by the notary himself, who held the fifth key. The *redolinos* contained in the first purse were then emptied into a silver basin and a child extracted one, following the method already described for the city of Huesca. The notary read the name selected out loud before resealing the wax ball. The child was then tasked with re-counting the number of balls and making sure that this figure corresponded to the number on the list (the *libro de matrícula*). The notary then put all of the *redolinos* back into the purse, and the purse back into the chest. This operation was repeated for each of the purses. The ceremony's purity was highlighted by its use of religious ritualism, including the presence of the child and the symbol-ism of the clear — almost holy — water and silver basin. The process was

---

3   Or *insaculació* in Catalan.

also public and documented by the notary (Sesma, 1978, pp. 49 *sq.* and 503 *sq.*).

Selection by lot was likewise adopted in the Kingdom of Castile during the same period of time. During the Revolt of the Comuneros (1520–21), which saw many of the Kingdom's cities rebel against the rule of Charles V, sortition was used, with a number of sources more-over attesting to the involvement of a young boy. In addition, starting in the 16th century, some communes introduced the use of selection by lot to designate their communal representatives (the *procuradores*) to the *Cortes*. The method used for sortition was a somewhat simplified version of the Aragonese procedure. In Cordoba on 9th December 1575, the 24 members of the commune's executive branch thus met to select the two *procuradores* from their midst. They each wrote their name on a piece of paper, which they then placed into a kind of silver nugget that ultimately went into a clay vase. The vase was emptied a first time: the nuggets were counted out to make sure they numbered 24, and then placed back into the vase. A young boy of eight or nine years old named Salvador shook the vase and extracted the two nuggets that would select the two *procuradores*. The procedure had the merit of appeasing competition between the leading families and was pre-served, at least partially, until the middle of the 17th century (Weller, 2010, pp. 117–138).

Swiss practices

In Switzerland, although sortition appeared at a somewhat later date, it was also preserved until the first third of the 19th century. In 1640, the evangelical *Landesgemeinde* (general citizen assembly) in Glaris decided to put an end to corruption and intrigue by ruling that, for each public office, eight citizens would be nominated, from which a random selection would be then conducted publicly. The ceremony combined a number of elements that had already been used elsewhere: 'The eight elected individuals presented themselves in the *Ring*, and a child distri-buted eight balls wrapped in black cloth to them, seven of which were silver and one of which was gold. The individual who received the gold ball was elected' (Rambert, 1889, p. 226). The selection was then progressively operated among all citizens. The use of sortition was only abolished in 1837 (*ibid.*, pp. 225–228 and 276–277).

During the election of some important public offices in November 1691, the first time that sortition was used in the Republic of Geneva, a fairly similar formula was used:

> So that all the people can see, six balls or boxes of the same size and outer colour are placed in front of trustees; two of these balls are black

on the inside. A young child of six or seven years old — in this case, little Léonard, the son of the public prosecutor Jean-Pierre Trembley — draws each ball out of the purse, one by one, and distributes them to the six nominees according to their rank. Each nominee opens his box: the first and the fourth are black inside, and Jacob de la Rive and Jean Sales are thus excluded from the nomination. At the end of the voting between the four candidates remaining, André Dunant and Pierre Lect were finally elected as auditors. (RC 191, 10/31/1691, 11/01/1691, pp. 316-320, see Barat, 2020, pp. 260-261)

This ritual would have a very long lifespan, giving rise to many variations along the way. Under the Helvetic Republic created following the French invasion, sortition was thus used to select the grand electors responsible for electing deputies and judges. Each village of at least one hundred inhabitants held a primary assembly to appoint an elector for every hundred inhabitants. The names of those elected were then sent to the national prefect who, with the help of the president from each competent local authority, proceeded to publicly exclude half of the elected names through random selection. The procedure was governed by a number of very strict rules:

> The municipality of the capital city shall make arrangements before-hand so that two intelligent children shall enter the room, neither of which shall be older than six years of age. These children shall open the ballots. One shall be placed in front of the national prefect and the other in front of the president of the administrative chamber. After drawing the ballots on which the names are written down, one after another from one of the purses, the first child shall hand over the ballots drawn to the president of the cantonal court, who shall open them and read them aloud. The secretaries shall then write down each name on a register, which shall again be read out loud immediately after being written down. The other child, drawing the ballots designating whether the electors shall remain or be eliminated, shall immediately after hearing the name read by the first child, likewise draw a ballot from the second purse, and hand it over still closed to the president of the cantonal court, who shall immediately open it and read it aloud. (*Handbook of Resolutions of the Great Grand Council*, session dated 31 August 1799, 16-20, quoted in Mellina, 2020, p. 286)

Ballotines in England

In England, selection by lot was used in several cities at the local level. In Great Yarmouth, a procedure rather similar to that used in Venice, Aragon, and Switzerland and called the 'inquest' was implemented; it remained in effect from 1491 to 1835. Here again the figure of a young child played a role: during an open assembly, the names of the magistrates in office were put into hats, six names to a hat. Three names were then drawn from each hat by an 'innocent person', usually a young boy, and the persons thus selected formed an electoral commission. These individuals would meet in a closed room, without the right to eat, drink, light a fire or candles, or communicate with the outside world. As a group, they had to elect the new magistrates, each one requiring a qualified majority of nine votes (Palmer, 1856, quoted by Dowlen, 2008, p. 139).

The young boy drawing lots could claim an illustrious pedigree, with James Harrington as one of the authors contributing the most to disseminating republican ideas across the English-speaking world, citing in particular the example of Venice. Circa 1600, Harrington published a short pamphlet titled *The Manner and Use of the Ballot*, which was reprinted in several editions and also incorporated into the main editions of Harrington's magnum opus, *Oceana* (Harrington, 1977, pp. 361–368).[4] Harrington advocated for a mixed designation system (which he called 'ballot') that combined the Venetian election model ('suffrage') with sortition ('lot'), according to a highly codified procedure involving 'ballotines'. The latter's role was not, however, to extract balls or slips of paper, but rather to handle the boxes in which councillors placed their ballots and to empty those boxes into basins lined up for that purpose (cf. illustration 5). It is remarkable that the pathos formula of the child drawing lots could thus be combined with an entirely different voting method. It must be noted, however, that the engraving cited was clearly based on two others (cf. illustrations 6–7), drawn from a highly successful work describing and analysing the Venetian system that had been published by the republican intellectual Donato Giannotti a century earlier, around 1540 (Riklin, 1999). Similar illustrations can be found in numerous works on Venice: the role of the *ballottini* was in fact to draw lots but also, more generally speaking, to collect votes.[5] As we have seen above, the two procedures were linked rather than opposed in Venetian practice. Until 1492 (Mueller, 2013), the year when special urns were introduced, composed of two or three vertical tubes and one horizontal tube into which individuals had to insert their arm before dropping their ball into the vertical tube of their choice (for, against, abstaining—the procedure thus ensured that the selection remained secret), the same instruments were generally used for both voting and selecting by lot. It is thus largely unsurprising that Harrington, an ardent admirer of the Venetian system, followed this tradition.

---

4   I would like to thank Raphaël Barat for drawing my attention to this point.
5   I would like to thank Claire Judde de Larivière for her insight on this point.

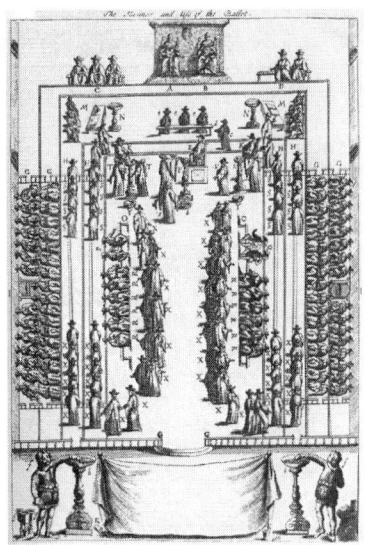

Illustration 6. James Harrington, *The Manner and Use of the Ballot* (1660), in Harrington (1977, p. 361).

Illustrations 7–8. Donato Giannotti, *Dialogi de repub. Venetorum* (1642).

The American colonies

A number of other examples can also be found on the other side of the Atlantic. In 1731, South Carolina adopted a law confirming the 'old practices' and imposing random jury selection. The method was considered to be 'fair, neutral and impartial', a guarantee of the smooth operation of justice. Harking back to Venetian traditions, it was once again a young boy (under 10 years old) who was tasked with randomly selecting the names of the future jury members, before these were announced alongside trumpet fanfare in the streets of Charleston (Trott, 1736, pp. 503–506, quoted by Dowlen, 2008, p. 176).

In 1809, during the uprising against the French occupation of Spain, the colonial territory of New Spain (now Mexico) was invited to send delegates to the capital's Supreme Central Junta. They embarked on this procedure by combining election and selection by lot, the latter being called upon to avoid the 'spirit of partisanship that tended to dominate in such cases' and to 'ensure the intervention of Providence in matters of human choice, as the ultimate guarantee of the social order' (Guerra, 2000, p. 192). The fourteen or fifteen provinces of New Spain each selected a representative. Three of those were then elected by the Viceroy and the Supreme Court (the *Real Audiencia*) to form part of a limited list. Once this list was complete, the names on it were written down on slips of paper and dropped into an urn. A young boy named Florencio Ruiz proceeded to extract one of these slips. The paper selected had the name Miguel de Lardizábal written on it: the latter thus became the Mexican representative to the Supreme Central Junta (Ávila, 1999, p. 85, quoted by Serafín Castro, 2019). After gaining its independence, the Mexican Empire subsequently continued to widely use selection by lot until the 19th century: the procedure functioned as a tie-breaker when no candidate in an election managed to obtain an absolute majority. A small child also seems to have been frequently involved when this method was used (Serafín Castro, 2019).

Identifying the pathos formula

These examples (and a number of others: for example, the elections to the consulate of Aix-en-Provence from the end of the 16th century until the 18th century; see Martemyanova, 2020) undoubtedly present a kind of pathos formula, where a male child is responsible for drawing lots. Not yet having reached the age of puberty, the young boy operates in a highly ritualized context that involves a number of other ceremonial elements depending on the variation: a silver bowl, a golden ball, holy water, etc. As Claire Judde de Larivière (2020) observes with regard to the Venetian procedures, the ritual and public nature of selection by lot was essential: this statement can be applied to all of the procedures discussed herein. The 'pathos', to use Warburg's term in a somewhat metaphorical sense, stems from the fact that this formula is designed to elicit the public's voluntary compliance with a procedure conducted by an innocent being who benefits from the presumption of neutrality and impartiality. It is likely that in contexts where politics were closely interwoven with religion, such as in New Mexico, the child's actions could be perceived as an extension of the hand of God, but this interpretation was not widespread; it could not, at any rate, be explicitly supported, due to the fact that the Church had formally condemned divination.

Significant discrepancies can be observed between the formula and how it was implemented in reality, however (Muir, 1981, pp. 279 *sq.*). The *ballottini* needed to be monitored, as they were the best placed to falsify election results. In 1496, the chronicler Domenico Mailipiero (1843, p. 701) thus recounted the story of how a young store clerk who played the role of the *ballottino* boasted to his boss that he and a friend 'had done their duty' by putting all the balls allowing individuals to be elected in one corner of the urn. The young boy's employer immediately reported this misbehaviour to the doge, arguing that the boy's actions warranted hanging. The two young boys were arrested before the Council of the Ten met to deliberate. The patrician who had benefited from this manipulation, a certain Mr Bon, was arrested while at the helm of the armed galleys stationed on the Tuscan shores. According to the chronicler Sanudo (*Diarii* 1 col. 303), Bon was the inventor of the whole stratagem. While Bon denied the allegation, one of the *ballotini*, Hironimo Friso, replied by saying: 'You're the one who made me do it.' The consequences were severe for Bon, who was banished from Venice and forced to spend the rest of his life in Famagusta. The two boys were likewise banished and sent to Rethymno, on the island of Crete, while a number of other accomplices were also convicted.[6] Although these kinds of transgressions have no doubt occurred countless times throughout history, they only serve to highlight the ideal norm contained with the pathos formula of the young child drawing lots.

It is nonetheless evident that this pathos formula does not represent 'the' formula for random selection in politics. While children often play a role, they are not always part of the set-up. For example, children are

---

[6]   In this passage, I closely follow the observations made by Claire Judde de Larivière in a hitherto unpublished manuscript that she was kind enough to share with me.

not mentioned in Athenian and Roman uses of the procedure; they are far from being omnipresent in the Middle Ages or the Renaissance (in particular, no mention of children is made in Florence, where ad hoc magistrates called the *accoppiatori* were tasked with the extraction procedure), or in Imperial China. Similarly, the involvement of a young 'innocent' is quite rare in contemporary instances of sortition, a topic to which we shall return later. We can therefore conclude that while the pathos formula was somewhat widely disseminated, it was not a historical constant.

Connected Histories

However, the formal similarities that exist do require genealogical investigation to understand the transfers (Espagne and Werner, 1988; Fontaine and Chollet, 2018) and connections (Subrahmanyam, 2014) that can account for the massive dissemination of this pathos formula. There is little doubt that the Italian communes and Venice in particular were a source of inspiration for many other governments. The spread of Italian practices and methods was encouraged by networks of trade, learning, and politics, as well as by transnational reflections on the political and divine order that took place within Christian circles, starting with the Franciscans. Few sources address the question of such transfers, however, and archival research of this nature would require a level of teamwork that is outside of the scope of this chapter. At this stage in the inquiry, however, our genealogical investigation invites us to go outside the traditional bounds of politics — more specifically, of what we define as politics today — in order to see if the use of a child in political sortition was not at least in some cases an element transferred over from other spheres and practices.

Four kinds of practices

In the 21st century and in a country like France, we automatically believe that politics represents a relatively distinct sphere of action, separate most notably from religion and entertainment. But this has not always been the case. In medieval Europe, the important division between the secular use of chance and the use of divination only appeared gradually. It was not until the 13th century that Thomas Aquinas theorized the cleavage between *sors divisoria* and *sors divinatoria*. By adopting a slightly modified and expanded version of this division, we can thus distinguish several uses of random selection according to ideal types (Grottanelli, 2001). Random selection can be used to allocate goods or functions (*sors divisoria*); it can also be wielded as a tool for divination (*sors divinatoria*), whether revealing one's destiny or operating as an intermediary for divine will; finally, random selection is also the basis for games of chance. Historically, there were countless transfers across these three domains, with their boundaries being much less rigid than they are today. When used judiciously, however, this tripartite structure has significant methodological value, as it provides a number of cardinal points for our research while simultaneously pushing us towards greater clarity and systematization.

Using this interpretative framework and expanding our formal investigation of the use of children in random selection procedures outside the sole realm of politics has led to the identification of four major sets of practices: secular practices of popular divination (from the Egyptians and the Etruscans to the 21st century); the Christianization of these pagan traditions into the practice of 'biblical lots' (from the 4th to the 8th century AD), and in the election of the pope of the Coptic Church (until the 21st century); political sortition (essentially from the 13th century to the beginning of the 19th century); and finally, games of chance, in particular lotteries and the drawing of lots for the Twelfth Night cake (from the 15th to the 21st century). We have already examined the use of selection by lot in politics in the first half of this chapter; let us now turn to the remaining three sets of practices.

The child and sortition in secular practices of popular divination

Practices of *sors divinatoria* calling for the involvement of a child were at times widespread throughout the European, Mediterranean, and Middle-Eastern world. The historian of religion Cristiano Grottanelli (1993, 2001) conducted a masterful study of the subject, finding traces of such practices in archaic Greece as well as in Egyptian papyruses dating back to the first centuries AD. Tracing these roots down to their contemporary practices in certain villages today, Grottanelli identifies two main forms. On the one hand, there is the child-soothsayer, who delivers an oracle whose meaning must be deciphered, often by individuals specialized in the art of interpretation. In such cases, the child is thus seen as a divine medium; a figure that anthropologists, in the wake of Marcel Mauss, have compared to simple-minded individuals living on the fringes of society like shepherds, strange women, and entertainers. As the old proverbs would have us believe, 'out of the mouths of babes and sucklings come grains of truth' and 'children and fools always speak the truth'. It should be noted that, in this variation, the sex of the child is less important than in the political sphere. Young girls can replace young boys, the important thing being that the child in question is still pre-pubescent. The child as supernatural medium can manifest itself in a prophetic fashion — that is, spontaneously — when the supernatural unexpectedly intrudes on everyday life. More frequently, however, children are used in practices that are properly divinatory, that is, entailing a ritual during which the divine is questioned about human endeavours (Grottanelli, 1993, pp. 67–68 and 24–25). In *The Night Battles,* Carlo Ginzburg provides one of the most striking examples of this. While the divinatory ritual that he presents possesses some specific traits, it takes place against a vague background that uses the child as a medium for the voice of the supernatural. During the trial of Giuliano Verdena held in Mantua in 1489, we thus learn that the defendant

> was accustomed to tell fortunes by filling a vase with water (sometimes holy water), setting it beside a lamp and then getting a boy or girl to gaze into it and murmur a well-known magical formula ('*White angel, holy angel, etc.*'). The proceedings were the customary ones, but the purpose of the spell was unusual, inasmuch as Giuliano only rarely permitted himself to make the reflections of the perpetrators of petty thefts appear on the water of the vase. Usually, he read from a book, while he urged the children to pay close attention to what they would see form on the surface of the water: and the children might say that they saw 'many, many who seemed to be Muslims' or 'a great multitude of people some of whom were on foot, others mounted, a few without hands', and sometimes 'a large man seated with a servant on either side.'(Ginzburg, 2013)

Although political procedures almost never called for the involvement of a child-soothsayer, the pathos formula that we analysed by looking at the Venetian *ballottino* can on the contrary be identified in a number of practices where children did not speak any words but were limited to drawing lots. This is the second variant that involves children as a sort of gateway to the supernatural. Phenomena of this ilk were documented in Etruscan culture as early as the 5th century BC (Bagnasco Gianni, 2001), and are also attested to as early as the 4th century BC in Palestrina, a city thirty or so kilometres from Rome and which functioned as the Roman Republic's main centre for divination. Cicero (2008, II, 41) describes this procedure at length in its late-Republican version. The epigraphy (Champeaux, 1982–1987) shows a child tasked with drawing the *sortes*, in this case oak tablets stored in a well, on which messages are inscribed that must be deciphered by soothsayers (cf. illustration 8). A similar procedure was used in Ostia, Rome's harbour city, while yet more examples can found throughout the ages.

Illustration 8. Divination by lots in Palestrina. (Source: Champeaux, 1982–1987.)

The child and 'Biblical lots'

During the first few centuries of their existence, Christian churches usually appointed their leaders by consensus; sporadically, however, they turned to selection by lots in cases of disagreement. In doing so, the early Christian churches were relying on a practice that had deep roots in the Greek and Roman worlds (Prescendi, 2010). The word for the clergy is in fact derived from the Greek noun *kleros*, which signified both the object used in casting lots as well as what was obtained by lot —i.e. one's 'allotment', especially in the context of succession arrangements (Ehrenberg, 1923, pp. 1467 and 1490; Demont, 2010). This practice was justified using references to the casting of lots from the Bible, in particular the Old Testament (Buchstein, 2009). In the New Testament, the designation of Matthias as the twelfth apostle to replace Judas came to justify selection by lot as a legitimate Christian practice (*Acts*, I, 26). However, the Bible makes no mention of a child being involved in any of the numerous instances where lots are cast.

And yet, despite the fact that divination practices had been banned by the Council of Vannes in 462, pagan traditions that associated the presence of a child with the expression of the supernatural were largely assimilated into Christian practices in the Western world from the 4th century until the 8th century AD. The selection by lot of Matthias to replace Judas was thus said to have been conducted by a child—an interpretation that left traces even in the modern era (cf. for example Leti, 1697, I, p. 75). A series of Christian texts linked the use of sortition in a religious context to the presence of a *puer*, and for a time this figure became inseparable from the use of 'Biblical lots' (Courcelle, 1953). The main inspiration for the association came from a famous episode in Book VIII of *The Confessions of Saint Augustine* (354–430) known for its iconic use of the expression '*Tolle, lege*' (cf. illustration 9). In this passage, young Augustine of Hippo recounts an incident where, wracked with doubt and torn between his old dissolute ways and the prospect of converting to a rigorous Christian life, he began to weep in his garden. 'So was I speaking and weeping in the most bitter contrition of my heart, when, lo! I heard from a neighbouring house a voice (*vocem*), as of boy (*pueri*) or girl (*puellae*), I know not, chanting, and oft repeating. "*Tolle, lege! Tolle, lege!*" [which is generally translated as "Take up and read" but more precisely includes an element of drawing lots]. Instantly, my countenance altered, I began to think most intently whether children were wont in any kind of play to sing such words: nor could I remember ever to have heard the like. So checking the torrent of my tears, I arose; interpreting it to be no other than a command from God to open the book, and read the first chapter I should find.' Opening up the Holy Book to a random page, Augustine came across this passage: 'Not in rioting and drunkenness, not in chambering and wantonness, not in strife and envying; but put ye on the Lord Jesus Christ, and make not provision for the flesh, in concupiscence.' At this point, all of Augustine's doubts vanished and he pledged to follow the path of sexual continence (Saint Augustine, 1909, Book VIII, Chapter XII, 29).

Illustration 9. Tolle, lege, tolle lege (St Augustine's Priory, Fulham Palace Road, London).

Saint Augustine's conversion involved chance at two different moments: the first is the appearance of the child-soothsayer, whose voice is overheard by accident and subsequently interpreted (cledonomancy), while the second is the opening up of a book to a random page, in this case the Bible (bibliomancy). This incident thus belongs to a much broader tradition of religious practices involving the presence of a child as a soothsayer or caster of lots.

A number of sources attest to the fact that Saint Aignan, Bishop of Orléans (358–453), was selected through a process that involved a *puer* randomly drawing from ballots with the candidates' names written on them. The procedure was clearly miraculous, because after extracting the slip, the child, who had not yet learned how to speak, read the name of the new bishop out loud. The result was then verified by opening three sacred books up to a random page: all of which landed on passages that confirmed the choice of Saint Aignan (Courcelle, 1953, pp. 201–202). A similar procedure was also used to select Saint Ambrose as bishop in 374. Gregory of Tours (539–594) likewise reported episodes where sacred books were consulted at random by a *puer*. In Friesland (the coastal region of the Netherlands that extends to the Weser river, today in Germany), a well-known collection of laws called the *Lex Frisionum* (734) was published after the region was converted to Christianity; the law code mentioned the use of a procedure wherein a priest, or failing that an innocent child (*puer quilibet innocens*), would draw lots (*tollere sortibus*) to discover who had committed a crime. The parallels drawn between the innocent child and the pure, neutral figure of the priest could go even further, as the word *puer* was sometimes used to refer to the young clerks who were planning to enter the priesthood and a life of chastity (Courcelle, 1953, pp. 203–209).

These practices nonetheless began to die out after the 8th century AD, especially after the *Decretum Gratiani* (1139–1158), a compilation of Canon law, clearly condemned divination practices as a whole. Starting in the 13th century, a veritable chasm began to separate religious practices and political ones: selection by lot quickly spread throughout the Italian communes at the same time as Pope Honorius III prohibited random selection for the nomination of bishops (1223) and then, two years later, for all other ecclesiastical positions (Keller, 2015; Maleczeck, 1990, pp. 129 *sq.*).

This prohibition primarily applied to the Roman Church, however; a number of Protestant churches continued to view sortition with more indulgence (Buchstein, 2009, pp. 145 *sq.*). The Coptic Orthodox Church also refused to submit to this ruling. During the 5th century, following the outcome of the Fourth Ecumenical Council of Chalcedon (451), the Coptic Church formally separated from the Greek Orthodox Church and other Christian churches. Even today, the Pope of the Coptic Church is randomly selected by a blindfolded child who draws a ballot of wax wrapped around a name from a transparent chalice containing the names of all the most important figures of the Church from a preselected list. This procedure, which already existed in ancient times but disappeared for many years, was once again codified in 1953 and has since remained in effect. In 2012, 'the hand of God' thus selected the man who would become Pope Tawadros II, through the medium of a pure and innocent child. This ritual's formal parallels with the *ballottino* —and more generally with the pathos formula studied above—are striking. Both are practices where *sors divisoria* and *sors divinatoria* are closely intertwined; in addition, the formula here echoes the representation of the blindfolded goddess Fortuna that would become standard during the Renaissance (cf. illustrations 10 and 11).

Illustration 10. Andrea Previtali, The Goddess Fortuna (around 1490), Gallerie dell'Accademia, Venezia. (Source: Wikipedia.)

Illustration 11. Election of the new pope of the Coptic Orthodox Church by the drawing of lots, 11/04/12. (Source: AFP/Getty Images.)

The child in games of chance

The fourth set of practices that combine the figure of the child and the role of chance can be seen in certain games of chance. While, since the dawn of time, children and adults have played various games of chance, we shall narrow our focus here: we shall look specifically at the use of a child to draw lots within a context of play (it should be noted that the figure of the child-soothsayer does *not* appear in the context of games). We shall look at two practices in particular: the cake slice selection during the French Epiphany celebration (Twelfth Night) and lotteries.

In France, and in other regions of Western Europe, it is customary to *tirer les rois*, or literally 'randomly select the kings', when eating cake for the Epiphany at the beginning of January. The origins of this tradition date back at least as far as the Feast of Saturnalia, the most popular Ancient Roman festival. Carnivalesque in nature, Saturnalia took place after the winter solstice, during the 12 days that existed between the solar and lunar cycles. Banquets and orgies proliferated during this time, as the usual social norms were suspended. In particular, games of chance, including dice games, were permitted during Saturnalia, while they were usually forbidden. Slaves would eat at their master's table; sometimes the masters would even serve the slaves. Free men randomly drew a King of Saturnalia (*Saturnalicius princeps*) who gave farcical orders to his subjects (Nilsson, 1923). However, while Saturnalia celebrations did not involve children in particular, (Prescendi, 2015), contemporary Twelfth Night festivities transform the child into the central actor. Families buy cakes, generally filled with an almond paste, with a fava bean hidden inside. The youngest child in the family slips under the table and has to answer an adult who points to each slice of cake asking, 'who is this one for?' The person who receives the slice of cake with the fava bean in it is crowned the king or queen of the day.

As early at the 15th century, and perhaps even earlier, the Feast of the Epiphany began to include a child in a way that foreshadowed current French customs. A miniature illustration contained in the manuscript of the *Heures d'Adelaïde de Savoie* (cf. illustration 12) thus depicts a child underneath a table, attributing each slice of cake one by one while reciting the ritual words that would find their way into literature over a century and a half later under the pen of Étienne Pasquier:

> The night before, we began not to pray to God, but to feast on good food. The master of the banquet bakes a cake with a fava bean hidden inside, a cake that is cut into as many slices as there are guests at the

feast. That being done, a small child is placed under the table, who the master calls Phoebus [Phoebus being an epithet for Apollo, the god of oracles, whose main site of worship was at Delphi], as if by virtue of his young and innocent age, the child could act like an Apollonian oracle. After being questioned, the child responds with the Latin word *Domine* [Master, lord]: at this point, the master beseeches the child to attribute the slice of cake that he holds in his hand to one of the guests; the child randomly names each guest without taking into account their relative importance, until one individual is given the slice of cake with the fava bean inside of it. In this fashion he [who receives the fava bean] is named the king of the feast, no matter his actual rank. And everyone eats, drinks and dances to their fill. There is no respect for anyone's nobility, the day's festivities call for it to be this way. (Pasquier, 1621, Book IV, Chapter IX, pp. 375-376).

This is indisputably a new variant of the pathos formula that we have analysed above.

Illustration 12. Miniature from the *Heures d'Adelaïde de Savoie* (1450–1470).

The other form of gaming that significantly involves both children and chance is the lottery. Documented as early as the Han Dynasty in China (i.e. from 206 BC to 220 AD), state-run lotteries were also widely practised during the Roman era. They disappeared around 222 AD, only resurfacing in the Western world around the 15th century (Pardieu, 1865, p. 759). Starting in the middle of the 15th century, however, lotteries quickly spread throughout Europe, radiating out from their first centres of popularity in the Netherlands and the northern Italian communes, the two regions being the most advanced in terms of trade and finance (Wykes, 1964; Belmas, 2006, pp. 308-328; Näther, 2008, pp. 99 *sq.*). Lotteries were especially popular in Venice and

Genoa, where they were frequently organized by private individuals and where the ancestor to today's modern game of lotto was invented.

In the Netherlands, a 17th-century engraving depicts children involved in the general lottery of the United Provinces (engraving by B. Mourik, *Drawing of the general lottery of the United Provinces*, Royal Library of the Netherland, reprinted in the Dutch version of Wikipedia under the entry '*Loterij*'). With the advent of the 18th century, accounts of lotteries being organized begin to crop up all over Europe. In England, the first official lottery was held in 1566. While the figure of the child does *not* appear in an engraving from the following year, it is nonetheless very present in 18th-century representations of the procedure (cf. illustrations 13 and 14).[7] In Germany, a drawing from the beginning of the 18th century likewise portrays two children extracting numbers from large bags during the lottery drawing of the city-state of Hamburg (cf. illustration 15). Also in the 18th century, another engraving depicts the lottery wheel in use at the time being operated by a young boy wearing a blindfold (Allemagne, 1905, pp. 101 *sq.*). In France, an engraving from the early 18th century also shows a 'foundling' (very likely drawing its inspiration from the Venetian *ballottino*) at the reins of a royal lottery (cf. illustration 16). A century later, a certain Delion would organize private lotteries for which he created public advertisements once again depicting a blindfolded child drawing numbers (*ibid.*, pp. 118–119) (cf. illustrations 17 and 18).

Illustrations 13 and 14. Drawing a state lottery in Guildhall, London, 1739 and 1765 (Source: Hilary Morgan/Alamy stock photo.)

---

[7]   I would like to thank Olivier Christin for sharing these illustrations with me.

Illustration 15. Lottery drawing in the city-state of Hamburg, 1716 (source: Wikipedia, German version); *Illustration 16.* Nicolas de Larmessin, *Tirage des loteries royales par un enfant trouvé* [Drawing of the royal lotteries by a foundling), 1706 (copyright BNF)].

Illustrations 17 and 18. Thumbnails decorating the brochure printed by Delion, France, circa 1810 (the second thumbnail is a close-up). (Source: Allemagne, 1905, pp. 118–120.)

In many countries, this practice endured until the 20th century, only disappearing when manual drawing was replaced by electronic systems in the 1960s and 1970s. One photograph thus portrays children drawing the French National Lottery as late as 1950 (cf. illustration 19); another depicts the first drawing, on 9th October 1953, of what is now a very popular lottery in Hamburg called the '6aus49'. This lottery drawing was done by a young girl named Elvira Hahn (http://www.mopo.de/ 22980512; cf. also Wykes, 1964, p. 238). In Luxembourg, another photograph also shows a child being used for the Grand Duchy's lottery in 1945 (cf. illustration 20). In Italy, lotteries were very popular in the decades that followed the Second World War, with many drawings being broadcast live on television (cf. illustration 21). In the 21st century, the practice is still widespread in Spain (where the first state-run lottery was only introduced in 1763); it is moreover significant that one of the country's main lotteries is called the *Lotería del Niño* (i.e. the lottery of the child). This lottery takes place on 6th January, for the Epiphany, a celebration that has preserved a great deal of importance in Spain and is almost on par with Christmas. The moment of extraction receives quite a bit of publicity on television and in the press (cf. illustration 22). Much like for the French Twelfth Night cake, the pagan origins of this celebration did not prevent its assimilation into Christian traditions, in particular when combined with the theme of the child Jesus and, in the case of the lottery, its commercial use in mass media.

Illustration 19. Drawing for the 35th bracket of the French National Lottery, Figeac, 6th September 1950 (source: Ladepeche.fr, 29th January 2017); *Ilustration 20.* Drawing of the National Lottery of Luxembourg, 1945 (source: https://www. loterie.lu/content/portal/fr/decouvrez-la-loterie-nationale/historique-organisation. html); *Illustration 21.* Contemporary Italian lottery, drawing from 30th September 1959 (Istituto Luce, http://fondazionerrideluca.com/tag/lotteria/); *Illustration 22.* Spanish lottery 'of the child' (*lotería del niño*), drawing of the first prize of the year 2017 (RTVE, 6th January 2017).

Another variation on the lottery, a game called *ozieri*, is common in Sardinia and in an area that stretches from the Balkans to Spain. The game usually takes place during New Year's festivities and involves a young boy or girl drawing from a number of objects deposited by each of the participants. Every time an object is extracted from the rest, it is accompanied by a short song predicting good or bad fortune: with the caveat that the number of good portents must equal the number of ill omens (Grottanelli, 1993, pp. 47–48).

From a formal approach to genealogical analysis

While the figure of the child-soothsayer is specific to the realm of divination, it is on the contrary striking just how crosscutting the pathos formula of the child drawing lots is with regard to politics, religion, and games. This pathos formula can even be found, albeit in a much more fragmentary fashion, with regard to the distribution of property. Just a few decades ago in Sardinia, it was still common practice for a child to divide up the portions of wild boar that had been killed during a hunt. The child would face a wall while an elder would point to each portion of boar with a stick, asking 'who is this share for?' until all of the participants had been called. The practice evolved over the years, with each portion subsequently being numbered and the child drawing those numbers randomly (Padaglione, 1989, pp. 195–201, quoted in Grottanelli, 1993, p. 47).

In short, the major types of practices that combined the figure of a child with the role of chance are presented below (cf. Table 1).

Using this formal framework, developed through morphological study, we shall investigate whether it is possible to advance other genealogical hypotheses that might allow us to further identify and nuance the various transfers and forms of filiation between these different uses of the child.

Distribution of goods and functions: distributive sortition (*sors divisoria*)		Cleromancy: divinatory sortition (*sors divinatoria*):	Games of chance
Distribution of goods in lots	Distribution of functions	Reveals a destiny or expresses a divine will	
Sporadic: distribution of the portions of wild boar after a hunt in contemporary Sardinia	Selection by lot in politics (13th–19th century) Sporadic reappearance in the 21st century	Popular divination practices (from the Etruscans and Romans to the modern day) Christianization of these pagan customs (4th–8th century AD): the figure of the child and Biblical sortition Selection by lot of the pope of the Coptic Orthodox Church	The Twelfth Night cake (15th–21st century) and lotteries (17th–21st century) Lottery variant: The game of *ozieri* (contemporary Sardinia)

Table 1. The figure of the child in various sortition practices. (The most important practices are presented in bold.)

Philippe Ariès (1973, p. 109) argues that the procedure behind official lotteries was doubtlessly inspired by the role of the child in doling out slices of the Epiphany cake, a hypothesis that cannot be dismissed out of hand. The sources that I have found attest to the presence of the child drawing lots as early as the mid-15th century for the Epiphany cake, whereas the oldest mention of such a practice with regard to lotteries that I have found was in a 1697 volume by Gregorio Leti titled *Critique historique, politique, morale, économique et comique, sur les loteries anciennes et modernes, spirituelles et temporelles des états et des églises* [Historical, political, moral, economic and comic critique of ancient and modern lotteries, both spiritual and temporal affairs of the Church]. However, this book mentions a practice that it presents as traditional in reference to a much older institutional invention—a matter to which we shall return in a moment. At any rate, the involvement of a child to distribute the slices of cake was more or less contemporaneous with the first lotteries, as both emerged around the middle of the 15th century. It is moreover documented that the sphere of dissemination of the Epiphany cake was largely limited to France and that lotteries were imported from Italy during the reign of Francis I during the first half of the 16th century. Although we cannot formally disprove Ariès' hypothesis, it therefore remains highly unlikely.

On the other hand, in his admirable overview of the figure of the child and the use of divination, Cristiano Grottanelli makes the striking admission that he has 'not been able to find examples of the involvement of children in the selection by lot of civil servants or magistrates in the modern era' and that he therefore cannot demonstrate 'a historical link between divination by lots in Palestrina (and in the Middles Ages) and lotteries', although this link is very probable (Grottanelli, 1993, p. 45).

Thanks to the findings of our research, however, we are clearly able to make the hypothesis that political sortition as operated by the hand of a child does in fact constitute the historic link between divinatory practices and Biblical sortition in Antiquity and the Middle Ages on the one hand, and contemporary and modern games of lottery on the other. In reality, popular practices involving children in divination and prophecy were never interrupted and they acted as a cultural breeding ground for periodic innovation in the realm of politics or games. It is nonetheless likely that these practices alone are not enough to explain the marked resurgence of this pathos formula in modern times.

Sources do not tell us why selection by lot in politics emerged with such vigour in the Italian communes at the beginning of the 13th century, nor why the pathos formula that involved the figure of a child was so frequently invoked. A variety of different elements could have served as inspiration, from divinatory practices and Biblical sortition to the few ancient texts known at the time. The fact remains that random selection was so popular in the world of the communes that it has rightfully been highlighted as the most significant and unique contribution of that era (Keller, 2015). During the late Middle Ages, and even more during the modern era, random selection was the main source driving the dissemination of the pathos formula of a child drawing lots. Venice and Genoa were at the centre of this phenomenon. Venice saw its selection procedure for the doges, in place since the 13th century, publicized throughout all of Europe. While playing a more modest role in the history of political ideas and practices, Genoa also made a decisive contribution to the dissemination of this pathos formula during the period when lotteries spread throughout the European continent. In 1528, three years before the Republic of Florence would definitively collapse under the rule of the Medici family, Genoa followed the suggestions of Andrea Doria and reformed its political system, with a view to defusing the conflicts that traditionally pitted the city's two major families against each other. The reform consisted in awarding major public offices, including the position of the Doge and members of the *Signoria,* for two-year terms rather than for life; in alternating members of the old patrician families with newer clans for the most important positions; and in combining election and selection by lot in a procedure that was even lengthier and more complex than its Venetian counterpart. The reform met with great success and remained in effect with only a few modifications until the French invasion in 1797.

The new system established in 1528 also stipulated that the eight persons who composed the *Signoria* alongside the Doge would be renewed in pairs every six months, with each individual completing two full years in office. These members were selected from amongst the 120 members of the aristocratic Great Council. Random selection was used as follows: 'After having put all the names in one urn, we have a young boy, in charge of the Holy Relics, draw two names, either to chase the Demons away or to simply serve as ornamentation' (Leti, 1697, p. 112). As the practice spread, the 120 names began to be printed ahead of time and bets were placed on the results of the selection procedure. After trying in vain to combat this betting, the Senate finally came to publicly endorse it and even transform it into an official practice in 1643–44, with many deriving 'great benefit' from it (*ibid.,* p. 140; Grottanelli, 1993, p. 43).

It is therefore highly likely that the pathos formula that stems from the political uses of selection by lot was transferred to lottery practices, with the city of Genoa doubtless playing an influential role in the process. Relatively similar transfers possibly occurred in Spain as well, as that country also relies heavily on the pathos formula of the child drawing lots in its contemporary lotteries. Moreover, it is telling that in his *Critique des lotteries,* Leti (1697) grouped civil practices and games together in the same category. One of the editions of this popular book also includes an engraving that depicts a blindfolded child or perhaps young adolescent turning the lottery wheel (cf. illustration 23). In the 18th century, the practice seemed solidly established in several European countries. If Grottanelli did not realize that, that was because he connected random selection procedures conducted by a child in Genoa with lotteries, without seeing that this form of selection already belonged an ancient tradition of political practices.

Illustration 23. Lottery drawing, illustration from an edition of Gregorio Loti's book, *Critique des lotteries*. (Source: Reprinted in Allemagne, 1905, p. 120.)

The origins of the random distribution of Epiphany cake slices by a child are more difficult to track down, however. Lamenting the assimilation of pagan traditions, Étienne Pasquier rightly refers to the Roman feast of Saturnalia to identify the carnivalesque roots of the Twelfth Night celebration. He emphasizes its direct filiation with divinatory practices, as evidenced by the reference to Phoebus/Apollo, and once again correctly identifies a link with a Greek procedure, used during the time of Socrates, to select magistrates by drawing a fava bean (Pasquier, 1621, Book IV, Chapter IX, p. 376). Referencing Xenophon (1923, Book One, Chapter 2, 9), Pasquier cites Eramus's *Adagia* (1500) and explicitly compares the fava beans to 'ballots', which would have been an unmistakable allusion to Venetian and Genoese practices, among others, for his learned audience. If Pasquier is right, we could conclude that the type of political sortition used for the attribution of major public offices from the Ancient Greeks to the Venetian doges in fact played a notable role in the syncretism that presided over the invention of selection by lot for the Epiphany cake slices.

Conversely, as procedures involving selection by lot have once again become relevant in the political landscape since the end of the 20th century, the pathos formula of the child drawing lots has made a marginal reappearance (cf. illustrations 24 and 25).[8] It is likely that the influence of this pathos formula on games of chance played a role in

---

[8] I would like to thank Dimitri Courant for having drawn my attention to this topic.

this regard, given the instrumental hybrids that can be observed across both fields (Sintomer, 2020).

Illustrations 24–25. Selection by lot of jury members in Arc-les-Gray, France (*L'Est républicain*, Vesoul-Haute-Saône edition, 15th June 2016); Random selection of the members of the advisory committee in La Montagne, France (*Ouest-France*, Pays de la Loire edition, 10th February 2015).

Conclusion

As we near the end of our necessarily partial investigation, we can nonetheless point to a number of significant results. Firstly, we have identified the existence of the pathos formula involving a child drawing lots across a variety of different fields. We have described its primary manifestations throughout the ages: popular divination practices (from the Etruscans to today); the Christianization of these pagan traditions (from the 4th to the 8th century AD in terms of Biblical sortition, and until today with the selection by lot of the pope of the Coptic Orthodox Church); the Twelfth Night cake and lotteries (from the 15th to the 21st century); and the random selection of public offices (from the 13th to the 19th century). Finally, we have discovered a handful of genealogical links that reveal where transfers occurred between these various practices, with political sortition doubtless playing a crucial role.

Naturally, although the pathos formula we have identified is not the only way that children and chance were linked, as the manifestation of the supernatural can also be conveyed by the presence of the child-as-soothsayer, it is nonetheless the most widespread. It also exhibits several different variations. In the most popular variant, the child directly operates the drawing of lots. In other cases, the child reads names out loud (as in the case of the Twelfth Night cake and some wild boar hunts in Sardinia) or numbers (again, in certain Sardinian wild boar hunts). The pathos formula used in the political sphere from the 13th to the 19th century also has a number of specific traits: it only involves the figure of the child drawing lots, and never the figure of the child-soothsayer; the child is directly in charge of extracting the ball or slip, which is not always the case in other variants; and finally, mirroring the political climate of that era, the child in question is always male (whereas in other forms of selection by lot, sex is generally less strictly defined).

One more characteristic must be stressed: generally, in divinatory sortition, strong emphasis is placed on the child's pre-pubescent purity (Prescendi, 2010). This is moreover why, in a Christian context, the child could be replaced by a young priest who had vowed to be sexually abstinent. From this point of view, impartiality could be seen as stemming from purity. In forms of political sortition that involve a child, impartiality is emphasized rather than purity; even though the latter can be mobilized, especially in societies where politics and religion are more closely intertwined (such as in Spain during the *Siglo de Oro*), it remains one of the preconditions for impartiality rather than a goal in itself. This is in fact why, in the Italian communes during the Middle Ages or even today, the child can be replaced by a priest but also, in some cases, by an adolescent (as was the case in Venice[9]). With the secularization of practices, the 'innocent hand' also changed in meaning. The ritual dimension of the act nonetheless remains very significant, which is why we can continue to refer to its pathos (cf. Table 2).

	Distribution of functions: distributive sortition (*sors divisoria*) in politics	Cleromancy: divinatory sortition (*sors divinatoria*)	Games of chance
Importance of the ritual	Ritual nature of the pathos formula	Ritual nature of the pathos formula	Ritual nature of the pathos formula
Role of the child	The child draws lots directly	The child draws lots directly	The child draws lots directly or reads the names or numbers out loud according to which lots are distributed
	—	The child-soothsayer	-
Sex of the child	Boy	Boy or girl	Boy or girl
Public or private nature	Public	Public or private	Public
Main logic	Mostly impartiality	Purity, impartiality	Mostly impartiality

Table 2. The pathos formula of the child drawing lots in different social realms.

---

9   I would like to thank Claire Judde de Larivière for having drawn my attention to this point.

A second result is noticeable. This pathos formula has allowed us to discover a handful of genealogical links that reveal where transfers occurred between various practices, with political sortition doubtless playing a crucial role. We have described its primary manifestations throughout the ages: popular divination practices (from the Etruscans to today); the Christianization of these pagan traditions (from the 4th to the 8th century AD in terms of Biblical sortition, and until today with the selection by lot of the pope of the Coptic Orthodox Church); the Twelfth Night cake and lotteries (from the 15th to the 21st century); and the random selection of public offices (from the 13th to the 19th century). French children would probably not choose the king or queen of the day under the table by distributing slices of cake during the Twelfth Night festivities if selection by lot implying the presence of a child had not been a widely shared practice in Italian communes.

A third result may also be put forward. The pathos formula that we have identified may have something to tell us about random selection in general. The figure of the child drawing lots implies both a form, described above, and a substantial logic of innocence and impartiality (the equivalent of the 'pathos' by Warburg). We have argued in the introduction that random selection in politics has no inherent meaning, as it can be used according to a wide variety of different logics: impartial resolution or at least reduction of conflicts, political divination, republican self-government and radical democracy, the common sense of the people in trial juries, and deliberative democracy. Nonetheless, of all its potential qualities, impartiality is the trait that can be found in almost all empirical examples of random selection. Impartiality is in most cases integrated, in a subordinate fashion, to all other forms of logic (cf. Table 3).

Divination in politics	Republican self-governance, radical democracy	Common sense (traditionally, juries in the judicial arena)	Deliberative democracy
Knowing one's destiny or the will of the Gods without human interference	Avoiding the creation of differences that would lead to hierarchies within a group, avoiding corruption, limiting the influence of factions	Avoiding judgment by anyone other than one's peers, avoiding the creation of unfair distinctions within members of a group	Allowing for the potentially equal participation of all social groups in deliberation through a representative sample or a fair cross-section of the people, limiting the influence of partisan interests

Table 3. Impartiality as a secondary dimension of other ideal-typical logics governing the use of political sortition.

While political sortition has no universal 'nature' or 'function', it may nonetheless have a particular elective affinity with impartiality. By taking this concept in its broader sense, we might even be able to say that the ritualized act of random selection in general (and not just its variants that involve the presence of a child) constitutes a pathos formula of impartiality in politics.

References

Allemagne, H.R., D' (1905) *Récréations et Passe-temps*, Paris: Hachette et Cie.

Aristotle (1944) *Politics*, Rackham, H. (trans.), Cambridge, MA: Harvard University Press.

Ariès, P. (1973) *L'enfant et la vie familiale sous l'Ancien Régime*, Paris: Seuil.

Ávila, A. (1999) *En nombre de la nación. La formación del gobierno representativo en México (1808–1824)*, Mexico: Taurus/CIDE.

Bagnasco, G.G. (2001) Le sortes etrusche, in Cordano, F. & Grottanelli, C. (eds.) *Sorteggio Pubblico e Cleromanzia dall'Antichità all'Età Moderna*, pp. 197–219, Milan: Edizioni Et.

Barat, R. (2020) The introduction of sortition in elections in the republic of Geneva (1691), in Lopez-Rabatel, L. & Sintomer, Y. (eds.) *Sortition and Democracy: History, Tools, Theories*, pp. 253–263, Exeter: Imprint Academic.

Belmas, E. (2006) *Jouer autrefois. Essai sur le jeu dans la France moderne (XVIᵉ–XVIIᵉ siècles)*, Seyssel: Champ Vallon.

Bloch, M. (2015) *The Royal Touch: Sacred Monarchy and Scrofula in England and France*, Anderson, J.E. (trans.), London: Routledge.

Bredekamp, H. (2015) *Théorie de l'acte d'image*, Paris: Éditions La Découverte.

Buchstein, H. (2009) *Demokratie und Lotterie. Das Los als politisches Entscheidungsinstrument von der Antike bis zu EU*, Frankfurt am Main: Campus.

Buchstein, H. (2015) Countering the 'democracy thesis' – sortition in Ancient Greek political theory, *Redescriptions*, 18 (2), pp. 126–157.

Champeaux, J. (1982–1987) *Fortuna. Recherches sur le culte de la Fortune à Rome*, 2 vols., Rome: École Française de Rome.

Chojnacki, S. (2000) Political adulthood, *Women and Men in Renaissance Venice*, pp. 227–243, Baltimore, MD: Johns Hopkins University Press.

Cicero (2008) *On Divination, Book 1*, Wardle, D. (trans.), Oxford: Clarendon Press [44 BC].

Cordano, F. & Grottanelli, C. (eds.) (2001) *Sorteggio Pubblico e Cleromanzia dall'Antichità all'Età Moderna*, Milan: Edizioni Et.

Courcelle, P. (1953) L'enfant et les 'sorts bibliques', *Vigiliae Christianae*, 7, Amsterdam: North Holland Publishing Company.

Demont, P. (2010) Tirage au sort et démocratie en Grèce ancienne, *La Vie des Idées*, 22 June, [Online], www.laviedesidees.fr/tirage-au-sort-et-democratie-en.html.

Dowlen, O. (2008) *The Political Potential of Sortition: A Study of the Random Selection of Citizens for Public Offices*, Exeter: Imprint Academic.

Ehrenberg, V. (1923) Losung, in *Paulys Real-Enzyklopädie der klassischen Altertumswissenschaft*, pp. 1451–1504, Stuttgart: Metzler.

Espagne, M. & Werner, M. (eds.) (1988) *Transferts. Les relations interculturelles dans l'espace franco-allemand (XVIIIe–XIXe siècles)*, Paris: Éditions Recherches sur les civilisations.

Fontaine, A. & Chollet, A. (2018) Introduction. Le tirage au sort, une histoire de déclinaisons et de transferts, in Chollet, A. & Fontaine, A. (eds.) *Expériences du tirage au sort en Suisse et en Europe (XVIe–XXIe siècles)*, pp. 11–24, Bern: Schriftenreihe Bibliothek am Guisanplatz.

Giannotti, D. (1642) *Dialogi de republica Venetorum*, Elzevir [1540].

Ginzburg, C. (1991) *Deciphering the Witches' Sabbath*, Rosenthal, R. (trans.), Chicago, IL: University of Chicago Press.

Ginzburg, C. (2013) *The Night Battles: Witchcraft and Agrarian Cults in the Sixteenth and Seventeenth Centuries*, Tedeschi, J. & Tedeschi, A.C. (trans.), Baltimore, MD: John Hopkins University Press.

Gracia, E.B. (2006) Documentos acerca del funcionamiento del sistema de insaculación en la aljama judía de Huesca (siglo XV), *Sefarad*, 66 (2), July–December, pp. 309–344.

Grottanelli, C. (1993) Bambini e divinazione, in Niccoli, O. (ed.) *Infanzie*, pp. 2–72, Florence: Ponte alle grazie.

Grottanelli, C. (2001) La cléromancie ancienne et le dieu Hermès, in Cordano, F. & Grottanelli, C. (eds.) *Sorteggio Pubblico e Cleromanzia dall'Antichità all'Età Moderna*, pp. 155–196, Milan: Edizioni Et.

Guerra, F.-X. (2000) *Modernidad e independencias. Ensayos sobre las revoluciones hispánicas*, Mexico: MAPFRE/FCE.

Harrington, J. (1977) *The Political Works of James Harrington*, Pocock, J.G.A. (ed.), Cambridge: Cambridge University Press.

Keller, H. (2015) Electoral systems and conceptions of community in Italian communes (12th–14th centuries), *Revue française de science politique*, 64 (6), English edition, November.

Judde de Larivière, C. (2020) Ducal elections, institutional usages, and popular practices: Drawing lots in the republic of Venice, in Lopez-Rabatel, L. & Sintomer, Y. (eds.) *Sortition and Democracy: History, Tools, Theories*, Exeter: Imprint Academic, pp. 219–234.

Leti, G. (1697) *Critique historique, politique, morale, économique et comique, sur les lotteries anciennes et modernes, spirituelles et temporelles des états et des églises*, Amsterdam: Chez les amis de l'auteur.

Maleczek, W. (1990) Abstimmungsarten, in Schneider, R. & Zimmermann, H. (eds.) *Wahlen und Wählen im Mittelalter*, Sigmaringen: Jan Thorbecke.

Malipiero, D. (1843) Annali Veneti, *Archivio Storico Italiano*, VII.

Martemyanova, E. (2020) La représentation 'imparfaite' en Provence au XVIIIe siècle, in Hayat, S., Péneau, C. & Sintomer, Y. (eds.) *La représentation avant le gouvernement représentatif*, Rennes: PUR.

Mellina, M. (2019) The use of random selection in the Helvetic Republic: The turning point for chance, in Lopez-Rabatel, L. & Sintomer, Y. (eds.) *Sortition and Democracy: History, Tools, Theories*, Exeter: Imprint Academic.

Mueller, R.C. (2013) Nel segreto dell'urna. La riforma della procedura elettorale adottata nel 1492 dal Consiglio dei dieci di Venezia, *Quaderni veneti*, 2, pp. 219–228.

Muir, E. (1981) *Civic Ritual in Renaissance Venice*, Princeton, NJ: Princeton University Press.

Näther, U. (2008) 'Das Große Los' — Lotterie und Zahlenlotto, in Badisches Landesmusuem Karlsruhe, *Volles Risiko! Glückspiel von der Antike bis heute*, catalogue for the eponymous exhibition, Karlsruhe.

Nilsson, M.P. (1923) Saturnalia, in Wissowa, G. (ed.) *Paulys Real-Enzyklopädie der klassischen Altertumswissenschaft*, Stuttgart: J.B. Metzler.

Padaglione, V. (1989) *Il cinghiale cacciatore. Antropologia simbolica della caccia in Sardegna*, Rome: Armando.

Palmer, C.J. (1856) *The History of Great Yarmouth*, Yarmouth/London: L.A. Mead & Russell-Smith.

Pardieu, E. de (1865) *Trattato delle imposte considerate sotto l'aspetto storico, economico e politico in Francia ed all'estero*, Turin: Stamperia dell'unione tipografico-editrice.

Pasquier, E. (1621) *Recherches de la France*, Paris: L. Sonnius

Prescendi, F. (2010) Children and the transmission of religious knowledge, in Dasen, V. & Späth, T. (eds.) *Children, Memory, and Family Identity in Roman Culture*, pp. 73–94, Oxford: Oxford University Press.

Prescendi, F. (2015) *Rois éphémères. Enquête sur le sacrifice humain*, Geneva: Labor et fides.

Rambert, E. (1889) *Études historiques et nationales*, Lausanne: Librairie F. Rouge.

Riklin, A. (1999) *Die Republik von James Harrington*, Bern: Wallstein.

Saint Augustine (1909) *The Confessions: The Confessions of Saint Augustine*, Bouverie Pusey, E. (trans.), Edinburgh: PF Collier & Sons [397–400].

Serafín Castro, A.D. (2019) Représentation politique et tirage au sort au Mexique (1808–1857), in Lopez-Rabatel, L. & Sintomer, Y. (eds.) *Tirage au sort et démocratie. Histoire, instruments, théories, Participations*, special issue.

Sesma, J.Á. (1978) *La Diputación del reino de Aragón en la época de Fernando II (1479–1516)*, Zaragoza: Imprenta librería general.

Sintomer, Y. (2020) *Between Radical and Deliberative Democracy: Random Selection in Politics from Athens to Contemporary Experiments*, Cambridge: Cambridge University Press.

Subrahmanyam, S. (2014) *Aux origines de l'histoire globale*, Paris: Collège de France/Fayard.

Trott, N. (1736) *The Laws of the Province of South Carolina*, Charleston, SC: Lewis Timothy.

Warburg, A.M. (1999) *The Renewal of Pagan Antiquity: Contributions to the Cultural History of the European Renaissance*, Los Angeles, CA: Getty Research Institute for the History of Art and the Humanities.

Warburg, A.M. (1979) *Ausgewählte Schriften und Würdigungen*, Wuttke, D. (ed.), Baden-Baden: Valentin Koerner.

Weller, T. (2010) Repräsentation per Losentscheid. Wahl und Auswahlverfahren der procuradores de Cortes in den kastilischen Städten der Frühen Neuzeit, in Dartmann, C., Wassilowsky, G. & Weller, T. (eds.) *Technik und Symbolik vormoderner Wahlverfahren (Beihefte der Historischen Zeitschrift)*, Munich: Walter de Gruyter.

Wykes, A. (1964) *Gambling*, London: Aldus Books/W.H. Allen.

Xenophon (1923) *The Memorabilia*, Todd, O.J. (trans.), Cambridge, MA: Harvard University Press.

Yves Déloye

From One
Materiality to Another
Random Selection through
the Lens of the Electoral Process

Translated by Sarah-Louise Raillard

Is it possible to compare the electoral process to the practice of random selection? Just the mere fact of asking this question means challenging traditional analyses of the modes and processes of selection used to legitimately appoint individuals to positions of power or authority. Past research has in particular sought to *essentialize* the devolution of power by theoretically attributing to both of these mechanisms (election versus random selection) a number of immutable traits. Elections were seen as encouraging greater competency and the recognition of different skills, by allowing for the competitive and deliberate selection of individuals that possessed the necessary knowledge, know-how, and expertise to accomplish political tasks — hence its aristocratic and conservative dimensions, alluded to by Alexis de Tocqueville at the time of the widespread (albeit male) experiment with 'universal' suffrage in France around the middle of the 19th century.[1] On the other hand, random selection[2] had long been associated with the neutralizing effects of chance. Since the days of Ancient Greece, sortition had been touted as promoting democratic equality and impartiality (principles whose purity was nonetheless often exaggerated).[3] Studies conducted in this vein have thus overlooked the numerous hybrid forms and

---

[1] For an in-depth discussion of this aristocratic dimension, see the now canonical analysis by Manin, *Principles of Representative Government* (1997 [1995], chapter 4).

[2] For an overview of the theoretical virtues of random selection, see Stone, *The Luck of the Draw* (2011).

[3] For a recent critique of this essentialist interpretation of the mechanisms and processes of the devolution of power, see Bonin (2017, pp. 3–23).

institutional arrangements that represented the reality of practices involving the devolution or delegation of power in different societies throughout the ages. In short, traditional analyses forget to systematically *historicize* the various conditions — cognitive, material, cultural, and political — that inform the mechanisms and provisions which regulate access to positions of power, majesty, and authority.[4]

Edited by Liliane Lopez Rabatel and Yves Sintomer, this collective volume offers a valuable counterpoint to such essentialist studies. First, because it meticulously contextualizes the many diverse uses of random selection in the political realm, as well as its numerous judicial, administrative, and religious applications. By providing a variety of experiential accounts (from the Ancient World to more contemporary uses of random selection), comparing different historical moments, and combining historical analysis with more theoretical considerations, this volume depicts the whole panorama of practices, rituals, and material formats that historically accompanied the effective implementation of random selection. Far from being reducible to an 'essence' or 'nature', or even to a stable principle, random selection is in fact revealed to be systematically embedded within ritualized institutional arrangements and historical configurations as well as individual cultures (often inherently religious or political), which always place their unique lens on sortition practices, thus preventing any sort of global understanding or overarching study of the procedure as such.

While paying attention to the historical configurations, political debates, and philosophical considerations that surround every performance and use of random selection procedures, as well as their associated iconography and other forms of representation, this volume also provides an inventory of the — sometimes overlooked — parallel and competing elements between the history of random selection and that of electoral processes.[5] These are not merely two different techniques used to distribute power. In fact, this book highlights the importance of the historical combinations of and clashes between the two practices. The chapters devoted to the experiments conducted in Italian cities during the medieval and modern periods, in particular in Venice, confirm the importance of cross-cutting experiments that combined both elections and sortition. In the Italian case, the combination of both mechanisms was justified as a means to compensate for the flaws of one technique (its divisive nature, for example, or the acts of

---

[4] For an argument in favour of historicization, and in particular regarding the electoral process, please see Déloye and Ihl (2017, pp. 595–644).

[5] On the history of selection by lot, see the seminal work by Sintomer (2020).

corruption that could undermine its results) with the alleged virtues of the other.

The medieval period of experimentation has echoes in a number of more recent political configurations that also attest to the possible overlap between these two techniques. For example, let us cite the episode described by Margarita Lavinia Anderson in her study of the development of electoral practices and culture in 19th-century Imperial Germany (Anderson, 2000). Her work examines what happens when universal male suffrage, a potentially egalitarian institution, is adopted by a society that remains otherwise deeply hierarchical by virtue of its attachment to noble lineage and a number of other social cleavages. Throughout the land of the Kaisers, Junkers, and generals, the desired effect of this new political technology (marshalling the electoral deference of the masses) was far from being a foregone conclusion. In the face of the new political uncertainties engendered by this partially unprecedented electoral mechanism, many concerns were expressed and many sources of pressure arose. How should electoral competition and the common destiny embodied by the emperor be reconciled? How could freedom coexist with authority, or quantity with quality? Those were questions whose complexity led some observers at the time to praise the apparent merits of random selection. This was notably the case of one schoolteacher, aged about 60 years old, who wrote to the Imperial Council (*Bundesrat*) in 1882 to call for the abolition of universal male suffrage. This schoolteacher, who was seen in France at the time as being responsible for the military and political might of the German Empire, recalled the calm, peaceful days of solidarity 'prior to 1848'. In his eyes, introducing the parliamentary principle and its translation into electoral mechanisms had completely destroyed that 'sweet tranquillity'. Hence his proposal, striking with regard to European history, to replace (partly universal) suffrage with a simple lottery. The aforementioned schoolteacher came back to Aristotle's original line of reasoning: with a lottery, 'all kinds of men can play. They win or they lose.' But—and this is the crux of the argument 'they will stop hating and pillorying each other.' Like many times before in history, mitigating and putting an end to the violence of 'factions' and avoiding the fragmentation of interests were the primary concerns that justified the clash between different political selection techniques in Imperial Germany.

A combination that can also—and perhaps primarily—be explained by the various competing interests of the elites and their constant preoccupation with selecting the procedure that will best enable them to maintain their control over society. A combination that can likewise be justified by the close ties that exist between these procedures and ritual arrangements of religious origin or inspiration. Both voting and random selection in fact owe much of their effectiveness to the overlap between the sacred and the profane, and to the fact that their performance often comports a religious dimension, an aspect justly underscored by many of this volume's authors. In so doing, this work harks back to the early intuitions of writers like Léo Moulin (1953)[6] and follows in the vein of more recent scholars like Olivier Christin (2014, in particular chapter 3), who insist on the need to take into account the religious origins of modern political technologies.

As can be seen from the number of chapters contained in this book, organizing the physical performance of random selection does not solely entail defining its ritual and symbolic protocol. It also involves anticipating and setting parameters on how social competence and political instrumentation co-exist at the heart of any act of political selection. Most of the authors in this volume invite us to peruse the various practices and forms of knowledge that shape the historically situated relationship to instruments of delegation and selection. For elections are not merely a means to enforce a dominant opinion through the aggregation of results, no matter what today's commentators may say when chagrined by recent electoral outcomes. Nor is random selection naturally or automatically an impartial instrument of chance. Both mechanisms are first and foremost social rituals whose material history produces political effects. Whatever their other differences, both techniques involve a number of elements — spatial arrangements, the distribution of bodies and objects in the space dedicated to the implementation of election or sortition processes, the furniture and physical instruments deployed such as vases, urns, balls, ballots, tablets, and lottery cabinets — which all heavily influence the nature of the selection that is consequently operated, and even more profoundly shape the symbolic performance and its effectiveness. Technique, materiality, and politics do not therefore play out on different stages with regard to random selection and electoral processes. The control over selection technologies and their potential instrumentalization for political aims have emerged as major political considerations time and time again. In other words, nothing is neutral or anecdotal in selection mechanisms. Nonetheless, it must be recognized that some of the success of these technologies stems from their physical presence and its associated symbolism. Far from being defined in the abstract,

---

[6]   See also Calvez, Hamon, Moulin and Voyé (1992 [1989]).

the performance of these mechanisms depends on the uses through which each political moment is socially and politically configured. From this point of view, the authors contained in this volume also share a desire to scrutinize the whole range of (more or less standardized) technologies and (more or less ritualized) practices that endow each choice made with its political signification.

Hence the importance of a number of archaeological discoveries which, at least in terms of Greek Antiquity, have allowed us to find the historical trace — and sometimes even physical remnants — of the sortition machines (*kleroteria*) used to allocate political offices at the time, thus impeding the professionalization of such offices and fostering their rotation between different individuals.[7] The true importance of the instruments of random selection can be found at the intersection between their different forms and practices; this is also where we can discover the full significance of the historically situated conventions which governed the use of vases, balls, and other instruments to ensure a legitimate procedure of selection to designate political responsibilities.

In short, this book, like many of those devoted to the electoral process,[8] rejects the reductive arguments introduced in the 1950s by the science of political behaviour. By divorcing the processes of political selection from their fundamental dimensions, this reductionism has in fact mutilated the knowledge that we have of such mechanisms.[9] The strength of both voting and sortition as selection mechanisms depends on a number of different relationships. This strength is established through the interaction between regulations, which are already subject to a variety of socially differentiated uses (let us allude here to what Pierre-Étienne Will wrote about the political uses of sortition to appoint civil servants in China at the end of the Imperial era), and the forms of knowledge and know-how involved in operations of random selection. Examining the practices that shape a society's relationship to the various mechanisms of political selection opens up a fruitful new path for research in the social and political sciences, so long as — like the authors contained in this volume — we consider the origins and

---

[7] During the conference held at the French School at Athens from 29 to 31 October 2015 (a conference which marked the origin of many of the chapters in this collective work), Liliane Lopez Rabatel presented a reproduction of a lottery machine, modelled after those used at the end of the 4th century in Athens and sometimes manufactured according to a standard template. On this project, see her chapter in this book. See also Lopez Rabatel (2011).

[8] See Déloye and Ihl (2008). See also the recent work by Le Gall (2017).

[9] On the topic of voting, see Saltman (2008 [2006]).

functions of each technology along a continuum rather than discretely: so long as we investigate the relationship between their social requirements and the historical tensions and transformations that affect the specifically political space where struggles for power and authority unfold. Another obligation also imposes itself: we must always be careful to preserve the ritual dimension, no matter how slight, of institutions involved in the devolution of power.

It is likewise in light of these scientific convictions that criticism of contemporary democratic processes may become relevant (see the chapters in the last section of this work). Only then can criticism wrestle with the uniqueness of lived experience, where democratic theories are endlessly confronted with experiences both past and present, where democracy is not merely an internationalized standard or ideal, but first and foremost a practice. In short: a material history.

References

Anderson, M.L. (2000) *Practicing Democracy: Elections and Political Culture in Imperial Germany*, Princeton, NJ: Princeton University Press.

Bonin, H. (2017) Sur la 'nature' du tirage au sort en politique: dialogue entre hasard et élection, *Politique et sociétés*, 36 (1), pp. 3–23.

Calvez, J.-Y., Hamon, L., Moulin, L. & Voyé, L. (1992 [1989]) *Organisations et mouvements politiques ou religieux. Mode d'acquisition du pouvoir et de l'autorité*, Brussels: M. Moulin.

Christin, O. (2014) *Vox populi. Une histoire du vote avant le suffrage universel*, Paris: Seuil.

Déloye, Y. & Ihl, O. (2008) *L'acte de vote*, Paris: Presses de Sciences Po.

Déloye, Y. & Ihl, O. (2017) La sociologie historique du vote, in Déloye, Y. & Mayer, N. (eds.) *Analyses électorales*, pp. 595–644, Brussels: Éditions Larcier.

Le Gall, L. (2017) *A voté. Une histoire de l'élection*, Paris: Anamosa.

Lopez Rabatel, L. (2011) *Klèrôtéria. Le tirage au sort dans le monde grec antique: machines, institutions et usages*, Doctoral thesis in languages, history and civilisation of the ancient world, Lyon 2.

Manin, B. (1997 [1995]) *Principles of Representative Government*, New York: Cambridge University Press.

Moulin, L. (1953) Les origines religieuses des techniques électorales et délibératives modernes, *Revue internationale d'histoire politique et constitutionnelle*, 10, pp. 106–148.

Saltman, R.G. (2008 [2006]) *The History and Politics of Voting Technology: In Quest of Integrity and Public Confidence*, New York: Palgrave Macmillan.

Sintomer, Y. (2020) *Between Radical and Deliberative Democracy: Random Selection in Politics from Athens to Contemporary Experiments,* Cambridge: Cambridge University Press.

Stone, P. (2011) *The Luck of the Draw,* Oxford: Oxford University Press.

About the Authors

Raphaël Barat is associated researcher in Early Modern history at the Historical Research Center Rhône-Alpes (LARHRA). He has published *Les élections que fait le peuple (République de Genève, vers 1680–1707)*, Genève: Droz, 2018, and coedited *Histoire(s) d'élection(s). Représentations et usages du vote de l'Antiquité à nos jours*, Paris: CNRS editions, 2018.

Wolfgang Blösel is professor for ancient history at Duisburg-Essen University. His research focuses on oligarchy and democracy in Greek and Roman history, especially on internal politics and the writing of history. He has among others published *Die römische Republik. Forum und Expansion*, München: C.H. Beck, 2015, and *Themistokles bei Herodot: Spiegel Athens im fünften Jahrhundert. Studien zur Geschichte und historiographischen Konstruktion des griechischen Freiheitskampfes 480 v. Chr.*, Stuttgart: Steiner, 2004.

Julie Bothorel is associate professor of Roman history at Sorbonne University. She is writing a PhD thesis about 'Sortition of the Provinces from the End of the Roman Republic until the Beginning of the Principate (227 BC–AD)', supervised by Fr. Hurlet at University of Paris Nanterre.

Antoine Chollet is senior lecturer in political thought at the Centre Walras-Pareto, Lausanne University. He studies theories of democracy and contemporary political thought. He has published on nationalism, direct democracy, the temporality of democracy, and presently focuses on populism. He is the leading researcher of a research project on experiences of sortition in Switzerland from the 17th to the 19th century, funded by the Swiss National Fund for scientific research (FNS).

Dimitri Courant is a PhD student at Lausanne University, Institute of Political, Historical and International Studies (IEPHI), and the Paris Center for Sociological and Political Research (CRESPPA), Paris 8-Saint-Denis University. His PhD thesis is *Le nouvel esprit du tirage au sort. Représentation et principes démocratiques au sein de dispositifs délibératifs contemporains*. He has coedited (together with Yves Sintomer) a thematic issue of *Participations*, on 'Le tirage au sort au XXIe siècle' (2019/1).

Yves Déloye is professor of political science at Sciences Po Bordeaux, and director of this institution. He focuses on the sociological history of politics. He is director of the *Revue française de science politique*. He recently published *Sociologie historique du politique*, Paris: La Découverte, 4th edition, 2017, and *Analyses électorales* (coedited together with Nonna Mayer), Brussels: Bruylant, 2017.

Paul Demont is emeritus professor of Greek language and literature at Paris Sorbonne University. His publications focus on Greek archaic literature and philosophy, history of ideas, ancient medicine, and the reception of Antiquity in later periods.

Oliver Dowlen is an independent researcher affiliated to Sciences Po. His work is in the random selection of citizens for public office. He is DPhil. New College Oxford 2002–06, Joint winner of PSA Sir Ernest Barker award for best doctoral thesis in political theory 2006–07. He has among others published *The Political Potential of Sortition*, Exeter: Imprint Academic, 2008. His recent work includes a study of (randomly selected) Citizens' Parliamentary Groups in UK and Australian constitutional contexts sponsored by the new Democracy Foundation.

Aurèle Dupuis is a PhD student at the Centre Walras-Pareto, Lausanne University, in the frame of a research project financed by the Swiss National Fund for scientific research (FNS). He is a historian, focuses on the constitutional history of the 17th and 18th century, and is currently writing a thesis on sortition in Switzerland.

Jean-Michel Fourniau is senior researcher at the French Institute of Science and Technology for transport, development and networks, in the Economic and Social Dynamics of Transport Laboratory (Dest-Ame-Ifsttar). He is a sociologist, member of the group of pragmatic and reflexive sociology, and teaches at the School of Advanced Studies in the Social Sciences (GSPR-EHESS). His research focuses on conflicts and citizen participation in decision-making processes, and ecological democratic experiments. He has among others coedited *Le débat public: une expérience française de démocratie participative*, Paris: La Découverte, 2007, and *Inventer la démocratie du XXIe siècle. L'Assemblée citoyenne du future*, Paris: Les liens qui libèrent, 2017.

Virginie Hollard is assistant professor in ancient history at the Lumière Lyon 2 University, and member of the research center History and Sources of the Ancient World (HiSoMA, CNRS/Lumière Lyon 2 University). Her research focuses on the history of the vote in Rome, Roman public law, and the history of Roman political institutions. She has among others published *Le rituel du vote, Les assemblées politiques à Rome*, Paris: CNRS, 2010, and coedited *Histoires d'élections, Représentations et usages du vote de l'Antiquité à nos jours*, Paris: CNRS, 2018.

Claire Judde de Larivière is assistant professor at the University of Toulouse Jean Jaurès. Her research focuses on Venetian society, working-class groups, and ordinary forms of politicization at the end of the Middle Ages. She has among others published *The Revolt of Snowballs: Murano Confronts Venice, 1511*, transl. Thomas V. Cohen, London: Routledge, 2018.

Yann Lignereux, former member of the École Normale Supérieure de Fontenay/Saint-Cloud, his 'agrégé' in history, and is professor for modern history at Nantes University. His research focuses on political practices and imaginaries in French Europe and North America from the 16th to the 18th century. He is member of the Research Center in International and Transatlantic History (CRHIA), Nantes University, and Associate Member of the Research Center American Worlds.

Liliane Lopez-Rabatel is associated researcher at the Research Institute on Ancient Architecture (IRAA, Lyon, CNRS—AMU). She has written a PhD thesis on sortition in Ancient Greece. She focuses on political history and on the architecture of the political in the Ancient Greek world, and on the Ancient Greek vocabulary of the city. She has coedited *Voter en Grèce, à Rome et en Gaule: pratiques, lieux et finalités*, Lyon: Maison de l'Orient et de la Méditerranée, 2019.

Romain Loriol is assistant professor in Roman literature and history, Jean Moulin Lyon 3 University, and member of the research center History and Sources of the Ancient World (HiSoMA). His research focuses on the one hand on Roman religion at the end of the Republic and during the Empire—and especially on divination—and on the other hand on the formation and uses of lists and catalogues in Ancient times, from an anthropological perspective.

Arnaud Macé is professor of philosophy at the University of Franche-Comté. His research focuses on the knowledge and practices of Archaic and classical Greece. He has recently published (together with Lorenzo

Ferroni) *Plato, Ion, édition, traduction et commentaire*, Paris: Les Belles Lettres, 2018.

Maxime Mellina is a PhD student at the Centre Walras-Pareto, Lausanne University, in the frame of a research project financed by the Swiss National Fund for scientific research (FNS), and the Paris Center for Sociological and Political research (CRESPPA), Paris 8-Saint-Denis University. His PhD thesis focuses on the experiences of political sortition in Switzerland in the 18th and 19th century, especially during the disappearance of random selection practices.

Lucio Milano is professor of ancient history of the Middle East at the Ca' Foscari Venice University. He has recently published (together with Westenholz, Aage) *The 'Shuilisu Archive' and other Sargonic Texts in Akkadian*, CDL Press, vol. 27, 2015.

José Luis Moreno Pestaña is associate professor of moral philosophy at Grenade University, and researcher in the Excellence Cluster FiloLab-UGR. His research focuses on body, work, and the social philosophy of democracy. His last publication is *Retorno a Atenas. La democracia como principio antioligárquico*, Madrid: Siglo XXI, 2019.

Yves Sintomer is professor of political science and researcher at the Paris Center for Sociological and Political Research (CRESPPA, CNRS/ Paris 8 University), and Associate Member, Nuffield College, Oxford University. His most recent books include *Participatory Budgeting in Europe: Democracy and Public Governance* (with C. Herzberg and A. Röcke), London: Routledge, 2016, and *Between Radical and Deliberative Democracy: Random Selection in Politics from Athens to the 21st Century*, Cambridge: Cambridge University Press, 2020 (forthcoming).

Julien Talpin is a full time research fellow in political science at the CNRS, Administrative, Political and Social Research Center (CERAPS, Lille University/CNRS) and co-director of the GIS Democracy & Participation. His research focuses on the political participation of the urban poor and the role of democratic countervailing powers. He has published *Schools of Democracy: How Citizens (Sometimes) Become Competent in Participatory Budgeting Institutions* (ECPR Press, 2011).

Lorenzo Tanzini is associate professor of medieval history at Cagliari University. His research focuses on the history of institutions and on the political culture of Italian cities during the Middle Ages, especially on communes. His publications include *A consiglio. La vita politica nell'Italia dei comuni*, Rome, Laterza, 2014.

Pierre-Étienne Will is emeritus professor at the Collège de France, Paris, and at the École des hautes études en sciences sociales (EHESS). His research focuses on the history of institutions, society, and economy in late Imperial China (16th–20th centuries), and on the policies of hydraulic planning during the same period and during the Chinese Republic. He has among others edited (together with Mireille Delmas-Marty) *China, Democracy, and Law: A Historical and Contemporary Approach*, Leiden: Brill, 2011. *Handbooks and Anthologies for Officials in Imperial China: A Descriptive and Critical Bibliography* will be published by Brill in 2019.